W9-CUJ-198

Henry Goulburn, 1784–1856
A Political Biography

Brian Jenkins's impressive biography documents Henry Goulburn's long and successful political career during the first half of the nineteenth century. Rescuing Goulburn from unmerited obscurity, Jenkins reveals that he was at the centre of far-reaching political and economic developments during a turbulent period of British history.

Between 1812 and 1821 Goulburn worked in the War and Colonial Office, where he effectively administered Britain's far-flung possessions. Appointed chief secretary for Ireland in 1821 – a Protestant to offset a "Catholic" viceroy – Goulburn was at the heart of the final rearguard action by the opponents of Catholic emancipation. As chancellor of the exchequer for the Duke of Wellington (1828–30) and Sir Robert Peel (1841–46) he participated in such momentous decisions as Catholic emancipation and the repeal of the Corn Laws. An opponent of parliamentary reform, he worked closely with Peel, his lifelong friend, to build the Conservative Party and served as a champion of the Established Church. Jenkins examines the conservative values Goulburn held, and the moral dilemma of an essentially good man who depended on the institution of slavery for his private income.

A modest man and a loyal lieutenant, Goulburn himself allowed that he had been content to walk in the shadow of political giants. This self-effacement helps account for the lack of wide recognition generally given him but does not detract from his significant contribution to British history. *Henry Goulburn* accords a remarkable politician his rightful place.

BRIAN JENKINS is professor of history, Bishop's University, Lennoxville, Québec.

Henry Goulburn as statesman emeritus, in which the artist George Richmond
(1809–1896) expresses his ideal of "the truth lovingly told."

Henry Goulburn,
1784–1856

A Political Biography

BRIAN JENKINS

Liverpool University Press

© McGill-Queen's University Press 1996
ISBN 0-85323-641-0 *cased*
ISBN 0-85323-651-8 *paper*

Legal deposit first quarter 1996
Bibliothèque nationale du Québec

Printed in the United States on acid-free paper

Published simultaneously in the European Union
by Liverpool University Press

This book has been published with the help of a grant
from the Social Science Federation of Canada, using
funds provided by the Social Sciences and Humanities
Research Council of Canada. A grant was also received
from Bishop's University in support of the publication
of this work.

McGill-Queen's University Press is grateful to the
Canada Council for support of its publishing
program.

British Library Cataloguing – Publication Data

A British Library CIP Record is available

This book was typeset by Typo Litho Composition Inc.
in 10/12 Baskerville.

In memory of James W. Alexander

Contents

Preface

The writing of political biography is a daunting challenge, for even some of political history's champions have been suspicious if not sceptical of this particular form. The obvious and ever-present danger is that of distortion by focusing on an individual. On the other hand, the subject must be a significant figure in actions or connections "and the biographer must combine breadth of knowledge with balance of interpretation." Henry Goulburn met his part of that standard. He was a major Conservative politician of his generation and was widely regarded as Robert Peel's *alter ego*. Yet one member of the school of "high politics" has dismissed him as a "coming man who never quite came." However epigrammatic, this is a harsh judgment. Admittedly, Goulburn never climbed to the top of Disraeli's "greasy pole," but he did lay the foundation of the modern Colonial Office; he served as chief secretary in Ireland for almost six years, and under the most trying of circumstances; and he briefly held the seals of the Home Office between two important stints as chancellor of the exchequer. And during a decade of opposition, he worked closely with Peel rebuilding the Conservative party while serving as a parliamentary champion of the established church. Late in life, he was regarded as one leader behind whom the divided Tory ranks in the Commons might reunite. Further, this full career was long complicated by his ownership of a Jamaican sugar plantation, which was worked until 1834 by a small army of slaves. These were not the most enviable of possessions for a public man of the early nineteenth century.[1]

If Henry Goulburn offers a biographer a life full of incident and interest, he is himself partly responsible for the curious fact that he has for so long been ignored or depreciated by historians. He was too content to labour in the shadows cast by two giants – Wellington and Peel. Modesty, a dislike of public speaking, and a reluctance to enter the spotlight, born as much of insecurity as of humility, encouraged a natural reserve that reflected a self-consciousness concerning his lack of true rank or station and his dependence for a private income on the institution of slavery. Thus this infuriatingly discreet and elusive figure illustrates John Kenyon's conclusion: "We try to reconstruct men's motives from their statements and actions, and the remarks of other people about them, but this is really only conjecture."[2]

Goulburn was unlikely to attract historical attention so long as the triumphant march of the liberal and democratic state was the dominant trend in British historiography. Moreover, the interpretive wheel has, of late, taken another decidely Whig turn. Renewed interest in Grey, studies of Althorp and Morpeth, and more general examinations of Whig/Liberal government have tended to diminish Peel and the Conservatives while re-establishing liberalism as "the dominant political force of Victorian Britain." A die-hard opponent of the Reform Bill of 1832, Goulburn might all too easily be dismissed as an anachronism in his own lifetime. Other contemporary trends, however, have been far less unfavourable to the reputation of early-nineteenth-century Conservatism. A growing scepticism on right and left of the beneficent state, a deepening disillusionment concerning the benefits of its interventionism and social engineering, contributed to the rise of the "high politics" school. Its students were determined "to rid the study of politics of the prevailing liberal highmindedness" and to emphasize the existence of "the visible world of impotent institutions and the invisible world of power." As a classic insider, spending his life at Westminster and scornful of popular opinion, a politician deeply respectful of the past and profoundly suspicious of the future, Goulburn would appear to fit this mold. But he had entered public life more as a vocation than in a fit of ambition. Nor was he an intriguer. Moreover, he was genuinely committed to advancing what he understood to be the welfare of the nation. This could only be assured, he believed, through the agency of the minimal state. Nevertheless, he was also involved in the determined effort to ensure both capable government and liberal economic policies. The hope was "that efficient, clear-sighted central government promoting equitable and expedient laws could best promote the nation's prosperity, international position and internal stability."[3]

If Goulburn was as reticent as many another liberal Tory on matters ideological, renewed interest in the impact of evangelicalism on the social and economic thought of his era has again placed him at the centre of the discussion. One critical and well-placed contemporary described him as a very clever man but "the most furious Protestant that ever was," while more than one historian has singled him out for the depth of his evangelical commitment. Yet his support of several of the policies most closely identified with the moderate evangelicals, whether emancipation, free trade, or bullionism, was often qualified. In this sense he personifies the reservations that have been expressed concerning the extent of evangelical influence. Indeed, he gives point to a recent caution concerning parties within the Church of England early in the nineteenth century. Instinctively orthodox in so many things, Goulburn was one of those Anglicans who blurred the edges of "orthodox" churchmanship and evangelicalism. He was certainly embraced by the definition of the former as "an attachment to the Church of England on purely doctrinal grounds and a conviction in favour of its divine authority and spiritual independence." As for the latter, his brand was never remotely Calvinist. He supported both orthodox and evangelical voluntary societies, drawing as he did a sharp distinction between moral and economic paternalism. In short, his religious affiliation serves as a reminder of his complexity and elusiveness as a man if not as a public figure.[4]

A gentleman, Goulburn was loath to speak ill of the living as well as of the dead. He was ever scrupulous as well as discreet. Even in his private correspondence with his wife and his closest political friend, he would reserve any matters he considered sensitive for discussion when they met. His diary was rarely more than an engagement book and an accounting of personal expenditures. Consequently, he presents a special problem for a biographer. Nor is the challenge reduced by a self-effacement that rarely brought the eyes of contemporaries sharply into focus when they did fall upon him. As a result, this account of his life and public career, which he considered as one, is heavily dependent on the work of others. There are, however, two collections of Goulburn Papers, the most substantial of which is to be found at the Surrey Record Office. Quotations are with the kind permission of the Surrey Record Office and the depositor. A second collection, dealing exclusively with Goulburn's negotiation of the Treaty of Ghent, is located in the William L. Clements Library of the University of Michigan. The library kind lent me a microfilm copy of these papers.

There is a substantial Goulburn correspondence in the papers of Sir Robert Peel, held by the British Library. I wish to thank the library for access to the Peel, Babbage, Bathurst, Gladstone, Hardwicke, Herries, Holland House, Huskisson, Liverpool, Perceval, Ripon, and Wellesley papers. A second Peel collection forms part of the Royal Archives at Windsor Castle, and quotations are from the microfilm edition with the gracious permission of Her Majesty the Queen. Quotations from the Trevelyan Papers are with the permission of the Robinson Library at the University of Newcastle upon Tyne and the Trustees of the Trevelyan Family Papers. I wish to thank the Earl of Harrowby for permission to quote from the Harrowby Manuscripts, Lord Sidmouth for permission to quote from the Sidmouth Papers, and the Department of Manuscripts and Special Collections, Hallward Library, University of Nottingham, for permission to quote from te Newcastle Manuscripts. Quotations from the Charles Wynn Papers in the Coed-y-Maen archive are with the permission of the National Library of Wales, and those from the Whitworth and Knatchbull collections with the permission of the Centre for Kentish Studies. I wish to thank Lambeth Palace Library for access to the Christopher Wordworth Papers. The records of the Bank of England are quoted with permission. Quotations from the Graham Papers are from the microfilm edition and with the permission of Sir Charles Graham. Those from the Adams Papers are from the microfilm edition and with the permission of the Massachusetts Historical Society. The Gallatin and Monroe Papers were also consulted on microfilm. Finally, I wish to express again my appreciation of the kindness of the late Major Richard Gregory, who loaned to me the Gregory collection, which is now held by the library of Emory University. Similarly, I wish to express special thanks to the Lord Hamilton of Dalzell who made available the copies of the Goulburn portraits which illustrate the text.

In closing, I acknowledge the staff of the Surrey Record Office, and I thank my friends Jim and Betsye Alexander who found for me a sabbatical haven in Georgia, where I wrote this book. My wife kept faith with this project even when that of the author wavered.

The youthful Edward Goulburn, Henry's brother.

St Peter's Church, the Alley, where Goulburn's slaves worshipped.

"The Moving of the Address to the Crown on the meeting of the first Reformed Parliament ... 1833," by Sir George Hayter (1792–1871). Peel and Goulburn sit close to the Speaker following displacement from their seats in the unreformed Commons. Peel is the figure in the light waistcoat, three seats to the left of the Speaker. Goulburn sits on his immediate left, partly overshadowed, as ever, by his friend. (National Portrait Gallery, London)

Henry Goulburn at age 49, a detail from Sir George Hayter's mass portrait of the meeting of the Reformed Parliament on 5 February 1833, given by the artist to the family.

Harry Goulburn. This incomplete portrait serves as a metaphor for a life cut tragically short. The artist is Thomas Wageman, who specialized in watercolours.

In this centennial depiction of the formal conclusion of the negotiations at Ghent, Henry Goulburn is the figure who has turned his back on the proceedings.

Henry Goulburn, 1784–1856

CHAPTER ONE

A Promising Young Man

Henry Goulburn exhibited little interest in his family tree which, notwithstanding its transplantation to the tropics, had produced a less than luxuriant foliage and all too few blooms. He understood that his ancestors had come from County Chester before migrating to Jamaica in the late seventeenth century. Had he been more concerned with his origins, he might have traced their roots back a further four hundred years when two of the sons of David de Malpas, lord of the moiety of the barony, had assumed the name of the manor of Golborne David. In styling themselves David de Golborne and William de Goulbourn, they were founding a tradition of variable spellings of the family name – Goldberne, Golburn, Golburne, Golbourne, Goulbourn, Goulbourne, and Goulburn. Further, the migration to Jamaica appears to have been led by two brothers, Edward Goulbourn and Henry Goulburne, and somewhat later than Goulburn understood. Their absence from the list of plantation owners compiled in 1754 suggests that they arrived on the island after that date, and so does the fact that they established themselves in the southern parish of Vere, for its development as a sugar producer occurred during the thirty-five years prior to the American Revolutionary War. However, they may have been distantly related to an established pair of landowners, George Goulbourn and Thomas Goulbourne.[1]

The Goulburn brothers were two in a seemingly endless line of adventurers and adventurous entrepreneurs who saw in the West Indies an opportunity for riches and ultimately for station. They evidently possessed capital, for they purchased a medium-sized estate of several hundred acres together with a small army of slaves. Astutely, they divided their labours. Edward raised the livestock to work a plantation, together with its feed, while Henry raised cane and produced sugar on the nearby estate of Amity Hall. Located alongside the Rio Minho, it was less than ten miles from the southernmost tip of the island and conveniently close to the port of Old Harbour.

Edward Goulburn married Thomasin Roberts, the daughter of an American merchant, and she bore him three children. Of their two daughters, the elder died in infancy, but in March 1758 Goulburn was presented with a son and heir, who was christened Munbee. Six months later Edward Goulburn was dead. Under the terms of his will, his brother assumed control of the livestock pen, working it in trust for his young nephew. At his own death in October 1765, Henry Goulburn – married but childless – made modest provision for his widow and settled a substantial sum on his niece Sarah, who had also been provided for in her father's will. "And all the rest of his estate both real and personal he gave unto his nephew M. Goulburn & his heirs, with remainder in case of his death before 21 years of age" to his niece "in tail general." But Henry's widow, a strong-willed and capable woman, declined to accept a mere £400 and the use of their dwelling house as full satisfaction for all her dower or thirds. Instead, under the laws and customs of the colony, she secured one-third part of her husband's real estate and "subsequently deducted and retained to her own use one third part of the net proceeds" of the properties. Further, as the sole executor of Henry's will and as the appointed guardian of her nephew and niece during their minorities, she remained in possession of the entire estate until Munbee came of age. Meanwhile, Thomasin Goulburn had remarried.[2]

The young heir was packed off to England for his education. The absence of schools had long been identified as "one of the principal impediments" to Jamaica's effectual settlement. On the other hand, the schooling received in England was scorned as entirely inappropriate to any useful employment in the colony. Moreover, the sons of wealthy planters had a distressing tendency to neglect their studies and "waste their patrimony in a manner that redounds not in the least to the national profit, having acquired a taste for pleasure and extravagance of every kind, far superior to the ability of their fortunes." All too often, in short, they behaved as if they had been sent "home" to "pass away their time agreeably, and that it is not meant they should perplex themselves with dry and obtuse literature, and their fortunes will enable them to live independent of science and business." Very few of them returned to the island.[3]

Munbee entered Eton in 1771, at a time when the school was in the midst of a decline. Enrolments were falling sharply even though Eton was then a less socially exclusive institution than it became in the nineteenth century. The children of ambitious tradesmen rubbed shoulders with aristocratic sprigs. Perhaps Munbee's most notorious fellow entrant that year was Richard Wellesley, the eldest son of a well-established but undistinguished Irish Ascendancy family, who had been expelled from Harrow for participation in a riot. Two generations later, the Goulburns and Wellesleys were again to be thrown together. Munbee Goulburn matriculated at Oxford at the age of seventeen. Although a young man of some academic ability, with a "more than average amount of literary acquirements," he appears to have been less interested in education than in the formation of useful social connections. He had to overcome the prejudice with which those whose fortunes had been made in the Indies, East as well as West, were regarded by the society to which they sought admission. Thus he spent lavishly on the pleasure of those persons whose company he sought and whose acceptance he craved.[4]

On coming of age in 1779, Munbee confirmed to his aunt "his satisfaction of all her transactions in & about the estates … with the accounts thereof kept by her during his minority." He had reason to be doubly grateful. She now surrendered to him her own real estate holdings, together with slaves, cattle, and stock, and released "all her dower or thirds & other claims at law & equity" in return for a modest annuity and the payment of some £9,000 to her estate. It was, he gratefully acknowledged, a generous arrangement on her part. Now a young man of considerable wealth if obscure origins, he was an eminently acceptable suitor for the daughter of a minor lord. A good marriage would be a significant step towards gentrification.[5]

The Chetwynds were a Staffordshire family whose ornate Jacobean hall at Ingestre had been set in grounds landscaped by Capability Brown. However, property and title had parted company on the death of the second viscount. The magnificent hall had gone to his daughter, who carried it into the Talbot family. Subsequently, the impecunious fourth viscount had been obliged to take up residence on the Continent, while his heir accepted a humble clerkship in the Home Office. The task of making a suitable match for the viscount's elder daughter, Susannah, therefore promised to be a challenge. She was not a young woman of obvious accomplishments, for her education had been neglected. What she did possess was a beauty that attracted the unwelcome attentions of the libertine Prince of Wales. More importantly, she proved to be a woman of fortitude and character. A strong mind, harmonizing as it did with a "nice perception of right and wrong," her admiring eldest son later recalled, well equipped her not only to resist the temptations of a dissolute society and to educate herself and ultimately acquire a "deep knowledge of religious truth," but also to carry her successfully through a life of both "chequered prosperity and adversity."[6]

The union of Munbee Goulburn and Susannah Chetwynd was very much a business transaction, but a mutual anxiety to effect the alliance induced a certain carelessness on the part of the negotiators for the bride and recklessness on the part of the groom. The young couple were introduced during the winter of 1781–82 at the London town house of a relative of the Chetwynds. There also Goulburn made his offer of marriage, and the attractions of the match were obvious. He estimated his annual income at never less than £5,000 and implied that the charges upon the sugar estate were negligible. Thus the Chetwynds accepted the proposal without hesitation, and the settlement was signed and sealed on 21 May 1782. Munbee, having specified the bequests of his father and his uncle to his sister, covenanted "that the Estate is free of all charges & incumbrances." There was no mention of his aunt's charges, an omission that he later blamed on his solicitor. Not that this explanation convinced everyone involved. The concealment of the claims amounted to "a Fraud upon the parties interested under the Settlement," one member of the Chetwynd family later deposed; the inadequate protection afforded Susannah Chetwynd arose from "the want of candour and veracity in the said Munbee Goulburn in not disclosing to the Parties interested, the real and just state of his affairs."7

The Goulburns had three children, all sons. The eldest, born in London on 19 March 1784, they christened Henry at the parish church of Marylebone. Although it had been rebuilt only forty years earlier, this plain brick oblong was by general consent too small and unprepossessing for the capital's "largest and most opulent" parish. There was not even a font for baptisms, merely a common basin set on the communion table. All too often, godparents were squashed together in such a disorderly fashion "that it was impossible for the minister to see many of them, or address and require them to make the responses, which the Rubrick directs." Limitations of space even on occasion obliged the living to share pews with the dead awaiting burial. As a result, "all reverence for the sacrament of baptism; all solemn and awful reflections from hearing one of the finest services ever composed, and on occasion the most interesting to the heart that can be imagined, are entirely done away, and the mind filled with horror and disgust." Not that the Goulburn baptism was celebrated in this macabre fashion. Instead, a parish clerk ruefully recalled twenty years later that he toasted the infant so often that he fell down and broke a thumb. But infancy proved to be a characteristically perilous time for Henry. A nurse sat on him. This accident left him with not only an indentation of his head but also permanently defective vision in his right eye. Hence Thomas Creevey's later cruel description of him as "cockeyed." Subsequently, he was carried off to France by his parents. They remained there for approximately two years, living first in Paris and then in Toulouse. Henry claimed that his earliest memory was of the packet boat carrying him back to England. By 1787 he had a brother, Edward, and Frederick was to be born the following year.[8]

The Goulburn family took up residence in Gloucestershire, renting Prinknash Park, which was owned by a family that was well connected in Jamaica. Here was an idyllic environment for an increasingly active child, anxious to explore his immediate world. A small manor house, it had been in turn a mill, a hunting lodge, and a residence of the abbots of Gloucester before the dissolution of the monasteries; parts of the building dated from the thirteenth century. There was a small chapel with painted glass and "many angels in their coronation robes," several "good rooms," and the promise of many nooks and crannies for an intrepid young explorer. The estate was as attractive as it was secluded. Set on the side of a horseshoe-shaped Cotswold hill, commanding a magnificent view of Gloucester four miles distant, whose cathedral tower could clearly be seen rising above the city, the house was surrounded by parkland and stood in its own "little forest of beech." It was here that Munbee, with the assistance of the local curate, set about the task of educating a first son who spoke better French than he did English. This was not an easy task, since the young Henry was by his own account a "passionate" child much given to tantrums. For them he suffered the traditional punishment of being locked in his room for extended periods, and like generations of children he exhibited considerable ingenuity in escaping from this form of confinement. Nevertheless, when his father dispatched him at the age of seven to Dr Moore's School at Sunbury, Henry found himself fully the equal of boys his own age in English and Latin. His difficulties remained behavioural. Still wilful and ill disciplined, his fits of temper brought merciless treatment at the hands of his fellow pupils. Then, on 29 November 1793, his father died suddenly.[9]

Munbee Goulburn's finances had become ever more complicated during the years of his marriage. He succumbed to the temptation of so many absentees – to live beyond his means. He mortgaged his estate on several occasions to cover his debts. He borrowed heavily from a Liverpool merchant, William Goore, to pay off the mortgage necessitated by his marriage settlement, and contracted in return to employ Goore as the agent for the sale of his produce at the northern port. Goore's claims against him at the time of his death approached £4,000. Further, Munbee had obtained land and slaves from his mother for which he ought to have paid her some £500 Jamaica a year, but content with her annuity from the estate of her second husband she had never claimed these monies. However, at her death in 1784, her bequests to her daughter raised the very real question of whether Munbee's sister was entitled to these arrears. Nor had he been any more successful in clarifying the situation left so murky in his marriage settlement – the substantial sums owed to his aunt and settled by her on his sister and another beneficiary. In 1791, as he struggled to service and even reduce his debts, he gave serious thought to ordering the entire sugar crop for the year shipped over to pay the trustees of his sister's marriage. Munbee's ultimate folly was to die intestate.[10]

Susannah Goulburn was as ill prepared for her husband's death as she was ill equipped to handle the consequences of his financial recklessness. Moreover, her health had already so far collapsed that she and Munbee had been planning to winter in Lisbon. Instead, she suddenly found herself besieged by his creditors and made the frightening discovery that the marriage settlement under which she was guaranteed at least £800 a year was "altogether a nullity." Alarmed and bewildered, she sold her husband's personal property and threw the family's affairs into the Court of Chancery. While the complicated problems at issue were being resolved, she assumed that she would be provided at least with the means both to maintain herself respectably and to educate her children. But the court was a notoriously dilatory and expensive institution.[11]

One immediate consequence of this crisis was severe domestic economies. Servants were released and the house that Munbee had acquired in Great Cumberland Place, Marylebone, was surrendered in favour of far more modest accommodation. The Goulburns moved first to a relatively small if recently constructed house in Manchester Street, a short distance north and east, and then to the outlying retreat of Acton. A rural area, five miles to the west on the Uxbridge Road, part of its appeal for Susannah Goulburn may have been the three wells of mineral water that had once made it fashionable. Meanwhile, Henry remained at Sunbury and was joined there by his brother Edward. However, when he fell victim to a severe eye infection that resisted medical treatment and temporarily deprived him of sight, he was withdrawn from the school and dispatched to Worthing, where the sea air eventually proved to be as therapeutic as his desperate mother had hoped. He was placed in the care of one of her sisters. With his recovery and the arrival of his brothers (for Susannah Goulburn could no longer afford to keep Edward at Sunbury and was then too unwell herself to care for her children), Henry temporarily assumed responsibility for the education of his siblings. In the process, he greatly improved his own grammar and his understanding of the less difficult Latin authors. After several months they returned to their mother's household, where they were provided with a tutor, though they did not benefit particularly from this more conventional arrangement. Perhaps because of their mother's reduced circumstances, their instructor possessed both limited knowledge and precious little teaching skill. After two years he was dismissed, and the decision was made to place Edward in the Royal Navy as a midshipman. Henry continued with his self-education, though he read only what interested him and initially demonstrated little aptitude for those fine arts, music and drawing, in which his mother sought to ground him.[12]

Throughout this difficult and trying period, Susannah Goulburn waited impatiently for a decision from the Court of Chancery. It mattered little that the members of the family disclaimed any wish to contest questions "unnecessarily" or that the widow and mother indicated her desire "to avoid the expense of a hopeless suit, particularly if any part of the costs would probably fall on the personal Estate." The court's taste was for "mature deliberation," and in this case, as in so many others, there were all too many opportunities to indulge it. There was a need to take the opinion of persons "conversant with the Laws of Jamaica" and the "acts of the Legislative assembly there." Then again, until it received a full accounting from the colony of the debts to be charged to the estate, and they had been settled, the court could not decide either Susannah Goulburn's or her children's shares of the personalty. Yet the manager of the plantation had forwarded such an accounting by the end of 1794, though a considerable period elapsed before he completed the inventory of personal property in Jamaica. Similarly, it was the end of 1796 before the emblements were finally and officially ascertained. The decision was then taken to sell sixteen slaves – that is, those over and above the number specified in the marriage settlement – to pay off Munbee's personal debts in the colony. Nevertheless, this essential information reached neither Susannah Goulburn nor the court in reasonable time. She long assumed that the source of this infuriating delay was in Jamaica, but eventually discovered that her many misfortunes included an inefficient and dishonest solicitor. As one defender of the much-abused court later observed, "the perplexity of Chancery details," the "tempers and objects of the parties, and the skill, activity and honesty of their respective agents" were the elements of the "real delay" in individual cases.[13]

Susannah Goulburn quickly turned her tangled affairs over to another solicitor, and her hopes of more rapid progress towards a settlement began to rise. However, she soon made a second disheartening discovery: the court would continue to proceed at its own time-consuming and income-generating pace. The Chancery Office was open so rarely that although she travelled up to town frequently, she found little opportunity to consult the master. Nevertheless, by the summer of 1800 it appeared that this frustrating business was at last coming to a close. But her optimism was misplaced. Before the year was out, she was dispiritedly complaining that "nothing can be more wearing than these unforeseen delays." The inventory of stores had been returned to Jamaica because it had not been submitted on stamped paper or been properly witnessed and sworn. Yet a few gains were made. Susannah Goulburn and her brother were appointed guardians of the children, and her sons' allowances were finally settled. Furthermore, in that brief flush of optimism, she had returned to Great Cumberland Place. While this decision soon became another source of financial embarrassment, as the proceedings in Chancery dragged on, it was to have a profound impact on the life of her eldest son. For it was during their brief second residence there that he came into contact with the Montagu family.[14]

Matthew Robinson was a younger son of a minor lord in the Irish peerage. Although ultimately to succeed to the title as the fourth Baron Rokeby, he had long since been more than happy to ensure his own and his family's fortunes by taking the married name of his paternal aunt. The widow of Edward Montagu, a grandson of the fourth Earl of Sandwich, she had been left a considerable estate by her late husband. Yet Elizabeth Montagu was a woman of distinction in her own right. The author of *Dialogues of the Dead* and *Essays on the Genius and Writings of Shakespeare*, she was one of a trio of London hostesses who determined to hold receptions at which intellectual conversation replaced the more fashionable diversion of card playing. Dramatists, orators, lawyers, clergy, ambassadors, and visiting foreign men of letters were all to be encountered at her gatherings, where she displayed her delicate social skills. She kept "us in constant good humour with ourselves, consequently with everything else," wrote one who knew her well. She had "quick parts, great vivacity, no small share of wit, a competent portion of learning, considerable fame as a writer, a large fortune, a fine house, and an excellent cook."[15]

With her seriousness of purpose, Elizabeth Montagu showed a lack of concern for convention with respect to "full dress," and thus one regular at her breakfasts and assemblies chose to wear grey or blue worsted rather than black silk stockings, a practice that led to the epithet "blue stockings" being attached to those who attended the gatherings. No less famous were her annual May Day receptions for the city's chimney sweeps, which were held in the extensive and well-wooded gardens of her mansion in Portman Square. It was another tribute to her good taste. She had been quick to recognize the talent of James Stuart, a fan painter turned architect, providing him with one of his earliest large commissions. His design for Montagu House combined Athenian grace with an attention to detail that impressed even the most discriminating visitors. On her death in August 1800 at the advanced age of eighty-six, Elizabeth Montagu bequeathed to her nephew not only this "noble, simple edifice" but a princely annual income. Dutifully, he edited and published four volumes of her epistolary works.[16]

Without exaggerating her literary attainments or overlooking the extent to which she was "oppressed by the load of her own superiority" (which led to the cold-shouldering of Dr Johnson for his "irreverent treatment" of her writings), Montagu celebrated his aunt as a "superior woman" and an example of the beneficial effects of education. Indeed, the education of both women and the lower orders was valued as a spur to the further improvement of the men of the higher orders. In short, although it was necessary "for the maintenance of their just authority, or what comes to the same thing, for the good of society, that the rich should be superior in knowledge to the poor, and men to women," there was no need for "recourse to artificial means to keep the storehouse of learning under lock and key, to prevent this order being subverted."[17]

Great Cumberland Place was only a short distance west of Portman Square, and since Montagu and Susannah Goulburn were already acquainted, perhaps as a result of her earlier residence there, the two families quickly developed an intimacy. Montagu interested himself in her legal problems and induced his friend Spencer Perceval to investigate her plight. An established lawyer and rising politician, Perceval had transferred his practice from King's Bench to the far more remunerative Chancery in 1802. His advice, given freely, was not to be scorned. Similarly, Montagu took a close interest in the future of Susannah's eldest son, who played so often with his own children.[18]

The early death of his father had accelerated Henry's transformation from wilful and self-centred child to adolescent. His sense of responsibility had been heightened by his role as his brothers' tutor and by his mother's growing dependence on him as the young man of the family. During her prolonged bouts of ill health, he had increasingly participated in the absentee supervision of the Jamaican sugar estate. In short, he had been obliged to act the part of the young adult. Denied the guidance of a father, he appears to have found a substitute in the person of Matthew Montagu. Montagu's integrity and trustworthiness inspired confidence, just as his high-mindedness invited emulation. It was Montagu who recommended that Henry Goulburn be prepared for admission to university. Education was an important element in the preparation of a gentleman for a life of social usefulness.

The college of choice was Trinity College, Cambridge, which both Montagu and Perceval had attended. A college fellow then residing in London for his rheumatism was employed as a tutor. He was the young man's first real instructor since leaving school at Sunbury, and his erudition and urbanity made a deep and lasting impression on his pupil. Excited by the world of knowledge to which he was exposed, Goulburn cheerfully commuted to the capital from the house his mother had taken on Ham Common for the summer of 1800. Lying on the edge of Richmond Park, directly across the Thames from Twickenham and Strawberry Hill, and famed for its "umbrageous walks" down to the river, the area was another secluded country retreat for gentry, successful businessmen, and literati. "Gardens, hedgerows, village churches, houses and walls with ivy growing about them, met the eye in all directions." Yet it was a long trek to town, some nine miles to Hyde Park Corner, and one that Goulburn repeated three times a week, though he returned home by coach in the evenings. Armed with a pocket edition of Horace, he read as he walked, and he always attributed his remarkable knowledge of that author to the passages he committed to memory during these hikes.[19]

Goulburn matriculated in 1801 at the age of seventeen and was duly admitted to Trinity. It had recently won recognition as the "first of the Cambridge colleges." He entered as a fellow-commoner, though he was later to regret the decision to enrol him in a class regarded as one of "rank and dignity." There was a clear hierarchy of undergraduate standings to which were attached a corresponding hierarchy of privileges. Fellow-commoners were only marginally less privileged than noblemen, being the offspring of gentry or commercial magnates. They were excused attendance at lectures and the great majority of college exercises. As a group, they enjoyed a well-deserved reputation for wealth and idleness. Certainly, there was a leisurely quality to their academic lives. At Trinity, they dined in hall at 2.30 PM and spent much of the rest of the day in coffee houses or engaged in a variety of sporting activities.[20]

Some did devote at least part of their time to learning, and Goulburn was one of them. An anxiety to impress his mentor and to assure his mother that her financial sacrifices on his behalf were not being wasted must surely have encouraged his diligent attendance at lectures. As a result, he was somewhat better prepared than most of his colleagues for the more rigorous examinations that had recently been instituted with the establishment of the Senate House tests. Goulburn was in the first class of each of the annual college examinations and he won a declamation prize. However, during his third year he relaxed. His rank, or so he later concluded, denied him the competition so important as a stimulus "to diligent exertion." He abandoned the study of mathmatics and chose to attend only those lectures that interested him or were given by lecturers he liked. Increasingly, he occupied himself with sports, principally shooting and rowing, and his vacations were no longer passed in study but were spent touring the dramatic landscape of North Wales and the Lake District. When Goulburn returned to the Senate House for his final year examinations, he was more concerned with keeping warm – for the weather was cold and there were no stoves to take the bite out of the air – than in parading his knowledge.[21]

The humiliating experience of now being bested by those whom he had passed earlier in his career served belatedly to goad Goulburn to greater intellectual effort, and he remained in college during the last long vacation to apply himself to composition and English history. But it was too little and too late, and he graduated without particular distinction in 1805 and took his MA in 1808. Goulburn's university career had done little, therefore, to correct those educational deficiencies that were the result of his family's fluctuating fortunes. He had gone too long as a child without a competent tutor. By his own admission, he left Cambridge with an inadequate knowledge of mathematics and a mere smattering of anatomy, chemistry, and physics. In short, Goulburn was all too aware of his modest educational attainments, and this self-consciousness no doubt played some part in explaining why, when he turned to politics for a career, he long proved to be a hesitant and ineffectual speaker in the Commons. Certainly, he later regretted that he had not been better fitted by his education for the duties that devolved upon him. On the other hand, he belonged to the first generation of young men to be exposed to heads of colleges who had rediscovered their didactic purpose. They reinforced the prestige of church and university and thus strengthened the resistance of the young to "the metaphysical subtleties which [had] thrown half of the nations of Europe into confusion." Goulburn appears to have been one of those young men who, raised against a background of political turmoil and war, and suffering from considerable personal insecurity, was drawn instinctively to conservative values as a bulwark of order and stability.[22]

Goulburn's religion was to enhance these values. He had been raised in a pious household, and the duty of daily attendance at chapel was for him no burden at Cambridge. More importantly, his faith now acquired an evangelical hue. There were several outposts of evangelicalism in the university, with William Farish based at Magdalene and Isaac Milner presiding over a transformed Queen's College. But the heart and soul of the movement was Charles Simeon, who had been a contemporary of Munbee Goulburn at Eton. Whether from his pulpit in Holy Trinity

Church, in his university sermons, or privately in his rooms at King's College, Simeon influenced successive generations of undergraduates. Perhaps Goulburn was one of that body of gownsmen whom Arthur Young noted in the congregation of Holy Trinity when he visited Cambridge in 1804. Almost certainly, he was a participant in Simeon's conversation classes. For Goulburn was later to be described as a "saint" who had given "lectures" in his rooms at Cambridge through which he "caught several young men."[23]

Simeon was at the height of his powers, physical and intellectual, by the time Goulburn arrived at Cambridge. He was an evangelical who spoke more often of joy than severity, who deplored extremism, and carefully distanced himself from the doctrine of predestination by preaching that salvation was available to everyone. He insisted that his zeal was entirely consistent with "the rules of order of the Church." The fact that he was a parish clergyman as well as a college fellow symbolized the attachment. Significantly, he was hostile to Dissent and opposed Catholic emancipation. He stressed the primacy of the Bible but venerated the Prayer Book, "because he found that it was soaked in the spirit and steeped in the language of the Bible." Similarly, his sermons were vehicles for teaching scriptural truth and thus were prepared with painstaking care.[24]

Henry Goulburn's own requests to God were that his religion be made deeper and more serious, that he be humbled with true feelings of repentance, that all his thoughts, words, and actions be regulated according to Christian standards, that he be delivered from a listless spirit and protected from the enervating effects of home life, and that he be blessed with a genuine desire and the self-denial to be useful. And like Simeon, his authority was the Bible supplemented by the Book of Common Prayer. The importance he attached to sermons was later reflected in the instruction to his eldest son to take notes on those to which he listened. Nor could there be any doubt of Goulburn's "loving obedience to his Church." Indeed, he was both evangelical and orthodox. He was to subscribe not only to the Eclectic Society, the Church Missionary Society, the Bible Society, and the Prayer Book Society, but also to the Society for the Propogation of the Gospel and the Society for the Promotion of Christian Knowledge. Similarly, while he made a commitment to good works (the "only sure evidence of conversion"), and while his choice of charities attested to an evangelical's belief that assistance to the needy ought to be founded on the recipient's moral worth, his philanthropy was invariably connected with the establishment. Indeed, it might be said of Goulburn, as it was much later of his closest political friend, Robert Peel, that "his piety was genuine, but neither complex not articulated." Never "an abstract theorist," he always considered himself "a pillar of the Church of England and of the established constitution."[25]

There was another and more traditional way in which Cambridge served Goulburn well. He formed friendships and connections that in some cases were to prove lifelong. Among his closest friends were Frederick Robinson, a future prime minister; Hugh Percy, a future bishop; Lords Clonmel and Royston; and, for several years, Henry Temple, who had just succeeded to his Irish peerage as the third Viscount Palmerston. He and Goulburn were fellow members of an exclusive debating society, drawn at the time from their respective ranks, nobleman and fellow-commoner, and their respective colleges, St John's and Trinity. The political nature of their discussions and papers ensured that it remained a "private" society, for the university authorities discouraged such activities during wartime. Thus Goulburn's membership suggested both a growing interest in political issues and a youthful willingness at times to challenge authority. Simultaneously, he put his patriotism on parade. He secured a captaincy in the Duke of Gloucester's volunteer infantry and was surely a member of the militia organized by the undergraduates.[26]

Throughout her son's undergraduate years, which coincided with what remained of his minority, Susannah Goulburn continued to find herself financially embarrassed. Although the Court of Chancery did eventually free her modest jointure, she declined to dip into the liberal allowance provided for Henry's education other than to pay his actual expenses. She even paid his private tutor's salary, though it amounted to almost half her personal income. Consequently, she was always in difficulty. She was temporarily rescued by her sister, who advanced in the form of a loan, secured by a life insurance policy, her entire fortune of £5,000. Unfortunately, the cost of the insurance, and the charges for the dilapidation of the house in Great Cumberland Place, which she had again to give up, still denied her any sense of financial security. So, in 1802, accompanied by a single maidservant, a young orphan girl she had raised, Susannah Goulburn moved to Britton's Lodgings, Hampstead. She took rooms large enough to accommodate both her youngest son, Frederick, and Henry when he returned home from college. The attraction of the village for a chronic invalid was its reputation for clean air, which often saw doctors prescribe a period of convalescence there. Since it was a fashionable summer resort frequented by the "respectable and rich" and therefore also favoured, not surprisingly, by artists and authors, residence there would not automatically be regarded as evidence of reduced circumstances, though this was the case with the Goulburns.[27]

While in Hampstead, Henry Goulburn continued to associate with persons of rank and wealth in London, who were unaware that he was obliged to perform the duties of a butler by cleaning his own clothes and even preparing the family breakfast. If the fear that his friends would discover this secret heightened the young man's reserve, which increasingly saw him mask his innermost self, he manfully bore the public indignity of supervising the sale of much of his mother's plate. He went along to a shop in Cockspur Street to watch as each item was taken from the plate chest, weighed, appraised, and the price affixed. The proceeds of the sale, together with a small contribution of his own, of which his mother remained unaware, and his success in persuading his aunt to forgo the insurance policy on her loan in return for his guarantee to repay the debt when he came of age, allowed him finally to guarantee his mother a constant and adequate income. It was sufficient to permit her to take a house in Phillimore Place, Kensington, where she was to remain until her death in 1818.[28]

Goulburn's financial arrangements on his mother's behalf did not resolve the family's problems. Edward had soon tired of life in the navy and had secured a commission in the Royal Horse Guards, or "Blues." There he promptly fell into bad company and debt. His was the familiar story of the very young man – he was still only sixteen – who succumbs to the notorious temptations of a military life. Henry came to his rescue by agreeing to settle with his creditors as soon as he himself came of age, but there was little he could do when his irresponsible brother landed himself in a legal scrape. Edward had published a satyrical poem, which cast his fellow officers in so unflattering a light that they had launched an action for libel. Happily, he escaped with only a week's detention, but he continued to be a sore and expensive trial to his elder brother. His gaming debts and tradesmen's bills invariably exceeded his income, part of which he chose to invest in racehorses, and on more than one occasion he had to be bailed out of custody and saved from importunate creditors. Yet when in 1805 Henry was at last in a position to aid his brother, he made the disappointing discovery that his expectations of wealth had been inflated. He had calculated that his plantation was producing £4,000 a year after all charges and thus that a very large sum must have accumulated during the twelve years when the income had largely been locked up in Chancery. Hence his dismay when he realized that almost half this sum had been eaten up by expenses. Still, he was able to repay his aunt's loan, to discharge his brother's debts, to rent a house in Upper Seymour Street, off Portman Square, and then to return to 2 Great Cumberland Street for the season. He threw himself heartily into the social round of balls, assemblies, and the opera. He had come to love music, the enjoyment of which he considered entirely consistent with his evangelical Anglicanism. Also, he was enabled to purchase a seat in Parliament.[29]

The general election of 1806 had seen Goulburn's friend Palmerston stand for the parliamentary borough of Horsham, Sussex. This borough was an electoral anachronism, even in the early nineteenth century. Less than four score of the more than three thousand residents were voters. Moreover, the franchise was attached to specific pieces of property, however humble, and to plots of land that in Horsham varied in area from a few square feet to several acres. No matter how many of these "burgages" an individual held or occupied, he could cast only a single vote for each of the borough's two seats. Therefore, just before an election, there were formal but temporary transfers of burgages to trusted agents, who were thereby enfranchised. Alternatively, long freehold leases might be offered at insignificant rents, though this device threatened to render the voter dangerously independent. Indeed, it was unclear whether the vote was vested in the landlord or the tenant, and there was considerable confusion about whether votes could be multiplied by the simple device of subdividing burgages. Furthermore, in Horsham the control of this valuable piece of political property by the Irwin family was being contested by the Duke of Norfolk, a Whig, who was the lord of the manor. His challenge in 1790 had been beaten back on the strength of the Irwins' split burgages.[30]

Palmerston agreed to pay the Irwins the current asking price of four thousand guineas (while the duke was willing to sell to a fellow Whig for the lesser sum of four thousand pounds). The four thousand guineas bought Palmerston the seat for the life of one Parliament, if he was elected. There was also a clear understanding that, in return for an advance, the costs of fighting any challenge would be borne by the Irwins and that full payment would not be expected until Palmerston was securely seated. This proved to be a prudent piece of insurance. Norfolk had been quietly dividing burgages and thus greatly increasing the number of votes under his control. Conversely, having concluded that divided burgages were of doubtful legality, the Irwins had been steadily consolidating their former parts into whole burgages. The upshot was an apparent victory in November for Norfolk's candidates. The result was immediately challenged by the Irwins' agents, on the grounds of the illegality of divided burgages. Although the bailiffs who served as returning officers were the duke's men, they had no desire to expose themselves to costly damages by ruling against the Irwins, so they declared all four candidates elected and left it to the House of Commons to decide which two should be seated. The Commons struck a committee, which in January 1807 unanimously decided in favour of Norfolk's candidates. For Palmerston, the disappointment of this reverse was soon eased by the dissolution of May 1807. Had he been declared a victor, he would have paid well over £1,300 for each month that he sat in Parliament.[31]

In 1807, Goulburn decided to try his luck and tax his purse in Horsham. Like Palmerston, he contracted with the Irwins and insured himself in the same manner. He went through the farce of canvassing those who claimed to be independent burgage holders, though, as he later recalled, his "pretensions to represent the Place" were founded less on his political principles than "on the question whether entire or divided burgages conferred the right of voting." After the poll on 11 and 12 May, the returning officers declared Norfolk's Whig candidates duly elected. The Irwins again challenged the result, and the Commons again investigated. Witnesses were again summoned to London at considerable expense to appear before the committee, which began its hearings on 11 February 1808. The members heard "the same questions and answers, put and obtained by almost the same Counsel." However, this time the Irwins' case was argued more skilfully. Their agent persuaded a majority of the committee that it should recognize only those divided burgages that had been duly registered some time before the election. Not unexpectedly, a sufficient number of those who had voted for the Whigs were discovered not to have been so registered, and the result was therefore reversed. One advantage of this belated return was Goulburn's escape of the traditional and boisterous post-poll "chairing" of successful candidates. Significantly, at the end of his life he opened his memoir with his election to Parliament, for this was the event which in his opinion "gave the colour to the whole" of his future life.[32]

A gentleman of means, Goulburn had neither the need nor the inclination to turn to a profession such as law. Instead, like his mentor Montagu, who enjoyed something of a reputation as "a frequent and tolerable good speaker in Parliament," he intended to fulfil the obligation of wealth and privilege – public service. Goulburn was convinced that God had cast his lot in public life, and Simeon had taught that service to God required "proper everyday conduct *in* the world." Moreover, the "opportunities for usefulness which were open to a politician seemed almost unlimited." "What a glorious place is the House of Commons. What an arena for the display of intellectual powers," gushed one political matron. "What a glorious field for the understanding, to see the ablest and best informed members of Society using their utmost means to do their *best*." Goulburn had been offered a seat in the previous Parliament, but carrying as it did the condition of support for the Whiggish government of Lord Grenville, he had declined a nomination that was so "inconsistent" with his "views of Public Policy." The Whigs did not profess a "sentimental loyalty to the Crown as the symbol of constitutional order and to the established Church as representing the highest ideal of national life." Further, their willingness to tamper with the constitution, not least by making concessions to Roman Catholics, whose number within the Protestant state had been greatly increased as a result of the recent union with Ireland, excited fears that they might prove mere stalking horses for radicalism. Finally, their ambivalent response to the long struggle against France left them vulnerable to the charge of defeatism. Their fall from power in 1807 and the appointment of the Portland ministry, in which Spencer Perceval was recognized as a dominant figure, suddenly made entrance to Parliament a far more inviting proposition for Goulburn.[33]

Goulburn's attachment to Perceval, as to Matthew Montagu, was both personal and political. Although disparaged by some critics as a small man with a small mind, the new chancellor of the exchequer provided a model for a serious, sober, and evangelical young man. As the acerbic Sydney Smith later recalled, Perceval was everything that John Bull admired – moral, religious, a devoted husband and father, quiet, meek but with the heart of a lion, and able to make "oppression and humbug respectable by his decent character and admirable demeanour, and his skill in debating." Exemplary in his private life, good humoured and unassuming, Perceval was "personally one of the most attractive figures of his age." As another observer wrote, he was well suited to a nation that accepted private virtue as a substitute for almost any political defect. The personal attraction for Goulburn was enhanced by the assistance Perceval had given to his mother. Politically, Perceval was a Pittite who regarded the late statesman as the nation's saviour during the turmoil and danger of the French wars. Yet his own conservatism was sharper edged than that of his master. He gloried in the balance of the constitution, which he considered to be endangered not by any action of the crown but by the turbulence of the mob. Furthermore, he shared the monarch's views on the simmering Catholic question to a degree that Pitt never had. Parliament had a responsibility to exclude from authority and office persons whose religious opinions it considered a threat to the constitution. Yet in proclaiming his opinion that "the Dissenter of any kind has *no right* to office," Perceval was careful to avow "that dissenters of all kinds have the most perfect right to toleration." On the other hand, he saw no injustice in requiring Roman Catholics to support the Protestant establishment. Equally, he reasoned that to concede the injustice of tithes on grounds of conscientious scruple would provide a powerful and persuasive precedent for any person required to support an establishment he did not like. These were the opinions of a "devoted adherent of the Crown, and a pious son of the Church," and the young Goulburn was quick to embrace them. Although he may have first been attracted to conservatism by a need for security at a time of great anxiety, both personal and national, it was Perceval, and to a lesser extent Montagu, who offered him a reassuring ideology – "the defence of the monarchy, the established church and private property."[34]

However evolutionary the "conservative case," it had received a revolutionary spur. Conservatives defined themselves and their ideology more sharply in opposition to the doctrines espoused in France after 1789 and against the course of the events in that country. Certainly, throughout his life, Goulburn professed to have been profoundly influenced by his youthful recollections of the French Revolution, which excited in him "a perfect horror of Republican propagandism" and "Democratic principles." Pitt had excoriated the Rights of Man as a monstrous and subversive doctrine. The majority had no right to alter the structure of a society that rested "upon an immutable moral standard that emanated from God." As for apparent social inequities, they were counterbalanced by the reality of the "mutual dependence" of all ranks. For example, the working poor were invariably blessed with good health, while the rich suffered the "disappointment, disgust, and indisposition both of body and mind" induced by luxuries. Moreover, people's natural inequalities, physical and intellectual, ensured that the advantages they derived were also unequal. Hence the value of the law to the weak – it defended them against the strong.[35]

If society protected both persons and property, the security of the latter became a fundamental tenet of the emerging conservative coalition. Property was wealth in all its forms, but especially in land. The greater a man's property, the greater was his interest in the defence and progress of the state that protected it, and therefore large property holders were natural governors. A government founded on property "guaranteed stability, equal civil rights and proper reward to industry and skill." Thus it mattered little how few were the electors who returned the present members of Parliament, or that many of them purchased their seats or were nominated by great landed proprietors. What was more important was that they provided "virtual" representation for all classes of Britons and were united by a common interest in good legislation. Conservatives genuinely believed that the electoral system did return the men most likely "to promote the general interest."[36]

What then of liberty? Liberty was "the permission, or right, to engage in any activity which did not injure the property and interest of any other individual, or the general interest of society, to use one's talents and labour to acquire property of one's own, and to be protected in the use and enjoyment of that property." The rule of law was thus essential to the enjoyment of liberty, and conservatives saw the existing constitution as its mainstay. They also valued religion for teaching subordination and providing another bulwark both of social control and of the existing social hierarchy. The founding of charity schools and then of Sunday schools drew strength if not inspiration from the conviction that docility could be taught to the children of the poor along with piety. The difficulty, as some observers uneasily noted, was how to restrict the poor, once they had acquired a rudimentary education, to reading only selections from the Bible and the tracts that flowed from the inspired pen of that evangelical champion of the established order, Hannah More.[37]

Goulburn's faith bolstered his political ideology. Most evangelicals were natural Tories, convinced as they were of humanity's sinfulness, fearful as they were of "the loneliness of liberty," and craving as they were for authority and obedience. They considered the social order itself to be God given. To challenge it was evidently an admission of doubt of God's providential goodness. For his part, Goulburn later claimed that from the moment of his entry into political life, he sought "to maintain the established institutions of the Country, to advance the cause of Religion and Learning, and to uphold, as essential to both, the interests of the University and of the Established Church." This credo indicates his affinity with the "rising generation of conservative scholars who emerged at Oxford and Cambridge from the 1790s onwards." These "Noetics," as they came to be called at Oxford, emphasized the "attainment of virtue through moral discipline" and the peculiar attributes of the higher orders of society. Only the rich could "exercise the higher virtues, such as benevolence, which are motivated by duty *alone.*" In brief, they believed in a strict social hierarchy as well as political conservatism.[38]

It was appropriate that Goulburn entered Parliament in 1807. William Pitt's supporters had coalesced to oppose the Grenville ministry in a systematic way that their dead leader would never have sanctioned. After all, he had always described himself as an enemy of "party." In the general election, they skilfully polarized opinion on the issue of the king's resistance to a confused and bungled ministerial effort to effect a minor measure of Catholic relief. The Anglican clergy, as a "distinct interest," was galvanized as never before, and the party labels, Tory and Whig, were again freely employed. The year 1807 also witnessed the beginning of a surge in evangelical membership of the Commons. Indeed, Goulburn might also have been represented as one of those "new men" now entering Parliament whose wealth was rooted in either commerce or industry. But like so many others of that class, he was closely bound to the traditional landed elite. His mother's family may have been impoverished, but she provided him with valuable links to the ruling class into which he was soon to marry; though his connections did not save him from being regarded with lordly disdain by at least one aristocratic upstart and a Whig magnate.[39]

In his anxiety to be sworn as a member, Goulburn rode down to the House of Commons only to be halted at the door for a breach of etiquette. He was wearing boots, and they were reserved for county members. Embarrassed and annoyed, he was obliged to borrow a pair of shoes from a colleague in which he was then admitted and duly sworn. He found himself surrounded by a number of familiar faces. Matthew Montagu was there, as were, from his own generation, Palmerston and Robinson, together with several other college friends and acquaintances, such as Robert Milnes and Charles Manners Sutton. Before long they and a number of other young men, who eventually included Robert Peel and John Wilson Croker, began "to live much together" and to dine at the Alfred Club each Wednesday. Well equipped, with a library and subscriptions to the major periodicals, the Alfred was one of those clubs of the "higher order." "We are the most abused, and most envied, most laughed at, and most canvassed society that I know of," one member later remarked, "and we deserve neither the one nor the other distinction." Theirs was an association not "for mere conviviality, but for intercourse upon a broader scale; political, literary, scientific, dramatic, and objects more diversified." This group of new young members was united by political sentiments and literary tastes, composing poetry as well as exchanging opinions. They were to be mocked for their earnestness and for their addiction to political gossip, but in their own minds they were merely taking their duties seriously. Perhaps looking to the future, they were consciously preparing themselves for the additional responsibilities of office.[40]

To that end, the Alfred became a haven of a liberal Toryism in economic matters. Coming down from the two old universities, its members were influenced by evangelicalism and the doctrines of Noetics. Moderate evangelicals, such as Goulburn, had a neutral conception of providence, and they reasoned that if God ran the material world with a minimum of interference, men could do no better than follow his example. "They were confident that *laissez-faire* policies would reveal a providential order and that the order would be a just one." Similarly, the Noetics, with their novel combination of natural theology and political economy, sought to "maximize economic development without shaking the social or political *status quo*." But the importance of ideology as a driving force of change as of personal conduct should not be exaggerated. No less important was the recognition that the long conflict with France had necessitated a significant enlargement of the state and a dramatic increase in its responsibilities. At the same time, "there was a growing awareness that Britain's ability to defend herself against larger powers depended critically on the pace of economic development" and that this in turn had been fostered by a considerable measure of freedom. Cheap government and freer trade were regarded as fundamental to the capitalist expansion, which guaranteed strength and promised social stability. And as advocates of a smaller, more efficient state, of liberalized trade and less economic paternalism, of retrenchment and debt reduction, these emerging liberal Tories could claim to be the heirs of the pragmatic Pitt.[41]

Goulburn attended the House faithfully and was soon placed on the Election Committee. He also exercised the right to attend any private committee and to vote on any matter that was referred to it. He intended at this early stage in his career to keep a meticulous record and explanation of every vote he cast, but this resolution proved to be as transitory as those made every new year. Slowly but surely he acquired an understanding of parliamentary procedure and business. And it was during this period that he made the acquaintance of the future Duke of Wellington, Sir Arthur Wellesley, who, between military commands, was serving briefly as chief secretary of Ireland. The two men often dined together in the kitchen, which was then the usual place of parliamentary refreshment, and it was there that they laid the foundation of an association which endured until Wellington's death and which Goulburn described as the "most fortunate circumstance" of his life.[42]

Goulburn dutifully supported the government. It was not until 24 February 1809, however, that he delivered his maiden speech. The occasion was an opposition assault on the failed military expedition to Spain led by Sir John Moore, a failure which the Whigs attributed to ministerial mismanagement and a lukewarm commitment to the enterprise. Goulburn rose to his feet at the same time as George Canning, and the foreign secretary gave way to him as a new member, perhaps recalling that moment fifteen years earlier when, fortified with "a bit of cold meat and a glass of white wine" as an antidote to "a sensation of *sinking* and emptiness," he had faced this same ordeal. Trembling with nervousness, Goulburn feared that he had lost both sight and understanding as he glanced down at his notes. But he managed to get through his short and intensely partisan speech. He excoriated the opposition: "The accusation of failure ... came with bad grace from individuals whose Administration was a succession of failures." And he defended the campaign as one that was productive of far from inconsiderable benefits – the army had acquired valuable experience, and

Europe had been reminded that Britain was formidable on land as well as at sea, while she had demonstrated her ability to produce commanders fully capable of matching "the titled minions of Bonaparte." Finally, he denounced the call for an inquiry on the grounds that it would serve only to paralyse the country. Writing to the king, Spencer Perceval drew George III's attention to this promising young man. But despite the congratulations of friends and the compliments of colleagues, Goulburn was not persuaded of the quality of his effort. In his nervousness, he had omitted what he considered the best part of his argument. Nor did the parliamentary reporter consider it worthy of inclusion in the record of the debate. Still, Goulburn was able to count himself fortunate in one respect. Soon after he sat down and Canning again rose, word reached the Commons that the Drury Lane Theatre was on fire, and before long "the immense blaze of light from the conflagration shone in at the windows of the House, as strongly as if it had been in the Speaker's garden." Here was a distraction with which no inexperienced speaker could possibly have contended. Witnessing the tumult, Goulburn offered up a silent prayer of thanks that he had been spared this bedlam.[43]

That there were limits even to his loyalty to Perceval, Goulburn soon made clear. He refused to enlist in his leader's gallant if misguided effort to protect the Duke of York, the commander-in-chief of the army, from the consequences of the scandalous and corrupt activities of his mistress. The evidence that several of the ministry's "staunchest friends," notably Goulburn, were planning to vote for crippling amendments to Perceval's supportive motion induced one member of the government to argue that only the duke's resignation could stave off defeat. In the event, Perceval secured from the Commons a resolution declaratory of the duke's innocence, and with this face-saving statement York resigned his post.[44]

As the session neared its close, Goulburn decided to travel to Portugal and Spain in order to see firsthand the progress of the Peninsular War in which Arthur Wellesley was so distinguishing himself and Goulburn's younger brother Frederick was serving. Before sailing, he was obliged to try yet again to restore some order to his other brother's finances. Edward had again run up substantial debts, and Goulburn suffered the acute embarrassment of being mistaken for him and briefly being arrested by one of Edward's creditors. He now agreed to pay off some £2,000 for which he was liable as a guarantor of Edward's notes, but he issued a stern warning: "I never will again pay down a sum of money for the discharge of your incumbrances." What he did agree to do was to pay Edward a regular allowance that was sufficient to keep him from "the extremity of distress" until he was able to support himself. These payments were to begin from the moment Henry left for the Iberian Peninsula, and during this absence he suggested that Edward seek refuge from his creditors on the Isle of Man. In making this arrangement, Goulburn re-emphasized the extent to which his brother's constant irresponsibility was exhausting his patience and running down his account. "I confess myself unable to discover the utility of ruining myself because you are ruined already," he wrote, "or of blasting all my hopes and prospects forever in feeding a disorder which I am more and more convinced every day is in you incurable." This attempt at shock therapy did not succeed. Indeed, in the opinion of his ever-indulgent mother, it drove Edward ever deeper into the arms of the "worst kind of society."[45]

Goulburn set out from London on 3 July 1809, travelling slowly and uncomfortably by coach through the undulating countryside of southwest England. His destination was the port of Falmouth, where the tattered remnants of Sir John Moore's command had landed six months earlier. Sourly, he dismissed it as the dirtiest town he had ever seen and his inn as the worst in England. "You cannot conceive the gratification it would be to meet some face that one had seen before," the urbane young politician confided to his mother. "Everybody here is dirty and it is impossible not to wish oneself anywhere else." At least his vessel, the *Princess Elizabeth*, inspired confidence. She was reputed to sail superbly, and her armament of ten guns promised security against any roving French privateer. Goulburn boarded her on 8 July with his companion William Ponsonby, a member of the prominent Whig family, who also had a brother serving with Wellesley. With the assistance of a brisk northerly wind, the ship made good time. Apart from the inevitable initial queasiness, Goulburn survived the voyage without discomfort, and on 14 July they sighted the rock at Lisbon. The state of the tide prevented them from immediately passing the bar, but the following day they stood in for the port. Goulburn was pleased by his ability to make himself understood by the Portuguese pilot, though it had been on his Spanish that he had worked hard in preparation for the expedition.[46]

The city was attractively situated, built on a series of hills, but the narrow and rough streets lined by lofty stone buildings gave areas of it a "sombre" appearance, or so Goulburn thought. Thus walking was "no slight fatigue" and was destructive of one's boots. These were not his only complaints. "Everything is thrown out into the street," he wrote to his mother, "and the stink is what you cannot conceive easily." "Had my nose possessed that sense of smelling which yours does I must have died of anything but aromatic pain." He attended a dramatic production with an appropriately patriotic plot, but was impressed neither with the play nor the performers. "The Ballet shewed nothing more than that those whom Nature seems to have interdicted from moving are capable of dancing in a way to please the Portuguese." As for the ordinary people, he considered them somewhat exotic. All were surprisingly dark complexioned, the women were unattractive, many of the "lowest orders" were "decorated with old cocked hats," and some strode around in "great cloaks," while others were not "overburthened with clothing at all." Happily, the capital was blessed with a British hotel, which not only commanded magnificent views of the entire area but was kept by an Englishman, was staffed largely with English servants, and was "totally comfortable."[47]

Late in the afternoon of 20 July, after four days of exploration and sightseeing, Goulburn and Ponsonby set out for Cintra. This town was notorious in Britain because of the generous convention with the French to which it had given its name, but Goulburn discovered it to be a place of surpassing beauty. Hills covered with fruit trees, and gardens filled with orange groves, vines, and geraniums all added to its natural beauty and perfumed the very air. "It is a perfect land of Goshen," he noted, "no mosquitoes here and scarcely any flies." Were it but in England, this young nationalist added, "it would be the most charming place in the world." From Cintra they advanced northwards in easy stages, a few miles each day on mules, usually travelling in the relative cool of the late afternoon. The first stop was Mafra, then on to Tôrres Vedras, which was soon to be rescued from obscurity by Wellesley. They paid a flying visit to the battlefield of Vimeiro, where they were amazed at the absence of destruction, before retracing the line of Wellesley's advance in 1808 – Roliça, Obidos, Caldes. At the last town, a spa whose waters Goulburn likened to those of Harrogate (and considered nearly as disagreeable in smell), they had the good fortune to meet up with the British ambassador to Portugal, John Villiers. Gratefully, they accepted his invitation to accompany him as far as Oporto. Goulburn had quickly realized that among the inconveniences of travel in the peninsula were the difficulties of finding comfortable accommodation and appetizing food. Once they joined the ambassador's party, they were assured of greater security en route, a colourful reception in each town and village, even to the extent of a twenty-one-gun salute in Oporto, and adequate food and accommodation. Even so, Goulburn found himself on occasion expected to sleep three in a room, "which is a portuguese custom adopted in the best houses." [48]

Oporto impressed him. "The town is in every respect the best I have seen," he recorded. "It is as well built and much cleaner than Lisbon and not inferior to it in beauty of situation. The shores of the Douro rise perpendicularly on each side of the town." The river provided an alternative means of transportation as they headed inland to the fortified town of Almeida. In travelling upriver, progress was slowed by a series of natural obstacles. Consequently, the two Englishmen had time to admire the grapevines, which appeared to grow even on rock and yet yielded the wine that occupied "the whole of the attention of the inhabitants of these provinces." Goulburn sampled the local product but confessed that he had no taste for wine – a discovery that did much to ease his subsequent conversion to a life of temperance. He was astonished "that so little pains should have been taken to improve the navigation of a river on which so material a branch of Portuguese trade" depended. Perhaps there was some truth to the claims of shippers, whose large share of the profits of the trade excited such envy among the growers, that the costs of transportation in Portugal were disproportionately high.[49]

At Almeida Goulburn heard the first detailed reports of the battle of Talavera, which included the disturbing news that his brother's regiment had suffered heavy casualties. Anxious for more information and thinking that he would obtain it in Perales, where William Beresford's Anglo-Portuguese force was understood to be headquartered, he hurried on into Spain. However, he and Ponsonby encountered a Portuguese commander whose difficulties with English prompted them to resort to their fluent French rather than halting Spanish, and this heightened the commander's suspicion that they were spies. Happily, their passports and a stroke of good fortune – their encountering Beresford's ADC – saw them safely through this experience. Even more welcome was the ADC's information that both their brothers were uninjured. At Taryar, they caught up with Beresford and the greater part of his army, and shortly afterwards they at last made contact with elements of Wellesley's force near Caceres. Henry found his brother Frederick fit and well.[50]

The troops that Goulburn and Ponsonby joined were evidently in retreat. Scornful of the conduct of the Spanish commander Cuesta and his men, and increasingly frustrated by the failure of the Spanish authorities to provide him with promised provisions, Wellesley had become alarmed for the security of his communications with Portugal and had begun a slow withdrawal from Spain. His temper was not improved by Spanish complaints that he had failed to follow up the success at Talavera and that his men were plundering the supplies intended for their troops; and he was further enraged by Cuesta's abandonment to the French of 1,500 wounded British soldiers who had been entrusted to his protection. Even Cuesta's fortuitous removal from command as a result of a stroke failed to ease the tension or halt the British retreat. Wellesley (who was now on the eve of his elevation to the peerage as the first Duke of Wellington) and the main body of his men paused at Badajoz, and it was there that Goulburn eventually caught up with them.[51]

Goulburn's experiences and observations in Portugal and Spain shook his confidence in his nation's Iberian allies. In Lisbon, he had concluded that the admiration of the British rested on no more secure a foundation than the population's perception that they were the stronger side in the war. "Were any reverse experienced," he added, "there are many who would be very ready to court the conquerors by sacrificing the conquered." Nor was he impressed with the ill-clothed and, in his opinion, ill-disciplined and unreliable Portuguese army. Once he crossed the border, he was quick to give voice to the all-too-common British disdain for the Spanish. They were "indolent and insolent," too "idle" to get you something from the next room, and so "imposing" as to attempt to cheat you when giving change. Similarly, lacking any true understanding of the political and military consequences of the national uprising of 1808, he was scornful of a Spanish army whose officers appeared without cravats and whom he likened in their dress to gentlemen who had been awakened at five o'clock in the morning by shouts of fire and had hurried into the street wearing whatever came to hand. Not surprisingly, he fully accepted the harsh criticisms levelled by his fellow countrymen at the military performance of the Spanish soldiers. Listening to accounts of Talavera, he was unable "to refrain from indignation" at the behaviour of the Spaniards, "who never during three days made the least attempt to assist our army. Their artillery indeed behaved well but no other part of their force was engaged." Inevitably, he concluded that all his hopes for the early liberation of Spain were doomed to disappointment. Yet he refused to lose heart in the face of this setback and the equally depressing news that Napoleon had crushed the Austrians at Wagram. As befitted an evangelical, he looked to "the particular protection of Providence." He was also cheered by the military capacity of his fellow countrymen after the victory at Talavera and was confident of the French Empire's eventual dissolution into "separate and independent" states. He recognized that nationalism was Napoleon's nemesis.[52]

Goulburn's own nationalism was sharpened by this first foreign expedition. To his mind, the Portuguese and Spanish served by their very faults to illustrate manly English virtues. Rationality, good taste, honesty, integrity, industry, efficiency, dependability, and personal cleanliness all seemed to be conspicuously absent from the national character of so many of the people with whom he came into contact. On meeting a body of Cistercians, he was distracted by the fleas hopping over their white habits. He complained of the "abominable filth" of the Capuchins, whose famous cork Convent he visited near Cintra, and was surprised at the inability of members of monastic orders to converse with him in Latin. He saw little to admire in the conduct of a group of men who entered a bullring armed only with cloaks. His sense of fair play was violated by the apparent unlikelihood that any of the men would receive serious injury, for the enraged animals were always distracted from one quarry by other assailants. "Eight bulls were let loose successively and only one had the good fortune to knock down a man," he snorted, "which arose more from the extreme awkwardness of the man than from any other cause." He was astonished by the number of beggars. "They look upon an Englishman as certain plunder," he reported to his mother, "but I am determined to undeceive them as far as I am concerned and am become inexorable."[53]

National prejudices were briefly driven from Goulburn's mind by personal crisis. He parted temporarily from Frederick at La Roca on 25 August without being unduly alarmed by Frederick's complaints of a severe headache and fatigue. They arranged to meet again at Montigo, but when Henry arrived there four days later he found his brother delirious with fever and without attendants save the young boy he had employed as his personal servant. Henry was able to turn to a British army surgeon in a neighbouring town for advice and assistance, but Frederick's condition discouraged any thought of moving him. For three weeks Henry nursed his brother, during which time he himself fell victim to dysentery. Lodged in a single room in a "miserable" cottage in a "detestable village" that was as "barren of intelligence" as it was "destitute of food," Goulburn's only diversions were the copies of the Bible and of Juvenal that he had brought with him on the journey. At least he improved his classical knowledge by committing the greater part of Juvenal to memory. At last, on 18 September, Frederick was fit enough for them to set out for Badajoz. Taking their time, they arrived two days later and reported to Wellington's headquarters. Henry was invited to dine, but Wellington was too unwell to be present at the meal. Nevertheless, Henry subsequently met with the British commander and agreed to carry to Seville dispatches for the eldest Wellesley, who had just taken up residence there as the new British ambassador. So, on 21 September, Henry and Frederick went their separate ways.[54]

Goulburn was received "most civilly" by Ambassador Lord Wellesley, with whom Ponsonby was already staying and whose offer of accommodation he gratefully accepted. After all, everything was "in the handsomest style" and was therefore "such as an *English* Ambassador ought to keep up." Among the members of the hypochondriacal marquess's household to whom Goulburn was introduced was Wellesley's personal physician Sir William Knighton. Goulburn could not have imagined the extent to which he would be thrown together with both these men later in his career. On 27 September he and Ponsonby took their leave of Wellesley and Seville, the city having proven a great disappointment. Goulburn considered it duller than he could ever have conceived "possible for the seat of any Government." By 2 October they were in Grenada admiring the Alhambra and lamenting the actions of those "barbarous Christians" who had defaced some of its Moorish ornamentation with whitewash. From there they inched their way northwards to Valencia via Murcia. But Goulburn was already growing restless, anxious to return to England and his political responsibilities. "I am too eager to attend to my Parliamentary duties not to return to the meeting of the Honorable House," he wrote home at the end of October. Ponsonby's correspondence suggested that the opposition was in high spirits because the Portland ministry showed signs of decrepitude and division. They received reports of another embarrassingly unsuccessful military expedition to the Low Countries, and then the startling news of a duel between two senior ministers, George Canning and Lord Castlereagh. "The Opposition will have a fair joke against a fighting administration," Goulburn mordantly observed. The incident promised to make such an alteration in the state of affairs at home that he was keener than ever to be back in time for the opening of the session. He and Ponsonby therefore abandoned all thought of journeying on to Sicily and Malta.[55]

At Valencia, they decided to about-face. By the time they reached Gibraltar they would have travelled 1,500 miles on mule and on foot. Before quitting the city, however, they were invited to meet with the provincial junta. Goulburn dismissed the experience as "a most absurd and ridiculous exhibition." They were ushered into a room where twenty-five men, mainly generals and clergy, sat around a central table on which two candles provided the only illumination. Groping their way to it, they were seated in a pair of velvet chairs only to be shown a portrait of Ferdinand VII, which they duly admired before being bowed out.[56]

Their departure from the city was delayed by Ponsonby's poor health, stricken as he was by severe headaches. Finally, on 1 November, they set out. On their return through Grenada, they passed two agreeable days engaging in the kind of "rational conversation" with former Cambridge acquaintances which was "never to be found" in Spanish society. At Málaga, Goulburn heard the cheering news that the Portland ministry had been largely reorganized under the leadership of Spencer Perceval. "I rejoice that Perceval is at the head of affairs," he informed his mother. "I think we shall go on much better. Mr. Montagu will be a warmer defender of the administration than ever." He also found comfort in the news that Lord Wellesley had been summoned home to enter the government as foreign secretary. "Whatever may be the difference of opinion respecting his conduct [as governor general] in India," Goulburn observed, "all must allow him to be a man of great knowledge as well as talent."[57]

On 1 December they left Málaga for Gibraltar, only for Goulburn's health now to give cause for concern. He spat blood, a disturbing symptom that was to recur throughout his life. Indeed, when Ponsonby decided to cross the bay from Gibraltar to Algeciras, Goulburn did not feel "stout" enough to accompany him. Heightening his anxiety at further delays was a letter from Perceval expressing a wish to see him, as well as suggestions from friends that it would be worth his while to return to the capital. The hint of office was especially tantalizing to a young man whose ambition to be of service was nourished by an awareness of his current standing as a marginal member of the ruling class. Hence his impatience as he was obliged to kick his heels on the Rock until offered a passage to Cádiz. There he eventually secured passage for England on a seventy-four-gun man-of-war, the *Renown*. She put to sea on 19 January 1810, but the voyage home proved to be long and tedious. Goulburn diverted himself by reading Maria Edgeworth's "tales of fashionable life" and in the evenings played whist. It was 13 February before they lay off Beachy Head. Since the ship was held in quarantine for a further three days, Goulburn did not reach London until 18 February, by which time the parliamentary session was already under way. He was immediately offered and accepted an under-secretaryship at the Home Office, joining – or soon to be joined by – Palmerston, Peel, Croker, Robinson, and Manners Sutton as junior members of the government. The leading lights of the Alfred Club were now on the path to power.[58]

CHAPTER TWO

Slave Owner

Henry Goulburn's Jamaican inheritance proved to be a lifelong burden. A property which at the time of his birth was generally regarded as one of the most enviable of assets had by the time of his death become a crippling liability. Throughout his adulthood, he had reason constantly to regret the extent to which his material comforts were tied to the profitability of Amity Hall. In the changing climate of opinion with respect to slavery, which as fate would have it coincided with his own development from youth to maturity, possession of a sugar estate and ownership of its workforce became a political encumbrance as well as a moral burden for a public man. Goulburn's personal response was to endorse the amelioration of slavery and belatedly its gradual abolition. With the triumph of emancipation, he strove tirelessly but ultimately unsuccessfully to prove that sugar could be produced profitably by free labour.

At the time of its seizure from the Spanish in 1655, the island of Jamaica had been thinly populated and of strategic rather than economic value to Britain. The population began to grow as substantial numbers of whites of humble origin but grand ambition migrated there from the Lesser Antilles. But their notorious reputation tended to discourage settlement by persons of quality, who were further deterred by the natural disasters, the tropical climate, to which Englishmen seemed peculiarly ill suited, and the diseases to which they proved all too susceptible. Little wonder, then, that dreams of wealth and the reality of an alien and alarming environment encouraged "a hectic mode of life that had no counterpart at home or elsewhere in the English experience." Increasingly, settlers saw in the production of sugar the quickest route to the fortune that would enable them to return "home" and there live in some style.[1]

The annexation of Jamaica coincided with the beginning of that lengthy transformation of sugar from a luxury into a staple of every

English family's diet. First Barbados and then Jamaica fed this appetite and helped bring the sweetener within reach of ordinary people. The growing popularity of three essentially bitter beverages – coffee, chocolate, and tea – created an ever-expanding market. Liberally sweetened tea provided a welcome energy supplement to the diet of the poor. By the mid-seventeenth century, sugar from Barbados was already returning a handsome profit, and when Governor Thomas Modyford was transferred from there to Jamaica in 1664, he brought with him eight hundred settlers and a determination to initiate the commercial production of sugar on the larger island.[2]

Within fifty years, Jamaica had overtaken Barbados as a sugar producer and had won recognition as "England's premier Caribbean colony." In addition, it produced rum from by-products of the refineries. West Indian merchants actively fostered the spirit's popularity in Britain, advertising its patriotic wholesomeness as an alternative to French brandy. It was distributed freely at elections, was recommended highly as a remedy for colds, and in diluted form it became a welcome and ritual part of the daily routine of British sailors. Thus legal imports of rum, which at the end of the seventeenth century barely exceeded two hundred gallons, multiplied ten thousandfold within three generations.[3]

Meanwhile, sugar production steadily expanded throughout Jamaica. Among the most valuable and productive lands were those in the southernmost parish of Vere. Largely flat and featureless, this area was invariably hot and frequently arid. The failure of a timely rain was a source of anxiety for all planters, but the fertility of Vere's soil was generally regarded as providing its cultivators with a more than adequate compensation. The lands of the parish, and especially those around the Rio Minho, such as Amity Hall, "are so productive, and yield sugar of so excellent a quality," an early historian observed, "that the planters are so well satisfied with their profits, if they lose one crop in three years." The soil also produced bountiful crops of guinea corn, which in this parish became the principal food of the armies of plantation slaves. Elsewhere, slaves were provided with provisions grounds on which they raised their own crops, most commonly plantains, bananas, and yams. Although the recurrent droughts in Vere had discouraged any such arrangement there, Munbee Goulburn sanctioned the establishment of such grounds at Amity Hall.[4]

The development of the sugar industry did little to encourage British planters to put down roots in the island. After all, it remained a perilous place in the eighteenth century, as the fate of the two Goulburn brothers illustrated. The absenteeism of more than half the colony's most successful families necessitated a system of plantation management that was heavily dependent for its staffing on those whites of humbler origin and means who were compelled to remain longer on the island in pursuit of the dream of affluence. A hierarchy of officers descended through the attorney to the overseer to several bookkeepers, alongside whom practised a doctor and also the occasional craftsman. By tradition, the attorney was recruited from the ranks of experienced overseers or was a merchant. He was responsible for the mercantile affairs of the estate, such as shipping and insurance, together with its general management, the purchase of local supplies, and the ordering of supplies that had to be sent out from Britain. He was expected to make detailed regular reports to the owner. However, since he usually managed more than one estate (for the man who had the management of several was regarded as being "in the way to realizing a rapid fortune"), he rarely lived on the property. When he did visit, he exercised the privilege of putting up at the "great house" and being attended by slave servants. For his remuneration, an attorney usually claimed a commission on all sales and purchases. More rarely, he received a fixed salary.[5]

The infrequency and brevity of the attorney's visits enhanced the position of the overseer, who had usually begun life as a bookkeeper and was paid a fixed salary. He operated the estate, with bookkeepers and tradesmen executing his orders. Slaves, livestock, fields, buildings, and utensils were all "committed to his attention and care." Clearly, these were arduous and important responsibilities, and much depended on the overseer's education, skill, temper, and habits. He could behave like an "unfeeling tyrant" or like a "mild, considerate, and equitable governor," but the temptation of personal and administrative irresponsibility were ever present and all too often proved irresistible.[6]

This system of management excited criticism. Attorneys were accused of spurring the "impolitic and unfeeling zeal" of overseers in order to maximize production, whether to prove their ability as managers or to fatten their commissions. Overseers were condemned in turn as footloose and thus lacking a vested interest in prudent management. They were accused of failing to develop a "settled rule or method" of cultivation, of abuse and thus exhaustion of the soil, of a want of initiative, and of being generally resistant to "improvements." Their reluctance to resort to the humble plough became the symbol of their alleged conservatism. Here was an implement, the contemporary historian Edward Long argued, which in skilled hands could prepare as much land for canes in a single day, "and in a much better manner," as a hundred slaves "could perform with their hoes in the same time." In short, it would save labour, permit the cultivation of a larger area, and produce more productive canes.[7]

That the production of sugar as traditionally undertaken was an expensive, harsh, and labour-intensive enterprise no one disputed. The business was a sort of adventure, wrote another influential contemporary, "in which the man that engages, must engage deeply." There was a rule of thumb that an investment of £30,000 was required "to embark in this employment with a fair prospect of advantage." Capital had to be invested in land, buildings, equipment, livestock, and labour. To manufacture sugar, the planter required at least one mill, if not two, a boiling house, a curing house, a distillery in which to produce the rum that was a profitable ancillary enterprise, and a storehouse. One way to help raise this capital was through a judicious marriage, and it may be no coincidence that one of the Goulburns married a merchant's daughter. As for the return on this investment, planters expected to earn 10 per cent per annum.[8]

The job of planting was a cruel one. To save their own slaves, some planters hired "jobbing gangs" for this back-breaking task. The fact that the canes required a full eighteen months to mature necessitated careful planning in order to minimize the danger of crops being damaged if not ruined by a lack or an excess of rain. Too little moisture reduced the sugar content, while too much caused the canes to rot. The time for harvesting was the dry season between the end of the calendar year and late spring. Slaves organized in gangs cut, trimmed, and bundled the canes for cartage to the mills. The roots of the original plants then sprouted, and the new growth ("ratoons") was harvested again and again. After several such crops, perhaps three but as many as five, the ratoons were exhausted and new canes had to be planted. Although the ratoons were inferior in juice content to the original plants, usually proving only half as a productive, they saved the labour of more frequent planting. Ratooning was particularly successful in Vere.[9]

Livestock were needed to haul the canes, to power the mills, and to cart the hogsheads of sugar and the puncheons of rum to wharfs for shipment. Craftsmen had to be employed – carpenters, coopers, mechanics, potters, and smiths – to make running repairs and to maintain the machinery. If the craftsmen were white, they expected to be well paid. In Britain, a planter needed to employ an agent to dispose of his produce. The Goulburns were somewhat unusual in their employment of two, one in London and another in Liverpool. Agents received a standard commission of 3 per cent of the value of the sales. The balance was placed in an account on which bills of credit might be drawn and to which was charged the cost of the plantation supplies – locks, screws, nails, hoes, augers, chisels, axes, hammers, hoops, pots, pans, paints, lead, pills, salts, candles, soap, oil, turpentine, cloth, bedding, crockery, cheeses, barrels of fish, pork, beef, butter, and hogsheads of porter – whose return shipment from England and Ireland the agent also organized.[10]

These supplies, and the commissions and salaries paid to the various agents and employees, were only a few of the charges against the gross profits. The so-called "island expenses," or "contingencies," included local taxes and the purchase of slaves, livestock, food, and lumber. It was the hope of every planter that these would be more than covered by the proceeds of the rum sales. Other costs were those of freight, warehousing, insurance, and brockerage. In all, depending on circumstances, the expenses might absorb from one-third to one-half of a planter's gross sales. Hence his complaints that the real profits from sugar production were less princely than was popularly believed. Nevertheless, planting remained a highly profitable enterprise for the man who conducted his business with care.[11]

Planters were shrewd guardians of their profit margins. They both limited production and established a monopoly control of the rapidly expanding metropolitan market. This achievement was evidence of their long-standing political influence in London, where they allied with merchants to form a powerful lobby that was well represented in Parliament. Trade and tariff legislation gave them immense advantages over their competitors, while the construction of the West India Docks at the turn of the nineteenth century was proof of the importance of their trade. Indeed, sugar was now so widely regarded as a necessity that the inability to purchase it was established in a number of English parishes as a test for poor relief in 1792. Yet the colonies were also valued as a market for manufactures, as purchasers of North American provisions and timber, thereby financing Canadian imports of British goods, as a conduit for smuggling goods into Spanish America, and as the customer for slaves, whose export from West Africa sustained that region's importations from Great Britain. Not surprisingly, therefore, Jamaica had lost little of its allure for British investors, particularly as the slave rebellion on the French sugar island of St Domingue in 1791 removed the most successful producer from the marketplace. With the outbreak of war with France in 1793, Britain was in a position to exploit this advantage further. As the French share of the sugar market withered, that of Britain burgeoned, and Jamaica's production and exports surged. More slaves were imported, more productive varieties of cane were planted, more fertilizer was spread, more ratoons were cropped, and the annual rate of profit increased sharply.[12]

Yet storm clouds were gathering on the horizon. The profitability of sugar naturally spurred its production elsewhere, notably in Brazil and Cuba. The government's desperate need for revenues during the

French wars saw it impose ever-heavier levies on this popular commodity, until in 1806 they amounted to almost two-thirds of the wholesale price. Inevitably, both consumption and profits were affected. At the same time, deteriorating relations with the United States, a neutral victim of the Anglo-French conflict, threatened to inflate the cost of provisions and lumber. Finally, the campaign to abolish the slave trade had taken on new life. The danger this cause posed to the sugar planters' interests had long been recognized by the West India lobby, for slavery was the very cornerstone of the plantation economy.[13]

The link forged between sugar and slavery in the Old World proved more than strong enough to extend the chains clear across the Atlantic to the New. The Spanish and Portuguese both imported black slaves from Africa, having already experimented successfully with plantations on their Atlantic islands. But it was the British who established this economy in Jamaica and turned to Africa for their workforce. Between 1655 and 1809 some 600,000 African slaves were transported to the colony of Jamaica alone.[14]

The "striking correlation between the soaring importation of African slaves and the unprecedented wealth of the sugar colonies" was too obvious to be missed by contemporaries. Driven by greed, the British slave system quickly earned an unenviable reputation for severity. Barbados enacted a slave code in 1661, founded on the twin if somewhat contradictory notions that blacks were both a "brutish" people and mere chattels. Thus a grudging concession of the slaves' humanity established a limit to an owner's otherwise absolute authority over his property and dictated that some legal provision be made for the slaves' care. This code then served as a model for that adopted by the Jamaican assembly in 1664, following the arrival of Governor Modyford from Barbados, though subsequent modifications tempered the severity somewhat and paid greater lip service to the slaves' welfare. In particular, masters were liable to a fine for a failure to clothe their slaves adequately, and they were urged to offer them instruction in Christianity. If these modest amendments suggested "that Jamaican slaves were generally better off than their brothers in Barbados," fear of rebellion in a society that was now overwhelmingly black long discouraged any significant improvement of their lot.[15]

Resistance to enslavement was common to most slave societies, and it took various forms, of which flight and rebellion were merely the most obvious as well as the most perilous. Jamaica's remote and largely inaccessible backcountry offered a relatively safe haven to runaways. Moreover, the island's population included the maroons, who were the descendants of runaway Spanish slaves and those who had fled their

British masters. They had fought for and won recognition of their freedom, and even though they accepted employment as slave catchers, and as military auxiliaries in the suppression of slave revolts, they "continued to provide an admired example for rebellious slaves."[16]

If the slave system's severity bred resistance, it also provided some contemporaries with a simple explanation of a chilling demographic statistic. The first three-quarters of the eighteenth century had seen 500,000 slaves transported to Jamaica, yet the colony's slave population had increased by less than one-third that number. The slaves' obvious inability to sustain themselves may have appeared all the more remarkable to Britons, who were increasingly aware of the steady growth in their own numbers. As for the reasons, planters anxious to make their fortunes as quickly as possible had concluded that it was less expensive to replenish their stock of male slaves periodically than to attempt to preserve a sexual balance in the hope that infants born of slave unions would survive and grow to adulthood. But there were other factors contributing to a low birth rate: the "extremely high incidence of sterility among African females in the West Indies," a result of "dislocation, stress and overcrowding" on slave transports; their greater age on arrival; the ill-health, hard work, and poor nutrition that was their lot; the extended period of lactation during which sexual intercourse was taboo; and even the sinking of blacks, under the terrifying strains of enslavement, into a state verging on "sexual anarchy." Moreover, many infant deaths went unreported. In short, low fertility was often a mask behind which there lurked a far more alarming rate of mortality.[17]

Children were especially susceptible to infections, and the rate of infant mortality among slaves approached 50 per cent throughout the eighteenth century. Perhaps four out of every five of the doomed newborn died within the first fortnight of life, many falling victim to tetanus. Poor diet, malnutrition, hardship, hard work, inadequate shelter, unhygienic conditions, even the want of footwear, all contributed to the slaves' vulnerability to deadly diseases and a broad range of debilitating respiratory ailments. Eventually, this "terrible waste of human life came to be questioned on grounds of self-interest, morality and religion." Some planters, even before they found themselves assailed by humanitarian critics, realized that money invested in the improvement of their slaves' living conditions would return a worthwhile human dividend and free them "from dependence on the African slave trade, and cut costs."[18]

Motivated by this enlightened self-interest, some planters provided their slaves with adequate clothing, improved their diet through the introduction of more fish and the allocation of plots of land on which to raise provisions, and delivered a rudimentary health care. Slave hospitals were erected and doctors were employed, though the physicians were rarely the best-qualified members of their profession. Nor were their European prescriptions of great benefit to victims of tropical diseases. Further, they often found themselves in conflict with the overseers, who were all too ready to dismiss the sick as malingerers. However, from 1788 on, an act of the Jamaican assembly required physicians supervising the care of slaves to make annual reports on all deaths. The same act offered financial inducements to managers and owners, direct in one case and indirect in the other, to foster slave births. The Consolidated Slave Act, passed four years later, promised even larger financial rewards to overseers whenever births resulted in a net increase in the slave population; it exempted from all hard labour slave mothers with six children living and excused owners all taxes on these fecund females; it obliged overseers to submit annual lists of births and deaths to the parish vestries; and it required planters to cultivate one acre of provisions ground for every ten slaves.[19]

The policy of amelioration was also a response, in no small measure, to the burgeoning antislavery movement. For centuries, slavery had been an accepted and unquestioned institution. Then, from the middle of the eighteenth century, it came under sustained attack as an immoral anachronism. In Britain, where there had been a steady rise in the number of slaves employed as servants, thought was given to slavery's place in a "progressive" society. In 1772 the lord chief justice concluded in a test case that an institution so odious required the support of positive law and could not rest simply on inference. This decision did not set free all slaves or declare slavery illegal in Britain, but it did liberate the single slave in question. The power of forcible removal back to the colonies, which the slave's master had sought to exercise over him, was declared unknown in English law. And the fact that the right of deportation had been the masters' principal means of discipline meant that this limited decision delivered "a deadly blow" to slavery in Britain. Nevertheless, "slaves continued to be bought and sold," and a number of deportations still took place.[20]

With the end of the American Revolutionary War there arrived in Britain blacks who had been promised freedom in return for support of the imperial cause, and also slaves accompanying Loyalist masters. Once again the issue was pushed to the fore. Simultaneously, humanitarians were able to exploit the appalling revelation that one slaver had thrown overboard and drowned his human cargo. One response was the creation of the Committee for Relieving the Black Poor, which eventually sponsored a settlement on the west coast of Africa at Sierra Leone. More than four hundred blacks and some sixty whites were shipped out in 1787 to settle a small piece of territory acquired from a local chief. Not only did the expedition demonstrate the limitations of this form of philanthropy, for the party was no more than an insignificant fraction of Britain's poor blacks, but it also illustrated the perils. Within a few months, disease had carried off almost all the whites and more than a quarter of the blacks. More successful, ultimately, was the abolition society formed that same year – 1787. Moreover, by this time "it was generally assumed that slaves arriving in Britain were free."[21]

If the loss of the thirteen American mainland colonies "simplified the problem of British abolitionists and emancipationists by narrowing the range of vested interests with which they had to contend," they were able to draw intellectual strength from the Enlightenment, while their passion was fired by faith. Quakers, their sensitivity sharpened by their own experience of persecution, repudiated the physical force on which slavery was founded. Anthony Benezet, the American Friend, exercised far-reaching influence. His writings inspired Granville Sharp, who won fame for his efforts to halt the sufferings of blacks. John Wesley's decision to join this humanitarian crusade owed much to the writings of the American. His conversion carried with it the Methodist organizations in Britain and America, thereby adding further institutional strength to the campaign. Indeed, evangelicals of various hues saw in abolition a focus for their response to God's mercy, from which they had benefited, and as a means of repaying the debt they owed for their own redemption from sin. They brought to the movement an unprecedented intensity and fervour. Finally, the secular case – that slavery was an "economic anachronism" – had been developed forcefully by Adam Smith in *The Wealth of Nations* (1776). As a result, there was by the late 1780s "little serious defence of slavery" on either intellectual or moral grounds. "Religion, economics, philosophy and political studies" all pointed to its undesirability.[22]

The organization of the London Abolition Society in 1787, followed by the establishment of a network of corresponding provincial societies, signalled the commencement of a political campaign to end the slave trade. The trade, rather than the institution it sustained, was selected as the target because it was "an infinitely more manageable, practical and less complex problem." The planters would have greater difficulty setting up the cry that their private property was under attack. Further, to sever the supply would surely compel planters immediately to treat more humanely those slaves they already owned even as the institution was slowly poisoned at its roots. This moderate and gradualist strategy paid a handsome dividend in gaining the support of figures such as William Wilberforce and Charles James Fox. The former was the leading Anglican evangelical in Parliament and a friend of the prime minister. The latter was the leading Whig in the Commons. Tactically, the abolitionists sought to impress Parliament with the extent of public support for their cause. They dispatched lecturers on tour, circulated the printed word, and organized massive petition campaigns. In 1788 alone more than one hundred petitions were submitted to Parliament, and four years later the number was five times greater.[23]

As the antislavery campaign in Britain gathered momentum, it was paralleled by the work of similar activists in France, while the Danes announced in 1792 their intention to close the slave trade to their islands within a decade. It seemed that the triumph of the cause was simply a matter of time. In Britain, a bill was passed in 1788 that sought to make the transatlantic passage less dangerous for slaves by discouraging overcrowding and encouraging their better care, and this cause was further advanced eight years later by a legal decision that denied shippers the right to claim insurance cover for deaths resulting from ill-treatment or neglect. In 1792 the Commons voted for the gradual abolition of the trade, only for the Lords to block the legislation. This proved to be a fateful setback, for the tide of events had suddenly turned, and the abolitionists found themselves crusading in a far less promising environment.[24]

The frighteningly radical lurch of the French Revolution in 1793, followed by war with France and by mounting fears of Jacobinism in Britain, led to abolition's being popularly tarred with the brush of radicalism. This association was strengthened by the conduct of some Radicals in yoking together the abolition of the slave trade and political reform. Compounding these problems were the events in St Domingue. Graphic accounts of the slave rebellion on that island even induced some sympathizers with abolition to draw back. The massive destruction of property and the slaughter of hundreds of whites excited fears for the safety of both in Jamaica. No doubt the desire to prevent the spread of the upheaval to their own territories played a part in the British decision to dispatch an expeditionary force to conquer the French island. Its decimation did little to generate renewed sympathy for slaves.[25]

The opponents of abolition sought to capitalize on the turn of events. In Jamaica, successive revisions of the slave laws were evidently intended to demonstrate a deepening concern for the slaves' welfare and thus the institution's successful adjustment to the higher standards of an enlightened age. In London, the West Indians could count on the support of a significant number of members of Parliament, perhaps as many as three dozen, who were in one way or another involved with the trade of the islands. In the provinces, meanwhile, the Society of Planters and Merchants financed a counter-campaign of petition and public information. Slaves were depicted as enjoying a degree of domestic comfort that was well calculated to excite envy and resentment among the British lower classes. The slave system's harsh discipline was likened to that of the armed forces, while even more insidious appeals to racism promised to be all the more effective in the light of the reported savagery in St Domingue.[26]

Theories of human origins dividing humanity into separate species invited the establishment of a hierarchy of races in which Europeans and Africans occupied the highest and lowest positions, respectively. From here it was but a short step to the assertion, or assumption, that the latter were subhuman. Edward Long's richly informative and thus influential *History of Jamaica* (1774) was deeply infected by notions of black inferiority. His bestial Africans were civilized by enslavement. At the same time, he was careful to stress the wealth that the slave trade, and the sugar production it made possible, created for Britain and all her peoples. However pervasive such racism was – and it may have had a stronger appeal for the governing classes than the governed – it did not deny that blacks possessed souls. Nor did it raise insuperable obstacles to "humanitarian action against slavery and the slave trade," though the apologists for the trade conspicuously lacked the moral fervour of its critics. Aware of their continuing vulnerability, the West Indians, in the person of Charles Ellis, an absentee proprietor, introduced into Parliament in April 1797 a motion that professed to initiate gradual abolition through encouragement of the policy of amelioration. Of course, the intent was to reinforce slavery, not to put it on the road to extinction. Following passage of the motion, the secretary of state for the colonies instructed governors and legislatures on the necessity of enacting measures to promote religious instruction and foster childbearing among the slaves. But emphasizing as it did the role of the colonial legislatures, this action "represented a major political victory for the West Indians and their supporters." Other victories quickly followed, not least the defeat of a succession of abolition bills introduced by Wilberforce.[27]

As the nineteenth century opened, the policy of amelioration appeared to have seen off the abolitionists. The London antislavery committee had simply ceased to meet. The slave transportation bill of 1799 had established a far more effective and rigorous standard than that in place since 1788. One immediate result was a significant reduction in the average number of slaves carried in British vessels and thus an appreciable rise in transportation costs. Not that this slowed the trade. British subjects continued it under foreign flags. Moreover, the government even entered the market for slaves in order to fill out the ranks of the black West India regiments. In short, there was precious little evidence of a decline either in slavery or the slave trade. In fact, both appeared to be flourishing if not expanding. If this was sufficient to convince many abolitionists that amelioration was a fraud, they were supplied with documentary evidence by James Stephen, a lawyer and West Indian resident. He forwarded to Wilberforce convincing evidence that planter-inspired amelioration had never been more than a strategy to defeat abolition and that it afforded scant real protection to the slave. In several of the islands, including Jamaica, he reported that legislatures were even seeking to impede missionary activities among the slaves. At the same time, the development of coffee production had created an even stronger demand for slaves to undertake the harsh labour of clearing lands.[28]

A resurgence of abolitionism was evidently under way. France's attempts to restore slavery to its empire meant that abolition of the trade "could almost bear the colour of patriotism." The arrival of one hundred Irish members of Parliament in 1801, following the Act of Union, brought to Westminster a substantial number of fresh recruits, while outside the House the London Abolition Society had been reinvigorated. Wilberforce and his supporters now argued persuasively that it would be unwise to permit the importation of slaves into territories that Britain had seized during the war but might well be forced to surrender in a peace. Why should Britain promote the development of potential competitors of her own colonies? The Pitt administration agreed and issued a proclamation in 1805 which prohibited British subjects from importing slaves into the captured colonies. Then, in February of the following year, Pitt's sudden death resulted in a Whiggish coalition ministry taking office which was somewhat more sympathetic to the cause of abolition.[29]

Lord Grenville, the new prime minister, had long been a supporter of abolition, and his commitment had been strengthened by his deepening personal faith and the re-establishment of his friendship with Wilberforce after a lengthy period of estrangement. But Grenville presided over a cabinet that included one fixed opponent of abolition and several lukewarm supporters of amelioration. As a result, he was obliged to move cautiously. His first step was to give "statutory force" to the proclamation issued by Pitt the previous year. Subsequently, under pressure from Wilberforce, he agreed to the introduction of a resolution pledging the administration to seek full abolition in a future session of Parliament, and he followed this with a bill designed to prevent, in the interim, any acceleration of the shipment of slaves to the British West Indies.[30]

The West Indians watched these developments with undisguised dismay. The Society of Planters and Merchants eventually appropriated £500 to finance another propaganda campaign, and they were aided by the East India interest and a number of provincial manufacturers. Among the latter was the cotton magnate Robert Peel, and it was to counter his intervention that Manchester abolitionists organized a petition in the spring of 1806. Theirs was but one of the many that again flooded into Parliament. Moreover, when a general election was held during the late autumn, abolition became an issue in a number of contests. With his own position strengthened, Grenville successfully steered an abolition bill through the Lords during the late winter of 1807. Not surprisingly, it sailed through the Commons. Shortly afterwards, the government fell.[31]

The crucial period for the British West Indian sugar industry – which began with the collapse of its principal rival, St Domingue, and culminated in the abolition of the slave trade – found the Goulburn estate less well placed than most others to capitalize fully on the opportunities or respond promptly to the pressures. Munbee Goulburn had long neglected his property, failing to provide careful supervision or to invest in improvements. Only in the last year of his life did he belatedly bestir himself, following the receipt of a new attorney's sobering account of the condition of Amity Hall. Too little replanting had been ordered by his predecessor, James Craggs reported, and therefore the crop from over-ratooned "pieces" was chronically short. There was a serious shortage of pasturage for the livestock because of lack of attention to the planting of grass, and much of what had been grown had been eaten out by wild cattle because of a failure to maintain the fencing around it. A similar inattention to the Goulburn animals had seen a number of them drift off into the herds of wild cattle, even though a shortage of stock was one of the estate's principal deficiencies. But Craggs's most alarming observations concerned the estate's small army of slaves. They were too few in number to complete the cropping before the onset of the rainy season, he warned. The result: lost production and income, and chronic overwork. Several of the slaves were "constant runaways," and one woman refused to work despite repeated punishments. Craggs's immediate response was to make an example of the recalcitrant by selling them to the Spanish, a fate much feared by all slaves. Equally revealing, however, was his warning that the influenza from which much of the island's population was then suffering might in the opinion of the estate's doctor ravage a people who were already "weakly." Clearly, amelioration had made little headway on Amity Hall.[32]

Munbee Goulburn's response was to order sixty acres of new plants each year and to insist that one mill properly worked and supplied could process a good crop. By his own estimate, however, he required a workforce of three hundred slaves and a stock of ninety steers and seventy mules. Therefore, he authorized Craggs to purchase the score or so slaves required to bring the force up to the desired strength. But before these instructions could be followed, Munbee was dead. His death intestate meant that important and even urgent decisions had first to be cleared through the dilatory Court of Chancery. The management of the estate was further complicated by the outbreak of war with France, which drove up insurance premiums and interrupted supplies of provisions from Ireland, necessitating the purchase of high-priced local provisions for slaves and feed for stock. Yet another complication was the prolonged drought, which began in Vere in 1796 and extended into the next century.[33]

Meagre crops and plentiful costs were an unwelcome combination. In this situation, it was frustrating and damaging to have to wait so long for Chancery permission to invest in additional pasture lands and other necessities, including the purchase of slaves. By 1798, Craggs was obliged to hire at least twenty-five slaves to help take off the crop, and this at a time when demands for labour on the new coffee plantations had driven up the cost of jobbing gangs. More to the point, he warned that the Goulburn slaves "were wearing out for want of a regular supply of new negroes as none have been purchased for some years." Craggs totalled up for Susannah Goulburn the cost of the various delays. Slaves who might have been bought a few years earlier for £90 each now commanded £120, and the sellers could demand prompt payment, whereas they had then been offering credit for up to two years. Cane holes that could have been dug for £7 an acre had in fact cost almost £10 because of the expense of having them dug by hired slaves. Cattle that might have been purchased for £20 a head could only be had for double that price, and the same was true of mules.[34]

The new century began in much the same fashion as the old had ended. Nature continued to restrict production on Amity Hall. The costly drought was succeeded by the flooding of the Rio Minho, which left forty acres of cane pieces waterlogged. The loss of the ship *Britannia*, carrying forty hogsheads of Goulburn sugar, added another disaster to this catalogue of misfortunes. The disadvantages of the estate being in Chancery were further illustrated by the master in Chancery's patriotic decision not to permit Craggs to purchase essential supplies, including timber, from the United States. Instead, he was instructed to purchase the more expensive products of British North America. Urgently, the attorney sought authorization to construct a new still house (which would increase rum profits and thus eventually cover the higher cost of contingencies) and a new hospital to improve the care of an exhausted slave force, and to purchase more slaves. "We have so few negroes on the Property they are obliged to be worked very hard which will wear them out sooner than if there was a proper strength to do the necessary work," he warned. Unimpressed, the court plodded along. It demanded sworn affadavits in support of all proposed expenditures. Finally, in 1801, the master authorized the improvements to the buildings and the purchase annually of sufficient slaves to increase the present workforce. Ironically, Craggs succumbed to a fever within a few months of this decision, and the choice of his successor obliged the Goulburns to confront the awful responsibilities of slave ownership.[35]

The position was sought by Thomas Samson, who boasted fifteen years' experience, twelve of them under Craggs and eight of those as the overseer at Amity Hall. He promised to continue Craggs's form of management and confidently predicted an annual production of five hundred hogsheads. Even more encouraging, he estimated that with the recently strengthened slave force, the estate was capable of an even greater level of production. The introduction of Bourbon canes gave additional credibility to this optimistic prediction. The only cautionary note he sounded concerned the stock. The number of animals would have to be increased, he advised, to compensate for the distance of many cane pieces from the mill. The news that Samson was under consideration for the position of attorney evoked both an anonymous and a signed protest. A "friend of humanity" warned Susannah Goulburn that "a fine healthy, well looking, and, generally, well disposed people" had already been reduced to a "sickly, poor looking, and wretched ill disposed sett [sic]" by the overseer's "wanton and savage cruelty." Nowhere in Jamaica were deaths higher, births lower, and runaways more numerous than on Amity Hall, this informant alleged. It was a charge that appeared to be disturbingly consistent with Craggs's complaint two years earlier that there were "a very great number of ill disposed People on the Estate, constantly running away from their work."[36]

This "Friend of humanity" recommended Alex Moir for the position. Moir, who was suspected of being the anonymous correspondent, wrote to Susannah Goulburn over his own name to caution her against Samson as well as to advertise his own candidacy. He had served at Amity Hall as a bookkeeper and then as Samson's immediate predecessor as overseer. Although dismissed, allegedly for "bad behaviour," this had not prevented him from being appointed attorney to another estate. Clearly, he was well acquainted with the Goulburn property, and he forwarded to Susannah Goulburn a list of twenty-eight runaways, who would readily return to Amity Hall, he said, if promised fair and humane treatment. He also noted that Samson was jobbing his own slaves to the estate, charging upwards of £1,200 a year for their labour.

These serious charges notwithstanding, Samson was appointed to act as attorney for a year while also continuing as overseer. He was instructed, however, not to work the slaves too hard in his desire to produce large crops. It would be "much more advantageous," Susannah Goulburn wrote, "that the property should make smaller crops and preserve the stock of negroes without diminution than to obtain large crops by overworking the slaves and obliging them to run away that they may obtain relief from their labour. For the slaves are the most valuable part of the property and unless they are treated with prudence and humanity the estate can never thrive." If this injunction indicated a primarily pragmatic interest in humanity, she did require that Samson report by every packet and submit "proofs" of humane treatment that would "divest" her mind and that of her son of "every apprehension."[37]

One of Samson's "proofs" was the testimonials he secured from neighbouring planters. Another was the confidence Craggs had always placed in him, even to the extent of visiting Amity Hall less frequently than any of the other estates under his charge. Samson also assured the Goulburns that he did not permit any bookkeeper to beat the slaves with sticks and that he alone decided how to deal with those they recommended for punishment. But the foundation of his defence against the charge of cruelty was the "weak-handed" condition of the workforce. There were now only 237 slaves on the plantation, 125 men and 112 women, or more than 40 fewer than at Munbee Goulburn's death. The low birth rate and high death rate were entirely attributable to this situation, Samson argued. Overwork impaired the ability of the women to bear children and overtaxed the elderly, thus a natural decrease would result without "the smallest instance of inhumanity." The solution was to buy slaves, and Samson claimed that the addition of forty would "prevent jobbing and make the labour for the others go on easy." "All the hardships on the slaves will be done away with by the purchasing of negroes," he insisted. It was an argument that neatly shifted responsibility to the owner, and it was one Susannah Goulburn readily accepted, given her late husband's conclusion that a force of three hundred slaves was required to work the estate efficiently. She instructed Samson to buy twenty slaves immediately and another score early in the new year. He purchased ten that summer, eight of whom were men because he was unimpressed with the quality of the women. An equal number, but these evenly divided by sex, were obtained much later in the year. Yet when Samson reported on the slave population in March 1803, the numbers had failed to increase proportionately. The totals of 136 men and 118 women plainly indicated that there had been no immediate improvement in the ratio of births to deaths.[38]

The controversy over Samson's appointment provided Susannah Goulburn with a timely reminder of the difficulties of absentee ownership, "for one is much embarrassed when property is at such a distance and one hears of anything going wrong how to form an opinion." However convoluted her syntax, she was clear minded in her determination to protect the interests of her son during his minority and in her acceptance of the duty to ensure that slaves on the estate were treated "with consistent humanity." To this end she initiated a discreet investigation of Samson's fitness. One of her brothers wrote to the military governor of the colony for additional information on the manager's character and system of management. She addressed the same inquiry to at least two knowledgeable Jamaicans. They sent reassuring replies. The estate's Liverpool agent, William Goore, wrote for information to Alex Falconer, who had temporarily taken charge following Craggs's death. He admitted that Samson's regime was more severe than was necessary but conceded that Amity Hall's slaves probably required "a strict Rein." Whether or not the estate was adequately manned he declined to say, pleading limited knowledge, but he pointed to the declining strength of the slave force on most properties since the end of the American war. "Properties in general many years ago had a larger proportion of Negroes on them than at present," he informed Goore, and "no estate can go well unless the cultivators are equal to the Labor or Task that is allotted to them, [and] even then 4% should be bought yearly to keep up the numbers." Lastly, he reported that Samson was regarded as a moral man and that his neighbours spoke well of him. This was sufficient for Goore, who recognized the difficulty of ever finding "a Person possessing all the qualities one could wish." He was confident that after all that had passed, Samson would be "circumspect" in his conduct. Nor did he forget to total up for Susannah Goulburn the other side of the balance sheet. Amity Hall regularly produced one of the best crops in the parish, and credit for this had to be given to Samson. He was "quite indefatigable in performing his duty and consequently keeps the slaves very close to work which cannot be so agreeable to them altho' it is advantageous to your son's Pocket, but whether he uses more severity than their conduct calls for it is not easy to ascertain." Perhaps to remove some of the personal temptation to drive the slaves so hard, the Goulburns decided not to offer Samson the standard commission but to pay him a fixed salary.[39]

Samson had not bought the full number of new slaves he had been authorized to purchase in 1802. Continuing dry weather had resulted in a poor corn crop, and he had cautioned that it would be very expensive to feed additional mouths. The times were "alarming and distressing," he repeated early in 1803. One year later, he was complaining of the poor quality or bad reputation of the slaves who were up for sale. They were the mere "refuse" of cargoes or "Congos," and their price was too high. By this time, it may have crossed the minds of the Goulburns that Samson's inactivity in the market was connected to his renting of his own slaves to the estate. But Henry Goulburn, who was increasingly active in the distant supervision of his property, was watching with some anxiety the revival of the campaign to end the slave trade. He urged Samson to purchase females, at least until their number equalled that of the men. The aim was to place his slave population in a position to maintain itself naturally, now "an object of serious consideration to all persons who have West India Property." Samson initially chose to misinterpret this as an instruction to purchase equal numbers of each sex, and this he did at the beginning of 1805 when he added five men and five women to the stock of slaves. Significantly, he advised the Goulburns that he required the same number again if he was to avoid the expensive employment of jobbers during crop, and a total of forty in order to bring the slave force up to strength. There were still only 260 slaves on the estate, he complained. As a result, it was "by far the weakest handed of any of its magnitude" in the parish. The purchase of an additional ten slaves during the summer, all freshly imported from Africa and "very fine women," therefore went only partway towards meeting the deficiency.[40]

On coming of age in 1805, Henry Goulburn took full control of his property. He would certainly have been better informed of the actual conditions on Amity Hall had he and his mother undertaken the visit to Jamaica which they had planned before he went up to university. But his mother's delicate health and the fear of yellow fever had seen that plan set aside. By the same token, his personal evangelicalism and the mounting assault on slavery failed to weaken his attachment to the institution. Since he possessed no other private income, it would have required a monumental act of moral courage for him to have taken up the cause of abolition. He was dependent on Amity Hall to maintain his position in society and to ensure a measure of comfort for his mother in her declining years. Yet he could not ignore the slave problem. He accepted the humanitarians' argument that the slaves' ability to sustain if not increase their number was the only valid test of their treatment. On the other hand, his anxiety on this subject was even more deeply rooted in the need to maintain an adequate workforce once the supply line to Africa had been severed. Therefore, in looking over estate lists which revealed that there were now nearly as many women as men under the age of forty, he expressed surprise "that the number of children born each year bears no reasonable proportion to the number of these negroes." On the basis of his own investigations, he concluded that there were but two possible explanations. Either "the intercourse between the two sexes" was "too promiscuous" or "the pains of childbirth and the little care taken of women when pregnant" made them reluctant to bear children or induced them to procure "abortions." By way of a remedy, Goulburn proposed that Samson actively promote monogamous relationships. He hastened to add that it was not his intention that every man be compelled to live with a woman, but rather that when two slaves had formed an attachment they should not be permitted to separate or take other partners. As an added inducement to form nuclear families, he recommended that couples who raised four, six, or eight children "should according to the number be either partially or totally exempted from labour except during the time of crop." In an effort to reduce miscarriages and infant deaths, he urged that no woman with child be employed in field work for a month or six weeks before and after delivery. "This is absolutely necessary both for the health of the Mother and the infant and is no less required for our own interest than for the sake of humanity." In brief, then, Goulburn believed that he could produce a self-sustaining slave population by making his negroes understand "that the more children they can bring up the more liberty they have to be idle." It was a misguided belief, rooted in the common prejudice that blacks had an ill-developed sense of family and were a naturally indolent if not promiscuous race. Beyond this there lurked another assumption – that blacks required the discipline of slavery in order to labour.[41]

Goulburn's low opinion of African slaves and the timidity with which he advanced his ameliorative measures surely encouraged his manager to ignore him. After all, he feebly admitted that his "hints" might be "unreasonable." Viewing Goulburn as an earnest, well-intentioned but naive young man, Samson skilfully exploited his willingness to attribute the estate's labour problems to black promiscuity. Thus one evangelical concern served as a counterweight to another. A "plurality of wives" constituted the slaves' "greatest luxury arising from natural habits," Samson replied, and to restrict a male slave to one partner on Amity Hall was to encourage him to visit neighbouring estates. He reminded Goulburn that the existing slave law exempted from hard labour females who had six surviving children, and he opined that moderate work during pregnancy was in fact beneficial. The frequency of abortions or miscarriages resulted not from overwork, he said, but from the slaves' natural indolence, which saw them attempt to avoid even the light tasks on which they were set to work. As for infant deaths, most of them occurred during the first nine days of life when the newborn were especially vulnerable to the many dangers of life in the tropics. There was but one proven way of managing slaves, Samson advised the owner, and that was to reward or recognize those who behaved well and to chastise moderately those who were badly behaved. Of course, it was essential always to maintain "strict discipline when they infringe on the rights of one another," for this introduced "equality of conditions and protection which makes them bear many other hardships, and begets in them confidence and security in their little property." With the passage of time, Samson added reassuringly, slaves were "becoming daily more civilized by getting richer and more anxious to remain at home at their labour and occupations to preserve that property." He concluded: "If you were here you would find all speculative reasoning on these subjects illusive."[42]

Impressed with Samson's "considerable attention to the nature and disposition of the Negroes," Goulburn welcomed his "insights" into "some points of their character." He expressed dismay at the news that they were irredeemably licentious and voiced confidence in the efficacy of rewards to those who behaved "better." Nor did he question the need for "strict discipline," though he did insist that Samson forbid "any severity to be exercised more than is absolutely necessary for the promotion and maintenance of good order: for improper severity is productive of more bad consequences than is generally imagined." Subsequently, as the closing of the slave trade neared, Goulburn authorized his manager to give priority to the strengthening of the slave force. "I should therefore recommend to you to purchase negroes in preference to every other improvement," he wrote. And he continued to turn over in his mind schemes to discourage flight and licentiousness. Education appeared to him to be the answer. If a little learning would make the poor of Britain less dangerous, it would surely serve to improve the slaves. Children should be removed from "vicious" parents at the age of two and instructed in those customs necessary for the good regulation of society. "By pursuing some plan of this sort," he added, "we may be able in the course of about twenty years to cultivate the estate by means of Negroes who from their education would have imbibed as strong a bias in favour of good behaviour as the present slaves appear to have in favour of bad."[43]

Samson patiently explained to Goulburn that "vicious" slaves were no less attached to their children than the "better" ones were, and that they would surely steal them back and thus instruct them in "more ruinous habits." The irony of this admission was unintentional and was lost on Goulburn. The problem of runaways was a chronic one, the attorney continued, springing as it did from the blacks' "aversion to labour." However, in an effort to discourage it, he was continuing to enforce the policy of "making an example of some of those who are irreclaimable." They were either put on trial in slave courts or sold off to the feared Spanish. "As to Education being introduced among slaves, it would lead them to ... revolt to a decided certainty," for "of all the classes of people they are the least capable of gratitude." He warned darkly that all attempts to reform slaves had not only brought total ruin to the estates involved but had necessitated the resort to "double severity" in order to reintroduce "subordination."[44]

However persuasive Goulburn found Samson to be on the subject of slavery, he continued to fret over the low birth rate on his property. The figures for 1807 revealed a single birth and nine deaths. The following year there was only a handful of births in a population that still hovered around 260. Samson admitted that he had again been "rather unfortunate with children," there having been three abortions and two infant deaths before the end of the first week of life. Very few estates were able to keep up their number, he reported by way of explanation, and in the case of Amity Hall the situation was even more difficult because of the large number of elderly slaves. A further decline in the population in 1809 saw him hasten to report that most of the dead had been invalids and thus "only a tax on the Estate."[45]

Samson's admission the very next year that there had again been but a single birth finally goaded Goulburn into a more forthright statement of his opinion. After all, as a public figure and now a junior minister, he could ill afford a reputation for tolerating a harsh regime at Amity Hall. There was a hint of posturing in his fresh instructions to Samson, referring as they did to earlier communications on this subject. It was as if he was seeking to establish a record of concern for the material well-being of his labour force. "Accidental cause may in one year make the number of Deaths considerably greater than in another," he observed, "but the vast disproportion between the number of Negroes on the estate and the number annually born can only arise from overwork or from neglect of the women when pregnant or from some bad system of management." From such a distance it was impossible for him to determine which of these was the actual cause, he noted, but he could and did "seriously recommend" that Samson pay "the utmost attention to this for the future," because he was "convinced that the increase in the population" on the estate was " a far better proof of its prosperity than any increase of the crop." In the meantime, fearful that the continuing decline in Amity Hall's slave population had reduced the total on the estate to a number "almost insufficient to its proper cultivation," he again instructed Samson to make purchases. Similarly, the overriding concern to maintain the strength of his labour force saw him reject Samson's request for the manumission of five mulatto children, who no doubt were the offspring of the attorney/overseer. Goulburn explained that he was "not partial to any proceeding

which tends to deprive the estate of slaves which have been born upon
it and to supply their places by strangers."[46]

Alive to his employer's heightening concern and mounting frustration, the attorney now revealed that nine women had been carrying
children but that four deaths during the first week of life and four
abortions had produced the disappointing total. To remove any suspicion from Goulburn's mind that the pregnant women had been the
victims of "mismanagement or overhard work," Samson disclosed that
four of them had been domestics. Of course, domestic work was not
necessarily light. Also, he reminded Goulburn that it was traditional
not to record births unless the infant survived beyond the ninth day.
Consequently, the actual number of births had always been higher
than those reported. "I beg leave to assure you that every attention in
regard to their accommodation compatible with the interest of the Estate has been all along paid to the Negroes," he wrote in November
1810. "I think this year if there is no actual Increase then there will be
no diminition [sic] in their number." In short, an investment of £4,200
in forty slaves, especially female slaves, had over the past three years
achieved precious little. Deaths had so exceeded births that the forty
purchases had raised the total by barely half that number.[47]

Just as persistent as Samson's refrain about the need to increase the
stock of slaves was his call for the outlying land of St Iago to be developed into a fenced pasture. He also recommended the construction of
a "breeze" mill. St Iago would be an excellent spot for cattle that were
exhausted after crop or were to be fattened up for sale, he repeatedly
advised. A breeze mill was closely related to the livestock question, for
it would save much of the considerable annual expense on animals.
Fewer steers would be required to power the mills. No less attractive
was the promise that a breeze mill would speed up the grinding of
canes and thus make possible the processing of the entire crop within
the dry season. But the master in Chancery was unwilling to sanction
the additional expense.[48]

As noted above, Goulburn had expected to find more than £40,000
awaiting him when he came of age in 1805. After all, his Liverpool
agent alone had paid £41,000 into Chancery since his father's death.
Of course, the half of the sugars that went annually to the London
agent, Joseph Timperon, purchased the supplies sent out from London and Cork, and the cost of these had risen dramatically at the turn
of the century. From an average of £900 a year between 1794 and
1798, they had ballooned to almost £1,600 annually over the next five
years. The salaries paid to the staff of Amity Hall, the freight and insurance charges, and the commissions claimed by Goore and Timperon
all ate deeper into the gross profits. So did the investment in new

slaves, which had been significant. In addition, Susannah Goulburn and her children had been paid allowances from the income. Finally, the estate had had to bear the heavy expenses of a Chancery judgment. Thus, in totalling up the net profit over a ten-year period, the master, John Simeon, arrived at a figure of £25,933, which he ordered invested in 3 per cent consols and bank annuities. Although this represented a return of no more than 8 per cent on the estate's capital value, and that during a prolonged sugar boom, it was an impressive figure considering the exceptional circumstances of this case. But the disappointed and cautious owner immediately sought economies.[49]

Goulburn may well have doubted the wisdom of sinking his capital in further improvements to Amity Hall. Certainly, Goore had recommended that he invest his fortune in a substantial property in England. Drawing Samson's attention to the enormous cost of supplies, which he put at more than £2,000 in both 1802 and 1803, Goulburn demanded economies. He called for a report detailing areas where retrenchment was possible. He deferred a decision on the breeze mill until the security of the island from French attack was assured, and in the meantime he demanded to know how Samson would make up the loss of manure as the dependence on animals lessened. He also sought information on how breeze mills had "answered on other estates where they have been erected." And fearful that yet another crisis in Anglo-American relations would disrupt the flow of American provisions, especially corn and timber, he suggested that more of the estate's uncultivated lands be planted and that its trees be felled.[50]

Samson's continuing inability to get the crop off and process it during the dry season, at least with the current strength of slaves and stock, had been underlined in 1805. The estate was still short of slaves, steers, and mules. Operations were incomplete at the beginning of August when the canes were yielding only half the quantity of juice they had given before the return of the rains. With the opening of the new crop season only four months away, yet faced with the need to harvest the corn and clean the pastures, Samson advised Goulburn that it would be impossible to devote to the canes the attention they required. Only the construction of a breeze mill, which would permit them to produce forty hogsheads a week, get the canes off quickly, and save the stock, could rescue the situation. So, late in 1805, Goulburn grudgingly sanctioned this additional investment. Unfortunately, progress was now delayed by Samson's fear that to rush the work would put too much strain on the steers used for hauling timber. Nor could Goulburn's misgivings have been removed by the unwelcome news of such poor prices for rum that it was barely worth producing. As a result of the drop in price, the island expenses, which the rum profits normally covered, depressed his income. Not surprisingly, he was in no mood to accept Samson's proposal that he convert an outlying parcel of land into a coffee plantation. Nor did the breeze mill solve any problems. Although it was up and working in 1808, Samson made the belated discovery that wind was not a reliable source of power. Consequently, the steers had to be kept at full strength if the estate was to operate at full capacity whenever the sails were still. Even when it was working well, the breeze mill simply magnified the livestock problem, for the canes had to be hauled quickly from pieces, otherwise they deteriorated.

In view of all these problems, at the end of the first half-decade of his full control of the property, Henry Goulburn found himself forced to consider selling part of it in order to raise the funds to invest in other needed improvements. His short experience had given point to his father's weary admission: "Whoever has a property in the West Indies must make up his mind to these sudden transitions from good to indifferent news." Further, Goulburn had hesitantly committed himself to the amelioration of slavery on Amity Hall. Yet his belated insistence that an increase in the estate's population be accorded priority over the production of even more sugar appears to have been motivated by material rather than moral considerations. He was responding much as the abolitionists had reasoned planters would to the imminent closing of the slave trade.[51]

CHAPTER THREE

War and Peace

Henry Goulburn owed a debt of gratitude to Matthew Montagu which he knew he would never be able fully to repay. Montagu had come to the assistance of his mother; Montagu had welcomed him into his home, treating him as a member of the family; Montagu had taken his education in hand and ensured that he was prepared for a life of public service; Montagu had encouraged him to enter Parliament, introduced him to his close friend Spencer Perceval, and enrolled him in the Tory leader's coterie of personal followers; and it was to Montagu's seat for the Cornish patronage borough of St Germans that Goulburn would succeed in 1812 when the Irwins sold complete control of Horsham to the Duke of Norfolk. Finally, it was surely Montagu who promoted Goulburn's claims for advancement when Perceval formed his administration in 1809. Nor was it a coincidence that Goulburn's appointment was to the Home Office, as an under-secretary to the self-effacing Richard Ryder. There were two Ryders in the cabinet, and with the senior of the brothers, Dudley, first Earl of Harrowby, Montagu had a friendship of exceptional intimacy which dated from their Harrow schooldays.[1]

When Henry Goulburn sought a wife, he selected the third of Montagu's daughters. As a suitor, he had already excited the ridicule of society. His courtship of the "beautiful" and "amiable" Lady Selina Stewart had been conducted with an ineptitude which the malicious attributed to his squint. Betrayed by passion in this instance, he did not repeat the mistake. "I am always afraid of marriages that arise out of excited feeling or sudden impulse," he later avowed. He had known Jane Montagu for all of her eighteen years, and the Montagus had worried that he thought of himself more as sibling than suitor. Matthew Montagu had every reason to be "particularly gratified in bestowing his daughter upon a young man whose worth and merits he is so certain of." Similarly, Susannah Goulburn welcomed the alliance enthusiastically. "You have the best prospect before you that a man can have with such a mind," she assured her son, noting that other attributes "however agreeable are fleeting but Principle and mind remain."[2]

Jane Montagu was "a captivating little soul," her diminutive stature and retiring nature prompting intimates to dub her "wren." One of her more feline acquaintances commented on her good fortune in securing "the protection and attachment of a man so calculated to perfect all the delightful promise" of her "youthful mind." Goulburn would make her what she "*ought* to be, a very superior as well as a very happy woman," for his "appearance and manner" announced "everything that is gentlemanlike and amiable." He certainly possessed all the virtues of an eligible bachelor – "honour, dignity, integrity, considerateness, courtesy," and a handsome income. He "is one of the best esteemed young men of the present times," wrote an envious friend of the Montagus. And shortly after the announcement of their engagement, Jane Montagu modestly wrote to Henry: "I feel every day more conscious how undeserving I am of the happy lot which awaits me & how much will be expected from me by all your friends who feel so rightly your value." For his part, Goulburn was undoubtedly doing what was expected of him by those to whom he was already deeply attached and heavily indebted. He was formally entering the Montagu family. On the other hand, he was attracted by his bride's "strength of intellect, her warmth of affection, her strong religious feeling." They were already as one in their faith.[3]

The Goulburns were married on 20 December 1811, and the Spencer Percevals made their house available to the newlyweds for a brief honeymoon over Christmas and the New Year. A few miles from London, set in extensive grounds on the edge of Ealing Common, it provided privacy, comfort, and convenience. Under the terms of the marriage contract, Montagu settled £5,000 on his daughter, and the groom agreed to contribute a like sum. The total fund was to be held in trust, and the income was to be available to either Henry or Jane, should she survive him. Following their decease, it was to be divided between their children in whatever way they specified. In addition, Henry undertook to provide his wife with £250 a year in pin money and to make provision for a jointure of £1,500 a year. Finally, while his estate was to be held for the use of the eldest son of the marriage, Goulburn was empowered to mortgage his lands up to the amount of £12,000 and even to sell his estate in Jamaica, on condition that the proceeds be invested in government or real securities in Britain. Evidently, his wife was to be better protected than his mother had been. Moreover, with his annual income still averaging almost £6,000, and with his wastrel brother Edward at last showing every sign of having found a suitable profession in the law, Henry Goulburn and his young wife appeared to be comfortably set.[4]

Jane Goulburn saw little of her husband, at least during the week. His had long been regarded as one of the relatively few "efficient working offices," and he was keen to impress his superiors. The calls on his time were seemingly endless. Even his decision to let his home on the west side of Great Cumberland Street, only a stone's throw from the Montagu residence, and to rent 30 Great George Street – which, by virtue of its proximity to his office and the Commons, held out the hope of a more satisfactory family life – failed to improve the situation materially. Following Jane's difficult first confinement, which resulted in a miscarriage during the summer of 1812, Susannah Goulburn explained to her daughter-in-law: "Henry's occupation must necessarily separate him from what is most dear to him." But a less than gregarious wife was not easily reconciled to her husband's constant absence. You "now and then thought I scolded you, when you left me to my own cogitations," she admitted to him, "which if I did was quite natural as I have enough of my own company unavoidably, when you are at the office and worse than that, at the House of Commons." Before long, her concern that he was overtaxing his weak eyes, as a result of working by candlelight late into the evenings, was superseded by her increasingly frequent complaints of debilitating migraines. Goulburn's absences were not entirely the result of his evangelical resolve to avoid the enervating effects of home life – or even a desire to please the secretary of state. They also arose from a heavy administrative burden.[5]

If Richard Ryder lacked the ability and knowledge that in Goulburn's opinion so distinguished Richard's brother Harrowby, "he had a clear judgment and had attained a proficiency in general knowledge beyond that usually possessed by a well educated Gentleman to which he added a knowledge of the law which he had previously practised." However, what most endeared Ryder to his young under-secretary was "the superiority of his moral qualities," his "honesty of purpose," his "utter absence of selfishness," and his "constant consideration of the feelings of all with whom he was either privately or officially brought into contact." Here was a worthy model for an ambitious and intelligent junior, at least in the art of human management. On the other hand, Ryder admitted to being ill equipped and ill prepared for an important portfolio. He had held but a pair of minor offices in the past. Thus, in proffering his support to his friend Spencer Perceval, he had reminded him that he possessed neither the mental ability nor the physical stamina for demanding responsibilities. A powerful sense of duty and personal loyalty eventually saw him accept the Home Office, if only with great trepidation. Another victim of nervous headaches,

Ryder was a hypochondriac, "badly lacking in energy," and "liable to collapse at moments of crisis," and he happily delegated much of the work of his office to his two juniors.[6]

The Home Office, whose seals Goulburn was himself briefly to hold almost a quarter of a century later, had been created in 1782 as part of a restructuring of the duties of the king's senior ministers in an effort to simplify and render more efficient the administration of domestic and foreign business. To these same ends, a third secretaryship of state was revived in 1794 to handle the increasingly heavy responsibility for war. Seven years later, colonial business, which had been conducted from the Home Office, was transferred to the third secretary. Thus the home secretary's responsibilities were more clearly defined as the "internal government of Great Britain." His duty to maintain domestic peace and security saw him armed with "an enormous police power" during disorders. He administered the Alien Office, which had been established in 1793, ostensibly to control the entrance to and movement within Britain of foreigners, but which also served as "the administrative office for the first comprehensive British secret service in the modern sense"; he oversaw the affairs of the Channel Islands, whose proximity to France gave them a somewhat higher profile after the outbreak of war in 1793; he supervised the volunteers and the militia; finally, he served as an essential channel of communication with the monarch on a wide range of appointments.[7]

By the time Goulburn joined the administration, Britain boasted perhaps the most effective central government in Europe. The population explosion, together with the transformation and expansion of the economy, had been agents of change, as had the demands and pressures of war. The "fiscal-military state" was now at its apogee. Some 10 per cent of the adult population was under arms, and the national debt was in the process of quadrupling in little more than two decades. The civil establishment was increasing by a more modest but still costly 50 per cent. And if during this national crisis the younger Pitt's several measures to centralize the bureaucracy "and make it a more effective and less expensive instrument of executive authority" had stalled, the Home Office had not witnessed any dramatic surge in its central establishment. The secretary of state commanded a modest staff of thirteen clerks, and he had the assistance of two under-secretaries. They decided which matters required his personal attention and then took his directions and drafted his responses. Routine business they handled themselves. They also conducted many of the interviews with the seemingly endless stream of callers at the office. Despite the humdrum nature of such duties, a politician as acute and relentlessly ambitious as George Canning had earlier aspired to the position in the belief that it would give him the opportunity to enlarge his general information and cut a figure in the Commons. Only later did he conclude that to add parliamentary to administrative duties was to overburden such men of business.[8]

Henry Goulburn's fellow under-secretary was John Beckett. He could have served as the mold from which later senior civil servants were to be cast. A lawyer by training, and thus better equipped than his young colleague for the task of drafting legislation, he was discreet and unobtrusive. He personified the strengthening commitment to "service" in the quest for efficiency and responsibility. And while a proposal to designate one of the under-secretaries as permanent had been formally rejected in 1795, it had effectively been honoured. Beckett was the "stationary" under-secretary, and Goulburn the parliamentary one whose tenure was tied to the minister or ministry he served. Not that this distinction prevented the two men from establishing a close relationship. Goulburn found Beckett "a most kind and able coadjutor." Equally important, they were ideologically compatible. Occupying senior positions in a department which by the very nature of its concern with public order and domestic security was inherently conservative, they were as one in their "zealous and consistent" conservatism.[9]

To streamline business, it was divided broadly into two classes, each under the supervision of an under-secretary. Goulburn's demesne was that of the volunteeers and the militia, though he often had to venture beyond it. Indeed, he suffered something of a baptism by fire. Barely had he taken office than the government decided to make an example of Sir Francis Burdett, radical gadfly and MP for Westminster, who had taken up the cause of the secretary of the British Forum Society. The secretary had been imprisoned – despite his abject apologies when summoned to the bar of the House – for the society's public criticism of the Commons' decision to clear the public galleries during the parliamentary inquiry into a bungled military expedition. Burdett had been absent from the House at the time of this action, but his subsequent denunciations of what he termed an abuse of privilege exposed him to a similar punishment. At Perceval's prompting, his colleagues duly voted that he be committed to the Tower. The Speaker made out a warrant, and it fell to Goulburn to direct the sergeant-at-arms, General Colman, to execute it. The hapless old soldier, without troops to command, was intimidated by the mobs that took to the streets in support of the popular member, and he was paralysed by the fear that he would himself be liable to prosecution if he broke down Burdett's door. After several days of disturbances and opera *bouffe*, and emboldened by a small army and a government promise of legal indemnity, Colman finally hauled Burdett off to the Tower, where the MP remained until the end of the parliamentary session. Predictably, Ryder collapsed under the strain as both will and health again failed him. For his young deputy, however, the object lesson of this episode was the unreliability of military men in civil crises. A man who had commanded a brigade in battle had plainly been overcome "by the novelty of his situation and the dread of the responsibility imposed on him by giving him direction in a civil struggle."[10]

Goulburn knew no such dread, which was just as well, for on several occasions and for extended periods during his first year in office he was left effectively in command of the department. Both Ryder and Beckett were on vacation or leave. The young under-secretary handled the problems that inevitably arose with surprising aplomb, whether it was a matter of finding mobile artillery for the exposed Channel Islands, of encouraging the desertion of French officers by recommending that they receive the pay of their equivalent British rank, or promoting a scheme to facilitate the rescue of shipwrecked mariners by placing equipment and stores at strategic and secure locations around the coast. However, his principal duty remained the time-consuming and tedious administration of the volunteers and militia.[11]

Following the outbreak of war with France in 1793, successive administrations had struggled to provide an effective system of home defence while ensuring a constant supply of recruits to regiments of the line. Yet the welter of patriotic establishments, among them the volunteers and the militia, were less a tribute to martial energy than a reflection of "poverty of thought and of power in organization." The unrealized ambition was to create an ever-larger national pool of trained men. The creation of the local as distinct from regular militia, which within a year was almost 200,000 men strong, failed to solve the acute and closely linked problems of army recruitment and the maintenance of a force adequate for home defence. Thousands of men continued to be drawn from the regular militia, and these losses were never completely recouped. Similarly, while the local militia absorbed, as was intended, many of the volunteers, the expiry of the first four-year enlistments saw a government, which was anxious neither to lose the services of men who had received a rudimentary training nor to replace them *en masse* with men entirely untrained, abandon the principle of rotation that was so vital to the creation of an ever-deeper reservoir of men. Instead, it offered bounties to encourage re-enlistment. The men who did re-enlist were thereby serving as substitutes for those who would otherwise have been inducted. So instead of supplementing each other, the regular and local militias were in competition for men. Meanwhile, the recruiting machinery of the army was grinding to a halt.[12]

Goulburn's task was that of facilitating the flow of recruits from the regular militia to the regular army in order to compensate for an annual "wastage" of some 23,000 men. His solution was the obvious one. He simply reduced the size of the militia establishments which the counties were required to maintain, thus freeing more men for annual harvest by the line regiments. In this way, or so he believed, he had established a precedent whereby in subsequent periods of national crisis, disciplined men would swell the ranks of the army. At the same time, he sought to upgrade the military quality of the local militiamen by initiating a scheme whereby they were provided with experienced drillmasters. Further, he devoted his vacation in 1810 to the consolidation and amendment of the various militia statutes. He welcomed the exercise as valuable experience in the art of drafting legislation. As he recalled years later, at the time "there was no legal officer whose duty it was to draw Acts of Parliament & assistance was only occasionally obtained from a Barrister himself engaged in extensive Private business & acting as Counsel to all the officers Military and Civil." Nevertheless, Goulburn's bill "proved generally acceptable to those connected with that force and passed through Parliament without opposition."[13]

Goulburn also played a large role in freeing a portion of the garrison of regulars in Ireland for service with Wellington in the Iberian Peninsula. Why not substitute British militia for those regulars, he suggested, and replace them with Irish militia? Ryder quickly recognized the merits of his young deputy's commonsense proposal, and it was strongly supported by Castlereagh, who was to return to the cabinet as foreign secretary early in 1812. Unlike earlier legislation, the Militia Interchange Bill of 1811 envisioned a permanent arrangement and thus "a total change in the Constitution of the Militia of both Countries." Moreover, the British militiamen who agreed to service in Ireland soon exceeded the 8,000 regulars they were to relieve. Another 4,000 militia were therefore assigned to replace that number of regulars stationed in the Channel Islands. On the other side of the ledger, fourteen regiments of Irish militia volunteered for service in Britain. All in all, the interchange was adjudged a vital innovation, and the *Quarterly Review* hailed it as "the most important and beneficial [measure] to the empire which has been proposed since the union."[14]

The smooth progress of Goulburn's life and career was suddenly endangered in 1812. For some time, he and the other senior members of the Home Office had watched anxiously the gathering storm clouds of economic dislocation and social discontent. A decline of trade (the result of Napoleon's Continental System and of difficulties with the United States), a series of bank failures, and a succession of poor harvests were the elements of an economic crisis. Industrial districts were especially hard hit, and it was in these areas that Luddism appeared in 1811. The unemployed, together with those fearful for the future of their skilled occupations, resorted to violence, largely as a result of their inability to secure relief or protection through peaceful appeals and petitions. Sometimes operating in well-disciplined parties, occasionally in disguise, they destroyed machinery and attacked mills, while other protesters participated in the more traditional food riots.[15]

At the Home Office, a preoccupation with the maintenance of public order and the preservation of domestic security inevitably coloured the interpretation of events. The importance of want, fear, and frustration as the nutrients of discontent tended to be discounted in favour of more sinister factors. The reports Ryder received from the disturbed districts certainly hardened his conviction that a vast conspiracy existed among the lower orders. So money and pardons were offered for information, and local communities were urged to organize reliable elements of the citizenry into mutual defence associations to protect private property. Draconian measures were piloted through Parliament, such as that which made frame breaking a capital crime, and the police powers of the magistracy were greatly if temporarily enlarged. Ryder also placed great stock in the Watch and Ward Act, which permitted the police to conscript the entire male population of a town. Several of the larger communities were indeed put under watch and ward, only for some magistrates to remind the Home Office that the act's implementation in their localities would amount to putting weapons into the hands of the disaffected. The main emphasis, therefore, was on the use of troops to overawe the disorderly.[16]

The lords lieutenant of counties and the military commanders were reminded that the local militia might be called out to suppress "existing Riots and Tumults." Inevitably, this drew Goulburn, by no means unwillingly, into an area of business from which he would normally have been excluded. He demanded a full investigation of a report that a number of privates of the South Hants Militia, while on their way north to the troubled textile districts, had declared that if required to act against the rioters of Manchester, they would fire over rather than into the people. He endorsed the decision of the lieutenant colonel of the Oldham local militia to supply muskets to industrialists for the defence of their works, but only on condition that the weapons were surplus to the needs of the militia and that they would be issued to those "manufacturing Houses of Eminence" where there was every reason to believe they would be put to good use and be well guarded. And to temper the resistance of local militiamen to the unpleasant duty of suppressing disturbances, he ensured that it would be credited against their fourteen days of annual training.[17]

In the midst of this excitement, Spencer Perceval was murdered. On 11 May 1812, John Bellingham waited for him in the lobby of the House of Commons and shot him at close range. Instability and insanity were part of the assassin's family history, and his mind had become unhinged as a result of a personal disaster while acting as the agent of a British firm in Russia. Some members of society feared, however, that this terrible deed was the signal for a revolution. Among those who ignominiously fled the capital was Henry Goulburn's friend and fellow member of the government, Frederick Robinson. The Goulburns were taking a late afternoon drive in St James's Park when they heard the awful news. For both of them, the prime minister's murder came as a shattering personal blow. Jane had long been a favourite of the Percevals, and since his marriage Henry's own relationship with Spencer Perceval had grown more intimate. The young couple hastened home, and once his wife's "first burst of grief" had subsided, Goulburn hurried to his office. There he found himself briefly alone with the assassin, who had been brought to the Home Office to be interrogated personally by Ryder. Late in life, Goulburn recalled that his initial thrill of horror gave way to compassion as he observed Bellingham's "haggard countenance, his glaring eye, quivering lip, and considered how short a time was to elapse before he would be called upon to answer before God for the crime which he had committed." Bellingham was "taken, committed, tried, condemned, executed, dissected, all within one week from the time that he fired the shot," despite applications for delay so that evidence of his insanity could be produced.[18]

The task of reconstructing the government proved to be a testing and time-consuming one. Goulburn was pessimistic that he would survive it, even though a caretaker administration led by Lord Liverpool remained in place. On the other hand, a bitter breach between the Prince Regent and his erstwhile Whig friends precluded any thought of the opposition simply being invited to take the reins of power. "Every crooked path will be tried in preference to the right road," the *Morning Chronicle* predicted. The prince's initial preference was for a coalition led by Richard Wellesley or Lord Moira, but neither man commanded sufficient support or respect, and by the beginning of June there was growing restlessness in the Commons at the delay in forming a government. This was a time of acute national crisis. The war with Bonaparte ground on, while relations with the United States continued to deteriorate. But all the manoeuvrings suggested that the next ministry would at least be a little more liberal than the last. As one of the dozen members of Parliament most closely identified with the very conservative Perceval, Goulburn fully expected to leave office with his immediate chief. Richard Ryder was going to depart no matter what, for his friend's murder and the stress of events had driven him back to his sickbed.[19]

Fate again intervened. The Prince Regent invited Lord Liverpool to remain as prime minister. While the continuation of a Tory government headed by a distant relative on his mother's side and containing his mentor's closest friend, Harrowby, greatly enhanced Goulburn's prospects of retaining office, his personal performance merited his inclusion in the new administration. He had shown himself to be energetic, diligent, hard working, efficient, and innovative. Equally important, he had exhibited a refreshing willingness to accept responsibility. In brief, he was earning a reputation as an excellent "man of business." Although these were the very qualities on which the new prime minister had built his own career, Goulburn's retention at the Home Office presented problems. Ryder's successor, Lord Sidmouth, had the position of under-secretary in mind for a member of his own family. But Liverpool soon found another spot worthy of Goulburn's talents and industry. He promoted Robert Peel, his former under-secretary at war and colonies, to the demanding office of chief secretary for Ireland and replaced him with Henry Goulburn.[20]

An empire disrupted by one revolutionary war had prospered during another. Britain had gained seventeen colonies during the recent conflict; and few of them, as one powerful interpreter of British imperialism argued, were acquired simply to create markets or to corner resources for industrialists. Dutch and French islands in the West Indies, the Dutch East Indies, Ceylon and Mauritius in the Indian Ocean, the Dutch factories in India, the Dutch colony at the southern tip of Africa, and the Ionian Islands together with those of Malta and Sicily in the Mediterranean had all been seized to deny them to the French, to weaken France's allies, or to enhance the security of Britain's territories. This sudden and remarkable proliferation of dependencies scattered around the globe, few of which had much in common save "small population, undeveloped resources and political and economic subordination to Britain," sparked a reconsideration of the value of empire. The new economic orthodoxy associated with Adam Smith taught that colonies were a drain on the resources of the mother country. On the other hand, national pride, not to mention the political influence of those with a vested interest in the empire's preservation – and of these the "gentlemanly capitalists" of the City of London have recently been elevated to a leading position – provided effective counterweights to intellectual theorizing. "If we cast our eyes on the map of the world," the *Quarterly Review* boasted, "we shall find, that the sun, in

its daily course, never sets upon Englishmen." The heightened nationalism of the period, the strength of evangelicalism, even the sharpen-
ing of racial attitudes, had helped to infuse many Britons with a new
sense of their imperial and civilizing mission.[21]

Empire was also a means of diminishing social misery and thus political discontent at home. Although T. Robert Malthus in his influential
Essay on Population – at least in its revised and weightier form published
in 1803 – warned that emigration offered only transitory relief from
the consequences of a population outgrowing its ability to feed itself,
others were greater enthusiasts of this solution. Henry Brougham, writing in the *Edinburgh Review* in the same year as the appearance of
Malthus's second edition, criticized Adam Smith for devaluing empire.
Colonies would provide markets for British goods, fruitful places of investment for surplus capital, and a haven for those Britons unable to
prosper at home, he maintained. Similarly, Patrick Colquhoun's *Treatise on the Wealth, Power and Resources of the British Empire* (1814) dwelt on
the contributions that settled colonies could make to the development
of the British economy. There was no hint here that all of these commercial advantages might be secured through "informal" empire.
Even political Radicals – who warned that the retention of colonies was
merely a device to protect the interests of the few at the expense of the
many – grudgingly conceded the value of colonies as a human safety
valve.[22]

Tories were imperialists, extolling the contributions that colonies
made to British security, naval power, commerce, manufacturing and
agriculture. Not only were colonial supplies vital, but the colonies provided the decisive counterbalance to Bonaparte's "immense population" and "immense continental dominion," and their identification
with naval might was "deeply embedded in the minds of the British ruling class." The glorious role of the Royal Navy during the French wars
ensured that the connection was a popular one also. Moreover, it was
an association which influential vested interests, both financial and
mercantile, had every reason to cultivate and exploit. The "main dynamic" of the City's gentlemanly capitalists was the "drive to create an
international trading system centred in London and mediated by ster-
ling." The British North America timber trade, for example, involved
"one-seventh of all British shipping" in 1820. This fact made an imperial enthusiast of the Society of Shipowners, "perhaps the best organized commercial association in early nineteenth-century Britain."[23]

Nevertheless, imperial pride, imperial mission, and the association
of the colonies with naval supremacy and commercial power could not
entirely overwhelm an ambivalence nourished by fear of the size of the
national debt and resentment of the high level of taxation. The costs

of administering and defending the expanded empire caused some disquiet. The size of the colonial bureaucracy – and a suspicion that it was deliberately bloated in order to provide a rich source of patronage for ministers – prompted parliamentary investigations. Not that Parliament ventured into colonial affairs either confidently or systematically. As yet, few members exhibited more than a spasmodic interest in them, and colonial policy was at this time rarely a partisan issue.[24]

As for policy, the lessons of the American Revolution had not been forgotten. There was danger in any attempt to impose the metropolitan will on those peripheries that possessed their own legislatures. Further, the cause of colonial self-government was certain to be espoused by domestic reformers. Lord Liverpool, for one, worried that an alliance of English Radicals and "factious and disaffected" colonials would see the American experience repeated. In short, there was far more caution than some historians have acknowledged in the exercise of metropolitan control. Nevertheless, there were colonies in which the establishment of representative institutions seemed peculiarly imprudent or inexpedient. Direct and "illiberal rule" seemed fully justified whenever "a colonial society was so backward or so divided by race, nationality, religion, wealth or servitude, that no group capable of working the old representative system was likely to provide good government in the interests of the population as a whole." The penal colony of New South Wales was an obvious case in point. In holding fast to this position, ministers were assured of the support of a well-organized and passionate phalanx both within and outside Parliament.[25]

The abolition of the slave trade had brought no slackening of interest in the condition of slaves. Two cases of appalling brutality, which had gone unpunished locally, galvanized metropolitan humanitarians into renewed activity. In 1811 Henry Brougham set up a cry in the *Edinburgh Review* for more effective British intervention in the affairs of the slave colonies. It was a call repeated in the Commons, where the "Saints" began to demand reports on conditions in the slave colonies and to expose the failings of colonial officials. Here, then, was one aspect of colonial policy that excited considerable and sustained parliamentary interest and concern. And while the government remained loath to attempt to coerce the old colonies and their legislatures, demands that the benefits of representative institutions be extended to new possessions, such as Trinidad, could be resisted in the sure knowledge that the "Saints" would firmly support this stand. In fact, at their prompting, an order in council was issued in the spring of 1812 establishing a slave registration scheme in Trinidad. A regularly updated and detailed registry of slaves seemed the best guarantee against their illicit importation.[26]

The men charged with the supervision and administration of the empire occupied a modest house built by George Downing in the seventeenth century at the St James's Park end of the street that bore his name. Dark, damp, and draughty, the War and Colonial Office afforded scant physical comfort. The swelling volume of incoming correspondence and a shortage of adequate storage space merely added to the crammed and cluttered appearance of the interior. There was a library but few books, though a copy of Colquhoun's *Treatise* was purchased, and the maps on hand were too general to be of real value. Even the system for dispatching the department's mail was cumbersome and inadequate. More important still, the staff was chronically overworked, having benefited little from the growth of the bureaucracy.[27]

In 1812, in addition to the minister and his two under-secretaries, the establishment included a chief clerk, thirteen clerks, six full-time extra clerks, a private secretary, a précis writer, a librarian, and several translators. By his own admission, the private secretary's position was a sinecure. The same could be said of the Arabic translator, since the Polish emigré who held this position was entirely unfamiliar with the language. As at the Home Office, the functioning members of the staff had long since been divided into distinct groups in order to expedite the handling of business. An under-secretary and eleven of the clerks and extra clerks were assigned to colonial affairs. Nevertheless, the combining of War and Colonies had created an unbearably heavy workload for the secretary of state. The intent in 1801 may well have been to guarantee him sufficient employment following peace with France, but with the renewal of hostilities he had little time for imperial concerns. This had been Liverpool's own experience there. It was a little surprising, therefore, that he asked his successor at War and Colonies, Earl Bathurst, to act as foreign secretary during Castlereagh's frequent expeditions to the continent. In consequence, Bathurst followed his predecessor's lead and devolved ever more responsibility for colonial affairs on his capable under-secretary.[28]

Henry Bathurst celebrated his fiftieth year in 1812. A devoted Pittite, he had occupied a series of junior and undemanding positions before Portland appointed him to the presidency of the Board of Trade. Under Perceval, he had continued in that position and acted as temporary custodian of foreign affairs until Richard Wellesley could be summoned home from his ambassadorial posting in Spain. Elevation to the secretaryship of War and Colonies now thrust Bathurst into the limelight after years of less conspicuous and more pedestrian administrative labour. This may help explain his elusiveness as a political figure. Disliking controversy, he masked his thoughts so well behind a screen of unending wit and humour that he could easily have been taken for an essentially shallow man. Yet even his critics admitted his abilities, while his admirers lauded his efficiency, his quick grasp of difficult subjects, and his lucidity of thought and expression. Moderately ambitious at best, happy to delegate, he had an amiable disposition and a considerate attitude towards his staff that earned him their affection and loyalty. With Henry Goulburn in particular, he quickly established a paternal relationship, which later prompted the younger man to describe their decade-long association as one of the most satisfying of his career. It was founded on an identity of qualities. Both men inspired the same confidence in their colleagues as they did in each other, for they were intelligent, sensible, honourable, trustworthy, loyal, and efficient. Traits such as these were very rarely found in combination.[29]

Goulburn's fellow under-secretary was Colonel Henry Bunbury. The son of an unsuccessful artist who had found a measure of financial security as a member of the Duke of York's official household, Bunbury had benefited from his father's royal connection. Commissioned in the Coldstream Guards, he had subsequently been appointed an aide-de-camp to the duke. An earnest and high-minded young man, he was appalled at the laxity and corruption that characterized York's entourage. In 1800 he resigned his position to enter the military college at High Wycombe, and he subsequently joined the quartermaster general's department. He was, then, an adminstrative rather than a field officer, though he did see limited action. In 1809 his military experience and knowledge, together with his administrative skills, saw him appointed under-secretary for war. A man of "conscientious diligence" with a "talent for business," he immediately buckled down to the task of reforming the department's "incredible disorders." The strain eventually took such a toll on his health that early in 1812 he offered to resign, only for Bathurst to insist that he remain.[30]

The business of the office was so distinctly divided, Goulburn later wrote, that "I knew no more of what was going on in the War branch than any stranger unless during the absence of my Colleague." The fact that Bunbury was cursed with ill health meant that Goulburn was involved rather more deeply and frequently in military matters than would normally have been the case. "No week occurred during 1813 and 1814," he recalled, "in which some messengers from some of the scenes of conflict did not arrive in Downing Street and measures were in many cases to be taken immediately." At times he was almost the only official left in town. "All the Cabinet Ministers are at their villas or even a greater distance from town," he reported to a close friend in September 1813, "and in the time of General Holiday I have only to brood over the impossibility of complying with the earnest requisitions for troops which we receive from all quarters and which we unfortunately are not able to comply with."[31]

Even when he was able to concentrate on colonial matters, Goulburn encountered unexpected obstacles. The simultaneous arrival in his office of a bag of dispatches from Gibraltar and his friend and vice-president of the Board of Trade, the hypochondriacal Frederick Robinson, produced a farcical episode. Obsessed with the fear that the correspondence had been exposed to the plague, Robinson suddenly left Goulburn's office only to return with a jar of vinegar, in which he "so completely immersed the letters as to render them in many instances altogether illegible." A bemused under-secretary recalled that Robinson "lives entirely with Dr. Pym who is appointed Physician to the board of Trade and has already evinced his talents by curing a boil on the Vice-President's nose which was supposed to have been occasioned by too much attention to infected papers."[32]

Bathurst's membership of the House of Lords meant that Goulburn had to serve as a departmental spokesman in the Commons. Nor was this inappropriate, since from the date of his appointment in mid-August 1812 he was in everything but name the minister for the empire. At a time when the cabinet gave little attention to colonial affairs, except when they intersected with the compelling issue of slavery, leaving policy as well as administration in the hands of the secretary of state, Bathurst exercised only the most general form of supervision over his energetic and capable junior. The war preoccupied him. Some incoming letters were put aside for his personal attention, and he signed most of the outgoing dispatches, but more often than not this was simply the case of the senior man putting his name to his deputy's drafts. Thus the conduct which Goulburn explained and defended in the House was invariably his own. For this reason alone, the role of spokesman added significantly to the weight of the burden he was already carrying. In his case, the strain was increased by the growing parliamentary interest in colonial affairs and his lack of confidence as a debater. He was a pedestrian speaker.[33]

Goulburn was unexceptionably Tory in his imperialism. He valued the colonies primarily for the power and prestige their possession conferred on the mother country. They were, he declared, "one of the greatest sources of our glory, and one of the great supports of our power, affording resources in war, and increasing our commerce in peace." Personally connected as a West Indian planter to the burgeoning services of the City – banking, insurance, and commerce – he extolled the Empire as "an extended field for commercial enterprise, additional markets for our produce and manufactures, and the employment of an annually increasing mercantile marine." In the conquered colonies alone, new markets to the value of £3 million were opened to British manufactures in 1814 and some £1.5 million in revenues furnished to the mother country. Nor did Goulburn overlook strategic considerations or the traditional connection between empire and naval supremacy. "From the very extension of our territory, and the increased employment which trade with ... [the colonies] afforded to British shipping and seamen, we had always within our reach the means of commanding a naval force without delay." Like his fellow members of the Alfred Club, he had "a powerful conception of the national destiny."[34]

Welcoming Goulburn to the chair he was vacating, Robert Peel provided him with the "detail" of his "future occupation." One surprising chore was the supervision of the secret service account. Much of the money was disbursed in the form of payments to French royalists and in financing the intelligence-gathering operation conducted out of the Channel Islands by Prince Bouillon, a former vice-admiral of the royal French navy. Not that Peel valued the investment, sceptical as he was of the quality of the information gathered by the agents smuggled into France. It "generally reaches us in the papers before it arrives from the spy," he advised his successor.[35]

Turning to the colonies, Peel assured his friend that there was "ample field" for him to "range in, extending from Botany Bay to Prince Edwards [sic] Island." He would be required to superintend the entire correspondence with all of the British colonies around the world, save for those in the Mediterranean, which until 1816 were administered by Bunbury. Lest this daunting prospect should unnerve the new under-secretary, Peel hastened to add that "the quantity of writing which you have bears no proportion whatever to the quantity of reading." Invariably, decisions could be deferred. There were few acts relating to the colonies with which Goulburn would need to familiarize himself, Peel noted by way of further reassurance, other than the navigation laws regulating the trade of the West Indies and the Canada Act of 1791. Questions of trade and commerce should be referred to the Board of Trade, where they would "afford a pleasing recreation to Robinson." However, the primacy of the Colonial Office in all colonial matters was by this date being effectively established and the continued referral was largely a formality.[36]

The more pressing issues were those that concerned the conquered territories. Which of these territories should be retained? Should Britain follow the Roman precedent "of compelling the conquered to adopt the laws, the language and the manners of the conquerors"? Should the government hold out "every encouragement for the superabundant population of the mother country to emigrate to the newly conquered" settlements? What contribution ought each colony to make towards its own protection? More specifically, a decision could not long be delayed on which of the Dutch colonies should be retained, and Goulburn was assured that he would immortalize himself if he managed to frame a constitution for Trinidad. "It has baffled all your predecessors who have uniformly left it as they found it, governed by Spanish laws and petitions for English," Peel reported.[37]

The metaphor Robert Peel coined for Trinidad was that of the unfortunate patient in a country hospital on whom new surgical procedures were tested. Those that succeeded would be repeated elsewhere. The man named as chief surgeon was James Stephen the elder, a former resident of the West Indies, a lawyer and Tory member of Parliament, who had been a literary scourge of American neutral trading during the French wars and was the brother-in-law of Wilberforce and a relentless campaigner against slavery. Wilberforce and Zachary Macaulay were to be occasional consultants. "The poor patient has to go through some very severe operations," Peel remarked ironically, "she is now actually bound down for a most painful one – a registration of slaves with penalties upon penalties on those who fail to observe the regulations of an order in council prescribed by Dr. Stephen."[38]

Goulburn was relieved to discover on arrival at his new office on 15 September 1812 that Stephen and Wilberforce were out of town. "I have a little time to prepare for the consultation on the subject of Trinidad which I hear from all quarters awaits me on their return," he remarked. His anxiety was heightened by an awareness of the personal suspicion with which they regarded him as a slave owner, though he considered this distrust unfair. After all, his views on slavery were very much those of the administration in which he was serving. He regarded it as an institution to be ameliorated rather than abolished, as indeed did the "Saints" at this time. Of course, this was a moderate public position that coincided with his private interest. But he was careful to keep his distance from the West India Committee, which all too often served merely as an apologist for slavery. Moreover, he was soon employing the younger James Stephen, the third of the abolitionist's sons, to examine the legislation enacted by colonies that had assemblies. Disallowance of their legislation was the principal means by which Downing Street exercised a measure of control over these colonies, though this was regarded as an "extreme remedy" and thus not to be applied lightly. The younger Stephen's appointment ensured an unprecedented scrutiny of the old West Indian slave colonies.[39]

The order in council establishing the system of slave registration in Trinidad had been issued on 26 March 1812 over the signature of Goulburn's cousin, Lord Chetwynd, the clerk to the Privy Council. It was an imposing document. Running to twenty-eight printed pages, it detailed the form of the registry, the procedures to be followed, and the qualifications of the registrar of slaves. However, delays in compiling the register, which were locally attributed to the ignorance of "coloured" slave owners, necessitated successive extensions to the period specified in the order. Another problem was the appointment of commissioners to visit plantations in order to ensure "better protection and security of infants, married women and lunatics, and all other persons under any disability or incapacity." There were simply too few respectable persons willing to go off to outlying areas, the governor explained. None of this sat well with the zealous and impatient elder Stephen, who interpreted all delay as obstructionism and demanded that the legal penalties be enforced. Further, noting an increase in the number of registered slaves from those entered on earlier returns, he emphasized the "urgent necessity" for the "strict execution of a law which can alone prevent the contraband importation of slaves into the colony."[40]

In this instance, Goulburn left to Bathurst the task of responding to Stephen. First, however, they sought additional information from Trinidad. They were advised that any enforcement of the penalties for "neglect and disobedience" would cause serious hardship if not ruin to "the aged and ignorant owner of one or two Domestic slaves," whose only crime was ignorance of the law, great distance from the town, or a traditional and "total indifference" to those orders of the government "which do not happen to suit some object of personal convenience." Beyond this, the governor denied the existence of any significant illicit trade in slaves and protested that he had instituted the most active measures for its detection and punishment. Nor did he overlook the difficulty some owners unavoidably encountered in making their annual returns within the ten days specified by the order in council. As he explained, it often took three weeks to communicate by boat with outlying districts. Therefore, a period of one month would be more reasonable. Meanwhile, to prevent any abuse of extensions, he was requiring the minority of slave owners who submitted late returns to be examined under oath by the chief judge. Finally, he challenged the accuracy of earlier returns, arguing that, unlike the register, they had not been founded on a strict census. This explanation seemed plausible to Goulburn and was forwarded to the elder James Stephen, but it failed to shake his conviction that many slaves had been illegally smuggled into the colony since the proclamation of the order in council. Significantly, Goulburn publicly rejected the extension of representative institutions to Trinidad in language calculated to reassure the "Saints" of his good intentions. In the slave colonies, the "British Constitution" amounted to throwing all power into the hands of a white oligarchy who then tyrannized the population, he declared in the House. And while there was little prospect of modifying the form of government so "improvidently granted" to a number of the old colonies, "he could not consent that any further extension should be given to this evil."[41]

Goulburn also found a way to appease those merchants and planters who had coupled demands for the "British Constitution" in Trinidad with pleas for the establishment of a more recognizably English judicial system. They objected to the use of the Spanish language, Spanish laws, and Spanish institutions of justice, charging that this policy discouraged investment and damaged credit and commerce. The appointment of a new governor in 1813 provided Goulburn with an opportunity to set in train a number of mollifying changes. All acts of the *cabildo*, an important part of the institutional inheritance from Spain, were now to be recorded in English as well as Spanish. Next, he directed that English be used in all courts and legal proceedings, and authorized the compilation of "an Epitome of the Spanish Laws in the English Language." The appointment of a chief judge, who while ignorant of Spanish law and the language was willing to learn something of both, offered additional encouragement to British merchants and residents without alienating the former Spanish subjects.[42]

With an eye to appeasing another group of zealous members of Parliament – the "economical reformers," who were alarmed by the growth in public expenditures and the consequent likelihood of more waste and corruption – Goulburn sponsored the establishment of a board of colonial audit in 1814. He also promised a more spartan bureaucracy in the colonies, and he sought to strengthen an earlier measure restricting absentee office holding in the colonies. Despite all these measures, Goulburn did not receive the credit he believed he merited as a reformer. As the opposition was quick to point out, his bill was prospective in its nature and left current absentees in their profitable places. The under-secretary's claim that this measure would compel respectable persons to reside in the colonies in order to keep their offices, thus improving the quality of colonial society, impressed few of his listeners. Nor did he enjoy greater success when he attempted to persuade the old Caribbean colonies to shoulder a greater share of the financial burden of their defence. But as important as all these issues were, the most urgent problem awaiting Goulburn in mid-September 1812 was the defence of Canada. He arrived at the Colonial Office soon after an American declaration of war, and there could be no doubt where the Americans would strike.[43]

On 1 June 1812, President James Madison had sent a war message to Congress detailing his nation's grievances against Britain: the impressment of crewmen serving on American vessels on the high seas; the plundering of American commerce "in every seas" under the license of orders in council; the evidence of British interest in New England separatism; and British involvement with "the savages" who had renewed their frontier warfare against the Republic. This lengthy bill of indictment was returned by a far from unanimous congressional grand jury. More than one-third of the members of the lower house voted against war on 4 June, while the eventual majority in the Senate was even slimmer. Indeed, the opposition Federalists and some dissidents in the president's own party attributed the war to imperialism. Not content with nibbling on Spanish Florida, they charged, the administration wished to devour Canada. Madison may have believed that military victory against Britain in North America was assured and would bring her quickly to American terms, but the targeting of Canada lent a certain credibility to the claims that his war was one of expansionism.[44]

The governor general of Canada was Sir George Prevost, a professional soldier and experienced colonial administrator. By nature a cautious man, for Swiss blood ran in his veins, he was defensive minded. The strategic necessity of holding on to Quebec at all costs, the small force of British regulars at his disposal, the lingering possibility of a diplomatic settlement even after the American declaration of war, and the evidence of popular opposition to the war in New England all disposed him to remain passive and seek a truce with the local American commander. "In the present state of Politics in the United States," Prevost reported to Downing Street in mid-July, "I consider it prudent to avoid every measure which can have the least tendency to unite the people of America." He considered American disunity the best insurance against a successful invasion.[45]

Command in the neighbouring and even more vulnerable province of Upper Canada was held by Major General Isaac Brock. He was the other side of the military coin, being both dynamic and aggressive. He had long since concluded that the only hope of successfully defending the colony was to seize the initiative and attack exposed American outposts before the United States could organize and bring to bear its overwhelming superiority in numbers and materiel. Moreover, immediate success in the west would probably bring the native people into Britain's camp. So he authorized the capture of the American fort at Michilimackinac as soon as he received word of the declaration of war. Furthermore, he had little option other than to fight when an American army advanced into Canada from Detroit on 12 July 1812, but he had secured the vital support of the Shawnee Chief Tecumseh as a result of the capture of Michilimackinac. "A more sagacious or more gallant warrior does not, I believe, exist," Brock reported to the Colonial Office.[46]

Many of the native people had sided with the British during the Revolutionary War, largely out of fear of the aggressively expansionist Americans, only to be betrayed in the peace treaty. Subsequently, the Republic sought to reduce the tribes to the lowly rank of economic dependents while inducing compliant chiefs to cede more territory. Here was the issue on which first the Prophet and then his half-brother Tecumseh sought to revive Indian unity and resistance to American expansion. The result had been an inconclusive military engagement at Tippecanoe in November 1811, following an ill-managed pre-emptive advance by the territorial governor of Indiana, but Brock was impressed with the native people's resolve "to continue the contest until they obtain the Ohio for a boundary."[47]

Tecumseh's alliance with the British completely demoralized the commander of the American invasion force, William Hull. Fearful for the security of his lines of communication, he immediately retreated to the safety of Fort Detroit, only to surrender that strongpoint when Brock hinted that he might not be able to control his Indian allies if forced to take it by storm. The surrender was a demoralizing blow to the United States and a correspondingly large boost to the morale of the people and militia of Upper Canada. Moreover, it drew the Indians even closer to the British. In this sense, Brock welcomed the Americans' termination of the truce negotiated by Prevost in the eastern theatre. He had worried that "however wise and politic," it would dishearten the Indians and excite their suspicion of British intentions. Yet as he prepared to counter a second American invasion, Brock conceded that offensive operations would ultimately prove counterproductive. "A spirit would probably arise from the invasion of the United States territory that would compel me to relinquish even the hope of being able to keep possession of this province," he privately acknowledged. So he prepared for a defensive battle in the onerous knowledge that defeat would surely result in the loss of Upper Canada. At Queenston Heights on 13 October 1812 he died at the head of his troops, but they won another decisive victory.[48]

In Britain, the deteriorating relationship with the United States had been a cause of concern to a war-weary and tax-burdened nation. Ministers remained confident that an "immediate rupture" would be avoided, heartened as they were by reports of dissension within Madison's official family and obstructionism in Congress. Moreover, their string of conciliatory gestures had culminated in the suspension of the orders in council, which Madison had only recently proclaimed to be his nation's essential grievance. Even when word reached London at the end of July of the American declaration of war, the fact that this step had been taken in ignorance of the latest concession gave grounds for optimism that it would soon be retracted. Instead, proposals for an armistice foundered on the rock of Madison's insistence that the war could not be terminated without some resolution of, and redress for, the practice of impressment.[49]

The British reacted bitterly to the American government's grim resolve to soldier on. Many Britons no less than American Federalists dismissed as mere window dressing the grievances itemized in Madison's war message. Recalling the Republicans' history of francophilia and the president's recent acceptance at face value of an obviously fraudulent revocation of the French restrictions on American commerce, the Tories suspected that "a secret understanding existed" between Madison and Bonaparte. Similarly, the recent American seizure of pieces of Spanish West Florida and the subsequent invasion of Canada confirmed their suspicions that Madison was bent on a war of conquest. Certainly, Henry Goulburn subscribed to the "stab in the back" analysis of American conduct and was in little doubt that Canada was "the real object of the war on the part of the United States." The fact that the war would be principally fought in Canada also meant that "its detail fell to the Colonial Department" and thus to him.[50]

Goulburn brought to this duty precious little military knowledge or experience. Service as a captain of volunteers, the administration of the militia, and occasional involvement with general military policy in Bunbury's absences from the department scarcely equipped him for the task at hand. His initial response to this "unexpected" war was to scratch around for additional supplies for the heavily outnumbered forces in North America. Clothing and equipment for eight hundred men were sent out early in August, while one of two transports laden with arms and ammunition and destined for the Mediterranean was diverted to Canada. At the same time, to encourage colonial volunteering, Goulburn authorized Prevost to promise 100 acres of land to each man who enlisted. As for Britain's native auxiliaries, "to prevent the commission of those excesses which are so much to be apprehended from their Employment," he issued instructions that they be employed only under the direction of the experienced officers of the Indian Department.[51]

By 1 October unsettling reports of defeatism in Upper Canada and of limited resistance to militia service in Lower Canada had reached London. Hence, Goulburn's relief to be awakened in the middle of the night only six days later by the special messenger from Canada carrying the first accounts of Brock's remarkable victory at Detroit. At the very least, vital time had been won in which to reinforce the colony's defences and counteract the effects of colonial indifference and disaffection. Unfortunately, the coincidental arrival of the news of a stunning naval defeat at the hands of the Americans completely over-shadowed the success in Canada. "The feeling in the British public in favor of the Navy," Goulburn admitted, "rendered in their eyes the military triumph no compensation for the naval disaster." Even joy at the defeat of the second American invasion force was dampened by the news of Brock's death. Goulburn composed an eloquent tribute to the fallen general. The crown had lost not only "an able and meritori-ous officer" but one well equipped "to awe the disloyal, to reconcile the wavering, and to animate the great mass of the inhabitants" to re-sist the enemy. Brock fell "too prodigal of that life of which his emi-nent services had taught us to understand the value."[52]

Brock had urged the home government to assure his native allies that they would be embraced in any peace, arguing that such a guarantee would attach them to Britain "forever." Prevost seconded the recom-mendation. The most cursory examination of the map, he remarked, would reveal "how extremely important it is to the future security of Upper Canada that the Indians should retain possession of the lands they now occupy and thereby form as long as we remain in friendship with them a formidable barrier" to American expansionism. Not that the notion of an Indian buffer state in the Northwest was an original one, having been advanced by successive British governments during the 1790s. This may explain the alacrity with which the Colonial Office now accepted the generals' recommendation. Before year's end, Pre-vost had been authorized to inform the native people that whenever peace negotiations were entered into, "the security of the Indian pos-sessions" would be neither compromised nor forgotten.[53]

Another war aim was the maintenance of that British naval suprem-acy on the Great Lakes which had been the basis of Brock's military suc-cess. At Prevost's suggestion, Goulburn ensured that control of the vessels on the lakes was transferred to the navy, and he sought to up-grade the poorly trained and inexperienced provincial marine through the introduction of "proper officers" and skilled seamen. But it was the spring of 1813 before the initial batch of three hundred officers and men could be sent to Quebec. Most of them had recently served with the flotilla defending Riga and were therefore regarded as peculiarly well suited to service in Canada. Shortly after their arrival, however, the British squadron on Lake Erie suffered a disastrous defeat. This com-pelled the troops operating along the western frontier to retreat to-wards the interior of the province, but they were severely mauled by the Americans and among the dead was Tecumseh. The western region of Upper Canada was now in American hands, though through ingenuity and hard labour an alternative line of supply was kept open to the tribes of the Northwest.[54]

The catastrophe on Lake Erie dumbfounded Goulburn. Several senior officers together with four hundred sailors had been sent to Canada since the spring, and an additional six hundred were ordered there in August – half of them dispatched from Britain and the other three hundred transferred from the fleet operating along the Atlantic coast. Of course, very few if any of these experienced men had reached the unfortunate commander on Lake Erie. Shocked by this unexpected turn of events, Goulburn impressed on Prevost the need to bend every effort over the winter to put a force back on the lakes by spring. In his words; "The reduction of the Enemy's present superiority is of such importance with a view to the preservation of Upper Canada, and maintaining a Communication with the Indians, that nothing but its absolute impracticability could justify its not being attempted." By dint of hard work, naval supremacy was regained on Lake Ontario in 1814, but there was every evidence of the Americans' intention to match British naval construction. The price of supremacy promised to be unending expense.[55]

The loss of naval supremacy on the Great Lakes in 1813 provided Downing Street with a fresh incentive to launch diversionary campaigns along the Atlantic seaboard. All military and naval stores were to be destroyed by the raiders, but individual citizens might purchase immunity for their private property. On one species of private property, however, the commander of the raiding force received specific instructions. He was to do nothing to encourage "servile insurrection," though slaves who exposed themselves to the possible vengeance of their masters by giving assistance to the British raiders were to be taken away and encouraged to enlist in one of the black corps serving in the West Indies. "You must distinctly understand that you are in no case to take slaves away, as slaves," the order continued, "but as free persons, whom the public becomes bound to maintain. This circumstance, as well as the difficulty of transport, will make you necessarily cautious how you contract any Engagement of this nature, which it may be difficult for you to fulfill." The following year, in an effort to tighten the screw on the Americans further, a proclamation was issued which, while it made no mention of slaves, offered transportation to persons who wished to emigrate from the United States in order to serve with the British forces or be sent "as FREE settlers" to British colonies. This caused panic among slave owners, for many slaves accepted the offer.[56]

Mounting naval pressure all along the Atlantic coast, as the blockade and raids disrupted trade, was to be coordinated with a more aggressive campaign along the Canadian frontier. Goulburn had accepted – albeit with unmistakable signs of frustration and irritation – Prevost's passive attitude, which the general continued to justify largely in political terms. By inaction, he hoped to increase the unpopularity of the war in the United States and "to add to the depression of the public credit." But 1813 witnessed a military build-up in North America as the steady erosion of Napoleon's empire at last allowed Britain somewhat greater freedom of action. A long period of westerly winds throughout the spring delayed the initial embarkations, but by the summer Goulburn had reason to believe that the governor general commanded sufficient men to take the initiative. Further, an additional four regiments of battle-hardened men would be on hand before the commencement of the next campaigning season. Prevost's response was entirely unexpected. He protested the "inadequacy of the means afforded him" and complained of a failure to provide him with detailed instructions on "the mode of conducting" the campaign. The opening of 1814 found him calling for reinforcements simply to maintain his lines of defence.[57]

Prevost's excessive caution brought a sharp rejoinder. The absurdity of attempting to direct a campaign from Britain was obvious, hence the decision not only to give him all aid possible but also to allow him the full exercise of his discretion. As for the insufficiency of the reinforcements either dispatched or already on their way, he was pointedly reminded that they exceeded the number he had himself specified as adequate only a few months earlier. From London it appeared that he had fallen under the influence of "overanxious individuals." He was urged to be more vigorous in seizing every reasonable opportunity to attack the Americans and disrupt their plans. Within a few months, however, the collapse of Napoleon's regime had freed even more experienced troops for service in North America and had facilitated the planning of more ambitious and destructive raids along the American coastline.[58]

Convinced that the governor general had enough men to wage offensive operations, Goulburn detailed the objectives that would ensure "ultimate security to His Majesty's Possessions in America." The hope in Downing Street was that the Americans' base at Sackett's Harbour on Lake Ontario would be destroyed, together with their naval establishments on Lakes Erie and Champlain, thereby guaranteeing British supremacy on these inland waters. The retention of Fort Niagara and surrounding territory, the reoccupation of Detroit, and the restoration of the whole of the Michigan country to the native tribes would also evidently improve the British frontier, as would occupation of any part of the territory between Lower Canada and Lake Champlain. To the east, meanwhile, Sir John Sherbrooke was to advance across Maine to the line of the Penobscot in order to establish a se-

cure land communication between Halifax and Quebec and to resolve the disputed ownership of the Passamaquoddy islands. These
were Britain's territorial objectives as peace negotiations at last got under way in Europe. Consequently, Bathurst and Goulburn were infuriated by Prevost's apparent willingness to enter into another armistice
while these negotiations were being conducted. "It is the wish of His
Majesty's Government to press the war with all possible vigour up to
the moment when Peace shall be finally concluded," the governor
general was instructed. An armistice would be contrary "to this system, and would leave it too much at the option of the American Government to protract or terminate the armistice as it best suited their
Preparations, and the hopes they might entertain of countenance and
protection from the European Powers." By this time, the summer of
1814, Goulburn was about to set out for Ghent to attempt to reach a
settlement with the Americans.[59]

The negotiating team was commanded officially by Admiral James
Gambier, an officer of evangelical belief and associations, who was
well connected politically. Although he was more naval administrator
than sailor, he had served in North America. Accompanying him was
William Adams, a successful lawyer who enjoyed a high reputation as a
legal technician and thus promised to be useful as the draftsman of
articles. Goulburn was not the first choice to complete the commission, but when George Hammond declined the appointment, reminding the prime minister of the intense hostility he had aroused in
the United States as Britain's first minister to the former colonies, the
under-secretary's name came to the fore. After all, the principal objective was to enhance Canadian security. Nor were Goulburn's American adversaries in any doubt that he was the plenipotentiary "most in
the confidence of his Government."[60]

Britain's position appeared to be a strong one. An offer of Russian
mediation had been fended off in favour of direct negotiation, and the
issue of maritime rights had emphatically been excluded from any general discussion of European peace. This minimized the danger of American problems becoming entangled in the settlement of the larger
conflict. Napoleon's abdication and exile had resulted in the restoration of a Bourbon regime in France, which gave every indication of being less than sympathetic to the Americans, and Britain's might could
now be concentrated in North America. Even the selection of the medieval Flemish city of Ghent as the site of the conference seemed to offer
the three Britons an advantage, since its proximity to London allowed
them to remain in close touch with their masters. But the task Goulburn
and his colleagues were undertaking was likely to be far more taxing
than either they or their government imagined.[61]

They were confronted by a five-man American commission led by Albert Gallatin, the former secretary of the treasury. Honourable, pragmatic, and resourceful, he was a skilled negotiator. He was ably supported by John Quincy Adams, the son of the second president. Adams was energetic and erudite as well as choleric and thin skinned, and was unrivalled in his international experience. No less impressive was Henry Clay, a spokesman for the western elements whose land hunger had done so much to alienate the native people and whose voracious appetite threatened Canada. Jonathan Russell, the U.S. minister to Sweden, and Senator James A. Bayard, a moderate Federalist from Delaware, completed the team. In short, the Americans were rich in ability, intelligence, and political skill. And while the strong personalities and disparate ambitions of these men led Castlereagh to conclude that they would never be able to agree among themselves, the Liverpool cabinet's long delay in dispatching commissioners to Ghent gave the Americans valuable time in which to reach some working understanding and to settle on a limited and realizable diplomatic objective.[62]

Although the British trio was appointed in mid-May and although the Americans were assured that the three would soon be on their way to Ghent, they made no move for another ten weeks. An expectation that the military reinforcements would soon effect the desired border adjustments in Canada's favour and that the arrival of thousands of regulars would induce the Americans to be reasonable surely helps explain this lack of urgency. No doubt there was also a desire to await Castlereagh's return from Europe so that he could draft the commissioners' instructions, and there was probably a disinclination to see Goulburn absent from the Commons at a time when colonial questions were exciting interest. Indeed, Liverpool could ill afford to see the Treasury bench further depleted even after the foreign secretary reappeared in the House. Thus it was only after the end of the session that Goulburn and his two colleagues departed.[63]

In the meantime, the Americans had reassessed their nation's position. An earlier visit by two of them to London, in the guise of tourists, had plainly revealed the unreality of the terms framed in Washington – a "satisfactory arrangement" of neutral rights, a more precise definition of blockade, an end to impressment, the exclusion of the British from all dealings with Indians living within the United States, and "a transfer of the upper parts and even the whole of Canada to the U.S." The astute Gallatin was quick to conclude that "the status ante bellum" was the most they could expect to achieve, for this was an objective that would exploit British war-weariness. The people would surely refuse to sanction continuation of the war once they understood that the

United States was demanding nothing from their nation. This realistic assessment was promptly endorsed in Washington, and the five Americans were authorized to settle for the *status quo ante bellum*.[64]

By contrast, Goulburn, Gambier, and Adams were expected to seek a "final arrangement" of maritime rights, the frontier, and the fisheries, and to impress on the Americans that "an adequate arrangement" of the native people's interests was "a *sine qua non of Peace*" and that Britain required not only that the Indians "shall be included in the Peace, but that a full and express Recognition of their limits shall take place." Indeed, Castlereagh's observation that a guarantee of Indian territory would provide "a useful barrier" between British and American settlements strongly implied that the creation of a "barrier" was the *sine qua non*. Of course, Goulburn and his superiors ought to have realized from the outset that the Americans would regard such a proposal as no more than a clumsy effort to deprive their nation of a large segment of its territory. The American revolutionary government had contemplated the creation of a native buffer state in 1782 to "allay Spanish fears about American expansionism," only for this French-inspired proposal to be disregarded by the American negotiators in France, prominent among whom was the father of John Quincy Adams, who smelled a "plot to rob [their] ... country of its hinterland." Similarly, one American defence of the unpopular treaty signed by John Jay with Britain in 1795 had emphasized its indirect discouragement of British efforts to establish an Indian buffer state between the Republic and the British North American provinces.[65]

Following a round of social visits in London, Goulburn set off for Ghent early in August. He was accompanied by his wife and their young son, Harry, who was just fifteen months old and still recuperating from "infantile fever." Arriving on 6 August, they put up temporarily at the Hotel Lion D'Or before taking more permanent quarters in a converted Carthusian convent. Part of the building – as befitted the residence of the representatives of the world's premier industrial nation – was being used as a textile manufactory. Here was a reminder that Ghent, sitting at the confluence of the Schedlt and the Leie, and with the twin rivers connected by a network of canals, had once been a thriving commercial centre. Not surprisingly, it was adorned with magnificent buildings. But the Goulburns were dismayed to discover that society had already retired to the country for the summer and there would thus be little public amusement until these families returned in November.[66]

A visit from Edward Goulburn caused some welcome excitement, bringing as he did the news that he was engaged to marry, though this pleasure was briefly diminished by the evidence that he was also taking a vacation from his law studies. Happily, he was to be called to the bar the following year. Another diversion was provided by a local dignitary who invited the Goulburns to lunch at his villa. Unfortunately, when their host came to greet them at the door, the short-sighted Jane mistook him for the butler; and on entering, they discovered that the house was sparsely furnished. Much as they enjoyed the meal, they hurriedly returned to their well-appointed apartments, resolved never "to make a longer visit to a house where comfort appears to be so ill understood." The onset of autumn, which proved to be even wetter and cooler than usual, did little to lift their spirits. There was an excursion to Antwerp, where they trudged up the dark and winding staircase leading to the top of the magnificent Gothic cathedral; another to Malines, where they collected a set of the celebrated china at an enviable price; and one to Brussels, where they were reduced to staying in a garret room in a city already bursting with English visitors.[67]

Goulburn deplored the late hours, hard drinking, and heavy smoking of this expatriate society. He gave even freer rein to his evangelical censoriousness in commenting on the scandal that had overtaken his friends the Bouveries, stimulating as it did the puritan's prurience. Bartholomew Bouverie, younger son of an earl and a fellow member of Parliament, had given his second daughter to the Earl of Rosebery in 1808, only to see her now elope with her dead sister's widower. "With so good natured a husband, so fine a family and so much in point of rank and circumstance to gratify her, I do not conceive it possible that she could have reduced herself to so low a pitch of degradation," a bewildered Goulburn observed. His assumption that she would never be able to regularize her new relationship proved incorrect, for Rosebery quickly divorced his errant spouse, and the lovers were married by special permission of the King of Württemberg. Nevertheless, a didactic Goulburn identified a moral lesson in this sad affair. Here was "another proof of the very great danger which attends beauty living in the world without principle or understanding."[68]

As for the negotiations, Goulburn quickly impressed the Americans as not only the most influential but also the "most inveterate" British representative. He certainly arrived at Ghent ill disposed to any compromise with them, convinced as he was that the United States had "declared war for the sake of annexing our Dominions." He abhorred Americans, and the more he saw of them following the opening conference on 8 August, the more he loathed them. He was irritated by petty slights, such as their failure to stand at a public concert during the playing of "God Save the King" and their unsubstantiated accusation that British naval officers had carried off American slaves in order to sell them in the West Indies. He regarded this charge as a gratuitous national insult. He bridled at their contesting of every point, "even the most trivial," with great hostility. "They seem to have come here with the belief that we should be willing to yield to America on every point under consideration," he reported to Bathurst. Moreover, their "insolence" was equalled by their vulgarity. With the exception of Gallatin, he considered all the Americans ill bred, and the social savagery of J.Q. Adams and the coarseness of Clay merely reinforced this opinion. "As an instance of their vulgarity what think you of their turning up their coat sleeves at the commencement of dinner as if they intended to act the part of the cooks rather than the guests," he remarked to family and friends, and he warned Peel that "living in American society is a misery which you have yet to come."[69]

There was not a little irony in the private grumblings of such evident anglophobes as J.Q. Adams and Henry Clay at Goulburn's "rancorous hostility" towards their nation. Yet in order not to prejudice the negotiations, both Goulburn and his colleagues punctiliously let pass remarks to which they could have given a "sharp answer." As one of the Americans admitted, the Britons were "extremely affable and courteous in their personal demeanour." Yet the issue of the Indians quickly tested Goulburn's temper and his government's tenacity. He was acutely sensitive to any betrayal of the commitments he had authorized Prevost to make to the native people during the dark days of 1812. He wanted to hold out for a self-denying ordinance under which the United States would agree never to seize Indian lands even in war, believing that this alone would guarantee the natives' territories. But Castlereagh declined to endorse this hard position when he passed through Ghent on 18 August. Instead, in the face of American resistance, the Liverpool cabinet hastily backed away from the creation of an Indian "barrier" as a *sine qua non*.[70]

During an icily polite conversation with J.Q. Adams on 1 September, Goulburn argued that the Indians were independent nations with whom the United States had long made treaties. In reply, the American declared that the Republic would never permit a few thousand savages to impede the irresistible progress of white civilization. For good measure, Adams slyly observed that those Indians who occupied lands recognized as part of the United States in 1783, but who were allies of Britain in the present conflict, were in much the same position as the Irish who had rebelled in 1798. They stood in need only of amnesty. And when Bathurst stated that the government would be content with an arrangement that embraced the Indians in the peace and restored to them all the rights and privileges they had enjoyed before the war, Goulburn expressed his dismay at this acceptance of a limited version of the *status quo ante bellum*. "I do not deem it possible to make a *good* peace now as I should not consider that a *good* peace which left the Indians as they are at present at the mercy of the liberal policy of the United States," he sarcastically observed to Bathurst on 16 September. "I had till I came here no idea of the fixed determination which prevails in the breast of every American to extirpate the Indians and appropriate their territory."[71]

Goulburn had intended to break off the negotiations following the Americans' rejection of any Indian "barrier" state, but he was instructed to pursue discussion of the topic. Dismissing as preposterous the American counter proposal of peace on the basis of the *status quo ante bellum* – which amounted to a refusal to enhance the security of Canada in order to make its annexation more difficult at some future date – his reponse to the Americans' cavilling over the details of the modified British proposal on the Indians was again to prepare for a rupture. Instead, Liverpool and Bathurst sought to disguise a further weakening of their position on the Indians by ordering its presentation in the form of an ultimatum. The United States would be required, following the ratification of peace with Britain, to end all hostilities with Indian "tribes or Nations" and to restore to them "all the possessions, rights and privileges" to which they had been entitled or had enjoyed before 1811. As the five Americans readily grasped, this wording had stripped the British principle "of some of its most exceptionable features" and would leave their nation free to deal with the Indians as it wished. From this point on, the British government's retreat soon resembled a diplomatic rout. They attempted a brief stand on the principle of *uti possidetis* before capitulating to that of the *status quo ante bellum.*[72]

Goulburn and his colleagues were steadily demoted from the rank of plenipotentiaries to the status of clerks and messengers, though this was less a commentary on their performance and more a reflection of the cabinet's anxiety to be rid of the American war. Castlereagh was critical of the way they had fought the opening rounds of the negotiations, suggesting that Britain's terms had been presented in too decisive a manner. But the prime minister revealed the fundamental weakness of the British position when he grumbled that "Goulburn and our other commiss[ioners], evidently do not feel the inconvenience of the continuance of the war." Fears that disagreements at Vienna, where a European settlement was being thrashed out, would degenerate from acrimony into hostilities, that an alienated tsar might retaliate by entangling European and American problems, or that an internal explosion in France might plunge the Continent back into full-scale war all influenced the cabinet's irresolute handling of the Americans; so did the generally disappointing military news from North America. Convinced that only the repulse of another Yankee advance in the Niagara region and the capture and burning of the American capital had induced the negotiators at Ghent to accept the ultimatum on the Indians, Liverpool and his ministers were disinclined to hold out for better terms on other issues when they heard that the attack on Baltimore had failed but the victor of Washington had been killed, and that Prevost's long-awaited campaign against Plattsburg had ended in a humiliating withdrawal. This turn of events would surely generate renewed popular support for the war in the United States just as the British people were plainly wearying of it.[73]

The prime minister was increasingly preoccupied with domestic concerns. "The continuance of the American war will entail upon us a prodigious expense, much more than we had any idea of," he advised the foreign secretary shortly before the reopening of Parliament in early November. The diplomatic implications were subsequently spelled out for Goulburn by Bathurst. "You must understand that we are anxious as ever to bring the Treaty to a conclusion," he wrote. "Meetings are beginning to petition against the Income Tax & we have difficulty in keeping the Manufacturers particularly at Birmingham quiet." In this context, Liverpool had no wish to expose himself further to the "rancorous" assaults of the Whigs by allowing the Ghent negotiations to fail over territorial questions. This was especially true when the Duke of Wellington not only avoided the North American command as a replacement for the discredited Prevost, but also offered the bald opinion that Britain had "no right from the state of the war to demand any concession of territory from America." Nor was Liverpool's predicament eased or his embarrassment lessened by the republication in London of the American accounts of the government's opening demands at Ghent. The Whigs welcomed this fresh ammunition for their charge that the conflict was being prolonged for the "aggrandizement and alteration of the boundary."[74]

Preparing Goulburn in late November for the final capitulation to the Americans, Bathurst admitted that the peace would not be "very creditable" when compared to their initial and well-publicized objectives. But he argued that it was the best thing that could happen in the circumstances. That the negotiations dragged on for another four weeks was largely the result of confusion and indecision in both camps as the cabinet sought a few fig-leaves with which to cover the nakedness of its concessions. This explained the inability of Goulburn and his colleagues to exploit at the beginning of December the link the Americans had accepted between their denial to the British of free navigation of the Mississippi and Britain's curtailment of their fishing privileges in British waters. Eventually, the cabinet accepted Goulburn's sensible suggestion that these problems be evaded by omitting the article from the treaty. This had the added benefit of exluding, as part of the same article, an agreement on the border west of the Lake of the Woods which would have cost Britain the best pass through the Rocky Mountains. An article was included providing for "the more effectual Abolition of the Slave Trade." And thanks largely to Goulburn, the Passamaquoddy Islands were excluded from the *status quo ante bellum* and were to continue to be occupied by the British; for when the Americans had indicated that they could not accept this, he had "lost all control of his temper." In the words of one less than generous American adversary, "He has always in such cases a sort of convulsive agitation about him, and the tone in which he speaks is more insulting than the language that he uses." It was, of course, more a matter of his releasing the long-bottled-up frustration over the less than heroic role he had been asked to play. Thus when Gallatin archly alluded to the advantage the Britons had enjoyed of referring every detail to their government, Goulburn was sufficiently stung to reply sharply that had this not been the case, the negotiations would have long since failed.[75]

The Treaty of Ghent was signed on 24 December 1814. It ended hostilities and established a process for resolving the disputes over the boundary line drawn in 1783, but this settlement was a far cry from what Goulburn had expected to achieve. Of course, this could also be said of the Americans, as the Tory press loyally emphasized. The United States had neither compelled Britain to abandon the practice of impressment nor driven her from North America. Even the American commissioners privately acknowledged that the terms of peace were "undoubtedly not such as our Country expected at the commencement of the war." They consoled themselves with the thought that their nation had emerged from the conflict with an enhanced international reputation. And a total if belated victory over the largest and most impressive of the British raiding forces, which under the command of Wellington's brother-in-law attempted to seize New Orleans, permitted Americans to luxuriate in this triumph of their arms and forget that at Ghent their government had abandoned the professed objectives of a war that it had conducted with astonishing ineptitude.[76]

The British were initially less fortunate. The scornful judgment of the Whig *Morning Chronicle* reflected the general opinion that this was peace but not necessarily with honour. Pragmatic Tory assessments that, considering all the circumstances, the settlement was "wise and necessary," and compliments on his Passamaquoddy article did not lessen Goulburn's sense of failure. He had gone to Ghent to obtain a more secure frontier for Canada and to elevate the native people to the status of independent nations complete with defined territories safe from American annexation; and he had been obliged to accept the *status quo ante bellum*. No doubt he feared that he had negotiated merely a truce rather than an enduring peace. Certainly, he did not sense its long-term significance for peaceful Anglo-American relations. Thus he was understandably keen to escape the scene of his disappointment. Even the opening of the Ghent social season failed to restore his spirits, and the local celebrations of the peace were a sore trial for him. Was it mere accident that an artist's depiction of the signing of the treaty, based on pencil sketches of the signatories, showed Goulburn with his face averted? Unlike his colleagues, Goulburn accepted neither honours nor honoraria for his services. Yet he had done nothing to damage his reputation among his superiors. He had stoically followed their orders constantly to retreat in the face of an American refusal to admit defeat. Galling as this was, as were the American allusions to his running a telegraph office, he had swallowed his pride and seen the unpleasant business through to the end.[77]

There was one additional ordeal to be faced – the parliamentary debate on the treaty, which would have to await news of its ratification by the United States. This was received in March, along with the accounts of the disaster at New Orleans. This promised to be an unfortunate juxtaposition of events. But just as the Madison administration had been rescued from political embarrassment by that victory, so was the British government now assisted by dramatic developments in Europe. Criticisms of the New Orleans military fiasco and the terms negotiated at Ghent were quickly overborne by the sensation of Bonaparte's return to France. The mounting crisis in Europe provided a distracting background to a desultory American debate on 11 April 1815. The Whigs duly charged the government with "gross misconduct," contrasting its initial demands with the terms accepted, and they protested that peace on this basis could have been secured much earlier at a saving of both lives and treasure. To all of this Goulburn made an effective reply, insisting that it had required considerable time to persuade the Americans to leave controversial questions undecided. He also sheltered behind "the friendless and unprotected Indians," admitting that their inclusion had delayed a settlement. Further, and a little disingenuously, he insisted that a quest for a better Canadian line had been nobly laid aside for the purpose of restoring to the Indians the privileges and territories they had possessed before the war. Of course, the wisdom of having made peace with the Americans, even on the terms reached at Ghent, was difficult to contest at a moment when Napoleon was again seated on a French throne. Moreover, memories of the ignominious conclusion of the always peripheral American conflict were soon erased by the triumph of British arms at Waterloo.[78]

CHAPTER FOUR

Slavery and Empire

It was a disconsolate pair of Goulburns who returned to London early in the new year. Henry's sense of diplomatic failure was matched by his wife's apprehension of domestic isolation once he returned to his office. She had grown used to his company in Ghent; but the candles were soon burning long into the night at Downing Street, following Bonaparte's reclaiming of his French throne in March. Troops had to be found to form the army which Wellington was now to command in Flanders. Many of Wellington's peninsular veterans had already been dispatched on the ill-fated expedition to the United States, while others en route to Canada could not be quickly recalled. The Portuguese refused to release the army "which had been formed by British energy, paid by British gold," and led to victory by the very British general who was now in desperate need of seasoned soldiers. Wellington thus found himself at the head of men "mostly inferior to those which he had hitherto commanded." Not surprisingly, many in London doubted his ability to best Bonaparte. Reports from Dover on 18 June that an artillery cannonade could plainly be heard across the Channel heightened tension in the capital, and the tension increased with the arrival in London of the first travellers to have quit Brussels on the morning of the battle, for they spoke with "positive assurance of the Duke's defeat." In this crisis, Goulburn later recalled, Bathurst "almost alone retained his confidence." Goulburn himself was sitting anxiously at home late in the evening of 21 June when Wellington's courier delivered to him the victory dispatch. He rushed to the office to circulate the document, stopping off briefly at a colleague's house several doors away to announce the good news to a large party at dinner there.[1]

Bonaparte's defeat, second abdication, and second exile excited in Goulburn twin regrets. Twice he had missed a place in history. First, he envied those members of his family, among them his brother Frederick, who had "seen and partaken of such a splendid victory the most brilliant and severe of all of the Duke of Wellington's achievements." Second, he was disappointed that his military colleague Henry Bunbury was dispatched to Plymouth to inform the captured French emperor of his fate. Nor was his frustration eased by his inheritance of the thankless task of supervising the administration of St Helena, Bonaparte's second, more secure and desolate island prison. The task was made all the more tiresome by a prolix military jailer.[2]

The spring of 1815 had found Goulburn conducting a second negotiation with the Americans, as well as helping to organize the army with which again to dethrone Napoleon. Gallatin and his associates had given notice in Ghent of their nation's desire "to treat concerning the general commerce of the two Countries." Not that they had expected any response from Britain until she received word from Washington of the ratification of the Treaty of Ghent. By that time Napoleon was back in France. His return promised to assist them. As one of the Americans hopefully noted, "The probability of renewed War in Europe places the subject of the Commercial treaty on more important ground; as in that event all questions which have hitherto arisen between the two Countries may come up again."[3]

First to arrive in London was the bumptious Clay, though he was soon followed by the gracious Gallatin. They realized that "the weightier concerns of Europe" preoccupied the British, but they did meet with Castlereagh in mid-April to resolve a tragic incident at Dartmoor prison, where several American prisoners-of-war had been killed earlier that month during the suppression of a riot. The foreign secretary defused this potentially explosive issue by expressing regret and proposing a joint inquiry into the tragedy. Later, on receipt of the commissioners' findings, the British government expressed "disapprobation" of the conduct of the troops involved and offered to compensate the families of the victims. Castlereagh delegated to Goulburn the task of meeting with the Americans to arrange the transportation home of the survivors. As for commercial negotiations, he insisted on preliminary and informal discussions to determine whether "it were likely that some general principles could be fixed upon to form the basis of such a Treaty."[4]

Sceptical of Britain's desire for a worthwhile commercial settlement, Clay and Gallatin were irritated at the passage of more than three weeks without any follow-up of Castlereagh's proposal of informal discussions – a delay that must surely have reminded them of the time they had spent cooling their heels in Ghent. They therefore found a way to get the discussions moving: they declined an invitation to dine at the foreign secretary's with the explanation that they had already booked their passages home at a prior date. This news brought an immediate invitation to call at the Board of Trade, where Frederick Robinson was vice-president and effective head. He was to lead a team of which Goulburn and William Adams were the other members.[5]

The three Britons were content to listen to the two Americans at an initial meeting on 11 May 1815. Gallatin and Clay separated the issues into two broad classes – commercial relations in times of peace and neutral rights during war. With respect to the former, they proposed a liberalization of trade founded on the "most favoured nation" principle. More specifically, they sought access to the West Indies, a clearer definition of the "inland intercourse" with British North America, the opening of India, and the abolition of discriminatory duties. Turning to neutral rights, a problem that had bedevilled Anglo-American relations since the beginning of the French wars in 1793, they suggested that an agreed definition of blockade would be "convenient," requested clarification and liberalization of their trading rights with the colonies of Britain's enemies, and urged that Britain abandon the claim of impressment in return for America's legal exclusion of her seamen from the American mercantile marine. Through all of this the Britons maintained a studied reserve. They declined "to discuss in detail any or either class of these propositions" and "purposely avoided such a discussion as applied to the second class." Their immediate purpose was to establish whether the Americans intended to make a commercial agreement dependent on a settlement on neutral rights. No doubt they took comfort from an evasive reply.[6]

At a follow-up meeting, Goulburn and his two colleagues announced their willingness to discuss all the issues but without any apparent expectation of resolving them. Moreover, their observation that they would expect an equivalent for the opening of India to American traders, perhaps in the form of "some accommodation in the Fur trade," immediately raised the Americans' hackles. They suspected the Britons of seeking to recover the ground abandoned at Ghent by re-establishing commercial and thus political relations with Indians living in the territories of the United States. No renewal of the former connection would be permitted, the two Americans emphasized. Nevertheless, sufficient progress was made to move on to formal negotiations.[7]

Another three weeks elapsed before these negotiations began, the Britons explaining with admirably straight faces that an attack of gout had prevented the lord chancellor from affixing the Great Seal to their commissions. By that time the impatient and homesick Americans were all for turning the entire business over to John Quincy Adams, who arrived in London on 25 May to take up his posting as American minister to the Court of St James's. At a meeting with the new minister four days later, Castlereagh made it clear that the two nations would be unlikely to reach an understanding on the sensitive issue of impressment so long as one of them permitted naturalization and the other held to indefeasible allegiance. Ever the diplomat, however, he sought to soften this blow by announcing the Admiralty's intention to issue fresh regulations that "would prevent all cause of complaint on the part of the United States."[8]

Although Clay and Gallatin decided to postpone their departure and pursue the negotiations, they resolved to seek a commercial agreement only. J.Q. Adams would have to handle the trickier problems of neutral rights. But when the two sides met again in Robinson's office at the Board of Trade on 7 June, it was clear that they had differing recollections of the preliminary discussions. Clay and Gallatin professed to have understood that the India trade would be thrown open "without hesitation or qualification," whereas the Britons distinctly recalled having stressed the need for some equivalent. And the Americans now ambitiously proposed not only the opening of India but also the mutual rejection of discriminatory duties, a "reciprocal liberty of commerce and navigation" between the United States and the British dominions in Europe, the acceptance of the "most favoured nation" principle, and recognition of an American right to navigate the St Lawrence down to Montreal and from there to Lake Champlain. Significantly, the British were to be denied access to the lakes that were under exclusive American jurisdiction.[9]

From this starting point, negotiations advanced at a snail's pace. Both parties believed that the other had more to gain from a settlement, a fact that discouraged any concessions. For Robinson, Goulburn, and the British Adams, there was another reason for caution – the conviction that their adversaries were not above sharp practice. Somehow the Yankees always managed to cheat them, Goulburn believed. "The real fact is that they will not be satisfied with a Treaty of mere reciprocity," Robinson warned Castlereagh, "but are resolved to get, if they can, some gratuitous concessions out of us." The upshot was a month of haggling, punctuated by a round of social activities in which the Goulburns played their full part. There was also the diversionary excitement and pageantry of the celebrations of the victory at Waterloo, while Bonaparte's final abdication served to release the pressure that had been building behind the issue of neutral rights. At last, on 3 July, the six commissioners signed a modest document. The liberalization of trade between Britain's European possessions and the United States had survived the tedious bargaining, as had a reciprocal abolition of discriminatory duties and the adoption of the "most favoured nation" principle, together with the opening of India to Americans trading directly with the United States. But the convention had a short lifespan, a mere four years, because the British believed that they had not received an equivalent for the Indian concession.[10]

"Well, this is the second good job we have done together," Goulburn remarked to John Quincy Adams at the conclusion of the negotiation. However limited the convention's commercial value, it built upon the modest success at Ghent and thus gave grounds for optimism that more amicable relations would slowly develop. "The convention, such as it is, must, so far as it relates to them, be considered as an evidence of a friendly disposition," Gallatin conceded. On the other hand, the morbidly suspicious Adams concluded that it had "shewn how very few points there were upon which any agreement could be made" and how little the mutual animosities had subsided.[11]

Whatever the long-term consequences of his diplomatic labours, Goulburn had earned his vacation in 1815. He had again taken a house with the Ryders at Cowes on the Isle of Wight, which was becoming something of a summer tradition, and was looking forward to the charm of that "ever varying yet tranquil scene." He and his family remained on the island for six weeks and were blessed with unusually fine weather. In mid-September, they set out for London, taking the journey in easy stages and stopping off to visit friends. Goulburn welcomed the opportunity to catch up with society gossip. Lady Abdy, a natural daughter of Richard Wellesley, had run off with Lord Charles Bentinck. "Every body is surprised by her taste in selecting a man notoriously so stupid," Goulburn reported to his sister-in-law Kate Montagu. The story was "that they eloped in a Tilbury and that on the road to Salt Hill they had so violent a quarrel that she set out on her return to her deserted lord [Sir William Abdy] who however had already had too much of a good thing to admit her again to his house."[12]

Suddenly, in the spring of 1816, Goulburn's health failed him. He had been almost completely free of illness since a crisis shortly before his wedding but was now felled by "a bilious fever." Confined to his bed for several days, he felt the effects for several months. Yet this was the very time when his burden of work was about to be greatly increased as a result of the abolition of the second under-secretaryship in the department. Anxious to regain his strength, recognizing the benefits of regular exercise and periods of relaxation, and determined to acquire one of the essential symbols of his class, Goulburn went in search of a country estate reasonably close to London. He settled on Betchworth House. Situated midway between the Surrey towns of Dorking and Reigate, an area famed for its chalk pits, and only twenty-six miles south of the capital, the house stood in an attractive park through which the River Mole meandered. Sturdy rather than elegant, substantial without being grand, it provided a peaceful and comfortable retreat. In addition to the house, he purchased an estate of 850 acres valued at £2,400 a year.[13]

Ironically, as much as Goulburn enjoyed his new residence, it quickly became another source of financial anxiety and domestic tension. Having given more for it than he could truly afford, he fretted that his tenants would quit the estate with the change of ownership. The rents were regarded as high at a time of depressed postwar agricultural prices. So he promised to pay £30 to each of them if prices did not recover by the following harvest season. He reduced the size of the domestic and estate staff, and let the home farm and park, retaining only twenty acres of grassland for his own use. Not that these economies sufficed. "I cannot say my affairs look comfortable in this respect and I have every fear of being drawn into expenses upon which I had by no means calculated," he admitted to his wife later in the year, "but I shall do my best to avoid them."[14]

Throughout his life Goulburn kept detailed accounts of his personal finances. They reflected his fear of following in his father's footsteps by living beyond his means. In 1816 his expenses, excluding those incurred with the purchase of Betchworth but including his mother's jointure and Edward's allowance, exceeded £6,000. Substantial as this expenditure was, it was almost balanced by his income from Amity Hall. Thus with his salary of £2,500 as an under-secretary, he remained safely within his total income. But over the next three years his expenditures rose sharply, until they neared £9,000 in 1819. What made this development all the more alarming was the simultaneous collapse in the receipts from his sugar plantation.[15]

Somehow Henry Goulburn had found the time even at Ghent both to keep an eye on his Jamaican estate and to conduct much of the "heavy business" of the Colonial Department. In fact, these two activities were not entirely unrelated. The "Saints" had decided for tactical reasons at the end of the French wars to concentrate on the international abolition of the slave trade, but when the results of this campaign proved disappointing, Wilberforce and his zealous friends returned to waging indirect war on slavery in the colonies. This struggle again placed men such as Henry Goulburn in an uncomfortable position. "Absentee planters in Great Britain, especially those who were active in public affairs, were highly vulnerable to antislavery propaganda and likely to support measures for ameliorating slavery."[16]

For Goulburn, the frustrations of plantation ownership appeared endless. Almost every year, or so it seemed, high hopes of princely profits were cruelly dashed by natural disasters, which in other circumstances he would have considered providential. The year 1811 had produced a reasonable yield of more than four hundred hogsheads, despite an undependable wind that frequently left the breeze mill motionless. The following year violent storms, heavy rains, and an earthquake severely damaged buildings and left many cane pieces waterlogged. Expectations that the loss of sugar might be offset by a higher production of rum proved illusory, and productivity was further reduced by the decrepitude of the still. A new one, dispatched from England, sank as it was being floated ashore. In 1813 there was a drought which further injured the canes. Then the livestock fell victim to disease. More discouraging still were Samson's reports on the condition of the slaves.[17]

A "dreadful disorder" carried off a handful of them in May 1811, and a smallpox outbreak in the neighbourhood subsequently necessitated the inoculation of all of the children. Indeed, the returns for the year again listed fewer births than deaths. Worse news soon followed. "The Negroes have been sickly and many of them laid up from measles," Samson reported early in 1812. On neighbouring estates a great many slaves had died of a mysterious disorder which began as a throat infection and developed into pleurisy. "What with measles and this malady," he added, "I have hardly been able to keep the mill going." Before year's end, he was obliged to hire a white carpenter and a jobbing crew of five blacks to build a new slave hospital.[18]

It had long been Samson's contention and excuse that the estate was undermanned. He took every opportunity to remind Henry of his father's calculation that a labour force of 300 was necessary to work the estate efficiently, yet by the end of 1811 the slaves numbered only 236. "We are much in want of more Negroes," Samson had written earlier that year, and Goulburn accepted his suggestion that he sell off a remote parcel of land and invest the proceeds in the purchase of slaves. Eventually this was done, although the money raised did not cover the cost of the twenty-five purchases. Moreover, within a month, the estate had lost the services of its doctor, who died while attending the slaves of a friend. "I have not yet engaged another as the present ones have too much Practice and do not attend regularly," Samson explained in March 1813. This decision soon seemed peculiarly ill advised. Of eleven pregnancies that year, six had failed, and there had been thirteen deaths. All too aware of Goulburn's long-standing concern for pregnant women and his wish that they not be worked too hard, if at all, but equally aware of the owner's belief in the slaves' promiscuity, Samson attributed this latest setback "to their favourite, wanton, Excessive, unsalutary, promiscuous amusements." However convenient, this explanation was by no means entirely implausible. Many of the women disliked the prospect of motherhood, and the incidence of abortion was on the rise. Equally, promiscuity had become deeply "imbedded" in the slave culture, and the diseases associated with it were all too prevalent. Beyond this, Samson gloomily insisted that declining slave populations were now inevitable. The closing of the slave trade had cut off the supply of young females.[19]

Alarmed, Goulburn pressed his manager to "use every endeavour" to remedy an evil of which he had "so often had occasion to complain." On the other hand, his own inquiries among knowledgeable persons in Britain had persuaded him that a declining population was almost inevitable on a sugar estate. Only on cotton and coffee plantations, where the labour was "less severe," had slaves been able to increase their numbers. Goulburn did propose, however, that every effort be made to lessen the severity of labour on Amity Hall. Samson responded much as he had a decade earlier: the slave force had to be strengthened. This was all the more necessary, he added ominously, because of the large number of aged and infirm blacks. Writing from Ghent, Goulburn authorized him to purchase the twenty-two slaves who had come onto the market. He expected the costs to be covered by the proceeds of rum sales. However, since the profits from the distillery were barely covering contingencies, Samson recommended the sale of another remote portion of the estate. Unfortunately, by the time these steps had been taken, there were all too few good slaves up for sale.[20]

A second option was to make greater use of technology. Goulburn's decision to send out ploughs in order to lessen the back-breaking work of hoeing was given a lukewarm reception by his attorney. Samson coolly recommended that Goulburn also send out a steady middle-aged man to provide instruction to the slaves. His own preference was for a steam engine to power the mill. He estimated the cost of iron-works and freight at £1,400, though to this expense would have to be added that for the assembling and housing of the machine. As for the benefits, they would include a "great saving" of stock and slaves. Perhaps as many as thirty steers might be sold to help defray the expense, he guessed. These arguments had an all too familiar ring, having been employed several years earlier in support of the breeze mill. Indeed, Samson claimed that the two mills in combination would allow him to delay cutting canes until the optimum time and would thus maximize their yield. They would also do "a great deal more justice to the canes." Thus persuaded – or convinced that he had no other choice – Goulburn ordered an engine in 1816. With another heavy investment in the offing, he was understandably eager to make economies elsewhere, and he challenged the quantities of coarse linen on order, only to be informed that the supply of Osnaburgh was "as small as possible." "We cannot give the negroes less clothing," Samson reported, for they were "sufficiently clothed and no more."[21]

Fate – in the form of a serious illness, which sent Samson home to recover his health – led to shocking revelations. In 1812 Goulburn had taken the customary precaution of issuing a "dormant" power of attorney. His choice had been George Richards, an English barrister who had migrated to Jamaica and was already serving as attorney on another estate. Samson had been less than enthusiastic about the selection, though he conceded that Richards was "a very kind and tender master." Now acting during Samson's sick leave, Richards sought to explain the disappointing crop in 1816. He criticized not only Samson's limited planting of new canes but also his treatment of the workforce. Half starved, he reported, the slaves had little interest other than to plunder and devour canes in "incredible quantities." A combination of undernourishment and hard usage explained the relentless decline in the estate's population, he charged, and it was to his reversal of Samson's severity that he naturally attributed a small but significant increase in the number of surviving births. "Well fed and better treated the people are moreover doing more work than they ever did before," he boasted, "and the Estate in every department of its business is in a state of much greater forwardness."[22]

This was not an assessment that Samson endorsed on his return to the island at the end of August 1817. He complained that nothing had been done to erect the steam mill and that Richards's plan to purchase materials and job the task of construction would have increased the expense unnecessarily. Indeed, everything was in a "backward state," he reported. Not until February 1818 was he able to announce that the steam mill was working well. With this additional incentive, he now undertook a rather more energetic search for slaves, and before the end of the summer he had purchased forty-one at a total cost of more than £3,000. To cover this expense he disposed of more outlying land; and although he obtained Goulburn's asking price, he granted the purchaser extraordinarily favourable terms of repayment.[23]

Long before payment was made, Samson had been dismissed. Richards's earlier report had finally pricked Goulburn's conscience. He surely recalled how Samson's fitness had been challenged before the overseer was promoted to attorney on the death of Craggs. In any event, Henry asked his soldier brother to visit the island and investigate conditions at Amity Hall. Frederick's regiment having been disbanded in Canada, he travelled down the Mississippi, no doubt in one of the new steamboats plying its waters, to take passage from New Orleans to Jamaica. He then spent much of the first two weeks of February on the estate or in the neighbourhood. Among the persons he consulted was George Richards, and he was much impressed with Richards's indictment of Samson's "blundering and defective" system of cultivation. What most struck him about the estate, however, was the "abominable" condition of the slaves.[24]

Frederick offered a severe commentary on Samson's conduct and, if only by implication, of his brother's absentee supervision of the property and its workforce. "Your negroes' houses are miserable huts huddled together without any regard to regularity or comfort," he reported. "Your negroes themselves bear every appearance of being badly fed and shew every sign of being much discontented with their present Attorney." He was clearly outraged by the discovery that each slave received only a miserable weekly ration of guinea corn and a handful of fish for more than half the year. The slaves were expected to provide for themselves during the remaining five months. They grew provisions on an area of some eighteen acres, on which the village also stood, and were permitted to use a strip of approximately one acre beside the river. But one-half of the provisions ground had been set aside, an incredulous Frederick noted, for the cultivation of vegetables for the white staff. "All this for the subsistence of two hundred and fifty negroes for a space of five months," he observed. During his brief tenure, Richards had converted an additional fifteen acres from cane pieces to provisions grounds and had almost doubled the corn ration. Yet this had still been little enough for subsistence. "The simple consideration of what one would order to be given to a horse after having ridden him a ten mile stage," Frederick commented sardonically, "will help one in deciding in favour or against Mr. Richards." Further proof was to be found in the dramatic increase in births during his management of the estate. It was simply a matter of food, the younger Goulburn argued a little naively.[25]

Considerations of humanity mixed with political self-interest (for if word of these conditions reached the "Saints," he could expect to be publicly pilloried) now led Henry Goulburn to commit himself fully to amelioration. He dismissed Samson and appointed Richards in his place. The new attorney's first act was to release a runaway who had been held for five weeks in stocks, his legs locked and his wrists shackled. Such "enormities" were by no means unusual on the island, Richards admitted, notwithstanding the assertions to the contrary "from respectable authority." He also discovered that Samson had recently denied slaves the land on which to raise provisions, and had even failed for several months to issue in full the meagre corn ration. As a result, he had found slaves lying in the fields from sheer debility or gnawing on canes from hunger. Indeed, it was in response to the conditions he discovered on Amity Hall that as a member of the assembly

Richards subsequently introduced an amendment to the slave laws in an effort to guarantee provisions grounds to all slaves.[26]

"It is quite refreshing, Sir, to hear such kindness expressed by a master for his people as your letter contains, and where that kindness is made the basis of his directions for their management, and for the management of his affairs," the new attorney wrote in accepting his appointment. He and Goulburn were in full agreement "that the proper and merciful treatment of negroes is entirely consistent with a prudent and economical management." With an eye to such treatment, and no doubt the protection of his public reputation, Goulburn resolved to send out a member of the Moravian Church to attend to his slaves' spiritual welfare. Richards was again supportive. "Be assur'd," he added, "that this and every other attempt to better their condition must proceed from England. Here there is nothing but pretence, acts of Assembly in barbarous jargon of goodwill and humanity, and enactments for their protection barefacedly not carried into execution." Unfortunately, a series of delays, in part inspired by fears for his health, kept Goulburn's missionary from sailing for the island.[27]

To Goulburn's dismay, the new and more benevolent slave regime failed to produce "economical management." Initially, responsibility for the disappointing news from Amity Hall could be laid at Samson's door. Richards attributed to his predecessor's neglect of basic husbandry the disappointingly small yield that year, while the careless omission of the damper during the assembling of the steam engine had seen it consume more cane trash as fuel than it produced. But as Goulburn watched his income shrink alarmingly, until it was barely one-third of the £6,000 it had averaged during the last seven years of Samson's administration, he began to have misgivings about his managerial change. Increasingly, he suspected Richards of lax supervision. Nor was he entirely reassured by the attorney's insistence that he kept a close eye on affairs through occasional visits, through correspondence with the overseer, and through interviews with responsible slaves summoned to his nearby home for the express purpose of being interrogated on the quality of life. From Goulburn's vantage point, this policy of "benign neglect" lacked even the merit of reversing the decline in the slave population. The dramatic spurt in births in 1816, which had helped Richards secure the permanent position, looked increasingly and dishearteningly like an exception rather than the rule. Yet when at the end of his life Goulburn privately expressed regret that he had been so influenced by Richards and his brother, he overlooked the political value of his actions. Assailed later by a leading "Saint" for the treatment and condition of his human property, he indignantly cited chapter and verse of his material sacrifices in the cause of humanity.[28]

One immediate consequence of the halving of his income in 1818 was Goulburn's refusal of promotion. He was Liverpool's choice to succeed Peel as chief secretary of Ireland when the latter resigned that office. And while several considerations dictated Goulburn's decision to remain at the Colonial Office, the worrying state of his personal finances was undoubtedly decisive. In his own words, "After every calculation I found that I could not bring the expenditure down so low as not to require addition to the official salary of more than my private income." However, this decision did not impede the development of a friendship that was to be the most important in his life.[29]

Goulburn had been acquainted with Robert Peel as a fellow member of the Alfred Club and had succeeded him at the War and Colonial Office. Their friendship now blossomed into a lifelong intimacy rooted in mutual respect and admiration. Shortly before Peel's marriage, he wrote to Goulburn: "Your perfect enjoyment of every domestic blessing and natural preference of retirement to what the world generally considers the advantages of office and public life have separated us to a degree quite inconsistent with the sincere regard I have ever felt towards you – and that unqualified respect in which I have ever held your character." There was, he said, "not a man in existence of whose attachment and good opinion I am more proud nay I may truly say, so proud as I am of yours." Peel was even more revealing to his future wife. He valued Goulburn's attachment "as much as that of any *man* on earth," he explained to her, for of all the men with whom he was acquainted, Goulburn approached "nearest to perfection." Goulburn not only fully reciprocated such sentiments but was increasingly overawed by Peel's intelligence and political brilliance. "I am really quite astonished at the rapid advance Peel has made in all branches of useful knowledge and in the development of his most superior understanding," he confided to his wife early in 1819. Already, he saw his friend as a man "fit to be placed some day or other in the Government of this Country." In short, he acknowledged Peel's right to lead and was content with a supporting role for himself.[30]

Peel's observation notwithstanding, Goulburn's enjoyment of every domestic blessing was less than perfect. He continued to put duty and responsibility before family, and the purchase of Betchworth in a sense worsened the problem. Now his wife and children – for Edward was born in 1816, Frederick the following year, and young Jane in 1820 – were physically separated from him. They remained in the country, whereas he had to be in London throughout the week even when Parliament was not sitting. Invariably, he was in his office in Downing Street by nine in the morning, and there he remained until six in the evening. Even those days that he did spend at Betchworth were devoted largely to the reading and drafting of dispatches. It was his proud boast that over the course of six years, between 1815 and 1821, he was never absent from the office for more than seven consecutive days, and for that length of time on two or three occasions only. His example helped inspire his staff, he believed, thus enabling him "to carry on the Colonial business with an establishment far below what was either before or afterwards deemed absolutely necessary."[31]

Goulburn was all too aware of the fact that he was almost a stranger to his young family, except in moments of crisis – though he was not an alarmist even about matters of health. When his wife wrote in near hysteria of the infant Edward's violent crying, Goulburn diagnosed from London the baby's inability to feed at his mother's breast because of a cold that prevented him from breathing through his nose. Goulburn suggested that his wife give Edward a little of her milk on a spoon, put his feet in warm water, and dose him with castor oil; and he promised that if the child failed to respond to this therapy, he would consult Sir William Knighton, the capital's most fashionable doctor, and bring his opinion down to Betchworth. Ultimately, however, he placed his trust in providence. "Pray calm your anxiety and do not anticipate evils which are not of necessary occurrence," he wrote in the midst of another domestic crisis, "but which if they do occur are for our good by teaching us the uncertainty of our enjoyments and by inducing us to look for other better support than our own." Yet he realized how unfairly he was treating his wife. "I am always doomed to use you shabbily but not willingly," he admitted on another occasion. "There is however so much to be done and so little time to do it that you must make some allowance for me." Inevitably, Jane Goulburn's health tended to collapse under the strain of responsibility and isolation.[32]

Goulburn's close relationship with Bathurst, his willingness to shoulder the responsibilities which the secretary of state so cheerfully delegated to him, and his anxiety to please the older man, who evidently regarded him with paternal affection, go far to explain his inability to find more time for his family. Goulburn served as Bathurst's eyes and ears on domestic political developments, he reported to him the more interesting items of news from the colonies, and he saved him "much labour" by providing him with a précis of important incoming dispatches, for on some days there were "immense arrivals." He also composed briefing papers on problems likely to be raised in the Lords, and he drafted the instructions to colonial governors. Some of these drafts were sent to the secretary of state in rough form, to be amended and returned with a blank signature, but others were submitted in fair copy simply to be signed. A signature intended for one dispatch was sometimes used by Goulburn for another. When

Bathurst's instructions on the government of Malta threatened to see the military command there devolve on an officer who was "quite mad and utterly unfit to have command for a single day," his under-secretary altered them. Similarly, he reversed Bathurst's decision to remove the military governor of Demerara, explaining that the problem was more complicated than the secretary of state had assumed. He conducted the discussions with Frederick Robinson at the Board of Trade which eventually brought a liberalization of the trade of the West Indian islands, in an effort to relieve their deepening distress. Finally, from 1816, the entire domestic correspondence of the department was in his hands. Although routine matters were handled by the chief clerk and his staff, Goulburn remained responsible for communications with all other ministries. He it was who met with the agents of the colonies and the merchants engaged in colonial trade. Thus it is not surprising that he saw so little of his wife and children. "I am really hurried and worried with business till I have no time to write to any body and can only give you a line," he wrote to Jane in 1816.[33]

The value Goulburn placed on the colonies did not lessen with the final defeat of France. He continued to regard them as militarily, commercially, and financially important to the mother country. Colonial development was one obvious strategy for expanding the economy and thus getting to grips with the legacy of debt bequeathed by four costly wars in little more than two generations. But the extent to which the diverse and widely scattered colonies were "subject to the supervision and direction" of the imperial government was a moot point. The "Saints" exaggerated imperial control as part of their amelioration campaign. Conversely, in defending himself and Bathurst from attacks for a want of zeal in the coercion of recalcitrant slave colonies, Goulburn protested that those with their own legislatures were part of a separate system of government, which was both different and inferior. Yet the crown's influence even in these colonies was not inconsiderable, controlling as it did the executive and appointments to the legislative council. Moreover, colonial laws were still subject to imperial review and veto. Furthermore, Goulburn firmly upheld Parliament's admitted constitutional authority to regulate colonial trade, and he stoutly defended a form of enlightened "colonial despotism" in the recent conquests. "Where a people have been accustomed to institutions having even a shadow of freedom it may be practicable to extend to them to a great extent the power of governing themselves," he conceded, "but where their whole idea of liberty is to confer upon one class the power over their inferiors which had been previously exercised by a despotic government over all, great caution is necessary to guard against a democratic tyranny under the name of liberty."[34]

In the development and implementation of policy, Goulburn had necessarily to be mindful of the issues that most excited his fellow members of Parliament. The demand for retrenchment was constantly made in the Commons, where a prolonged campaign was under way to dismantle the war state and thus lighten the burden of taxation. The annual examination of military estimates invariably led to the charge that the cost of maintaining the empire far exceeded its economic value and was an expense the nation could ill afford. Assaults on the Colonial Department as an expendable luxury saw Goulburn make a pair of unusually effective speeches in defence of the third secretaryship of state. "Bad government was no economy," he reminded the Commons, "and it would be bad government to reduce an office which had the care of so valuable a portion of our possessions as the colonies." Correspondence, as measured crudely in the number of pages, had recently quadrupled, he announced, while that connected with the abolition of the slave trade alone fully occupied an entire office. Indeed, the increase in public business was "beyond all former precedent" and "rendered it impossible to dispense with a separate department devoted to such purposes." Yet his denunciations of "pernicious parsimony" could not prevent savage economies in personnel. In 1816 the second under-secretaryship and a number of clerkships were abolished, though the total annual savings were derisory. The result, however, was that Goulburn administered the entire empire with the assistance of eleven clerks. Ironically, by his efficiency and dedication he made possible the resort to the parliamentary paring knife. Similarly, his personal success at both the Home Office and the Colonial Office did nothing to shake his belief in the virtues of the minimal state.[35]

Another parliamentary concern was slavery, and Goulburn was obliged always to handle the "Saints" with kid gloves. When Wilberforce called to see him to request that the Colonial Office arrange for "negro girls" living in the neighbourhood of Sierra Leone to be "purchased" to accommodate the men of a black regiment who had been freed and settled there, the under-secretary responded positively but placed his decision within a broader imperial context. "Something of this sort must be done both there and Honduras or otherwise the settlements will go to ruin," he informed Bathurst. "I wish we could send some of our reforming countrywomen," he added facetiously.[36]

Another interest group that commanded attention and respect was the merchant community. Thus, when licences were granted to a number of Dutch shippers in 1815 authorizing them temporarily to continue trading with Demerara and Berbice, Goulburn actively sought some compensatory commercial concession from Holland in order to forestall protests from London and Liverpool. Yet as important as trade and philanthropy were in the formulation of colonial policy, so also was the desire to promote "good government." Thus Britain's task in Ceylon, the *Quarterly Review* asserted, was to "endeavour to fix the stability of our conquest on the affections of the natives, by instilling into the minds of the rising generation the true principles of morality and religion; and ... 'to promote extensive industry and consequently improvement, by giving the people an interest in the soil, and by instituting amongst them an acknowledged claim to the possession of the lands, that they may be induced to labour for their own profit and advantage.'"[37]

In few colonies did instruction in the true principles of morality and religion, and the promotion of industry and improvement seem more necessary than in New South Wales. The loss of the American colonies had obliged the government to look elsewhere for suitable "receptacles" for criminals sentenced to transportation, and Australasia had been its choice. The threat of being shipped to the end of the world promised to provide a new deterrent to crime, and at first the voyage itself proved in all too many cases to be a capital sentence. By the time Goulburn moved to the Colonial Office, the penal colony harboured some 10,000 souls, and the population more than doubled during his tenure.[38]

Goulburn recognized that the unique character of these settlements, founded neither for territorial nor commercial reasons, meant that they could not be "administered with the usual reference to those general Principles of Colonial Policy" that were "applicable to other Foreign Possessions of His Majesty." They were also set apart by the vast distance that separated them from the mother country. Well over two years often elapsed between the issuing of an instruction and the receipt in Downing Street of the governor's response. This situation justified investing the governor with greater authority than that possessed by any other colonial executive. "The materials of which that colony was composed were so extremely combustible," Goulburn reminded the Commons, "that it required a strong compressive force to prevent them from bursting into flames."[39]

Although he defended the necessity of an authoritarian form of government in New South Wales, Goulburn's arrival in Downing Street was quickly followed by a series of decisions that were plainly intended to foster a stable and more normal society in the colony. He was responding, at least in part, to the report of the select committee on transportation. Thus the policy of discouraging wives from following their transported husbands to the other side of the world was discontinued. However, the considerations of economy which had determined the earlier decision were not ignored. The governor, Lachlan Macquarie, a career soldier, was ordered to report promptly on the wives' ability to support themselves, "as the further extension of this measure will depend on the result of the present experiment." In much the same spirit, Goulburn had already acted on Macquarie's advice to dispatch forty female convicts to Hobart. He was careful to instruct the lieutenant-governor of Van Diemen's Land (as Tasmania was then called) to ensure their proper treatment. But his efforts to achieve a better sexual balance, and thus to civilize as well as to people, were doomed by the fact that the vast majority of the convicts transported were men.[40]

The abstemious Goulburn enthusiastically backed the governor's decision to check the excessive consumption of rum, which contributed to the colony's unruliness. Macquarie resolved to control the spirit's importation more strictly, even though a parliamentary committee had recommended the establishment of a local distillery in an effort to stimulate agricultural development and discourage illicit distillation. Mulling over the statistics forwarded to Downing Street, Goulburn found no evidence of an existing surplus of corn production. Consequently, legal distillation threatened greater scarcity of corn for food. As for illicit distillation, he reasoned that it could only be effectively discouraged by a virtual free trade in untaxed legal spirits. This he rejected on the grounds that "there is too much reason to apprehend the consequences which may result from the reduced price of an article, the injurious effect of which upon the morals and health of the inhabitants is only equalled by the avidity with which it is required." Even Macquarie's subsequent conversion to the cause of local legal distillation failed to shake the under-secretary's resolve.[41]

These initial and modest efforts to rescue the settlement from its unsavoury reputation were accompanied by measures that looked to the creation of a society less alien to British traditions. A two-tier court structure was put in place, one to deal with minor civil actions, the other to hear major civil actions and criminal cases. Lawyers were sent out from Britain to staff it. However, that "distinguished feature of the British Constitution," trial by jury, was withheld on the grounds of an insufficiency of true "peers." Harsh police regulations were moderated. The virtually unlimited power granted by the governor to magistrates to inflict corporal punishment on persons convicted of "idle and disorderly" conduct was rejected as objectionable, and the punishment was criticized as excessive. Similarly, the guards of convicts were denied a free hand to punish "incorrigible rogues." Again the objection was the danger of an abuse of power. Goulburn was also more cautious than Macquarie on the controversial subject of the full readmission to society of convicts who had "redeemed themselves for past transgressions." The governor's forgiving policy was approved in principle, but he was cautioned to be sensitive to the hostility it generated among free settlers. There must be no jeopardizing of his authority "by exerting it on a subject where Resistance may be so well cloaked under a rigid sense of virtue or of a refinement of moral feeling."[42]

Goulburn's intent was to assimilate this peculiar colony's regulations as far as was possible to the enactments of British statutes. But the governor continued to govern without the assistance of a council, for Downing Street doubted the presence there of persons fit to fill it and feared the development of a factionalism that would weaken "the higher authorities in a Society composed of such discordant materials." Goulburn supported Macquarie in a conflict with the new judicial officers, who were recalled. Nevertheless, the governor was no longer permitted to operate in quite the same unfettered way as before; his right to issue pardons was withdrawn and that to grant tickets of leave was subjected to closer scrutiny; and when he deprived a resident of his land grant and official position simply for signing a petition to Parliament critical of him, he was sternly rebuked for interfering with a hallowed right of all British subjects. Summing up the achievements, Henry Goulburn claimed in 1816 that better regulations had been adopted for the prevention of crimes and the promotion of virtuous habits. The number of crimes in the colony had decreased, he informed the House, punishments were less severe, marriages more frequent, and there was every hope "of the progressive amelioration of the colony."[43]

Another of Goulburn's successes was to improve the survival rate among the criminals being transported. Impressed by a colonial report on the need for naval surgeons and careful attention to hygiene aboard the transports, he implemented the proposals. In addition, a system of classification was introduced, separating young offenders from mature convicts. On at least one vessel, an energetic chaplain established a school in which thirty convicts were taught to read and write, religious duties were enforced four times each week, and the use of profanity was discouraged. "In no case was there a great degree of neglect," Goulburn boasted in the Commons, "and in many cases an extraordinary degree of attention was paid to the convicts."[44]

In 1819 John Thomas Bigge, the former chief justice of Trinidad, was sent to New South Wales as a special commissioner to examine and report on the colony. His instructions, which Goulburn surely drafted, revealed a willingness to re-examine all aspects of policy following the law officers' opinion that the government did not possess the "power to raise taxes or customs duties in a settled colony except through a representative assembly." On the one hand, Bigge was to consider how the colony could be revived as an object of peculiar terror to persons sentenced to transportation. On the other, he was to report on those issues that touched on its attractiveness to free settlers. To this end, he was to judge the adequacy of the judicial system, the severity of the police regulations, and the possibilities for diffusing education and religious instruction, always bearing in mind the fact that "these two branches ought in all cases to be inseparably connected." Inevitably, perhaps, governor and commissioner clashed. This time Goulburn came down against the governor, but Macquarie had already decided to resign. He was replaced by Sir Thomas Brisbane. Subsequently, Bigge's three reports "were made the basis for the first Australian constitution, embodied in an act of parliament in 1823."[45]

Another colony that presented Goulburn with problems that were both peculiar and pressing was Canada. Here his preoccupation was with a different form of security – protection from an ambitious and expansionist neighbour. The hope of creating an Indian barrier state between Canada and the United States had been dashed at Ghent, so the Colonial Office increasingly concentrated on the creation of an alternative human "barrier." Even as the negotiations sputtered along in the Flemish city, the Canadian authorities had been authorized to offer inducements to soldiers serving in North America to settle there at the end of their service. They were to receive one hundred acres of land, the implements with which to work it, free transportation of their families across the Atlantic, and rations for a period of at least six months. Settled at strategic points, they would act as a barrier to further American incursions. "I have been long alive to the extraordinary encroachments of the American Government on every one of these frontiers," Goulburn assured one alarmed correspondent.[46]

The efficacy of this policy was open to question, however. Would a former soldier make a good settler? Habits of "idleness" and "dissipation" were too deeply entrenched to be easily overcome, one senior military officer warned. Moreover, there was evidence "that an unsettled country immediately on the frontier affords better defence than any population that could be placed there." The inexpensiveness of a wilderness policy certainly enhanced its appeal in London, and the Colonial Office was soon voicing dismay that the vital area between Montreal and Lake Champlain had not been left in a "state of nature." It ordered that additional settlements be prevented, that settlers be encouraged to exchange their holdings for those farther from the frontier, and that the construction of roads be discouraged and those now open be permitted to fall into disrepair. Yet the security provided by an impenetrable wilderness could be overstated, as Goulburn recognized. On the other side of the line, he reminded the Commons in 1816, "the forests had disappeared – the natives were withdrawn – a numerous American population was spread along the shores of the Lakes – and the opening of roads and canals had brought the enemy at once in contact with our frontier."[47]

One obvious response to the burgeoning population and power of the United States was more rapid settlement of Canada. Thus Goulburn drafted a scheme of assisted emigration in the immediate aftermath of the disappointing settlement at Ghent. Initially, he sought to divert to British North America the steady stream of Irish and largely Ulster emigration to the United States. These emigrants were offered inducements and benefits similar to those already extended to demobilized soldiers. "I believe if we intend to preserve those Provinces it is the only method by which we can hope to do so," he explained to Peel. Subsequently, the scheme was extended to Scotland and England.[48]

The results were disappointing, and this bold program did not long survive. Delays in its implementation while the Colonial Office awaited word of American ratification of the Treaty of Ghent – for emigrants were to be carried out in the empty transports dispatched to bring back the troops – resulted in the disruption of the entire process when Napoleon's return to France created a new military emergency. The transports sailed without waiting for the emigrants to be assembled. Further, the Colonial Office's sensible precaution of demanding a bond, in order to ensure that persons transported at public expense to Canada did not immediately migrate to the United States, discouraged some applications. Less than one hundred families persisted, and they were transported to Canada too late in the year either to be settled immediately or to fend for themselves. They became a public charge. By this time also, the scheme was falling victim to the mounting pressure for economy. The prime minister had long since made his support conditional on the government's being involved "in as little expense as possible," and early in 1816 the cabinet fixed on assisted emigration as one area where savings might be made.[49]

Nevertheless, Goulburn did not abandon a policy he considered vital to the survival of British North America. October found him requesting from the governor general a report on the principal difficulties encountered by emigrants and seeking suggestions not only on how to solve them but also on "the best and most economical mode" of conducting settlements in future. And he was quick to implement several of the eminently practical suggestions. He withheld letters of recommendation from those seeking to embark late in the year and thus denied land grants to them. He accepted that the job of surveying lands be undertaken as a matter of some urgency, but on the understanding that the costs would be borne by the provinces. He sanctioned the use of crown reserves and endorsed the creation of more compact settlements close to existing communities, where immigrants could "either derive assistance in clearing their own lands or procure the means of subsistence by labouring for those who have the means of employing them." And while in the current penny-pinching climate there could be no general or generous issues of rations to settlers, he did sanction continued relief to the needy.[50]

The official policy throughout 1816 and 1817 remained the meagre one of providing emigrants with a parcel of land and a supply of farm implements. Only in a number of exceptional cases was free transportation provided, though some emigrants were transported on credit – they agreed to repay the government "as soon as possible" after their settlement. Increasingly, Bathurst and Goulburn staked their hopes of success on inducing "capitalists to take grants of land and carry out cultivators under their protection and superintendance." Each "capitalist" would have to lead out at least ten "cultivators" in order to qualify for the standard land grant of one hundred acres for each individual. Further, he would be required to put up capital at the rate of £20 per person and advance half of it as a form of bond before passage. This would be repaid once the party was settled, thereby ensuring that emigrants possessed "some means to purchase the articles of which they may be in need." For although they were to receive free passage across the Atlantic, they were required to bear the cost of their food and supplies. This scheme also held out the promise of the re-creation in the colonies of that class of gentlemen who had contributed so much to the political and social stability of the mother country. Along with this more ambitious general policy went more generous land grants to former soldiers, especially officers and sergeants, who would be particularly helpful in the reorganization of the provincial militias, a task of some urgency in view of the Americans' efforts to improve their force.[51]

The wisdom of providing, in Goulburn's words, "very trifling" public assistance to emigrants and of focusing on those with the means of maintaining themselves for a reasonable time after their arrival was strongly endorsed by a newly appointed governor general. "Pray stop the emigration if possible," the Duke of Richmond wrote in August 1818, "unless for those who can bring a little money." His appointment amounted to a significant upgrading of the governor generalship. Aristocrat, soldier, diplomat, politician, a former viceroy of Ireland, and Bathurst's brother-in-law, he promised to bring unprecedented prestige and influence to the office. He did not bring his duchess, however. He could not stomach the thought of her "alarms at sea," and he had no desire to risk having his life in Canada made miserable by her certain dislike of the colony.[52]

Richmond was alive to the tensions between the largely French-speaking population of one province and the English who dominated the other, a situation that went far to explain why so few of the recent immigrants remained in strategically vital Lower Canada. Yet he favoured a union of the provinces. A united Canada would surely be a harder nut for the Americans to crack. "Whether an union could now be brought about is another question," he conceded. How, then, was the colony to be made more secure in the short term? Richmond outlined a program of fortifications and public works similar to that recommended two years earlier by separate naval and military commissions. At the time, the Colonial Office had been intimidated by the cost. Now, with Wellington's support, it endorsed Richmond's proposals for Quebec. Over the next few years, considerable sums were to be spent on fortifications in Lower Canada. Within a few months, however, Richmond's influential presence had been lost. Bitten by a rabid animal, he suffered an agonizing and terrifying death. By then, a more radical form of defence was being attempted – friendlier relations with the United States.[53]

The Treaty of Ghent, the commercial convention of 1815, a prudent British defusing of the occasional crises over the fisheries, Britain's careful restraint of the Indians, its prompt response to the Americans' complaints of interference with their vessels on the Great Lakes, and the signing in 1817 of a convention severely limiting armed vessels on those lakes (which gave the Americans an obvious advantage in the event of another conflict) all indicated a growing commitment to "amity and friendship." Nor was the government unaware of the commercial significance of the American market, which at this time was "the most important single factor in bringing prosperity or depression to British export industries." Consequently, Liverpool again chose to conciliate the Americans when they threatened to disrupt British trade in retaliation for their merchants' continued exclusion from the trade of the West Indies. Anyway, the limited convention of 1815 was soon to expire.[54]

Castlereagh received a new American minister in July 1818. He was Richard Rush, who had been born during the Revolutionary War, had held high office during the War of 1812, and as acting secretary of state had given his name to the convention limiting arms on the Great-Lakes. Rush possessed all the social graces that his predecessor in London (and the new secretary of state) John Quincy Adams not only lacked but scorned, and he made a favourable impression on his hosts. Among those who paid him "high" compliments was Henry Goulburn. The two men were of a similar age and not dissimilar in character. Able, companionable, and loyal, they were both seemingly content with secondary positions. But Goulburn's favourable assessment would not have survived exposure to Rush's private opinions of Britain and her people, which appear to have been formed following a conversation with the under-secretary's father-in-law. The American concluded that Tory and Whig were as one in their fundamental dislike of the Republic and were motivated by a "deep seated Jealousy" of its prosperity and power. He contemptuously dismissed Britain as a cramped little island inhabited by a swindling people. "We are cheated here all around the circle," he reported to President Monroe; "the cook, the coachman, the footman, the butcher, the fishmonger, the green grocer, all cheat us; and if we change, the new ones cheat us worse."[55]

To ensure that his nation was not short-changed in the general negotiation which Castlereagh, to his surprise, agreed to open, Rush leaned heavily on the knowledge and experience of his fellow negotiator Albert Gallatin. He had served under the older man at the Treasury and held him in high esteem. Now American minister to France, Gallatin was sceptical of their obtaining "any reasonable arrangement" from the British, even though he acknowledged that within the ministry there was "a more favourable disposition towards the United States than had existed at any former period." The American invasion of Florida, he fancied, would strengthen Britain's bargaining position by allowing her to regain her influence over Spain. The execution of two British subjects by the commander of the invading force and hero of New Orleans, Andrew Jackson, seemed certain to complicate matters further. Nor were Gallatin and Rush confident of being able to exploit Britain's evident anxiety to renew the commercial convention. Their own nation's desire for its renewal was no less obvious.[56]

Castlereagh turned again to Frederick Robinson, who was now president of the Board of Trade and a member of the cabinet, and Henry Goulburn to conduct the new negotiations. Their familiarity with the issues explained their selection. Before departing for Aix-la-Chapelle, Castlereagh gave matters a pleasantly informal helping hand by gathering the four men at his country retreat in Kent to engage in a general discussion of the issues. Only one of the problems was considered in any detail – impressment. The foreign secretary had surprised the Americans by adding it to an agenda that already included renewal of the commercial convention, trade between the United States and British territories in the West Indies and North America, the fisheries, the boundary between the Republic and British territory west of the Lake of the Woods, the conflicting claims of the two nations to the Columbia River country in the Pacific Northwest, and American demands for compensation for slaves carried off by the British alledgedly in violation of the Treaty of Ghent.[57]

Formal negotiations opened at the Board of Trade on 27 August 1818, but the initial meeting was notable only for the Americans' half-hearted attempt to link the other points at issue to a renewal of the commercial convention. This Robinson and Goulburn bluntly rejected. The conferences then dragged on throughout September and into October. Meetings were postponed at the request of the two Britons – no doubt, as the Americans suspected, in order to allow them to obtain additional directions from the cabinet. Robinson and Goulburn were also inclined to delay any settlement until they had received from the United States some satisfactory explanation of the executions of the two British subjects in Florida. On this point they received no more than lukewarm support from the foreign secretary. He saw no reason why this "unpleasant episode" should impede a renewal of the commercial convention and expressed his confidence that the Monroe administration would give them "the means of an honourable explanation." Goulburn's participation was then briefly interrupted by the death of his mother, who had long been in failing health, but he returned to duty almost immediately, on 13 October 1818. By this time the negotiations had fallen into a frustrating and fruitless pattern. "Projects and counter projects transcribed I know not how many different times, to comprehend the numerous modifications, substantial and verbal, which each side from time to time has to propose," Rush complained privately to Monroe. "It is all full of interest, but would seem to be intrinsically incompatible with expedition."[58]

The negotiations were suddenly energized by Gallatin and Goulburn, when they met on 16 October. In an at times heated review of the issues, the American declared that the only topic on which they seemed likely to agree was renewal of the commercial convention, "and he regretted that the convention had been opened at all, as Mr. Rush had been authorized to agree to that renewal by itself." He concluded with the announcement that he wished to set out for France in five days. Goulburn kept a grip on his temper and maintained his composure throughout this outburst, responding calmly and perhaps infuriatingly that their work would surely prove useful in "subsequent proceedings of the two Governments." Nevertheless, he and Robinson were sufficiently galvanized by Gallatin's outburst to secure from the cabinet permission to settle swiftly. At their next full meeting, on 19 October, the four men quickly arranged most matters. The subjects on which the prospects of agreement were "hopeless" – impressment, and West Indian and North American trade – were set aside. But after some additional skirmishing, they managed to compromise on the remaining issues. The American claim for compensation for slaves illegally removed after the Treaty of Ghent was to be adjudicated by a friendly sovereign. The Americans were given access to a somewhat larger area of the fisheries than their instructions from John Quincy Adams had demanded, but they did not secure the restoration of the privileges they had enjoyed before 1783. Nor were they able to obtain a specific guarantee that these rights would remain unaffected by another war. Instead, they had to be content with the insertion of the word "forever" in the article. In return, they formally renounced all claim to fishing grounds outside the prescribed areas. The boundary west of the Lake of the Woods was to be drawn along the 49th parallel as far as the Rocky Mountains, Goulburn and Robinson having predictably failed in a half-hearted attempt to barter this for renewed access to the Mississippi. Across the mountains, they were equally unsuccessful in their quest to strengthen their nation's grip on the northern bank of the Columbia River. Instead, the disputed territory was to be open for ten years to the citizens and vessels of both nations without prejudice to the territorial claims of either. Finally, the commercial convention was renewed, also for a period of ten years.[59]

At the formal signing ceremony on 20 October, Henry Goulburn remarked that "the pen of Gibbon, who was once a member of the board of trade, had often been used at the table" over which their discussions "had been carried on." If this comment revealed his sense of history and reverence for tradition, it was not inappropriate, given the historic importance of their achievement. The successful arrangement of several long-festering disputes had placed Anglo-American relations on a more secure foundation, and the price in concessions had not been particularly high. Moreover, much as Goulburn disliked and distrusted the United States and was generally disdainful of Americans, though he was impressed with both Gallatin and Rush, he had played a significant role in this important international development.[60]

The pressure for economies, which helped persuade the government to seek additional protection for Canada in better relations with the United States, had long since emerged as a determinant of general colonial policy. Before 1815, the incentive had been the crushing financial burden of the war effort. Thus in Ceylon the Colonial Office had been prepared even to overlook the atrocities committed on British subjects by the still independent King of Kandy. A retaliatory war would cost too much in European lives and imperial treasure, the governor was informed. The news that he had already defeated the king, swiftly and inexpensively, was welcomed in London as an opportunity to reduce the island's military establishment. Across the Indian Ocean in Mauritius, an expensive system of government slavery inherited from the French was ordered to be dismantled, more as a cost-saving than humanitarian measure. The slaves were to be encouraged to enlist in black regiments serving in Ceylon or the West Indies, or to be apprenticed locally, on condition that security was given for their good treatment and that an inspector was appointed to ensure that they were not mistreated. Similarly, the escalating expenses of the colony's administration saw the governor rebuked. The system adopted by the French "may have been in some instances oppressive or defective," Goulburn sarcastically observed, "but it was at all events, as far as economy was concerned, one well deserving of your imitation."[61]

Calls for economy became even more insistent after 1815. Liverpool had long expected to encounter difficulty securing the renewal of the property tax once the French war had been won, and Goulburn had the misfortune to be the most senior member of the government present in the Commons on 1 March 1816 when the House sought to discuss the avalanche of petitions demanding relief from the tax. His explanation that the senior ministers were all indisposed, save the chancellor of exchequer, who simply could not be located, brought the mocking retort from Henry Brougham that they were all surely sick of the property tax. Subsequently, the Commons delivered a severe blow to the government's finances by refusing to renew the tax. Now the pressure for additional reductions in expenditures seemed certain to be irresistible. One immediate consequence was the rash pruning of Colonial Office staff. Another was a colonial circular demanding "a minute investigation" of all sources of public expense and a report detailing every item "however minute" where savings might be made. Surplus revenues resulting from retrenchment were to be applied against the costs of military establishments that were essential for security.[62]

Hand in hand with this instruction went a request that the colonies assume a larger proportion of the costs of their defence. The Colonial Office announced that the imperial government would continue to carry the entire burden throughout the current year, 1816, but warned that "it will in future years be impossible to maintain an equal force unless some part of the charge be defrayed by the colonies themselves." Unimpressed, the colonies rebuffed or rejected the request. They pleaded poverty or stagnant economies, and some of the West Indian islands took this opportunity to remind the mother country of their direct payments to the imperial treasury through taxes on their produce, especially sugar, and their indirect contributions as a result of their exclusive purchase of British goods and use of British ships. This was the argument Goulburn himself employed in the Commons when he sought to put the best face on the evasive or hostile colonial responses. A guiding principle of colonial policy, he declared, was that the mother country compensate the colonies for a monopoly of their commerce by maintaining their civil and military establishments.[63]

Nevertheless, the Colonial Office continued to demand a critical scrutiny of civil and military expenditures. Governors were required to complete and return a printed questionnaire that provided Downing Street with information on the tenure, duties, and emoluments of offices and indicated whether they were occupied by principals or deputies. Goulburn then pressed governors to shrivel those bureaucracies that he considered bloated. He imposed severe restrictions on the hardship pensions paid to the families of public servants who died while in service. Public works projects, except those that were clearly necessary for security or were to be financed entirely from colonial resources, were disallowed. The great object, colonial executives were reminded, was the equalization of their revenues and expenditures. Success in this would be regarded as the most "convincing proof" of their zeal in the king's service.[64]

The desperate desire to economize left imperial authority vulnerable to colonial challenge, as in Canada, where annual votes of supply were withheld by legislatures that were locked in struggles with the executive. It also prompted a hardening attitude in Downing Street towards the distribution of provisions and presents to the Indians who gathered like vagrants around government stores, though the evangelical Goulburn insisted that this economy would also expose them to "less temptation to continued indolence and intoxication." The news from Ceylon of an insurrection in Kandy saw the fears of ever-swelling expenditures again dressed up in more appealing garb – the concept of an empire founded on the acquiescence of the peoples who constituted it. If the insurgency was rooted in a desire to return to an ancient form of government, the governor was advised, and if it "proceeds therefore from a general indisposition to remain under His Majesty's Protection, it will be on every account unfit to persist in the contest."[65]

That the zeal for economy might nevertheless be pursued altogether too zealously was evident in Mauritius. There, the elevation of an energetic but impulsive and ham-fisted general to the temporary governorship was followed by a frenzy of retrenchment, which set off a storm of protest by its victims. Hence the Colonial Office was almost grateful for the general's folly in suspending the chief judge and personally assuming judicial authority. The general was dismissed. On the other hand, he had identified a number of serious abuses and had drawn attention to a swollen bureaucracy. Nor was there any reason to believe that Mauritius was unique in this respect.[66]

If Goulburn's unrelenting efforts to reduce the costs of empire were all too often defeated or evaded, they were accompanied by the more positive policy of encouraging the colonies' economic development. To the extent that colonies were self-sufficient, they would be less dependent on the imperial treasury. Goulburn approved a state tobacco monopoly in Ceylon as a means of emancipating producers from a brutal private monopoly, though he cautioned the governor to regard this pragmatic deviation from economic liberalism as a "temporary expedient" only. After all, wrote this graduate of the Alfred Club seminars, it could not "be easily reconciled to the just and enlightened principles which prevail in those parts of the world where the real interests of commerce are best understood." Before long, the growth of the export trade in tobacco permitted the termination of this form of public interference. The essential task in this colony, Goulburn concluded, was to promote the cultivation of provisions rather than the production of cash crops, thereby freeing the Treasury from the necessity to purchase foodstuffs because of their scarcity. Elsewhere in the empire, where the food supply was already assured, he recommended that they concentrate on the production of goods for export. It was wines, for example, at the Cape Colony in southern Africa. A colonial preference for Cape wines in terms of duty – which Goulburn did not consider inconsistent with his emergent liberalism in economic matters – and their increased consumption in England encouraged optimism in Downing Street that any improvement in the quality of these wines would allow them to compete successfully with those of Spain and Madeira. Thus the governor was urged to give "every possible encouragement to the improvement of the vineyards and of the manufacture of their produce."[67]

Another instrument of economic development was immigration. The scheme that Goulburn had drafted in December 1817 to promote the settlement of Canada had been shaped by the evidence that isolated individuals, lacking the financial means to provide for themselves at least for several months, had become burdens on the colony. Many, disheartened by their difficulties, had "left their lands in disgust and proceeded to the United States." Such desertions vitiated an emigration policy that had been given an additional fillip by amendments to the shipping regulations governing the carrying of passengers, which resulted in inexpensive fares to Canadian ports.[68]

Emigrants organized in reasonably well-financed groups offered an assurance of a less-dispersed pattern of settlement and a greater measure of mutual support, while the capital which the organizer had at his disposal ensured both cultivation of the land and the maintenance of those under his charge for the first difficult year. Equally, this system would promote gentlemanly values and protect the colonies from "an inundation of idle persons" possessed of neither the energy nor the means to make use of the lands provided to them. Goulburn made it clear to British parishes willing to ship out their poor that he had no interest in providing overseas dumping grounds for their paupers. In 1818 his new policy saw only a few hundred emigrants transported to North America, though some organized parties did go out at their own expense. The following year, 1819, the offer of free passage was withdrawn. In 1820 and again in 1821, organized parties of distressed Scots who paid their own way to Canada were provided with free transportation to their places of settlement, as well as periodic small cash advances to help them weather the first year on the land. Politically motivated, this decision was taken by the prime minister and the chancellor of the exchequer, and was not one of which Goulburn approved. By this time, however, the principal thrust of emigration was being directed elsewhere, for the Colonial Office was seeking to channel the continuing stream of emigrants to the Cape. This may partly have been a response to Richmond's urging that all emigrants to North America be discouraged unless they carried with them a minimum of £50 in cash; it was also a result of the growing stability of the relationship with the United States, which saw in 1821 the withdrawal of the prohibition on settlement and road construction in the strategically important area between Montreal and Lake Champlain.[69]

Goulburn had always regarded his scheme of group emigration as the basis of "some regular plan for settling the waste lands of the Crown in the several British colonies," and in terms of the advantages to individuals and the general prosperity of the country, he had had the Cape specifically in mind. For other members of the government, deepening distress and swelling discontent among the "lower orders," especially the manufacturing classes, provided the spur in 1819 to launch a program of state-assisted and capitalist-led emigration to the Cape. To his credit, Goulburn sought to discourage the use of his plan for this particular purpose. He recognized the limitations of the colonial safety value. When approached by the Duke of Newcastle, who wished to know whether to advise distressed operatives to take advantage of the program, he replied frankly, "Generally speaking [they] succeed the worst. Their ignorance of agriculture is in itself a most serious obstacle and as far as my observation goes I would say they are less patient of inconvenience and therefore more easily disheartened." Yet the Cape promised to provide a better haven than Canada, given its more favourable climate and the fertility of its soil. To enhance the emigrants' chances of success, Goulburn once again called on the knowledge gained from North America. The departure of the emigrants was carefully timed to ensure that they arrived at the beginning of the planting season. The governor was instructed to provide them with prompt transportation to their places of settlement. He was also to ensure that their lands had been previously surveyed and divided into lots, and was urged to provide them with the assistance of intelligent soldiers to instruct them in hutting. They were to be located as close as possible to good fishing. Rations were to be readied for distribution, though these and additional supplies, together with farm implements, were not to be given out free; they were to be provided at cost price. It was essential, Goulburn argued, to require "on the part of the settlers that due diligence and exertion of labour for the means of subsistence which experience has pointed out to be utterly incompatible with a gratuitous distribution of provisions."[70]

These and other wise precautions notwithstanding, the immediate results of this substantial enterprise were disappointing. The largest settlement was located on lands better adapted to pasture than arable farming. Moreover, too many of the emigrants were artisans entirely ignorant of agriculture, and as Goulburn had feared, they soon wandered off to towns where their skills were more marketable. Nevertheless, they did improve the colony's security and promote its anglicization. To this end, Goulburn and the governor were keen to replace Dutch schoolmasters with Englishmen of "a superior class." Here was the "best means of making the English language more general in the Colony and improving the manners and morals of the people."[71]

No system of education could succeed in this essential task, Goulburn believed, unless it was rooted in religion. Long a supporter of missionary activities, he saw the empire as a fit field of work. Thus, in Ceylon, the natives' indulgence in "promiscuous intercourse" meant that education and religious instruction were required. Here was further evidence that "man was degenerate in his spiritual essence until rescued by the atoning grace of Christ." Young clergy were recruited to go out to the colony, and Bibles and prayer books were forwarded there. "Nothing, I can assure you, can give me more gratification than to be from time to time informed of the Progress of Religion in the Colony," Goulburn wrote encouragingly to his first clerical recruit. To facilitate the task of recruitment, Parliament subsequently passed a bill temporarily enabling the archbishops of Canterbury and York and the bishop of London to admit to Holy Orders persons willing to serve in the colonies.[72]

Yet the empire's sectarian diversity dictated a measure of religious pragmatism. Insurrection in Kandy could be grasped as an opportunity to expel Buddhist priests, but Protestant zeal had to be restrained elsewhere. A pragmatic Goulburn was both careful and sensible in his dealings with sizable Roman Catholic communities, even though the Catholic Church was one he devoutly detested. In Mauritius, a former French colony, the Roman Catholic clergy were removed from the jurisdiction of the archbishop of Paris and placed under the authority of an

English chief curé. "He has been strongly recommended to me by persons whose opinions I highly value," Goulburn advised the governor, "and what I have seen of him is favourable to his loyalty and attachment to this Government." Nevertheless, the appointee was quickly disabused of any notion that he might expand the influence of his church in this part of the empire. The current establishment would be maintained and supported, and churches would be repaired, but there were to be no ecclesiastical visitations to other colonies.[73]

The situation was even more delicate in British North America. The French-speaking and Catholic residents of Lower Canada had long since been guaranteed a measure of religious equality, and theirs was the predominant voice in the provincial assembly. Thus the "great object" was to prevent "Demogogues" from making "the Roman Catholics the instruments of mischief." To this end it was necessary to conciliate the Catholic bishop, given the power he wielded over the clergy and the influence they in turn exercised over their flocks. His territorial title was acknowledged, even though this was a dignity reserved elsewhere in the empire for members of the established church, and he was invited to sit on the Legislative Council. Such deference and recognition were angrily disputed by a new Anglican bishop of Quebec. Following an interview with Goulburn in Downing Street, he complained that the under-secretary had let slip an intention to concede to the Roman Catholic Church in Canada a pre-eminence to which it was not legally entitled. Bathurst leapt to Goulburn's defence, reminding the bishop of the Catholics' legal rights. The duty of the government, he observed, was "to encourage as far as circumstances will admit, the religious instruction of all classes of His Majesty's subjects in Canada." In the same spirit, the Colonial Office rejected the bishop's demand that Catholic proselytism be discouraged. There would be no interference so long as clergy confined themselves to "the legitimate means" that all sects possessed "under the free toleration allowed them."[74]

As devout Anglicans, Goulburn and Bathurst did, however, provide discreet support to the established church. They approved the Anglican bishop's request for the legal establishment of parishes and rectories; they endorsed his proposal for the founding of "a more fit establishment" for the education of Canadian youths; they cooperated with the Society for Promoting Christian Knowledge in a campaign to ensure that the Protestant "lower orders" in both provinces had an adequate supply of Bibles and prayer books, though they made plain that these were not to be forced on anyone; finally, they denied state support to Protestant dissenters. Indeed, when the chief justice of Upper Canada interpreted the province's organizing legislation to mean that public support had been extended to all Protestants, Goulburn cited chapter and verse, quoting from the parliamentary debates held at the time, to establish that the clergy reserves had been exclusively set aside for the Church of England. Moreover, noting that the judge was himself a dissenter and thus "naturally not impartial," he recommended to Bathurst that the judge's ruling should not be attached to their request to the English law officers for a legal opinion. He had always found that lawyers had "a great repugnance to give opinions adverse to those of members of their own profession."[75]

One region of the empire where the established church ought to have been assured of fairer weather was the Caribbean, but even here it risked a severe buffeting. Methodists and other missionary dissenters had been far more successful than the more reserved Anglican clergy in establishing an intimacy with the slaves and influence over them. Goulburn saw the slave rebellion in Barbados in 1816 as an opportunity to reassert the leadership of the established church. The purity of its doctrines were better calculated than those of any other persuasion, he told the governors of the slave colonies in a circular issued in April 1817, "to impress upon its communicants a strong sense of moral obligations, a cheerful submission to the Laws, and that cheerful Resignation to the will of Providence which lighten the Burthens of Life by rescuing affliction from the bitterness of Discontent." Moreover, the missionary activities of other persuasions were to be tolerated only so long as they gave instruction in "the leading doctrines of the Gospel" and did not disturb an "infant Faith with polemical discussions."[76]

The zeal of the established church and the depth of its concern to meet the spiritual needs of the vast black population were questions to which Goulburn constantly sought answers. The responses he elicited – on the number of churches and parsonages on the different islands, the diligence of the clergy in the performance of their sacred duties, especially the essential sacrament of baptism, the fees they charged and who paid them, planters or slaves, and the extent to which slaves were accommodated in churches – were so haphazardly organized that the information was of limited value. Goulburn wearily accepted the returns as evidence of the clergy's diligence but encouraged governors to continue to animate them. His hope that the largest and wealthiest colony, Jamaica, would make provision for a resident bishop, thereby enhancing ecclesiastical discipline while countering the decision of the Roman Catholic Church to place its clergy under episcopal supervision, was dashed by a penurious assembly. He then suggested that a bishop be appointed to one of the existing livings, only to have the governor quash this proposal. A rector's income arose principally from "the Christenings and Burials of the Coloured Population," the Duke of Manchester explained. "And it would certainly ill become the station of a Bishop to attend at the Houses of these persons when they celebrate the Christening of their illegitimate children."[77]

A sabbatarian, Goulburn was keen to discourage merchants from working and employing their clerks on Sundays. Since their justification was the need to prepare for the regular Monday sailings of the packet to England, he persuaded the postmaster general to change the weekly sailing to Saturdays. Goulburn viewed "neglect of religious ordinances, and more especially the Sabbath," as "the great check to the religious instruction and improvement" of *all* classes in the West Indies. Hence his urging that the slaves' practice of holding markets on Sundays be more closely regulated. He did not suggest that the markets be banned, fearing that this might stimulate "idleness and dissipation," but he called for their restriction to certain hours that did not conflict with divine services. Moreover, since there was already an admitted problem in providing blacks with adequate accommodation in most churches, he scouted the possibility of additional services being scheduled in the larger towns at times convenient to the slaves.[78]

Manchester scotched this well-intentioned initiative. He warned that any meddling with market days would be "highly imprudent," recalling that an earlier decision to close the Kingston market in the afternoon to allow slaves to attend a special service conducted by the rector had excited so much dissatisfaction that it had been abandoned. Yet the governor was careful to offer reassurance that the religious education of the slaves was not being ignored. Additional services had already been established in Kingston and a number of other centres, he wrote, and in the regions of the island where there was no town in which slaves might trade, they were attending church. The assembly had made provision for the appointment of curates to assist parish priests in propagating the Gospel to the slaves, and there was a scheme "in contemplation" to establish special places of public worship for blacks where curates would officiate. Much hinged on the discretion of these curates, Manchester cautioned. Any hint of "intemperate zeal" would renew prejudices that were "nearly extinguished, and would defeat the exertions of those who are really disposed to do what may be practicable, but still to do it with care and moderation." Since this reflected Goulburn's own conservative approach to problems, he had to be content with it.[79]

The rebellion in Barbados, which Goulburn had attempted to turn to the advantage of the established church, was widely attributed to the slaves' misunderstanding of the objectives of the "Saints." The continuing horrors of slavery and charges of clandestine importations received a regular airing in Britain. There were demands for the closer supervision of the slave colonies by the Colonial Office, for the enactment of general legislation to promote amelioration, and for the establishment in every slave colony of a registry modelled on that already in place in Trinidad.[80]

When Wilberforce personally presented this last demand to the prime minister on 1 March 1815, he was informed that the ministry "could not support the Register Bill for want of proof of actual smuggling." His brother-in-law, James Stephen, who was all too aware of the boost the slave trade was likely to receive from the ending of the Napoleonic Wars, resigned his government-controlled seat in Parliament in disgust and published a long and passionate pamphlet, which again made the case for slave registries. Wilberforce introduced a registry bill late in the session, though he could not have expected it to pass in the face of both ministerial opposition and that organized by the West India interests. In vain Stephen protested to Bathurst the absurdity of the imperial government countenancing "the monstrous pretension" of petty assemblies to independence.[81]

Wilberforce did not revive his bill in 1816. The hope of a diplomatic settlement with the slave-trading nations and the outbreak of the rebellion in Barbados – responsibility for which the well-funded West India lobby sedulously sought to lay at his door on the grounds that slaves had understood his bill as an act of emancipation – contributed to his decision, as did private assurances from Bathurst that the ministry would act the following year if the West Indians ignored its advice now to act themselves. But Wilberforce maintained his private pressure, especially when he read the secretary of state's response to a Whig motion that called on the Colonial Office to recommend measures of amelioration to the colonies. Bathurst had defended the government's record on suppression of the slave trade and then expressed doubt that any slaves were being smuggled into British territories. Was he unaware of the evidence from Jamaica used by Stephen in his pamphlet? Wilberforce asked.[82]

In its politic anxiety to secure the suppression of the slave trade, the Liverpool ministry had initially been willing to bribe the defeated French to embrace abolition. The restored monarchy was offered the choice of a sum of money or the transfer of that new jewel of the British empire – Trinidad. When the French proved obdurate, successfully holding out for the temporary revival of their trade in slaves, the issue was carried to the general peace congress in Vienna. Unfortunately, that gathering was content to adopt a declaration that was long on noble sentiments but short on action. As a result of such setbacks, the ministry was roundly condemned for "gross mismanagement" of the negotiations and "lukewarmness" towards the cause of humanity. It ought to have bartered the restoration of France's empire for French abolition of the trade, Whigs argued. To some extent, however, Liverpool and his colleagues were rescued from this embarrassment by Napoleon's return from Elba. Following Waterloo, abolition was written into the second Treaty of Paris. But this entire episode, and the astonishing success of a petition campaign to protest any revival of the trade, had greatly strengthened the hand of those demanding a slave registration bill.[83]

One objection to any simple extension of the current limited slave registration was the additional burden it would impose on an already sorely overworked Colonial Office staff. A visit to Downing Street persuaded Stephen that Henry Goulburn realized "that it would be impossible for him and his clerks" to handle the material. "Not a sale, or mortgage, or assignment of slaves will be executed or agreed for in this country, without a search to see that they are duly registered," Stephen observed. To undertake this task, a full-time staff and supervisor were indispensable, but there was no immediate prospect of securing the necessary legislative authority to create this new bureaucracy. In the meantime, the Colonial Office cautiously pressed on with amelioration. Goulburn sought to ensure that the residents of Mauritius were prevented from smuggling slaves. And when the governor requested copies of the various sets of West Indian regulations governing the treatment of slaves, an ironic Goulburn responded, "I am not aware that their adoption in Mauritius would materially improve the situation of the slave." He did, however, promise to furnish the governor with "such information as may be best calculated to satisfy the laudable anxiety" that he had "evinced for improving a Code of Laws the perfection of which is, in every particular, so extremely desirable."[84]

As another spur to amelioration, Goulburn pressed the governor of Trinidad to award "honorary distinctions" to planters and overseers whose slaves were judged on examination "to be in point of comfort, Health, and general Improvement in the best state." The tests of the slaves' condition were to be the increase in births, the abolition of night work, the introduction of mechanical equipment and other means to lighten labour, the regular instruction of slaves, and the practice of evening prayers. Moreover, the candidates were to be classed "so that in no case should a sugar estate be brought into competition with a Cotton, Coffee, or Cocoa Plantation, or these with any but those of their own class." Elsewhere, amelioration was pursued through the introduction of slave registries modelled on that of Trinidad. By 1816 the system had been extended to St Lucia and then to Mauritius, though in the latter colony it had excited such open defiance that the military had to be called in. That same year also saw a registry established in the Cape Colony, where it had seemed all the more necessary given the unsavoury reputation of the "Dutch boors" for "harshness" in their treatment of "their slaves and Hottentots."[85]

The revolt in Barbados did not deflect Bathurst and Goulburn from the task of convincing the colonies to introduce a registration scheme. Nevertheless, the circular issued on 28 June 1816 emphatically disclaimed any intention on the government's part "to propose an emancipation of slaves." What it did bluntly assert was Parliament's right to legislate for the colonies, and the wisdom of voluntary colonial action before imperial intervention became necessary. Indeed, there was a none-too-subtle reference to the danger of such interference being again "misunderstood" in the "present agitated state" of the populations of the slave islands. One way or another, registers were going to be established, and the circular outlined the provisions that all colonial measures should contain. They were to require a description of the registered slave, though not in the minute detail proposed by Wilberforce. Violations were to be punished with a fine of at least £100 in each case, with half being paid to any informant, while the alleged owner of an unregistered slave would have to prove that he or she had not been imported illegally and was his bona fide property. Finally, authentic copies of the registers were to be forwarded to London. With their domestic flank thus seemingly well guarded against the charge of foot dragging, Bathurst and Goulburn awaited the colonies' responses.[86]

The news early in the New Year that the two most important islands – Jamaica and Barbados – had enacted legislation, followed as it was by the acts adopted in St Vincent and Antigua, was welcomed in Downing Street. Any satisfaction was shortlived, however, for the legislation framed by both Jamaica and Barbados gave the impression that effectiveness had not been the object. The mood of the assembly in Jamaica had been particularly surly. Protestations of a genuine desire to contribute to the "comfort" and "advantages" of the slaves rang hollow, the governor admitted. There existed a "disinclination to adopt new regulations adapted to the improved state of civilization to which the negroes have arrived." Dissatisfied, Wilberforce delivered a long and passionate indictment of the Jamaicans in a letter to Bathurst at the beginning of 1817. Clearly, Bathurst and Goulburn could expect fresh parliamentary assaults on their persuasive rather than coercive policies towards the slave colonies.[87]

Informed that a planter in Jamaica had been permitted to escape justice after having shot one of his slaves, Goulburn reacted indignantly and sternly. He drafted the dispatch that went out over Bathurst's name instructing the governor to dismiss the coroner for failing to hold an immediate inquest and to deliver a severe reprimand to the magistrate who had been unaccountably slow in issuing a warrant for the arrest of the culprit. Credited with ignorance rather than deliberate misconduct, the magistrate was to be put on notice that a second serious error of this kind would result in his removal from the bench. Goulburn also acted swiftly to ensure the more careful locating and humane treatment of Africans rescued from vessels illegally engaged in the slave trade and settled in the West Indies as apprentices. He applauded the continuing efforts of the authorities in Mauritius to suppress the trade there, but noted the absence "of any instance in which the [local] parties concerned in it, have as yet been brought to trial for felony." When the temptation to commit crime was so strong, he wrote, "nothing short of the utmost severity of the law can be expected to counteract the evil." And he added that if the governor considered it impossible to secure a conviction in the colony, he was to send the accused to Britain for trial. Subsequently this was done.[88]

Simultaneously, the Colonial Office was exerting pressure on Jamaica and Barbados to make amendments to their laws that would appease critics by plugging obvious loopholes. Significantly, Downing Street objected to a clause in the Barbados law bestowing immediate freedom on any African slave omitted from the register. Fears that the sudden emancipation of slaves would be followed by disorder were heightened in this instance by the knowledge that those freed would have been embittered by their recent abduction from their African homelands. Then again, it was false humanity to free someone who possessed neither the means of subsistence nor the information and habits essential for self-support. Such persons should be turned over to the crown, Downing Street directed.[89]

That the Colonial Office's campaign to cajole and coerce the laggard colonies into action did not satisfy the most enthusiastic proponents of amelioration was soon all too obvious. Responding to Wilberforce's call in the House for more information on colonial measures to improve the conditions of slaves, and to Samuel Romilly's questions concerning reported acts of extreme cruelty on Nevis, Dominica, and St Christopher, Goulburn was reduced to pleading for more time for the policy of persuasion. He also voiced the opinion "that the day was not far distant when such a change would take place in the condition of the black population of the colonies as would be most beneficial to them, and highly honourable to the character of this country."[90]

The claim was made that on the island of Jamaica the proprietors generally, and the legislature in particular, had endeavoured to promote the policy of humanity. Apologists cited the acts providing for the furtherance of the abolition of the slave trade, for more accurate returns of slaves, for their better subsistence, clothing, regulation, government, and protection, and for the appointment of curates to attend to their spiritual needs. But a general law applicable to all the West Indian islands could no longer be avoided, and Goulburn introduced it on 8 June 1819. Not only would every colony be required to compile a detailed and triennial slave registry, but it would also have to send authentic copies to the special office established in Britain. Goulburn conceded that "his bill would be more restricted than the bill of his hon. friend [Wilberforce]," but "the colonial legislatures had made it unnecessary to pass a more extended law." Indeed, he said, he had submitted to the Commons two months earlier copies of satisfactory measures adopted in Berbice, Dominica, Grenada, Nevis, and Tobago.[91]

Colonies slow to forward to London the copies of their registers were reminded of the inconvenience this would cause their planters; for no purchases could be made in Britain or monies raised there on the security of slaves unless these copies had been deposited in the Office of the Registrar of Slaves by 1 January 1820. Similarly, an accurate register was seen by Goulburn as the principal means of suppressing the persistent slave trading in Mauritius. New slaves would surely be discovered every three years, he argued, and their instant forfeiture would chill enthusiasm for this trade. He concluded that "we must look for the prevention of the Trade more to the conviction of its being a bad branch of trade than to any higher motive." If this suggested his final acceptance of the argument of the ameliorationists, he soon had reason to question anew the efficacy of any law that did not command broad local support. Thus in Mauritius the trade in slaves continued. The result was a series of supplementary measures: the more careful scrutiny of returns from the parts of the colony where illegal importations were most prevalent; renewed authority to ship the culprits to Britain for trial on felony charges; the thoroughgoing reform of an evidently corrupt police force; the purchase of a number of small vessels to assist the navy by patrolling closer to the shoreline; and an agreement with the ruler of Madagascar, from whose territory most of the illegal slaves came. By 1821 there was good reason to hope that the trade was finally being suppressed.[92]

On the very eve of his departure from the Colonial Office, in December 1821, Henry Goulburn was still wrestling with the problems of slavery – in particular, the need "to cook up something which may be satisfactory" with respect to Demerara's imperfect register. There were also instructions to be issued to the commissioners who, in response to a House of Commons address, were about to be sent to the Caribbean to investigate the condition of Africans liberated from slavers and slavery. The investigators were ordered to report on the condition of negroes given into the crown's care; on the fate of female Africans who had been assigned as wives to enlisted blacks or as servants to officers, for it had been reported that some of the latter had reduced them to slavery; on the fate of Africans who had joined the armed forces on the promise of full freedom; on the extent to which apprenticeships prepared Africans for freedom by equipping them with skills; and on the reduction of any apprentices to slaves. If they did turn up cases of enslavement, the commissioners were ordered to make immediate representations to the local government. They were to do so discreetly, however, for it would not do to implant in the minds of slaves the idea that they had been sent out to the West Indies to effect emancipation.[93]

Goulburn later composed a brief, modest, and somewhat defensive assessment of his handling of this, the moral imperative of colonial policy. In the various measures adopted to improve the conditions of the slaves, "I bore a willing part," he wrote. "I introduced and carried the Slave Registration Bill to which the abolitionists attached great value. Orders in Council were passed for the Crown Colonies. Legislatures of the other colonies were induced to pass laws abridging the hours of labour and restricting corporal punishment." If anything, he understated his contribution to the cause of amelioration. He had proven to be, after all, an energetic enforcer of the law to abolish the slave trade. In his opinion, that was "the first point from which an amelioration in the condition of the slaves must follow." He had certainly sought to mitigate the evils of slavery on his own estate, though his motives remain opaque. Humanitarian concerns at times seem to have been no more influential than a desire to protect his public reputation and to maintain his income. However, reputation and morality eventually took precedence over income, as the appointment of Richards as his attorney attested. Goulburn was also diligent in seeking to promote the religious education of slaves; for he, no less than other evangelical Anglicans, was convinced that the conversion of heathens "was part of God's providential plan for human history." At the same time, he was ever mindful of the need to vindicate and enhance the position and role of the Church of England.[94]

More generally, Goulburn had drafted and implemented a new emigration policy for an empire that had grown substantially during the French wars – and it was a policy designed to provide colonies with settlers rather than to relieve the British Isles of paupers. He had pursued a sensibly pragmatic economic policy. His emergent Tory liberalism in this respect was always qualified by the peculiar circumstances of individual colonies. Confronted by a revival of protectionism in Europe and the United States at the conclusion of the French and American wars, he was one of those policy makers who were "as much agreed on the need to maintain protected colonial outlets for goods and services as they were on the importance of liberalizing the domestic market."[95]

Even more impressive was his success, with precious little clerical assistance, in initiating the transformation of the "ramshackle structure of the old colonial system" into something approaching a modern administration. The "Goulburn era" saw the Colonial Office set about the task of arming itself with the information that was so necessary for the development of coherent policies. Governors' requests for guidance no longer went unanswered even if, as in the case of New South Wales, the replies were often less than prompt. Given the enormous distance of that colony from Britain, Goulburn tended to allow as many as eight dispatches to come in before drafting one comprehensive response. Nevertheless, his efficiency encouraged colonial executives to write more frequently and more informatively. Perhaps the best testament of his achievement was the warning that one observer issued to Goulburn's successor: "You will receive no active assistance in getting through your business, which is beyond belief lonesome and laborious – nothing can equal the stupidity and prolixity of your Colonial Correspondents and you will be assailed with documents of bulk immeasurable without one interval of repose." Yet by his performance in office, his efficient handling of business, his ability to do more with less, Goulburn lent credibility to the demand for a return to a more minimal state. He appeared to confirm that retrenchment was not inconsistent with effective administration and good government. On the other hand, he recognized the danger that this zeal might be carried too far, to the point of "pernicious parsimony," which would result in "bad government."[96]

CHAPTER FIVE

A Fit and Able Man

The third decade of the century opened discouragingly for Lord Liverpool. Both he and the administration he led were showing signs of wear and tear. The death of George III early in 1820 finally brought the Prince Regent to the throne, and with him a retinue of complications. A floundering economy ensured that the political disenchantment was palpable, even though the government survived the obligatory general election, and in this context George IV's demand for a more regal allowance was characteristically inopportune. The opposition had campaigned almost to a man for a reduction of the Civil List. His ministers' refusal to humour him did little to ease the new monarch's strained relationship with his first minister. For his part, Liverpool realized that accession would merely heighten George's desire to be rid of the wife he hated. Thus the queen's unexpected return to England, in June 1820, from her form of exile merely precipitated the unedifying (if at times titillating and ultimately unsuccessful) parliamentary proceeding to dissolve the marriage. The prime minister slowly sank into a political and personal depression, for these public miseries were overlaid by private anguish as his wife's health inexorably declined.[1]

The king's flirting with the opposition became all too public in November 1820, and Goulburn was not alone in the belief that the ministry's days in office – and thus his own – were numbered. The resignation of the restless, resentful, and ambitious Canning underscored the administration's weakness in the Commons. Depressed though he was, Liverpool instinctively sought to bolster his position in the Lower House. W.C. Plunket was approached soon after his signal triumph in securing a Commons majority for Catholic relief during the spring of 1821. "The strengthening of the present Cabinet, by the accession of Persons favourable to ... [the emancipation of Catholics from their remaining disabilities] does not appear to me to be impracticable," Plunket advised his office-hungry Grenvillite associates, "because if its adversaries yield to such an accession, they in fact give up the question." His reasoning was as self-serving as it was flawed, but the advantage for Liverpool in an arrangement with this faction was their baker's dozen of votes in the Commons and the limiting of the king's options should he undertake a more determined search for an alternative ministry. Even as these negotiations were unfolding, the executive officers were replaced in Ireland.[2]

There, incessant rain had revived fears of famine in a society already cursed with extensive and deeply ingrained poverty. Intractable problems and a refractory population made for a volatile mixture, and growing social unrest exposed all too nakedly the failings of an ill-matched team at Dublin Castle. The conservative viceroy, Lord Talbot, had long been at odds with his liberal chief secretary, Charles Grant, and their inability to pull together in this crisis saw them both dismissed. Senior ministers eventually settled on Richard Wellesley as Talbot's successor. His appointment would facilitate the ongoing negotiations with the Grenvillites, for he had a liberal record on religious issues. Further, his intelligence and ability were widely recognized. But he had squandered both wealth and reputation through excessive ambition, vanity, scandal, and arrogance, and an administrative inefficiency rooted in indolence and nurtured by hypochondria. Not surprisingly, the cabinet withheld his nomination until "*a very capable* secretary" had been found to accompany him to Ireland.[3]

Liverpool had offered the post to William Huskisson, a Canningite. He declined. Anyway, with the provisional selection of Wellesley, the appointment of an advocate of Catholic relief to the chief secretaryship was no longer feasible. The Protestant Ascendancy – secular as well as sectarian – which had been alienated by Grant, needed to be conciliated, and not least by a government which since its formation in 1812 had professed "neutrality" on the divisive Catholic question. Thus that devout "Protestant," Henry Goulburn, rapidly came to the fore as the best possible choice. "Goulburn is not only invaluable in himself, but he is just the man to be Sec[retar]y to Lord Wellesley," the prime minister observed. "His purity and correctness of character make amends for the defects of the other." Goulburn was as industrious as Wellesley was idle, as steady as the older man was erratic. The problem was to persuade him to accept this promotion. After all, it had been his for the taking in 1818. Then he had been deterred largely by financial considerations, and they remained the principal obstacle to acceptance now. "They are to me very important in every sense of the word," he explained to both Liverpool and Bathurst. In truth, he was increasingly pessimistic of ever being able to afford promotion to "the higher stations" of political life. His income from Jamaica had continued to shrivel. However, the prime minister found a "most honourable" solution to this difficulty. Goulburn was awarded a modest pension of £1,000 a year for his long years of service as an under-secretary. Not that this relieved him of all anxiety. "My state is this," he informed Peel early in the New Year, "I am ruined already by non payment of rents, by the decay of my West India Property and by an office which does not pay its expenses." Indeed, the extent of the shortfall was soon painfully evident, and over the course of the next half-decade his private funds were drained away at an average rate of £2,000 a year.[4]

What was the office Goulburn accepted at such cost? The legislative union between Great Britain and Ireland had left in place an Irish executive government. Headed by the viceroy, it included a Privy Council, a distinct legal structure presided over by a lord chancellor and including an attorney general and a solicitor general, and a full score of administrative departments employing a small army of public servants. There was also a military department, which provided for the needs of a substantial military garrison. In short, instead of being fully integrated into a United Kingdom, Ireland was administered not unlike a colony. Was this another reason for Goulburn's selection?

Although the lord lieutenant remained the senior officer, clothed as he was in viceregal trappings, his chief secretary was emerging as a power in his own right. He divided his time between supervision of the administration in Dublin and attendance at Parliament in London. These latter duties brought him into frequent contact with the prime minister, the home secretary, to whom he reported on the state of Ireland, and other senior members of the ministry. Without doubt, his was a challenging and taxing office, and its weight was in no way lightened by the frequency with which the problems of Ireland thrust themselves onto the parliamentary agenda. Not surprisingly, therefore, it was increasingly seen as a testing ground for young men of promise. At the age of thirty-seven, Goulburn was no longer a young man, but success in this office would surely open other doors to him.

The knowledge that Robert Peel was about to return to the ministry as the secretary of state for home affairs helped persuade Goulburn to accept what he recognized as "one of the most difficult and laborious offices under the Government." He was also actuated by his well-developed sense of public duty and by partisan considerations, willing as he was to sacrifice personal comfort in the "general interest of the party." And no doubt, for all his self-effacement, he was vain enough to be flattered by the attention he received from Liverpool and other senior ministers as they sought to overcome his reservations. Nor would he have been human if he had ignored the opportunity to advance his career. Finally, he was a resolute protector of the Protestant establishment. His opposition to Catholic relief had not weakened over the years. He was determined to resist it "to the utmost of his power." It was his opinion that Catholics had slowly but surely secured an ever-larger share of the privileges of citizenship. Unless this incremental strategy was frustrated, he feared that all too soon they would be in a position to undermine the establishment. He was "the most furious Protestant that ever was," remarked one observer, and would therefore start "with a great degree of unpopularity." Certainly, the leader of the Catholic agitation in Ireland described him as "our mortal enemy."[5]

Goulburn was sworn into the Privy Council on 13 December 1821, carefully noting that it had cost him £30. The next day he set out alone for Dublin. His wife and children were to follow later. He travelled via Lulworth Castle in Dorset, in order to consult with Peel and be briefed on the principal figures with whom he would soon have to deal. Peel also sought to allay his financial concerns by confessing his own mistake in 1812 of wasting time and money on an unnecessarily large establishment. Perhaps heartened, Goulburn journeyed on to Bath to pass a weekend with the prime minister. He listened to Liverpool's explanation of policy, and they discussed the measures which the Irish government might adopt. Then it was on to Holyhead to take the ferry to Dublin. He reached the Irish capital on 20 December and the following morning held a tense meeting with Talbot and Grant. The former, a distant relative on his mother's side, was especially bitter, insisting that he had been dismissed and that this indicated the government's determination to pursue a different policy. He offered to conduct the formalities of appointing Goulburn chief secretary so that he could press ahead with its implementation, but the sensible Goulburn decided to await Wellesley's arrival. However, he did what he could to smooth the transition by kindly honouring a promise of place made by the departing Grant.[6]

Another of the delicate commissions entrusted to Goulburn was that of easing William Saurin out of the Irish attorney generalship. An enduring symbol of the Protestant Ascendancy, Saurin was anathema to Irish Catholics and their English sympathizers. To cushion the blow, he was offered the loftiest position on the bench, and ermine in the form of a peerage. But "vexed and annoyed" by his dismissal, Saurin rejected both. "The Government therefore will lose his assistance altogether and I shall lose the opportunity which official connection gave of cultivating the friendship of the man for whom your good opinion of him led me to entertain the highest respect and esteem," Goulburn sadly observed to Peel. Saurin's vexation stemmed from a sense of repudiation, which was inescapable given his successor – Plunket. Much admired as a parliamentary orator – and not a little feared, for his "satire was, at times, of that corroding yet witty nature, that no patience could endure the junction" – Plunket's appointment was an integral part of Liverpool's arrangement with the Grenvillites.[7]

First appointed Irish attorney general in 1805 and continued in office by Lord Grenville, Plunket had resigned with the fall of the Talents' Ministry and had been succeeded by Saurin. Now their fates were reversed, but Plunket's recent emergence as the leader of the Catholic cause in the Commons certainly added insult to the departing Protestant champion's sense of injury. In the opinion of Peel, the exchange was a poor one. He did not believe that Plunket would be of much assistance to Goulburn in the Commons, suspecting that on many critical issues the Irishman would equivocate. Peel's advice was therefore simple and direct: "Do not let Plunkett [sic] interfere with you – Put a stop to that at first." This injunction did not discourage an ever-sensible Goulburn from approaching his new colleague in an effort to ensure that in spite of their profound differences on the Catholic question, they went "on well together."[8]

This hope was not shared by Plunket's parliamentary associates, whose political allegiance Liverpool had purchased at what was initially a low enough cost, though one wag remarked that everything had recently fallen in price except the Grenvillites. The pair of Grenville nephews who had kept the faction alive as an independent clique were rewarded. The Marquis of Buckingham was elevated to a dukedom, and Charles Wynn was appointed president of the board of control, with a seat in cabinet. Equally, it was understood that on Irish issues Plunket would be consulted as if he belonged to the cabinet. Hence the Grenvillites' discomfiture at the announcement of the "anti-Catholic" Goulburn's appointment. They scurried to protect themselves from the accusation that in bartering their support, they had sold their principles. As a first step, Liverpool agreed to acknowledge publicly that they had been unaware of Goulburn's promotion when they agreed to support his ministry. Next, he privately conceded to Wynn the right to originate Irish measures at any time of his choosing. Leaked to the press, this authority did little to enhance that of Goulburn and served to remind him of the hostility with which he was regarded by these recent recruits. But this was only one of the many difficulties he had to face. Even more important and pressing was the need to establish a working relationship with Wellesley.[9]

The wisdom of yoking a "Catholic" viceroy to a "Protestant" chief secretary, following their complete failure when placed in the reverse sectarian order, was widely questioned. A virulently Protestant member of Parliament grumbled that no two men could be more dissimilar, though he expressed the hope that the chief secretary would claim more authority and influence than he thought his principal was "likely to allow him." This did not seem probable, for even before he left London, Goulburn was given a foretaste of viceregal arrogance as Wellesley sought to demonstrate to mocking Whigs that he would not "suffer himself to be clerk-ridden." Moreover, while the new chief secretary was at Lulworth, the new viceroy was closeted with Lord Grenville. On emerging from the meeting, he announced his intention to place particular confidence in Plunket. To counter this alliance and to prevent his isolation in Dublin, Goulburn could depend on Peel. No less essential, however, was the loyalty of the other important figure in the Irish administration – the under-secretary.[10]

Able, astute, discreet, and industrious, William Gregory had a command of the detail of Irish administration that was unmatched. He had been appointed under-secretary in 1812, shortly after the arrival of Peel, to whom he quickly became deeply attached. This resolute Protestant was master of the whole machine of government for that half of each year when his chief was in London. And with Goulburn he established an instant rapport. Peel had much to do with this, for he enthusiastically recommended each man to the other. Thus, to Gregory, he was unstinting in his praise of the chief secretary: "You have often heard me speak of him, and it is therefore unnecessary for me to say what I think." What he thought was that Goulburn possessed almost every virtue: "firmness, temper, industry, knowledge of business, and the highest principles." In his public and private character Peel knew "not a single defect in him."[11]

Peel's unqualified recommendation, and the knowledge that Goulburn came on a mission to defend the Protestant Ascendancy, guaranteed him a warm and sympathetic welcome from Gregory. Yet their harmony owed much to Goulburn's qualities. His ability to earn the confidence and gain the affection of older superiors, such as Ryder and Bathurst, without ever sinking into obsequiousness was now complemented by a capacity to win the admiration and respect of his juniors, no matter their age. In part, this was a question of temperament. As most people who came into contact with Goulburn admitted, he was "a most agreeable man." No less important was his efficiency. The word was soon circulating in Dublin that Goulburn had amply repaid his subordinates "for the additional labour of a change [of masters], by his method and intelligence of doing business." In the words of one knowledgeable observer, "He has judged well in choosing to follow Grant, rather than Peel; for the contrast, whether of official or social habits, will now be greatly to his advantage; tho' it was a terrible mistake to select an Irish Secretary who drinks *no* wine."[12]

Gregory tolerated Goulburn's temperance, for his own brand of evangelicalism had not prevented him from laying down an excellent cellar of "carefully bottled hogsheads of claret." Early in February 1822, as his chief set out for London and the new session of Parliament, the under-secretary was writing enthusiastically to Peel: "I feel much obliged by the manner in which you made Goulburn and me acquainted, and I assure you he has fully answered the character you gave him. I have found the greatest satisfaction in transacting Business with him, and in private he is everything to be wished." This assessment stood in stark contrast to his opinion of the viceroy. Kept at arm's length for more than five weeks by Wellesley, the under-secretary informed Peel that he would have been "wounded to the quick" had he received such treatment from a man he "knew and esteemed."[13]

One political benefit that Goulburn derived from this friendship and respect was the knowledge that, even when in London, he would always be well briefed on events in Ireland. "My wish is to protect you from being worried in the house by repeated Questions, without being able to return any answer from Authority," Gregory assured him. Of course, all such communications were for the chief secretary's "private ear," though Gregory assumed that Peel would be privy to everything that came from him. In return, Goulburn granted the under-secretary an extraordinary measure of discretion.[14]

His lengthy absences from Ireland again obliged Goulburn to make domestic sacrifices. Understandably, he was reluctant to uproot his young family each winter. "I can only again repeat the pleasure I felt in having determined to leave you in Ireland," he reported to his wife after one especially unpleasant trip, "for, as to attempting a winter journey with you and the children, I have seen enough of the roads and weather to be quite decided against doing anything of the kind." The sea crossing from Dublin to Holyhead was invariably a trial at that time of year, and Goulburn soon had reason to fear that he had lost his immunity to seasickness. Less violent yet exhausting was the overland portion of the long journey by carriage. He usually strove to complete it as speedily as possible, stopping only briefly to catch a meal and sleeping as best he could in the carriage. With his family in tow, he would have been compelled to travel at a more sedate pace, putting up at inns. Similarly, financial worries discouraged him from bringing his family over to London during the spring, when the weather was usually less to be feared, for the "season" drove up the price of rental accommodation.[15]

Goulburn was unable to find a suitable house near Parliament, one that would serve as both office and home. Just as scarce were smaller houses adjoining each other, "which would give effect to the same object." Alternatively, a simple residence would have to be paid for entirely out of his own pocket, and the "exorbitant" rents their owners demanded persuaded him "that it would be absolutely a waste of money even if one had it to take one on the chance of a two months occupation." He simply could not afford 900 guineas for a house that would barely hold them, and he did not believe that a hotel was likely "to be more reasonable in point of living." As a result, each year he undertook a search for an affordable and conveniently located house, only to conclude that whatever was suitable was far too expensive. "I think it might be better to make up our minds to remain as we are this year," he wrote to Jane in 1826, "and to compensate the evils of our separation by a knowledge that we are husbanding our resources or at least avoiding unnecessary involvement."[16]

The physical separation from his family was of an order, in distance and time, far greater than that to which he had grown accustomed at the Colonial Office. "I am heartily sick of living a Bachelor life and long more than I can express to see you and the children again," he admitted to his wife in March 1824, only one month after leaving Dublin. His uneasiness was heightened by the knowledge that Jane's health had long been hostage to his sense of public duty. He wearily noted that there "is almost always a fatality in my absence as it generally brings with it some attack of illness to you." A victim of "violent" headaches and a variety of other pains, she resorted to opium for relief, though she was fully convinced "that rest and idleness" were the only effective remedies. For his part, Goulburn attempted in his letters to raise her spirits with diverting anecdotes and the latest society gossip. He passed along the stories circulating in London in the spring of 1824 of Lord Brudenel's activities. Here was a gentleman so keen to fight a duel that he had already issued eleven challenges, and when he eloped with a Mrs Johnston, he sportingly offered her husband prompt satisfaction; hence his mortification when the cuckold waspishly replied "that having taken off Mrs Johnston he could give him no greater satisfaction." The gossip was less amusing, of course, when it involved members of one's own family. Reports that Edward Montagu had been discovered kissing Lady Harrowby excited considerable mirth. For as Croker acidly remarked, she "is, or may be, a Grandmother and even when she was young, the Duke of Beaufort christened one of his horses Susan, on account of their resemblance."[17]

Goulburn attempted to write frequently, even if it was only a "shabby note" following the breaking up of the House in the early hours of the morning. As he explained to his wife on one occasion, revealing that humorous side to his nature which he all too often suppressed, "A writer of Epigrams has said: 'When Theseus Ariadne left in bed / The lady married Bacchus in his stead' which Allegory to my way of thinking means that deserted ladies take to drinking. Now lest my deserted lady should follow this which is represented to be the general rule I think it advisable to ply her with my correspondence." Much of their correspondence concerned family or politics and was of an uplifting nature. "I perfectly agree in all you say as to the difficulty of understanding the excessive inequality of happiness in the present life," Jane granted, as they pondered the meaning of the death of a relative after four years of agony. Of course, the suffering of a child was more difficult to understand or to rationalize. It had to be viewed as an exercise in faith, as well as in evangelical resignation, which would even in some mysterious way ultimately be beneficial. A Christian determinism continued to influence Goulburn's public as well as private life. "Doing however the best as I think we are," he remarked in the midst of one crisis, "I trust that we are fulfilling the will of Him who works through our inferior instrumentality, and makes even our errors subservient to the accomplishment of his great purposes." Even his infrequent illnesses were invested with providential meaning. "Health has its own temptations, and we are less sensible of the blessings of air and exercise and of the goodness of him who gives us the power of enjoying them if we are not occasionally compelled by health to abstain from the enjoyment."[18]

Goulburn did, however, fret over the health and education of his children. News that his young daughter Jane had contracted measles put him out of sorts for days. Such worries merely increased the pressure on his neurotic wife. He urged her to summon Philip Crampton, the most respected of Dublin's doctors, whenever she was alarmed over the health of the children. For the more common childhood complaints, they maintained a file of traditional remedies. Bowel disorders were to be treated with the rather strong natural medicine of rhubarb. At the first sign of croup, the victim was to take an emetic every fifteen minutes until vomiting was induced, then a dose of calomel was to be taken, the legs and feet were to be immersed in warm water and the throat rubbed with a linament. To ease dental problems, they kept a powder on hand of which the main constituent was the magical oil of cloves. Goulburn took an appropriately conservative view on the extraction of teeth that were not evidently decayed. "Art may be useful occasionally," he allowed, "but in the long run nature deals better with us than any operator."[19]

He corresponded with his children. To Harry, he wrote in French as well as in English. He also tested his Latin. "I send you the letters of Cicero to his friends in order that by reading and translating them you may acquire a habit of expressing yourself in English as justly and elegantly as he does in Latin," he explained. He dwelt on the importance of studies to a life of usefulness and personal happiness: "Always bear in mind that this is the only end of learning and be diligent." However, when the letters were returned replete with errors attributable to negligence, this man of business sternly repeated one of the maxims of his own life: "Attention is of all things the most indispensable and the want of it what I least like to observe."[20]

There was little doubt that the first-born Harry was the Goulburns' favourite child. Henry's letters to him opened "My dearest boy," while those to his two other sons were addressed to Freddy and Neddy. Jane Lydia, born in 1820, was as yet too young to be interested in notes from her father. Indeed, Harry imitated his father in his neat arrangement of things and in his efforts to save his mother trouble. "He is so like you in that and in his style of writing," she reported to Henry, "that it gives me the greatest satisfaction in the hope that the resemblance may equally hold good in all essentials. I wish the younger boys were more like him, but one has no right to expect them all to be equally rational." Edward, in particular, was a trial. He was both irritable and volatile, perhaps the result of sibling jealousy, but his father applauded his literary skills. "It is singular how with all his deficiency of application and industry," he remarked to Jane, "he contrives to do what he does so clearly and so well." Nevertheless, it was to Harry that Goulburn dedicated most of his free time, and it was in his achievements that he took the greatest pride. "He is a great favourite & I think deservedly so," he proudly reported to Jane during a visit to friends, "for nothing can be more modest, unassuming & proper than his conduct in every respect." Thus Harry grew into a competitive and industrious young man, anxious not merely to do well but to excel – all to please his parents, especially his father. Admirably devout and exceptionally serious, he dutifully recited his prayers several times a day, and at his father's insistence he kept notes of the sermons through which he sat. Yet Henry's response to his son's declaration of love was affectingly reserved. "The expression of your affection is a most agreeable return for the anxiety which I always feel for your happiness and welfare," he avowed, "and if I beg you to cultivate it, it is not more for my own gratification than from a conviction that the cultivation of that love will lead to the permanent comfort and happiness of us both."[21]

Unfortunately, there was all too little comfort and not a great deal of happiness in Goulburn's official life. The workload proved to be even heavier than that he had carried at the Colonial Office. In London, there were bone-wearying days of office drudgery, meetings, and parliamentary sittings. He usually lodged with his in-laws and would breakfast alone in Portman Square, pen and ink in hand. Fortified by "sky blue milk," ash-leaf tea, alum bread, and hogs' lard butter, he would set out for the Irish Office. From there he usually went on to see Peel and frequently the prime minister. No doubt it was Peel who advised him of Canning's return to the cabinet as foreign secretary and leader of the House in September 1822, following the suicide of Castlereagh. But the subsequent promotion of his old friend Frederick Robinson to replace Nicholas Vansittart at the Exchequer was completed without his knowledge. This alarmed Jane. She feared that a more far-reaching ministerial shuffle was being contemplated, one that would see her husband dealt out of office. Goulburn was quick to set her mind at rest. "Nothing could be more cordial and friendly" than his reception by Peel he reassured her, explaining that his friend had been placed under an injunction of strict secrecy by Liverpool. And following a private dinner and frank discussion of Irish matters, he added, "You will be glad to know that we agree perfectly in our views and ideas and whatever may be the result of the present turmoil it will not occasion any difference of opinion between us but will rather unite us more closely together." Unknowingly, he was outlining his entire future political career when he added, "I shall act in concert with Peel because I feel with him and he feels with me."[22]

Even Goulburn soon began to complain, however, of the remorseless daily grind. He was "beset by bores" at the office. The fact that cabinet was beginning to meet more regularly meant that he was frequently summoned to its discussions of Irish policy. He had also to attend the numerous parliamentary committees on Ireland. "I have really so much to do that I am in a constant worry and get nothing done," he fretted. The days appeared to fly by, while most evenings were spent in the Commons. There he often found himself a victim of the order of business. "I unfortunately had just business enough to oblige me to wait until a long discussion on turnpike gates was brought to a conclusion," he reported to his wife at the end of one long and particularly frustrating evening. But it was "the attending to the debate with a view to speak or reply" that most taxed him. He was still neither a confident nor a polished speaker, and it was a struggle for him to find anything original to say on major issues that had long been debated. Listening to Canning and Peel, he was all too conscious of his own failings and of the advantages of a good classical education, at least when it came to expressing oneself elegantly and swaying a sceptical audience. "I never satisfy myself and after I have done therefore am always very thankful to those who say anything civil on the subject," he admitted.[23]

Prolonged separation from his young family and the seemingly ceaseless demands on his time caused even London and its glittering social life to pall. In the winter, he complained of fog so thick at times that it was impossible to see across the Thames and thus so dark that it was necessary to work by candlelight even in the middle of the day.

The strain on his inferior eyesight was severe. Even the passion for "improvements" in the capital excited his ire. The demolition of old houses to make way for the new and the ripping up of pavements in preparation for their macadamizing made life increasingly inconvenient for the pedestrian. Goulburn was scornful of the alterations to Hyde Park, especially the felling of young trees that were just beginning to give shade. He was increasingly reluctant to dine out, fearful as he was of sinking ever deeper into arrears with his work. On occasion, however, the experience proved diverting. One host was so overweight that he could not see his own feet and thus made a habit of standing painfully on his guests' toes. And while Goulburn was ever willing to indulge his love of music, this delight was blighted in February 1825 with the discovery that the Opera House was structurally unsound.[24]

Goulburn's return to Ireland at the end of each parliamentary session took him back to a troubled land and a divided administration. Poverty and violence appeared to be endemic in large areas of the countryside, at least as viewed from the vantage points of Dublin Castle and the Irish Office. Yet the roots and the relationship of these twin blights were matters of dispute. Some observers attributed the disturbances to a broad range of social and economic factors: the rapid increase in the population and consequently the subdivision of landholdings into ever smaller plots; the lack of any true sense of landlord responsibility for the tenantry; high rents; the injustice of local taxation as levied and expended by landlord-dominated grand juries; the tithing of the Catholic poor for the support of the Protestant establishment; the unwillingness of Parliament to complete the emancipation of Catholics; and the chronic inadequacies of the traditional agents of good order. All too many of the gentry were absentees, the police were inefficient, and the magistracy was incompetent if not corrupt. The obvious solution was to redress these grievances. At the very least, the financial and administrative system of Ireland required purification. But most conservatives had an entirely different order of priorities. Reports of "plunder, menace and murder" were so startling, Goulburn allowed, that Englishmen would suppose "if the narrative were not fabulous, that it related events which had taken place amidst barbarous tribes in the heart of Africa." The first duty of the state was therefore to discipline the disorderly and suppress lawlessness. The second was to root out the causes of evil, and the third was to determine the "real grounds of complaint" and inquire "as to a proper remedy." Only then would the government be in a position "to come to parliament for such measures as promised to supply a permanent cure."[25]

Goulburn had landed in Ireland fully expecting to find an unfamiliar land and people. Like so many Englishmen, he assumed that his country had achieved "a state of civilization far more advanced" than that of her sister island. In England, people obeyed the law "not from fear of the power of compulsion with which it is armed, but from a feeling of respect and attachment." He quickly concluded that even Irishmen of the better sort almost always "act blindly ... with little regard to principle and little knowledge of their ultimate interests." The scenes he described during a tour of the countryside implied much about his view of the great mass of the Irish as a semi-civilised peasantry. He reported seeing naked children playing with pigs, and families eating potatoes out of a pot with their fingers rather than dirtying the utensils on the table behind them. However stereotypical this image was, it reflected Goulburn's conviction that Ireland could not be administered in the same manner as other parts of the realm. Although he conceded that errors had earlier been committed by "English government," he was firmly of the opinion that much of "the difficulty of Ireland had grown out of the habits of the natives," out of the difference of feeling between England and Ireland, "and from the embarrassment which the legislature had felt in applying laws, framed for the government of one country, to the peculiar circumstances of the other." In his opinion, there was scant prospect of quickly bringing Ireland "to any state at all corresponding with that of England." Yet as exceptional as Irish circumstances evidently were, and not least the extent of the poverty, Goulburn remained evangelically averse to state intervention. His own experience in office had done nothing to undermine his faith in the minimal state. Moreover, recent reports of better crops than predicted, and encouraging estimates that the supply of provisions and fuel would be adequate, allowed him to procrastinate. He quickly concluded that it would be inadvisable for the government "to stir."[26]

In contemplating the daunting tasks at hand and ahead, Goulburn recognized that he would be better placed if he had a "master of another description." Wellesley failed to inspire respect. He became the butt of popular ridicule and a source of administrative frustration. Widely suspected of having accepted the viceroyalty and its regal income in order to rescue himself from improvidence, his parsimony was cruelly abused by a Dublin populace that had jeered at his predecessor for riding around in a humble gig. Rumours that he intended to repay his English creditors with Irish offices and that even a fishmonger had been offered a place as full payment of the viceregal account further damaged "the good fame and dignity" of his high office. Then again, Wellesley's "childish vanity" and taste for pageantry were ludicrous and comical. For example, he received the sacraments in the viceregal chapel while wearing the sword of state.[27]

Few of these "eccentricities" were "relieved" by the conduct of Wellesley's "confidential coadjutor," his natural son and personal secretary Edward Johnston. Even those observers who were willing to make every allowance for Johnston's youth and inexperience could not abide his "presumption and want of judgment." His relationship with undersecretary Gregory was especially strained, as the older man feared for his position under a liberal viceroy and resented the influence of this meddlesome natural son. In his blackest moods, Gregory gave serious thought to resignation, but he was dissuaded by Peel and Goulburn, whose concerns were the man, the office, and the defence of the Protestant Ascendancy.[28]

Mutual distrust, itself the product largely of fundamental differences over Catholic claims, had always threatened to condemn the new Irish executive to the fate of its predecessor. Yet, for a short time, affairs went along surprisingly well. Cooperation was facilitated by Wellesley's immediate decision, in which Plunket acquiesced, to soft-pedal the divisive Catholic issue. He let it be known that he was of the opinion that until Catholics conducted themselves with more "temper," it would be "highly dangerous to concede to them further power." On the other side, the fervently anti-emancipationist Peel sought Goulburn's advice on how to handle the prickly Wellesley. "If you can throw in anything of a compliment to his talents in his former public situations it will render your letter still more agreeable for there are few persons possessing his talents who look more to have them acknowledged," an ironic chief secretary replied. Finally, Wellesley's subordinates were pleasantly surprised by his businesslike and thorough approach to his responsibilities. Even Gregory admitted that the viceroy was "very diligent in minutely and attentively reading every paper connected with the state of the country, and never delaying to return them, beyond the time necessary for consideration." Unfortunately, this uncharacteristic diligence proved to be all too transitory.[29]

On being sworn in as lord lieutenant on 29 December 1821, Wellesley had immediately signalled the change of regimes. He had commuted a number of death sentences and ordered the dismantling of the defences that his embattled predecessor had hastily thrown up in Dublin when advised that an uprising was being planned. Before long, however, Wellesley acknowledged that any network of secret associations was certain to become a "just object" of suspicion; meanwhile, fearful Protestants were warning darkly of similarities between the current situation and that which had prevailed in 1798 on the eve of the rebellion. Goulburn quickly made up his mind on what needed to be done. The first essential was to obtain the extraordinary but temporary powers of the Insurrection Act and a suspension of habeas corpus. As a longer-term solution, he wished to strengthen the agents of law and order by creating a general police force, which could be reinforced in emergencies by the Peace Preservation Force organized by Peel during his service in Ireland. The cost of the "Peelers" had made them too expensive as a permanent system, Goulburn realized, so he planned to create a force that would be cheap and effective.[30]

His first task was to win Wellesley's support for resolute action. This promised to be difficult, given the viceroy's knowledge that his own appointment had been widely viewed as the inauguration of a more conciliatory approach to the Irish problem. Thus three weeks elapsed before Wellesley was "fully convinced" of the need for additional powers "to put down the evil which is spreading over the country." Even then, he wanted to see only a modified Insurrection Act introduced, since all too often in the past landlord/magistrates had abused their larger powers by arbitrarily punishing obnoxious tenants. But Goulburn and Peel resisted any tampering with the Insurrection Act. They argued that a gentler law would be less effective and yet no less objectionable constitutionally, and that there would be an even greater clamour for its frequent use. Here was an argument well calculated to appeal both to conservatives and to limp liberals such as Wellesley.[31]

The Insurrection Act and the suspension of habeas corpus were introduced soon after Parliament opened in February. The task fell to Castlereagh, for neither Goulburn nor Peel had yet arrived in London. Following a tried and true formula, Castlereagh recounted a story that could be guaranteed to shock English gentlemen from the shires; he described how sixteen policemen had been trapped in a house by a large mob, who had then set it on fire. Over the protests of some Irish Whigs, the bills were hurriedly passed by the Lower House. However, both measures were limited to six months. The Lords handled the legislation with similar dispatch. To those members of the opposition who demanded that the government go to the source of Ireland's problems, Liverpool responded with a metaphor that may have been inspired by the incident described in the Commons: "When a house was in flames, the first object was, to extinguish them; the next, to consider by what means a repetition of the conflagration was to be prevented."[32]

As the author of strong measures, Goulburn was at pains to ensure their discreet enforcement. His faith in the efficacy of "severity" as an antidote to violence was not that of the zealot. He insisted that "the greatest caution" be observed whenever it was thought necessary to imprison anyone without benefit of habeas corpus. Similarly, the death penalty was only to be carried out in cases of murder or for such atrocities as rape. Gradually, the situation improved in the most disturbed county, Cork, only for trouble soon to erupt in Limerick and Kilkenny. The Insurrection Act was proving less effective than Goulburn had hoped. Despite an encouraging and appreciable decline in the level of violence with the onset of spring, experienced observers were far from sanguine. There could be no suspension of the "terrors" of the act, Gregory counselled, and during April it was extended to a barony in Westmeath that was already being policed by the "Peelers."[33]

Meanwhile, Goulburn was under mounting parliamentary pressure to bring forward a more constructive policy than the repression of violence. His immediate predecessor as chief secretary, Charles Grant, moved the House with a sympathetic and impressive analysis of Ireland's plight and needs. He recited the familiar litany of miseries and grievances and called for the introduction of the equally familiar catalogue of reforms – police, magistracy, tithe, education, and emancipation. Such a generous policy, he asserted, would diffuse "a spirit of reciprocal kindness." In response, Goulburn made a flying visit to Ireland early in May to confer with the viceroy. He found him looking far from well, afflicted as he now was with an eye infection that provided him with a "valid excuse" for his failure to write. If the viceroy was in truth again sinking into inactivity if not indolence, at least he remained cooperative. He concurred in the proposals Goulburn intended to introduce in the Commons – an extension of the Insurrection Act, a police bill, the weeding out of incompetent magistrates, and an interim arrangement on the contentious tithe. Here was a modest program of reform consistent with the chief secretary's belief that all demands for change should be examined from the vantage point of the Protestant minority, whom he credited with holding Ireland "fast to the British connexion." The expediency of conciliating dissidents, especially Celtic Catholics, must never overwhelm the inutility of alienating loyalists.[34]

That Ireland required an effective regular police force few observers disputed. The traditional local constabularies had long since fallen into disrepute as mere sources of local patronage, while the "Peelers" were organized to serve only as flying squadrons in disturbed districts. Goulburn now produced an ambitious plan to create a permanent, regular, armed, and national force of some four thousand men. There would be four provincial inspectors general, and every county would have several detachments composed of constables and sub constables, each commanded by a chief constable. Furthermore, he provided for the appointment of police magistrates, or stipendiaries, whenever the local magistrates neglected their police duties. All appointments were to be in the hands of the Castle. Naively, he thought that this measure would pass without serious difficulty. But several Irish members of Parliament, supported by Charles Grant, denounced this new species of gendarmerie as an assault on constitutional freedom and an invitation to executive tyranny. They demanded restoration of the hallowed principle of local control, and thus the retention of their patronage. Those Irish magistrates who had exercised their discretionary power to provide the existing constabulary with a generous increase in pay, ostensibly in order to attract better recruits, assailed Goulburn's bill as a breach of faith with men who had been promised pensions if they served for twenty years. One Irish Whig complained that the chief secretary, like his predecessors in office, "came over from England totally ignorant of the country he was to govern" and that "like them, or most of them," he had "seen no person from whom to collect information but the clerks of the Castle or the needy expectants who endeavour to recommend themselves by misrepresenting the people." Although the bill weathered second reading with the powerful assistance of Peel and Plunket, Goulburn decided to compromise with his critics: although the senior officers would be appointed by the Castle, the appointment of constables would be restored to local magistrates. Goulburn also retreated on the stipendiaries: a request signed by seven local magistrates would be required before a police magistrate could be appointed.[35]

Characteristically, Wellesley dismissed the amended legislation as worthless and announced that tranquillity depended entirely on the reinforcement of the military garrison. Yet the Constabulary Act represented a significant achievement. Thanks to Goulburn, every county of Ireland was now assured of effective policing. Moreover, the surrender of central control over the appointment of constables quickly proved to be more symbolic than real. Before year's end, the magistracy in several counties had relinquished to the inspectors general the nomination of constables, "thereby admitting in fact the propriety of the Provisions of the original Bill which they all opposed and which they all now profess to wish for." Nevertheless, the confusion over the primary allegiance of the new force – whether to local magistrates or to the Castle – constituted "the chief flaw in Goulburn's constabulary."[36]

Goulburn's concessions to local autonomy emphasized the importance of removing from the magistracy the inactive, the incompetent, and the invisible. Here, he had inherited from Grant a sensible plan to cancel the existing commission of the peace and to issue another from which "objectionable names" had been deleted. Months were to pass, however, before this tortuous procedure was completed. By early 1823 some six hundred magistrates had been weeded out, amounting to one-sixth of the total. Not that this achievement drew universal applause. One critic grumbled that many of the new men were as unfit as their predecessors. By and large, however, Goulburn was reasonably well satisfied with the results. "We coaxed, threatened & flattered them into a discharge of their duties," he recalled, "and among other inducements we gave them a constantly attending and well organized Police obedient to their orders in all criminal matters."[37]

One cause of the disturbances that had overwhelmed the old police and threatened to occupy the new police fully was the tithe, which the Catholic peasantry, in particular, objected to paying to the Protestant clergy. Irish Whigs had long considered this tax to be a Catholic griev-ance that should be redressed, and they evinced every determination to revive the issue. Goulburn realized that the House would not be sat-isfied "without some proposition on the subject of Irish Tithes or some evidence on the part of the Irish government that they are bona fide preparing to make some proposition on the subject." To do nothing was to invite a parliamentary committee, whose investigation of the problem would be difficult to control. This was a point that he, Liver-pool, and Peel individually and collectively impressed on the Irish bishops attending Parliament, and the viceroy was requested to convey the same message to those remaining in Ireland – though Wellesley had no wish to share the responsibility for framing such controversial legislation.[38]

As ever, Goulburn simply buckled down to the task. Of course, he was motivated by a determination to defend the Protestant establish-ment and by the knowledge that the non-payment of tithes had already impoverished many members of the Protestant clergy. Members of Par-liament had to be made to understand that this was a question of prop-erty, and that although it might now be expedient to meddle in its administration, "that interference ought to be as delicately and as carefully measured by the necessity of the case where tithes are con-cerned as it would be if the landed property of certain Country Gentle-men were the object of it." Moreover, any argument that applied "to the subversion of the Church of Ireland and the diminution of its dig-nity" would apply equally well "to the subversion of the Church of En-gland." Here were arguments calculated to diminish any English appetite for radical reform, even in Ireland. The scheme that took shape in Goulburn's mind was voluntary rather than compulsory. It ex-empted all potato plots from tithes but compensated clergy for this loss by establishing an acreable assessment on all other lands in the parishes concerned; it permitted the leasing of tithes for twenty-one years; and it sought to encourage landlords to assume the charge, in-stead of having it fall on the occupiers of the land, on the understand-ing that they might recover it in the form of increased rents. In this way, peasant resentment of the Protestant clergy might at least be diverted. These were the essential provisions of the bill that Goulburn introduced with repeated warnings that he would not be a party to any "spoliation" of the property of the church.[39]

That this modest measure would never suffice was widely predicted. Indeed, the claim was made in October that not a single lease had yet been signed. Few landlords had any interest in accepting a charge which they had good reason to fear they would never recover. They had trouble enough already collecting rents. Equally, Irish bishops had no desire to spend their time examining and approving scores if not hundreds of leases. Then again, agricultural prices were certain to rise eventually, and this discouraged clergy from entering into long leases at a time when prices were depressed. Finally, under persistent questioning from the opposition, the government had revealed that a plan of general commutation was in the offing. This news surely encouraged all concerned to stand fast until the details were published. As a result, popular resistance to payment of the tithe continued, and by the autumn many clergy were reported to be "nearly in a state of ruin."[40]

Not surprisingly, Liverpool concluded that Ireland would be a preoccupation of the upcoming session of Parliament. Nor was he in any doubt that the most important of the Irish questions remained that of the tithe. "I think it will be quite impossible not to do something more effectual on this subject, than what was intended to be done by the Bill of last session," he advised Peel. "I should very much regret that so delicate a question should be thrown loose on a Committee of the House of Commons, composed as it would be, in a large proportion, of Members, who, if not hostile to the Establishment itself, would certainly be ready to sacrifice its interests to their own." The Irish executive was instructed to revisit the problem.[41]

Goulburn was pessimistic of ever reaching a satisfactory settlement of this contentious question, convinced as he was of the grim determination of the great majority of Irish to "defraud" the church of her due. The war on tithes was being waged by "*all* classes," he subsequently reported to Peel. He directed his thoughts, therefore, "more to the discovery of some arrangement which by being one of real commutation should guard the Church against plunder than to any which shall in fact operate to get rid of the tythe." He had a faithful ally in Gregory, who denied that tithes were the load under which the poor sank. Rents were ten times more oppressive, the under-secretary argued. The draft proposal bore the Goulburn imprint. Commutation was to be the basis of reform, though out of deference to the Irish clergy's dislike of the term, it was styled a composition. In the first instance the composition was to be voluntary and to be negotiated through a special vestry, but in the event of no agreement being reached it was to be rendered compulsory through the introduction of an arbitrator. Once again, the period was to be limited to twenty-one years. "To a compulsion such as I have adverted to, coming after an attempt at voluntary composition, I believe many of the Clergy here would accede," Goulburn reported to Peel. The draft also revived the scheme of transferring payment to the landlord.[42]

A healthy respect for the landed gentry – and perhaps a concern that a principle once applied in Ireland would be invoked in England – led the cabinet to reject a transfer of payment. Also, ministers were sceptical of finding sufficient qualified arbitrators when voluntary composition failed, and they worried about consistency in decisions made across the length and breadth of the island. The qualifications of the members of the special vestry was yet another concern. Moreover, the prime minister preferred the adoption in Ireland of the English solution – an exchange of tithes for land. Patiently, Goulburn explained the essential differences between the two countries. There was precious little common land in Ireland from which to compensate tithe holders, he reported. Thus land would have to be obtained from proprietors, but how was this to be effected to the satisfaction of the clergy? That is, how were they to secure a block rather than several scattered parcels of land? An attractive alternative, he countered, was to purchase in each parish an estate that would produce something more than the amount of the tithe composition, and assign it to the incumbent as a glebe in full satisfaction of the tithe. The composition might then remain as a land tax payable to the government. But this radical proposal generated little enthusiasm in London. Equally discouraging was the cabinet's refusal to establish rent, or the value of a landholding, as the tests for membership of the special vestries. All in all, Goulburn feared that whatever tithe bill now emerged would be a clumsy arrangement at best.[43]

Compelled to give ground on the tithes, Goulburn had also been obliged to abandon his initial position on the related issue of public relief. That resistance to the tithe had mounted with the deepening distress in Ireland appeared to be no coincidence. Yet Goulburn continued to insist that government action to relieve the misery caused by a partial failure of the potato crop should be deferred for as long as possible; namely, until "there was real and immediate danger of absolute famine." Like so many of his contemporaries, he believed that "self-help" was the only enduring solution to the chronic problem of poverty. The fear of want, the desire to escape its clutches, would motivate people to improve themselves. His position was much the same as that to which a friend and fellow Alfred Club member later gave expression, with an appropriate allusion to the Book of Common Prayer. "It is meet and right, and our bounden duty, to help the weak, and to alleviate distress, as far as our means allow," John Wilson Croker wrote. Nor was the availability of means Goulburn's only qualification of this Christian duty, though it always figured largely in his mind. To inform the poor that any power could relieve them of their state of want and dependence was to impugn "the dispensations of Providence, and to disorder the frame of society." These were the "mischievous results" of any "meddling with the natural means of supplying the market."[44]

Goulburn had reason to be fearful of the enormous expense that might be involved in relieving Irish distress. One of the resident gentry of County Clare, where the peasants had lost their crops and were too poor to purchase potatoes, estimated that £400,000 would scarcely supply the wants of the suffering population. Even William Gregory's more careful calculations produced a figure in excess of £100,000. Moreover, intervention on this scale in County Clare would be bound to "excite clamorous demands from other Districts." With only £41,000 (the balance of an earlier parliamentary grant) on hand, Goulburn would have to return to Parliament for another appropriation if he sanctioned extensive relief operations. And yet, as the under-secretary asked, "Are so many thousands to be left to the Chance of perishing for Want?"[45]

Recognizing that assistance could no longer be withheld from the people of Clare, Goulburn's overriding concern was "how to afford it in the most sparing manner and so as to excite the least possible attention." In his opinion, nothing could "be more impolitic than to encourage an expectation that the Government will annually feed the poor during three or four months of the year." Anxious to head off appeals from areas where the distress was less severe, he followed a course suggested by Peel. Public funds would initially be provided only to a limited extent and as a supplement to sums "subscribed by the neighbouring proprietors." For this purpose, Gregory was instructed to lay his hands on any sum within his reach. Goulburn's continuing reluctance to go to Parliament for monies was motivated by a concern that this action would "stop all private charity" and "have every gentleman throughout the Country pressing his claim to a share of the vote for his own tenantry and neighbours." Nevertheless, the House was assured that he would soon propose a vote of credit to enable the viceroy to make advances, rather than grants, in order to expedite public works. At the same time, seed potatoes, biscuit, and oatmeal were quietly forwarded to Ireland for distribution and sale to the poor, who were now being put to work. Employment was the most acceptable means of giving the poor bread. Further, a private subscription was opened in England which eventually totalled £250,000.[46]

The Poor Employment Bill that Goulburn introduced in mid-May 1822 authorized advances from the consolidated fund in order to expedite road building and other public works already voted by grand juries. An additional sum of £50,000 was made available to the viceroy to spur employment in the same way. Pointing to this paltry sum, one critic scornfully calculated that it would provide only one shilling for each individual who was in desperate need of assistance. This criticism was echoed by reliable observers on the ground, such as the archbishop of Tuam. He forwarded a chilling description of the conditions in Galway and Mayo, and dismissed as a "literal drop in the ocean" the £1,000 he had received from Dublin to supplement the private subscription he had organized. Unless thousands of pounds were sent into Galway and Mayo immediately, the archbishop warned, thousands would "die of actual hunger." Wellesley's assessment was equally grim and unnerving. More money must be granted without delay – at least another £50,000 – he announced. Goulburn was finally persuaded that expense must be a subordinate consideration. "In the present state of things economy must be put out of the question," he replied to the viceroy, "and I am sure that Parliament will not be satisfied unless every exertion be made to feed a starving population wherever it is found."[47]

"You must excuse my anxiety about the state of the country," the chief secretary wrote to the loyal Gregory in mid-June, "for I am persecuted nearly to death both in and out of Parliament and am supposed to be the most inhuman and unfeeling of men because I have not given an assurance that the Government of Ireland can and will feed all the people." Herein lay the ever-present danger – that Goulburn's aversion to state intervention would result in a lack of compassion for those of the poor who were simply unable to help themselves. However, he fully accepted that it was the duty of government to prevent its citizens from starving. So he arranged for one thousand bags of biscuit to be sent from the naval stores at Plymouth to the archbishop of Tuam, and he claimed the entire £100,000 that had already been voted for advances and relief. Indeed, wherever there was an "actual scarcity of provisions," Goulburn ordered that food as well as money was to be provided and that the commissioners of relief were to be impressed with the importance of meeting the evil in time. But with the notion of "self-help" still firmly in mind, he continued to emphasize that "the more employment and the less gratuitous relief" given, the better.[48]

Newspaper reports in July of 140 deaths from starvation in a single parish saw Goulburn swiftly order an investigation both to determine

their accuracy and to identify ways of preventing such calamities. Yet
Gregory was soon offering the usually well-informed opinion (for he
sat on the central board administering relief) that there was no longer
any justifiable fear of a want of provisions. "There is food sufficient,"
he reported in mid-July 1822. Goulburn resolved, therefore, to call a
halt to all direct relief on 1 September. "There is every appearance of
an early and abundant harvest and if under those circumstances the
Country cannot maintain its population it never can," he advised Peel.
"And you and the Government must make up your minds how you will
permanently maintain them."[49]

But misery and want continued to haunt areas of the countryside.
The commissioners charged with the supervision of relief reported an
increase in distress as the season advanced. An unusually wet July had
served to retard both ordinary labour and the potato crop. In more
mountainous regions in particular, they warned, a continuation of relief was essential. Unfortunately, evidence of distress competed with
tales of abuse. There were the all-too-familiar stories of public assistance being "infamously jobbed." In some baronies the persons relieved exceeded the total population as enumerated in the recent
census, and there was a strong suspicion that local gentry saw relief as a
means of guaranteeing the payment of rents. Persuaded that there was
a general abundance of provisions yet severe distress in localized areas,
Goulburn resolved to practise what he had earlier preached. The suspension of direct relief would go ahead as planned, but public works
would continue in particular areas as a means of providing the poor
with the money to purchase the available food. Of course, the investment in road building had the added benefit of improving communications and opening formerly isolated areas that had provided havens
for the lawless.[50]

As 1822 drew to a close, Goulburn had reason to reflect on his performance as chief secretary. After all, in fending off opposition attacks
in the House during the spring, he had pleaded for more time to remedy the evils of centuries. What had he accomplished? He had restored
a much-needed administrative efficiency to the Irish government and
had established a close relationship with the under-secretary while
maintaining a satisfactory one with the viceroy. He had achieved a significant reform of policing and was completing the "purification" of the
magistracy. In short, he had taken a long step towards ensuring that
each county of Ireland possessed the means of protecting the peaceable. His efforts to protect the revenues of the Protestant establishment
had been far less successful, however. Even appeals to the "sacred"
rights of private property had proven far from effective in discouraging
a tampering with the tithes that was evidently intended to lessen popu-

lar discontent rather than to protect the clergy from hostility or guarantee their incomes. Goulburn's sense of foreboding on this score was paralleled by his uneasiness at being obliged to compromise on the issue of public relief for the distressed. Perhaps a little depressed by his self-assessment, he was mortified by the consequences of a sudden eruption, at year's end, of Wellesley's foolishness.

The viceroy had been aware from the moment he landed in Ireland of the suspicion with which "the Orange Party, especially the Corporation of Dublin," regarded his appointment. Yet he flattered himself, as he was wont to do, that he had overcome this distrust. Nevertheless, as the summer season of Protestant triumphalism approached, the Orangemen rejected his request that they forgo the traditional and provocative decoration of King William III's statue in Dame Street. The Protestants' celebration of James II's defeat at the Boyne was therefore marred by the equally traditional sectarian brawls. As the next high day of the Orangemen neared – the commemoration of William's birthday early in November – Wellesley showed himself determined to act. But his chief secretary's attitude was more ambivalent. The previous year, Goulburn had welcomed the Orange decoration of King William's statue in St James's Square, London, and he acknowledged the order's loyalty to the crown. Nor did he wish to establish a precedent that might oblige the executive to intervene to prevent other Protestant celebrations in a land where "even the most innocent ceremony" seemingly led "sooner or later to a breach of the peace." On the other hand, he deplored the "absurdity" of the Orangemen's attitude towards the lord lieutenant. His position was best expressed by Peel, who explained to the viceroy, "I wish to maintain in force those laws by which Roman Catholics are excluded from any material share in the direction of public affairs, but for this very reason I ought to feel and do feel anxious that the mortification inseparable from exclusion, should not be increased by any irritating ceremonies." Thus Goulburn wished to discourage the Orangemen from decorating the statue without humiliating them. His solution was to give them an opportunity to claim that they had yielded to force.[51]

Peel had long since suggested a way of proceeding – persuade residents near the statue to swear that they apprehended a riot, and then have the magistrates ban the decoration on that ground. Unfortunately, the Irish lord chancellor, "with his usual discretion," began to tell people that any interference with this annual rite would be illegal. "When there are so many persons anxious to have a good reason for violating the law this course of conversation on his part is not very prudent nor agreeable to those who are to enforce it," an irritated Goulburn privately complained. Nonetheless, on 29 October he instructed the mayor in the viceroy's name to ban the decoration in the interests of public peace. This the mayor did two days later. The appearance of his proclamation induced a group of men to halt their painting of the statue, but it inspired a member of the Common Council and his associates to take up the work. Although they were dispersed by force, they had the satisfaction of knowing that they had prevented the day passing off without incident. Yet there was a lingering suspicion that the Castle had accorded the decoration of the statue a notoriety it had never before enjoyed. Certainly, there was an unprecedented decoration of the city on 4 November with the "outward signs of its inward absurdity."[52]

Elements of the city's Protestant community were still seething with resentment when Wellesley, together with Goulburn and other senior members of the administration, attended a performance of *She Stoops to Conquer* at the New Theatre Royal on 14 December 1822. The viceroy was greeted with a conspicuous lack of enthusiasm. From the crowded gallery there soon came chants of "No popery" and "No popish government," and the catcalls were followed by missiles – a coin, handbills denouncing "popery," oranges, part of a bottle, a short stick, and a watchman's rattle. The last narrowly missed Jane Goulburn and Lady Anne Gregory, who, together with their husbands, were occupying the box next to the viceroy's. Eventually order was restored, and several men were either arrested or ejected by police.[53]

Notwithstanding his wife's narrow escape from serious injury, Goulburn quickly recovered his sense of humour and of proportion. After this his first visit to an Irish theatre, he observed that never before had he heard so much of the audience and so little of the players. Irony aside, he agreed that the men responsible for this gross insult to the lord lieutenant should be severely punished. Unfortunately, Wellesley's reaction to the information that there had been a conspiracy to insult him lacked both humour and proportion. Convinced that Orange conspirators had intended either to assassinate him or to drive him from Ireland, he demanded that the culprits be indicted on capital charges. It required the combined representations of his confidential and official advisers, together with the debilitating effects of a cold, to dissuade him from this folly. And when the crown preferred indictments on lesser charges, a grand jury packed by an Orange sheriff nullified them. As the chief law officer, Plunket was therefore obliged to proceed on the basis of "ex officio information." Meanwhile, Wellesley's melodramatic depiction of himself as the target of a murderous plot excited widespread scorn, not least among his former admirers, who appreciated that a "dignified, discreet and temperate" exploitation of this incident might well have placed them in a position

finally to secure the suppression of the Orangemen. In these circumstances, Wellesley would have been well advised to allow the episode to
fade from the public's memory once the ex officio prosecutions had
been dismissed. Instead, he exposed himself and his administration to
even greater ridicule.[54]

Toasts to the viceroy's health had long raised scarcely a cheer in
Dublin's clubs, so the silence that greeted this ritual during a meeting of the Beefsteak Club in February 1823 was by no means exceptional; nor was the enthusiastic applause that accompanied the toast
to his predecessor, Lord Talbot. Just as wounding to Wellesley's inordinate vanity was a report that his health had been mockingly drunk
to the tune "Now Phoebus Sinketh in the West." The fact that the
lord chancellor, the commander of the military forces, and three
members of the viceregal household were present and participated
in the festivities in no way diminished Wellesley's sense of outrage.
He promptly dismissed the three members of his household, one of
whom was an elderly and popular figure. In Dublin, this "inhuman
proceeding" caused the ladies of the best society to resolve to boycott
Wellesley's drawing room whenever he got around to holding a reception. In London, the reaction was ridicule rather than outrage. A
lord lieutenant who had gone to Ireland to put an end to party had
done it so well that he would not "allow even a dinner party." The
general opinion was summarized by one of his original supporters
for the viceroyalty, who observed, "There never was such an ass."[55]

Wellesley's behaviour brought Goulburn to the brink of resignation.
"I find that discretion is an ingredient which enters into the composition of very few Irishmen indeed," he complained to Peel. Now, from
Gregory, who began to muse again on the attractions of retirement, he
received the warning that the clamour against Wellesley was not a transitory phenomonen. It was the result of a profound hatred "which exists amongst all the higher classes of the kingdom, whether they are
supporters or opposers of his Majesty's Cabinet." To a weary and har-
rassed chief secretary it seemed that the viceroy had now made difficult if not impossible his task of reconciling the Protestant community
to the new regime at the Castle and its program of moderate reform.
Fearful that all his hopes of good government and of achieving an improvement in the country had been dashed, Goulburn was strongly
tempted to resign. His wife steadied him. She sympathized with him,
recognizing the uncomfortable situation in which he had been placed
by Wellesley's "intemperate conduct," but she reminded him of how
happy she was in Ireland and how reluctant she would be to leave. She
concluded with an appeal to his well-developed sense of duty. "I trust
your own natural calmness of temper for preventing your deciding on

so important a step without serious reflection, and altho' I cannot but wish your master were changed, I do not see how the public good is to be advanced by your withdrawing yourself from your situation."[56]

CHAPTER SIX

Chief Secretary

Goulburn returned to London early in February 1823 to find the capital locked in an arctic embrace and the streets deep in snow. He was given a warm welcome by the Peels, and after an evening with the dramatically beautiful but conversationally limited Julia, he gallantly concluded that his own fireside was worth two of that of his friend. The parliamentary session also promised to generate heat, for the government was pledged to the introduction of additional measures "to promote and secure the tranquillity" of Ireland and "to improve the habits and condition of the people." The new chancellor of the exchequer, Frederick Robinson, soon tinkered with taxes in a way that won the applause even of Irish Whigs, though they urged that these "salutary measures" be accompanied by the suppression of the Orangemen. Wellesley and Plunket favoured this step, not surprisingly, but Goulburn balked. He wished neither to alienate the Protestant gentry further nor to apply against loyalists a law enacted to suppress rebels. The irony would be too bitter. Nevertheless, the issue was forced in Parliament, and on 5 March 1823 he was obliged to announce his intention to introduce an unlawful oaths bill. He tried to placate the Orangemen by emphasizing that although their secret association was "open to grave and serious objections," they had been as loyal to the state as the Ribbonmen had been treasonous. But this "cold defence" failed to temper Orange resentment or to diminish Catholic pleasure. The bill made it "an indictable offence to belong to any society bound together by an oath." "This coming from a no Popery man as Mr. Goulburn is, strikes deeply into the Orange," a gleeful Daniel O'Connell chortled.[1]

Goulburn also introduced a pair of tithe bills, one for the temporary composition of tithes and the other for their permanent commutation for land. Both were assailed by Ireland's Protestant hierarchy. They complained of a lack of consultation and protested the ominous distinction now being drawn between the churches of Ireland and England, whose unity had been a "fundamental article" of the Union. The angry bishops warned that the very essence of the Irish establishment was being destroyed "by an invasion of its property, and by the consequent subversion of its independence." Sympathetic as Goulburn was to this argument, he realized that moderate reform was the soundest defence against radical change. Therefore, the churchmen had to be protected from themselves.[2]

Goulburn drafted legislation incorporating his preferred solution – the exchange of tithes for glebes purchased with loans advanced by the "Commissioners for Reduction of the National Debt" – but in England commutations for land had already transformed the resident clergy into nonresident landlordry, and this was a problem that required no exacerbation in Ireland. So this bill quietly disappeared from the parliamentary agenda. What remained was a complicated and cumbersome procedure for temporary compositions. It alarmed the wealthy landowners, who resented its termination of their dodge to escape the tax – the exemption of pasture from tithes – and were fearful that clergy would claim the monetary equivalent of the full tithe rather than the fraction they had traditionally collected. Deftly, Goulburn exploited their concern to secure a modification of the principle of compulsion, which he still regarded as a violation of the right of property. Irish clergy compelled to surrender property in the name of public good, he argued, ought to be granted "full value of the property forcibly surrendered." The bill's compulsory features were hastily deleted. And as amended by him the following year, to correct errors in the initial drafting, to circumvent the obstructive tactics of the grassland interest, and to reintroduce a more palatable compulsory aspect, the reform had much to recommend it. The tithe system had been simplified and the poor had been relieved of the irregular, heavy, and uncertain rate of the tax. On balance, the measure was generally adjudged a success even though it was evidently no more than a "temporary expedient."[3]

Wellesley described tithe reform as an integral part of a "general system of combining relief of the People with the enforcement of the law of Ireland." To this same end, he and Goulburn sought to rescue law enforcement from a reputation for partiality and sectarianism. "If men do not get their complaints listened to and justice done in a way that seems to themselves or their neighbours satisfactory," Goulburn taught his sons, "the power of the community is undermined and angry passions are fostered." Catholic lawyers were now appointed to the important position of assistant barrister of quarter sessions; strong encouragement was given to the practice of local magistrates meeting regularly in petty sessions, instead of hearing cases individually; the ranks of the new constabulary were opened to Catholics, and the employment of these policemen in the collection of rents or tithes was discouraged; and sub-sheriffs were put on public notice that the corrupt among them would be pursued and punished.[4]

Widespread disturbances during the spring convinced Goulburn in mid-May to seek an extension of the Insurrection Act. He tied a carrot to this stick, offering free transportation to the colonies for one thousand emigrants from the disturbed districts. His hope was that this scheme "would produce an impression that some good is intended" and would "induce the lower orders to adopt a more peaceable line of conduct." Although he was able to report before year's end that outrage "rarely occurs in any part of the country," he opposed any reduction in the military establishment. He was anxious to avoid placing too severe a strain on his new police force. Moreover, having accepted the direct link between distress and disturbances, he worried that "great distress" if not famine would soon rear its ugly head. Dismal weather again threatened the vital potato crop, and his first thought was quietly to stockpile substitutes over the winter; by discreetly entering the market through private agents, the government could purchase rice or oatmeal at an excellent price. But Peel vetoed this prudent proposal, willing as he was to face parliamentary criticism for inaction rather than "run the risk of creating undue alarm and encourage improvident consumption during the winter, by those who will be taught to rely on the assistance of government in the time of necessity."[5]

When Parliament reopened on 3 February 1824, Goulburn discovered that there was "more disposition to cavil and to grumble" on the opposition side of the House than he had anticipated, and not least on the subject of Ireland. No fewer than twelve motions had been fixed for different periods before Easter. One prominent Irish Whig raised the sensitive issue of the denial of Catholic funerals in Irish churchyards. Another moved for returns showing the religious affiliation of Irish office holders. There were calls for the public funding of Catholic schools for Ireland's Catholic poor, whose natural loyalty some younger Whigs believed had been corrupted by ignorance. Finally, they gave notice of their intention to seek a select committee on the state of the island. Sensibly, Goulburn seized the initiative. He secured passage of a bill "to compel, as far as was possible, the residence of the clergy of Ireland upon their benefices." His amendments to the previous year's tithes bill made steady progress, despite complaints that they were unfair to landlords and too generous to clergy. Meanwhile, he happily relinquished to Plunket the thankless task of managing the proposed compromise on the churchyards. "Our Burials Bill seems to be in universal disfavor," he mordantly observed. "It has however afforded one subject on which Roman Catholics and Protestants can agree."[6]

When the Whigs finally moved in mid-May for a select committee, Goulburn was prepared. He successfully limited the inquiry to the disturbed areas, though he indulged his taste for irony by pointing out that this offered the investigators a broad enough field. At the same time, he sought to counter the charge that Catholics had been systematically excluded from office. Fully one half of the 1,800 constables already appointed under his recent police bill were Catholics, he announced. But the fact that he seemed to lose the thread of his argument in the midst of his speech, and abruptly sat down, not only detracted from the effectiveness of this performance but exposed him "to numberless jests." Nor was he pleased by the composition of the select committee, for a clear majority of its members regarded Catholic relief as essential for the pacification of Ireland.[7]

On education, which he regarded as an instrument of "amelioration and improvement" and a means of "placing the humbler classes of the Irish community on a level with the people of Great Britain," Goulburn secured a commission instead of the committee the Whigs were demanding. Their intent, he believed, was to substitute sectarian education for the professedly nondenominational instruction provided by the publicly funded Kildare Place Society. Although its schools had been accused of proselytism, Goulburn suspected the Catholic hierarchy of being opposed to any system other than one "wherein the Gospel morality was explained according to the tenets of the Roman Catholic Church." How else was he to interpret their warning that Catholic children would be discouraged from attending any school where the master was of a different religion or where a religious instructor named by them had not been admitted?[8]

If the Catholic bishops were less than candid on this subject, Goulburn was disingenuous. "I can assure you that I have no other wish than that the poor of all classes should be educated together, that their education should be conducted on Christian principles but that all reference to the peculiar religious tenets of any particular sect should be most carefully avoided," he informed the hierarchy. But he secretly hoped to advance the cause of conversion through nondenominational education, certain as he was that to educate "the people of Ireland on Christian principles" was to work "effectually for the overthrow of the Roman Catholic persuasion." Catholicism could not "stand against the light of the Gospel," and children who read the Bible rather than Catholic interpretations of it would eventually be won for the reformed faith. "If however you attempt directly to convert them, you arouse every feeling of the parents against you and I am anxious therefore on all occasions to disclaim any proselytising or any direct attempt at conversion." Clearly, he would have preferred to avoid an inquiry on education altogether. But as one seemed unavoidable, he considered a commission "less mischievous" than a committee and persuaded his Grenvillite friend Frankland Lewis to chair it. The addition of Anthony Blake allowed him to argue that Catholicism had been afforded "a reasonable counterpoise" to the Protestantism of the other members.[9]

Throughout the session Goulburn received reports from Gregory on the distress in Ireland, and he must have had second thoughts about the wisdom of Peel's rejection of his scheme to stockpile provisions. Hurry "the business through Parliament as fast as you can," the under-secretary advised in late May. Already, frantic appeals from Connemara had induced Wellesley to forward seed potatoes to the region, and the price of the tuber had fallen. Nevertheless, as cheap as potatoes currently were, "the poor could not buy them as they had not the money." The second week of June brought more than two dozen fresh applications for relief, and the suffering afflicted large tracts of nine counties. Even Gregory, who remained firmly opposed to government intervention in cases of partial or merely local crop failures, recognized the cleft stick in which he and Goulburn found themselves. How long could they ignore the plight of a poor unable to earn the money with which to purchase the available provisions? Lack of employment was evidently a no less serious problem than want of food.[10]

There was mounting alarm in England that unless steps were taken to "improve" Ireland, her poverty would be the financial ruin of Britain. Frederick Robinson had made another small but helpful concession in his budget by finally repealing all the remaining Union duties. And when Goulburn was visited by a worried merchant from County Clare who was seeking a program of public works to put money into the pockets of the poor, he ordered an immediate investigation of the alleged distress. Yet, as usual, he intended to "be very cautious of letting the Gentlemen know that whenever they discover a practical want of provisions in any part of the Country they are immediately to have the poor employed by the Government – the Gentry are certainly bound in such cases to provide for the poor around them."[11]

Optimistic crop predictions towards the end of June saw Goulburn and Wellesley agree to resist appeals for aid except in the most special circumstances. If ever there was a time to revert to a "sound state of things" and to try the experiment "of letting people trust to their own resources aided by the Charity of their neighbours," this was the moment, Goulburn concluded. He was confident that any suffering would be short-lived, for the soon-to-be harvested crop of potatoes promised to be so abundant that prices were certain to fall. Equally, the parliamentary recess afforded them an opportunity to try this experiment without fear of daily denunciations. No less important, to continue public support of the distressed would strengthen the position of those who wished to extend to Ireland the expensive Poor Law that had long been in place in England. Like many a Tory, Goulburn was later to acquiesce in the Whigs' harder-hearted reform of this institutionalized form of assistance.[12]

In August, Goulburn made a personal tour of distressed districts. He travelled through Limerick, Tralee, Killarney, and Mallow before following the valley of the Blackwater. What he saw came as a pleasant surprise and reinforced his scepticism of local reports of dire need. The condition of the people was much less wretched than he had expected, with "great numbers possessing that superabundant luxury of shoes and stockings." The dwellings of the poor, except those in the bogs, were not as bad as the miserable "tenements" in the vicinity of Dublin and were better furnished than he had imagined. Another surprise was the employment provided by spinning, especially in Limerick. Just as encouraging was the growing fashion "of attending the poor, of providing them more comfortable dwellings and of educating them which cannot fail to promote improvement." The better sort were evidently meeting their social responsibilities.[13]

By year's end Goulburn had noted a great improvement in every branch of industry and a corresponding increase in the prosperity and comfort of all ranks of society. Large capital investments in cotton manufacturing continued to be made along the eastern coast but particularly in the north, and this was being reflected in a sharp rise in exports. And in a country where land remained the principal if not the "only necessary of life," there could not be "a more certain indication of prosperity than the degree of readiness" with which rents were paid and land was rented. Admittedly, rents had been much reduced, but their lowering had been reasonable and essential. He could not defend their "exorbitant" level at a time "when the value of money rose and the value of produce decreased in proportion." Moreover, as the economic outlook brightened and the number of disturbances decreased, Goulburn had progressively withdrawn the Insurrection Act, which he continued to regard as "in some degree a departure from the principles of the constitution."[14]

For all of this good news, something close to panic gripped elements of the island's religious minority as the nights of 1824 lengthened and darkened with the approach of winter. For the deadline was also fast approaching for the fulfilment of "Pastorini's Prophecy" of the extirpation of Protestants. Christmas was the widely rumoured date, and as it approached, the more hysterical members of the Protestant Ascendancy began to behave as if a modern St Bartholomew's Day Massacre were being plotted. They demanded protection. Neither Wellesley nor Goulburn found cause for immediate alarm, the latter imaginatively reading popular songs for clues to "the disposition of the people," but he did view with disquiet "the new and complete organization of the country" under the banner of the Roman Catholic Association. As organized by the charismatic, complex, captious, and demagogic Daniel O'Connell, it agitated not only for emancipation but for redress of an entire catalogue of peasant grievances. And through the device of associate membership purchased with a modest subscription, the poor were enrolled in large numbers, thus generating a substantial weekly income.[15]

Attracted by the association's commitment to emancipation and by its allocation of a portion of its income to the support of Catholic education and the construction of chapels and presbyteries, many priests willingly served as recruiting agents and exhorted their congregations to join almost as a religious duty. Catholic bishops provided other agents with the returns of local priests, thereby greatly facilitating the collection of the "Catholic rent." These were the developments that alarmed Goulburn. But Peel's hopes of obtaining a clear recommendation from the Irish executive on how to proceed in the face of this challenge so skilfully thrown down by O'Connell were doomed to disappointment. For here was an issue that cut to the quick of its split personality. Wellesley was mired in a bog of self-pity, constantly complaining of being unappreciated and betrayed. Moreover, for advice on the legality of the association and the adequacy of the existing law, he naturally turned to the "Catholic" attorney general. "It is a great inconvenience to have an Attorney General residing out of Dublin and a Lord Lieutenant who is so uncertain as to the days on which he can do business," a frustrated and resentful Goulburn explained to Peel. Nor was the situation improved by Wellesley's insistence on conducting business in person. For the chief secretary, this meant long hours cooling his heels in the viceroy's antechamber and then, when finally admitted to the august presence, listening to this classical scholar's latest composition. Wellesley's poetic style was not celebrated for its "compression." As for the problem at hand, Wellesley and Plunket were soon manoeuvring to escape responsibility for any action that might further tarnish their liberal reputation. Plunket indicated that he could not support any measure to suppress the association which did not extend to the reviving Orange Order. This did not sit well with Goulburn, who believed that the challenge to legal authority came

only from the former. To rank the two organizations as equally dangerous would be "a great proof of undue partiality for the Roman Catholic Body." As another season of Protestant triumphalism approached,
however, he did urge the avoidance of "all offensive displays."[16]

Meanwhile, the Roman Catholic Association continued to prosper.
Goulburn worried that its growth in membership, especially of noblemen and gentlemen, among them members of Parliament, together
with some of the more senior members of the Roman Catholic clergy,
had given it even greater stature in the community at large. He feared
that other Protestants, seeking the support of an overwhelmingly Catholic electorate at the next election, would also join the association and
that those landlords who did not lend a sympathetic ear to the cause
would face an electoral revolt. More disturbing still was the ever-length-
ening reach of the association, as its agents taught the people to look to
it as the guardian of their religion and protector of their interests. It
"apes the form and assumes the authority of Parliament," Goulburn
warned Peel. But level-headed as ever, he carefully distanced himself
from the more excitable members of the Protestant ascendancy, who
were predicting rebellion and demanding that the yeomanry be
brought up to strength and called out. To raise this ill-disciplined Protestant force would inevitably heighten sectarian tensions. The association has "no military organization; no adequate supplies of arms, no
pecuniary resources or regular leaders, without which nothing in the
shape of a general insurrection could be planned or undertaken,"
Goulburn reported. To his way of thinking, it was more of a "prepara-
tory" organization. The difficulty was how to suppress a body that
could, if necessary, continue most of its activities under the cloak of a
charitable society. One glimmer of hope was the possibility that the association, by its recent formation of several general committees, had acquired a sufficiently representative character to violate the Convention
Act. Another response was to prosecute for seditious libel those editors
who published the "inflammatory proceedings" of the "Popish Parliament." If it achieved nothing else, this action would at least "remove
the foolish impression which exists that the Government either ap-
proves or is afraid of it."[17]

Demands for action were also being made by the monarch. His
brothers York and Clarence had so frightened him with the implications of the Catholic rent that he now threatened to withdraw his consent to emancipation remaining an open question in cabinet. Of
course, this was an expedient that was essential to the unity of the Liverpool ministry. Peel pondered the legislative options. The government could either seek a new law framed against all such societies in
general, but with the association in particular in mind, or it could pro-

pose a measure directed specifically against the association. He could see the pitfalls – a general law could all too easily be evaded by the ever-artful O'Connell, while a specific one promised to evoke an outcry in Britain from the more liberal elements.[18]

The cabinet eventually plumped for a measure applicable to all "unlawful" societies. If this amounted to a concession to the Grenvillites and to Wellesley, Peel manoeuvred to ensure that the viceroy and Plunket were closely identified with suppression. He insisted that the bill be drafted in Dublin. Nevertheless, they continued to wriggle to free themselves from the hook of responsibility. Indeed, the attorney general appeared to draw a distinction between his ministerial duty to draft the bill and his personal opinion of its merits. Moreover, as chief secretary, Goulburn would introduce it. As the appointed day neared, he grew ever more nervous. There was every reason to suspect that he would "face a storm" in the Commons. Then he began to sneeze and feared that he was falling victim to the influenza that had already laid low Peel, Robinson, and Huskisson. But when he rose in his place on 10 February to open the debate, he spoke for two hours and to some effect. He followed the line agreed in cabinet. This new measure amounted merely to an amendment of the Convention Act of 1793 and of the recent bill to discourage the Orangemen. He emphasized the Roman Catholic Association's interference with the regular administration of justice, the massive involvement of the Catholic clergy, the intimidation of those who opposed the Catholic rent, and the deepening sectarian animosities.[19]

"You will be glad to hear that what I said yesterday was satisfactory to my friends and was attentively heard by the House," Goulburn reported to his wife. Especially gratifying was the praise of his Irish friends. However, management of the bill soon threatened to be fully as arduous a task as he had feared. Plunket made a fine speech on the second night of debate, reaffirming his belief in emancipation but supporting suppression of the association. This delicate balancing act merely confirmed Goulburn in the opinion "that a man who means to lead a quiet life ought not to change his party and accept office at the same time." The Whigs protested that the only "proper" way to put down the association was to redress Irish grievances by granting emancipation, and they denounced the legislation as "partial" since it did not also seek specifically to crush the Orangemen. Eventually, in the early hours of the morning of 16 February, the bill passed first reading with relative ease. "I believe no man alive recollected a debate so protracted on leave to bring in a Bill recommended by a King's Speech," one participant recorded. "I never recollected the House so attentive to every speech during the whole discussion."[20]

Instead of this being the preliminary skirmish in a long and bloody struggle as Goulburn had anticipated, the bill progressed with surprising ease. Second reading was given less than a week after the first, and by much the same majority. Nor was the bill delayed in committee. By 9 March 1825 the Unlawful Societies Bill had received royal assent. Yet its swift and relatively comfortable passage had less to do with Goulburn's skilful management than with the revival of the larger but related question – Catholic emancipation. Supporters of this measure reasoned that their chances of success would be "materially injured" if they brought it forward while the other bill was still before the House. Although Goulburn welcomed the "unexpected relief," he was pessimistic of again successfully resisting this fundamental concession. His position remained what it had been ever since his entrance into public life as a follower of Spencer Perceval – that it was "inconsistent with the existence of a Protestant established Church to admit Roman Catholics to political power." Yet there could be no escaping the evidence of a weakening resistance. An issue that bound Goulburn ever more closely to Peel separated them both from old colleagues in the Alfred Club. He detected a growing indifference among many English MPs. He fancied that out of sheer boredom with Ireland and its problems, they might be tempted to try any experiment to shorten or avoid debates, unless their constituents evinced sufficient hostility to this particular measure to induce them to oppose it. Should emancipation carry, he believed there would be a "material change" in the government. His own inclination would be to resign, but much would depend on the conduct of Liverpool, Peel, and others with whom he acted in public life.[21]

The Commons debate on Catholic emancipation opened to a drumbeat of conflicting testimony before the ongoing select committee on Ireland. Irish Tories and the clergy of the established church denied that this concession would solve Ireland's many problems; they warned that the "mere mass of the population" equated emancipation with Catholic supremacy. A second parade of witnesses, among them Daniel O'Connell and other leaders of the Roman Catholic Association and representatives of the Catholic hierarchy, offered the assurances which the liberal majority on the committee plainly wished to hear – that it would tranquillize the island, remove the priests from politics, and save the Union. But O'Connell admitted that the chief secretary had been falsely accused of being an Orangeman – and the emotive charge was too often on his tongue in Ireland, where with sly wit he frequently referred to the home secretary as Orange Peel. Nevertheless, the Catholic leader remained confident that the tide had finally turned in England. Never given to false modesty, he claimed the credit for this. "If I had not been here, nothing would have been done," he boasted.[22]

In the House, a preliminary motion for a committee on Catholic claims carried with a majority of thirteen, and a gloomy Goulburn predicted that it would swell as actual legislation progressed. He himself had not spoken. He was suffering from yet another head cold and had difficulty thinking clearly, and was convinced that he would have made little impact. And while he expected the bill to perish in the Lords, he fancied that even there passage could not be delayed indefinitely. Indeed, there were rumours that the prime minister was ready to give way on the question. This would mean the disintegration of his ministry, for neither Peel nor Goulburn, nor any other "Protestants," were yet ready to participate in a retreat. Consequently, Liverpool took care to contradict the reports. Meanwhile, both Goulburn and Peel were consulting William Gregory, whom they regarded as an authentic voice of the Protestant ascendancy. They sought his opinion on the situation in the Commons and on the Protestant securities, or "wings," that the House appeared likely to attach to any relief bill – state payment of the Catholic clergy and the disfranchisement of the great mass of Catholic voters, the forty-shilling freeholders.[23]

Gregory did not disguise his sense of betrayal by English Protestants. He dismissed the proposed securities as worthless, doomed to be removed one day "for the same wise purpose that their Claims are now admitted, viz. to satisfy the Catholics." Those Irish Protestants who could flee would do so, he forecast, leaving behind to fend for themselves only the "hapless residue" trapped by age or circumstances. He took some comfort from the assurances of Goulburn and Peel that they would not compromise, and he counselled them to resist the state payment of Catholic clergy. To pay and thus to acknowledge a Catholic "establishment" without securing the right to nominate its members would be "madness." As for the contemplated disfranchisement of the "wretched, famished, perjured" forty-shilling freeholders, he urged his two friends to oppose or support this measure "as may best serve the protestant cause, by dividing the ranks of the Enemy on the question."[24]

During the debate on the second reading of the relief bill, Goulburn briefly restated his opposition to it. He charged that the legislation amounted to the "first recognition of the Roman Catholic church of Ireland" and complained that there was "no one provision which he could discover, that went to preserve the established episcopal church of England and Ireland, as it was recognized at the Union." On the "wings," he steered the course already plotted by Gregory. He opposed both payment of the priests and disfranchisement of the freeholders in the hope that defeat of the securities would erode support for emancipation. Speaking late at night, shortly after midnight, he failed to hold the attention of tired members, but he took heart when the relief bill cleared third reading by an unexpectedly narrow margin. The "wings," it seemed, had proven as much of a liability as an asset in the gathering of votes. Attention now shifted to the Lords.[25]

There, the decisive role was that of the prime minister. Although talk of his temporizing continued to swirl around the capital, Liverpool's resolve to hold fast to his long-standing if at times less-than-fervent opposition to emancipation drew strength from the fact that the concession was clearly unpopular in the country. Liverpool was also influenced by the surprisingly small majority in the Lower House, by the Duke of York's announcement as heir apparent that he would never assent to claims that violated the Coronation Oath, and by Peel's determination not to acquiesce in the concession. Liverpool advised his confidantes that in such circumstances, he would have no alternative but to resign with Peel. He then delivered his "first violent speech" against emancipation, and the bill went down to defeat on second reading by a larger majority than had been anticipated. "The division in the Lords will have sufficiently shewn you that there is still a feeling for the constitution as it stands in that body," a relieved Goulburn wrote to Gregory.[26]

Briefly, it seemed that Liverpool might fail to hold his administration together. Rumours were rife in Dublin and London that Goulburn was to be replaced. There was no change, however. The size of the majority in the Lords, which avoided the embarrassment of the bishops providing the margin of victory, had lessened the likelihood of Peel, Liverpool, and thus Goulburn quitting office. Equally, the removal of Goulburn would surely have prompted Peel to resign, acutely sensitive as he already was to his isolation as the only senior minister in the Commons who was opposed to emancipation. Indeed, after some posturing by Canning, the cabinet rallied behind the less-than-heroic policy of muddling on as before. "As each individual however has reserved to himself the full right to act upon a different principle whenever he thinks the circumstances require it, the duration of the Government is necessarily uncertain," Goulburn advised an anxious Gregory. "But I see no reason to believe that it is more so than it has been for some time past." [27]

Goulburn did not expect an eruption in Ireland in reaction to this latest disappointment, though huge crowds of the "hereditary bondsmen" turned out to give O'Connell a rousing welcome home. "Many causes as it appears to me operate now to produce tranquillity which have in former periods been wanting," he wrote confidently to the viceroy late in May. Indeed, the Irish were soon completely free of the repressive provisions of the Insurrection Act. The reform of the magistracy and the creation of an efficient force of police even generated optimism that peace might be maintained under the ordinary laws. But, of course, the island was never entirely tranquil; magistrates were reminded of the illegality of the traditional Orange demonstrations organized for 12 July. Under the terms of Goulburn's bill, the Orangemen were compelled once again to dissolve their revived organization. Meanwhile, Goulburn was skilfully winding up the select committee. He outmanoeuvred the members who were seeking to prolong its life. Determined to demonstrate that Ireland was not being governed by a Commons committee, he secured a "short and plain" report that left "all important questions open for the decision of the government." They had ample time before the reopening of Parliament, he judged, in which to prepare an agenda of ameliorative measures.[28]

The commissioners on education had already presented Goulburn with a copy of their first report. They recommended that public support be withdrawn from several of the organizations which Catholics suspected of proselytism, and they urged that care be taken to ensure that these organizations did not receive indirect funding through the Kildare Place Society. Further, they suggested the creation of a government education board to superintend the management and control the finances of schools, and they proposed dual "literary" instruction in schools where there were significant numbers of Catholic children. One of the instructors in such mixed institutions should be a Roman Catholic, and all of them were to use a common text that was to be "doctrinally neutral." The commissioners also favoured separate religious instruction. Goulburn duly suspended all new grants to schools, while the Kildare Place Society was advised to inform any of its schools connected with proselytizing societies to sever the tie on pain of losing their funding.[29]

Following his return to Ireland in July – and having had time to think through the commission's recommendations and to discuss them with leading Irish Protestants – Goulburn concluded that no subject was likely to cause him greater embarrassment when the House next met. Protestants condemned the proposed periods of doctrinally neutral literary instruction as inherently unfair, since this meant the use of materials acceptable to Catholics. Thus Catholic children would go to their religious instruction fully prepared, whereas Protestants would have to return to basics. Indeed, there was an impression abroad, Goulburn warned Peel in September, that the commissioners' object had been "to consult R. Catholic feeling alone." In an effort to finesse a report he could not reject without setting off a political storm, Goulburn artfully suggested that the government announce a willingness to experiment with the new system while maintaining the old. He was fully prepared to brave charges in the House that he was sustaining proselytizing and Orange institutions in order to uphold the Kildare Place Society as "the established machine of Scriptural education." It was a response that was evidently influenced by his own proselytism and his profound distrust of the Catholic clergy, whose real object, he believed, was to keep their flocks in a state of ignorance. "I despair of their willing approval and support of any system of education which does not give them a separate and complete controul," he privately admitted. Therefore, it was essential to maintain the existing schools for several years.[30]

Although Goulburn had received, as always, an effusive welcome from the viceroy, their relationship remained an uneasy and trying one. Wellesley continued to shirk his responsibilities with the plaintive cry of ill health, though this did not prevent him from suddenly announcing his intention to risk the fatigues of a wife. His betrothed was a youthful American widow of great beauty who had long been hunting a nobleman. The difference in their ages sparked uncharitable comment, but more worrying to Goulburn was the bride's religion. "Her being a Roman Catholic & a bigotted one will prove a serious inconvenience here as he will I presume be as much under her influence as he has heretofore been under that of Mr. Johnston," Goulburn wearily commented to Peel. Yet he was soon obliged to concede that the marriage had been celebrated correctly – a public service according to the rites of the established church and a discreet Roman Catholic ceremony in the privacy of the lady's chamber.[31]

Meanwhile, a new Catholic Association appeared to be making a mockery of the recent law. By year's end the Irish law officers were of the opinion that both its regular gatherings and its general meeting were illegal. Wellesley was tempted to issue a proclamation enjoining all to abide by the law, but he soon abandoned such a futile exercise. He then proposed that those members of the new association who were also members of the gentry should be approached privately in an effort to convince them to quit it. Goulburn strenuously and successfully opposed any such proceeding, arguing that it amounted to an unworthy deference to certain members of an illegal organization simply on the basis of their rank or station. Furthermore, he was sure that the only practical result would be a modification of the association's activities in order to make it even more difficult to attack. On the other hand, a legal assault was discouraged by the English law officers, who were still unconvinced that the law had been broken.[32]

While Goulburn prepared for what would be the final and abbreviated session of Parliament before a general election in June, he also had to cope with some unseemly squabbling. In Dublin, the viceroy's household was in turmoil as a result of the long-predicted collision between Wellesley's bride and his natural son, Edward Johnston. The amazing accounts of the conflict that were soon circulating proved damaging to the "Lord Lieutenant's respectability in the country," observed Goulburn, and he pleaded with his superiors in London to recall Johnston to his post in the Stamp Office. The recent events were "the most extraordinary instance of power obtained & maintained by an unworthy person," he protested. But neither Peel nor Liverpool – nor even Wellington – was willing to intervene in this domestic dispute. Anyway, Liverpool had to contend with squabbles enough within his own official family. Moreover, the notoriously peevish prime minister was preoccupied with the nation's economic troubles.[33]

The new parliamentary session began "very harmoniously," or so Goulburn reported to Wellesley on 4 February. The members had made the happy discovery that Ireland was generally regarded as the "bright part of the picture." This unusual if not unique perception was an indication of the gathering gloom in a Britain gripped by financial crisis and deepening industrial distress. In December, several banks had failed largely as a result of their speculation in the South America market. There was alarmist talk of credit being ruined, and by the second week of February the funds stood a full twenty-one points lower than their level exactly one year earlier. The "despair" in the City was matched by that of silk weavers and glove makers as they contemplated their market being thrown open to French competition. At least the distress in Britain diverted attention from Ireland, much to Goulburn's relief. "We shall therefore have a troublesome session," he judged, "but not an Irish one."[34]

In this confident mood he set before the House, which had long been accustomed to a rich diet of Irish measures, a menu that was conspicuously devoid of Hibernian epicurean delights. His earlier suggestion that the report of the education commissioners be implemented only on a limited basis was now adopted as government policy. Opposition protests against an increase in the public funding of the Kildare Place Society made little headway, for this organization had a host of influential admirers and apologists. The Whigs also criticized the continued public support of the educational activities of other societies accused of proselytism, and they made much of the statistical evidence of religious discrimination in education by reminding the House that fully nine-tenths of the 400,000 Catholic children in school were being educated without benefit of public aid. However, the presentation of a petition from Ireland's Catholics, "praying for a grant of money for the Education of Catholics in Ireland in their own way," worked to Goulburn's advantage. It excited another "anti-popery" spasm in the Commons and lent credence to his charge that Catholics would never be content with anything less than sectarian schooling.[35]

In the Lords and the Commons, respectively, Liverpool and Goulburn had committed the government to the introduction of two legislative measures in response to the findings of the select committee. Evidence of the misappropriation of the church rates levied by Protestants in vestry on an overwhelmingly Catholic population demanded action. Reluctantly, under insistent prodding from the opposition, Goulburn made explicit the discretionary authority granted to vestries to provide monies for the construction and repair of Catholic chapels as well as Anglican churches. The second bill was a subletting act, which ostensibly sought to discourage the subdivision of lands into the uneconomic plots that were widely regarded as a source of Ireland's chronic poverty. However, its invalidating of all subleases entered into without the prior approval of the landlord clearly facilitated evictions. Not surprisingly – and not unreasonably – the bill was suspected of being inspired as much by political as economic considerations. On the eve of a general election in which Goulburn expected the Roman Catholic Association to challenge landlord control of enfranchised tenants, the hand of property had been somewhat strengthened.[36]

The dissolution of Parliament threatened to be delayed, however, by the continuing distress in England. Goulburn noted that widespread unemployment in the textile industries had given "rise to the folly which always animates the lower orders under such circumstances of destroying the Machinery by which we have created so great a demand for the manufactures of the Country & the labours of the people." A panicky cabinet first recalled troops from Ireland and then began to tamper with the Corn Laws. The stick of military might was to be paired with the carrot of cheaper bread. Observing the furious response of the powerful agricultural interest in both Houses of Parliament to any lessening of protection, Goulburn privately grumbled that the government had merely "aroused against them a great many of their best friends," and he professed not to understand how men "possessed of sense and experience" could get themselves into such a "scrape." "How to get out of the difficulty is not easy to define," he acknowledged. Liverpool's solution was to permit a severely limited importation of cheap corn and to "stake the existence" of the government on the passage of the measure.[37]

England's economic miseries were speedily surpassed by those of Ireland. The financial panic crossed the Irish Sea, where the effect of this virus was all the more debilitating, given the patient's chronically weakened condition. Distress was most acute in Dublin and among the cotton weavers of Drogheda, but private subscriptions in aid of the poor fared poorly. Whether this was the result of a general lack of wealth, as Wellesley believed, or whether as Gregory argued, it was because of a conviction among "the most worthy inhabitants" that the crisis originated in the growing influence of trades unions "which ought first to be broken up," it caused the Castle to forward modest public grants to Dublin and Drogheda.[38]

By the time Parliament adjourned on 31 May (to be formally dissolved two days later), Goulburn was not only reading all-too-familiar reports of acute distress in Ireland but was also deeply committed to a bitterly contested election at Cambridge. The attractions of the ancient university seats were personal prestige and inexpensiveness. Peel was the proud holder of one of Oxford's two seats, and Goulburn was no less ambitious for the "high distinction" of representing his university. He had first tested the waters – though only very gingerly – in 1822, when the death of a sitting member had necessitated a by-election. The victor had been a Tory and a "Protestant," William Bankes, who had joined another Tory and a "Catholic," Palmerston, in the Commons. Goulburn, who had decided not to stand, concluded from this result that the university had forsaken its traditional party balance in favour of a new religious equipoise.[39]

His decision to contest Cambridge in 1826 was therefore somewhat surprising, and it had far-reaching personal and political consequences. Both the sitting members supported the government, and although Palmerston was a "Catholic," he was also a long-serving junior minister and a personal friend. Further, the free-spending Bankes had made the seats less financially attractive by the precedent he had set in 1822 of paying the travel expenses of nonresident voters. His rivals had been obliged to match his generosity. Yet Goulburn doggedly persisted with his own candidacy. He was probably encouraged by evidence that "antiliberals" were now dominant at the formerly Whiggish Trinity College and surely shared the ambition of fellow "Protestants" to capture both seats. Publicly, Goulburn was careful to cast his intervention as a challenge to the unpopular Bankes and not to his friend and colleague Palmerston. Certainly, Peel carefully divided his sympathies between them. But Goulburn was able to count on Bathurst employing his "little interest" exclusively on his behalf, while Liverpool proclaimed "neutrality." Hence Goulburn's dismay when Peel warned him that the Duke of York, at the instigation of John Herries, then a secretary at the Treasury, was heavily supporting Attorney General Copley, another "Protestant," another Trinity man, another member of the government, and another of the unsuccessful candidates in 1822. Goulburn angrily complained that he had as much "claim to the support and assistance of the Government as the Attorney General," and he protested that his exile "in the most disagreeable office under Government" ought not to operate as a "disqualification" or induce it "to give assistance to others."[40]

Shortly before Christmas 1825, Goulburn travelled down to Cambridge to attend the commemoration of the Benefactors of Trinity College and thus make himself known to as many eligible voters as possible. He established committees in Cambridge and London to continue the canvassing. The four candidates now in the field were dubbed by one wag "Profligacy, Roguery, Bigotry and Folly," and as clever as Goulburn regarded this characterization, he was being stigmatized as a fool. Yet he had powerful supporters. He was described as "the idol of the Saints, a prime favourite of Simeon's, and a subscriber to missionary societies." The endorsement of Charles Simeon, who had visited Ireland in 1822 to promote evangelicalism within the church, was one to be treasured. Similarly valuable was the aid that Goulburn received from one of the "saintly" scions of the wealthy and influential Thornton family. Ironically, this evangelical connection proved to be his undoing. Fearful that Bankes would withdraw from the contest and throw his support to Goulburn, another "Saint" and his son intervened on behalf of the only candidate committed to Catholic emancipation – Palmerston. Zachary Macaulay, who three years earlier had relaunched the crusade against slavery, now undertook, with the assistance of his son Thomas, an insidious campaign to discredit Goulburn in order to encourage Bankes to remain in the field and thus inadvertently play the role of a spoiler.[41]

The elder Macaulay attacked Goulburn in a series of letters addressed to prominent Cambridge figures, such as the president of Queen's, and abstracts from them were then more widely circulated to Simeon and other evangelicals. The indictment was especially damaging in view of the university's petition to Parliament in 1823 for "the mitigation and abolition of slavery." Macaulay charged that Goulburn had permitted his 250 slaves to live in ignorance of religion, without benefit of marriage, to labour day and night without distinction of sex, and to suffer under the lash. He assailed the former under-secretary for his reluctance to speak out in Parliament against slavery and for his failure to exploit the "peculiar facilities" of his position at the Colonial Office to promote reform even in the crown colonies. The claim that Goulburn had furthered amelioration was entirely unproven, Macaulay went on. Instead, he had permitted colonies to mutilate the measure providing for registries of slaves. Here were charges so serious that one of Goulburn's canvassers approached him with a request for a statement on the treatment of his slaves, without revealing the detail or author of the accusations, perhaps because he was unaware of the extent of Macaulay's campaign. In his defence, Goulburn produced letters to prove his concern for the welfare of his labourers and to demonstrate that he had "made the greatest sacrifices of income to ensure their convenience and comfort."[42]

The coincidental revival of the slavery question in Parliament saw Goulburn still offering cautious public support to measures of amelioration. His circumspection was dictated less by the old constitutional fear of fatally alienating the colonies with assemblies than by the delicate state of West Indian affairs. "I am satisfied that slavery ought at any price to be abolished as soon as it can be done with consistency & due regard to the interests of the slaves themselves," he advised his wife, "but I have my doubts whether it can be effected without the ruin of all who have anything to do with W. India property. Come however what may it cannot & must not be resisted further than is necessary to effect it with prudence." In short, he had (if only in private) finally committed himself to gradual abolition. His position, then, was honourable but conservative.[43]

In mid-May Goulburn was presented with the full particulars of the bill of indictment that had been brought against him. The president of Queen's forwarded an abstract of Macaulay's charges, without identifying the author. Goulburn attempted to refute them by again detailing his efforts to reform the management and improve the treatment of his slaves: the equalization of the sexes; the introduction of labour-saving technologies (windmill, steam engine, and plough); measures of moral and educational improvement; the appointment of a liberal attorney; and the setting aside of an area of the estate on which slaves could grow provisions. He boasted that he had shown himself to be "perfectly prepared to make any sacrifice of income to secure the comfort of the negroes." He had also intended to employ a missionary to supervise the religious education of his slaves, but the appointment had been delayed by the onset of the sickly season, and the idea was abandoned with the collapse of his income and the assurance that his slaves were regularly attending the nearby parish church. Goulburn observed that if his people had been improperly treated, this had occurred against his orders, without his knowledge, and in spite of his surrendering of four-fifths of his income. As for his public conduct, he expressed surprise that the bill establishing slave registries was now denounced as worthless though at the time of its passage the opponents of slavery had made no effort to amend it.[44]

At the insistence of his worried advisers, who feared an erosion of support, Goulburn attended the annual meeting and dinner of the Society for Promoting Christian Knowledge. It promised to be a very dull affair, for the postprandial entertainment was "a long exposé" on the state of the society. But Bankes, who also was present in search of votes, provided an unexpected diversion. He made a complete ass of himself by jumping to his feet to boast that he had founded a branch in Cambridge, only for it quickly to become embarrassingly evident that he had confused his societies. No doubt the malicious pleasure Goulburn found in his rival's discomfiture had much to do with Bankes's attack on him as a tool of the government – that he was standing simply to divide the "Protestant" vote in order to ensure the return of Palmerston. In fact, Goulburn was still hoping to triumph. He remained in London after the dissolution of Parliament rather than making the long journey to Ireland, for he was determined not to lose the chance of the seat for "want of attention." As he told his wife, he diligently wrote to people whom he cared "nothing about but whose votes are of value." By the end of the second day's poll, however, there could be no doubt of Goulburn's defeat. He was firmly in last place. He consoled himself with the thought that he had laid the groundwork for a more successful campaign in future. Besides, he knew that he had already been returned for an Irish constituency. The government had reserved Harwich for him in the event of his defeat at Cambridge, but the primate of the Church of Ireland had called on him in London to inform him that the church, as a mark of its appreciation of his services, would return him for the city of Armagh. This had permitted him to release Harwich, thereby strengthening his claim to government consideration at some later date. Additionally, as he wrote to his wife, it was "not a little gratifying I confess to have one's endeavours to be usefully appreciated & I therefore indulge my vanity in making you aware of it."[45]

Goulburn's decision to go to the poll at Cambridge had worked to Palmerston's advantage, but this failed to prevent him from complaining of mistreatment at the hands of Liverpool and his ministerial colleagues. Convinced that he had been the target of a "Protestant" conspiracy, Palmerston relished his victory without being appeased by it. He was satisfied that he owed his re-election to the support of the Whigs, who had, he said, "behaved most handsomely to me." Although he continued to look to liberal Tories for his allies, the campaign marked an important moment in the shift of Palmerston's political allegiance. Equally, his long friendship with Goulburn had been chilled by this experience. For his part, Goulburn was busy totalling up the financial cost of the campaign. He had spent £1,500 that he could ill afford.[46]

The state of Goulburn's personal finances continued to be a source of anxiety, and his wife fretted that too much strain was being placed on shoulders that were already carrying a heavy burden of private cares and public responsibilities. She urged him to take whatever measures he considered necessary with respect to her allowances, adding supportively that her confidence in his "judgment, prudence & kindness" was "unbounded." Goulburn's brothers, on the other hand, were proving more troublesome. Edward's spirits were improving. The year 1824 had found him mired in a depression, having recently been bereaved. He was ill adapted to the solitary life of Chambers but did "not feel himself rich enough to marry a poor woman," while a rich one was no easy catch. His solution was to marry his cousin, Esther Chetwynd, a daughter of the fifth viscount, which he did in 1825. Yet when Goulburn secured for him the offer of the solicitorship of the Excise in Scotland, worth £2,000 a year, he refused to accept "exile" to Edinburgh. Meanwhile, through the good offices of Bathurst, Frederick had been appointed colonial secretary to the governor of New South Wales. He had accepted exile there only to find himself at the centre of an unpleasant controversy. He was accused of shipping female convicts to an isolated outpost to service men. Although Frederick was exonerated, the controversy merely added to Goulburn's worries.[47]

The general election did little to revive his flagging spirits. He gloomily predicted that there would be "a very blackguard set" in the next Parliament. The "anti-popery" cry had been set up in Britain but not to any great effect, as Goulburn could personally attest. From Ireland there came discouraging accounts of unprecedented priestly political intervention. The most startling return was in Waterford, where those Protestant Goliaths, the Beresfords, had been felled by a tribe of Catholic Davids. Not that Goulburn shed tears for them, despising as he did almost all the members of a family that was notorious for arrogance, intolerance, and greed. His one consolation was that his absence from Ireland had isolated him from these sectarian contests.[48]

Goulburn was followed to Ireland in mid-July 1826 by an account from Peel of the cabinet's first post-election meeting. The home secretary reported difficulties with the United States and the persistence of distress domestically. Against a backdrop of a declining revenue and rising unemployment, there was a deepening popular suspicion that "the principles of free trade seem entirely to work for the benefit of foreigners." As ever, the situation in Ireland was no better and was arguably far worse. A harassed chief secretary certainly did not relish the task that awaited him, complicated as it still was by the viceroy's constant indisposition and his meddlesome natural son. "I give Goulburn great credit for his temper," Peel wrote to the prime minister, "and the credit which he deserves also for his sense of public Duty. Nothing but the very rare combination of those qualities could make any man with a decent competence submit to such a worthless coxcomb as Mr. Johnston exercising an influence over Irish affairs."[49]

Goulburn found Ireland more bitterly divided than ever along sectarian lines, with priests triumphant and Protestants sullen. Nor was he entirely unsympathetic to the latter's complaints of the Castle's "partiality" for Catholics. After all, Orange processions continued to be suppressed under a law which the new Catholic Association successfully evaded. Adding to the ferment and heightening the likelihood of conflict were reports of priests employing pulpits as podia and organizing boycotts of Protestant merchants. As for O'Connell, Goulburn concluded that he was seeking to excite irritation and hostility "to the highest possible pitch short of actual violence" in the hope of achieving his ends by intimidation. After nearly five years of attempted conciliation of the Catholic majority, little appeared to have changed, a weary chief secretary noted. No less chronic was the troubled state of the economy, which had brought fresh misery to Dublin as unemployment and a desperate strike put thousands of angry men onto the streets. The exhaustion of the funds at the executive's disposal, coupled with the continuing inadequacy of private donations, had brought an intensification of the suffering, a worsening of the squalor, and an epidemic of disease. Typhus was abroad. "Our metropolis therefore is not either agreeable as a residence or consolatory as a specimen of prosperity of the country," Goulburn mordantly observed. The condition of the countryside gave additional cause for concern. Although the wheat crop was likely to be an excellent one, drought had ruined both flax and oats, and the barley had been seriously damaged. Goulburn could only keep his fingers crossed and hope that the recent rains would save the potatoes.[50]

Alarmed by this sombre assessment of the condition of Ireland, Peel supplied a little of the same "oil" that he had already applied to the squeaking "machine" in England. He was hopeful that two or three months would see the economy begin to gather fresh momentum, for the stocks of manufactured goods on hand were so low that industrial production seemed certain to rise soon. Determined as he was to avoid the "quackery" of "direct interference of the Government," he therefore authorized the chief secretary discreetly to spend up to £4,000 on the containment of the fever epidemic and a further £3,000 on relief for the distressed. These authorizations proved timely, for the appalling conditions in Dublin's "liberties" saw 5,000 people pour out of this area on a summer's evening early in August and raid food stores. "The disorder has now assumed a shape which requires instant and vigorous coercion," an overexcited viceroy commented. More measured in his response, Goulburn announced a "Royal" donation to the Dublin relief committee and forwarded to outlying manufacturing towns modest sums in aid of local subscriptions. Simultaneously, steps were taken to ensure increased accommodation in hospitals and the construction of temporary shelters for fever victims, while a vigorous sanitary program cleaned both houses and streets of the filth in which the disease flourished.[51]

The harvest, especially that of potatoes, remained the matter of overriding concern. Should it fail, there would be no alternative to direct government intervention to relieve the distress. Goulburn took some comfort from the early crop. It would sustain the peasantry until the late one rescued by the rains was harvested, he reported on 25 August. "Scarcity in particular districts will undoubtedly be felt," he conceded, "but there will not be that extensive famine which I in common with many others apprehended a fortnight or three weeks ago." Indeed, having noted again the excellence of the wheat crop but the dismal prospects for oats, barley, straw, and hay, he predicted that distress would be most evident in parts of Munster and Leinster, less in Ulster, and least of all in Connaught. Before the month's end, a good potato crop was safely in. Nevertheless, the Castle welcomed the cabinet's decision to open the ports of the United Kingdom to provisions in which the Irish harvest was most deficient, primarily oats, and it was further reassured by Peel's promise of additional financial aid should that become necessary.[52]

The heaviest expenditures continued to be in Dublin, where the unabated severity of the fever epidemic compelled Goulburn to dip deeper into public funds. And when his resistance to calls for the direct distribution of food to the poor saw him charged inevitably with callousness, he provided more generous assistance to the victims of typhus. "We thought it right therefore to make more ample provision for those who are absolutely sick than might on the whole appear reasonable," he explained to Peel, "in order to satisfy the public that our resistance to the plan of feeding the poor was one founded on principle not an indifference to their suffering." Private and community contributions were the proper means of affording food relief to the healthy in cases of localized distress, he continued to assert.[53]

Overlying the economic troubles were the island's sectarian animosities. Goulburn was convinced that the Catholic priesthood was now dictating not only to the "mob" but also to the gentry and magistracy. It was an analysis which served to harden, if that was possible, his opposition to emancipation. "To my mind their conduct presents a foretaste of what we may expect, when those who are their puppets (for after all the first Roman Catholics are nothing more) have all the power they desire." While he refused to be panicked by ordinary disorders or even by crimes of an "insurrectionary character" such as thefts of arms, he did fear the existence of a power that was independent of and had more popular authority than the regular administration. It could "at any moment direct against the Government a mass of poor, ignorant, unemployed, and discontented population," he warned. In response to Peel's request for an accounting of the force at his disposal, he itemized a total of 26,000 troops and armed police. These he judged adequate to maintain order so long as there remained in England a military reserve that might rapidly be shipped to Ireland in the event of a crisis.[54]

The new Parliament opened on 26 November 1826 with a Speech from the Throne that made no mention of Ireland. The essential purpose of the session, Canning explained in the Commons, was to indemnify the government for the emergency relief measures it had adopted since the dissolution. "It is not our intention at present to bring before parliament any specific measure respecting Ireland," he announced, "but that will not prevent any individual member from agitating the subject." Ambiguous as this statement was, it reaffirmed the government's uneasy neutrality on the issue of emancipation. However, among those individuals who accepted Canning's invitation to agitate was Henry Grattan. Clearly, Catholic relief would again be placed on the agenda when Parliament reassembled in February. This disagreeable prospect surely encouraged Peel to suggest to Goulburn in mid-December that the time had come to suppress the new Catholic association, sensing as he probably did O'Connell's intention to stage massive demonstrations in support of emancipation. But the home secretary received little support from the Irish executive. Wellesley and Plunket counselled against prosecution. Surprisingly, Goulburn offered the same private opinion. He considered the association no more formidable now than it had been at the beginning of the year, when on legal advice they had remained inactive; moreover, its suppression would do nothing to rein in the rampant priesthood. "They are a body more fitted for business, admirably disciplined and acting more secretly," he observed, "and whether the Association exist or not they will as I believe continue to direct Roman Catholic affairs in the Country with more mischievous effect and with equal unity of object."[55]

Goulburn arrived in London from Ireland on the evening of 9 February 1827, the only memorable event on the tiring journey being his night crossing of Thomas Telford's latest engineering masterpiece linking the island of Anglesey to the mainland. Far beneath he could see the shimmering waters of the Menai Straits, and he felt not a vibration on the suspension bridge, which had been built high enough to allow naval vessels to pass beneath it. Chilled by a bitter easterly wind, he developed a heavy and persistent cold. He was not alone in his misery;

several of the dignitaries in attendance at the recent funeral of the Duke of York had succumbed to chills, and Canning's serious and worrying illness was laid at the same bier. In Goulburn's opinion, the Duke of Clarence, now heir apparent, had behaved with characteristic "want of feeling and decency" both at and after his brother's burial. Two days after the interment he had given a dinner party and expressed a desire that his guests attend out of mourning. "These are the people that make radicals and republicans," Goulburn grumbled. "His only excuse is that he is not sane. He is not enough of the contrary however to prevent his doing mischief."[56]

One week after Goulburn's return to the capital, the prime minister was felled by a stroke from which it was soon apparent that he would never recover. Goulburn saw only the bleakest of futures beckoning for him personally and for the conservative cause that Liverpool had led. Who else possessed the authority to fend off jobbers and radicals, to prevent "wild alterations in the constitution and habits of the Country"? Had not the path to the highest office in the land been fatefully cleared for the brilliant but untrustworthy Canning? Even a king whose long-standing enmity for the Irishman was notorious had recently succumbed to his charm, wit, and shameless flattery. There remained, of course, the providential possibility that Canning's health might fail him at this moment of triumph, but in the short term it seemed much more likely that Liverpool's removal would be followed by Catholic relief. Already, some members of the government who were "liberals" on this issue were reputedly talking of turning out all the "Protestants." In these circumstances, Goulburn saw little alternative to resignation but decided to act, as always, in concert with Peel. Yet he would regret leaving office, for it had permitted him to contribute more than would otherwise have been possible to the "comforts" of his family and friends. "Independently of these considerations," he gallantly wrote to his wife in an effort to put the best face on the approaching setback, "I shall not regret having more time to enjoy your society and to attend to the education of my boys."[57]

Jane Goulburn responded tearfully to the news, disinclined as she was to leave a place where she had been happy. Nor did she expect Goulburn to understand her agitation, since he was blessed with a "serenity" of mind. He promptly apologized for having upset her. "It is one of the miseries of separation that it deprives us mutually of the power of assisting each other in moments of difficulty when our judgment fails & our feelings are too strongly excited unless corrected by mutual discussion and advice," he replied by return mail. He reminded her of how painful she had found the initial move to Dublin, so with "God's blessing" another change might yet again prove "a source of new & unexpected happiness." Finally, he stressed the attractions of a period of calm reflection after so long a "season of pleasure & incessant employment." He had held demanding and unusually arduous offices for fifteen continuous years and was undoubtedly weary if not mentally exhausted. Whether or not it was her recognition of this fact or her husband's assurances that there was little danger of an imminent breakup of the government, Jane Goulburn quickly recovered her composure.[58]

The debate on Catholic relief was reopened on 5 March 1827 by Sir Francis Burdett, but the "Catholics" were defeated by a majority of four after two long nights of debate. Goulburn had prepared for the battle by engaging in a fruitless search for something new to say on this old question. He complained that speaking had left him hoarse, with both a sore throat and a sore chest. The only memorable moment in the debate was a sharp collision between Plunket and Peel, of which the former complained privately to an unsympathetic Goulburn. Such personal antagonisms notwithstanding, Goulburn convinced himself that the government ought somehow to be kept together. However, he doubted that the principles of both parties – those of the "Catholic" Tories led by Canning and those of the most determined "Protestants" such as Peel and himself – could "be brought to coincide on some important points." It was probably the strain of so many years of hard labour, together with the tension of this extended period of crisis and uncertainty, not to mention the gnawing fear of losing his salary, that caused the intestinal disorder that plagued him for weeks. According to the doctors, he was suffering from a "foulness of the bowels which irritates the stomach and makes it refuse to do its duties properly."[59]

When the king finally commissioned Canning to form a government, the principal "Protestants," led by Peel and Wellington but including Goulburn, took their leave despite assurances that the existing policy of neutrality on emancipation would continue. The object of the "Parti Conservateurs" was to rescue the crown "by Moderation, by Consistency, by Firmness, & Good Temper" from the mischief with which it was threatened, Wellington privately observed. In his opinion, Canning did not "possess one particle of any of these qualities." Yet in quitting office largely because of their profound attachment to the Anglican constitution and their distrust of the new prime minister, these "Protestants" were leaving the intensely ambitious Canning with few options. He recruited a number of Whigs who expected to achieve Catholic emancipation, and thus initiated something of a political realignment. That this was slow to develop was partly because of the hostility with which many of the younger Whigs regarded Canning, and partly because of an uneasy reunification of the Tories following Canning's premature death. However, the ranks of the party had been disrupted, and for this Wellington and Peel bore a large portion of the responsibility. They were to divide it further by subsequently effecting, ironically, the very measure which their resignations now ostensibly protested. And Goulburn, despite his long-held belief "that we should all keep together," dutifully followed the two men to whom he looked for leadership on their tortuous path.[60]

His more than five arduous years in Ireland had burnished Goulburn's reputation as an excellent man of business – at least among his conservative associates. He had won golden opinions for soldiering on in the company of an indecisive, indolent viceroy with a meddlesome natural son, and an attorney general who was preoccupied with the protection of his "liberal" reputation. Further, Goulburn had restored efficiency to the Irish administration without any sacrifice of its integrity. In the management of parliamentary business – which, in the virtual absence of communications from Wellesley, was left almost entirely to his discretion – Goulburn had necessarily employed the patronage at his disposal. Yet there were larger considerations at work here than that of simplifying his life in the House. "I may say that there is still enough of difficulty in managing the Country Gentlemen of England," he reported to the viceroy in 1822, "to make us desirous of consulting the best means of securing the support of the Irish Gentlemen in case of need." Nevertheless, he upheld basic standards of competence in important patronage appointments, such as assistant barristerships, and scornfully rejected Plunket's example of filling practically every valuable office within his grasp with family and friends. "I determined never to gratify any private wish of my own by the smallest Irish appointment," he commented to Peel. "There is nothing half so disgusting as the personal monopoly of honours and offices by those to whom the distribution of them is entrusted." He honoured the gentleman's code, "which placed duty before self-advancement."[61]

As a conservative, Goulburn was convinced that the suppression of disorders must precede any redress of grievances. This did not prevent him, however, from piloting through Parliament a number of important reforms. His police and tithe bills were constructive measures. His response to Irish distress, once he was convinced of its extent and severity, had been decisive if not compassionate. Pragmatic as he had shown himself to be, even to the extent of proposing a form of intervention that was too far-reaching for Peel's taste, he had not weakened in his resolve to resist the state's permanent acceptance of a responsibility to assist the island's legions of poor. The cost would have been enormous. He had given effect to Wellesley's desire to lessen sectarian bitterness by providing more even-handed local justice and by reining in the provocative Orangemen. Yet he had also contributed to the aggravation of sectarian feelings. His success in reviving Protestant confidence in the executive, his support of a discreet proselytism through education, his profound distrust of the Catholic clergy, and his unflinching resistance to Catholic emancipation had been ill calculated to win the confidence of the overwhelming majority of the Irish people.

CHAPTER SEVEN

Chancellor of the Exchequer

Tragedy and farce were the leading productions of the political stage during the autumn of 1827. Canning's death within weeks of his finally being cast in the starring role saw Goulburn's old friend Frederick Robinson, now Lord Goderich, nervously enter the spotlight. While Goderich's sympathy with Catholic emancipation had seen him join Canning's ministry, he was ill equipped to hold together the fractious coalition of Tories and Whigs. "I can perfectly understand fourteen persons of very moderate abilities, carrying on a government provided they have one common feeling and were bound by attachments or habits to each other," one well-placed observer commented, "but here is not the case; what one wishes the other dislikes, what one proposes the other objects to, and no business whatever is doing in any department." A struggle over the chancellorship of the exchequer, an attempt by the Whigs to increase their representation in cabinet, and a dispute over the chairmanship of a select committee on finance eventually drained Goderich's small reservoir of self-confidence. A tremulous, weeping figure, he fled the stage in December.[1]

Goulburn, watching his old friend's trials with wry amusement, heard welcome whispers that the king, tiring of the farce, would soon send for Wellington and Peel. This summons was not issued until early in the New Year, when the duke was escorted to Windsor by the lord chancellor, Lord Lyndhurst. Following a royal pantomime on the recent ministerial crisis, in which the old trooper paraded his thespian skills, Wellington loyally accepted this new commission. His first call for assistance went out to the indispensable Peel, but an invitation was also dispatched in quick order to Goulburn at Betchworth. Arriving in the capital on the evening of 10 January 1828, Goulburn called immediately at Peel's home, where he received instructions to go on to Apsley House. There he found Wellington, Peel, and Lyndhurst.

They had kept a portion of their meal hot for him, and as soon as he was warmed and filled they got down to the task at hand. Goulburn's advice echoed Peel's. He urged Wellington "to bury animosities" and endeavour to reunite all those who had acted together under Liverpool. In short, abandon any thought of forming a "Protestant" administration, for there were not enough men of experience and ability in the Commons to staff it. Wellington decided to do as they suggested, but before setting off to recruit the Canningites, he offered Goulburn a seat in the cabinet. He did not specify a portfolio. "I presume that I shall have an office of hard work at all events," Goulburn reported to his wife, "in which if I can make myself useful I shall be satisfied."[2]

Goulburn placed his political association with Wellington alongside that with Peel as the most important of his life. They had become acquainted soon after he first entered Parliament, and like so many other young men of his generation Goulburn not only stood in awe of the soldier who had vanquished Bonaparte but was fascinated by his personality. "There is something so frank and open in his manner and so straightforward in his modes of thinking," he explained, "that it is impossible not to be captivated with him." He was understandably flattered by the great man's unfailing civility during their service together in the Liverpool administration. As for Goulburn's qualities, they were those highly valued by a soldier long used to issuing orders: competence, energy, loyalty, deference, and obedience. Finally, the two men had an ideological affinity. They both saw themselves as defenders of the constitution, preservers of social stability, and promoters of the true happiness of the people. When Wellington avowed his determination to maintain "the prerogatives of the Crown, the rights and privileges of the Church and its union with the State," he held aloft a standard under which Goulburn was ever ready to enlist.[3]

The duke soon experienced the frustrations of political command. He encountered a cavilling monarch, surly Ultra-Tories disillusioned by his moderation, and skittish Canningites. The last now looked to William Huskisson for leadership, and on 11 January he indicated his willingness to enter the cabinet along with several friends. No doubt it was with an eye to their enlistment that Wellington mentioned to the king the very next day his intention to name Goulburn chancellor of the exchequer. For any thought of reappointing John Herries, who had been Goderich's chancellor, was quickly banished. The bitter dispute in which he and Huskisson had then engaged had created too deep a reservoir of ill-feeling for him to be restored to the office. Instead, he received the Mint. Hence Wellington's fury when Huskisson and his three friends – Dudley, Palmerston, and Grant – suddenly presented him with a list of conditions that included the exclusion of

Herries from the Exchequer. Also, they demanded the honouring of Canning's promise of a select committee on finance and the appointment to it of Lord Althorp. The duke resented this posturing, having already assured Huskisson that Herries would not be returning to the Exchequer. Nor did he consider Althorp's membership of the finance committee an appropriate subject "of any preliminary discussion in the formation of our Government," and not least because he was the Whig leader in the Commons and had been at the centre of the conflict between Herries and Huskisson. Wellington was further incensed by the subsequent demands of this faction, growing as they did out of Goulburn's appointment to the Exchequer.[4]

"I recollect that (as far as we know) the four places which among them dispose of the whole of the domestic patronage of the Country are to be held by decided Anti-Catholics," Charles Grant reminded Huskisson on 17 January. "I mean the Chancellorship [Lyndhurst], the Premiership, the Home Secretaryship [Peel], and the Chancellorship of the Exchequer." An assurance on the subject of patronage was all the more necessary in view of Goulburn's nomination, Palmerston added. They were equally insistent that the viceroy and chief secretary of Ireland should practise neutrality on Catholic emancipation. At the end of the day the four of them entered the cabinet, even retaining their former high offices; Althorp was made a member of the finance committee, and the "Catholic" pairing of Lord Anglesey and William Lamb continued in place in Ireland. Yet the price of success was high. Wellington already regretted their inclusion in his government, for which mistake he blamed Peel: the home secretary had insisted on being surrounded by "speakers" in the Commons, the duke complained privately. Not surprisingly, there was a conspicuous lack of camaraderie among the ministers who assembled at the Royal Lodge, Windsor, on 22 January, to kiss hands and receive their seals of office.[5]

From humble medieval origins, the office of chancellor had grown slowly but steadily in importance with the emergence of the Treasury as the most powerful department of government whose "First Lord" was the prime minister. By the early nineteenth century, "the First Lord of the Treasury and the Chancellor of the Exchequer [had] it in charge to provide for the maintenance and due distribution of the public revenue, and for the integrity of all those sources of navigation, commerce, manufacture, internal trade and industry, from which such revenue must be derived; and, finally, (in cooperation with other Boards appointed for this special purpose) they [had] to provide for the naval and military defence of the empire, and the maintenance of the docks, arsenals, ordnance etc. in all the means and material of future operation." Of course, the chancellor was very much the second fiddle to the first lord. However, whenever the prime minister was a member of the House of Lords, the chancellor's prestige grew, since he was the principal financial spokesman in the Commons.[6]

Under the strains of the American and then French wars, the Treasury had been one of the major departments reorganized in an effort to streamline business and promote administrative and tax-gathering efficiency. Among other changes, the position of assistant secretary was created. The first appointee, George Harrison, transformed the position in the course of two decades from little more than a superior clerkship "to that of confidential adviser to the prime minister with a wide administrative and even political discretion." Further, he worked assiduously to extend Treasury influence over other departments in matters of expenditure and audit. Yet by the time Goulburn entered the Exchequer in 1828, the department was characterized by low morale and inefficiency. Because there were only four chief clerks to handle six divisions, there had been a blurring of roles and a shirking of individual responsibility. A lack of attention to the education of the staff meant that junior members were usually ill prepared for promotion to senior positions. These and other problems, together with a program of remedial measures, had been carefully detailed in a report drafted by one of the junior staff members, but it is unlikely that Goulburn ever saw it. In any event, he focused on the nation's fiscal problems rather than on the administrative deficiencies of his new department.[7]

Although Britain was in the process of establishing a commercial and industrial global supremacy, this satisfying and rewarding development commanded less attention than her mountainous debt. A generation of warfare had seen the national debt more than triple, until by 1815 it stood at the staggering sum of approximately £800 million. A redemption scheme, the Sinking Fund, had been inherited from William Pitt. Annual surpluses were to be applied to the purchase of government bonds, which were to be held and the interest they earned employed to make further purchases. Compound interest would thus painlessly pay down the debt. Whatever its virtues during peacetime, this scheme had proven another liability during the long French wars. Governments had borrowed in order to meet their obligations to debt redemption. However myopic this course, the idolized Pitt's authorship of the fund long discouraged debate of its wisdom. Meanwhile, there was an ongoing discussion on how best to strengthen the economy, relieve distress, and reduce the immense burden of debt in order to lighten the weight of taxation. For many participants, the writings of Adam Smith provided inspiration. These had been established as Tory doctrine by Pitt and then elevated to the touchstone of economic orthodoxy. Three separate editions of Smith's *Wealth of Nations* between 1805 and 1814 were testament to this fact.[8]

Balanced budgets and retrenchment were two of the economic orthodoxies of those determined "to restore the confidence of investors and other property-holders in the credit system and hence in the credibility of government." The resumption of specie payments was their currency equivalent. Payments had been suspended in 1797 to prevent the Bank of England's bullion reserves from being bled completely away, but in 1819 a Commons committee chaired by the young Robert Peel had recommended their resumption. Perhaps the members who once again embraced the gold standard were "seduced by its moral force as a symbol of truth and stability, of immutability and impartiality," but many advocates of resumption were motivated by the practical belief that it would inhibit the speculation which they held responsible for depressions. One economist credited with influencing this decision was David Ricardo. He and his followers in the Political Economy Club also argued that prosperity depended on the transfer of resources to manufacturing. But, of course, observant ministers did not require instruction in theory to recognize the progressive shift in the economy from agriculture to manufacturing, and the relationship of foreign trade to prosperity. However, the "re-adoption of the gold standard, the rigorous discipline exercised over governmental expenditure and even the initial moves towards free trade" have also been identified with the emergence of a gentlemanly capitalist élite, who illustrated Britain's "status as an international service centre" rather than "her position as the world's workshop."[9]

Others, among them many liberal Tories, including members of the Alfred Club, appear to have travelled a parallel path but with their eyes cast heavenward. Few of them understood the abstruse arguments of Ricardo. Their commitment to liberalized trade was rooted in evangelicalism, as they sought to employ "competition as a means to education rather than to growth." Not that they could ignore growth. Parliament's action, in 1816, of refusing to renew the property tax, thereby compelling the government to begin in earnest the demobilization of the "military-fiscal state," meant that more than 70 per cent of revenues were again drawn from indirect taxation. Consequently, the expansion of trade and increases in consumption were of immediate and material significance, as well as of long-term and moral significance. Led by Frederick Robinson during the early 1820s, the Liverpool ministry had cautiously sought to encourage both by relaxing the Navigation Laws and lowering tariffs. Unfortunately, the implied promise of greater prosperity and stability had not immediately been honoured. Instead, a banking crisis in 1825 had almost precipitated a general disaster.[10]

Critics of the liberal trade policies were quick to blame them for a deepening crisis, but the prime minister took aim instead at the country banks. They were charged with irresponsibility for issuing excessive amounts of small notes, and with a structural weakness arising out of the restricted nature of their private partnerships. Legislation was introduced to restrict and ultimately to eliminate the circulation of small notes, at least in England and Wales. The Bank of England's privileges were also trimmed. Its monopoly of joint-stock banking was limited to a radius of 65 miles from the capital, though the directors did cautiously accept an invitation to establish provincial branches. These would facilitate the circulation of the bank's notes, give the bank greater control over the entire paper circulation, and help protect it from the competition of the new and presumably larger provincial joint-stock banking companies.[11]

The Corn Laws were another pressing concern and a dangerous political problem. Since 1815, they had provided farmers with a good measure of protection in the hope of creating domestic self-sufficiency. However, at a time of declining employment and thus declining wages, popular demands for a lowering of the price of bread grew ever more insistent, and criticism of the laws as an example of the selfish political power of the landed interest became ever more strident. In the spring of 1827, Huskisson had sought to move the nation gently towards freer trade in corn. Importations of foreign corn were no longer to be prohibited. Instead, a new and moderate pivot price was to be set, beneath and above which a sliding scale of duties would come into play. As the price fell, so the duty was to rise, and vice versa. The bill had been derailed in the Lords by Wellington, who had successfully moved an amendment to prevent the release of bonded corn until the average domestic price was significantly higher than the pivot. The frustrated Liverpool government abandoned the measure, accepting a temporary arrangement on the understanding that a permanent one would be introduced in the next session. As a result, a corn bill was one of the first items on the agenda of the Wellington administration.[12]

Committed to tackling this sensitive problem and to the final implementation of the banking reforms, the new cabinet was also confronted in 1828 by the mountain of debt and the farce of the Sinking Fund. The sensible decision in 1819 to apply only genuine surpluses to its redemption had subsequently been vitiated as a result of Robinson's ambitious scheme to allocate annually £5 million to the fund. The government's income, fluctuating sharply as it did with the growth and contractions of trade and consumption, could never produce the permanent surpluses on which the success of this policy hinged. Consequently, the Treasury had continued to borrow to pay down the debt. The new chancellor did not inspire confidence as the man to master these complex problems. Goulburn's apparent unfamiliarity with economic and financial matters was one reason for the incredulity with which the announcement of his appointment was greeted; he was mocked for not "knowing much more than that two and two make four." The gossip was that Huskisson had engineered his selection in order to ensure his own control of economic policy. Even Jane Goulburn feared that this office was one of "such difficulty and responsibility" that her husband would be unable "to fulfill the duties of it, with ease and satisfaction to himself." She believed him the equal of any of his competitors for the position but doubted whether it was within the power of anyone "to go on comfortably in it."[13]

Goulburn was not the first – nor was he to be the last – chancellor to enter the Exchequer lacking a reputation as an economist. His intellectual preparation for this office was probably confined to a reading of Adam Smith, a study of the career of the younger Pitt, and membership of the Alfred Club. But his own brand of liberal Toryism was more deeply rooted in his evangelicalism. He accepted as inevitable if not providential the economy's cyclical turns. "It seemed to be the rule of the affairs of mankind," he observed, "that blessings should not be showered down, without a corresponding visitation of depression." Consequently, he laid much emphasis on "patient forbearance." He was keen eventually "to make an experiment of reducing taxation on some articles ... with a view to an ultimate increase of the consumption, and a future increase of revenue," but this was always qualified by his horror of deficit financing and his determination to lessen the debt load. No person holding this office ought "lightly to hazard a large amount of duties, which had been long continued, and was easily enforced and collected." The preservation of the tax base, retrenchment, and the promotion of the minimal state were all instruments of the state's creditworthiness. "In relieving the burthens of the people," he cautioned members of Parliament, they "ought not to forgo the greater advantage of sustaining public credit, and of supporting the future energies of the country." He viewed the resumption of specie payments in the same light.[14]

Goulburn was a bullionist, and one who briefly dallied with bimetallism. He rejected as "the greatest folly" the "unlimited circulation" of paper notes alongside the gold payments resumed almost a decade earlier. Was there any man, he asked rhetorically on one occasion, "who looking to general principles, and taking the result of experience and history, could doubt that a metallic circulation was essentially the interest of the country?" But he disclaimed, in the best liberal Tory tradition, adherence to any particular economic theory. He proclaimed his attachment to "expediency," with its echoes of Burke, which he was quick to define not as some immediate transitory advantage but as a policy of a "higher character," one that looked to "what had happened, and consulted what was likely to come hereafter." In short, he was avowing a "pragmatism" that made him an heir of Pitt as well as Burke, and in Ireland he had practised what he now preached. Strong as his attachment was to the minimal state and the personal responsibility of the poor, he had bent before the force of that island's peculiar predicament. But he had not changed his view that public expenditures could never solve the problem of chronic unemployment. Whatever the state spent on relief had been drained from the reservoir of potential private investment.[15]

Goulburn's Christian economics probably played little part in Wellington's selection of him for the Exchequer. The duke was surely more impressed with the depth of Goulburn's administrative experience and his abundant good sense. Also, Wellington recognized that he possessed "the evolving twin criteria of probity and efficiency." They were founded in turn in the evangelical's "ideals of œconomy, frugality, professionalism, and financial rectitude." Moreover, the new chancellor was promptly enrolled in a crammer course on the arcane details of public finance as a member of the agreed select committee. Not that either he or his colleagues required additional tutoring in "the absolute necessity of reducing expenditures." The time had come, Peel announced as leader in the Commons, to examine the nation's accounts "fully and fearlessly." There was some surprise, however, when he announced the membership of the committee. The ministerial representation was initially confined to Goulburn, Herries, and Vesey Fitzgerald. Huskisson had declined to serve. Under some pressure in the House he relented. The nomination of Sir Henry Parnell to the chair, and the representation of the several shades of political opinion, won general approval. But the committee made such slow progress that in mid-May Goulburn reversed his earlier decision to postpone discussion of the estimates until it reported. He successfully steered fifty-one estimates through the House in a single evening, which was no mean achievement and reflected his growing assurance as a manager if not as a debater. Meanwhile, impatient members increasingly laid the blame for the delay at the door of Parnell's pedantry in "thinking of nothing but political economics, and of them very confusedly." More serious, because it was shared by Wellington, was the criticism that the committee had lost sight of its purpose. Instead of inquiring into alleged abuses and extravagance, it was accused of seeking to arrogate "the discretion and power of the executive Government."[16]

After more than three months of investigation and several weeks of wrangling, the committee finally issued four reports. These offered a qualified endorsement of the "experiment" of reducing duties in order to stimulate trade and consumption, and set in train the introduction of a more modern system of accounting in government departments. But the principal recommendations were to be found in the second report, released in mid-June. Here was the gospel of retrenchment. Painful "economical reform" was described as "absolutely indispensable" if the nation's finances were ever to be righted. Similarly, there was a rousing appeal for greater Treasury control of all departmental expenditures. This was astutely framed less as an innovation than as a return to an "old and constitutional" practice, which misguidedly had been "set aside." And to ensure the faithful enforcement of essential reforms, the Commons was summoned to hold "the Treasury responsible for every act of expenditure in each Department." These "first authoritative parliamentary demands for joint financial control by a responsible Treasury and a watchful House of Commons" proved to be "landmarks of the first importance."[17]

There was one other significant service performed by the committee. The absurdity of borrowing to pay down debt was fully documented in its fourth report. Robinson's annual fixed appropriation of £5 million for debt reduction clearly had to be abandoned. Yet Goulburn was anxious to have some specific sum applied to this purpose, if only to ensure that Parliament would continue to support a level of taxation that was at least sufficient to produce an annual operating surplus. His proposal was narrowly defeated, as was another moved by Huskisson that would have had much the same effect. Instead, the committee agreed to apply to debt reduction any actual surplus. Nevertheless, Goulburn and his colleagues did rescue something by calling for a planned annual surplus of at least £3 million.[18]

Even as the finance committee was grappling with "economical reform," the Wellington administration was wrestling with the issue of cohesiveness. The duke was ill suited to the leadership of a government, as he soon came to recognize. His austere personality, explosive temper, evident impatience with those whose performance he found wanting, and "extraordinary self-centredness," which often manifested itself as an astonishing insensitivity, were serious liabilities in the political world, where officers no longer jumped at his command. Instead of unquestioning obedience, he immediately faced a cabinet revolt, in which even the hero-worshipping Goulburn joined. For Wellington wished to retain command of the army on succeeding to the premiership. Constitutional proprieties aside, the cabinet realized the danger of providing the opposition with additional ammunition for the charge that the administration was infected with a spirit of militarism. Frustrated in this desire, an irritated prime minister was especially irked by the clannishness and arrogance of the Canningites. Their boast that they had not joined a Tory government but that the Tories had effectively joined theirs sat ill with him. Moreover, his public denials that he had conceded control of vital areas of policy to them merely advertised the fact that "these matters are not distinctly understood and settled as they ought to be for the security of the new Government."[19]

Disagreements soon surfaced. The Canningites struggled to vindicate their dead hero's Balkans policy, even though it remained anathema to Wellington. The cabinet cut a poor figure in its shuffling response to a Whig proposal to remove permanently the restrictions of the Test and Corporation Acts, under which Protestant dissenters technically laboured. As a practical matter, they were already free of them. It was on these grounds, and because they feared that permanent as opposed to annual relief would injure if not undermine the position of the established church and further the cause of Catholic emancipation, that cabinet "Protestants" such as Goulburn opposed the repeal of the Test and Corporation Acts. Huskisson, on the other hand, like Canning before him, feared that the conciliation of Protestant dissenters might prejudice the cause of Catholic relief. But when the cabinet resolved to resist, he and others then insisted on the right to distinguish their liberal opposition from that of their "Protestant" colleagues. However, a Commons vote demonstrated that this was a concession whose time had come. Huskisson and a majority of the cabinet then opted for acquiescence. Wellington and Bathurst alone remained opposed, Peel affected indifference, and poor Goulburn uncomfortably straddled the fence. After all, they had now abandoned the fundamental principle of "the establishment's legal and political superiority over the non conformists," while the Whigs had clearly sponsored the measure in the hope of promoting Catholic emancipation. Although the government sought to cover its retreat by requiring emancipated dissenters to disclaim any intent to injure or subvert the established church, this requirement was widely judged to be no more than face-saving nonsense.[20]

The cabinet disarray did not inspire public confidence. In this context, Wellington was in no mood to give way to the Canningites on the new Corn Law. The battle lines were quickly drawn. Grant and Huskisson revived the 1827 proposal, only for Wellington to demand a more protective law and the incorporation of his earlier warehousing amendment. There followed an extended cabinet struggle and crisis. When a majority of ministers, among them Peel and Goulburn, at last accepted a compromise proposed by Huskisson but amended to make it more palatable to the duke, who finally gave way, Charles Grant suddenly balked at the settlement. With the president of the Board of Trade absenting himself from cabinet meetings and with Huskisson indicating that he would be compelled to resign if Grant quit his office, Goulburn struggled to clarify the issues by drafting resolutions to serve as the basis of further discussion. He it was whom the duke commissioned to elicit from Grant whether or not he intended to introduce the legislation. Grant's last-minute capitulation – and he was under heavy pressure from his friends to be reasonable – saved the situation only temporarily. Wellington was plainly angered by this squabble, which had done nothing to repair his government's tattered reputation. His desire to be rid of the Canningites "or to break up their union" was hardening into a resolve.[21]

In launching the Corn Law debate on 31 March, Grant further fanned the flames of Wellington's dangerous temper. His peroration amounted to "a studied panegyric" to Canning's memory, which also infuriated the Ultra-Tories, who were still sore over their lack of representation in the administration. There followed a peculiarly ill-tempered cabinet dinner, during which too much wine was consumed, though Goulburn was a sober exception, having long since forsaken intoxicating beverages. Nor did the compromise Corn Law prove successful. Continued protection failed to guard the farmer against himself and a bountiful nature, while abrupt rather than gradual changes to the sliding scale of duties merely encouraged corn merchants to speculate by delaying the release of foreign supplies onto the market. In August an uneasy Peel sought information from Goulburn on the state of the crop, explaining that if a poor harvest were to bring an "extremely high" price, it would "be of importance to shew that the attention of the Government was at an early period called to this subject." The reply served as a reminder of the inexact and informal information on which ministers frequently operated. "It was only yesterday week," Goulburn revealed on 20 August 1828, "that I learnt from the greatest corn dealer in London that there was then no reason to apprehend a deficiency."[22]

Long before Peel's worries about the harvest, Wellington had rid himself of the troublesome Canningites. The decisive issue proved to be political reform. The proposed disfranchisement of two corrupt boroughs, Penryn and East Retford, would free four parliamentary seats for redistribution. The Canningites saw this as an opportunity to correct the "great scandal" of the lack of representation of the large industrial towns, whereas the duke and his more conservative ministers wished to transfer the seats to the neighbouring agricultural interest. Peel's obvious compromise proposal, a division of the spoils, brought him into conflict with Huskisson on which pair of seats to award to a large urban centre. Moreover, Huskisson had committed himself in the Commons to support a transfer to a "great town" if only one of the boroughs was ultimately disfranchised. With the Penryn case still before the Lords, Peel went ahead in the Commons with what he understood to be the cabinet's decision – to transfer East Retford's two seats to the agricultural interest. Huskisson, taunted with his earlier statement and smarting from Lady Canning's public accusation that he had betrayed her husband's memory, affected to believe that the cabinet had left the question an "open" one, and he voted against the measure. He was joined by Palmerston, the only other senior Canningite present. Peel, having been somewhat embarrassed during the debate by the precocious Edward Stanley, was furious. In the words of one observer, "Huskisson ought to have avoided an open abandonment of the leader."[23]

Acknowledging a breach of etiquette if not of faith, Huskisson submitted his resignation. He intended it merely as a formality and fully expected to remain in office, oblivious as he was to Wellington's profound dislike of a group who "all entertained an erroneous and exaggerated view of their own consequence" and whose departure would be greeted with rejoicing by many other Tories, who regarded them as "unprincipled and assertive jobbers." Furthermore, Peel now seemed willing "to try the House of Commons by himself." The duke therefore allowed the Canningites to depart. They were accompanied by William Lamb, the chief secretary for Ireland, and several junior ministers.[24]

Goulburn was at the centre of the proposed reconstruction of the government. The king suggesteded that Goulburn replace Huskisson at the Colonial Office and be succeeded at the Exchequer by Herries. The same arrangement also occurred to Lord Ellenborough, who hoped to fill the vacant chair at the Foreign Office. The Colonial Office "is one of great labour and importance, and there are many questions now pending which require much consideration," he noted, and Goulburn certainly knew "the business." But Wellington saw two insuperable obstacles to this change. First, it would place Goulburn in charge of colonial affairs "at the moment when there are several questions depending in Parliament respecting slavery, he being a proprietor of the West Indies." Second, to remove him from the Commons while he sought re-election "would be very inconvenient, if not impracticable." So Goulburn and Herries both remained where they were.[25]

Wellington promoted one of his Peninsular War veterans, Sir George Murray, to the Colonial Office. Another, Henry Hardinge, replaced Palmerston. The appointments served merely to bolster the opposition's charges of "military government." Aberdeen secured the Foreign

Office, while Ellenborough was subsequently, though only partially, appeased by being given the Board of Control. The highly regarded if inexperienced Lord Francis Leveson Gower, one of the minor Canning-ites, eventually withdrew his resignation and went to Ireland as chief secretary. Intended as a sop to the liberal viceroy, Lord Anglesey, and as a signal that a more rigidly "Protestant" administration had not been formed, the change seemed to offer little immediate prospect of a set-tlement of Catholic grievances. Although Wellington protested that he truly desired to find a solution, he "confessed he did not see daylight." Ironically, the cabinet changes forced the issue. The promotion of Ve-sey Fitzgerald to the presidency of the Board of Trade obliged this pop-ular landlord and political "Catholic" to return to County Clare to seek re-election. Unexpectedly, he was challenged by the charismatic Daniel O'Connell. The news created a "sensation" in London, for the exclu-sion of Roman Catholics from Parliament now seemed certain to be contested in a most direct and personal fashion.[26]

To the rumble of distant thunder warning of the gathering storm in western Ireland, Goulburn prepared and presented his first budget. He had advised his colleagues in April of the promising signs of eco-nomic recovery, as revenues ran far ahead of those for the previous year. Nevertheless, there were good reasons for caution. Industry was pervaded by "a general atmosphere of disappointment, unrelieved by the promise of rising prices and profits." A downward trend in prices, and severe competition, were matched by a substantial decline in the real value of exports. Investment also was falling, particularly overseas, and its dramatic slowing at home was all too evident in the organiza-tion of fewer railways and joint-stock ventures. Shipping was suffering, and shipowners were agitating for the restoration of the protection they had lost as a result of trade liberalization. The iron and coal in-dustries were both "relatively depressed." In brief, the recovery that had generated buoyant revenues in April soon had all the appearance of a false dawn.[27]

Concern for the condition of the economy was heightened by the looming deadline when small notes were to be withdrawn from circula-tion in England and Wales. A sudden and substantial decrease in the quantity of money in circulation, and thus a corresponding rise in its value, threatened farmers with lower corn prices and a more onerous burden of debt, while wage earners would not escape harm either. Fear-ful of worsening distress, some parliamentary economists argued for the continued circulation of the small notes. An alternative, which both the prime minister and the chancellor considered, was a compensatory coinage of silver. This the Bank of England foiled. The directors sus-pected another raid on the bank's privileges, even a conspiracy to convert the Royal Mint into a rival national bank. They therefore expressed all too unambiguously the opinion that there was already "sufficient coin in the country." Although sceptical of this response, Wellington was not inclined to lock horns with the bank. So when Goulburn rose in the Commons on 3 June to propose legislation to prevent the small notes that would continue to circulate in Scotland from flowing across the border, he had little alternative but to offer reassurance that the withdrawal of the notes elsewhere in Britain would not be disruptive. This he did by minimizing the total amount in small notes that would be affected and by pointing to a loophole in the law that would permit some notes still to circulate, thereby producing a gradual if not imperceptible cancellation. Moreover, he insisted that there were sufficient supplies of gold to replace the slowly disappearing small notes. A measure of his success was the brushing aside of a Whig motion to delay action.[28]

Goulburn presented a conservative and cautious budget on 11 July 1828. Both he and the prime minister were determined to operate with a healthy surplus in order to cover any "failure of particular branches of revenue" or errors in the estimates. Tax reductions would win an easy popularity, but such a policy often failed to consider "the ultimate benefits that might be derived from pursuing a course which involved some present sacrifice." The first task was to deal with the national debt. Forecasting a sharp rise in the surplus, to over £3 million, Goulburn announced that it would be applied to the Sinking Fund. In short, he was effectively implementing the strategy which the finance committee had declined to recommend. With a sharp eye to possible counterattacks, he dwelt on the administration's zeal for retrenchment and put the total savings from all sources at £1 million. He affected optimism with respect to the general health of the economy, citing the continuing growth in the quantity of exports without discussing their value. Productivity gains were already reducing manufacturing costs and thus cutting prices. He seized on the buoyancy of excise revenues as proof that consumption was expanding and thus that the comforts of the "lower classes" were improving. The productiveness of assessed taxes offered the same reassurance with respect to the rich, he noted. Evidently, there was no pressing need to reduce either duties or taxes.[29]

The opposition's praise of the "fairness" of Goulburn's financial statement did not inhibit criticism of his debt fixation. Parnell naturally pointed out the conflict with the report of the finance committee he had chaired, but the crux of his argument was that the taxes "will do a great deal more harm than this Sinking fund will do good." Any surplus of revenue "ought to be applied in reducing those taxes which fell on industry," he asserted. "Every thing depends on the progress of Industry and the accumulation of new wealth." Here was a fundamental disagreement over policy between a theoretical political economist and a pragmatic evangelical. Helpfully, the independent and increasingly influential *Times* praised Goulburn's abandonment of the Sinking Fund in its "old delusive form" and his application of a genuine surplus, "the only real Sinking Fund," to debt redemption.[30]

Goulburn enjoyed less success in his efforts to cut the cost of pensions by reviving, as the finance committee had proposed, a superannuation scheme funded by deductions from the salaries of public servants. The intent was to promote administrative efficiency and economy by making "officeholders more effective servants of the state and less obviously parasitic on the public." Hundreds of government clerks set up an effective opposition to his legislation. They claimed that it would amount to a "breach of compact," that it would fall unfairly on the shrunken staff of the civil administration and would amount to a salary reduction at a time when their additional labour merited an increase. Meanwhile, in the House, members objected to the scheme's retroactivity. In withdrawing the legislation, which he did with evident reluctance, Goulburn repeated the necessity to make savings in this area. Hence his decision the following year partially to effect his ends by decree. A Treasury minute was issued that was prospective, not retroactive. From the beginning of August 1829, all persons entering that department were to be informed that a deduction for superannuation would be made from their salaries and emoluments.[31]

The session had been a successful one for the chancellor, but at its close the king objected to two of the paragraphs in the speech his ministers had drafted for the dissolution ceremony, both of which touched on Goulburn's demesne. The Commons ought not to be thanked for the finance committee, the monarch complained, nor should the crown commit itself to additional reductions in expenditure. The first objection was accepted, for the Duke of Wellington shared the monarch's hostility towards the committee, but the second objection was not approved. The struggle to retrench went on throughout the autumn. Wellington raised the possibility of initiating negotiations for renewals of the charters of the East India Company and the Bank of England. His incentive was financial. The transfer of Ceylon to the company would save the public more than £100,000 a year, he calculated, and a like sum might be extracted in one way or another from the bank for an extension of its privileges. "It seems to me he is sacrificing future advantage to present profit, and all to make a good financial show next year," one cabinet member tartly observed. But it was Peel who dampened the duke's enthusiasm. He disputed the wisdom of tackling both charters simultaneously. Then, with the April deadline fast approaching for the replacement of small notes by coin, he impressed on Goulburn the desirability of a further postponement of discussions with the bank. "The subject will require very mature consideration," he cautioned.[32]

Goulburn continued the search for other savings. He challenged the decision to build a new Guards' barracks in the capital, only to discover that Wellington was committed to it. He wound up a commission on the revenue. He cast an economizing eye over the colonies, delaying loans and challenging expensive defence expenditures. Here again the prime minister occasionally frustrated him. "Why is all our economy to be applied to the means of defence of the Country which are in some instances null, and in all deficient," the querulous old soldier asked, "and never to the Civil, political, Religious and financial establishments which are known to be enormous?"[33]

Ireland also attracted attention. Peel sought Goulburn's assistance to disprove the Irish charge that the Scots had been more generously treated by Parliament than had they, for Anglesey was pressing for the funding of at least "some" of the projects advanced by the Society for the Improvement of Ireland. His principal concern, of course, was to calm a nation raised to fever pitch by O'Connell's dramatic electoral victory in Clare. Indeed, on the very day Goulburn delivered his budget statement, one of his colleagues noted in his diary, "The accounts from Ireland are awful." When, four days later, the defeated Vesey Fitzgerald proposed to cabinet that O'Connell's seat be declared vacated "on the ground of his declining to take the oaths," Goulburn joined his colleagues in rejecting this resolutely "Protestant" line lest it precipitate a "convulsion." With the viceroy emphasizing the need ultimately to make concessions, and with some "Catholic" cabinet ministers fretting over the possible consequences of allowing matters to drift, Wellington drew an alarming picture of Ireland for the king in order to extract from a peevish monarch permission to consider the Irish problem.[34]

The duke had assured the king that he would consult only Lyndhurst and Peel. Both men responded cautiously. As the prime minister realized, the home secretary's position was peculiarly difficult, given his long and powerful opposition to Catholic relief. Exactly when Goulburn was brought into the discussion is unclear, though perhaps it was during the third week of August when reports reached the capital of a startling speech delivered in Derry by George Dawson. Because of Dawson's connection to Peel and the government (he was a brother-in-law of the former and a minor member of the latter), considerable significance was attached to his statement that there was now little choice except to settle the Catholic question. Goulburn promptly complained to Wellington of Dawson's want of "discretion" and "consistency," to which the duke replied that the man "ought to be put in a strait waistcoat." Peel simply threw up his hands in dismay. How could anyone "blunder in everything with such sinister dexterity?" he asked.[35]

Goulburn surely did not long remain in ignorance of Wellington's capitulation to the inevitability of emancipation. He was too close to Peel, who still consulted him on Irish policy, and they had been too long united in opposition to this concession not to have conferred on their respective positions. The central issue for Goulburn was how to check the influence of the Catholic clergy. His suspicion of them remained as deep as ever. "The memorial of those reverend Gentlemen is like all others of a similar kind," he remarked of the hierarchy's recent paper on Irish education, "replete with insinuation and falsehood." Yet in the political activism of priests he found a glimmer of hope. The "miraculous" power with which they were invested by an ignorant peasantry and their claims to "abstractedness" from worldly concerns must eventually, he believed, be tarnished by their employment virtually as political agents. "The solemnity of the Chapel, the sanctity of Priestly office is outraged," he mused, and "in proportion as the Priest succeeds in his appeal to the passions of his hearers will he destroy his power over their imaginations." This same objective initially determined Goulburn's stand on the proposed disfranchisement of the forty-shilling freeholders who had given O'Connell his triumph. To reduce the size of the electorate, Goulburn argued, would simplify the priestly manipulation of it. Priests would be able to exert more traditional pressures on a small and largely middle-class electorate. Many shopkeepers, for example, were dependent on clerical patronage. So long as a priest was required to establish his control over a huge mass of voters, Goulburn reasoned, he would be inhibited by his need to resort to the demagoguery of which he himself stood in fear. "He is by religious belief an enemy to Liberty and yet he must invoke liberty. He must fulminate spiritual thunder at the risk of its being constantly proved ineffectual." To the extent that he was caught in such contradictions, the priest might yet be successfully challenged by the landlord in the battle for electoral influence.[36]

The opening of Parliament was set for the first week of February 1829, which obliged the cabinet to reach some agreement on Ireland early in the New Year. As 1829 dawned, Goulburn was in high favour with Wellington, who regarded him as one of the successes of his government. Goulburn had piloted a sensible budget through Parliament with a minimum of fuss and controversy, had exhibited a laudable if at times uncomfortable zeal for retrenchment, and was proving surprisingly cooperative on the emotional issue of Catholic emancipation. He dutifully accompanied Wellington, Peel, Bathurst, Lyndhurst, and Herries to see the king on 13 January. As the recognized "Protestant" ministers, they individually impressed on the monarch the need for the cabinet to confront an issue that appeared to depend on the state's securing the "willing moral obedience" of more than one-third of the population of the United Kingdom. With George IV's reluctant permission, and having replaced the obstreperous Anglesey with a more pliable and discreet viceroy, the cabinet turned to the task of thrashing out the terms on which relief would be conceded. Some members argued for securities, while others regarded them at best as an expedient to make the measure more palatable to the Lords. Goulburn, who at a meeting on 17 January declined to commit himself fully until he had seen the entire package of measures, was nevertheless added to the small group who drafted the King's Speech announcing this radical change of course. Once the monarch had consented to the draft, Goulburn was deputed to prepare the Irish primate for what he clearly considered the Hobson's choice of emancipation. A full-hearted Protestant government was no longer possible in a Commons where the majority in favour of concession was growing year by year, he reminded Archbishop Beresford. Nor was dissolution a valid option, launching as it surely would an O'Connellite electoral revolution in Ireland. "The only alternatives were to retire or to support a Government aiming at a rational settlement of the Roman Catholic question." Here was another statement of pragmatism, and he was speaking as much to his own position as to that of the Irish primate.[37]

When he rose in the Commons on 12 February to announce his painful about-face on emancipation, Goulburn frankly founded it on "expediency." He had become convinced, he said, "that a disunited administration, a divided parliament, and an excited people, were likely to prove much more prejudicial to the interests of the Protestant Church" than Catholic relief. Meanwhile, within the inner circle of the cabinet, he was one of those now demanding the disfranchisement of the forty-shilling freeholders. This amounted to a reversal of his earlier position and reflected the political need to erect eye-catching barriers against Catholic domination of Ireland. Disfranchisement appeared to be the most attractive of the securities on offer. In the absence of Peel, who was fighting an unsuccessful battle for re-election for the University of Oxford, having considered himself honour bound to resign the prized seat following his reversal on the Catholic issue, it fell to Goulburn to announce the government's timetable for the introduction of the relief bill.[38]

On 5 March, Peel (who was now sitting for the notoriously corrupt borough of Westbury) brought on the question with a monumental and majestic speech. Twelve days later, St Patrick's Day, the debate on relief and disfranchisement was formally opened. Goulburn spoke but made little impression on the House. His lack of enthusiasm for the measure, coupled with the residual effects of a heavy cold, impaired his performance. He laboured unconvincingly to square his current support of concession with his long-standing opposition to it by pointing to the "greater evils in the political state of Ireland." And he struggled manfully but without great conviction to establish that the bill "had mainly for its object to make the Protestant religion the ascendant." By restoring "the kindly intercourse" that had formerly existed between a Protestant rector and the Catholic residents of his parish, relief would allow the established church again to be employed "as an important engine in the moral improvement of the people," Goulburn declared. By the same token, to the extent that it reconciled the Catholic majority to the payment of tithes, emancipation would place the church "upon a solid and secure basis." Neither he nor his listeners truly believed any of this. By month's end the bill had been read for a third time in the Commons, and within an additional two weeks it had cleared the Lords and received royal assent. But the government churlishly denied O'Connell the distinction of being the first Roman Catholic to claim a seat in Parliament. He was required to return to Clare to be re-elected.[39]

The hope was that this concession would reconcile the great majority of the Irish population to the Union, thereby allowing a vigorous executive to maintain order and establish the stability that was so essential to the island's economic development. Prosperity would mitigate poverty and thus complete the integration of Ireland into the United Kingdom. Unfortunately, though, anti-Catholicism was on the rise, the result of a number of factors: the strengthening of Catholicism in Britain, which was most evident in areas settled by the rising tide of Irish immigrants; the "increasing assertiveness" of the Roman Catholic Church in general and the militancy of the Irish priesthood in particular; and the sense that Protestantism was "the fundamental essence" of the constitution but had been gravely weakened first by the repeal of the Test and Corporation Acts and now by emancipation. Not surprisingly, Ultra-Tories excoriated Peel as an apostate to the Protestant cause. But Goulburn avoided the obloquy heaped on his friend, perhaps because he was so evidently a mere supporting player in the drama. He also helped himself. He was quick to respond to concerns of the Irish primate, sitting as he still did for the borough of Armagh, and he took every opportunity to restate his conviction that the church "was an integral part of the Constitution, which was essential to the well-being of the people, and ought to be supported for the benefit of

the State, by the general contribution of all classes of the community."
In Ireland, this meant the continued payment of tithes by Catholics,
and to this position, at least, Goulburn resolved to cling. "We must not,
by impolitic abridgments," he insisted, "affect its wholesome power,
and impair its real dignity, so as to circumscribe its sphere, for the performance of its useful and essential duties."[40]

The most obvious and immediate consequence of Catholic emancipation, however, was the desertion of an important element of Wellington's political army. The splintering of Tory ranks, which had begun in
1827, had not been repaired by the duke's virtual ignoring of the Ultras in 1828, when he put together his cabinet. They were even surlier
after the passage of the Catholic relief bill. More than two hundred
MPs had defected at one time or another during that battle. The Tories' long political supremacy was clearly threatened, but its final collapse in 1830 has been attributed, at least in part, to the government's
handling of the economy. To the extent that this was true, Goulburn
shared the responsibility. On the other hand, it was his management of
financial policy, his contribution to the government's record for economy and efficiency, that did so much to sustain its "liberal" reputation
and thus facilitate its retention of power.[41]

Deceived by a brief surge in economic activity, Robert Peel ridiculed
early in 1829 warnings that industry was "cramped," that the labouring
sections of the community were on the verge of ruin, and that the
landed gentry were living off their capital rather than their income.
"Who, then, inhabits the new houses going up in every town?" he asked
Goulburn. "Why does a Leviathan in the funds, like Alex Baring, invest
a million in land?" Nevertheless, the economy was slumping. A poor
harvest had produced high corn prices, and it was some time before
they began to drop as warehouses were opened and farmers poured
their remaining supplies onto the market. Meanwhile, the value of exports was again declining. Higher food prices and less employment
brought disorder and riots to the textile regions of Lancashire and
Cheshire.[42]

With his eldest son proudly watching from the gallery, Goulburn introduced his second budget on 8 May 1829. He admitted that current
conditions "cast a partial gloom over the prospect before them," but
then announced the more cheering news that the surplus for the year
just ended had exceeded his prediction. He paraded the government's
unceasing search for savings, which had resulted in a further dramatic
reduction of the estimates, and forecast another large surplus. He then
made plain his determination to retain an income that would ensure
the avoidance of deficits. In short, he still considered tax reductions
neither prudent nor possible. Moreover, he betrayed an uneasiness

about the security of his revenues by now completing the abandonment of the Sinking Fund. He announced that no sums would be applied to the reduction of the national debt other "than those which were clearly and *bona fide* surplus revenue after paying all the charges of the country." This announcement was greeted with some gloating by the Radicals.[43]

Goulburn concluded his speech with a statement that confused many of his listeners and mystified others. He was going to convert unfunded into funded debt by offering a small premium to the holders of £3 million of exchequer bills to induce them to accept 4 per cents instead. Joseph Hume sarcastically complimented him on the clarity of his presentation. Althorp, the principal Whig spokesman in the Commons, accused him of effectively borrowing to pay down the debt, and he privately assailed this "very great blunder." It would have been more sensible, he claimed, to have applied the surplus immediately to redemption of £3 million of unfunded debt. Yet neither Hume nor Althorp did Goulburn justice. He was, in fact, carefully laying the groundwork for a more ambitious conversion scheme; but tradition dictated that he not tip his hand, and so he obfuscated. He had recognized that as the Sinking Fund sank as an instrument of debt reduction, greater attention would have to be given to a reduction of the debt by lowering the interest paid to bondholders. Moreover, the conversion and thus the modest increase in the funded debt indirectly advanced his conservative purpose of ensuring that there was sufficient taxation raised to cover debt payments. Finally, in the gloom of the current economic slump and with the very real likelihood of a shortfall in revenues, it would have been folly to apply the projected sum to the unfunded debt.[44]

In this mood, Goulburn pressed on with the unrelenting search for economies. Assaults on the abuse of pensions and less generosity in their award, the disposal of "redundant officers of the Customs," searching inquiries into charges that improvement projects in Ireland had been "fearfully jobbed," and further scrutiny of colonial expenditures were all testimony to the administration's economizing zeal. Even so, they did not indicate a witless commitment to retrenchment. Wellington and Goulburn continued to fund Charles Babbage's revolutionary calculating machine, which promised to produce the accurate navigational tables so essential for maritime safety; and at Lord Abderdeen's prompting, they found the money to purchase for the nation a pair of Greek bronzes, though the duke admitted to the chancellor that being so small, the bronzes made no great show: "For one person who *knows* that you have made a good bargain, twenty will think that you have paid extravagantly." Moreover, the prime minister endorsed Goulburn's emergency scheme to raise £2 million through an issue of exchequer bills to make loans for public works. "There cannot be a better and more economical scheme for the public," Wellington acknowledged. "We shall do exactly what is required. We shall supply the means, at a comparatively small expense, of laying out a large sum annually in works of permanent improvement, the execution of which will furnish employment immediately, as their completion and existence in the country will hereafter."[45]

As the hectic year of 1829 drew to a close, anxiety over the economy's health deepened. Huskisson privately expressed his alarm at the evidence of distress in every sector, which he traced to the financial and banking policies implemented since the restriction act of 1797; in particular, he cited the "exclusive privileges of the Bank of England" and the "huxtering manner" of their use. There was need of "a speedy and sufficient reform of the English banking system," the Tory *Quarterly Review* insisted. Meanwhile, Wellington was being inundated with unsolicited advice on how to respond to the crisis. The most popular remedy in the shires was the repeal of the taxes on malt and beer, even the introduction of free trade in that traditional beverage. This action would revive agriculture and perhaps revitalize the entire economy, magistrates and gentry claimed. On the other hand, there was evidence that the economic difficulties were regional rather than national. This information confirmed Wellington's roseate analysis of the situation, while those closest to him whispered that the distress was being deliberately exaggerated by the alienated Ultras in order simply to embarrass his government.[46]

The prime minister's reported "indifference" to the state of the country and his alleged insensitivity to the plight of "the people" did little to assist his ministers in the Commons. An attempt in the Throne Speech to pass quickly over economic difficulties as being regrettable but local and beyond the control of the government was not well received. Goulburn was obliged to protest that no one felt the sufferings of the people more keenly than he and his colleagues did. He repeated the claim that the distress was far from universal, though his singling out of Ireland as an example of comparative "ease" and "comfort" brought Daniel O'Connell leaping to his feet in protest. The Irishman sensed, not without reason, that this comment foretold an intention to seek more revenue from his country. Although the opposition amendment to the Address was comfortably defeated, the size of the majority did not impress Wellington's intimates. They blamed Peel for poor management, whereas he in turn was growing increasingly resentful of the lack of support he received from those who sat alongside him on the Treasury bench. Goulburn alone had come to his aid during the debate.[47]

The government's initial response to the impassioned demands for action was subdued. Goulburn repeatedly rejected suggestions that he tamper with the currency. There would be no reissue of the small notes recently withdrawn, he announced. There was ample gold in circulation, he added, and there had been a significant increase in the issue of notes of larger denomination. He also reiterated the administration's steadfast commitment to retrenchment even as he ridiculed proposals for truly swingeing reductions in expenditures. Yet it was obvious that an unflagging enthusiasm for economies would not still the criticism. There were three measures that would enable them to overcome all opposition, Peel argued: first, the "removal of all restrictions on the establishment by Charter of Banking Companies with limited liability"; second, the cutting of expenditures "to the lowest amount consistent with *public safety*"; third, a "commutation of the taxes bearing on the industry – and the comforts of the labouring poor – for other taxes reaching *Ireland – great capitalists* and *absentees*."[48]

For a month, from St Valentine's Day until the Ides of March, the cabinet deliberated. Ministers were united in their commitment to retrenchment. Similarly, the opening of negotiations for a renewal, at a higher price, of the Charter of the Bank of England commanded broad support. There was, after all, a distrust of a board of directors whom Herries accused of unprecedented "jealousy and suspiciousness," and there was confidence that the bank's unpopularity in Parliament would make it more amenable to a settlement on terms favourable to the government. Goulburn had outlined several possible strategies months earlier. The strength of the bank's position, he recognized, was its independent position as manager of the national debt. What he proposed, therefore, was that the government seek a relaxation of those artful restrictions on joint-stock banking which the bank had persuaded the Treasury to establish by decree in 1826, and a further narrowing of the circle around London from which such competitors were excluded. On the other side of the ledger, the bank's provincial branches might be extended and be made the only medium for remitting public revenues. In short, country banks would be deprived of this advantage. As for the compensation the government should demand in return for the benefits the bank derived from its connection to the government, Goulburn suggested any one of three alternatives: an annual contribution to the Treasury or an equivalent reduction in the bank's management fees; a lump sum payment; or a loan for a limited period at a nominal rate of interest.[49]

Wellington agreed that a principal objective in the negotiation should be the opening of "the whole system of private banking" to parliamentary consideration. In a joint letter to the bank's senior manage-

ment on 16 February 1830, he and Goulburn had sought an end to
the restrictions on other joint-stock banks. They offered assurances in
turn that such newly freed banks would be effectively regulated, and
they concluded with an implied warning that it would be unwise for
the bank to cling to its "exclusive privilege" for the three remaining
years of its charter. But the bank's principal negotiator, who was soon
to succeed to the governor's chair, John Horsley Palmer, proved to be
as formidable and skilful a defender of a strong position as Wellington
had been on many a battlefield.[50]

The directors declined to surrender any of the bank's existing privileges without first reaching an understanding on its "future position."
They detailed the "prejudicial effect" of the proposed changes, emphasizing the challenge that new joint-stock companies would pose to
private banks, whose virtues they suddenly extolled, and they warned
darkly of the likelihood of the new banks succumbing to the temptation to issue excessive amounts of paper money. A frustrated Wellington tried a little intimidation, but without success. He and Goulburn
were quickly reduced to asking the bank what it was prepared to offer
in return for an extension of its privileged position as the sole bank of
issue in London and the surrounding area, and its employment as
banker to the government as well as manager of the debt. To exert
more pressure, however, they demanded a full statement of the bank's
accounts so that they could determine for themselves the profitability
of these services.[51]

At a meeting with the chancellor on 16 April, Palmer proposed that
the paper money in circulation should "eventually" be that of the bank
operating through its branches. Given the existing resentment of the
bank's monopoly privileges, this was not a proposal Goulburn encouraged, and in a pair of meetings he laid out the government's terms.
The bank would remain the sole corporate banking body in the capital
but the exclusion zone would be reduced to a radius of twenty miles
from the metropolis. Ministers would retain the right, after renewal of
the charter, to propose additional measures of banking reform on the
understanding that these would not prejudice the bank's actions in the
sphere assigned to it. Further, on the basis of Goulburn's examination
of the charges for the management of the debt – and he criticized as
wildly exaggerated the accounting of the expenses involved – he proposed that the sum now paid be virtually halved. This would have saved
him £100,000 per annum. Palmer and his colleagues declined to settle
on these terms, and the negotiations were suspended.[52]

One attraction for Goulburn of a single large payment from the
bank in return for the renewal of its charter was the opportunity this
would afford him to experiment with tax reductions, the third of Peel's

options. The money would cover the "immediate loss" involved in lowering certain consumption taxes. Denied a modest savings on the bank's charges, and confronted by declining revenues, the ever-cautious Goulburn suggested to his colleagues at the beginning of March not only a number of possible tax reductions but also the reimposition of a modified income or property tax. Its revival had been an item on the agenda of the hapless Goderich ministry, and it was given fresh impetus by Henry Parnell in his pamphlet *On Financial Reform*. Significantly, Goulburn's liberal Toryism encouraged him to recommend a levy on landed and fixed property and on income from the funds and salaries, but to exempt the profits of industry and trade. He was determined to avoid any action that might jeopardize a revival of either. But this played into the hands of those – principally peers – who clustered around Wellington in self-interested opposition to the measure. They argued that it was unfair and would pinch hardest on the duke's natural constituency, the landed interest – an interest already complaining bitterly of the depressed condition of agriculture. Wellington also affected to believe that it would be impossible to carry this unpopular measure in the face of a predicted budget surplus. Indeed, he persuaded himself that Goulburn could remove or reduce taxes and balance the loss of revenue with the savings he intended to achieve by lowering the interest on a large portion of the debt and by imposing an increased duty on spirits and a somewhat larger charge on Ireland. After a week of discussion and argument, and perhaps private pressure from Wellington, Goulburn abandoned the idea of an income tax. It was a decision Peel greeted with dismay.[53]

Goulburn announced the government's decision to experiment with tax reductions on 15 March 1830. Admitting that revenues for the previous year had fallen short of his expectations, he informed the Commons that £2,400,000 of "surplus actually and really available" had nevertheless been "applied to the purpose of reducing the Debt." However, the forthcoming year would see the emphasis placed on the abatement of taxation. With unusual candour, he revealed that an income tax had been discussed in cabinet and rejected. As a result, his concern was to provide the greatest relief at the least cost to the revenue. A remission of the beer tax was cast in terms of Christian economics, as a means of weaning the lower orders off spirits with more wholesome and inexpensive beer. Virtuous behaviour would be encouraged even as the material well-being of the poor improved. Greater consumption of beer, which he proposed further to facilitate through its freer sale, would have the added political benefit of stimulating demand for malt. Similarly, the removal of the tax on cider, and more particularly that on leather, promised additional relief to the agricultural population. Yet by briefly delaying the implementation of these measures, he effectively diminished the loss to the revenue over the coming year. Indeed, by reducing by one-half per cent the interest paid on another portion of the debt, by increasing stamp duties in Ireland until they equalled those in England, by imposing a tax on tobacco grown there, and by raising the duty on spirits in Ireland and Scotland, together with that on corn spirits in England, Goulburn projected a surplus of £2 million. This, he fancied, would be large enough to guard against both any shortfall in revenues and the awful danger of "borrowing under disadvantageous circumstances."[54]

Critics were soon in full cry. The "Leviathan" of the funds, Alexander Baring, assailed the proposed reduction of the 4 per cents as a breach of faith with the public creditor. His, however, was a solitary voice. But the corn distillers complained bitterly that there had been no matching increase in the duty on rum; whereupon Goulburn, who was acutely sensitive to any suggestion that he had shown favouritism to an industry with which he was personally interested as a sugar planter, quickly promised to re-examine the issue. The Whigs damned him for the timidity of his tax reductions and, led by Poulett Thompson, who was both clever and knowledgeable in such matters, they demanded a committee to examine taxation.[55]

Peel, still hankering after the income tax, privately exerted additional pressure by voicing doubt about his ability to defeat the Whig motion. But his colleagues resolved to oppose Poulett Thompson's inquiry on the grounds that it would paralyse economic activity in all the areas where tax relief seemed possible. Goulburn, in developing this line of argument in the Commons on 25 March, carefully positioned himself as a practitioner of a Pittite fiscal prudence, and the Whig attack was easily beaten back. There was stiffer resistance, however, to Goulburn's proposal virtually to free the retail trade in beer. Licensed victuallers warned darkly that any increase in the numbers of retail brewers would be prejudicial to public morals, for in parts of Lancashire in particular the clergy had long since complained that Sunday was "a day of general drunkenness from the absence of all control." Protesting that his purpose was "to supply the public with a wholesome and nutritious malt beverage," Goulburn gave ground. He announced that those who sold beer only would require a licence from the Excise, whereas those who combined the beer trade with that in wines and spirits would continue to be licensed as before.[56]

Already hard pressed by the critics of his budget, Goulburn soon found himself under an even more severe strain, for he was forced to assume leadership of the Commons while Peel was drawn away from the House by his father's illness and subsequent death. Goulburn assumed the responsibilities at a peculiarly demanding time. He "is obliged to make the whole fight," a friend remarked, "and there is really business enough for a month on the paper for the week." Adding to his difficulties was the ill discipline not merely of the government's back-bench supporters but even of some of its junior members. At least two of them slipped out of the House before the division on first reading of a Jewish Emancipation Bill, leaving Goulburn to suffer an embarrassing defeat and to be charged with "illiberality" for his own opposition to this measure. Having admitted dissenters, he believed that Parliament ought at least to remain an exclusively Christian assembly. Peel later rescued the situation on second reading. As for the ill discipline of members, the harried chancellor blamed this largely on the grave condition of George IV's health.[57]

The likelihood of an early general election following a royal death and succession encouraged country gentlemen to position themselves for the forthcoming campaigns. Goulburn was obliged to withdraw a vote for repairs to Windsor Castle and to agree to a committee to consider the question, following vehement criticism of the constant escalation of the original estimate. Everyone "was against us," he explained to Peel. He had faced an unpleasant choice of embarrassments – accept defeat on the vote and see a committee appointed, or withdraw the vote and appoint a committee whose terms of reference he could define narrowly. "The same question will arise as to each vote objected to," the weary Goulburn warned, "and if the Country Gentlemen who usually support us behave as they did last night (and I see no reason why they should behave less shabbily), we shall have to make a choice between submitting ourselves to a committee on every point in which any discretion is to be exercised or giving up the conduct of public business altogether – As far as regards myself I should far prefer the latter alternative." So long as the monarch clung to life, one of Goulburn's colleagues cold-bloodedly remarked, there "would be no possibility of carrying on the money business in the House of Commons." Goulburn did have some successes, though. He fought off a Whig demand for removal of the duty imposed on coal imported into Ireland, and he succeeded in frustrating an inquiry into the pensions and emoluments of members of the Privy Council simply by swamping his harassers with information. "The game [of the opposition] is evidently to delay all business," he informed the still absent Peel, "and to take every opportunity of shewing strength and acquiring a popularity suited to Election purposes."[58]

Peel's return to the Commons brought no appreciable improvement in the management of government business. Aware that the ministers could neither resign nor dissolve Parliament during the monarch's protracted death, the opposition continued to torment them. Again, Goulburn found himself a principal target. Whig demands for the repeal of the taxes on soap and candles he resisted without great difficulty, but he was forced into a humiliating retreat on the sugar duties. The West Indians had been pleading for relief since the beginning of the year. Goulburn's initial budget proposals to cabinet in January had included some reduction in the duties on sugar, but rejection of an income tax had compelled him to turn to less costly remissions. In June, however, the sugar issue was revived in the natural course of events because the existing duties were to expire unless renewed. Charles Grant then gave notice of a motion to effect a general reduction, and Goulburn found himself facing the very real danger of a substantial loss of revenue.[59]

He first attempted to finesse the problem, offering as a "temporary and experimental" measure a sliding scale of duties on the coarser sugars consumed by the "lower orders." He planned to recoup the lost revenue – and appease some of the critics of his budget at the same time – by revising upwards the duty on Irish and Scottish spirits and by lowering that on English corn spirits while raising it on rum. The plan appeared "to have succeeded" until it was roasted in the House one week later, on 21 June, with Huskisson applying much of the heat. So on the last day of the month, less than a week after the death of George IV and the succession of his brother as William IV, when the Commons was facing imminent dissolution and there was thus no room in which to manoeuvre, Goulburn capitulated. The general reduction of duty that he had earlier resisted was now brought forward "as a temporary arrangement, not to lay down any permanent system of trade." This was a very small fig-leaf indeed.[60]

The black dress of mourning in which most members of the cabinet outfitted themselves for their first council with the new monarch accurately reflected their mood. The ministerial disarray in the Commons was exciting recriminations, with the duke's friends again blaming Peel and he in turn complaining of the burden he was personally carrying there. Wellington had briefly contemplated resignation in order to allow Peel to reconstruct the government according to his own wishes, but he had been dissuaded by intimates and by distrust of the liberal course that Peel might pursue. There remained, however, a pressing need to find some way to strengthen the Treasury bench in the Commons. Several ministers began to discuss among themselves possible changes, including the incorporation of moderate Whigs. Goulburn's name was frequently on the lips of those seeking to make room for recruits – not least, perhaps, because in his case retirement might be accomplished gracefully. He had expressed an interest in the Speaker's chair. Certainly, he was tired after so many years in office and was increasingly sensitive to the snide references to Wellington's "*parasites.*" Yet it was unjust to yoke him together with the hapless Sir George Murray as an "inefficient" minister, as Harriet Arbuthnot did, or not to exclude him from a sweeping indictment of ministerial performances in the Commons, as his mentally and emotionally exhausted friend Peel did. Henry Goulburn had been an effective chancellor of the exchequer.[61]

He ought, perhaps, to have held more tenaciously to his proposed income tax. It would have given him far more freedom in the selective reduction of other taxes. After all, he was assured of the resolute support of Peel and Herries. On the other hand, there had been no assurance that the Commons would revive so essential a prop of the "military-fiscal state" without evidence of an economic crisis equivalent to war. Goulburn had been budgeting for a surplus, while the current dislocation seemed to be temporary and far from universal. Nor were Wellington's political objections entirely unreasonable. Tories remained at odds with one another, and the landed interest to whom the prime minister looked as his natural constituency would certainly have assailed any income tax, let alone the modified version Henry Goulburn had in mind. "Why risk the complete alienation of one's supporters?" the duke's friends had asked. The only gainers would be the despised Whigs. Significantly, they were to lack the courage to introduce the income tax during their subsequent eleven years in power. And while it might be argued that they prepared the way for Peel and Goulburn to take this decisive step in 1842, that was only by bequeathing to them the full-blown fiscal and economic crisis that did not exist in 1830.

The chancellor had not been successful in his dealings with the Bank of England. He had failed to persuade the directors to accept a diminution of its privileges in the interest of strengthening the general banking system. Nor had he been able to extract a somewhat higher price, in the form of a reduced charge for managing public business, in return for a renewal of the bank's charter. Here again the stumbling block was the government's determination to retain the discretion to modify the existing structure of provincial banking. Bargaining from a position of strength – for there was still three years to run on the charter, and the bank remained relatively independent as the corporate manager of the national debt – the directors gave no ground. During an interview with the chancellor in mid-September, a hard-headed Palmer suggested that a "fair trial" be given to a gradual extension of the circulation of the bank's notes before any additional joint-stock banks with limited liability were established. Further, he proposed that any new joint-stock banks should be heavily restricted in the issue of their own paper. These were not terms that the Wellington government could accept.[62]

Disappointing as this outcome was, Goulburn could not have done much more than he did to bring the bank to a satisfactory settlement. Nor should this failure overshadow his real achievements. He had put an end to the folly of borrowing in order to maintain a sinking fund; and although he abandoned the concept of an annual fixed-sum redemption only with reluctance, because of his anxiety both to address the problem of the debt and to ensure a level of taxation sufficient to guarantee an annual operating surplus, he courageously compromised with reality in 1829. While the sums he had applied to the reduction of the debt amounted to a mere 1 per cent of that huge mountain, he had effected a substantial reduction of the annual charge on the funded portion of it.

With respect to other expenditures, Goulburn's contribution to the struggle to bring them under effective control was again a large one. Although he was frustrated in his effort to create a general superannuation scheme in the public service, he did establish a limited one that prepared the ground for more effective Treasury control of establishments and expenditures. Similar progress was made towards a clear and uniform accounting system and to putting in place procedures to weed out inefficient public servants. Even more striking were the victories in the field of retrenchment, where the duke liked to take personal command. In less than three years the estimates had been pruned by almost £3 million. In short, Goulburn had made a substantial contribution to the development of a smaller but more economic, more efficient, and more professional central government. Lastly, he had launched a characteristically careful experiment in tax reduction. His Whig successors at the Exchequer would have been well advised to emulate his fiscal caution.[63]

CHAPTER EIGHT

The Great Reform Bill

After a meal at Lord Ellenborough's Roehampton home, Henry Goulburn travelled to Windsor in the company of several of his colleagues to attend the royal funeral in the evening of 15 July 1830. Scandalized as he had been by the new monarch's bizarre conduct during the obsequies for his elder brother, the Duke of York, three years earlier, he was surely not surprised by William IV's unconventional behaviour on this occasion. Indeed, the royal dignity was frequently to be bruised. At William's first meeting of the Privy Council, a nervous clerk attempted to swear the councillors in the name of George IV. Then, when the moment came for Goulburn to kiss hands, the sovereign muttered to him; "D'ye know I'm grown so near sighted that I can't make out who you are. You must tell me your name, if you please." When the ministers assembled again on 24 July for a council for the dissolution, it became clear that not one of them knew how many days must elapse before the new Parliament was summoned, though as Charles Greville remarked, they had been in office "all their lives." Frantic research turned up the answer of fifty-two days.[1]

The midsummer general election offered little political comfort to the Duke of Wellington. Only a minority of seats were contested, but this statistic was misleading. "Those candidates who stood on the support of the Government found no advantage from it," one observer recorded, "but on the contrary were invariably obliged to abandon such ground for the ground of reform and economy, and are committed in almost every instance to conditional engagements on these points." A government effort to unseat the Canningites who were most vulnerable to its "influence" failed miserably, while personal identification with Robert Peel appeared to be a peculiar liability: two of his brothers and a brother-in-law went down to defeat. However, fears of serious losses in Ireland because of the anger aroused by Goulburn's budget and the duke's refusal to sanction a program of public relief proved to be exaggerated. The Tories held their own with the shrunken electorate. Yet nothing could mask the setback suffered in "popular elections." Barely one-third of the English county members were now enlisted in Wellington's political army. As for Goulburn, he decided not to contest Cambridge. Not only was he disliked by religious liberals, but he had yet to be forgiven by anti-Catholics.[2]

Against the backdrop of electoral reverses at home and political turmoil overseas – for France and Belgium had erupted in revolution – Wellington was inclined to reinforce his government. The performance of several ministers in the Commons had been waspishly criticized, Goulburn being a favourite target. The duke was accused of having appointed a chancellor "whom the House would not listen to" – not that his own limitations as an orator escaped ridicule. Wellington's choice in the aftermath of the election was either to seek a coalition with moderate Whigs or recruit individuals. Fusion with the former in the person of Earl Grey remained anathema to him, but his political flexibility, which had been manifest in the about-face on Catholic emancipation, now led him to seek a reconciliation with Huskisson. Something needed to be done – and in short order – if the ministry was to avoid finding itself threatened by a united opposition of Whigs, Ultras, and Canningites.[3]

The prime minister intended to sound out Huskisson during the ceremonial opening of the Liverpool-Manchester railway on 15 September. The Goulburns were not present, but an earlier and shorter journey into Manchester had left them impressed with the "rapidity of the motion" and charmed "with the perfection of the engines, and the apparent security of the whole arrangements." Tragedy struck, however, on the ceremonial occasion, when Huskisson stumbled into the path of an oncoming locomotive and suffered a mortal injury. Jane Goulburn consoled herself with the thought that his recent submission to dangerous surgery had fully prepared him for a premature death and that others would heed this providential warning and "endeavour to be in an habitual state of preparation." Earthier considerations dominated more political minds. Huskisson's death promised to dissolve the little party he had led, and this might in turn permit the duke to recruit an individual or two at "a less cost." He focused on Palmerston. The prime minister's inner circle, which included Goulburn, decided to sacrifice Sir George Murray to make room for the former minister. When Palmerston declined to come alone, Wellington was fully prepared to manoeuvre Herries aside to create a second vacancy, but Peel balked at this concession. Although yet another overture was made to Palmerston, his price had continued to rise. He demanded a more radical reconstruction of the

cabinet in order to include Whigs. The objective, Wellington concluded, was to force him to embrace parliamentary reform, the abolition of
slavery, and other "follies."[4]

Wellington's rejection of Palmerston's terms may have been eased, if
briefly, by his optimism that "upon the whole the people are satisfied."
Public opinion was steadily emerging as an important factor in politics.
The harvest had been good, corn prices were high enough to please
the most demanding of farmers, and manufactures and trade "were
never in a better state." Equally encouraging, "the misfortunes and follies of other countries" promised to prolong this happy state of affairs.
Further, Wellington hoped that just the fact that Parliament was meeting would tend "to tranquillize" a public that was uneasy about European turbulence and unsettled by the domestic agitation for reforms.
In this anodyne mood, he now approved a modest program of public
works in Ireland, and the cabinet discussed Goulburn's proposed
changes to the new monarch's Civil List. These promised some savings
on the allowance voted to his brother a decade earlier.[5]

Optimism proved as ever a delicate bloom that could not survive chilling evidence of disaffection in country and town. Rick burnings and the
smashing of threshing machines in Kent were initially dismissed by Wellington as the work of local smugglers, but the disorders soon showed a
disconcerting tendency to infect other counties. Simultaneously, unrest
erupted in the industrial areas of the North. Rising unemployment and
more expensive bread brought strikes for higher wages, to which mill
owners responded with lockouts and the government responded by re-
inforcing the garrisons in northern industrial centres. The Throne
Speech opening the new Parliament on 2 November included a pledge
to suppress disorders and to continue strict economy "in every branch
of public expenditures." With an eye to the unavoidable discussion of
the Civil List and the opening this would provide for embarrassing attacks on pensions and sinecures, the speech assured the members that
additional royal revenues would be surrendered. Not that Whigs or Radicals were appeased. Althorp made plain his intention to claim this
promising battleground. Yet it was less the desultory discussion in the
Commons than the remarks by Wellington in the Lords that created an
immediate sensation. In reply to Earl Grey's call for parliamentary reform, the duke absolutely rejected any tampering with the existing system of representation.[6]

Wellington's statement was not quite as inept as it seemed. Divisions
within the ranks of the reformers, who ranged across the entire political spectrum, had seen two moderate Whig proposals go down to defeat in the Commons earlier in the year. Not unreasonably, the prime
minister saw little prospect of Whigs, Canningites, Radicals, and Ultras

combining on this issue. Moreover, he was personally convinced that concession would set the Empire on the slippery slope to revolution, and he knew that the leading members of his cabinet shared his opinion. Robert Peel had informed his colleagues that he "would never undertake the question of Reform." If Goulburn was less forthright, his conservative position was equally clear. He had even opposed a modest proposal to increase the number of polling places in large constituencies, arguing that it would subvert the hallowed tradition of the candidate making himself available to respond to all voters' questions. During the debate on East Retford, he had warned of the peril of taking even "a single step" that was not sanctioned by the "sacred landmarks" of precedent. Such misoneism saw him ridiculed as one of those perennial, purblind children ever to be found "in the leading strings and go-cart of antiquity."[7]

The end came quickly. At the prompting of Wellington and Peel, who had been warned of possible trouble on the streets, the cabinet advised the king not to attend the lord mayor's banquet on 9 November. The decision excited considerable derision, though Goulburn alone of the senior ministers warned that the general feeling was against them in this instance. Then, on 12 November, the debate began on the Civil List. Goulburn outlined a reduction of some 10 per cent on the sum granted to George IV. However, he made an indifferent speech and concluded with the empty threat of an exhausted man, stating that he and his colleagues would resign with satisfaction if the House failed to support them. The Whigs laughed. Three days later, the Canningites and a band of Ultras joined forces with the Whigs to refer the Civil List to a committee. Peel, Goulburn, and Charles Arbuthnot carried the news of this defeat to Wellington, who was dining with the Prince of Orange, and convinced him that there was no alternative to resignation. Indeed, as the duke readily grasped, it was far "more advantageous" to go out on this question than on that of parliamentary reform. He may also have calculated that the Whigs would be unable to hold together on reform and that he would therefore soon return to office in a strengthened position.[8]

Goulburn genuinely welcomed liberation from the strains and pressures of official life. To an old friend he wrote: "I am by no means sorry for a change which has released me from a mental and bodily labour which was I felt beyond my strength to bear and which must necessarily have been increased by the determination of the then opposition to use every mode of vexatious delay which the forms of the House permitted in order to wear out their opponents." The strain had become almost unendurable in the Commons, where the lack of dependable support had recently made the task of carrying on business even more arduous. Goulburn was worn out by "nearly twenty years in hard work-ing office." Apart from the brief hiatus in 1827, he had been a mem-ber of every government since 1810, and he did not exaggerate when he described as peculiarly demanding the offices he had filled. "I think it profitable, at least I hope it will be so, to have time to dedicate to other studies and occupations of higher moment and of more perma-nent importance," he remarked. However conventional this declara-tion, Goulburn needed a respite from back-breaking administrative labour.[9]

He did not envy his successors. "Our state is one of very considerable perplexity and difficulty," he gloomily observed. "There is a species of servile war raging in some parts of the Country, and there is a general restlessness, spirit of commination and aversion to controul which does not hold out a pleasing prospect of future peace." Playing the part of the squire of Betchworth, a role all too often denied him by ministerial duties and parliamentary obligations, he hastened home to rally local farmers to stand against rioting labourers. He pressed his fellow land-lords to contribute greater sums to poor relief, and the promise of ad-ditional payments did have a calming effect. Not that his own financial position was any longer a comfortable one. Domestic retrenchments were the order of the day. At least young Freddy, who had responded to the disturbances by organizing his own band of "watchers" for rick burnings, found some humour as well as excitement in the situation. He joked that "we shall have nought but millet pudding for dinner," that "we must make our old jackets last a long time longer and not have any new ones for 2 or 3 years," and "we must go to church in ragged breeches. So much for politics."[10]

As ever, Henry Goulburn awaited the unfolding of the divine plan. "God that rules over all will dispose us as may be best," he observed. "We have only to pray that we may not be dealt with as we deserve." To prepare his eldest son for admission to Cambridge and to reinforce his faith in this evangelical truth, Goulburn placed the boy with the Rev. Henry Venn Elliott in Brighton. A Trinity man, a prominent evangeli-cal, and a member of the Clapham Sect, he worked his handful of charges "very hard and was extremely strict." Yet even Goulburn was concerned that his son was devoting too much of his time to religious studies. Thus, when forwarding at Harry's request several books on He-brew, he suggested that greater knowledge of history and a better un-derstanding of English poetry might "at present be more useful than the acquaintance of a language which necessarily occupies much time with no immediate benefit." While his father's acceptance of the cen-trality of religion was tempered by a measure of educational utilitarian-ism, Harry's mother was concerned that he pay more attention to his physical well-being. His consumptive appearance was giving his parents increasing cause for concern. But Henry Goulburn soon discovered that he could not practise the relaxation he and his wife preached to their favourite child.[11]

The new ministers claimed their seals of office from the king on 22 November, literally passing the departing chancellor and his colleagues on the way. Although the new government was commanded by Whigs, with Earl Grey as prime minister and Lord Althorp as chancellor of the exchequer and leader in the Commons, and although it was heavily dependent on Whigs and moderates for rank and file, it was in fact a coalition in which former Canningites were well represented. Even an Ultra found a place. The principal partners were committed to the restoration of order, a liberal commercialism, and a measure of parliamentary reform. The aristocratic Whigs' dedication to reform has been variously explained, and no doubt the motivations even of the party's leadership were complex. Grey provided a personal link to the traditional Foxite advocacy of measured civil and religious liberty. Althorp and some of the younger Whigs saw themselves as the moderate alternative to the extremes of Ultra-Toryism and Radical demagoguery. They hoped to persuade educated and respectable men, who might otherwise provide the discontented lower classes with leadership, to accept the existing social order, including leadership by the aristocracy. The time had come to alter and enlarge the basis of representation in order to restore the esteem of the Lower House by adjusting to the "increasing improvement of the people." In this sense the disturbances in town and country imbued the campaign with fresh urgency, for the lack of public confidence in the existing basis of government seemed all too plain.[12]

Henry Goulburn was deeply distrustful of all Whigs, many of whom had been equivocal in their response to the French Revolution and less than unflinching in their support of the French wars. His "fearful recollection" of that revolution explained his "perfect horror of Republican propagandism." At a time when Britain was seemingly enveloped "in a fearful cloud of violence and irreligion," he deplored any tampering with institutions that had been vindicated by their survival of the earlier and more virulent revolutionary plague. He abhorred "democracy," which he, no less than other Tories, regarded as the antithesis of personal freedom. The lesson taught them by the French experience was that increased popular participation in government led to a diminution of the fundamental right to dispose without molestation of one's person and estate. "To produce the greatest amount of personal freedom and security with the smallest degree of political power in the lower classes" was the great object of all good government, Tories insisted. Henry Goulburn was to remain faithful to the proposition that Britain should never be engaged in support of democratic principles.[13]

Wedded as he was to tradition and scornful of "cheap popularity," he deplored "mad enthusiastic feelings for reforms and changes." Instead, he and his associates professed a qualified commitment to change. They sought "real improvement of a definite nature" that was "compatible with the existence of the fundamental institutions of the country" – the crown and the church being the pre-eminent institutions. The appeals of others for the adjustment of institutions to "a new state of society" fell on deaf ears. To the Tories, all such reforms tended merely "to propogate themselves; each change producing a *newer state of society*, which [would] equally demand fresh reforms." Seemingly oblivious to the sincerity of the Whigs' long-standing commitment to parliamentary reform, Goulburn regarded concession as the worst kind of expediency and as altogether too pragmatic, for it threatened to set the constitution on the slippery slope to democracy. The Whigs' "willingness to rouse popular agitation," and their musings on the sovereignty of the people and the rule of pubic opinion, served only to heighten his concern that they were about to remove the finger from the dyke that prevented the enlightened minority from being inundated by mere numbers. Moreover, he could legitimately argue that the various gradations of society did participate in the existing political system to a lesser or greater extent; thus, in a narrow sense, the system was representative. Equally, the electorate was neither as small nor as docile as some detractors claimed, and general elections were vibrant affairs. Increasingly, candidates acknowledged an accountability to their constituents. The electors' right to hold them to that responsibility was Goulburn's excuse, after all, for his opposition to an increase in the number of polling stations. And while it was impossible to deny the existence of "infamies" and "vile management," even the notoriously corrupt boroughs often served a useful purpose. They gave young, affluent men a ready entrée to public life, as Goulburn could attest, and they made possible the immediate return to Parliament of essential men such as Peel in 1829. Yet as the *Times* remarked following Wellington's fall, it was "incredible" how little would have appeased the public's hunger or even satisfied its appetite for reform. Here was a commentary on the Tories' resistance to change.[14]

Henry Goulburn's family had hoped that his loss of office would enable them to enjoy somewhat more of his society. They were quickly disappointed, though a bout of ill health during the high summer of 1831, which cost him weight and drained away strength, did see him remain at Betchworth for an extended period of recuperation. He rode the fields in search of fitness and to restore some colour to his cheeks, though his wife observed in late August that he still looked "shockingly." However, he returned to the Commons as soon as he was physically able to do so, and before long he was again complaining that he rarely had a moment to call his own. Mornings were taken up with committees, including those on West Indian slavery and tithes. He was surely placed on them as a senior Tory and sugar planter in one case and as a zealous defender of the established church in the other. But it was his evening work in the House that initially and unexpectedly gave him the greatest satisfaction. The Whigs handed him a succession of minor parliamentary victories, beginning with their introduction of a Civil List that was not unlike his own ill-fated proposal.[15]

"I think we shall be able to beat them in debate as well as in information," he observed cheerfully, "and what is better, if we do but manage our proceedings with temper and discretion we shall have the feeling of the country soon with us." Already the City seemed to be losing confidence in the new ministers. Goulburn's optimism was given a further boost by the savage mauling of Althorp's first budget. The new chancellor and his colleagues lacked the political courage to revive the income tax, so they attempted a bold if not rash experiment in reduced taxation. Here was an early intimation that the Whigs' economic policies would not be unlike those of the Tories in their liberalism but that they would lack the caution in implementation that had characterized Robinson's term at the Exchequer and even more so that of Goulburn. Duties were to be repealed on a number of items, including seaborne coals and candles, and lowered on others. Colonial preferences also were attacked, in the shape of Canadian timber and Cape wines. The lost revenues were to be offset by a new imposition on imported raw cotton and a small tax on the transfer of landed and funded property. The added benefit in all this was the knowledge that these measures would pinch hardest on the commercial and monied interests identified with the Tories. Not surprisingly, Goulburn viewed them with a healthy cynicism. For three years he and Wellington had stoutly ignored the Marquis of Londonderry's pleas for a reduction of the duty on seaborne coal. As the nation's greatest mineowner, he stood to profit handsomely, and the Whigs had now provided him with this "immense boon." But the principal beneficiary was the prime minister's son-in-law. Similarly, Poulett Thompson, who as vice-president of the Board of Trade was widely believed to have influenced Althorp and had been dubbed "Tallow" Thompson, was suspected of feathering his own nest by cheapening the price of candles. His family, moreover, had long been involved in the Baltic trade, which would benefit from any erosion of the price advantage accorded to Canadian timber.[16]

In perhaps the best speech he had yet delivered in his parliamentary career, Goulburn launched a blistering attack on the budget. He chastised Althorp for gambling with the surplus, pointing out that he was projecting a perilously small one, and he ridiculed Althorp's claims that the tax reductions would benefit the lower classes. Most damaging, however, was his charge that the transfer tax amounted to a breach of faith with those who had invested in the funds on the assurance that they would not be so taxed. Not surprisingly, the City was in an uproar. Goulburn happily stirred the pot by meeting with deputations of outraged shipowners and indignant merchants. Assaulted from all sides, the government undertook a retreat, which rapidly resembled a rout. The transfer tax was abandoned, the question of Cape wines' preferences postponed, and the tax on raw cotton substantially modified. The timber duties were retained, only for the government subsequently to suffer the humiliation of a defeat in the House. In brief, the entire episode was a political and financial fiasco.[17]

Goulburn relished the prospect of the Whigs damaging themselves permanently with the monied interests of the City. Even their abandonment of the transfer tax failed to still criticism there. Now the charges were of "incapacity and indecision." His thoughts turned to the possibility of an unexpectedly early return to power, only to discover that Peel was in no mood to seek to capitalize on the Whigs' ineptitude. Unlike Wellington, who was striving to hold together the former ministers and their supporters in readiness for an early return to office, Peel stood apart, even aloof. He exhibited little interest in the activities of an organizing committee that was laying the foundations of what became the Carlton Club. Goulburn, on the other hand, was an enthusiastic participant. He realized that "it is necessary to meet political friends if we are to act together." Of course, the strength of Peel's position was his knowledge that no Tory government could be formed without him. However, to survive, such a ministry would require the support of the Ultras, and no one doubted that having been so abused by them, the thin-skinned Peel would ever solicit their aid. Nor was he by any means alone in the realistic opinion that the Whigs' inept handling of public business had come too early in the life of their administration to be fully exploited by a party that was still deeply unpopular in the country.[18]

All Tories were heartened, however, by the rumours of "great differences" among ministers on the subject of parliamentary reform. That, after all, appeared to be the only issue capable of rescuing this disaster-prone crew. The likely thrust of a reform bill was obvious, given the Whigs' long support of a more representative Parliament. They would disfranchise corrupt and nomination boroughs, two-thirds of which were controlled by Tories, and would transfer the seats to the great industrial towns. Equally likely was an attempt to curtail the crippling costs of fighting elections in the more populous counties, for Grey's personal purse had suffered from this tradition. The enfranchisement of the "respectable" would be another objective. Less obvious at this stage was the depth of the Whigs' commitment to enduring reform. By late January the cabinet had resolved to reduce radically the number of borough seats by applying a population test and to introduce a £10 householder franchise, which was expected to enlarge the electorate by at least 400,000. To make the Commons more manageable, they planned to reduce its total membership by 10 per cent.[19]

Lord John Russell introduced the Reform Bill on 1 March. Diminutive in stature and painfully shy in manner, he gave an indifferent performance. Nevertheless, the high drama of the moment more than compensated for his failings as a speaker. The far-reaching measures he outlined stunned many of the listening Tories. Peel seemed particularly upset. Even Goulburn, who had expected the Whigs to go "as far as they can in accordance with popular opinion," was beside himself with fury. "Never was any measure conceived with such wickedness," he wrote home, suspecting as he did that it had been inspired by malevolence. The Whigs expected to go out of office on the issue but not before making "it untenable for any successors." They intended to "leave a question which will be the foundation of perpetual agitation if rejected and of revolution if carried." Another problem of the Tory leadership – and one that helped to determine Peel's Fabian tactics – was the instability within the ranks of their supporters. "The cowardice of the Representatives of populous places will prevent many who will vote against it afterwards from opposing the first introduction," Goulburn gloomily predicted, "and under these circumstances we shall reserve our strength until the 2nd Reading." Here was an admission that the cause was a popular one and that the arguments in favour of reform were "plausible."[20]

As the debate got under way, Goulburn was far less confident of success than the Tory whips were, and he began to look ahead to the committee stage as the best opportunity "of reducing the mischief." When he eventually spoke, on the seventh evening, rather than charting new ground, he chose to follow the line already marked out by Peel. Pointing to the success and prosperity of Britain under the existing system of representation, he gave voice to the conservative's familiar protest against change: his objection to the removal of "that which he knew to be good, for the purpose of adopting something which he was merely told might be better." The elimination of so many nomination boroughs would jeopardize a truly effective opposition, Goulburn argued, for these boroughs provided a secure haven for ex-ministers who had adopted necessary but unpopular measures while in power. With a sarcastic allusion to Althorp's performance at the Exchequer, he suggested that the presence of knowledgeable and critical former ministers was essential for the efficient conduct of public business. Finally, he noted that one ironic result of reform would be the disfranchisement of many of the existing lower-class voters. In the judgment of one Whig, he had taken the "low ground."[21]

Writing to an anxious wife on the day he spoke, 9 March, Goulburn assured her that he was in no physical danger. There was rarely a throng in the neighbourhood of Parliament, he reported, and even the lobbies were less crowded than usual. He took heart from the modest attendance at rallies in Westminster and Marylebone, which reinforced his belief that popular interest in reform was lukewarm at best. He was deceiving himself. Nevertheless, capitalizing on Althorp's slipshod parliamentary management, the Tories defeated the government on the timber duties on 18 March, and Goulburn hoped that this victory would embolden sufficient waverers to ensure the defeat of the Reform Bill on second reading. Instead, fear of a dissolution and the loss of their seats – and thus fear of clearing the way for an even more radical measure – continued to paralyse some members. Further undermining Tory credibility and unity were those Ultras who, as Goulburn remarked incredulously, "would pledge us to an intent of reform little short of that which the Bill purports to effect." Similarly, when he approached the monied and colonial interests of the City, seeking declarations of hostility to the bill, he encountered the same want of "courage." His sole consolation was the conviction that second reading could be carried only by a majority so small that it would be tantamount to defeat. In this, at least, he was right.[22]

On 23 March the bill survived by a single vote in a tense House where the attendance was unprecedented. The impossibility of carrying the bill through the committee stage on the strength of this minimal majority saw Grey begin to press the monarch for a dissolution. On the other hand, the significance of 302 members voting for reform could not be ignored. Goulburn gloomily conceded that a "great evil" had been done "by so large a division in favour of the abolition of our existing constitution," and he complained bitterly of those "who from fear or other unworthy motive have deferred their better judgment to temporary popularity or who have abandoned the national interests to a cry raised by the Government for their own purposes." The ministers, meanwhile, made a number of expedient concessions to their opponents, but these failed to save them from defeat on a Tory motion to maintain the current total of English and Welsh seats. The king now granted Grey's request for a dissolution.[23]

The Tories had been preparing for an election since second reading, and they decided to put up Goulburn and one of Peel's brothers as "moderate" candidates for the University of Cambridge. Thus Goulburn was careful to identify himself as a qualified opponent of reform. He avowed a readiness "to concur in giving effect to some such moderate and well considered improvements in our system of representation as time and altered circumstances may have rendered requisite," but he assailed the Whig measure as "pregnant with danger to many of the best interests in the country and tending ultimately to the subversion of the Constitution." Aided by senior members of the established church and by his old evangelical allies – for clergy constituted a large segment of the electorate – and endorsed by an impressive slate of senior academics, Goulburn had good reason to be confident. Yet it was soon evident that this Cambridge battle was going to be as unpleasant as that of 1826.[24]

Goulburn's pension, which had been increased to £2,000 in 1825, was widely and scornfully publicized by the Radicals as proof of his better understanding of his personal financial interests than those of the nation. More surprising was the accusation that he was an enemy of "true religion." This was founded on the conduct of some of his supporters, who had allegedly violated the Sabbath in canvassing on his behalf. The charge was potentially damaging, given the high proportion of clergy among the electors, and it was patently unfair. Goulburn had long been a supporter of Lord's Day Observance legislation. Even his tolerance of those "innocent recreations" of the poor man that did not desecrate the most sacred of days but "invigorated his frame against the ensuing week of labour, and made him look up with more gratitude to the Great Author of all being," had not extended to places of "amusement" such as the British Museum. To those who claimed that its opening would discourage drunkenness by providing worthy diversions, he replied with "statistical facts" to prove "that in proportion as facilities had been afforded, even on lawful days, to the public to visit these places, drunkenness had increased." Here was further proof that statistics could be used to prove almost anything.[25]

The allegation that threatened to do the greatest damage to Goulburn's electoral chances was the old one that he was a friend of slavery. The economic depression with which he had had to contend during his last winter at the Exchequer had encouraged a revival of abolitionism among evangelicals, who were fearful that domestic distress was a divine judgment for the nation's continuing complicity in slavery. Led by Thomas Fowell Buxton and Zachary Macaulay, the general meeting of the London Anti-Slavery Society issued an address to the "people" on 23 April 1831, urging them to influence electors and interrogate candidates in an effort to ensure the return to Parliament of members who were genuinely committed to the "entire extinction of Slavery." The abolitionists had decided to yoke their cause to that of parliamentary reform. They also "unanimously adopted" a resolution that declared slaveholders "unfit" to serve. Less than a week later, a handbill was circulating among members of the university reminding them of Goulburn's ownership of more than two hundred slaves. Next, the charges of mistreatment levelled in 1826 were again put in circulation. But this time Goulburn was prepared. Warned several months earlier by a fellow member of Parliament of reports that his slaves were the victims of unnecessary severity, and recalling how readily such allegations were believed and how assiduously spread, he had armed himself well before the election with a sheaf of testimonials. Local planters, magistrates, the doctor, and the rector all attested both to the good condition of his slaves and to his genuine concern for their spiritual and physical welfare. He now made full use of this material, and almost from the outset of the polling it was clear that he was set fair for victory. However, his expenses still exceeded £2,000, so he was grateful when a group of friends opened a subscription to assist him.[26]

There was an unpleasant postscript to this triumph. Goulburn was determined to clear his name of the imputation of mistreatment of his slaves. He demanded from Thomas Pringle, secretary to the Anti-Slavery Society, an explanation of its failure to give him an opportunity to refute the charges before they were put in circulation. This exchange eventually flushed out their author, Zachary Macaulay. Initially, Macaulay avoided a confrontation following the death of his wife and with pleas of his own ill health. Nevertheless, he opened the door to additional controversy by rejecting any notion that direct proof was required of the abuse of Goulburn's slaves. Their plight could safely be inferred, he insisted, from the general condition of Jamaican slaves. This statement, forwarded by a third party, infuriated Goulburn. For want of a direct target, he first vented his spleen on the vicar of Harrow, one of his leading clerical canvassers. This unfortunate had not only withheld information from Goulburn in 1826, but he continued to defend Macaulay as a man of noble character and righteous zeal. But Goulburn's prey remained Macaulay, whom he eventually succeeded in drawing into a direct correspondence. What he sought from the old abolitionist was an admission of excessive zeal if not error in the assault on Goulburn's record as a slave owner. Instead, Macaulay artfully shifted ground and argument, forever slithering infuriatingly out of the politician's grasp.[27]

The likelihood, therefore, of this damaging charge being again brought against Goulburn "whenever an opportunity shall offer"

convinced him of the need for additional testimonials. From the
rector of the Alley church, St Peter's, which bordered his estate, he
sought further proof of the spiritual and physical care of his labour
force. Several months elapsed before he received a reply, this priest
having fallen victim to that ill health which had carried off five of his
predecessors in as many years. He eventually reported that the young
of Amity Hall were under the care of his curate, who visited the estate
twice each week to give instruction to the children. Indeed, during his
visitation in April, the bishop of Jamaica, now finally appointed, examined several hundred children before singling out for particular praise
those from Goulburn's estate. As for the adults, the rector reported
that Goulburn's slaves were as diligent in their church attendance as
those on other plantations. Even more helpful, he and the bishop confirmed that the past four years had witnessed a marked improvement
in their character and conduct.[28]

Goulburn's hard-earned victory at Cambridge provided Tories with
one of their few opportunities to cheer an election result. "It is an oasis
in the Desert and the only relief we have had in these desperate times,"
Wellington congratulated him. Fully three-quarters of the Tories who
had been returned in England sat for boroughs earmarked by the
Whigs for disfranchisement, and barely a handful of Tory loyalists now
represented English counties. The reformers were in complete command of the Commons. Their swollen ranks included the strengthened Radicals, whose success excited Tory fears for the security of
property, the colonies, the union with Ireland, and even the monarchy.
Wellington had no doubt of what needed to be done. They had to rally
their depleted forces and make a stand as soon as possible after the
opening of the new Parliament. "If that is done early it will be done effectually," he assured Goulburn. "If it is delayed we shall find Terror
preventing many from doing what they know to be right, and forcing
many to do that which they know to be wrong." Clearly, he opposed
any continuation of the temporizing tactics Peel had imposed on the
party during the spring.[29]

Here was the rub. Peel had created something of a sensation in London by his comments at a public dinner in his new constituency of Tamworth. He had attempted to lay claim, as Goulburn had at Cambridge,
to the middle ground of politics. He rejected at one "extreme" the
Ultras, who were opposed to all change, and at the other the Whigs/
Radicals, whom he dismissed as "advocates of too violent and sudden in-
novations." Still smarting from the savage personal criticism of his reversal on Catholic emancipation, he insisted that it was "impossible for any
statesman to adopt one fixed line of policy under all circumstances."
Did this comment signal an intention to compromise with the reform

spirit that was so popular in the country? The answer he gave to inquiring friends and concerned colleagues lacked the simplicity and clarity of Wellington's position. Peel intended to evade all responsibility for the passage of reform even as he disdained the politics of expediency. He would enter into no pacts of convenience with the extremes on his political spectrum simply to defeat the government. He remained of the opinion that there was "nothing half so dangerous as the man who pretends to be a Conservative, but is ready to be anything, provided only he can create confusion."[30]

Goulburn struggled to convince Peel to be more active. Only through "a perfect understanding and concert" of all those oppposed to the government's measure would waverers be reassured, the timid cheered, and the Whig rumour squelched that Peel would never "combine" with other opponents of the Reform Bill. "Without you we of course can do nothing beyond considering the various courses that are open to us," Goulburn admitted. "We have a good force and I think may do a great deal if we can direct it properly and in a body." The response he received was discouraging. Peel would "cooperate with any person of any party in resistance to the Bill," but expected to be defeated on its principle and was already looking to the possibility of mitigating "the evil of the details." However, he continued to reject any association with the Ultras, and he exhibited a morbid anxiety to avoid at all costs the charge of naked ambition. Nor was he unmindful of his limitations as a leader, not the least of which was his refusal to suffer political fools and bores gladly. Thus he subjected to withering ridicule a proposal that the opponents of reform sit down to a political dinner before the meeting of Parliament. He even declined to join Goulburn, Wellington, and a baker's dozen of other colleagues in establishing an official headquarters for the party's organizing committee. Nevertheless, the Tories soon had an office and a greater measure of organization.[31]

Examining the many new faces in the Commons when Parliament opened in mid-June, Goulburn judged that they were "not very good looking nor yet so bad" as he had expected. More attractive were the well-founded rumours of disunity within the ranks of the governing coalition. The Radicals were reported to be demanding a greater measure of reform, which Goulburn glibly attributed to a relentless pursuit of cheap popularity, while the Whigs and Canningites were riven by mutual distrust. Indeed, Lord Melbourne (William Lamb) was ill, and Palmerston was under the influence of Lady Cowper, "who is working toothe and nail to separate him from the Government." "Our best course undoubtedly will be to endeavour to break the connection between the Radicals and the present Government," Goulburn reasoned.

Not that he expected to effect a breach, persuaded as he was that the ministry was "more radical than the radicals." On 24 June, Russell's motion for leave to bring in the second Reform Bill was approved without debate. This new measure marginally increased the number of disfranchisements; among the boroughs now to lose both seats was the Cornish fishing village of St Germans for which Goulburn had once sat. Early in July the bill comfortably survived second reading, only for the Tories to resort to the ready arsenal of procedural devices in a vain but exhausting effort first to prevent the opening of the committee stage and then to prolong it. Members underwent an endurance test as the legislation inched along at a snail's pace in a hot and ill-tempered chamber. Ill health saved Goulburn from much of this strain and discomfort, at least during July and August, but whenever he did travel up from Betchworth he was in the vanguard of the government's harassers. His appetite for detail, which three years at the Exchequer had failed to sate, made him a formidable adversary at this level. He was quick to recognize and exploit apparent inconsistencies in the bill's many clauses, mocking the ministers for "legislating in the dark." He assailed their violation of an agreement on the time set aside for debate, thereby exhibiting "a total want of courtesy" towards members who had private business to transact. Not surprisingly, the bill's supporters were frustrated and infuriated by these guerrilla tactics and Goulburn became the target of much verbal abuse. "Really it is too bad that a member cannot be allowed to speak the truth when the prosperity of the country is at stake ... without being involved in discussions of a personal nature," Jane Goulburn complained.[32]

During the steamy and emotionally charged days of high summer, Peel at last began to assert his leadership of the opposition. He continued to throw cold water on Goulburn's enthusiasm for a temporary alliance with the Radicals, arguing that to defeat the ministry with such allies would not only throw on the Tories the responsibility of "making the bill more radical" but would also invite accusations of sacrificing principle to expediency. However, on the morning of 26 August he did attend a meeting at the party's new committee room, where the decision was taken to cease dividing the exhausted House until third reading. The hope was that they would then make a good showing before speeding the bill to the Lords. All of this Peel reported to a convalescing Goulburn. He then gathered his senior colleagues, including Wellington, at his Staffordshire home in early September to plot strategy. Goulburn's poor health again kept him away. And when Peel's extended absence from the capital during the late summer set tongues wagging, he was persuaded to return to the Commons for the final stages of the debate.[33]

Goulburn duly ceased the harassment of the government, which he had continued intermittently as his strength allowed. But the Tories had made a number of gains. The total membership of the reformed Parliament would be much the same as the old. The number of boroughs that were to lose representation had been reduced. More important still, the franchise in the counties had been successfully amended to increase the number of voters amenable to landlord influence. With these modifications, the bill was carried to the Lords on 22 September. Goulburn decided not to observe the debate in the Upper House, since the chamber was certain to be so full as to be uncomfortable. There, after five nights of drama, reform was defeated on second reading by a majority of forty-one.[34]

Defeat in the Lords saw the government's supporters in the Commons introduce on 10 October a motion of "unabated confidence" in its "integrity, perseverance and ability." Goulburn was first on his feet for the opposition in an unsuccessful effort to broaden the discussion from reform to Althorp's inept performance at the Exchequer. Bolstered by an immense majority on the confidence motion, the cabinet appealed for calm as demonstrations were held to protest the action of the Lords. Arriving late for that debate, an ironic Goulburn explained that he had been "overborne by an assembled multitude" marching through the capital. Nevertheless, ministerial assurances that another Reform Bill would soon be introduced had seemingly stilled much of the clamour when Parliament was prorogued on 20 October, only for the cities of Nottingham and Bristol to erupt. These riots convinced some persons of property that constitutional change was more perilous than inaction. Sensitive to the growth of such sentiment, the "cabinet were led to adopt a more conservative position."[35]

The government drafted a third bill. The number of boroughs to lose representation was again curtailed, and the Commons was restored to its full pre-reform membership. As a concession to the Radicals, more of the available seats were to be transferred to large northern towns. The government also made an approach to the Tory "Waverers." However, when their leader, Lord Wharncliffe, suggested to Peel that the Tories as a whole should cooperate with the government to enact this much-modified measure, he was left in no doubt that such an arrangement remained out of the question. Nor was Henry Goulburn, whom Peel kept advised of developments, in a more conciliatory mood. He expected another stormy campaign, "for the state of the country and of all our concerns foreign and domestic is such as to call forth every latent feeling of bitterness and hostility."[36]

The bill was introduced on 12 December, and five days later it swept through second reading with a majority that equalled the total vote of the opposition. Goulburn disagreed with Peel on the course they should now follow. He was pessimistic of their chances of stripping the bill in committee of its "objectionable" provisions, as his friend proposed. He suspected that the majority of the Commons would "vote as they are bid" and send it up to the Lords unaltered. Moreover, he doubted that any significant amendments would even be made in the Upper House. The peers simply lacked the stamina necessary to overcome "the dead weight of the Government" during their committee stage, he warned, while their fear of the people would deter them from a second outright rejection of reform. Therefore, the Tories in the Commons should make every effort to spur resistance and to encourage those committed to amendments also to oppose if their proposed changes were not adopted. Indeed, he backed the introduction of a substitute measure in the Lords, one that would pose little danger if passed yet would provide the peers with a peg on which to hang their defeat of the government's bill. "It is therefore bad policy in us to do anything which looks like encouraging an idea that we think the Bill as it is must pass."[37]

Peel's objection to any Tory bill remained what it had always been. "The author of the substitute does assume if not the whole, at least a very serious share of the future responsibility of his own act," he observed, whereas "the mitigator in Committee is absolutely free from any responsibility." Equally, Goulburn had omitted from his analysis the likelihood of the king being prevailed upon to create sufficient peers to ensure passage of the government bill in the Upper House. Under this threat, all that the Tories could reasonably hope to achieve was mitigation of the "evil" by nibbling away at the bill's edges. Furthermore, the government would be more vulnerable on the Irish bill. Goulburn had already embarrassed the ministers by drawing attention to the different principles that governed the Irish measure, apparently for no more principled reason than to deny cities such as Galway and Cork increased representation. "They have so blundered the whole business of Irish Reform without an excuse for their blundering," Peel remarked, "that I see no honorable escape for them from their embarrassment."[38]

As ever, Goulburn deferred to Peel. Perhaps he was further encouraged to do so by his friend's increasingly forceful leadership of the opposition. Peel was active in the essential business of ensuring a good attendance of Tories in the House; he was a full participant in the discussions that resulted in the abandonment of the modest committee room in Charles Street for a more imposing and well-funded Carlton Club; and in January he dined with Goulburn and Herries to concert a "plan of operation" in the Commons. They decided to focus on the ministers' weak handling of the nation's finances in order "to keep up a growing opinion in the public mind of the incompetency of the Government to conduct any real business." In this endeavour Goulburn naturally assumed a leading role. He had taken every opportunity to illustrate the Whigs' failings, and Althorp's frequent financial statements certainly provided no shortage of them. Goulburn's repeated warnings of the dangers of operating with only a miniscule surplus now acquired the aura of prophecy. He extracted from the Treasury the painful admission that a small projected surplus had been transformed into a somewhat larger actual deficit. "So much for Whig rule," one approving Tory listener remarked.[39]

By their "moderation" during the committee stage of the Reform Bill, the Tory leaders hoped to lull some of the government's friends into overconfidence. To the extent that they absented themselves from the often tedious proceedings, Peel and Goulburn might at least create the illusion on divisions of diminishing support for the bill. Not that this hope was realized. The series of motions they moved were all crushed. A recurrent theme of Goulburn's frequent interventions was the failure of the ministers to provide the Commons with adequate information on which to base important decisions. He called for more information on the way in which the fifty-six boroughs to lose all representation were selected; for more information on the choice of the thirty earmarked to lose a single seat; and for more information on the electoral divisions of the counties that were to receive additional seats. After all, he pointed out, if the divisions were to be geographical, the agricultural interest in Warwickshire, for example, would be swamped by the residents of Birmingham and Coventry. "Ministers appeared determined to decide the question first," he repeated time and again, "and give the necessary information afterwards." Implicit in this criticism was the charge that the cabinet was not above partiality in many of its decisions.[40]

A second theme of Goulburn's remarks was the bill's impracticality in the large towns. How was the £10 householder franchise to be enforced, he asked. It might be necessary to track a potential voter through five or six parishes. Difficult as this would be in metropolitan districts, what of the additional confusion in the all too likely event that houses were rated on different principles in different parishes? He mocked the requirement that lists of registered voters were to be posted on church doors, together with the revised lists necessitated by inadvertent omissions and successful challenges to persons who had been included. Where would they find doors large enough to carry this material? He contested the grant of a temporary authority to sheriffs to compel persons to serve as returning officers, arguing that it might be abused in order to disqualify potential candidates for election. When Althorp sought to answer this objection by freeing from any danger of compulsion persons with landed property worth more than £300 a year, Goulburn complained that the class of persons best qualified to fill the position was being excluded. Both he and Peel assailed the provision that charged the expenses of election officials to the poor rates. They warned that this would erode public support for this fund. And it was Goulburn who summed up for the opposition in the last act on the Commons stage on 26 March, Peel having spoken four days earlier. He made one final defence of the old system, arguing that it was representative of "every class" and was far less venal and corrupt than the reformers charged. He opposed the government's bill because it was "pregnant with danger to almost every interest in the State." The only remaining hope was that it would be rejected by the Lords.[41]

The bill was carried up to the Lords that same day, 26 March. In mid-April it survived second reading by a small majority. Yet the ministers fully expected to encounter serious resistance in committee. Their apprehension and difficulties were heightened by the monarch's backtracking on an earlier promise to create sufficient additional peers to guarantee passage of the bill, especially when news of his change of heart leaked out. So in response to a defeat on a Tory motion, the cabinet members offered the king a choice between their resignation and his creation of a substantial number of new peers. On 9 May he opted for the former and commissioned Wellington to form a government. During the several days of ensuing turmoil, Henry Goulburn also was obliged to make a choice – between Wellington and Peel as his leader.[42]

A soldier's sense of duty had ensured that Wellington would respond to his monarch's call, even at the cost of further damage to his political reputation. Some measure of reform would have to be enacted, he acknowledged. Yet to reverse positions again would expose all Tories to scorn, however high minded the motive might be. A savage attack on the duke in the *Times*, at the first whisper of his forming a ministry committed to a measure of reform, surely penetrated Peel's notoriously thin skin and contributed to his rejection of office. Equally unnerving was the outburst of public anger at this turn of events, which led to a run on the Bank of England's gold reserves. Ignoring these portents, some leading Tories excitedly speculated on the composition of a second Wellington administration. Goulburn's name was bandied around as an interim cabinet minister, perhaps holding the Home Office until Peel changed his mind, before being placed in the Speaker's chair. But the duke quickly discovered that even the loyal Goulburn, whose sense of duty and desire to rescue the king from his predicament rivalled his own, declined to serve.[43]

Goulburn was already under the Radicals' lash for his stinging criticisms of the Whigs' management of the nation's finances. They castigated him as "all hodge-podge, subterfuge and deception." This unpleasant public attention – for one of the advantages of operating in the shadow of greater men was the avoidance of the spotlight – may have influenced his answer to Wellington. Certainly, friends and associates assumed that, identified as he was with Peel as a prominent opponent of reform and having stood shoulder to shoulder with him while he executed his about-face on Catholic emancipation, Goulburn could ill afford now "to take a line that would expose him not only to the taunts of political adversaries, but to the bitter reproach of a comparison with Peel."[44]

Yet it was not a simple matter of Goulburn again following his friend's lead. He had concluded for himself that from the moment of the last dissolution, the king was pledged to a measure of reform far in excess of anything with which Goulburn could personally be identified. "It is to my mind quite clear," he explained to his wife, "that the King cannot be assisted at any sacrifice of personal character." Goulburn had recently assured an acquaintance that he "could be no party to introducing any bill of reform." Similarly, the state of the country and of the House of Commons, "infuriated as both have been by the acts of a democratic administration, put out of question any attempt to make an anti-reform or even a moderate reform administration." In short, Goulburn saw no honourable way of coming to terms with the present House and no prospect of "any advantage from immediate dissolution." "The result is melancholy to all who love order or real liberty," he allowed, "but I cannot say it is to me unexpected or other than the natural march of our revolution." The Reform Bill had to be passed, he now realized, before any campaign could be launched to turn out the government. Further, during an interview with the duke, he made plain his acceptance of Peel's leadership. He thought "that a united opposition to the Bill headed by Sir R. Peel gave a far better chance of modifying the Bill [than] any Government formed on the principle of modification could give."[45]

The refusal of Peel, Goulburn, and then several other leading Tories in the Commons to serve under Wellington dashed the duke's hopes of constructing a ministry. Not that Goulburn rested easy. The king had been left "to make such terms as he may with men who, having no regard for monarchy and no feeling for existing institutions, will not be very merciful in their triumph and will for a time march uncontrouled [*sic*] upon the revolutionary road which they have opened for themselves." His consolation was his faith that "we are in God's hands and he will dispose of all things." So with Grey back in office, fortified by the monarch's ironclad pledge to create as many peers as were necessary to carry the bill, the Tories abandoned the struggle, and the Reform Bill became law on 7 June 1832. The electorate was increased significantly in size; a total of eighty-seven boroughs lost representation, partial or complete; and the redistribution of seats began to correct the southern and rural overrepresentation in the Commons.[46]

Goulburn spent the summer attending the secret committee on banking and anxiously watching for signs that Wellington was recovering from the depression into which he had sunk following his humiliating failure to form a government. There was also a cholera epidemic to worry about, and there were preparations to be made for the first election under the reformed system of representation. More pleasant was the opportunity to luxuriate in the praise his eldest son was winning at Cambridge. Harry's performance as runner-up for a major scholarship was given unusual notice, but it was less this minor distinction than the manner in which Harry had accepted defeat that made his father swell with pride. "Honors may be easily attained," Goulburn observed, "but such absence of selfishness is the most delightful and most rare triumph."[47]

Harry Goulburn had gone up to Trinity in 1831 and was soon complaining, in the best undergraduate tradition, that the lectures were "stupid." The threatened arrival of cholera added both anxiety and excitement to his life. This terrifying disease had swept across Europe, travelling from India via Afghanistan to Russia. Following the traditional trade routes and carried by Russian troops into Poland and then by refugees from that unhappy country to other European centres, its advance had been watched with apprehension in England. As a precautionary step, the government had created an advisory board of health in June 1831 to draft regulations for the guidance of local authorities and their own advisory boards. The first case officially diagnosed in Britain was in the northeastern port of Sunderland, and from there it began its insidious march. By the end of November, Harry was reporting to his parents that rowing had been suspended at Cambridge for fear that if "there was any choleric tendency in the air there was no exercise or employment so likely to bring it into operation." Certainly, it was a water-borne disease.[48]

The Goulburns were briefly distracted from this general threat to health by mounting concern for the spiritual and physical welfare of their second son. Edward's slow growth suggested that he would be "very squat indeed," and his aversion to exercise contributed to his sickliness. "The poor boy means well, but his views and tastes want purifying, and I fear the real work is yet unbegun in his soul," his mother confided to his eldest brother. Jane Goulburn had recently organized a Sunday school at Betchworth in which sixty children were enrolled. Although the junior Goulburns were each required to lead a class, Edward was as reluctant to perform his religious exercises as his physical. Henry first thought of packing him off to the stern Rev. Elliott's in Brighton for tutoring. Next, he sought Wellington's aid in securing him a commission in the Grenadier Guards. The duke duly entered Edward's name on the list of candidates but cautioned that "everybody wants to have a Son or Relative" in the Guards and that the list was therefore long and "much time must elapse" before a candidate receives his commission.[49]

The appearance of cholera in the capital in February 1832 did not alarm Goulburn at first, limited as it largely was to the sordid slums of Rotherhithe and Southwark along the Thames. He reassured his anxious wife that "it does not extend itself rapidly and that it confines its effects mostly to the lowest order and to the dissipated and filthy even of that class, [so] that I do not apprehend that its existence in London need give any alarm to those who live in any dwelling and who are of regular habits." Complacency, and the belief that the disease was a form of punishment for those who were not only poverty-stricken but depraved, appears to have left Goulburn less sensitive than some of his less evangelical contemporaries to the appalling "moral and physical degredation" of so many of the lowest class. Thus one worldly observer noted that the "awful thing" revealed by the epidemic was the "evidence of the rotten foundation on which the whole fabric of this gorgeous society" rests. "Is it possible for any country to be considered in a healthy condition when there is no such thing as a *general* diffusion of the comforts of life?" Henry Goulburn admitted to no such doubts.[50]

Before long, however, the disease proved to be a respecter of neither class nor conscience. "It is frightful how much the complaint is spreading amongst the higher orders," Jane Goulburn observed. Goulburn now sought virtually to quarantine his family at Betchworth. He carried down from London supplies each week in order to avoid deliveries by local merchants. And he forwarded the latest medical instructions on how to respond if cholera was suspected. Not that these were calculated to inspire confidence. At the first sign of a bowel disorder, family and staff were to take a glass of port containing ten drops of laudanum. If the attack was accompanied by vomiting, the stomach was to be cleansed by a "spoonful of mustard in warm water." No less important was prevention, and to this end he ordered a much-reduced consumption of raw fruit and vegetables. Unlike other evangelicals, Goulburn did not subscribe to the belief that the disease was an exercise of divine retribution. He did not call for the closing of all places of public entertainment, and he was one of those who attempted to restrain the younger Spencer Perceval, the son of the assassinated prime minister, who rose in the House on the eve of a national day of fasting and humiliation to excoriate the nation and Parliament. Goulburn considered Perceval the victim of religious dementia; he was himself beginning to drift away from an increasingly divisive and intolerant evangelicalism. As for his evangelical son, to keep Harry out of harm's way, Goulburn gave him permission to spend the summer hiking through majestic Snowdonia, on the understanding that he would not be too adventurous in climbing the mountains. Harry had inherited his father's poor sight.[51]

The Goulburn family survived the first cholera epidemic unscathed, and by mid-August Henry was ruefully analysing political affairs. He marvelled at the lack of interest in the tumult in Ireland, mordantly supposing that members of Parliament had grown so used to considering "murder natural death in that country" that they regarded as "natural occurrences" riots and resistance to the law. He was critical of the ministers' involvement in Don Pedro's attempt to seize control of Portugal, fearing that the government would impose on that nation a monarch whom the people "and especially that portion of the Portuguese who are attached to England by their interests and feelings will not willingly receive." Of more immediate interest to him, with a general election in the offing, was the working of the Reform Bill. Goulburn saw no evidence that Betchworth men were hastening to claim the franchise, not least because of the one-shilling registration fee. And while he suspected that this might fuel demands for additional changes to the law, he was heartened by the thought that "the people of this country care more about being well governed than about sharing in the Franchise and this after all was the sound argument against Reform and was common sense."[52]

Thinking ahead to life in the reformed Parliament, some Tories turned over in their minds the merits of likely candidates for the Speaker's chair, which the incumbent had indicated he intended to vacate. The need for an experienced and respected parliamentarian was even more pressing in these exceptional circumstances. Approached by Charles Wynn, who was seeking support for his candidacy, Peel delayed replying until he had elicited Goulburn's "opinions, wishes and feelings." The position was one that attracted Goulburn, for it was "highly honorable in itself" and would afford "the means of providing for, or at least assisting" his posterity. Yet as Peel pointed out, there was scant likelihood of the Tories carrying the chair against the government; moreover, should the Tories unexpectedly triumph in the upcoming general election, he would want to have Goulburn in cabinet. All that the Tories could reasonably hope to achieve, therefore, was a decent showing in the contest for the Speaker's chair. To this end, and this end only, explained Peel, he was prepared to cooperate with the Radicals, and Goulburn would be far less attractive a candidate to them than Wynn, who had the reputation as something of a reformer. It was a line of reasoning that Goulburn loyally followed. "What feelings of ambition I may have had are gone," he explained, "and I only remain in public life because God has cast my lot there, and because I consider it the duty of every man to use his best endeavours in the station in which he finds himself to arrest the progress of evil; in other words to check the frantic career of the Government." This could only be achieved, he acknowledged, by keeping together the party that was opposed to the present ministers. He would thus do whatever "may best strengthen the conservative party."[53]

As it happened, the sitting Speaker, Manners Sutton, changed his mind and announced a desire to return to the chair. Indeed, he decided to stand with Goulburn as a candidate for the University of Cambridge. Although Goulburn initially questioned the wisdom of nominating two Trinity men, fearing the alienation of the large force of Johnians, the strategy worked. They met little opposition. And although the slavery question was again agitated effectively in many constituencies, Goulburn heard not a whisper of it in Cambridge. His dogged pursuit of Zachary Macaulay after the previous contest was paying a handsome dividend. Even his expenses were a mere fraction of those of 1831. Astonished by the ease of his success and of the assistance he received from former supporters of Palmerston and Cavendish, he was tempted to generalize. "Judging in short from what I have seen here," he reported to Peel, "I should say that conservative principle had gained great strength in the educated classes of the community." This may have been the case in Cambridge, but elsewhere they were overwhelmed by the new electorate. Only 147 Conservatives were returned. The silver lining to this dark cloud of defeat was the Tories' modest recovery in the English counties, where they had made much of their commitment to the protection of the landed interest.[54]

CHAPTER NINE

The Conservative Revival

Late in 1832, Henry Goulburn initiated a discussion with Robert Peel on Tory strategy for the upcoming session of Parliament. Theirs remained a friendship founded on absolute trust and mutual admiration. "I can never have any difficulty in stating to you without reserve my wishes and feelings upon any subject," Goulburn declared, "for I am confident that the same regard for me which would lead you to give due consideration to what I might state would equally prevent you being unduly biased by any ill-judged or erroneous opinions which I might appear to you to entertain." In this spirit, he emphasized yet again "the importance of perfect union and complete concert with all who called themselves Conservative, as the only hope of keeping a party together," and opined that "without a strong party, strong in union more than in numbers, there was no hope of our being of any use." The time had come, in short, to put past differences behind them and unite with the Ultras. Peel was unmoved. He even discouraged an opposition meeting "to arrange any course of action" before the opening of Parliament. Plans were liable to be "disturbed" by developments, he explained unconvincingly. Similarly, he continued to repudiate any association with the Radicals merely to frustrate the government. He believed that the "chief object" of a party of Conservatives was to resist radicalism, and to this end he was prepared to support the coalition ministry whenever it espoused their principles. "The party that interposes" between the Whigs and the Radicals "will have the greatest advantage, relatively I mean to its own intrinsic strength," he argued. Should there be no breach between government and Radicals, then they must oppose this united force with all their energy. His objective was the methodical reconstruction of a Conservative party undermined by reform. They would soon find "in circumstances a bond of union," he insisted, and would "ultimately gain the confidence of the Property and good sense of the Country."[1]

Goulburn was naturally disappointed by his friend's steadfast "unwillingness to unite cordially with the Ultras," for his private information indicated that the Radicals and the O'Connellites intended to "support the Government cordially." In the short term, therefore, Conservatives were likely to require every vote they could muster if they were to stall the party of "Mouvement." So he continued to hope that he could soften Peel's attitude towards the Ultras. Another problem and distraction was Peel's frigid relationship with the Duke of Wellington. However, the Tories who attended the Carlton Club in promising numbers on the eve of the new Parliament resolved to follow Peel's lead in the Commons. They would "lie by" in order "to allow the Ministers to fight it out with the Radicals, to punish the Whigs for their infamous conduct, and expose the Radicals to the world."[2]

When the House opened, both aspect and atmosphere seemed very different from earlier Parliaments. New faces were legion, and the leading Tories found their seats occupied by Radicals and O'Connellites, so they were obliged to move up nearer to the Speaker. This displacement seemed to be a metaphor for their diminished standing. The first weeks of the session appeared to confirm Goulburn's worst fears of a feeble ministry capitulating to its extremist allies. He deplored the Whigs' tolerance of the Radicals' "false attacks" on the "Higher orders." "The Government in fact are utterly incapable," he fumed, "and their ignorance as much as their want of principle accelerates the progress of revolution." More disturbing still, however, was the fact that "the grossest attacks were made on the clergy by the most popular members of the legislature." He feared that a sustained assault was going to be launched on the established church and on the Anglican exclusiveness of the two ancient universities where its clergy were educated. For him, as for the precociously gifted William Ewart Gladstone, who was just embarking on a career of public service, "the preservation of the Church and the triumph of Christian values" was the core of his political being. Thus in those urban areas "where dissolute habits were owing to poverty," he believed that "the best remedy for the evil was the providing the means of improving their morals" through church construction.[3]

Now well into middle age, standing "rather above middle size," his strong features showing the tell-tale marks of age, his hair receding, his countenance thoughtful, and his head leaning somewhat to the left side, no doubt because of his injured eye, Goulburn still cut a fine figure. "His appearance is much in his favour, and his manner of delivery is easy and graceful," remarked one observer admiringly. "He has a fine musical voice, and times his utterance with much judgment to the ear." Goulburn was now a more assured speaker, having discovered during the struggle over the Reform Bill that he did possess ability in the art of reply. Quick witted, only rarely at a loss for words, and blessed with a "faultless" command of language, he had at last found an effective role as a parliamentarian. However, the "favourable impression" he immediately made was to some extent "neutralized" by his "extreme" notions of church and state. On this subject, there were few "more zealous or decided Tories" in the House. Indeed, many of Goulburn's fellow Tories were increasingly reluctant to alienate the growing army of nonconformists by resolutely upholding all of the rights and privileges of the establishment. The situation was further confused by the emergence of the Oxford Movement, which added another strain to the existing tug, within the church, between the orthodox and evangelicals. Goulburn continued to keep a foot in each of these camps, though this became ever more difficult as their relations grew more hostile. His religious position had always been embraced by Samuel Horsley's inclusive definition of High Church, that is, "an attachment to the Church of England on purely doctrinal grounds and a conviction in favour of its divine authority and spiritual independence." Now Goulburn also passed the new test, which required a stern defence of the church against dissenters.[4]

In later life, Goulburn recalled that a number of the most energetic advocates of parliamentary reform avowed "that the perpetual exclusion of the Tories from office was one of its main objectives and advantages." In their pursuit of this ambition, he accused the Whigs of having closed their eyes to other consequences; in particular, the extent to which they made themselves hostages of a powerful group of supporters – "the various classes of dissenters." Certainly, the old alliance of Whigs and nonconformity was reinforced and reinvigorated by the struggle over this reform. Emancipated in 1828 (and further emboldened by the passage of the Reform Bill, which may have resulted in their constituting one-fifth of the electorate), most Protestant dissenters were startlingly open and savage in their attacks on the establishment. And while the leadership of the Methodists was reassuringly Tory with its commitment to the principle of religious establishments, the rank and file tended to vote Liberal. Similarly, in Ireland, far from reconciling the Catholic majority to the church, emancipation appeared merely to have whetted the appetite for a redistribution of its property. As for the oath which Catholic members of Parliament were required to take, pledging not to subvert the established church, Daniel O'Connell pointed out that they had not sworn to continue it.[5]

The church was vulnerable. The bishops' contribution to the defeat of the Reform Bill in the Lords in October 1831, the shortage of places of worship in the industrial towns and regions, the large number of parishes that lacked resident clergy, the extent of pluralism, the irritants of the tithe and church rates, the alleged wealth of the church, and the maldistribution of its income were all grist for Radical mills. Defenders such as Henry Goulburn knew that the church was acting to correct these evils and that it was doing so with a gradualism which he regarded as the essence of true and safe reform. A diocesan revival was under way, led primarily by the orthodox, while evangelicals had been in the forefront of the movement to establish Sunday schools, infant schools, and lending libraries, and to bring "the teaching of the Church to the door of the most distant cottage." However, evangelicalism had proven a source of even greater nonconformist strength. Similarly, some reforms had been less than effective. So many livings lacked residences that residence was difficult to enforce. Legislation to raise the stipends of curates had lowered the number of clergy living in abject poverty but had not addressed the larger problem of income inequity. On the other hand, since 1818 there had been a substantial investment of public funds in church construction and the repair and rebuilding of parsonages. However, the pace of reform was too circumspect and the abuses still too egregious for critics to be silenced.[6]

Their first attack seemed certain to be directed against the exposed Irish flank. At a time when members of the Church of England seemed to be in peril of being reduced to a national minority, the membership of the Church of Ireland was no more than a fraction of the Irish population, and yet the institutional edifice rivalled that of its sister church. Not surprisingly, many Irish clergy were redundant, while nonresidence and pluralism were all too common. The entire top-heavy structure was sustained by the hated tithe. Here was an institution which Radicals, dissenters, and Catholics considered "as anomalous and inefficient as any rotten borough." Yet its reform presented problems for the governing coalition. Edward Stanley and James Graham were the most prominent members of a faction determined to guard the unique role and property rights of the established church. Liberal Anglicans, on the other hand, "aided and abetted" by Lord Althorp and other evangelical Whigs, wished not only to maintain the church but also to redress religious grievances and even appropriate the surplus revenues of the Irish church for social and educational purposes.[7]

Goulburn vehemently objected to the new system of national education established in Ireland by the Whigs, for it excluded the Bible from periods of joint instruction of Protestant and Catholic children, and it deprived the established clergy of a supervisory role. He complained that this system would give "direct and open" encouragement to Roman Catholicism, and he warned that "if the Word of God was to be neglected, there was an end of all of the blessed effects which were generally attributed to religion." While Goulburn remained profoundly suspicious of all Whigs, many of whom he regarded as little better than Jacobins and infidels, he cooperated with Edward Stanley in 1832 in an effort to settle the problem of Irish tithes. The inability of many clergy to collect their income and the belief that the tax lay at the root of much of the rural violence in Ireland were reasons enough for a select committee to be struck. Goulburn served on the committee, which eventually proposed three measures: the permanent and compulsory composition of tithes and the transfer of their payment from tenant to landowner; their redemption, at something less than the nominal value, in the form of a single cash payment or commutation for land; and the establishment of an ecclesiastical corporation consisting of bishops and beneficed clergy to manage church finances. Only two measures were pushed through Parliament in 1832, however – the Composition Bill and an act authorizing the government to make advances to the hard-up clergy.[8]

Goulburn supported the government "in order to enforce payment of what is due to the Clergy," for the initial proposals were merely an extension of the measures he had introduced a decade earlier. Little did he realize, as he worked with Stanley, how far the cabinet was prepared to go in its reform of the Irish church. Nor was he alone. Edward Stanley presented far-reaching reforms to his senior colleagues in October 1832, only to be obliged to amend them at the insistence of Radical and Liberal Anglican ministers. The number of sees he had proposed eventually to extinguish was increased to two archbishoprics and eight bishoprics. The church rate was abolished, the revenues of two of the wealthiest sees reduced, and an income tax levied on the more comfortable livings. Stanley's commission to inquire into benefices and sinecures was now to be given the power to suspend new appointments to livings where divine service had not been performed for three years. Finally, the principle that monies saved were to be applied exclusively to church purposes, which the chief secretary had artfully sought to finesse, was further compromised. A portion of any savings might be applied to secular purposes.[9]

Althorp introduced legislation embodying these measures on 13 February 1833, and Peel and Goulburn lost no time making plain their opposition to many of them. Yet they were inhibited in their attacks by the Whigs' astute involvement of the Irish primate in the initial deliberations. Goulburn explained privately to his angry colleagues how Archbishop Beresford had been compromised – a task he performed to such good effect that Tory hostility towards the prelate was replaced by something approaching sympathy. Another restraint on them was the anxiety not to bring on a vote which, if lost, might well invite harsher measures. Nevertheless, Goulburn did have one "important victory for friends of the Church." He artfully substituted benefices for parishes in the returns of places in which divine service had not been conducted for the last three years. The former included unions of parishes, within most of which a service was far more likely to have been performed. Yet he continued to regard the bill as a spineless government concession to some of its allies and a stalking horse for "the destruction of Church property" in England as well as Ireland.[10]

That spring, Goulburn was unable to attend the House as frequently as he would have wished. First, his youngest son, Freddy, was struck down in mid-April by a feverish illness. Then he himself was felled in a severe bout with influenza, which left him as "weak as a cat" and again spitting blood. As late as mid-June his condition remained a source of anxiety to friends. Peel kept him abreast of developments and consulted him on tactics, and they took some credit for the "material improvement" of the Irish Church Bill. A number of incumbents had been exempted from the new tax on benefices, and the powers of the commission authorized to suspend appointments wherever divine service had not been performed for three years had been curtailed. Nevertheless, Goulburn remained unalterably opposed to several other features: the interference with the property of bishoprics and the possible appropriation of monies to other than church purposes; the grant of powers "in matters purely ecclesiastical" to lay commissioners; the reduction in the number of bishops, which would condemn parts of Ireland to the misfortune of never encountering a Protestant prelate; and the prohibition of the separation of parish unions or the building of additional churches in them. Goulburn returned to the Commons on 13 May to register his opposition and to reaffirm that in his opinion a true policy would promote the expansion not the contraction of Protestantism. Althorp gave ground, while Peel made headway with his unrelenting criticism of the possible appropriation of church monies to secular purposes. At Stanley's suggestion, this controversial clause was abandoned. Infuriated by this retreat, the Radicals indicated their intention to oppose third reading. Peel, who was ever averse to association with them and had been confidentially advised by Stanley of the divisions within cabinet, was tempted to accept the amended bill as the least objectionable terms likely to be obtained for the Irish church. But Goulburn held him up to the mark of opposition, for he was convinced that this was no "final arrangement," and he feared that Tory acquiescence in the bill's passage might deter the

Lords from amending it further. Holding their noses, the Conservatives entered the lobby with the Radicals on 8 July to vote against passage.[11]

Wellington's hostility to the bill, and the strength of the Ultra-Tories
in the Upper House, suggested that it was doomed either to destruction or mutilation there. The duke consulted Goulburn on possible
amendments. In the end, the Tory peers settled for a modest change to
the clause suspending appointments in benefices where no divine service had been performed in three years. Any monies so saved were to
be used for the building of additional churches and glebes. At least
this paid lip-service to Goulburn's demand that every opportunity
should be taken to promote the Protestant faith in Ireland. The peers'
unexpected discretion reflected the pressure brought to bear on the
duke by the king, who was committed to a measure of reform, by the
Irish primate, who warned of an impending financial disaster for the
Irish church in the absence of some settlement, and by Peel, who had
reopened direct communication with Wellington to warn him that rejection of the bill would prejudice an acceptable resolution of the tithe
problem. More than this, Peel feared that defeat would provide the
ministry with an excuse to resign at a time when Conservatives could
neither form a government with any hope of survival in the present
Parliament nor contest a general election with any prospect of making
sufficient gains to command a majority in a new one.[12]

Second reading of the Irish Church Bill in the Lords coincided with
second reading of the West India Bill in the Commons, for slave emancipation was the second great issue of the 1833 session. A resurgent antislavery movement had prompted the Tories to commit themselves to
amelioration in 1823, when Canning introduced a series of resolutions
to improve the treatment and condition of slaves. For the balance of
the decade, successive administrations had quietly urged the colonies
with legislatures to implement these resolutions and had issued instructions to the other colonies. At the heart of this commitment to
gradualism lay the conviction "that, if the abolition of slavery take
place in the West Indies before a very material improvement has been
made in the slaves themselves, it will either plunge them into lasting
barbarism, or compel them to struggle onward to civilization, after a
sacrifice of the present landed proprietors, through years of anarchy
and blood." Haiti clearly remained a powerful symbol and a useful argument. Emancipation of the mind, the Tory *Quarterly Review* declared,
must precede that of the body.[13]

The sullen acceptance of amelioration by colonies such as Jamaica
eroded metropolitan support for the policy. So did occasional acts of
horrifying brutality and the continuing decline of the slave population.

The return of the Whigs to office in 1830 gave fresh impetus to the movement for abolition, as distinct from amelioration. The success of parliamentary reform further advanced the cause by undermining the West India lobby – which saw its representation halved, heavily dependent as it had been on corrupt boroughs – and by bolstering the influence of dissent, which provided so many missionaries to the slave colonies. But the popular appeal of emancipation extended far beyond "the boundaries of nonconformity." The "people generally" revealed an "astonishing" interest in the slavery question during the 1830 general election, while the cholera epidemic was interpreted in some circles as divine punishment for continued national acquiescence in the sin of slavery. In 1831 the number of petitions to Parliament urging abolition had been double those requesting parliamentary reform.[14]

Henry Goulburn's personal commitment to amelioration had long predated its enunciation as government policy, and by 1826 he was privately acknowledging the necessity of eventual emancipation. To his credit, he was not one of those owners who were "mercilessly [exacting] as much labour from slaves as possible before emancipation." However, in 1825 he had replaced the liberal but ineffectual Richards as attorney. The new man, Alexander Bayley, soon submitted an all-too-familiar report – works in a state of decay, steam engine in a state of disrepair, buildings in a state of dilapidation, and cheerful and healthy slaves in a "state of idleness and licentiousness." Bayley planned to introduce a sterner disciplinary regime of exemplary punishments, but a dramatic spurt in the number of runaways compelled him to draw back even before he received word of Goulburn's disapproval of his measures. An overseer who was despised by the slaves for his rigidity and severity was quietly dismissed, and the exemplary punishments were discontinued. In an effort to reassert some semblance of his authority, Bayley made an example of a black driver who over the past few years had been "virtually in more authority than any of the white people." The driver was sentenced by a magistrate to four months in a workhouse for insubordination. In response, Goulburn restated his belief that by "continued steadiness of conduct without any severity the order of an Estate as well as the comfort of the people" would be maintained. He also sought further explanation of the slower but continuing decline of the slave population. Why had there been so few births? Bayley assured him that on no other estate did the slaves receive so ample and constant an allowance of corn, but few other properties were so undermanned, he explained. Lest this be interpreted as a euphemism for overwork, the attorney assured Goulburn that slaves who were required to perform "a proper and moderate degree of labour" were more likely to "thrive and increase" than those who were left to their own devices. It was an argument that appealed to the owner's faith in employment as a means of personal improvement.[15]

Goulburn had already forwarded to Amity Hall a copy of the detailed regulations approved by West Indian proprietors for the guidance of their managers. They were an elaboration of Canning's resolutions. Bayley dismissed most of them as either impractical or meaningless, and noted that others were already in place. For example, resort to the whip had been forbidden except in cases where an example was required, "but not in any instance among females." On the other hand, he suggested that Amity Hall was more the exception than the rule with respect to a declining population. Here was an embarrassing admission, especially for an owner who had long accepted that an "increase of the negroes" was the "best proof" of their good management. Goulburn repeated that the contentment of "his people" was his "first anxiety." The production and quality of sugar were always to be subordinated to the "improvement of the Negroes." A "kind and steady exercise of authority without severe or corporal punishment" would be mutually beneficial, he insisted. In his opinion, the "only rational mode of improving the negro condition" was "by instructing the younger in their duty and raising them gradually to a better condition in society." The steady contraction of the area of the estate under cultivation, together with disappointing yields and inferior sugar, and Bayley's repeated assurances, convinced him that his slaves were not being overworked. The conclusion he reached, with the Attorney's help, was the familar one that "profilgate habits and indiscriminate intercourse of the sexes" explained the decline in the population.[16]

Goulburn sought to halt the immorality which he convinced himself was the root cause of the problems on Amity Hall. The whites were to set an example to the blacks, and dismissal was to be the punishment for backsliders. He forbade the corporal punishment of women; those who committed offences were to be confined. Banned also was night work, because "the promiscuous assemblage of slaves during the night" facilitated "debauchery." Family relationships were to be encouraged through inducements such as better clothing and more time for recreation or for working plots of land. Of course, Goulburn devoutly believed "that it is only by making the negroes comprehend the truths of religion that permanent restraint can be imposed on the licentiousness of their manners." If the rector of St Peter's was unable or unwilling to attend to their religious education, a catechist was to be employed for that purpose. The children were to attend religious instruction for a period of two hours each day, and the adults were to worship in church twice on Sundays. Moreover, sabbatarian that he was, Goulburn prohibited his slaves from working their gardens on the Lord's Day. They were to be permitted to devote Saturdays to that task instead.[17]

A few weeks after Goulburn issued these instructions, a new order in council to much the same effect was on its way to the crown colonies. It also placed restrictions on the number of hours a slave could be compelled to work each week. Freer to work for wages, the slave (and presumably his master, too) would gradually become accustomed to a wage economy. As for the legislative colonies, they could expect fiscal and commercial coercion if they refused to adopt these directives. This evolution of amelioration did not, of course, satisfy those members of Parliament who deplored the continuance of "forced labour, and unpaid labour." These advocates of complete freedom were provided with additional ammunition by the Jamaican rebellion, which began on 27 December 1831.[18]

Declining sugar prices and rising absenteeism had seen many managers and proprietors extort more labour from their slaves even as they cut their supplies. These conditions became unbearable to slaves who mistakenly believed that their masters were withholding a freedom Parliament had granted them. This tinder was finally ignited by the charismatic Samuel Sharpe and other black Baptists, resulting in widespread violence. Surveying the wreckage of a large number of properties and infuriated by the loss of fourteen lives, vengeful white Jamaica was not easily appeased. More than 540 slaves were to die, the majority of them executed, while a campaign of terror and arson was waged against the nonconformist missionaries, whom many of the terrified residents held responsible for the disaster; ministers were assaulted and chapels put to the torch. The ferocity of this reaction excited horror and outrage in Britain, while the revolt itself suggested that slavery was no longer compatible with social order.[19]

Since leaving office, Goulburn had served as a Commons spokesman for a West India sugar interest that was afflicted by rising competition from Cuba, by a declining preference in relation to East Indian sugar, and by a deliberate violation of the colonial monopoly in the British market in an effort to aid metropolitan refiners. Prices collapsed and with them Goulburn's income from his estate. The government resorted to the traditional ploy of an inquiry into the distress, and the early months of 1832 found Goulburn not only sitting for a portrait by the fashionable Henry Pickersgill – whose work was distinguished more for the accuracy of the likenesses than for artistic merit – but also sitting on the select committee. The majority of the committee's members were unconvinced by the West Indians' argument that their competitiveness

had been undermined by rising labour costs, which were a result of amelioration. Furthermore, in the House, Althorp resisted demands that the
duty on imported West Indian sugar be reduced in order to encourage
its greater consumption. However, the narrowness of his victory on this
issue saw him subsequently hint at concessions to sugar colonies that cooperated full-heartedly with the policy of amelioration.[20]

The Jamaican rebellion hardened Goulburn's attitude towards "necessary discipline," even though his estate had escaped damage. If firmly, regularly, and humanely maintained, discipline was "as essential to
the improvement of moral Character as instruction or example," he
lectured Bayley. Nor did he welcome the appointment of another select committee, especially as it was to report on the possibility of rapid
and safe abolition. Goulburn worried that this step would "produce
most fatal consequences by giving rise to inordinate expectations on
the part of those who are slaves and exciting great alarm among those
who are the resident overseers of them." But his own gradualism with
respect to abolition undoubtedly owed as much to an anxiety to guard
what remained of his income as it did to a concern for the "improvement of the slave condition." Appointed to the committee, he anticipated its report. He instructed Bayley to prepare for sugar cultivation
by means other than slave labour, only to learn by return mail that an
experiment with free labour on Grenada had been a dismal failure.
Not a single free person had agreed "to engage in the cultivation of
Cane, even at ... enormous wages."[21]

The need to ensure a ready and reliable supply of plantation labour
was a dominant theme of the hearings of the select committee, which
sat throughout much of the summer. It heard conflicting testimony.
Proprietors and former attorneys, together with a few naval officers
who had served in the Caribbean, doubted the willingness of freed
blacks to work sugar estates. Clerics and missionaries, on the other
hand, exuded confidence that people who worked their gardens and
provisions grounds so diligently and successfully would happily enter
the wage economy if offered a "fair reward." The debate was peculiarly
relevant for Goulburn, who heard, shortly after the committee urged
the House quickly to take up the question, that Bayley had died and
that Amity Hall was again in a dilapidated condition. A reliable supply
of labour was essential if it was ever to be worked profitably again. A
common feature of the several plans of emancipation discussed by the
government were measures to oblige free persons of colour to labour.
Thus the Colonial Office reminded cabinet that the Irish peasant "is
not less lazy, and his wants are not more numerous or less simple than
those of the negroes, yet he considers it a favour to be supplied with
the hardest work at the lowest wages."[22]

The task of introducing emancipation fell to the conservative Edward Stanley, who had happily exchanged his office in Dublin Castle for a house in Downing Street. As colonial secretary, he was keen to conciliate the West India interest. Its members wished to see emancipated slaves bound as long as possible to their former masters, and for owners to be compensated for the loss of their human property. They also wished to retain their privileged position in the British market. But Stanley's plan, when revealed on 14 May, proved too conservative for the "Saints" and too radical for West Indians. Goulburn played little part in the debate, though he presented a petition, signed by 1,800 persons of "high respectability," including bankers and merchants, which expressed opposition not to emancipation but to the government's proposals. Speaking for himself, he called for compromise and warned against "premature measures, which would not only have a fatal influence on our own colonies, but by their failure serve as an excuse for continuing slavery in other colonies." This proved to be his final word on the subject. He was absent from the House for much of the summer, perhaps as a result of the lingering effects of the ill health that had dogged him during the spring. He was later privately to concede of his attitude towards slavery that he had "concurred in evil thro' want of courage to speak or to act." The settlement that emerged provided for a compensation fund of £20 million, thereby protecting the sanctity of private property. On the other hand, abolitionists won a substantial reduction in the period of "apprenticeship" during which former slaves would be obliged to labour for their former owners.[23]

The bill was carried to the Lords on 7 August 1832, where there was reason to fear for its survival intact. West Indians, who had powerful friends in the Upper House, were embittered by the government's halving of the twelve-year period of apprenticeship. In their minds, the bargain had been compensation for only twelve additional years of guaranteed labour. They looked to Wellington for help, but their position was one that even he could not defend. From 1 August 1834, all slave children under the age of six were to be free. Older slaves were sentenced to periods of apprenticeship – six years for field workers and four years for others. Thus full emancipation would not take effect until 1 August 1840. Apprentices were obliged to labour for just over forty hours a week but could not be compelled to work for a longer period. They were to be paid wages for any additional time they agreed to put in. Their masters were to continue to provide the basic necessities of housing, food, and medical care, and the apprentices were fixed to the land. They could not be sold other than with the estate to which they were attached. A special force of stipendiary magistrates was to be sent out from England to resolve disputes and to assist in the setting of a fair price at which an apprentice might purchase complete freedom before 1840.[24]

Goulburn fleetingly thought of going out to Jamaica personally to supervise the transition from slavery to apprenticenship, but his grim resolve to resist other Whig policies at home probably accounts for his abandonment of this idea. Moreover, the initial reports from his new attorney, Evan McPherson, were cheering. His slaves had behaved in an "orderly and peaceable manner" throughout the emancipation debate. McPherson voiced confidence in the apprenticeship scheme "provided we have a strong police to compell [sic] them to work," he wrote. Hence Goulburn's relief when the Jamaican legislature enacted a police bill. An accompanying vagrancy bill promised to be equally "useful." Nevertheless, McPherson understood the necessity for greater care and sensitivity in the management of the labour force. When Goulburn complained of the lengthening hospital list, he was advised that it was vital to attach "the people as much as possible to the estate and render their situations as comfortable and happy as we can." Consequently, it was only prudent to indulge slaves who fancied themselves sick and wished to spend a few days in hospital. Similarly, McPherson allowed them more time to work their gardens, confident that this would have a better long-term effect than an attempt to extract more labour from them.[25]

The first working day following the August celebration of conditional liberation found all apprentices present on Amity Hall. Even so, McPherson was not confident of working the estate successfully unless he could persuade them to part with a portion of the time they were legally entitled to claim for themselves. He fancied that a cask of rum would facilitate negotiations. It was soon clear, however, that the apprentices were reluctant to labour on the estate beyond the legal requirement. Adding to Goulburn's disappointment was the certainty that he would receive a less than generous award from the compensation fund. The assessors visited Amity Hall in September 1834, and their report indicated that he stood twelfth on the list of Vere's 171 slave owners. His human property, a total of 242 persons, of whom 26 were children under the age of 6, was valued at £12,885. He was later awarded barely one-third of that sum.[26]

It was to Ireland, not Jamaica, that Goulburn journeyed in the late autumn of 1833. He found scant political pleasure in the visit, convinced as he was that Stanley's successor as chief secretary, Edward Littleton, would be "little more than a tool in the hands of the Roman Catholic Party." So, he returned home via Drayton. He wished to confer with Peel on strategy in the forthcoming session of Parliament, which he was certain would witness another attempted raid on the church's property and privileges. The Irish Church Bill had not solved the problem of tithes. Relative tranquillity had been briefly purchased through the creation of a special fund from which clergy could claim a percentage of their arrears and thus avoid personal confrontation with tenants. Yet English taxpayers were unlikely long to tolerate this form of subsidy to the Irish clergy. Moreover, the Grey administration was evidently anxious to appease those nonconformist supporters whose alienation had been starkly illustrated at a recent by-election. They had itemized their grievances: Anglican control of the registration of births, the legal solemnization of marriage, and burials; the imposition of church rates on everyone; and the religious exclusiveness of Oxford and Cambridge. The government responded by introducing in 1834 a marriage bill, a church rate bill, and, most controversially of all, a proposal to admit the dissenters to degrees at Oxford and Cambridge.[27]

The leading role assumed by Lord John Russell served to deepen Goulburn's conviction that this was one more attempt to undermine the established church. He regarded Russell as a mere tool of the dissenters. Had he not stated in 1828 that he saw "no cause why the Dissenters should make any declaration concerning the Established Church." Cambridge, like Oxford, was in Goulburn's mind "a Church of England Establishment" intended for "the education of members of that Church." He feared that the admission of dissenters would necessitate the abandonment of the true religion fundamental to a worthwhile education. What distinguished Britain from other nations, he believed, was the fact that her men of learning and science were also "the most zealous advocates for that Church which their labours so greatly illustrate and maintain." But the sentiment in the Commons was plainly for concession, and when Goulburn doggedly attempted to restate his objections during third reading, he was drowned out by cries for the question. Once again, however, the Lords came to his aid. They threw out the bill. Nevertheless, he quietly urged the authorities at Cambridge to revise their ancient statutes in order to correct those anomalies which might expose them to renewed attacks as bastions of bigotry and discrimination. And he persuaded Wellington to recommend the same strategy to Oxford. Meanwhile, the bill to abolish church rates and transfer the cost of repairing churches to the Treasury proved more acceptable to Tories than to Radicals and dissenters. Embarrassed, the Whig leadership in the Commons lost its enthusiasm for this solution.[28]

Goulburn was struggling to bolster the church's defences on two fronts that spring, for Littleton had finally produced his plan of Irish tithe reform. The divisions within cabinet on the principle of lay appropriation of church funds were put on embarrassing display in the

Commons by the conservative Stanley and the liberal Russell. The Radicals moved quickly to exploit the situation, putting down a motion on the subject. Clearly, there was an opportunity here for the Tories. With Peel at Drayton, leadership fell to Goulburn, though this was not a role he welcomed. He recognized that he lacked his friend's "dexterity and management," as well as the rank and station that commanded support. He had no personal following in the Commons. Ever the partisan, he argued that they should "avoid everything that can have the effect of healing the existing differences" within the cabinet. He wished "to avoid also entering into the real subject of discussion which the Government in the first instance must deal with some how or other." If push came to shove, however, he was inclined to lend support to any ministerial procedural ploy to finesse the question.[29]

Still seeking to attract to the Conservative cause "the more moderate and respectable supporters of the present Government," Peel's overriding concern was to shun any association with the Radicals in the ousting of the Grey ministry. A triumph would be "very shortlived," he argued, if it resulted from such an alliance. He favoured a slightly more passive stance than that recommended by Goulburn. But when the cabinet attempted to mollify the Radicals with a commission of inquiry into Irish church revenues, Stanley, Graham, and the Earl of Ripon (Goderich) all resigned. Not that this dramatic development gave Goulburn an immediate reason to cheer. He was distressed by the king's apparent willingness to replace the three with more radical figures. Moreover, Conservative unity continued to be a source of unease. The rival ambitions of Peel and Wellington for the Oxford chancellorship had been resolved by Peel's declining to be nominated, but he was conspicuously absent from the festivities during the second week of June to celebrate Wellington's new academic eminence. Goulburn was present to accept an honorary doctorate as a champion of the church and of conservatism, and he was among those who received the most enthusiastic and noisy welcome from the student audience.[30]

The revised tithes bill, which was presented to the House in June 1834, did not provide for lay appropriation but did allow for the possible diversion of a portion of the revenues of the Irish church. This was sufficient to goad Stanley into a savage assault on his former colleagues, even though he had compromised on this sensitive issue in his own bill the year before. Meanwhile, the Tories sharpened their attack on the tottering government as a creature of the dissenters. Morale on the Treasury bench was further undermined by a collision with O'Connell over an Irish coercion bill. The ministry disintegrated. Grey, Littleton, and Althorp all resigned. Although the king would have preferred to see the formation of a coalition of the Tory leadership and conservative Whigs, he realized that his only immediate option was to accept Lord Melbourne at the head of a reconstructed Grey administration. Not that its foundations were ever secure. The king disliked the new appointments to the cabinet, which was fractious and unstable. Although Althorp, who was regarded as the indispensable man, agreed to return to office, he did so without enthusiasm. A coercion bill shorn of the provisions O'Connell disliked was passed in both Houses, only for the tithes bill to be rejected by the peers. All the while Goulburn was energetically challenging the ministry's fiscal credibility. He documented a proliferation of administrative appointments and offices, which betrayed the Whigs' traditional gluttony for patronage instead of their boasted appetite for economy, and he heaped scorn on Althorp's latest budget for its failure "to make an impression on the public debt."[31]

The Conservatives had reason for optimism that their time was coming. In mid-July, with the possibility of receiving a summons from the king, Peel finally did what Goulburn had long urged. He trimmed his sails on dealing with the Ultras; he sounded out Sir Edward Knatchbull, one of the architects of the defeat of Wellington's administration in 1830. Although the opportunity to take office failed to materialize, Conservative prospects did not dim. The administration inspired little enthusiasm in the Commons. All three measures introduced to conciliate the dissenters had been poorly conceived and were either defeated or abandoned. In the country, the Tories were profiting from their defence of the church, a defence in which Goulburn had played such a conspicuous part. And a series of well-attended public meetings served to remind the nation of the existence of a Conservative party in which those who did not like "the destruction of the institutions of the country" would find persons who held the "same opinions as themselves."[32]

In mid-October Peel set off in the company of his wife for a tour of Italy. A month later Althorp was removed from the Commons by the death of his father, Earl Spencer. Melbourne's proposal to appoint Lord John Russell leader of the House, apparently signalling as this did "further encroachments" on the established church, afforded the king both the opportunity and the incentive to dismiss his ministers. "We are all out; turned out neck and crop," one of them commented. William IV sent again for Wellington, who agreed to preside over a caretaker administration and to do so more or less single-handedly until Peel returned. Among those the duke hastily summoned to St James's Palace on 17 November to form a Privy Council and effect a formal transfer of power was Henry Goulburn. He was certain to be appointed to any Peel cabinet.[33]

Peel reached London on the morning of 9 December, by which time he owed a large debt of gratitude to Wellington. The duke had held the fort for more than three weeks. He had already taken steps to improve relations with the press, having belatedly recognized that the absence of such an effort had been one of the failings of his administration. He had set in train the planning for a general election and had sent letters of encouragement and exhortation to Conservatives to exert all their influence to secure the return of a majority of Tory members. Finally, he had composed a memorandum listing the members of both Houses who merited office or had a claim to some mark of distinction. Henry Goulburn's name was at the head of his Commons' list of obvious cabinet ministers. For his part, Goulburn had been soliciting opinions in an effort to assist Peel in framing policies. What he had discovered was "that the property of the Country desires a conservative and not an *Ultra Tory* Government" and "that the general feeling seems to be in favor of a union with Stanley etc both as a security against *ultra Toryism* and under an idea of his own importance and weight in the House of Commons." These were far from novel recommendations, and Peel's first act was to write to Stanley and Graham. To them, and to the small group of leading Tories who gathered at Wellington's home that first evening, he emphasized his commitment to moderate policies. But after nine nights of continuous travel he was soon packed off to bed. Not that he slept well, for the rumble of the carriage wheels appeared to have been trapped in his ears.[34]

Although Stanley and Graham declined to join the government, this disappointment was not without its compensations. "The Cabinet will be smaller," one Tory noted. "The party will be more cordially united. We shall be obliged to look ... before we speak." Further, the knowledge that the offer had been made would "show that Peel had done all he could to form a broad based Government." On the other wing of the political spectrum there stood Knatchbull, to whom Peel again offered his right hand – and it held the seals of the Home Office. However, this Ultra preferred the position of paymaster of the forces, an office that combined the least labour with the least anxiety. So Peel turned to the devoted and efficient Goulburn for a home secretary. Goulburn promised to be a reassuring figure for many Irish Protestants and for the established church in both kingdoms, while the word that he was ultimately destined for the Speaker's chair would console those of his more liberal colleagues who doubted the wisdom of the appointment. At a dinner that was attended by Goulburn and eight other new ministers on 13 December, Peel announced his intention to make a public declaration of the new government's moderate principles.[35]

His target remained that "respectable" element of society whose support he had long been cultivating. What he offered them was assurance – that there would be no attempt to turn back the clock on parliamentary reform but neither would there be any capitulation to radical democracy; that the essential institutions of church and state would not only be defended but would be strengthened through the reform of revealed abuses; and that all "real grievances" would be redressed. Even dissenters were assured of sympathetic and conciliatory treatment at the hands of the new government. On the issues on which Peel was clearly resolved to stand fast, such as respect for the property of the established church, whether in Ireland or England, there was a promise that the irritation would be soothed by tithe reform and a reorganization of church revenues. Lastly, he pledged economical and efficient government.[36]

These "principles" were discussed at a second cabinet dinner four days later, before being distributed to the press in the form of a letter from Peel to his Tamworth constituents. The "manifesto" created a "prodigious sensation," and at least one inveterate Whig wondered how Goulburn was "to swallow such Liberalism." Indeed, the vehemence with which Whigs assailed Peel's "humbug" suggested that he had successfully occupied the electoral high ground. Yet there was little immediate evidence that his manifesto was producing any movement in the public mind in the Conservatives' favour. However, the Tory leaders harboured only the modest ambition to make sufficient electoral gains to be able to cling to office until they could legitimately seek a second dissolution. Much would also depend, therefore, on the contents of the King's Speech. Peel sketched for his colleagues a series of proposals concerning marriages, burials, church rates, and admission to the great professions of law and medicine which were calculated to mollify dissenters. A small subcommittee was struck, which included Goulburn, to draft a proposal on dissenter marriages. He and Peel also patiently set about the task of persuading the episcopacy to cooperate in any church reforms initiated by their sympathetic government. What they had in mind was a strict law on pluralities and nonresidence, and the abolition of sinecures. The surplus revenues so generated were to be used in England to reform church rates and in Ireland to compensate landlords who had taken on the tithes which the tenantry still refused to pay. When Goulburn went up to Cambridge for his traditional Christmas sojourn there, he discreetly prepared the university community for reform along these lines.[37]

There was a perception, as the electoral campaign got under way, that the Tories had stolen a march on the Whigs not only with their manifesto and carefully nurtured alliance with the *Times* but also with their greater degree of party organization. They had amassed a central fund to aid candidates, and in several constituencies Conservative associations had been established. There was also a central committee to coordinate activities. Although not a leading organizer, Goulburn was consulted about party matters and was at times pressed into more active service. Granville Somerset, the principal organizer, turned to him for advice on whether he should urge Peel to address the rank and file before the opening of Parliament. The meeting was held. Of course, as home secretary, Goulburn took close interest in Henry Hardinge's management of matters in Ireland as chief secretary. There, Conservative voters, not least the Catholics among them, were the victims of "brutal vindictive violence." "So long as you have not acted partially in your protection of voters and in the maintenance of tranquillity it matters little by what name they denigrate you," Goulburn wrote reassuringly. In England, meanwhile, particularly in the boroughs, the Tories were making considerable gains, often with the assistance of the local parsons but not the dissenters. The victory at Leicester of Goulburn's brother Edward was regarded as an excellent omen. At Cambridge, Goulburn himself was returned unopposed.[38]

The Conservatives almost doubled their numbers and clearly constituted the largest single bloc in the Commons, but they remained well short of a majority. Peel was undaunted. "If what we shall propose to the House of Commons will not satisfy – who are the men that will propose that something which is to satisfy," he remarked jauntily. No doubt he expected to attract the support of many of the conservative Whigs who had been returned, and one of his ministers passed on a confidential assurance that the Whigs were not seeking immediately to oust the government. "You may stand therefore upon your measures," this well-placed informant wrote, "and be secure."[39]

As home secretary, Goulburn was returning to the department where his career had begun a quarter of a century earlier. He had now, at the age of fifty-one, reached the very highest level of government. Only Peel and Wellington outranked him in cabinet. Moreover, he seemed well suited to his new office. He certainly possessed the essential qualifications of "prudence, discretion, freedom from wild notions, conciliation, and, above all, a disregard of popularity." Another advantage was his affability, which would facilitate informal contacts with members. Nor could anyone question his industry and dedication, important qualities in a department where the business was so heavy that one of his successors complained of the lack of time to read a newspaper or write to friends. Since Goulburn's early days as an under-secretary, there had been a significant increase in the time-consuming, tedious, and arcane business of drafting legislation, which reflected "the ever growing range of subjects" for which the Home Office had become responsible. On Goulburn's agenda were the complex and controversial questions of church reform, tithes, and reform of the municipal corporations, and he sensibly coaxed Peel's former legal draftsmen, William Gregson, into accepting the position of under-secretary.[40]

Few issues were more inflammatory than the tithe. Goulburn arrived at his office on 15 December to find on his desk a report from Ireland of fresh resistance to the tax and a request from the Castle for guidance on the assistance to be afforded to legal officers seeking to collect it. Prudently, he elected to follow the practice of his Whig predecessors. He authorized the "presence of an adequate Civil or Military force not for the purpose of collecting tithe but for the preservation of the peace and the support of the law." He exhibited equal good sense in ignoring the provocative behaviour of the intensely nationalistic Roman Catholic archbishop of Tuam, John McHale, who had purchased a small farm in order to claim the franchise and had then announced his refusal to support the established church in any way. Goulburn was no less circumspect in his response to a bloody affray between the peasantry and the troops protecting the tithe collectors. He ordered an impartial investigation and demanded clarification of the claim that one of the magistrates accompanying the troops was the archdeacon whose tithes were being collected.[41]

The embarrassing discovery that two of the three magistrates present had a personal interest in the collection of the tithes simply added fresh urgency to the search for a "final adjustment" of the issue. So did a report submitted by the Irish primate, which documented widespread and at times intense resistance to the tax. Goulburn's bills in 1823 and 1824 had laid the groundwork for a settlement, to the extent that they had sought to fix definitively the amount to be paid in each parish for a number of years, to apportion the burden more fairly, and ultimately to transfer payment from occupier to landowner. Essentially permissive, these bills had been reinforced in 1832 by a measure of compulsion and a more effective transfer of payment to landlords. The defect of Stanley's bill, in Goulburn's opinion, had been its failure to make this transfer universal. As a result, composition was still being levied on persons who were ready "to avail themselves of the plea of a different religious creed, in order to evade or to resist the payment and who find no difficulty in enlisting in such a cause the feelings and the services of the lower Orders." To complete the transfer to the landowner and to allow him to recover the charge in rent was the immediate object. For advice on how to achieve this, Goulburn turned to the new lord lieutenant.[42]

The Earl of Haddington arrived in Dublin on 5 January 1835. His appointment had raised some eyebrows there, for he was regarded as a "half Liberal Canningite." He soon expressed personally to Peel his alarm at plans to appoint three stalwart "Protestants," one of them William Gregory, to the Irish Privy Council. This "could have a bad effect upon the public mind in Ireland, and lead to erroneous impressions as to the Policy of the Government," he cautioned. In response, the prime minister ordered that the appointments be made discreetly and individually. On the other hand, there was a need to retain the allegiance of the "more *vehement* friends of the Government." No doubt this concern contributed to the new viceroy's decision immediately to seek authority to pursue "the enemies of peace, security and order." Goulburn sanctioned the legal pursuit of those who attempted "to inflame the public mind, to encourage and sometimes to prompt the commission of crimes, and to excite resistance to the law." But, ever cautious, he urged that in the first instance prosecutors focus on one or two persons whose activities had a "direct tendency" to excite disturbances. Plainly, he had no wish to see the Irish government embark on a course of action that smacked of a crusade. Nor were any libels to be prosecuted until after the elections.[43]

Haddington admitted his difficulty in finding a way through the "maze of perplexity" that was the tithe. With desperate clergy pleading to be relieved temporarily of the obligation to repay earlier advances, he understood the gravity of the situation. Of course, the deepening crisis worked to his advantage to the extent that it disposed the clergy to make those sacrifices "necessary to save not only them, but the Protestant Religion in Ireland." Thus the proposals he forwarded to London envisaged a substantial loss of income by the clergy, first as a result of the conversion of the composition to a rent charge, and then by a redemption of the rent charge itself. Nevertheless, they were accepted as the skeleton of a settlement which a cabinet committee was struck to flesh out.[44]

Goulburn escaped service on the tithe committee. He had enough already on his plate. He was working with Gregson to draft a bill to regulate the marriages of dissenters. His twin aims were to guard effectively against "clandestine marriages" and to avoid any advantage accruing to those who chose to marry by licence rather than in church. If the former proved to be cheaper, he feared that "the lower orders" would "swell the ranks of the dissenters to save expense," whereas any advantages of cost and convenience ought to be granted to the Church of England. The upshot was a bill that permitted marriage as a civil contract but left registration with the parish clergy. Goulburn may have hoped that dissenters would opt for a church service once it was no longer compulsory, and he knew that a substantial minority of the magistrates who would preside at a civil ceremony were clergymen. All the while, of course, he was shouldering the traditional responsibility of the home secretary to uphold law and order. As in the matter of the tithe, he acted cautiously and conservatively. An appeal from a group of Hartlepool magistrates for a more centralized system of law enforcement, to replace ineffectual rural police and parish constables, evoked a cool response from this advocate of the minimal state. Local problems should be met by swearing in special constables, Goulburn replied, or by defraying the cost of obtaining on loan a group of experienced officers from the police force that Peel had organized in London half a decade earlier.[45]

The issue closest to Goulburn's heart was church reform; more particularly, how to strengthen the institution. His and Peel's chosen instrument was an ecclesiastical commission. Their negotiations with the archbishop of Canterbury were successful in securing the hierarchy's cooperation. What they had in mind was "a more equal partition" of the duties of the bishops, an examination of the state of cathedral revenues, limitation if not abolition of pluralities and sinecures, and the use of surplus revenues to promote the residence of ministers and "the efficient discharge of pastoral duties." The fundamental objective, Goulburn later declared, was to ensure the "proper religious instruction" that was so essential to the welfare of the nation's swelling population. This program was not unlike that advanced by Peel's brother-in-law, Lord Henley, in his *Plan of Church Reform* published two years earlier. By mid-January, both archbishops and three senior Bishops had agreed to serve on the commission. They were joined by Peel, Goulburn, and five other sympathetic laymen. The Ecclesiastical Commission got down to work early in February with an intensity born of political anxiety. Peel was anxious to demonstrate his government's commitment to genuine reform, while some of the clergy recognized the wisdom of completing as much work as possible while his sympathetic government clung to power. The first report was issued on 19 March 1835, and the commission proved to be the lasting achievement of the first Peel ministry.[46]

Even as the members of the cabinet toiled to prepare for the opening of Parliament – and one of their labours was to pare expenditures, for Peel was determined to establish his administration's claim to be the most economical in memory – there were ominous signs of a gathering assault by a Whig-led opposition. The day before Parliament assembled, "reformers" gathered at the invitation of Lord John Russell to concert their plans. One clue to the Whigs' seriousness was their selection of a candidate for the Speaker's chair who was acceptable to Radicals and O'Connellites. He narrowly carried the day over the government's nominee when the members of Parliament assembled on 19 February in the old peers' chamber, their own having been destroyed by fire in October. This inauspicious beginning promised to be followed by other setbacks once it became clear that Stanley would be unable to deliver all the votes of that significant minority of members who ostensibly looked to him for leadership.[47]

Peel had always seen the King's Speech as the principal instrument of survival, and the document William IV read on 24 February detailed an impressive program of reform. In the subsequent debate, Goulburn became a particular target of the Whigs' attacks as they disputed the sincerity of these commitments. Once again the government was defeated, this time on an amendment to the Address. But the ministers decided to struggle on, for the majority against them was not large and they had Stanley's support. Goulburn's introduction of the Dissenters' Marriages Bill on 17 March was something of a personal triumph, for while it did not entirely satisfy the nonconformists, it met with general approval. "Probably no measure could have been introduced which would be so injurious to the Whigs," Ellenborough gloated, "as we succeed where they failed, although they did all they could to satisfy their friends." On the other hand, the decision of Peel and Goulburn to reward their old friend William Gregory with the dignity of appointment to the Irish Privy Council gave added force to O'Connellite and Whig accusations that the administration had an Orange tinge. An untimely outburst of Orange triumphalism in Dublin did little to help them fend off this unfair and damaging charge. On 23 March the House appointed a select committee to investigate the activities of the Orange Order in Ireland.[48]

This was another of the humiliating reverses suffered by the government in the Commons. These setbacks appeared to demoralize Peel, and his apparent defeatism put him at odds with several of his colleagues and reopened that old wound which still pained Wellington. Indeed, the strain and tension were beginning to take their toll on the good judgment of other members of the harassed administration. At a reception given by Lady Bathurst, Goulburn charged that Earl Grey was egging Russell on in his attacks on the government in order to open the way for his own return to office. Lady Grey indignantly denied the accusation. Meanwhile, Wellington's cronies were privately assailing Peel for his want of "right conduct towards the King, the country, or his colleagues and party," and the two men engaged in a hot exchange on the issue.[49]

On 30 March Russell struck. He moved a preliminary motion with respect to the Irish Tithes Bill, which clearly opened the door to the lay appropriation of surplus church revenues. The debate afforded Goulburn another opportunity to come to the defence of the Church of Ireland, to remind the House of its missionary role in that kingdom, to warn that an attack on its property would set a dangerous precedent for other owners of private property, and to stake a personal claim to the title of moderate reformer. He wished to reform abuses when they came to light, he declared, whereas Russell sought to pull down the institution. Defeated by an unexpectedly large majority on this first trial of strength, Peel informed his colleagues that unless they could carry the vote in at least one of the three remaining divisions, he would resign. This time there was little dissent. "I think he was right to announce this and I think he will be right to do it," one former critic noted. Then, on 7 April, Russell successfully moved the decisive amendment to the tithes bill. As Goulburn explained to the master of Trinity College, by blocking any measure that did not provide for "the appropriation of Church Property to other than Church purposes," the Commons had prevented the ministers from effecting a reform "essential to the tranquillity of Ireland and to the recovery of any part of the clerical income in that country." In these circumstances, they had no alternative to resignation.[50]

Short as its life had been, the first Peel ministry proved of far-reaching importance to the revival and redefinition of Conservativism. Peel had finally asserted his leadership, and he had accommodated himself to the need for unity within the rank and file while providing them with an electorally appealing platform of moderate reform. More than this, he and his colleagues had proven that they could safely be entrusted with the reins of power and that they were not reactionaries whose appeals to the past betrayed a desire to return to it. Less obvious was the extent to which Peel had failed to conciliate the agrarian interest, which was so important to his party in the counties, as well as the extent to which he had disappointed militant Protestants, especially those in Ireland. Yet with the creation of the Ecclesiastical Commission, he had done much to buttress the position of the established church. For Henry Goulburn, this was the principal reward for his brief term as home secretary. He also took pride in his personal achievement in scaling one of the high peaks of government. His simple memorial tablet in Betchworth Church bears the inscription "Secretary of State."[51]

CHAPTER TEN

Return to Power

Many Tories were confident that Melbourne's second administration would be as short-lived as his first. To them, it appeared to be humiliatingly dependent for its Commons majority on the Radicals and the unpredictable Daniel O'Connell. This impression was strengthened by a spate of liberal appointments, which not a few observers interpreted as a signal that the prime minister had abandoned hope of a reconciliation with Stanley and Graham. Indeed, the latter was soon echoing Goulburn with his dismissal of the cabinet as a collection of Jacobins and infidels. As for public confidence in the new ministers, a stunning by-election defeat for Lord John Russell gave grounds for optimism that as shallow as it evidently was, it would quickly evaporate in the heat of political battle. Less obvious was the extent to which O'Connell was a captive of his association with the Whigs, given his determination to prevent Peel's return to power. Similarly, this Whig government possessed greater cohesion than Grey's coalition had done, thanks in part to the loss of the "half-Tories." Nor was Peel in any haste to topple it. He did not intend to try to govern again without an assured majority in the Commons, and he reminded Goulburn that the next rather than the current registry of voters would be more favourable to the "conservative cause." Consequently, they should be "very careful not to force dissolution until that cause can have that advantage."[1]

Recently, the Whigs have been credited with having had a political and intellectual coherence during the 1830s, with a concept of government that motivated them to strive to integrate and harmonize "different classes and interest groups within the political nation." This mission also embraced the several nations, and not the least of their challenges was that of binding Ireland "within a genuinely United Kingdom." Implied in much of this was a greater measure of government intervention in social questions than had characterized the Tories, with their commitment to the minimal state. Equally, from the partisan and naturally more cynical viewpoint of the opposition benches, the Whigs' national legislative agenda smacked less of nobility of purpose than of a taste for expediency in its basest form. Thus the introduction of another Irish Church Bill was greeted as a sop to their Irish ally. This time a surplus of revenues was to be ensured by closing down parishes that had nonexistent or miniscule congregations and by cutting off some of the monies applied to secular purposes. The tithe, meanwhile, was to be converted to a rent charge set at barely two-thirds of the nominal value. Goulburn sought to demonstrate, with the aid of some questionable statistics, that Protestantism was now to be abandoned in those very areas where it was most rapidly gaining ground. He denied that there was a genuine surplus to appropriate. "Was that the way to tranquillize Ireland," he asked scornfully, "to hold out a hope of pecuniary advantage, which, as there could be no surplus, could only be realized by the extermination of Protestants?" Resolutely opposed to lay appropriation, he and Peel calmly accepted defeat in the Commons in the knowledge that the Lords would wreck the measure.[2]

The Municipal Corporations Bill sought to sweep away the ancient and oligarchic urban bodies and replace them with elected councils. The government's intent may well have been to establish a more effective check to the growth of central power and to prod men of property into exercising local leadership, but the Whigs' motivation was open to another interpretation, for the existing unrepresentative corporations were largely Tory in sentiment, and they had used their patronage on behalf of Tory candidates in the 1832 elections. The reform also promised to enhance the influence of nonconformists, for in many parts of the nation they already formed an urban elite. Furthermore, elected councils had an obvious appeal to the Radicals, whose large representation on the royal commission of 1833 was reflected in its recommendation of this solution. Thus the Tories were quick to label the legislation another "contemptible" concession to the Whigs' allies. But Peel, with an eye to broadening the base of Conservative support by continuing to project an image of moderate reform, was temperate in his opposition. Hence his fury when the Tory Lords imprudently savaged the measure. He stalked off to Drayton, and there he remained for almost a month. So Goulburn assumed the role of intermediary. He met with Wellington and Lyndhurst in an effort to preserve some semblance of party unity by serving as a line of communication between them and his sulking leader. He forwarded the amendments which the Lords were proposing to make to the bill in committee, remarking that with a single exception they were consistent with the changes demanded in the Commons. Not the least important of these was the amendment that restricted to Anglicans on the reformed councils the control of local appointments to the established church. Peel replied that the peers were jeopardizing the closer ties he was slowly establishing with Stanley and Graham. Further, he had no wish to present the Whigs with an excuse to resign at a time when the Conservatives were still too weak to govern and he saw little prospect of them picking up the required seats in an election. Goulburn seriously doubted the Whigs' willingness to test their popularity, and as the weeks passed he warned Peel that the Radicals were gaining ground and influence. What should their attitude be when the bill came back to the Commons? he asked archly. Should they permit the Radicals and the government to settle matters between themselves, or should they re-enter the fray? Personally, he believed that there was "something very disagreeable in taking no part in a question which with reference to consequences may be of extreme importance." Moreover, the fact that the Lords had created little "sensation" by their conduct suggested that association with them on this question would not be at the expense of popularity.[3]

Goulburn did, however, distance himself from the Lords' half-baked proposal that a portion of the existing corporation in any municipality be continued as part of the new council, and he upheld the right of his Commons colleagues "to object to some of the Lords' Amendments." The peers had "an equal right to adhere to them or to yield to our reasons against them." What was most important, however, was that Conservatives in the two Houses work together. "Acting independently will certainly lead to more misunderstanding and to a wider separation which is above all to be deprecated," he reminded Peel. Eventually, these appeals and warnings had the desired effect. Advised by Goulburn late in August that the Whigs' decision on the amendments was at hand and that the one hundred Conservatives likely to be present in the House wished him to be at their head, Peel returned to the capital.[4]

The willingness of the Whigs to compromise (for example, the church patronage at the disposal of the corporations was to be sold) saw Peel announce his support of this settlement. Not that this action released the tension within his own ranks. He was adjudged to have thrown over the Lords. "Nothing could exceed the dismay and rage (though suppressed) of the Conservatives at his speech," one observer recorded. Goulburn's personal uneasiness was stilled by the evidence that the peers, at least, would swallow their pride in the name of party unity. They accepted their limited victory. But the autumn found him exerting pressure on Peel to consider the state of party morale before settling on tactics in the upcoming session of Parliament. Buoyed by a recent by-election triumph in Northamptonshire, yet alarmed by the

victories of Radicals and nonconformists in the new municipal elections, the rank and file would be keen "to be brought into conflict with
the enemy." Unless they were assured of some immediate battle, he
feared that they would not attend the House in large number. On the
other hand, Goulburn conceded that without the "cordial cooperation
of Stanley," any aggressive action "would be in every way impolitic."
Similarly, consultation with the Lords' leadership was essential if the
lingering resentment over the passage of municipal reform was to be
extinguished and cordiality restored.[5]

Peel duly summoned a war council at Drayton, which Wellington and
Harrowby attended, along with Goulburn and a handful of other senior
figures. Peel agreed to be in London before the opening of Parliament
to prepare the party for whatever measures the government introduced, and Goulburn made the necessary arrangements to ensure the
attendance of their "friends." But despite these careful preparations
and a decision to proceed cautiously, the session opened humiliatingly
for the Tory leader. The Lords forced his hand by moving an amendment to the Address, in which the government prudently acquiesced.
When Peel moved a similar amendment in the Commons, however, the
Whigs rallied their troops and allies to repulse it with disconcerting
ease. "Our proceedings in the House of Commons were not as satisfactory as many had expected," a disappointed Goulburn drily admitted.
Another embarrassment was in store.[6]

The introduction of an Irish municipal reform bill saw Peel decide,
in consultation with Goulburn and his other "Irish experts," to counter
with a motion to abolish all Irish corporations and make other provision for local government and the administration of justice. In this way
the Protestants would be protected if not appeased, and the Catholics
would be confounded, for they would inevitably dominate practically
every Irish borough where elections were held. Unfortunately, as Goulburn cautioned his colleagues, the Ultras regarded Peel's proposal with
as much dread as they did that of the government. This did not bode
well for a good showing in the division, since the Ultras were planning
to absent themselves and the Whigs were beating the bushes to bring
up every man. Nevertheless, the leadership decided that the question
was "of import too vital to admit of not resisting it to the utmost."
Heavily defeated, the Tories were again reduced to reliance on the
Lords. The Upper House adopted a proposal similar to Peel's and the
government abandoned the bill. Similarly, it was the peers who threw
out yet another Irish church and tithes bill incorporating the principle
of lay appropriation.[7]

An English tithes bill, on the other hand, passed with welcome ease,
meeting no resistance from the church. So did legislation governing

dissenters' marriages and the national registration of births. Goulburn objected to specific provisions but made little headway with his demand that the law offer advantages to members of the established church. Yet the first report on the new registration system lent some credence to his warnings that clandestine marriages would be facilitated and church baptisms discouraged. Somewhat more surprising was his breaking ranks with Peel to join with Lord Ashley in attacking the Whigs when they sought to water down the already modest protection afforded children in the Factory Act of 1833. As home secretary, he had taken seriously his responsibility for its enforcement, demanding that the miniscule inspectorate get on with the task of investigating the hours worked by children in textile mills. And when Ashley subsequently strove to strengthen the legislation which the Whigs had introduced with a conspicuous absence of enthusiasm, Goulburn was the most senior Tory again to offer him support. He continued to avow pragmatism and deny paternalism as his motive, insisting that the time had come for Parliament to reassert its authority in the face of wholesale evasions of the law. However, he did admit that it was "the duty of Parliament to exercise a control over the management of those children, in order to protect their comforts and their lives by diminishing the cruel demands made upon their labour." This deviation from liberal Toryism may have been a reflection of his mellowing evangelicalism, or of sympathy for the evangelical and severe Ashley, who had such difficulty working with most of his colleagues in the Commons. Alternatively, Goulburn's strong desire to promote Tory unity may have convinced him that he had a role to play serving as a bridge between the party's romantic and realist wings. The former rejected political economy.[8]

Goulburn did not quit the capital until mid-August of 1836. He had remained on hand to watch the progress of the Established Church Bill, which gave effect to a number of the recommendations of the Ecclesiastical Commission. And while he joked that his presence was necessary to help ensure rejection of "a proposition for making in future the knowledge of Welsh the only indispensable qualification for a Bishop in Wales," this provision was in any case struck out in the Lords. (Surprisingly, it did not cross Goulburn's mind that a requirement that bishops understand Welsh would have made the church more attractive in that principality, where nonconformity was closely associated with the national language.) Returning to Betchworth, Goulburn gave thanks for the evidence of a good harvest and thus abundant employment. Always welcome, such indicators were especially appreciated this year. The new and more rigorous Poor Law was now in place, and the counties on either side of his own had witnessed riots the previous year when relief in kind had replaced cash payments, and direct allowances to children had been reduced. Favourable circumstances were essential if the new law was to stand a chance of being seen to work "without apparent severity." Goulburn took the initiative in transferring the elderly from the local workhouse to lodgings in the village, believing they would be more comfortable there "than in a house of such mixed company." At the petty sessions, he and his fellow magistrates amicably settled the complaints of those villagers who, having avoided or escaped payment of the old poor rate, were hard hit by their loss of exemption under the new system. Last but not least, he found time to counsel his sons.[9]

Harry had graduated from Cambridge in 1835 with great distinction and honour, and he personified the ideal of the new generation of earnest young intellectuals – "godliness and good learning." He had settled on the bar as his profession, but it was understood that if he found the work "distasteful" he would enter the church. The only cause of parental concern was his health. Already stoop-shouldered and with a chronically weak chest, both perhaps signs of incipient tuberculosis, he appeared very unwell to his mother's anxious eye in February 1836. Goulburn sought to reassure her that this was true of practically everyone in the middle of winter, but he took pains to introduce Harry to a London specialist. He also insisted that the young man take an extended period of relaxation abroad. Meanwhile, Harry's perfection made late adolescence a peculiarly testing experience for his siblings. Edward had finally secured his commission in the Grenadier Guards, only to succumb to the temptations that had so nearly ruined his uncle and namesake three decades earlier. Goulburn decided to isolate him from the virus of frivolity by obtaining for him an appointment as an aide to the military governor of Malta. In Freddy's case it was a matter of preparing him for Cambridge. The task was not eased by his evident distaste "for exertion or for intense study."[10]

Goulburn's optimism with respect to the 1836 harvest had proven to be overexpectant, and in the gathering economic gloom of the autumn he was peculiarly susceptible to Peel's not entirely serious musings on the similarities of prerevolutionary France with contemporary Britain. "All the same wild opinions as to Government and Religion are now abroad," an uneasy Goulburn agreed, "and if any period of difficulty and distress should dissatisfy the mass of the community I confess that I contemplate with awful apprehension what may be the consequences." A failed harvest was certain to make it more difficult for them to persuade the people of the new Poor Law's ultimate benefit. He suspected that opposition to it would be made a test of parliamentary representation at the next general election. Nor were his spirits revived by the reports from the money markets. The demand for gold and lack of confidence in the Bank of England's directors reminded him all too vividly of the "wild speculation" of 1826. "Any catastrophe in the Money Market would be yet worse than a defective harvest," he fretted. As the bank rate rose and with it the danger of bankcruptcies, the Whigs adopted a number of corrective measures, which fended off immediate disaster but did not revive the economy.[11]

In the light of these developments, Peel acknowledged that they had to make up their minds on the major issues before Parliament met, and he reassured his loyal lieutenant that he was anxious to achieve a "cordial concert" with Wellington. However, Peel's departure for an extended vacation in France with his wife effectively halted discussion. In December, as the opening of the new session neared, Goulburn reached a limited understanding with the duke on tactics in the Lords, and he coaxed Peel into issuing a summons to their "friends." Already, he had taken steps to ensure that members who were abroad or were some distance from the capital were advised of the importance of a full attendance. On the eve of the session a party meeting was held at Peel's London home. But an unsually bland Throne Speech induced the Conservative leadership to sit back and wait on events, for there was no shortage of controversial legislation in the offing.[12]

The Anglican monopoly of the marriage ceremony and of the registration of births, marriages, and deaths had finally been broken in 1836. That year had also seen a charter granted to the University of London, where the absence of any religious profession allowed dissenters to obtain degrees. But the church rates remained a major grievance. The Whig measure introduced in March 1837 proved too radical by half. The rates were to be abolished, and the church's fabric was to be maintained out of a surplus to be generated by a more productive management of its lands. Denounced by the clergy, this scheme was vehemently opposed by the members of the Ecclesiastical Commission on the grounds that the existing resources of the church did not answer its needs. Goulburn's response was predictable, believing as he did that the welfare of the established church "was indeed the beginning and end of all legislative deliberation." Whatever the "evil" in the present system of support, the "real evil" was the inability of the church to provide adequate religious education for all the people. Relieving dissenters of an estimated £50,000 per annum in church rates was infinitely less important in his mind than "providing a million of the population with the means of religious instruction" so essential to the discouragement of vice, the elimination of dissension, and the promotion of social peace. Although the bill survived introduction with a small majority, it was in truth already doomed. When that majority shrank to a mere handful on second reading, the government effectively abandoned the bill.[13]

Goulburn cast his opposition to the revised and revived Irish Municipal Corporations Bill in the same light – defence of the established church. At a strategy meeting held on the evening before the debate, which opened on 10 April 1837, he and his senior colleagues agreed, in deference to Stanley's wishes, to call for a delay until the "other measures very materially bearing on the state of Ireland" had been brought forward. But in the House, Goulburn deplored the omission from the Irish measure of those "safeguards to the misuse of municipal power" that had been a feature of the English bill. Instead, the concession of the franchise to the "lowest ... grade of society," and the virtual powerlessness of Irish corporations, would merely ensure that they became "mischievous engines for exciting discord and inflaming the passions of the people." In particular, he feared that the advocates of lay appropriation of church revenues would be presented with "the means by which they might keep alive agitation, and render it difficult to realize the property of the Church." In short, the Whigs and their Irish allies were seeking, by indirect means, to achieve this long-frustrated objective. However fevered Goulburn's imagination might be, the introduction of another Irish Tithes Bill only three weeks later lent substance to his fears, for it included a 10 per cent tax on future holders of Irish benefices. The monies were to be used to to help finance education. This measure had scarcely cleared second reading (while the other bills were still stalled in the Lords) when William IV died and was succeeded by the young Victoria. The government happily threw up its hands and dissolved Parliament.[14]

The Tories entered the election in confident mood, for a recent by-election success in the former Radical stronghold of Westminster suggested "real" progress of "Conservative principles." Peel's growing national stature and his ever-closer alliance with Stanley and Graham further buoyed spirits, as did the wealth of issues to exploit. Of these, the familiar but effectve cry of the church being in danger, which was so often on Goulburn's lips, promised to be especially potent. The Conservatives' identification with Protestantism was certain to serve them well at a time of resurgent anti-Catholicism. Also, some of them were shamelessly determined to capitalize on the unpopularity of the Poor Law in which their leaders had acquiesced. This unpopularity had continued to grow as the economy continued to contract, and it was especially marked in the North, where clergy began to provide the opposition with leadership. Finally, the party was still profiting from the compromises made by the Whigs in the Reform Bill, which gave it a significant advantage in the counties and some of the boroughs. Reflecting on all this, Goulburn reached a characteristically measured conclusion. "I think that in the English and Welsh boroughs we shall either not lose at all or not more than one and what we may gain in the Counties will be clear advantage," he informed Peel in late July. "The extent of the loss in Ireland I cannot calculate. The progress of the elections there does not inspire much hope."[15]

Goulburn came to regard this election as a missed opportunity. "Had we been more aware of the extent of the reaction in our favor more might certainly have been done especially in Sussex but yet enough has been done to shew the real strength of Conservative principle in England." Ireland, as he had suspected, told a different story. The government's allies there ensured that it would still be in a position to control the Commons despite the Tories' gains. With an eye to the more effective marshalling of their larger force, Goulburn recommended to Peel that the popular, agreeable, and gregarious Thomas Fremantle be appointed to the vital position of whip. Fremantle's previous service as secretary to the Treasury gave him an acknowledged seniority, which lessened the danger of any of the unsuccessful candidates taking offence. Fremantle received the nod. It was difficult to resist the seductive notion that the Conservatives were "too strong for the existence of the Government in any respectable condition." After all, Melbourne seemed more vulnerable than ever. His majority had been reduced to barely a score of seats and those controlled by O'Connell. Not surprisingly, the more than three hundred Tory members who gathered at Peel's house before the opening of Parliament were in an ebullient mood. And indeed the early days of the session suggested that the Whigs had no other choice than to adopt conservative measures that would eventually alienate their "best friends."[16]

While Goulburn waited in 1837 for what he expected to be a not too distant return to office, he struggled to cover the demands on his income which, in the absence of a ministerial salary and in the face of the collapse of his revenues from Amity Hall, were disturbingly excessive. Edward's commission alone had cost £1,400. Goulburn raised £3,600 from the sale of exchequer bills and consols. The premature death of his younger brother Frederick earlier in the year had not only been a personal blow but was another source of financial frustration. Frederick had invested heavily in Australian mortgages during his service there, but Goulburn's efforts as his executor and heir to recover an estimated £7,000 were to drag on infuriatingly for several years. As a gesture of personal economy, he resigned from Whites, though he retained his membership of the Carlton and University clubs and the London Statistical Society. He had joined the last in 1834 at the invitation of its Trinity College organizers, who were seeking Tories to offset a distinctly Whiggish and ministerial colouring. He had been present at the organizational public meeting on 15 May 1834 and had moved the inaugural motion that "accurate knowledge of the condition and prospects of Society is an object of great national importance not to be obtained without a careful collection and classification of Statistical facts." Charles Babbage then moved the formation of the society, and Goulburn was elected to its council. However, he does not seem to have involved himself deeply in its activities or even to have been regular in his attendance of council meetings. He had a strong aversion to the liberal Anglicanism of several of its leading lights.[17]

The year ended with the Whigs in some disarray, having been frequently embarrassed by Goulburn and others in the House. They "will reap the harvest of men who do what is wrong and what they know to be wrong for a temporary advantage," he intoned sententiously. However, reports of rebellions in the Canadas, led by provincial reformers who had wearied of mere agitation, so added to the government's troubles that leading Tories feared that Melbourne would be turned out before they were truly ready to take power. In this sense the situation was further complicated by the growing impatience of many backbenchers, who wished to strike quickly against the tottering ministry. Nor did Melbourne's appointment of the Radical, Lord Durham, as governor general of troubled Canada gain his ministers much credit on either side of the Commons.[18]

The Canada Bill that the Whigs brought forward authorized the new governor general to summon a convention composed of persons untainted by rebellion to advise him on constitutional changes. The problem with this procedure, Goulburn advised Peel, was the likelihood that the selection process would alienate powerful forces in one or both of the provinces. "The object is clearly to unite … [the Canadas]," he added, "and it w[oul]d be better to do it by [positive] enactment than to have it grow out of a Convention formed as it is proposed to form this of Lord Durham under Royal instructions." Peel took "precisely the same view" and had already given notice of a series of amendments to the legislation. Unexpectedly, the government meekly accepted them all. Not only did this foster the impression of an enfeebled administration dependent on the opposition for survival, but it further strengthened the attachment of Stanley and Graham to the Conservative party.[19]

Their leader's triumph on this issue made Conservative back-benchers that much more difficult to control. In a series of divisions, the government found itself more often than not in a minority. On one occasion when Peel was absent, eighty-six Conservatives embarrassed Goulburn by refusing to follow his lead and support the government.

All of this made Peel extremely uneasy, for he remained less than confident of his ability to hold on to power himself. Hence his concern that a Radical motion of censure of the indolent and inefficient colonial secretary, Charles Grant, now Lord Glenelg, would pass. Together with Goulburn and a handful of other close advisers, he sought to avoid premature success. They decided to amend the motion, which Goulburn, for one, considered an unfair attack on an individual for what was a collective failure. Perhaps at Stanley's suggestion, the amendment was worded "*for the very purpose* of precluding Radical support." The government survived, but only at further cost to its reputation, while the clever tactics of the Conservative leadership had united its followers. Very few Tories were prepared to vote with the Radicals.[20]

Goulburn was one of 295 Conservatives who sat down at the dinner given in Peel's honour on 12 May 1838 at the Merchant Taylors' Hall, during which the latter explained his Fabian strategy and the former offered a suitably partisan toast to the nation's Conservative electors. Those in attendance had every reason to be well satisfied. Events in the House continued to lend credence to Peel's after-dinner boast that they had remained true to their principles and were effectively the government. An Irish Poor Law had recently passed, over the objections of O'Connell, only with their support. The Whigs had been obliged finally to abandon the principle of lay appropriation of any surplus revenues of the Irish church. In return, Goulburn and the other members of the Tory inner circle on church and Irish issues had acquiesced in the forgiving of tithe arrears and the conversion of the tax into a rent charge set at 75 per cent of its nominal value. Under this arrangement the Irish clergy would, for a time, be "better off."[21]

The control which the Tory leaders flattered themselves they exercised over the parliamentary agenda was less than perfect, however, especially as they were not always able to control their own rank and file. The abolitionists had long been campaigning within Parliament and without for a premature end to the apprenticeship system that had been created as a way station between slavery and freedom. On 22 May 1838, in a thin House, the parliamentary crusaders successfully carried a motion calling for its immediate end. Here was an issue in which Goulburn had a direct interest, and it was one on which he had charge of the opposition forces, whose support had been promised to the ministry in sufficient number to resist the motion. Instead, Tories provided the abolitionists with the margin of victory. However, responsibility for this piece of mismanagement rested largely with Thomas Spring Rice, who was in command of the Whig forces that evening. This vote was effectively reversed a few days later, with Peel again taking the lead and ministers meekly accepting his proposed resolutions as their own.

In any case, the colonial assemblies were already dismantling the system. In general, they were responding to planter disillusionment with it, though in Jamaica there had been an additional stimulus.[22]

Some planters had behaved both spitefully and harshly towards their apprentices, withholding supplies and extorting more labour. The stipendiary magistracy appointed to protect apprentices from such abuses had proven ineffectual. Undermanned and underfunded, the magistracy had been compromised by its close relationship with planters or their managers. Thus it was not surprising that abolitionist critics assailed apprenticeship as "a mitigated form of slavery." Not that the apprentices had been docile. They had resisted, had declined to cooperate with their former owners or overseers, and had skilfully exploited their strong bargaining position during "crop," when the need for their labour was most acute. Further, they had quietly lessened their dependence on employment by working plots of land on which they might subsist. Not surprisingly, "much of the violence and most of the disputes in the apprenticeship period involved mainly questions of working hours and condition during the harvest season." Was this true of Amity Hall?[23]

Initially, Goulburn's apprentices had shown themselves resistant to surrendering "one minute of their own time" even for "liberal wages." McPherson's response was to provide the local stipendiary with a re-decorated "Great House" at a modest rent. The apprentices soon agreed to extra labour for wages. Indeed, they signed a contract which bound them "for the whole crop." Yet the estate's rich potential remained unfulfilled, due primarily to the want of sufficient labour and stock. One solution was to import British labourers on short indentures, but Goulburn rejected this on account of the expense involved and his scepticism of the ability of the English "lower orders" to labour for long in the tropics, given their notorious "addiction to ardent spirits." Another possibility was to purchase apprenticeships, but Goulburn was hesitant to invest in labourers who might quit his estate with the end of the system in 1840, even if it survived that long. Moreover, he was discouraged by an unflattering account of the moral condition of his "people." His response was to approve the establishment of an infant school, but without any real hope of thereby saving the young. He ordered a return to inducements, in the form of more responsible and rewarding positions for adults who took religious instruction. Yet for all of his misgivings, which sprang in part from his suspicion that the Whigs would buckle under the abolitionist pressure for an immediate end of apprenticeship, he eventually purchased a pen with its 107 apprentices and 80 head of stock. Although the risk was great and the investment considerable, at more than £3,500, he reasoned that this

substantial enlargement of the estate's population would at least improve his chances of retaining an adequate labour force whenever full
freedom was granted. And his anxiety to foster among his apprentices
a deeper sense of attachment to Amity Hall saw him invest heavily in
large purchases of clothing, in lumber for houses, in tools, and in fish
to supplement the workers' diet.[24]

Another potential source of labour were children, who under the
terms of the Emancipation Act could be voluntarily apprenticed for a
number of years. Binding them to Amity Hall would discourage their
families from moving away after 1840. McPherson scotched this idea.
Parents would never apprentice their children, he reported, for they
regarded the system "as a species of bondage." Indeed, large numbers
of the young were growing up "in laziness, idleness and vice." Alarmed,
Goulburn sought to foster the work ethic. He proposed that parents be
offered additional wages or reduced hours of labour in return for permitting their children to be employed on simple tasks. Alternatively,
families might be assigned task work. Any extra labour they performed
after its completion would then be rewarded. The best preparation for
the end of apprenticeship, he concluded, was "to give to the Negro the
greatest possible interest in his labour, to give him a taste for pecuniary
payments & thus to make the balance of comfort be on the side of his
continuing regularly to work."[25]

The abrupt termination of apprenticeship proved to be Goulburn's
noblest hour as a plantation owner. Suppressing his indignation at the
loss of the precious capital he had so recently invested in additional apprentices, he immediately provided for those who from age or infirmity
were incapable of earning their own subsistence. "So long as the Estate
produces anything," he instructed McPherson, "I hold them to have a
claim to support and I should above all things be unwilling because the
Parliament has been unjust to be cruel and unjust to them." In the
same paternalistic spirit, he gave instructions that health care should
continue to be provided to the aged, the infirm, and in cases of necessity to labourers, even though this was no longer his legal responsibility.
At the same time, he sought an understanding with local planters and
managers on wages and rents in order to avoid any "inconvenient" attempts to outbid one another. He revived an earlier suggestion that
cane pieces be rented to "industrious negroes," who were to be guaranteed a price for the canes they delivered to the mill. Such an arrangement "might animate them to raise a greater quantity of produce than
they would otherwise be disposed to do." Yet there could be no escaping the uncomfortable and ironic fact that his hopes of again making
the estate pay depended on the actions of his former slaves. "If the negroes will work when emancipated we shall all ultimately benefit by the

change," Goulburn summarized. "If they will not our prospects are poor indeed."[26]

The "Amity Hall people" proved to be disconcertingly adept negotiators. They declined to discuss wages before the first day of freedom and then increased the pressure on the harassed attorney by taking the balance of the month as a vacation. When they did agree to discussions, McPherson discovered that they expected a full day's wage for as little as five hours of work. He received some assistance from the governor, Sir Lionel Smith, who on a visit to Vere stayed with him and advised the labourers to return to work. Also, he expected to be able to exert some countervailing pressure on them through the rental charges for their houses and provisions grounds. The rule of thumb that he and other managers were seeking to establish was two days' labour for a cottage and a plot of land. But he was prepared to sweeten this arrangement by halving the rent or forgiving arrears in return for a promise of six months' continuous labour. Within a few weeks, however, he was compelled to raise substantially the wages of field labourers, hauliers, and workers in the boiling house. Nor did these rates last long. A strike forced him to improve wages yet again. Even so, the labourers continued to spend two days on tasks that as apprentices they had completed in one. Furthermore, they refused to pay their rents. All of this, McPherson gloomily concluded, contradicted those abolitionists who had argued that free labour would be more productive than slave labour. To strengthen his attorney's bargaining position, Goulburn authorized him to exercise tighter control over the provisions grounds and to be strict in the collection of rents. "Ultimately I am satisfied that the best course will be to pay liberal wages and enforce proportionate rents," he declared.[27]

Goulburn decided to spend the autumn and early winter of 1838 on the Continent. His wife's chronic ill health – and rheumatism had recently been added to her catalogue of complaints – saw him agree to her wintering "in a Southern climate in the hope that if she can bear the fatigues of the journey she may afterwards return to England in a state more capable of enjoying it." Setting out early in August, they travelled by coach and rail from Antwerp to Wiesbaden, accompanied by their daughter Jane. After a fortnight's therapy in the spa's warm sulphur springs, they journeyed on to Switzerland and dallied for a month amid the lakes and mountains before heading south into Italy. Captivated by the beauties of nature and the achievements of man, Goulburn gave little thought to what might be happening at home. He was distressed to detect a decline of British influence on the Continent, for which he naturally blamed the Whigs. They had undermined foreign confidence in, or respect for, Britain's might by their swingeing cuts in defence expenditures at the behest of the Radicals, he complained, and by ceaselessly harping on the necessity of peace. The image of their nation, he advised Peel, was that of an enfeebled giant.[28]

Returning home alone in February 1839, Goulburn discovered that little of what had occurred during his absence was calculated to alter this foreign perception of Britain's paralysis. Durham had behaved with characteristic and predictable indiscretion in Canada, only to quit his office when the government nullified one of his arbitrary actions. However, there was a general expectation that Melbourne would go to practically any lengths to appease him on his return home. Indeed, the organization of the working classes in the Chartist movement for democratic reform and the founding in the nation's industrial heartland of the Anti–Corn Law League convinced many Tories that the Whigs would seek in such traditional Radical issues as the ballot and cheap bread the basis of an understanding with the surly Durham. Moreover, the Lancashire member selected by the government to second the Address in support of the Throne Speech used the occasion to call for repeal of the Corn Laws. Cheaper bread would allow manufacturers to reduce wages and would thus enhance British industrial competitiveness, he imprudently argued. His reward for such honesty, Goulburn wryly noted, was the cold shoulder of political friends and ouster from the chair of the Manchester Chamber of Commerce. But this was merely one in a series of Whig mishaps. The unceremonial and abrupt removal of Lord Glenelg from the Colonial Office and claims that the cabinet had unanimously approved the decision led to mocking suggestions that Glenelg had fallen asleep during the discussion only for his nodding to be interpreted as agreement. Even the Whig ladies at court added to Melbourne's tribulations. Lady Tavistock was reputed to be the source of the accusation that Lady Flora Hastings, a member of the household of the queen's mother and a Tory spinster, was carrying a child. Banished from the young queen's presence, she had subsequently to be readmitted when further medical examination authoritatively contradicted the gossip. "In short, nothing can be more contemptible & pitiful than the state of the Government," Goulburn concluded.[29]

Yet he did not expect the ministry to fall. The Whigs' attachment to office was so strong, he said, that they would "bear every insult and reproach that can be heaped upon them and not care how affairs go on" so long as they commanded a single vote majority. Their hold on power was so tenuous, Goulburn scornfully observed, that Russell was reduced to introducing a motion praising himself and his colleagues for their administration of Ireland in order to claim with its passage that they still enjoyed the confidence of the House. But their difficulties continued to multiply. In India, the natives had been excited to rebellion by "a most unjust infraction of existing treaties;" in America, the Yankees were talking "very big" over a number of recent border incidents; in the manufacturing districts of northern England, the people were in an uproar and were suspected of having gathered arms; and as if all this were not enough, the ministers had given notice of a motion to suspend the Jamaican constitution.[30]

Glenelg's departure from Downing Street had already caused Goulburn to "tremble for Jamaica," where "things" were going on "as badly as possible." He suspected that he had seen the last of any income from the estate. "I know not how I shall get on," he warned one son. "If we are to live at all we must all pull in our horns." Now, as punishment for the Jamaican assembly's obstructive and defiant conduct, the government was proposing to suspend the colony's constitution for five years in favour of direct rule by governor and council. This seemed certain to heighten confusion on the island, thereby further jeopardizing Goulburn's already faint hopes of again turning a profit on Amity Hall. This thought was surely in the back of his mind when he both opened and closed the Tory attack on the proposal. Without defending the Jamaican assembly, he carefully laid responsibility for the crisis at the government's door. A policy of vacillation had been too abruptly replaced by one of decisiveness. More than this, the Whigs were effectively proclaiming to the world "that the necessary consequences of negro emancipation was the abolition of free institutions."[31]

Melbourne's resignation, when his government's majority fell to five on this question, took both Goulburn and Peel by surprise. In sanctioning the attack, the Conservative leader had been seeking simply to mollify those of his followers who were increasingly impatient with his Fabian strategy. He had calculated that another government retreat would hold them in check by reminding them of their indirect control over the parliamentary agenda. Instead, he was suddenly called on to form an administration at a time when he still doubted his ability to do so successfully. Thus he was surely far from dismayed when the young queen refused to make the changes he sought within the ranks of her ladies-in-waiting. Victoria's personal attachment to Melbourne, who had counselled her on her response, and the Whig colouring of her household fully justified Peel's request for this mark of royal favour. In the face of her blanket refusal, he returned the commission and Melbourne returned to office. But although the Tory leader's explanation of his conduct and decision won high praise from most of his principal colleagues, Goulburn was critical of his friend's high-mindedness. In his opinion, Peel should have roundly condemned the ministers who had advised the queen.[32]

There was one other personal disappointment awaiting Goulburn. The Speaker's desire to retire had long been rumoured, and Peel had decided that Goulburn would be the best man to put up against the expected Whig candidate, Thomas Spring Rice. After all, the Irishman's unpopularity on his own side of the House and the Radicals' active dislike of him presented the Conservatives with another opportunity to show that they were effectively in control of the Commons. In the event, though, the election was held soon after Melbourne's unexpectedly swift return to office. Thus the contest assumed even greater importance as a test of strength, and the Whigs packed the unpopular Spring Rice off to the Lords with the "soaring title" of Lord Monteagle. In his stead, they nominated the far more popular figure of Shaw Lefevre, who scraped through with a narrow victory over Goulburn.[33]

Goulburn put the best face on his defeat. The party had united behind his candidacy, only three Tories missing the division. Moreover, the task of presiding in the Commons "with an adverse government whose supporters [were] always unwilling to submit to authority" would have been a peculiarly difficult one. Goulburn found additional solace in the Whigs' unpopularity, for they had regained office only as a result of the unreasonable conduct of the queen. The performance of the anthem "And They of the Household Divided the Spoil" during a service at the Chapel Royal, which was attended by the queen and her ladies, excited much amusement. "The words 'And they of the Household' were repeated over and over again in every variety of modulation," Goulburn noted, "so that by the time the Chorus came to 'divided the spoil' the application of the words to the actual state of affairs became evident to all and the Chapel was in a titter."[34]

Goulburn's conviction that religion was the core of all worthwhile education and that state-aided education in England should be controlled by the established church had seen him join the increasingly successful National School Society. Lord John Russell's decision to introduce a national scheme of education in 1839 may have been inspired more by his dislike of the society than his desire to conciliate his Radical and dissenter allies. But those of his proposals that threatened to diminish the society's burgeoning influence or advance the cause of nonsectarian education excited a storm of resistance. Members of the established church, Goulburn thundered, "would never consent to their children being sent to schools merely for secular instruction, and merely for general religious instruction." With the church and its devoted members lined up in opposition to them, the Whigs again retreated and abandoned much of their bill. What remained, essentially, was the provision for a secular supervisory board, and even this had subsequently to be amended in a way acceptable to the church.[35]

Goulburn derived almost as much pleasure in flaying the Whigs for their mishandling of the nation's finances. Over the years, he had enunciated a handful of principles which, in his opinion, ought to determine fiscal policy. First, the issues should be examined in terms of their long-term consequences rather than their immediate impact. Second, the public debt had to be kept in an easily manageable state. Third, "real economy did not consist in a niggardly reduction of the official establishment, so much as the careful husbanding of the means of the country." Fourth, tax reductions should be governed by two subsidiary principles, one of which was vaguely utilitarian and the other mildly progressive. The principal purpose of any tax reduction, he reasoned, was "to effect the greatest proportion of benefit to the greatest extent." In short, the interests of the whole community should always be paramount. Beyond this, the burden should "continue as much as possible upon the luxuries" and be diminished "as much as possible upon the necessaries of life." Of course, he had long warned "that reduction of taxation did not necessarily produce increased consumption, unless in the case where the reduction was large."[36]

The stagnating economy, which saw the nation afflicted after 1837 with falling commodity prices and chronic unemployment, with poor harvests and rising bread prices – and thus with mounting working-class discontent – had produced a succession of budget deficits. The Whigs' earlier and popular decision to cut direct taxation now returned to haunt them, for the indirect taxes on which the Exchequer was now largely dependent simply failed to generate sufficient revenues. The cost of compensating the slave owners and the expense of suppressing the Canadian rebellions were but two of the additional strains. Had the Whigs not pursued the foolhardy policy of cutting the military and naval establishments to the bone, Goulburn argued, the problems in Canada might have been nipped in the bud. At the same time, he ridiculed the government's repeated claims that the deficits were temporary, and he pointed to an ever-heavier burden of debt as an ominous consequence of the government's resort to borrowing to cover the deficits. In this gloomy context, he challenged the wisdom of the establishment of the penny postage.[37]

The innovation was popular among Radicals in the Commons, and the Whigs decided to offer it to them as another sop in 1839. "This will increase the number of idle scribblers," one old Tory complained, "be of little benefit to the lower classes, who seldom have occasion to write, and is likely only to advantage the commercial houses and bankers, who can well afford to pay the [current] postage." As both Goulburn and Peel were at pains to point out in the Commons, the ministry was planning at a time of chronic deficits to risk a revenue of £1,500,000 on the gamble of a massive increase in cheap mail. Significantly, Goulburn did not call for the rejection of this popular scheme, merely its postponement to give time for more deliberate consideration. Not that he and Peel were unduly distressed when they were heavily defeated on the issue. The opportunistic government had presented them with another hostage to fortune.[38]

The "derangement of the stomach" and "depression of the spirits," to which Goulburn fell prey in July, he attributed at least in part to anxiety over his irresponsible second son, Edward. He was too unwell even to make a final call on Peel before setting out for Naples with Harry as an escort to collect his wife and daughter. They sailed from Southampton to Le Havre, then travelled overland to Marseilles, where they took ship for southern Italy. In October, escorting the two Janes, they set out on a more leisurely return journey. In both Munich and Paris they encountered the young Benjamin Disraeli and his wife, who found the Goulburns "very agreeable" and with whom they became "intimate." They arrived in London on 8 November.[39]

Goulburn reported for duty soon after his return, though it took him several days to put his domestic affairs in order and to catch up with the news. Before long, he was directing Peel's attention to the questions they needed to consider before the opening of Parliament. The most important was the parlous state of the nation's finances. Goulburn was alarmed not only by the recurring deficits but also by their easy acceptance by so many people. This state of things, he wrote, "is slowly but surely doing the work of the Anarchists by gradually breaking up the foundations of our prosperity and thus ultimately involving all property and consequently all classes in corruption and ruin." They must recommit themselves, he held, in the best tradition of Pitt, to the principle of steadily reducing the national debt. They could not go on borrowing, relieving themselves of burdens at the expense of their heirs. The only solution was taxation to "bring up the Revenue to the expenditure & provide for an annual application to the liquidation of the debt." Goulburn added that alone among public men, Peel possessed the national "weight and authority" to implement this resolute and painful policy.[40]

Peel's response was characteristically pragmatic. There was little point in demanding an end to deficits without first considering which new taxes could be imposed, he replied. His caution reflected the debater's concern not to present opponents with easy points, as well as a belief that the Radicals were at the root of the problem. By encouraging deficits, they were able to exercise "greater control over a Government, and enforce reduction of establishments with greater effect." In mid-December Peel wrote again, seeking Goulburn's advice on their "line of policy" at the opening of the session. They had to find some way of relieving the pressure that was building on the back benches for another assault on the Whigs. Should they attack? How should they attack? When should they attack? and Should they make a concerted movement with the Lords? he asked. The danger of moving a confidence motion, as Goulburn realized, was that the government would secure a modest majority sufficient to enable ministers to ignore other defeats during the remainder of the session. Not that this checked his own desire for action, for he was far less sanguine than Peel of an imminent disintegration of the Melbourne ministry. The Whigs were too weak for the luxury of differences, he astutely observed, but unless they were ousted soon, their continued mishandling of the economy would present a Conservative administration with an ever more daunting challenge. Indeed, he submitted to Peel an estimate which indicated that the deficit for the current year would exceed £1 million. "If therefore the difficulties are to deter you now from accepting the Government or from attempting to drive out our enemies," Goulburn tartly observed, "I do not see when the period is likely to arrive at which the Government could safely be either attacked or displaced."[41]

Urged on by Goulburn and Graham (though Wellington and Stanley, whom he also consulted, were far less enthusiastic for action), and provided with optimistic assessments by his parliamentary and party organizers of the votes he would collect in the Commons and the seats he might capture in the country in an election, Peel sanctioned a non confidence motion. However, a spate of unexpected Liberal successes in by-elections left even the eager Graham pessimistic of the outcome. In the event, the Whigs' majority of twenty-one had the effect Goulburn had feared. They were safe for the session. Moreover, the Conservatives were acutely sensitive to the fact that the young queen was "so violent a partizan" of the Whigs. This she demonstrated yet again by her reluctance to invite Wellington to her wedding to Prince Albert. His crime had been his role in cutting the enormous allowance which Melbourne had foolishly recommended for the prince. When the queen was persuaded by the prime minister not to snub the duke in this most public manner, she petulantly excluded him from the wedding breakfast.[42]

The balance of the session passed without a great deal of excitement. Goulburn supported the ongoing reform of the church through the reduction of cathedral establishments and the use of the surplus revenues to increase and maintain parish clergy. He criticized the government's choice of taxes to be increased in its effort to balance the budget. To levy an additional 5 per cent on tobacco, tea, and spirits would not necessarily produce a similar increase in revenue, he remarked. However, a new chancellor, Francis Baring, was at least seeking to tackle the deficit and therefore deserved a short period of grace. The reform of Irish corporations was also finally effected, though on terms dictated by the Lords and consistent with Goulburn's earlier objections to a too liberal franchise. The union of the Canadas was treated as a nonpartisan measure, and the archbishop of Canterbury consulted closely with Goulburn in drafting a settlement of the clergy reserves in the colony that was "highly favourable" to the established church and "opposed to the principles of [the government's] supporters." For all of these minor victories in Parliament, the autumn found Goulburn filled with foreboding. Everywhere, a "spirit of restlessness and dissatisfaction" seemed to have rendered the task of government "if not hopeless at least dangerous and difficult."[43]

Goulburn's pessimism deepened with the news from the West Indies, and he indulged in some gallows humour with respect to his worth. The death of his attorney had brought yet another demoralizing assessment of the condition of Amity Hall. Cane pieces had been left unattended and were overrun, pasture was in poor condition, fences were in bad order, buildings leaked, the Great House was dilapidated and its furniture had disappeared, the stock of cattle was insufficient, and the cottages of the estate's workforce were in need of repair. Wearily, Goulburn responded to his new attorney: "I know that the Estate is capable if properly cultivated of making large crops in proportion to its extent. The proper cultivation therefore is the first and paramount object and under existing circumstances I must urge upon you to adopt whatever means may secure it and to consider how far any improvement may be introduced by which human labour may be saved."[44]

However sceptical he had become of ever deriving a worthwhile income from Amity Hall, Goulburn still enrolled in Thomas Fowell Buxton's Society for the Extinction of the Slave Trade and for the Civilization of Africa. He had, after all, long struggled to suppress the slave trade when he was at the Colonial Office. This new organization, which was dedicated to the promotion of legitimate commerce and Christianity along the West African coast through the establishment of prosperous communities, became so closely identified with the Tories that some Radicals declined to participate. That Goulburn did not play a more active role in its affairs was the result of the society's encouragement of nonconformist missionary work. While he wished the Baptists and Methodists well, he felt that in teaching "an imperfect form of Faith," they offered the natives only an "ambiguous boon." He demanded reassurance that he was advancing civilization and Christianity in the form of the Church of England before participating more heartily in the society's work. Moreover, the Niger expedition, which the Whig government agreed to subsidize in 1841 with an eye to reviving its old alliance with the antislavery movement, ended in death and disaster.[45]

Disaster also appeared to threaten Britain's economy. The cotton industry, which was so vital to the export trade, was sunk in depression, and high unemployment and the high price of bread brought distress and disaffection to the textile districts. The stalling of railway construction contributed to the slump in the coal and iron industries. The woollen industry was no better off. As the Whigs struggled ineffectually with the deepening economic crisis, some of them were reduced to hoping that the Tory party would "fall to pieces" either as a result of the aging Wellington's death or of his strained relationship with Peel. Instead, the Iron Duke's constitution proved less brittle than expected, and influential Tories quietly conspired to "effect the renewal of that intercourse [with Peel] which we all so fervently desire." Stanley and Graham, meanwhile, announced their candidacies for the Carlton Club.[46]

All the while, the Whigs' predicament grew worse. Wars in China and India, troubles in Canada, a swelling O'Connellite movement in Ireland for repeal of the Union, a program of rearmament under way in France, and a threatening United States all demanded "timely preparation." Where were the Ways and Means to finance preparedness? The tax increases introduced by Baring the previous year in an effort to come to terms with the deficit had proven "worse than productive." The cabinet's, having again rejected the income tax, decided that the answer was to plump for a reduction of protective duties, especially on colonial produce. The assumption was that this would so spur consumption that revenues would actually increase. The staff at the Board of Trade advocated this strategy, which had recently been given a full public airing by a parliamentary select committee dominated by free traders. But the confidential information coming Goulburn's way suggested that the Whigs' avowal of sweeping tariff reform and their attack on colonial preferences were motivated as much by partisan considerations as by fiscal difficulties. The colonial interests involved were still regarded as Tory in sentiment, while cheaper sugar, cheaper coffee, cheaper timber, and cheaper bread would surely prove appealing on the hustings. On the other hand, this chant would drive the agricultural interest deeper into a Tory embrace. No less important, the proposal greatly to reduce the duty on slave-grown foreign sugar would undoubtedly cost the Whigs the support of a large segment of the antislavery movement. Only the year before, 1840, the World's Anti-Slavery Convention had called for the permanent exclusion of slave produce from Britain.[47]

In the House, Goulburn exploited the Whigs' vulnerability. Speaking on 30 April 1841, he pointed to the critical situation in which the nation found itself as a result of growing expenditures and a constant reduction of duties. The following day, he and other members of Peel's inner group decided to concentrate their fire on the sugar proposal, which alone of the major issues promised success in the House without embarrassment at the polls. But Goulburn was disqualified from leading the assault by his recent campaign to preserve a preference for the producers of West Indian rum over their East Indian competitors. Nevertheless, he did speak in the debate, and to some effect. He pointed out that the proposed reduction in duty would achieve little with respect to consumption and revenue, for rarely over the past fifteen years had the price of sugar risen above that at which the foreign slave-grown product was now to be admitted. On the other hand, he protested that this action would so stimulate production in Brazil that the slave trade to that country would be given a fresh impetus. Therefore, it would be far better to forbear any reduction of duty until it was clear "that it might be done without injustice to our colonies, and until some reciprocal advantage to this country and to humanity was obtained from Brazil."[48]

Heavily defeated on the sugar proposal, the Whigs decided to appeal to the country. While their promises of cheaper bread and cheaper sugar might not save them from electoral defeat, these did offer the Whigs the best prospect of minimizing their losses. But in the manoeuvring for position, Peel proved to be more deft than the tired and discredited ministers. He introduced another nonconfidence motion, and amidst extraordinary scenes in the early hours of the morning of 5 June, which saw the desperate Whigs wheel in a member who was reportedly "in a state of total idiocy," it carried by the smallest of margins. But instead of resigning, Melbourne went ahead with the announcement of a dissolution and made plans to meet the new Parliament.[49]

This desperate electoral strategy worked in many of the old commercial centres and newer manufacturing districts, but the Whigs were overwhelmed in the English counties and small towns. The Tories stood for agricultural protection and Protestantism, appealing in centres such as Liverpool to an anti-Catholicism reignited by Irish immigration, and they again exploited the popular hatred of the Poor Law and the hopes for a humanization of the factory system. Their suspicion that the Whigs had gone to the country after the vote of censure "with the sole object of crippling the administration of their successors" was strengthened by the contents and tone of the Queen's Speech to the new Parliament. The Whigs' "wicked" references to the Corn Laws seemed calculated to create as much excitement as possible, and Goulburn even suspected that there was an intrigue afoot to foment enough popular agitation to make possible both the queen's early dismissal of a Conservative administration and a second dissolution. In this dark mood, the Tories moved an amendment to the Address, during which Goulburn made a spirited attack on the Whigs' financial record and announced that a Conservative government would balance the nation's accounts. The Melbourne ministry was overwhelmingly defeated and made an ignominious departure from office. "Our party is shipwrecked," one prominent Whig remarked of the unseemly scramble for pensions, "and every body lays hold on any plank that he can find and fights desperately for it."[50]

For Henry Goulburn, the ejection of the Whigs was a peculiarly satisfying and timely event. His partisanship had inevitably been intensified by a decade in opposition, but his contempt for his adversaries had deepened apace. In his mind, they had been unfit to govern, and the squalid nature of their exit did nothing to disabuse him of this notion. Indeed, it encouraged arrogance if not superciliousness. The leading lights of the Conservative party neither suffered fools gladly nor doubted their own superior fitness for high office. They alone could rescue the nation from the morass into which the incompetent Whigs had dragged it. This they would do by their integrity, efficiency, command of administrative detail, fiscal responsibility, and political courage. Goulburn also assumed that they would reverse the trend of the Whig years by preventing any further erosion of the church's privileged position and by providing it with additional state aid. But the reality of the situation, as Peel had acknowledged during his short administration six years earlier, was that the power of the dissenters obliged even Conservatives to treat them with consideration. Finally, ministerial rank was even more important personally to Goulburn in 1841 than ever before. The financial anxiety that had long gripped him and had seen him cast an envious eye at the comfort of the Speaker's chair tightened its hold on his mind with the collapse of Amity Hall as a profitable enterprise. He needed not only the income but the influence of high office if he was to make satisfactory provision for his family.

CHAPTER ELEVEN

Peel's Chancellor

Henry Goulburn fretted that ill discipline among the rank and file would bedevil the government, embracing as the Conservative party did the most zealous defenders of the church, an agricultural interest sure to resent liberal Toryism's preoccupation with commerce and industry, and paternalists averse to their leader's hard-headed if not hard-hearted attitude towards social issues. For his part, Peel increasingly saw the solution to working-class distress and disaffection in an expanding economy, which would create work and generate wealth. Full employment and full stomachs were the best remedies for radicalism.[1]

The executive that Peel led and expected his back-benchers dutifully to follow boasted a wealth of experience and talent. Goulburn's inclusion turned on the question of the speakership. Some partisans wished to place a Conservative in the chair, and Goulburn would certainly have claimed the nomination, but following consultations with colleagues, and having sampled back-bench opinion, Peel concluded that there was no general enthusiasm for the unseating of the popular Shaw Lefevre. The fact that the Whigs had retained a Tory Speaker when they took power more than a decade earlier swayed some members, while others were simply reluctant immediately to wage an intensely partisan battle. The prime minister duly reported these findings to Goulburn, who loyally accepted the decision not to fight. Of course, he was able to console himself with the Exchequer. Peel was not going to repeat the experience of 1834–35, of serving both as first lord and chancellor. Indeed, a wish to have the dependable, hard-working, knowledgeable, and level-headed Goulburn in this critical position as he struggled to get to grips with the government's daunting economic and fiscal inheritance may explain Peel's readiness to retain Lefevre in the chair.[2]

A cabinet that included Stanley, Graham, Wellington, Lyndhurst, and Aberdeen commanded respect, yet Goulburn was widely regarded as the prime minister's "most intimate friend." But observers who dismissed him as Peel's *alter ego* misjudged the man and the relationship. Goulburn had entered politics as a vocation, and the reach of his personal ambition had always been limited by his lack of rank or station. In many ways a modest man, and certainly one of ever more modest means, he craved neither a great name nor a great reputation. Rather, he hoped to leave public life with a general acknowledgment of his rectitude and useful service to the nation. His "statesmanship, industry [and] conscience" made him the quintessential Peelite, but his tendency to defer to Peel's political judgment out of respect for his friend's brilliance, both intellectual and tactical, ought not to be confused with subservience. His habit was to weigh the pros and cons of a course of action very carefully and then to indicate clearly the balance of his opinion. Moreover, he had gained in political authority over the preceding decade, and he possessed an undisputed mastery of the business of his office.[3]

Goulburn had remained true to the principles of moderate liberal Toryism that had guided him during his first term at the Exchequer. He was determined to balance the budget; this he expected to achieve through strict economy and increased taxation. He was equally determined to lighten the burden of debt. Further, he continued to harbour a healthy scepticism of any iron link between the reduction of duties and increased consumption. Thus his support of trade liberalization had always been qualified by a concern to ensure both ways and means. In "our eagerness to promote universal freedom of trade," he cautioned, "it would be well to remember financial considerations – so essential to the commerce because so important to the credit, of all trading communities." In short, he was no ideological free trader. "I do not adopt extreme opinions either on the one side or the other," he insisted. Instead, he put his "claim decidely to retain those duties which are essential for revenue purposes; to retain those restrictive duties which are essential for preserving public morals; and to retain those duties which may be necessary occasionally for the public safety." Of course, the formulation of economic policy was an interdepartmental task. On matters of trade, tariffs, and corn laws, Peel turned to the Board of Trade – over which the Earl of Ripon (Frederick Robinson) presided but in which young William Ewart Gladstone was the dynamo – and to Lord Aberdeen at the Foreign Office. Colonial duty preferences necessarily involved Edward Stanley as the secretary of state.[4]

Goulburn remained wedded also to the minimal state and to the cause of Treasury control of departmental expenditures. The govern-

ment's interference with commercial operations should always be severely restricted, he argued, for any general adoption of the principle
that the state ought "to make persons carry on their businesses hon-
estly and safely" would end in "intolerable tyranny." Predictably, other
departments considered no less intolerable the Treasury's efforts to
discipline their spending habits. But Goulburn found a zealous second in Charles Edward Trevelyan, who had been appointed assistant
secretary of the Treasury only the year before. Trevelyan's Whiggish
sympathies and his marriage to a daughter of Zachary Macaulay might
have been expected to prejudice his relationship with Henry Goulburn. Instead, whatever suspicions Goulburn initially harboured concerning his senior official's connections were quickly allayed by
Trevelyan's evangelical integrity and industry, and his commitment to
economy and efficiency. He took very seriously the Treasury's duty "of
looking after the pecuniary interests of the State."[5]

The immediate task was to find the monies necessary to carry the
government through to the end of the financial year in April 1842,
and to indicate the means by which they intended to meet the current
deficiency of £2,500,000. Goulburn's options were limited. The brevity
of the session discouraged any attempt to introduce additional taxes,
while the sale of government stock would put him at the mercy of the
City. Any significant shortfall in sales would expose him to Whig jibes.
So he raised £3,500,000 by encouraging the holders of exchequer bills
to deposit them for the purpose of being funded. "You have made provision for the deficiency and have lightened the floating debt by a million," one knowledgeable acquaintance congratulated him. "This has
been effected upon terms very advantageous to the public." Furthermore, he had the added satisfaction of explaining his strategy in what
was generally regarded as an "admirable speech."[6]

Goulburn moved with similar dispatch and decisiveness to uncover
and then limit the damage of an extensive fraud in the exchequer bills
office. An urgent investigation revealed that a large quantity of forged
bills had been issued. Together with Peel and Graham, Goulburn personally attended the examination of the senior public official involved
in the affair, and they then met hurriedly with senior members of the
stock exchange. To restore confidence in a shaken public credit, Goulburn ordered that all the bills in circulation be called in during daylight hours for examination. The genuine ones were stamped and
reissued, but the forgeries totalled £377,000. They had been of such
good quality that the assistance of an expert from the post office was required in order to identify them. To reassure a nervous public that procedures would be put in place to prevent any repetition of this crime,
Goulburn established a small commission to investigate and make rec-

ommendations. It also served to stifle demands for a full public disclosure of the details of the affair when the central figure pleaded guilty and was rapidly sentenced to transportation for life. Indeed, the commission subsequently provided Goulburn with the means of escape from the corner into which he had painted himself with his hasty refusal to provide compensation to the victims. His fear was that this would merely encourage the circulation of other securities of dubious authenticity; but in the face of a well-orchestrated campaign for the honouring of the forged bills, he found in the commission's recommendations the face-saving formula for making restitution in most cases.[7]

More ominous still was the parlous state of the nation's general finances. Goulburn and Peel were confronted by an accumulated deficit that exceeded £7 million, and there was every reason to fear that it would continue to grow. Military and naval expenditures were being driven higher by a host of foreign difficulties, while an inelastic revenue was dwindling in the face of stagnant trade, poor harvests, high inflation, and unemployment. Adding to the sense of anxiety and instability were the popular political movements. In Ireland, Daniel O'Connell was exhibiting characteristic skill and energy organizing a campaign to repeal the Union. In England, the depressed state of the economy threatened to see the Anti–Corn Law League and the Chartists emerge as even more formidable enemies of the established order. The challenge, then, was to restore fiscal and economic confidence. In mid-July, with electoral victory certain, and his return to power simply a matter of time, Peel had sought Goulburn's opinion on whether to resort to an income tax. Goulburn responded with a characteristically thoughtful and balanced memorandum, which James Graham cited as proof of the wisdom of his selection as chancellor.[8]

Although Goulburn had recently opposed the revival of the tax, arguing that such a radical change in taxation policy would further unsettle an already fitful economy, he carefully weighed for Peel its advantages and disadvantages. The fact that it would appear to fall only on the more affluent sections of society promised to be politically advantageous. On the other hand, to the extent that the affluent had less disposable income, the poorer classes would be indirectly pinched by a reduction in demand and thus of employment. The principle advantage, however, was the immense revenue likely to be generated. On the basis of an admittedly rough-and-ready estimate, Goulburn calculated that a modest rate of 2.5 per cent would produce some £4–5 million annually. This sum would not only erase the deficit but would leave a healthy surplus, which could be "applicable either to the reduction of debt or to supply deficiencies of Revenue occasioned by experimental reductions of taxation with a view to relieve the suffering classes or to increase consumption." In short, he envisaged the tax not merely as the means of balancing the nation's accounts but also as an instrument of social policy and economic growth. "The object was, by means of it," he later explained, "to remove from the public generally other taxes which were found to press on the industry of the country, and upon the consumers of several important articles." Certainly, the lowering of duties on a range of articles of general consumption would make the imposition of the tax "palatable with the working classes at least." His own preference was for a reduction in the sugar duties, which, besides being of benefit to a large mass of the population, would also help the hard-pressed West Indian producers, one of whom was himself.[9]

Goulburn was well aware that the tax would be unpopular with those on whose income it was levied; he was uncertain whether the reformed House would be willing to enact the measure without "the pressure of War expenditure"; and he knew that legislation of such complexity would have to be drafted with peculiar care. Because of all these factors, he recommended that they proceed with great caution. To curtail opposition and discourage complicated schemes of evasion, he suggested that the level of taxation be low, that its life span be limited, and that a preliminary inquiry be launched into other possible sources of revenue. Both Graham and Stanley joined him in urging the cabinet to tread warily. They endorsed Goulburn's deliberate approach, seconding his proposal of a thorough prior investigation of possible alternatives, such as further savings in expenditures and the more efficient collection of revenues. The result was an unpaid commission "for the express purpose of revising the charge of collecting the revenue in all its branches." Here was evidence of their determination to do "something effectual" and of their "desire to consider reductions" before proposing taxation.[10]

There was some ministerial resistance to the tax, though it was young Gladstone from outside the cabinet who brought forward the alternative of reviving the house tax. This suggestion attracted little support from ministers who were able to recall how unpopular the house tax had been in its time. Goulburn, in another of his thoughtful memoranda, pointed out that the houses of the "middle ranks" would bear the heaviest weight of taxation, for the "number of small contributors [was] the very essence of effective taxation." Large houses were simply too few in number for the tax to be restricted to them. An "excessive and unjust pressure" on one class of property and society would provoke "universal dissatisfaction," Goulburn warned. "This criticism struck at the very root of Gladstone's argument for the tax, and probably did more than anything else to reconcile ... [him] to the effectiveness of the income tax."[11]

The revival of the tax was therefore accepted in principle, and the details were thrashed out in a series of cabinet meetings during the winter. Meanwhile, planning was also under way for that return to liberal Toryism which the tax was always intended to facilitate. The tariffs were to be overhauled by the Board of Trade in order to give "a stimulus to the industrial energies of the people." Any growth of commerce promised a recovery of employment. But Goulburn's suggestion of a reduction of the sugar duties was abandoned in the short term. At a time when colonial producers were unable to meet existing demand yet continued to enjoy a virtual monopoly of the British market, "the remission of the duty would in a great degree be a boon to the planter at the expense of the Exchequer." Nor was anyone anxious to reopen debate on lowering the duty on slave-grown foreign sugar, given the party's resort to "anti-slavery arguments" during the assault on the Whig proposals. Ministers decided to do nothing, and Goulburn assured them that the price of sugar would drift down anyway.[12]

Closely allied to the question of tariff reform was that of the Corn Law. It was one thing for members of the Anti-Corn Law League to point to the rising challenge of German manufacturing as a reason for lowering the cost of bread and wages in order to improve British competitiveness, but it was quite another matter for a Conservative administration to tamper with agricultural protection. Many of the Conservatives' followers came from the shires, and they had recently campaigned against the Whig measure. Peel's freedom of movement on this controversial problem was restricted, for he had to worry about holding onto the two cabinet representatives of the landed interest – Edward Knatchbull and the Duke of Buckingham. He therefore submitted to his colleagues in January a detailed sliding scale of duties, which he believed would allow the agrarians a generously remunerative price. However, this concession was not sufficient to keep Buckingham in the cabinet.[13]

Parliament was opened by Queen Victoria on 3 February 1842, and the following week Peel held a meeting of the party to explain the intended changes to the Corn Laws. Many of those present might have wished for additional protection, Peel confidently informed the queen, but the great body of them would support the measure. Not that the landed interest welcomed a measure which, according to some estimates, would cost them 15 per cent of their rents. Nevertheless, the bill had a somewhat easier passage than even Peel had forseen, though unrest soon grew among the farmers of Rutland and Lincolnshire. Goulburn's interest in all this was primarily tactical. He did not wish to allow too long an interval between the announcement of the changes to the Corn Law and the introduction of the tax resolutions. Otherwise, the

"Corn Law opponents would combine against the [Income] Tax, and endless petitions and motions for delay would give time for them acting with all that were dissatisfied with any part of the plan."[14]

A bout of ill health and then an accident caused Goulburn to be unusually irregular in his attendance in the House during the first two months of the new session, yet he managed to play a full part in the successful passage of the income tax. He drafted the memoranda that served as the basis for the cabinet's discussion of the measure, modelled on Henry Addington's revision at the beginning of the century of the earlier tax introduced by the Younger Pitt. Thus there were to be five schedules, dealing with property and income in their several forms. The rate was eventually set at almost 3 per cent, and it was to be levied on annual incomes in excess of £150. The tax was limited to a period of five years. Ireland was to be exempted – for reasons that were evidently more political than fiscal – but it was to be assessed higher levies on spirits and stamps. The entire package of taxes, including the reimposition of a tax on exported coals, was brought forward by Peel on 11 March. The surplus of revenue over expenditure would be applied to a revision of the commercial tariff, he announced, with coffee and timber marked as the principal items for reduction. However, progress on the income tax was soon slowed by its opponents, who resorted to the procedural device of "vexatious motions for adjournment." "You will have seen that we made little progress in your absence," an exasperated prime minister wrote to Goulburn on 25 March, "excepting I hope in disgusting the Country with vexatious delays, and breaking up the concert of our opponents."[15]

Goulburn delivered three set speeches in support of the measure. Sensibly, he focused on a limited number of points: that the nation was confronted with a severe crisis as a result of Whig folly; that there was no real alternative to an income tax as an instrument for placing the country's finances "in a sound and stable condition"; that it was far more progressive than Whig consumption taxes, for the latter were "felt more keenly by the middle and lower than by the upper classes of society"; that this income tax would be less inquisitorial than its wartime predecessor; and that it would make possible "that relief to the commercial and manufacturing interests of the country which all concurred in believing to be necessary." Summing up at the end of the long-drawn-out debate on 31 May, he claimed that the nation backed the government. "He believed that there had been less petitions presented against [this] measure than against the toll on Waterloo-bridge."[16]

Goulburn assured the House that he would not create an expensive new bureaucracy to collect the tax. He intended to hand the task to the underemployed commissioners of assessed taxes and make use of superannuated officers. As a result, he expected to limit the additional administrative cost to £30,000. He was no less miserly in his response to appeals from persons who pleaded for relief on the grounds of peculiar hardships. When Peel forwarded one such plea, Goulburn responded, "There is no remedy ... the Income Tax makes no distinction between a Provident and improvident expenditure of income." Indeed, he soon wearied of queries. "If people would read the act," he snapped, "they would not ask absurd questions." On the other hand, he took care to guard against the emotive charge of harassment. Thus those who considered themselves unfairly assessed by the commissioners were provided with two levels of appeal. Nor was there to be any systematic examination of returns. Instead, a few doubtful cases would be investigated to discover whether improper deductions were being made, and only if the practice proved to be widespread would there be need for greater vigilance.[17]

Peel had spelled out in the House on 10 May "the general scope and object" of the proposed alterations to the tariff. There was plainly some uneasiness, even in cabinet, that he was going too far or too quickly towards free trade. But it fell to Goulburn to defend the unpopular tax on exported coals, which he did skilfully. He argued that monies that were currently finding their way into foreign coffers through import duties on the coal would now be diverted to the Treasury. It fell to him, also, to justify the disappointing decision not to tamper, at least for the time being, with the prohibitory duty on sugar. He could not forgo revenue until there was some assurance of a supply adequate to an increased demand, he explained. Beyond this, since most foreign-grown sugar was produced by slaves, its admission was dependent on the producing states making concessions with respect to the despised institution. The Tariff Bill finally cleared the Commons at the end of June, but the obstructive tactics of the supporters of the Anti–Corn Law League so stalled other essential measures that Peel was obliged to schedule a series of marathon sittings in early August in order to bring the session to a rapid close.[18]

This brought no immediate respite for the members of the cabinet. The previous October, Peel had circulated an alarming private letter, which Goulburn had received and forwarded, concerning the deepening crisis in Lancashire's textile districts. A substantial industrialist, who was both "an active opponent of the Anti–Corn Law League" and a "staunch conservative," told a chilling tale of "dreadful uncertainty" and warned that a combination of starvation and Corn Law agitation would soon excite unprecedented disorder. Disturbances, strikes, intimidation, looting, and death were all now being reported from industrial areas. The government had opened a public subscription for the distressed operatives in May, contributing £500 in the queen's name and advancing funds from the Treasury, but the ministers eventually persuaded themselves that the unrest was politically inspired. Following a meeting with magistrates who had come up to the capital to confer with them, they banned meetings and dispatched troops to Manchester, while Goulburn sanctioned the additional expenditures necessary to organize military pensioners as an auxiliary force. By late August calm appeared to have settled over the industrial centres, but Graham at the Home Office continued to warn that the discontent was widespread: "The working classes are dissatisfied with their Employers," he noted, "and have many just causes of complaint. In these circumstances the Government must be prepared."[19]

Graham's conviction that force alone could subdue the "rebellious spirit" saw him resort to Irish-style policing in northern counties and seek to bolster irresolute gentlemen magistrates with stipendiaries. This was one proposal in which Goulburn was not prepared to acquiesce, despite his introduction of it to Ireland twenty years earlier. He had powerful support from Wellington when he voiced dismay at the "growing tendency to withdraw the administration of business judicial, financial or administrative from the hands of the upper classes of society and to vest it in paid officers of the Government." He feared that such arrangements would ultimately undermine the very structure of the society which the Conservatives were committed to sustain. What would become of the gentleman who was relieved of the responsibilities and obligations of his class? he asked. Why, he would "degenerate into an idle and useless member of society living either in London or by the sea side according to the season of the year and failing on the one hand to exercise his proper duty to his dependents and on the other to ruin the respect which is now justly paid to him." How long would it then be possible to defend the privileges of class? The proposal was abandoned.[20]

Urban disturbances were accompanied by complaints of imminent rural distress as the price of cereals fell. Though Goulburn was unmoved, he was nevertheless all too aware of the political implications. "The outcry to which low prices will give rise," he remarked to Peel, "is preferable to that which results from a population in want of food though it may be more embarrassing to a Government whose support is to a great degree agricultural." For his part, the prime minister attempted to head off trouble on his back benches by insisting that low prices resulted not from the recent lowering of protection but from the poverty of the people. In damping down the fires of Tory resistance to his liberal policies, he was assisted by the fortuitous arrival of the news of a British dictated peace to the Emperor of China. "Our manu-facturers will get employment, our merchants will find a market and Goulburn will find money," one senior Whig predicted. At least it was a glimmer of light.[21]

The disappointing revenue returns still crossing Goulburn's desk that autumn merely confirmed the necessity of the income tax. Yet there was alarming evidence that these returns had "materially suf-fered" as a result of "systematic corruption on the part of the lower class of officers" at the Customs House and "systematic fraud on the part of merchants." Peel had no wish to see Parliament take up the is-sue in the next session, and he thought that the best way to avoid this danger was for the cabinet to announce its own inquiry. Having al-ready ordered a full investigation by the commissioners of customs, Goulburn initially resisted a second probe. He preferred to uncover those implicated in the scandal before attempting to decide the extent to which inadequate supervision and neglect of duty were factors. In-deed, he was reluctant to concentrate on this problem, overburdened as he already was with work at the Treasury, where he complained of being "almost alone." He was also distracted by the deteriorating health of his eldest son. Late in October, however, he prodded the chairman of the Customs Board into more vigorous activity and ar-ranged for Granville Somerset and his unpaid Revenue Commission to undertake a separate investigation.[22]

Surprisingly, with the reopening of Parliament in February 1843, the opposition showed scant interest in the Customs House frauds. In-stead, Whigs and Radicals dwelt on the persistent distress in Lanca-shire and elsewhere. A lacklustre debate was dramatically enlivened by Richard Cobden's suggestion that the prime minister was personally responsible for the suffering. A furious Peel, still shaken by the murder several weeks earlier of his secretary, whom the assassin had evidently mistaken for him, accused the Anti–Corn Law League campaigner of inciting acts of personal violence. When order was restored, both men rephrased and qualified their statements, but the episode revealed the prime minister's agitated state of mind. The subsequent acquittal of the killer on grounds of insanity did nothing to ease his concern for the security of public figures. And it was at Peel's insistence that Goul-burn applied to the Bow Street magistrates on 7 March 1843 for a war-rant against John Dillon.[23]

A former coastguard officer, Dillon had failed to secure what he con-sidered to be his just share of the prize money from the disposal of a condemned American vessel in 1822. By 1843, he had taken to stalk-ing Goulburn, both in Downing Street and around the House of Com-mons. He had also sent him a number of threatening letters. However,

Goulburn was far from convinced that the man was truly dangerous. Certainly, he did not reflect a broader social animosity towards the chancellor of the exchequer. Nor could Dillon be detained indefinitely, though Peel was assured that on his release every precaution the law allowed would be taken to prevent him from following through on his wild threats. No more was heard of him. Yet public figures remained vulnerable, as Peel explained to the queen. Herself a target the previous year, she expressed alarm over the security arrangements for a levee at which Prince Albert would deputize for her. Peel promised personally to check with police, and he said that he walked home every night from the Commons and, despite "menaces" and "frequent intimations of danger," had not met with any "obstruction."[24]

On 8 May Goulburn presented the budget, which had now begun "to take on a central political role." The task was a difficult one, for the rosy revenue predictions offered by Peel the previous year had failed to materialize. Goulburn revealed a deficit in excess of £2 million for the fiscal year just ended. However, in another solid, workmanlike performance, he adeptly defended Peel's sanguine estimates of 1842. He attributed the disappointing return from the increased duty on Irish spirits to the temperance crusade led by Father Matthew. "It is reported to me," he announced with a commendably straight face, "that on St. Patrick's Day not a single man was seen drunk in the streets in several large towns." His listeners surely took greater heart from deeper retrenchment, which promised savings of almost £1 million, and from the chancellor's uncharacteristic willingness to gamble. He was planning neither additional borrowing nor higher taxes. Instead, he was counting on a reviving economy to eliminate the deficit. Strangely, it was almost the end of the session before Russell reminded Goulburn and Peel of their earlier denunciations, in opposition, of the Melbourne administration's revenue miscalculations. This restraint was peculiarly welcome to Henry Goulburn, who was in the throes of a private agony.[25]

The doctors had confirmed in 1842 the Goulburns' worst fear: their son Harry was suffering from an "affliction of the lungs." They resolved "to live entirely with a view to his recovery." He spent that summer on the Isle of Wight, where he had been born and had spent many an idyllic holiday. His health showed some improvement, but he continued to cough and expectorate. On his return to London in the autumn, his doctors advised him not to return to his law practice, and he passed the winter in the bracing air of Hastings and Brighton. In this personal crisis, which saw Goulburn's wife prostrated yet again by apprehension and "violent headaches," Goulburn himself soldiered on with his political duties and sought strength and comfort in his faith.

"The only consolation," he wrote to the master of Trinity, "is that we are in the hands of Him who will rule all things for the ultimate benefit of those who like our sons have been from their earliest years his servants." The belated discovery that three winters earlier Harry had worn a "respirator" on his doctor's orders did little to ease the Goulburns' anxiety. There was a hint of foreboding in a father's letter to his ailing son in March, thanking him for his birthday greetings and for a touching offer of help with his personal financial difficulties. Two weeks later he was writing on the eve of Harry's thirtieth birthday, which Goulburn described as that day of the year on which he felt "most deeply the blessing which you have ever been to us all." But his anguish was palpable, and not least in the accompanying expression of hope "that we may continue for some years to be a mutual comfort to each other upon earth and that ultimately we may be united in heaven to partake for ever in each other's felicity."[26]

May found Goulburn labouring over the budget while his son's strength ebbed agonizingly away. Desperately, he and his wife looked for signs of improvement and found those that were not there. During a visit to Cobham, Surrey, Harry and his mother were caught in a shower while walking to church. His instinctive speeding up of their pace so exhausted him that he appeared to be more dead than alive during the service and had to be carried by a servant to a carriage at its conclusion. This "terrible evidence of his excessive weakness has deprived me of all the little hope I had been able to keep in my head," Jane Goulburn admitted. They returned to Downing Street, and there Harry passed the last days of his short life. He occupied himself with religious exercises and writing commentaries in a little notebook. As he grew ever weaker, his father sat with him at night, maintaining a vigil. In the early hours of the morning of 8 June, Goulburn's "best beloved son" became first speechless and restless and then quiet. At 4.45 AM he rallied sufficiently to write a brief note to his brother Freddy: "Don't grieve for me. There is hope and peace in believing." He died a few minutes later.[27]

Jane Goulburn constantly reproached herself for having left her dying son's side during the final hours of his life. She read and reread his final jottings and pleaded; "O Lord increase my faith which is too feeble to comfort that overwhelming sense of what I have lost"; she fretted that her surviving sons were insufficiently dedicated to religious study; she performed ever more faithfully her private devotions; and she became ever more of an invalid. For his part, Henry Goulburn undertook the heart-rending duty of settling his son's accounts, including those for pills and syrups which Harry had taken in such quantity and to such little effect. Meanwhile, he selected a "strong Elm coffin lined

and ruffled with rich white sarsnet," and ordered the large marble tablet. There had been much to celebrate in his son's life, but this merely
underscored the tragedy of Harry's premature death. Regarding his
first born as his posterity, Goulburn never truly recovered from this disaster, and there was to be precious little joy in his household from this
date.[28]

"I am not in a state of mind to give you much assistance in any public matter," Goulburn advised Peel on 9 June. He had continued to attend cabinet meetings almost until Harry's end, but had been more
laconic and withdrawn than usual. He did not participate in the debate
on the decision to permit the importation of Canadian corn at a nominal duty, which reawakened the landed interest's suspicions of Peel.
Nor was he deeply involved in the struggle over the education provisions of Graham's Factory Act, which, in conceding practical control of
factory schooling to the established church, aroused the dissenters to
vehement opposition. He did, however, concur in the cabinet's decision to drop the controversial provisions from the bill, even though he
saw no good reason why Wesleyans, at least, should not attend church
schools. Goulburn seemed unaware of the recent deterioration of relations between Anglicans and Wesleyans in the parishes, where high
churchmen were discriminating against the latter. In any event, the bill
was subsequently postponed until 1844, and the government continued to fund Anglican domination of elementary schooling through
the National Society. In the House, meanwhile, Goulburn successfully
resisted opposition demands for a small reduction in the duty on colonial sugar and greater access to the British market for foreign sugar.
And he refused to surrender £100,000 of revenue by tampering with
the duty on foreign wool in an effort to relieve the distress in and
around Leeds. A steady growth in trade and industrial production gave
him reason to hope that an economic recovery was finally underway,
while another excellent harvest promised relief from the anti–Corn
Law agitation. Hence his dismay when a Whig merchant with the back-
ing of the Anti–Corn Law League won a stunning victory in an autumn
by-election held in the City itself. Goulburn concluded after a flying
visit to the scene of this electoral disaster that Conservatism had in this
instance been betrayed by the indifference of its friends, many of
whom had declined to come up to the capital to cast their ballots.
They could not afford a second loss to the league or to "Democratic
principle," he warned Peel.[29]

Goulburn had passed through London on his way up to Cambridge
to serve as escort and guide to the young queen and her prince, who
were paying an official visit to the university. He reported a royal success. "There was no contretemps nor any accident and the weather was

beautiful." Victoria's visit provided Peel with a timely opportunity to announce the appointment of a Cambridge man to the vacant see of Litchfield. This selection reflected a growing concern with the pastoral responsibilities of senior clergy, as opposed to their scholarship or ability to perform well in the House of Lords. Goulburn, whom Peel consulted about such appointments, was particularly insistent on the primacy of this qualification, even though his faith was mellowing with age.[30]

He could still respond with evangelical horror to a proposal to celebrate the christening of the heir to the throne by throwing open London's theatres, with the government compensating their owners. Why incur this expense? he asked, especially when it was "for the gratification for a few hours of the very lowest and some of the most profligate classes of society in opposition to the feelings of many who conscientiously object to theatrical exhibitions as tending to the demoralization even of the more instructed or better disposed." He did not object, however, to a celebration in a "more rational way by contributing to the comfort of those who are now suffering, or by any exhibition approved by all and accessible to all and not tending to give additional opportunity to profligacy." On the other hand, his related sabbatarianism was increasingly tempered by social considerations. He resisted demands that country post offices cease issuing or paying money orders on Sundays. "In many cases (of servants especially) it would be very hard to prevent their transmitting these small payments on the only day on which they are able to write letters or go to the office," he explained to Peel. "Such payments are really works of charity and piety of a very high order." All he would countenance was a restriction of postal business to hours that did not interfere with divine service. Further, he was pulling towards the *via media* in the bitter conflict between Tractarians and evangelicals. He acknowledged that there was "good" in the doctrines and practices of both factions and wished to combine the better part of both. He wholeheartedly supported the archbishop of Canterbury in his proposal that an Oxford vacancy be filled by someone capable of teaching pastoral theology rather than biblical criticism. Not only did Goulburn consider the latter a source of the current "errors" of doctrine in the church, but he insisted that "it would be impossible to lecture on that subject without coming in conflict with the doctrines of one or other of the conflicting parties while Pastoral Divinity is the sort of Neutral ground on which both parties though rivals work common and universal good."[31]

Goulburn's recognition of the need to promote pastoral work led him to press for a modest state contribution to a program of church construction and extension, which appeared increasingly necessary in the teeming and turbulent industrial districts, where the unrelenting pursuit of earthly wealth had resulted in a neglect of the essential preparation for the hereafter. Although Peel had supported a parliamentary grant as recently as 1840, he was now too aware of the power of the dissenters to provide such assistance. "I dread for the sake of the Church and its best interests stirring up that storm which large demands from the public purse would inevitably excite," Peel explained. Of course, Goulburn had never proposed a "large" grant. Nor did he join Peel, Stanley, and Graham in exerting pressure on the primate to allow the Ecclesiastical Commission to exercise closer supervision over the management of church estates in an effort to generate internally the funds "to relieve spiritual destitution." In the end, all sides compromised, and the commission was authorized to create additional parishes out of an anticipated increase in its revenues from other sources. Indeed, Peel appealed to the affluent in the manufacturing districts to contribute to this cause and set a personal example by donating £4,000. Goulburn applauded such generosity and lamented his inability to emulate it.[32]

The arrival of autumn brought cheering evidence of the continuing growth of the national economy. Fears of a poor harvest during a wet July evaporated with the moisture as the weather turned fair in August and corn prices fell. Moreover, all branches of manufacturing were at last "exhibiting indications of improvement." The beginning of the New Year found the nation imbued with fresh optimism. The recovery of Eastern trade and a distinct improvement in exports, especially textiles, were important, but even more significant was the availability of inexpensive capital with which to finance the railway boom that was generating the real motive power of the general recovery. Increasing employment and the rise of real wages soon worked their magic on the working classes. "The internal condition of the country has undergone a great change," one cabinet minister commented shortly before the opening of Parliament.[33]

Goulburn moved quickly in the early spring of 1844 to capitalize on this favourable environment. He had long been planning to reduce the interest on the 3.5 per cent stock, which he had helped to create with his earlier successful funding scheme. This time, however, he quietly prepared the City for the operation. Not that there was much likelihood of resistance from that quarter, given the current low rates of interest in the markets, the high price of funds, and the bright fiscal and economic outlook. Significantly, Goulburn rejected the radical reduction of one-half of one per cent favoured by both Peel and the money men. The former was anxious to achieve the largest immediate saving, while the latter realized that Goulburn would need to offer a bonus, which might add as much as £12 million to the capital of the debt, in order to effect so large and abrupt a conversion. Instead, Goulburn set the interest rate at 3.25 per cent for the next decade and provided for its further reduction to 3 per cent in 1854. This would effect an immediate annual saving of £625,000 and would ultimately double that sum. The announcement was greeted with loud cheers and general support within the House, and the response of the financial markets was equally enthusiastic. Only a handful of stockholders declined to accept Goulburn's offer.[34]

Goulburn's triumph on 8 March had an immediate impact on the government's other business, as the House speedily passed the remaining estimates and a large supplementary vote. More contentious was the revived Factory Act. Although it offered a number of important concessions to the advocates of reform, and although the controversial educational provisions were omitted, there was no inclusion of the ten-hour day for which Ashley was campaigning. Goulburn, consistent with his past support for this lordly reformer, was one of a small minority of cabinet members who appeared willing to accept such a limitation – but Peel and Graham vehemently opposed any "confession of weakness." Their concept of executive government, their pique at the refusal of the reformers to acknowledge the bill's "liberal" provisions, and their contempt for the political myopia of those agrarian backbenchers whose support for the amendment seemed motivated by a thirst for revenge on the manufacturers who supported the Anti–Corn Law League all played a part in the cabinet decision to reject any compromise. The decisive consideration, however, was the possibility that a ten-hour working day would disrupt industry and stall the economic recovery by cutting the number of working days in a year and exposing British industry to formidable competition from countries where no restrictions were in force. Not forgotten, either, was the certainty that reduced hours would mean lower wages, thus increasing agitation against the Corn Laws.[35]

Goulburn acquiesced in his colleagues' decision to reject a compromise on the basis of an eleven-hour day, for he was influenced as much by Peel's refusal to bend as by the economic arguments. However, the defeat of both the government's proposal and Ashley's amendment saw the bill withdrawn. New legislation was introduced in April. Eventually, on 10 May, Ashley made his inevitable attempt to amend the bill by astutely setting a transitional daily limit of eleven hours on the way down to ten. Again, Peel and Graham refused to give ground. Moreover, the prime minister made clear his intention to resign if defeated on this occasion. His threat impressed his followers, and Ashley's amendment was eventually rejected by an "immense and unexpected majority." Significantly, it was Goulburn whom Peel commissioned to meet with Ashley in a vain effort to reconcile him to the passage of the government bill.[36]

One other factor that helped convince the cabinet not to show "weakness" on the factory legislation was the looming probability of "difficulties" on the back-benches over the Irish question. Daniel O'Connell's staging in 1843 of a series of monster meetings in support of repeal of the Union, and the prominent participation of the Catholic hierarchy and priesthood, had alarmed and intimidated many Irish Protestants. But Peel had responded coolly to their reflexive demands for firm government action. After all, his was a cabinet that boasted unusual familiarity with Ireland. Goulburn's experience rivalled his own, and three other former chief secretaries sat around the table. Nor were they blind to the inconsistency of suppressing O'Connell's association when they had for so long tolerated the activities of the Anti–Corn Law League. In the circumstances, it seemed sensible to apply to Ireland a policy not unlike that already in place in the disturbed industrial districts of England – resolution mixed with conciliation.[37]

Magistrates infected with repeal sympathies were dismissed, and an arms bill was passed that restricted possession of dangerous weapons. Troop reinforcements were dispatched to Ireland, along with orders that Irish soldiers be kept out of earshot of speakers at meetings, and provisions were stock-piled in barracks to be on hand in the event of an uprising. The latter did not seem entirely unthinkable following the proclamation of a giant meeting at Clontarf and the subsequent arrest of O'Connell on a charge of conspiracy. But this policy was disconcertingly expensive. "What is to become of the finance of the country," Peel fretted, "if after all our recent … adjustments of troublesome questions we cannot equalize expenditure and Revenue?" Consequently, he was doubly anxious to reassure the Irish that their peculiar problems could be solved within the Union that he was determined to uphold. He and Goulburn agreed to assist the construction of a railroad from Dublin to the south and southwest of the island and to encourage the extension of railway communication from Chester to the ferry station at Holyhead. The long-festering issue of tenant rights was referred to a small commission chaired by the liberal Lord Devon. Peel proposed that a reasonable equality be created in voting qualifications in Ireland and England. This had been another of the grievances exploited by O'Connell. Further, he recommended the expansion and improvement of the facilities and opportunities for higher education in Ireland, which promised to appeal to merchants, farmers, and the middle classes of Irish society in general. Of all classes, however, the Catholic clergy were recognized as the most influential. In an effort to separate them from O'Connell, Peel wished to facilitate the charitable endowment of the Catholic Church and to fund with far greater generosity the seminary at Maynooth.[38]

Goulburn objected to a substantially greater state endowment of Maynooth. He, along with Gladstone (who had entered the cabinet in the spring of 1843 following his elevation to the presidency of the Board of Trade), stressed the "great shock" this action would give to Protestants in an England where anti-Catholic sentiment had strengthened since emancipation. Yet as the debate within cabinet wore on, Gladstone eventually found himself alone. Goulburn came to accept Peel's twin arguments – first, that liberal concessions were the only means of protecting the Church of Ireland, by splitting the ranks of its enemies; and second, that any breakup of the government on this question "would be followed by the accession of a very democratic Ministry." As ever, loyalty to Peel and pragmatism shaped Goulburn's course, and he it was who received the commission from Peel to dissuade Gladstone from carrying his principles to the length of resignation. This task was eased, at least temporarily, by the cabinet's decision to postpone consideration of Maynooth until an inquiry into its condition had been conducted.[39]

Goulburn was more forceful in his objections to a proposed extension of Trinity College, Dublin, that would transform it into a national institution for the education of all faiths. If Catholics and other dissenters took degrees there, they would be qualified to vote in the elections for the two members of Parliament for Dublin University – who, as he pointed out, were "now the only representatives of the Irish Church." This would surely ignite sectarian conflict between Protestant and Catholic colleges. Far better, he reasoned, to create another university similar to that established in London, and one with associated colleges in the provinces. While these colleges would not possess any elective franchise, they would be able to confer degrees and would provide "an appropriate education and an equal means of competition for Honours and such emoluments as it might be practicable to afford to successful competitors." The Trinity proposal was abandoned. Meanwhile, in the Commons, franchise reform was withdrawn in the face of stiff Conservative opposition. Thus, of Peel's initial conciliatory measures, only the Charitable Bequests Act effectively remained. As for coercion, it had proven no more successsful. Even O'Connell's conviction had been overturned by the law lords on appeal, and he had been triumphantly liberated.[40]

Goulburn's preoccupation during the spring of 1844 was not Ireland but the budget. Clearly, the brightening economy and optimistic revenue projections meant that there was no need to increase the rate of the income tax as Peel had earlier contemplated. On the other hand, Goulburn considered the extension of its life from five years to six desirable if not essential. This would remove the issue of renewal from the next general election, which was likely to be called in 1847, and would lay the groundwork for the tax being made permanent. Further, such an extension might be justified easily enough by broadening the range of articles on which duties were reduced, thereby allowing the government to claim that more time was required in order to ensure that the losses of revenue would be offset by increased consumption. But, ever prudent, Goulburn counselled caution in the selection of such duties. Recalling the parliamentary revolt against the hated tax in 1816, he had no wish to surrender entirely other productive sources of revenue which, once abandoned, would be difficult to revive.[41]

Peel proved to be both more conservative and more political in his attitudes than his chancellor was. He dismissed the fear that a general election would endanger the income tax but shied away from an extension for the very reason Goulburn was proposing it – "the character of permanence." Peel preferred the safer course of initially seeking merely to continue the tax for the two additional years allowed for under the existing law. Even then, he expected to face resistance unless "popular reductions" were made in duties and taxes that would evidently benefit the great mass of the population. Since much of the current surplus would be absorbed by the deficit carried over from 1843, thus severely restricting the options in 1844, this strategy also dictated postponement of the issue of renewal until 1845, though the way could be prepared for this step through a reduction of the sugar duty. Goulburn and the prime minister were equally resolved to lower duties on coffee, wool, and vinegar. On cotton wool, Peel worried that any substantial reduction might reinvigorate the agitation for a shorter factory workday. "It would be thought that we unduly favoured the Manufacturer," he cautioned Goulburn, "if we *at the same time* protected him from the reduction of hours of labour, and relieved him altogether from the duty of the raw material."[42]

In his budget speech on 29 April 1844, Goulburn carefully laid the groundwork for a subsequent renewal and even extension of the income tax, and for an ambitious program of tariff revision the following year. He announced a number of modest adjustments in duties, which were plainly intended to benefit the lower classes and promote trade and industry. Some of these unspectacular changes, such as those to vinegar and currants, were greeted with mocking laughter on the opposition benches, whereupon Goulburn pointed out that the first was widely used by calico printers and the second was consumed by the lower classes. The upper classes preferred raisins. Goulburn, the Christian economist, announced a substantial reduction of the differential advantage enjoyed by colonial coffee over foreign, for it was "of utmost importance ... to extend the use of the beverage which is so great a luxury to all classes of the people, and supersedes other beverages detrimental to their health and morals." Lastly, he gave notice that there would be significant changes to the sugar duties when they came up for annual consideration later in the session. Colonial producers would no longer be conceded a virtual monopoly of the domestic market. Instead, they would be given a substantial preference over foreign-grown free-labour sugar, which with the imminent end of the commercial treaty with Brazil could at last be admitted without embarrassment. "We have arrested the downward course of a long-continued and increasing deficiency," Goulburn boasted in his peroration. "We have completely fulfilled the assurances given that the revenue of the country should be equalized with the expenditures." This was not a statement that won universal applause, but most of the criticism focused on the threatened extension of the income tax. Even his wife was dismayed at the prospect.[43]

In their quest to restore the economy to lasting health, Peel and Goulburn as liberal Tories did not overlook the necessity of ensuring a stable currency. The recurrent crises of the previous decade, the revival of opposition to the gold standard and the growing support for bimetallism, together with the approaching deadline for a renewal of the Bank of England's charter, served to focus their minds. Goulburn did not deny that commercial distress was usually the result of a combination of factors, but he believed that its principal cause "was the undue extension of the currency when it ought to be contracted." One possible solution was to establish a single bank of issue, and this idea had been scouted by the Bank of England's negotiators during their discussions with Goulburn almost fifteen years earlier. But he reminded Peel of the peril here: if the bank were to be the issuer, the cries of "self-interested monopolist would overwhelm it." Alternatively, the government could assume the responsibility. Goulburn's objections to this course were largely political. Not only would they be unable to exercise control without at times producing great losses to traders, but such an arrangement would call "forth combinations against the Government to effect improper extensions of the currency." The pressure would be such, he feared, that government would scarcely be able to function. In this dilemma, an automatic regulation of money and credit through the foreign exchanges had obvious appeal.[44]

Advocates of the "currency principle" insisted that a mixed currency of coin and notes could be made to work properly. The challenge,

Goulburn believed, was to make the currency "fluctuate precisely" as if it were "entirely metallic," to make it "gradually conform itself to the prices of articles, and to take care that the fluctuation should be gradual, and that the prices should never rise or fall so suddenly as to involve individuals in ruin, or to cast into danger the most important interests of the country." To this end, he privately admitted that the *ultimate* objective was a single bank of issue. Given the attractions of this solution to the Bank of England, it was not surprising that when Goulburn and Peel initiated discussion of a new charter, the bank made much of the running.[45]

The negotiations, largely conducted by Goulburn, were opened early in the New Year of 1844 and fell into two phases. First, there was a series of confidential meetings and exchanges during the opening three months of the year; then there was a carefully organized formal correspondence intended for presentation to Parliament. The path to a single bank of issue – and thus the silencing of the cries of "self-interested monopolist" – was to be slowly and discreetly cleared. There was to be a clear separation of the bank's ordinary operations from those of an issue department; any profits from issues were to go to the public; the right to issue notes was not to be granted to any new banks, and that of those already established was to be curtailed; any void was to be filled by Bank of England notes. As a sop to the other joint-stock banks, the prohibition on their drawing, accepting, and paying bills within a radius of sixty-five miles of the capital was removed. Further, the Bank of England was required to make a somewhat larger annual payment to the Treasury for its privileges. To ensure currency stability, the issue of notes was to be tied to the bullion and securities held by the bank.[46]

"The main object which Sir R. Peel and myself had in the arrangement made in 1844," Goulburn later recalled "was to ensure the convertability of the Bank note and to prevent as far as was in our power a return of the calamitous circumstances which had resulted from the suspension of cash payments of which we were both old enough to have witnessed the commencement and the close." They believed this could best be effected "by limiting the amount of notes issued on security to such a sum as would, if the note circulation approached that limit, necessarily bring back (from scarceness of circulating medium and consequent enhancement of prices) Gold into the country." They settled on £14 million, in addition to the private bank circulation, as the sum it would not be safe to exceed, and they abandoned the idea of permitting the government to authorize an emergency increase of the circulation for fear of exposing it to irresistible political pressure. Instead, all additional issues were to be backed by their equivalent in bullion. These were the essentials of the Bank Charter Act, which Peel introduced on 6 May and which he and Goulburn steered through the Commons. Ironically, the act and its fiduciary ceiling were greeted without enthusiasm in the City. Moreover, since the foreign exchanges were now supposed to regulate money and credit automatically, the legislation added force to the argument that sudden fluctuations in these exchanges had to be avoided. One cause of such fluctuations, argued a growing number of City men, was the operation of the Corn Laws. In the opinion of the *Bankers' Magazine*, their repeal was the "necessary complement" to the Act.[47]

Whereas the deficiencies and liabilities of the Bank Charter Act were only to become evident with the passage of time (though the Scottish and Irish bills passed in 1845 were somewhat less rigid), the government's proposed changes to the sugar duties precipitated an immediate crisis. Goulburn's approach to this difficult and controversial problem was characteristically deliberate and perhaps not entirely selfless. To increase consumption materially, they would need to lower the price, and to achieve this by any means other than a significant lowering of duty was to place in peril the West Indian producers. But to cut the duty at a time when there was scant prospect of an increase in supply would not result either in a substantial price reduction or in greater consumption. "The question therefore appears to me, to turn upon whether we can sacrifice half a million of Revenue for the time requisite to allow the introduction of E. Indian and Foreign Free labour sugar in sufficient quantity to affect price," Goulburn had observed in September 1843. Now, almost a year later, the situation had changed. He had reduced by more than £500,000 the national debt's annual charge on the Exchequer, and this made experimentation both easier and safer.[48]

Not that Goulburn ever contemplated a radical experiment. He remained a supporter of colonial preferences, insisting that the "real benefit" derived from the colonies far exceeded the expense to which British consumers were put "by differential protecting duties." Further, he was a gradualist. Interests that had grown up under a system of protection should in his opinion continue to receive a "fair protection," because "that could not be withdrawn without involving those interests in ruin, and with them the interests of the country." Thus the sugar proposal he had sketched out in his budget, and which he formally introduced in June, called only for a modest reduction in the duty on West Indian sugar. It also established a reasonable colonial preference over foreign free-labour sugar. And in an effort to forestall criticism, he emphasized its interim nature and exploited the unpopularity of the income tax. The government did not wish "to fetter the judgment of Parliament" on the renewal of the income tax in 1845 by making any substantial surrender now of its revenues.[49]

Goulburn was soon embarrassed, however, by an artfully designed and successful motion to lower the duty on West Indian sugar further and increase the preference. At a crisis cabinet meeting on 15 June 1844, an agitated Peel appeared set on resignation. Although Goulburn was one of a small minority of ministers who demurred, and although the decision was postponed (for several cabinet members were out of town), he was privately pessimistic of the government's survival. He shared Peel's fury and dismay at the defection and language of sixty of their "so called friends," the absence of eighty others, and the rumours that these dissidents had actually conspired with the opposition. Shaken by the evidence of back-bench disloyalty, Goulburn saw no easy escape from the predicament in which he and his colleagues found themselves. To seek an immediate reversal of the vote would not only be hopeless but would be "discreditable to the House" so soon after its about-face on the Factory Act under threat of Peel's resignation. To adopt the amendment, on the other hand, would be "disgraceful" after the way the ministers' "friends" had treated them. As for some entirely new plan of sugar duties, he dismissed it as "impracticable." All in all, on 15 June, Goulburn considered it "scarcely possible" that he and his colleagues could retain office.[50]

At a meeting the following day, the cabinet began to lean towards a reversal of the Commons' vote. By making a minor concession, they could provide the House with a fig-leaf to cover the nakedness of its humiliation. The ministers confirmed this decision when they met in the afternoon of 17 June, by which time some two hundred backbenchers had gathered at the Carlton Club to affirm their support of the government. But Peel's statement in the House, with its thinly veiled allusions to political treachery, did not endear him to his followers. Goulburn adopted a more matter-of-fact tone, insisting that it would be unwise to create a demand for sugar which could not as yet be supplied, though he did voice indignation at the vituperative character of Disraeli's assault on the government. Although the government survived, thanks largely to a tactful but forceful performance by Stanley, many back-benchers had made at best a sullen submission to the prime minister's will.[51]

The brief crisis over the sugar duties was another illustration of the difficulty that many Conservative members still had in coming to terms with Peel's concepts of political leadership and loyalty. Thus Peel was usually and revealingly at pains to draw to the queen's attention the number of his followers who opposed ministerial measures, for the traditional notion of the independent-minded member of Parliament had little appeal for him as party leader. Under the strains of office, he not only found less time to flatter his back-benchers, but he was growing more impatient with and resentful of their questioning of his policies. He expected them to defer to his administration's judgment, founded as it was on more detailed knowledge of a problem than any individual member could possess. One Whig, observing the events of 17 June, gloated, "The agony will be long and lingering as ours was. But dissolution has commenced."[52]

CHAPTER TWELVE

The Disruption
of the Conservative Party

As 1844 neared its end, Henry Goulburn sensed that his career did not have a long distance to run. He had celebrated his sixtieth year in the spring and was approaching the thirty-eighth anniversary of his entrance to Parliament. He had served "in various offices of more or less importance" for almost a quarter of a century. Like many other men "of uncertain fortune who embark in public life," his private affairs had "suffered prejudice" from his "attention to the business of the public." Naturally, he was anxious to provide for his family. In 1842 he had secured for his brother Edward one of the new commissionerships of bankcruptcy, a position to which the sergeant brought not only his legal skills but a fund of personal experience. Now he obtained for his son Freddy a vacant commissionership of customs. After an undistinguished undergraduate career, Goulburn's youngest son had been called to the bar, though he did not appear in court to plead. As Peel explained to the queen, the death of Harry had caused the Goulburns to be even more protective of the health of their surviving children. In the case of Freddy, "From weakness of the Chest it is feared that great and continued exertion of the voice might be injurious to him." Appointed to the Customs Board, which had survived the investigation of the frauds, Frederick Goulburn made the most of his opportunity and eventually rose to the chairmanship.[1]

The nation's finances were also very much on Goulburn's mind at year's end as he looked to the preparation of another budget. There could be no escaping "very large" military estimates. Relations with the United States were one cause of concern, for a dispute over the Oregon Territory in the Columbia River country had become an issue in the presidential contest. Both Britain and the United States had claims to the region. Even more unsettling was a crisis with France which, together with the revolution in naval warfare resulting from steam navigation, had drawn attention to the lamentable state of the defences at Britain's ports, dockyards, and naval arsenals. "One would suppose that each was at the mercy of a handful of men," an incredulous prime minister remarked to Goulburn in December. Evidently, the naval budget would have to be increased significantly. Although Goulburn was prepared to admit the need for additional expenditures, he disputed the wisdom of sinking them in fortifications. Fixed defences were "of minor importance as compared with the complete efficiency of the navy as to steam vessels and squadrons of Exercise and competent officers," he judged. Britain had always relied on her navy rather than on fortifications, he reminded Peel, and steam had added to the means of defence as well as to those of attack. Thus "naval efficiency" remained "the *first* point to be attended to."[2]

The substantial and unavoidable increase in military expenditures meant that unless the civil outlays were held severely in check, the government would have "to forbear repeal of taxes." Yet abatements were central to the strategy of economic growth and social peace. Therefore, monies could no longer be found for Charles Babbage's experiments, for Brougham's pet project of the publication of the ancient chronicles of Britain, or even for the appointment of a new officer to draft and correct bills. Furthermore, renewal of the income tax, which Peel had elected not to announce in 1844, required that he offer the House and the nation the sweetener of another dose of sweeping reductions in duties. One duty they were already committed to lower was that on sugar, but Goulburn was alarmed by Peel's suggestion that the use of sugar should be encouraged in British breweries and distilleries. To admit sugar for distillation, as a concession to the hard-pressed West Indian producers, would necessitate a drawback on whatever duty remained, since the grain that was currently being used paid no duty. This would multiply the opportunities for fraud. Equally, there would need to be some adjustment of the duty imposed on colonial rum, otherwise it would not be able truly to compete with the domestic product and thus prevent the latter from greatly enlarging its market at the expense of other domestically produced spirits. In all of this, Goulburn saw a serious loss of revenue and the danger of antagonizing that wealthy and powerful interest group, the distillers. He had no desire to tangle with them. Nor had he any wish to alienate unnecessarily the agricultural interest, which remained such a force, though a discontented one, within the Conservative party.[3]

From the reports reaching him, Goulburn feared that by the time Parliament met in February 1845 the agricultural districts would be experiencing such difficulties that members from the shires would be more than usually "jealous of any arrangement appearing however re-

motely to affect them." Any action that threatened to lessen the consumption of malt by increasing that of sugar was certain to fall into
this category. By the same token, malt and sugar would have to be
placed on terms of equality with respect to duty. Given the commitment on sugar duty, this would amount to a significant reduction of
the malt tax and a loss of perhaps £1,600,000 in revenues. Nor could
they, either consistently or in good conscience, seek to offset this loss
by reimposing the tax on beer, having refused to retain any part of the
tax in 1830 because it operated "exclusively on the beverage of the
Poorer Classes." Goulburn's wariness of offending the agrarian section
of the party also prompted his questioning of a correspondence with
the Prussian government, which appeared to have been written with
an eye to its production in Parliament. "It raises the question of the
Corn Law," he warned Peel. "It implies a pledge to reduce the duties
on Butter and Cheese and in fact would alarm every interest in the
House of Commons the ultra free traders excepted." Nor did he consider it wise, politically, to look to the free trade section of the opposition for support against their "Agricultural friends." That would be "a
painful and false position for the Government to occupy and would
probably be ultimately fatal."[4]

Peel bowed to Goulburn's arguments on sugar, but he did not share
to the same degree his chancellor's concern for the agricultural interest. Demands from that quarter for a reduction of the malt tax that
were quite independent of the sugar issue left the prime minister unmoved. He preferred to remit taxes in a way that would be more "generally advantageous," he priggishly remarked, and he was therefore
"quite prepared to resist any party combinations entered into either
with a view to embarrass, or bona fide to effect an improvident reduction of a Tax." However, contemplating a real surplus of approximately £4 million, Goulburn proposed to Peel that they first settle the
life of the income tax and then decide who should be relieved – the
consumers, the traders and manufacturers, or the farmers. Personally,
Goulburn believed that a lowering of the price of sugar would afford
consumers all the direct relief they could reasonably expect. As for the
farmers, he rejected their argument that a decrease of the tax on malt
would boost its consumption and revive agriculture. A change in public taste – away from malt liquors to tea, coffee, and cocoa – and a succession of barley crops that had proven indifferent for malting
purposes explained to his satisfaction the decline in demand. Consequently, fiddling with the tax was unlikely to reverse this trend. Goulburn did not, however, forget the politics of the situation. "If we are
careful not to affect the protection now enjoyed by Agriculture in
other Articles during the next session," he added, "I do not apprehend

that even with Lord John's assistance a motion for repeal of the Malt Tax would be successful." Thus, by a process of elimination, Goulburn favoured the reductions in duties that would aid British manufactures in their battles for foreign markets.[5]

Peel was in broad agreement with the chancellor's emphasis on the promotion of trade and manufacturing and the maintenance of a high level of employment through a selective remission of duties. A repeal of the cotton tax, for example, would help English manufacturers resist the competition of the highly profitable enterprises in New England. Beyond that, Peel was determined to make full use of the surplus to pursue the financial experiment "of ascertaining whether increased consumption under a lower rate of duty will give you equal or nearly equal Revenue." In this he was far less cautious than his Chancellor, who quietly recommended that they keep in hand some £1,500,000 to guard against unforeseen revenue fluctuations. Indeed, Peel doubted that it would be possible to secure the renewal of the income tax, that milch-cow of revenues, with such a favourable balance in the national accounts. Nor was he any more receptive to Goulburn's suggestion that they simply understate the amount of the surplus. They would be too vulnerable to embarrassment by anyone who carefully checked the figures, he countered.[6]

Peel again presented the budget, filled as it was with eye-catching provisions. Duties were to be abolished on more than half of the eight hundred articles still covered by the tariff. The income tax was to be renewed for an additional three years, thereby effectively extending its life as Goulburn had recommended the year before. But the chancellor's role in all this was essentially that of the Peel's second. He patiently explained, to those critics who deplored the government's failure to offer more direct relief to the consumer, that the principal thrust of the budget was the enhancement of purchasing power through the promotion of employment. He nimbly defended the preservation of a differential between colonial and foreign free-labour sugar, and the effective exclusion of sugar produced by slave labour. While he admitted that sugar produced by slave labour could "be raised cheaper than that which is raised by free labour," he stood on high moral ground, maintaining that Britons would never abandon their honourable antislavery tradition simply to reduce the price of the sweetener. On a more material note, he emphasized that the setting of a lower duty for the inferior of the two qualities into which sugar was now divided would maximize the benefit to the consumer. And to the Whigs who complained of the extension of the income tax, he made the obvious rejoinder that it would be in the power of Parliament to discontinue the measure in 1848. By Easter, the major provisions of the budget had been successfully steered through the Commons. Even resistance to the swollen military estimates had crumbled. This was largely the result of a blustering inaugural address by the new president of the United States, James K. Polk, who had been elected on a promise to secure all of the disputed Oregon Territory.[7]

"The Government here are as strong as ever, in spite of the undisguised discontent of many of their followers," Palmerston judged in mid-March 1845. But Peel was about to divide his followers as never before over his conciliatory Irish policy. His modest success in establishing a working relationship with a number of Irish Catholic bishops, following passage of the Charitable Bequests Act, had encouraged him to attempt to extend the government's influence over the priesthood by pressing ahead with more generous public funding of the overcrowded and dilapidated seminary at Maynooth. Yet Goulburn's annual visit to Cambridge during the last week of the year had convinced him that opposition to such a measure would be broadly based and virulent. He had found the university preoccupied with religious issues. Heightened fears of Tractarianism as the first step towards the revival of "Romish error," the surge in membership of the Catholic Church, due in no small part to Irish immigration as well as to population growth, and the failure of emancipation to allay Catholic "hostility" towards the Protestant state all contributed to the fevered atmosphere. The "liberal" master of Trinity College had delivered "a very Protestant sermon" on the anniversary of the Gunpowder Plot, and he warned Goulburn privately that additional assistance to Maynooth would be regarded as "putting arms into the hands of the enemy" and would thus "cause universal excitement in the protestant mind." Goulburn shared this concern. He recognized a "growing dread" of Catholicism among "the better class of the clergy" and feared that more generous support of the seminary would spur demands from England and Scotland "for increased means of education and religious instruction in an opposite direction to Popery." In short, he worried that sectarian animosities would be exacerbated. Indeed, he observed that if an important member of the government were to resign on this question – and Gladstone's position was all too clear – he would "not be surprised if the flame of real religious apprehensions of the consequences of the measure were to burn as fiercely as ever."[8]

Peel's resolve remained unshaken, though he sought to exploit Goulburn's possible difficulties with his Cambridge constituents in a final unavailing effort to dissuade Gladstone from resigning. At least, Gladstone promised not to provide leadership to the opponents of the measure. This was just as well, for the well-organized opposition proved to be fully as intense as Goulburn had predicted. Parliament was deluged with petitions, for there was a widespread and deep suspicion that this concession marked a significant advance towards concurrent endowment of the Irish Catholic Church. The Maynooth grant, the details of which were announced on 3 April, was "ridiculous as a finality, serious as a beginning," the *Times* charged.[9]

The ever-loyal Goulburn suppressed his private doubts of the wisdom of the measure, and he publicly lent it support and defended Peel. The principle of public funding having been conceded by the Irish Protestant Parliament a half-century earlier, he insisted that the only point at issue was the expediency of making the college "effective for the object for which Parliament originally established or endowed it." He dismissed suggestions that the bill was intended to increase enrolment at Maynooth or to prepare the way for state endowment of the Catholic Church. Instead, he said, the proposed grant would merely "make that establishment adequate to the maintenance of the number of priests now required for the religious service of the Irish people." In this sense, he emphasized the gratitude with which Irish Catholics had welcomed the measure and stoutly denied that the Church of Ireland was being placed in any danger. Much to Goulburn's relief, his Cambridge constituents were far from united in their opposition to the bill. But the division within the parliamentary party was far more ominous. Conservative ranks were split down the middle, and it was the Whigs who provided the government with its commanding majorities. Here was evidence that a "core of opposition to Peel and the liberal direction of his government" was quickly forming on the back benches. Was there to be another debacle like that of 1830, when the Ultras, angered by the Wellington government's about-face on emancipation, had conspired to bring it down?[10]

The second string to Peel's Irish bow was a bill to establish three university colleges, which would wean the adult youth "from vicious habits" and would "substitute knowledge for idleness and profligacy." To avoid the obvious sectarian pitfall, the colleges were not to include faculties of theology, but this omission excited ultra-Protestant denunciations of "Godless" institutions. The charge was soon repeated by the ultra-Catholics led by Archbishop MacHale, and the hierarchy's hostility eventually crippled this well-intentioned scheme of educational conciliation. Despite the setbacks and the evidence of a deepening and widening schism within Conservative ranks, one experienced Whig concluded that the best the opposition could hope for at the next general election was a halving of the prime minister's majority in the Commons. Peel had his own reasons for continued optimism. Trade and the revenue were prosperous, the monetary system was sound, the people were contented, the labourer was enjoying a higher standard of living than ever before, and the church was weakened only by "internal stupid differences and controversies." "But we have reduced protection to agriculture, and tried to lay the foundations of peace in Ireland," he wrote a little self-pityingly to one of his colleagues, "and these are offences for which nothing can atone."[11]

By the autumn, however, dark clouds were seen to be gathering on the horizon. One was the proliferation of railway schemes, for as many as a hundred additional private bills had recently passed Parliament. Not only was Goulburn disturbed by the speculative mania in shares, but he was apprehensive that if only a limited number of the projects went ahead, as much as £20 million might suddenly be withdrawn from circulation in the form of the deposits which promoters were required by law to make. This would "materially cramp Manufacturing and commercial enterprise for the time and greatly affect the value of public securities," he feared. His response reflected his aversion to legislative interference with commercial activities. The Railways Act of the previous year had sought to control the danger of local monopoly without disciplining erratic development. The regulatory state was to impinge as little as possible on personal life. As "indifferent spectators," ministers could "do little beyond observing the march of events" and preparing for the storm. However, at the prime minister's suggestion, Goulburn published a detailed statement of the dangers in the current situation, and by October he was prepared to consider allowing deposits to be made in public securities instead of money. But the fever broke later that month, as panic on the stock market sent prices plummeting. By that time, a second and even more ominous storm cloud had gathered overhead.[12]

In August, the prime minister had reported to the queen a first dividend on his politically expensive and conciliatory Irish policy. Roman Catholic priests were in many instances cooperating with the government in the maintenance of public peace, and the repeal movement appeared to be in a terminal decline. Here were reasons to hope that the foundation had at last been laid "not only for present Tranquillity but for a permanent improvement in the state of affairs in that unhappy Country." Soon, however, there were disturbing reports of a widespread failure of the potato crop because of a sinister disease, though its fungal nature was not immediately recognized. However, both Peel and Goulburn were personally familiar with the consequences of such failures in a land where a large proportion of the population was dependent for much of the year on this food.[13]

Recalling his own experience in 1822, Goulburn's initial response to the reports from Ireland was characteristically cautious. Yet he understood that "when it was stated that the people were unemployed, and that the potatoes on which they had relied were diseased, it was as much as saying that there was a total failure in the means of subsistence for themselves and their families." His evangelicalism served to restrain compassion, for he accepted that to "prevent altogether the effects of such a visitation is not in the power of man." Similarly, he believed that the Irish had contributed to their misfortune by their willingness to depend on public charity rather than on their own exertions, and by their chronic lawlessness. Capital that might have been invested in Ireland to produce a cultivation comparable in its efficiency to that of Scotland had been withheld because of the insecurity of life and property. Like his assistant secretary, Goulburn was incensed by the failure of some Irish grand juries to repay earlier Treasury advances to expedite relief works, and both men suspected that "jobbing" was a national occupation. Moreover, Goulburn's personal experience of Ireland had taught him to be sceptical of local reports of severe distress, while his acceptance of the obligation to assist those who were suffering had always been qualified by the state's capacity to afford the cost of relief. Irish poverty could not be allowed to imperil Britain's fiscal health. "He wished it to be understood," Goulburn declared on one occasion, "that he was not unwilling that ample aid should be given to the people of Ireland, so far as was consistent with the pecuniary burdens which pressed on this country." Finally, he had a powerful political reason to dispute the seriousness of the Irish crisis.[14]

Reports from an unnerved viceroy of a massive failure of the potato crop in large areas of the island convinced the prime minister in mid-October that he would soon be faced with desperate appeals for assistance. The cabinet should plan for intervention, he argued, if only to save precious time when it became necessary. As prudent as this recommendation seemed, what alarmed Goulburn was Peel's revelation that he was considering the "absolute repeal for ever of all duties on all articles of subsistence." There was no point in a mere suspension of the duties on corn, Peel reasoned, for in the present state of public opinion on this subject they could never be reimposed. On the other hand, there were several other possible steps short of this "momentous" one. Were any of the diseased potatoes salvageable by artificial means, for instance, or the sound portions of them convertable to potato flour? He dispatched to Ireland a small scientific commission, led by Lyon Playfair, a noted soil chemist, to investigate the possibilities of minimizing crop losses. The commissioners recommended the dry storage of sound potatoes (having mistakenly concluded that the blight resulted from cold and damp weather), and instructions to this effect were widely circulated. However, Playfair's private reports were far from reassuring. He and his colleagues estimated that half of the potato crop had been destroyed or rendered unfit for human consumption. Another possible response was for the government to encourage large importations of sound potatoes from distant and unaffected producing states. "The alarm is so great and is spreading so fast, in Ireland at least," Peel observed to Goulburn, "that we need not much fear the increase of it by the indications of Government interference."[15]

Goulburn's questioning of the urgency of the crisis was plainly influenced by Peel's evident inclination to grasp this opportunity to repeal the Corn Laws, for the chancellor knew that such an action would deliver a fatal blow to what remained of party unity. Goulburn knew also that oats were reported to be abundant in both Ireland and Scotland, that a greater acreage of potatoes had been sown this year than in earlier years, and that no reliable estimates of the losses would be possible until the late crop was dug towards the end of the month. Thus he clung to the hope that the disease would prove to be less catastrophic than Peel feared, for he saw little prospect of their supplying the Irish with potatoes. The tubers were too bulky and too liable to deteriorate to be shipped long distances, and the prevalence of the blight in Europe ensured that they would not be obtainable from neighbouring countries. Conceding that the people of Ireland might well need other foodstuffs, Goulburn noted that barley and oats might supply the deficiency, if at substantially higher cost. As for the task of importing and distributing food, that was better left to private speculators. Goulburn still subscribed to the opinion "that Government never embarks successfully in such operations" and that the interest of individuals is "a far surer ground of reliance for an adequate supply of any article." The government's responsibility was merely "to secure to the people by means of employment the means of purchasing the more expensive food to which they are compelled to resort." In the case of the Irish, this form of intervention was doubly necessary, since their taste for "rows" was frequently attributed to a boredom resulting from want of work. "The Head of an idle man is the Devil's Garret." Of course, both individual landed proprietors and grand juries would be expected to cooperate in this endeavour. Even the railway mania might work to the government's advantage. "The Railroads bona fide undertaken will afford much relief," Goulburn argued. But the essential preliminary step was to obtain accurate information on the potato losses and the stocks of barley and oats. Meanwhile, there must be absolutely no tampering with the Corn Laws. "I should decidedly object to any suspension of the Corn Law," Goulburn advised Peel on 21 October. It would amount to an admission of failure of the sliding scale put in place only three years earlier, he argued, adding that any unlimited importation of oats at this time would alarm domestic producers and lessen their ability and willingness to pay the wages on which the lower classes depended for the means to purchase food.[16]

The official information from Ireland which Peel presented to the cabinet on the last day of October suggested that the crop losses had in fact been underrated, not exaggerated. He then listed for his colleagues the precedents for government intervention and briefly outlined the current actions of foreign governments to control the movement of foodstuffs. He asked his ministers to mull over all of this and discuss the looming crisis among themselves before reassembling the following day. At that meeting there was general agreement that the traditional responses to distress, such as the prohibition of distillation from grain, would be "quite inadequate" to this emergency. In particular, Goulburn could not overlook the loss of revenue if the distilleries were stopped, thereby diminishing the government's ability to provide assistance. There was no similar consensus on the need to repeal the Corn Laws. Instead, the majority – seizing on information in several recent private letters from Ireland that the danger of the disease had been overstated – supported the temporizing policy Goulburn advocated. It was the opinion of the ministers "that there should be some further time and opportunity for inquiry before any decisive measures requiring immediate Parliamentary Sanction could be safely adopted," Peel reported to the monarch on 6 November.[17]

James Graham sought the more authoritative information from Ireland that his colleagues were demanding. At the same time, he authorized the creation of a broadly based Relief Commission, which could establish food depots in areas of acute distress and spur local committees to set in motion public works. He decided not to order the commissary general to Ireland at this time in case his arrival would be interpreted as a signal that public purchases of food were in the offing and would thus "paralyse individual exertion." Public aid of this description, Graham reminded the viceroy, "must be reserved for the last extremity and administered with a cautious and sparing hand." Just three days later, he, Peel, and Goulburn agreed to purchase a substantial quantity of Indian corn and meal in the United States. It was inexpensive and had been resorted to in earlier crises, and the fact that there was no substantial regular Irish trade in this food allowed the government to square the action with its ideological aversion to meddling with private commerce. Although Goulburn calculated that this purchase would keep a million people in food for forty days, the intent was less to feed the Irish than to be in a position to moderate food prices. Already, there were reports of private merchants importing large quantities on their own account. To mask the government's involvement – which, as soon as it became known, would drive up the price as well as "paralyse individual exertion" – Goulburn recommended that they employ the House of Baring as their agent. Significantly, he was now somewhat less inclined to leave it to individual enterprise to supply the needs of the Irish, and he acknowledged that the course they had taken was "right though at variance with general principles." Indeed, he privately approached the Admiralty, which maintained mills at its ports, to purchase as if for itself a large quantity of oats and to grind them into meal.[18]

None of this implied any abandonment by Goulburn of a cautious policy. He met with the deputy governor of the Bank of Ireland on 12 November and took the opportunity to grill him on the state of the island. The banker estimated that about one-third of the potato crop would prove useless as food, and he warned that the question of "great want" turned on the peasantry's prudent care of those potatoes they did harvest. As for the abundant oats, they had already risen steeply in price "from the alarm felt as to potatoes." What Goulburn recommended, therefore, was the identification of the areas of Ireland where there was the most immediate likelihood of great distress, and also of those more fortunate districts from which supplies of potatoes and grains might be secured; he urged that they seek to determine whether private works were already in progress in the distressed districts which might provide, perhaps with additional public funds, employment for a large number of the poor; that an investigation be launched of worthwhile land improvement and road construction schemes that might be implemented with government advances or partial grants; and that an attempt be made to locate possible safe storage points for provisions in the event that the poor were paid in kind. With this end in view, Sir Randolph Routh, the commissary general, was now sent to the island and added to the Relief Commission. His task was to supervise the purchase of food supplies, together with their safe and convenient storage and their effective delivery to local committees. These arrangements were to be governed by the need to "impose the smallest possible ultimate burthen on the Public." Finally, Goulburn proposed that they take precautionary steps to ensure adequate accommodation for those of the poor who fell victim to disease. Here was a cool and dispassionate response to the crisis.[19]

Goulburn continued to baulk at the repeal of the Corn Laws, and resistance characterized the cabinet as a whole. Yet public protests against the high price of provisions were already being staged, and the Anti–Corn Law League and the Whigs were clearly intent on exploiting the crisis. Moreover, the demand for the free importation of foreign grain had been one of those made at a recent public meeting in Dublin, and it was presented personally to Peel on 7 November. But

Goulburn continued to operate on the reassuring knowledge that the potato failure had been partial only, and he still could not see how tampering with the Corn Laws would afford relief to hungry Irish families. After all, it was next to impossible to demonstrate that repeal would give them more corn than they were likely to secure under the existing law, which had "produced steady prices below Peel's 'remunerating' price." This was an opinion shared by those in the trade who were not unfriendly to free trade, he reported to Peel. Indeed, it was arguable that repeal would make the existing situation worse by persuading neighbouring states that the crisis was more serious than they had been led to believe, thus prompting them to impose restrictions on food exports and drive up prices. A pragmatic anxiety not to encourage this foreign response, as well as an ideological aversion to the interruption in the free flow of goods, may well explain the short shrift given to another of the demands voiced in Ireland – a prohibition on the export of oats. However, the crux of Goulburn's opposition to repeal was personal and political. His and Peel's long support of the Corn Laws would be interpreted as the crudest political expediency if they suddenly abandoned them in such unconvincing circumstances. They would be accused of having upheld them earlier, as in 1841, merely as a weapon with which to vex and defeat political opponents. Charges of insincerity, deception, and treachery were certain to fly, as in 1829, and Peel would surely be their focus. The damage to his character and that of his colleagues "would be fraught with fatal results to the Country's best interests," Goulburn fretted. "In my opinion," he added, "the party of which you are the head is the only barrier which remains against the revolutionary efforts of the Reform Bill. So long as that party remains unbroken whether in or out of power it has the means of doing much good or at least of preventing much evil. But if it is broken in pieces by a destruction of confidence in its leaders (and I cannot but think that an abandonment of the Corn Law would produce that result) I see nothing before but the exasperation of class animosities, a struggle for preeminence and the ultimate triumph of unrestrained democracy."[20]

Yet for all his doubts and fears, Goulburn gave way before an adamant Peel. As he told his longtime friend and colleague, "I have such an habitual deference to the superiority of your judgment and such an entire confidence in the purity of your motives that I always feel great doubt as to my being right when I differ from you in opinion." And Peel believed that the dismantling of the Corn Laws would help reduce class animosities and would lower the pressure for radical parliamentary reform. So a majority of cabinet reluctantly agreed to support the measure in an effort to hold the government together. However, the continued opposition of Stanley and Buccleuch, and their announced intention to resign rather than acquiesce in repeal, prompted a careworn and resentful prime minister to throw up his hands in dismay and turn the problem over to Russell and the Whigs. Goulburn endorsed the decision to resign. By this time, he was prepared to concede the necessity of repealing the Corn Laws even at the price of the disruption of his party, for the reports from Ireland were of truly disastrous crop losses, but he believed that the repeal "ought to be, and could best be, done by others." Unfortunately, the Whigs had little taste for the task. Russell backed and filled for more than a week, seemingly more interested in evading the responsibility of forming a government than accepting it. Finally, on 20 December, he formally abandoned the attempt. As one Whig remarked, the failure "will do more good than harm. Peel is now forced to undertake the settlement of the question."[21]

The *Times* welcomed Peel back to office not as a Tory and "not even as a Conservative," but as a "popular Premier." The prime minister was determined to drive repeal through Parliament no matter at what political and personal cost. His taste for expediency, which had not escaped criticism in the past, was now less in evidence. Tired if not exhausted by his years of political leadership and government, ideologically committed to free trade, determined to halt the Anti–Corn Law League's dangerous class polarization of society, anxious to promote an adequate supply of wheat at a time of rising population and growing European scarcity – and by stabilizing food prices to end disruptive trade and currency fluctuations – and perhaps hoping to spur greater efficiency in British agriculture, Peel summoned his old cabinet to a meeting on 21 December to inform them of his intention. Only Stanley declined to follow him, though less from a faith in protectionism than from a desire to protect his own reputation for political consistency and to preserve the Conservative party from schism. In this last sense, he would have done better to follow the example of Goulburn and Wellington, who remained within the government. Dangerous though Stanley's defection was, the prime minister was cheered, as was Goulburn, by Gladstone's agreement to replace the departed minister.[22]

There were those who believed that the chancellor shared with Wellington the distinction of being in a uniquely uncomfortable position. Recalling Goulburn's qualified commitment to free trade and his recent opposition to repeal of the Corn Laws, one old friend remarked that the chancellor would now be obliged to eat his words "and become a cypher in his own department." Indeed, Goulburn felt compelled to offer a public explanation of his decision to rejoin the government. He had earlier misjudged the extent and depth of the crisis in Ireland, he admitted, but he now recognized the need for a permanent response to what promised to be an extended failure of the potato crop. They had to provide for the substitution of corn for that food, he informed the House. They could not wait "until the time of distress, famine and mortality arrives" before settling the question. Yet his support was also intensely personal, a reflection of his profound and abiding loyalty to Peel. "I acted in unison with him in every public question," he subsequently avowed. "There existed between us the most unreserved communication of sentiment and opinions; and at no time has he taken any important step in politics without my being privy to it, and fully acquainted with, the circumstances which regulated his conduct."[23]

Clutching at straws, Goulburn even began to hope that repeal might be effected without alienating the entire agricultural interest. An old acquaintance, for whom he had secured a small church living in Suffolk, reported that many farmers in that area were not unalterably opposed to repeal so long as they received compensatory relief from some of the heavy charges on the land. "There is a great change among the Farmers on the subject," this correspondent wrote reassuringly. By the same token, he insisted that many agricultural labourers believed that cheaper bread favoured them because its price promised to fall proportionately more than their wages. Similarly, the threat that unprotected farmers would reduce their workforce to cut their costs lost its menace when it was understood that already they did not employ one man more than was absolutely necessary. Heartened by this information, which he forwarded to Peel, Goulburn fleshed out a proposal for a simultaneous and gradual reduction in protection and a gradual redistribution of the burdens that fell upon the land. Thus the administration of law and order might become a general charge on the public purse; county rates might be lightened by removing the costs of maintaining bridges and gaols; there might be a more equitable division of the burdens of poor relief; and the land tax might be removed and the malt tax reduced. The protection of agriculture should be considered in the same manner as that of any other manufacture, Goulburn argued, since it was an industry "of which the raw material is the earth and the manufactured article is corn." As ever, Goulburn emphasized gradualism. If protection was suddenly withdrawn from the farmer, "no sudden change of taxation could be made to distribute among all classes equally what presses specially on him." In short, the "real difficulty" would be "to ensure the payment to Agriculture of the equivalent when the present advantages are withdrawn."[24]

The measure that Peel introduced five days after the opening of Parliament on 22 January 1846 had a Goulburn colouring, even though it was perhaps a little too bold for his personal taste. Corn was to be but one element in a general lowering and removal of duties, a policy vindicated by the success of the experiments of 1842 and 1845. Nevertheless, this declaration did not banish suspicions that Peel was capitalizing on the Irish crisis to implement a long-term strategy of free trade. The reduction of corn duties was to be gradual, spread over three years, and was to be accompanied by the lessening of the charges on the land and by assistance to high farming. Peel's long and pedestrian speech was "much cheered by the Opposition," but his own back-benchers "looked gloomy and cold in the extreme." There were a number of resignations from the Royal Household and other minor offices, and several members felt obliged to retire from their seats, though the prime minister took some comfort from the reports of divisions within Whig ranks. Only subsequently did he seek to set repeal more securely within the context of a looming disaster in Ireland.[25]

Goulburn gave Peel loyal and effective support in the House, which the beleaguered prime minister appreciated. Not even protectionists claimed that the Corn Laws were immutable, the chancellor pointed out, so when would change ever be more necessary than in the face of a failure of the potato crop? He made short work of those protectionists who argued that tampering with the Corn Laws was unnecessary because the situation in Ireland was not as serious as the government alleged. He ridiculed the financial proposals introduced by Lord George Bentinck, who had emerged as a leading Tory dissident, which amounted to a transfer of the tax burden back to customs duties. Indeed, Goulburn began to sound almost Mancunian with his avowal of free trade as an agent of international peace. Tariff wars had in the past all too often resulted in "the dissolution of ties of amity and peace," he argued, whereas tariff reductions were "calculated to lead to the best financial results, as well as to promote friendship between ourselves and the nations with whom we traded." But the comfortable progress of the corn and tariff bills through the Commons could not mask the government's weakness there. Two-thirds of the Conservative members voted against passage of the Corn Bill, and from that moment late in February, the Peel administration was dependent on the Whigs for its survival.[26]

In the midst of the ministerial crisis in December, Charles Edward Trevelyan, the assistant secretary of the Treasury, had assured Commissary General Routh "that the necessity, whatever may be the extent of it, of saving certain classes of the Irish from starving, will not be affected by any changes in the higher branches of the Administration." Although the two principal instruments of relief, the Commissariat and the Board of Works, were subordinate to the Treasury, the assertive

Trevelyan was careful to acknowledge the lord lieutenant's supreme authority in Ireland. The heads of these agencies were commanded to "obey any directions which His Excellency may at any time think necessary to give, even if they should differ from the instructions with which you may have been furnished from this office." Not that this discouraged the Treasury from seeking to exercise its supervisory authority. It was ever on watch for evidence of waste or of attempts to charge ordinary distress to emergency relief. Goulburn's preoccupation with the corn and tariff bills saw him delegate much of the day-to-day supervision of the crisis to his industrious and capable assistant secretary, but he kept a careful eye on what was being done in Ireland. His determination to secure the government "against the permanent maintenance of the Poor of Ireland out of the national purse" was reflected in Trevelyan's requirement that the Irish be taught "to depend upon themselves for developing the resources of their country, instead of having recourse to the assistance of the Government on every occasion." A firm stand had to be made against the "prevailing disposition" to take advantage of this undoubted emergency.[27]

This concern dictated absolute secrecy concerning the importation of food and preparations for its distribution, though such discretion did nothing to quieten popular alarm. Similarly, the Treasury continued to hope in February that the "evil day" of government relief could be put off for just a few more weeks until "vast numbers" of the able bodied found their usual seasonal employment. On the other hand, Goulburn's caution was always tempered by his acceptance of "the serious obligation and responsibility" to take "effective steps to provide suitable and adequate relief for every proved case of impending destitution in any locality." Moreover, Sir Randolph Routh, who headed the Commissariat, had some knowledge of Ireland, having been dispatched there two years earlier at the height of the repeal campaign to plan a supply system for troops in the event of an insurrection, and he was left in no doubt that the Treasury's "general principles of action" were not to prevent him from exercising his initiative in exceptional circumstances.[28]

Trevelyan suggested both private appeals and public exposure as ways of putting pressure on Irish landowners to shoulder their responsibility to contribute to relief. Early in 1846 he sanctioned the opening of government stores in distressed localities for the sale of provisions at cost price to boards of Poor Law guardians, local relief committees, and individuals. The intention was to deny local authorities and gentlemen any excuse for failing to perform their duty, and to discourage private provisions' dealers from exploiting the crisis. The food available for distribution was almost exclusively Indian corn and meal, for repeated suggestions that seed potatoes be imported and distributed continued to be rejected by Goulburn on the grounds he had given Peel earlier. He also rejected the proposal that the government offer a bounty to encourage their private importation. He argued that this would surely give rise to unpleasant disputes over the guaranteed disposal of all such potatoes. Equally worrying was the possibility that such a scheme would permit people to relax their efforts "to preserve or procure the necessary stock," efforts which the resort to substitute food in the form of Indian corn did not discourage. One of the essential duties of the Commissariat, Trevelyan reminded Routh, was to impress on the Irish people "the indispensable necessity of their preserving with proper care a sufficient quantity of potatoes for seed, *and that on this point the Government will not have it in its power to afford them any assistance.*"[29]

Similar cautionary instructions were issued to Colonel Harry Jones, the chairman of the Board of Works which surveyed, for the Relief Commission, local projects designed to provide employment. The board was ordered to draw a clear distinction between works which were "indispensably required" for the relief of suffering and those which, under the pretext of scarcity, were intended to serve other "incidental purposes." Jones was advised that the works should be confined to the distressed locality and be capable of being quickly terminated when the crisis passed, and that payments should be made in food as far as possible. Equally important, local landowners were to "be required in every case to pay their fair proportion of the expense." Treasury fears of possible abuse were heightened by the series of emergency measures introduced in February 1846 and speedily enacted by Parliament. They sought to stimulate public works through a more generous system of grants. Assistance with employment had long been Goulburn's preferred form of government intervention in the crisis, and the year ending in January 1846 had already seen £138,000 advanced from the Consolidated Fund and a further £89,000 made available for improvements to the Shannon. In order to make public grants – as distinct from advances – go as far as possible and to deter their misappropriation to projects of private advantage, the Treasury had for some time insisted that they be matched by private contributions. Indeed, any proprietor likely to derive a peculiar benefit had been required to make a proportionately greater personal contribution. The weakness of the Treasury's position under the new legislation was twofold. First, it was not empowered to compel individuals to contribute to the cost of works. Second, proprietors knew that the government could not "under any circumstances allow the People to starve." At Goulburn's direction, however, Trevelyan instructed the board to investigate and report on every application for a grant. For instance, did the state of actual or impending destitution in an area require an employment project? Would the labouring class in general find work, or would only skilled artisans so benefit? Would any particular proprietor gain more advantage from the works than other cess payers, and would he be willing to make a proportionate contribution to the expenses? These were by no means unreasonable queries.[30]

The grant system now in place was so much more advantageous than any other means of executing public works, Trevelyan noted, that if applications were automatically approved merely because they had complied with the provisions of the various acts, the Treasury would be obliged to undertake every improvement desired by influential persons for their own benefit rather than in aid of the poor. Nevertheless, requests from the influential for special grants to help finance extensive and expensive navigation and drainage schemes were not necessarily rejected. In several cases the public benefit was adjudged sufficient to merit assistance from public funds. But the Relief Commission's proposal of a temporary land tax to compel landowners to contribute to the costs of relief was vetoed by Graham, who feared that it would merely excite greater bitterness against Britain. Ireland was already bearing its share of taxation, he observed, and much of the island's land was heavily encumbered or its revenues were being paid to absentees. Another complication was the ever-louder English talk of Irish ingratitude, which had arisen in response to an Irish member of Parliament's complaint of unnecessary delays in the launching of public works.[31]

For the sake of Ireland, the *Times* bellowed, the kingdom had been convulsed, classes estranged, ministries broken up, and the sovereign embarrassed. "Beyond this, half a million of money has already been voted in one shape or another to find work for the Irish. A fleet of Indian corn has been brought from America for their use. The supply is already in their ports." The letters of the newspaper's special commissioner to Ireland, Thomas Campbell Foster, did nothing to soften British hearts. "The Irish peasantry will make a 'poor mouth' because they hope to get some of England's bounty, and to escape paying their rent," he warned. And although he acknowledged that the Irish would suffer "heavy loss by this calamity," he doubted that they would starve. To help prevent such sentiments from fostering resistance to additional help, the government laid on the table of the House a series of alarming papers and reports, which fully documented the extensive failure of the potato crop, the depth of the suffering, the spread of disease, and the inability of the Poor Law system to provide sufficient relief. There was nothing ordinary about the current level of scarcity and distress, Goulburn reminded the House. Potatoes had more than doubled in price in large areas of Ireland, and those that had been stored were all too often found to be unusable even for animal food. The human consequences were plain: "Dyspepsia, dysentery, and diarrhoea, caused by unsound food; cottiers ... without even tainted potatoes for food; many unemployed ... in a starving condition." Not surprisingly, the incidence of crime among a desperate people was again on the increase. The cabinet responded with a Life Protection Bill, which Irish members immediately retitled the "Coercion Bill." Its easy passage through the Lords was not expected to be repeated in the Commons.[32]

To simplify and expedite the machinery of relief, the viceroy's supervisory commission (on which all the interested authorities were represented, thus making it a somewhat cumbersome instrument) effectively gave way in late February to an executive committee of three, over which Commissary General Routh presided. The committee met each day and was empowered to decide on the nature and extent of assistance. There was some discussion with the Treasury of an adequate daily food ration. It was set at one and one-half pounds of Indian corn and half a pound of oatmeal. The addition of the oatmeal was intended to make the otherwise "heavy and unwholesome" corn more palatable to Irish tastes. Instructions were also drafted and circulated on how to prepare it. Another "essential point" was the price to be charged local relief committees or individual proprietors for the corn provided to them. To fix it higher than oatmeal would win the government little gratitude, but to set it much lower might well bring down the entire country on the commissary stores and injure private trade. Eventually, it was decided to charge one penny per pound for small amounts, and a somewhat higher price (to cover the costs of transportation) for bulk sales. Nevertheless, reports that large quantities of Indian corn had been introduced into Ireland by private dealers prompted the Treasury to order that government stocks be sold only in cases of unusual distress. "We must carefully avoid assuming the position of an ordinary Dealer," Trevelyan warned, "and confine ourselves to those exceptional cases where the operations of the ordinary Dealers do not work." Yet another reason to conserve supplies was the greater availability of normal employment during the current farm-labour season. When that season ended, the cost of provisions was likely to rise; and the greater the government stocks were, the more successful their agents would be in preventing speculators from charging famine prices.[33]

The arrival of Lord Lincoln in Dublin in March to succeed Thomas Fremantle as chief secretary was soon followed by a sustained and successful challenge to Treasury control of the relief effort. His first target was the Treasury's policy of paying those employed on public works projects in kind. The wisdom of this decision had already been queried by Routh, who pointed out that people who were used to earning at least eight pence a day for their labour were demoralized to receive a ration of food valued at less than half that sum. This did nothing for their pride or their fondness for Indian corn, he drily remarked. Lincoln took up the issue at the beginning of April, pointing out the administrative folly of seeking to establish a multitude of small food depots to issue rations to persons on numerous and widely scattered works. Equally important in his mind was the need to accustom the Irish to the receipt of money wages regularly paid. Of course, wages on relief works would have to be set below those offered by local private employers. Goulburn agreed to modify the policy, though the Treasury minute announcing the change predictably provided that the wage be, "as nearly as possible, limited to what is absolutely necessary for providing a sufficient quantity of food for the support of workmen and the helpless persons of their families."[34]

Goulburn's alarm at the quickening pace of expenditures grew in proportion to the multiplying requests for state assistance to undertake public works. He continued to suspect that some proprietors were capitalizing on the situation for their personal benefit, especially in the construction of roads, and this impression was confirmed by Colonel Jones at the head of the Board of Works. Consequently, Goulburn urged Lincoln to scrutinize all applications. Simultaneously, the Treasury directed the suspension of new projects until their necessity had been fully established. At this, the chief secretary exploded in anger. He accused Trevelyan of pursuing his own private policy in Ireland, and the Treasury of regarding everyone there as "jobbers" and of undermining the authority of the Irish executive. He predicted trouble in the Commons and in the Irish countryside, where "a great disposition to disturbance" had arisen when word of this decision spread. Lincoln was powerfully supported by Peel and Graham, both of whom protested to Goulburn "this interference of the Treasury with the progress of public works." It was vital to allow "a large discretionary authority to the Irish Government," Peel remarked. He argued that one good man on the ground, who had the power to act for the best, to check fraud and prevent starvation, would "do more, and at less expense in such an emergency as the present – than all our boards and regulations and protracted correspondence." The existing elaborate structure for administering relief was simply "too cumbersome a machine."[35]

Goulburn was stung by the criticism, which he regarded as unfair if not hysterical. Lincoln had been consulted before the Treasury's tests of the necessity of public works had been reissued in a minute, which itself had been intended to prevent further complaints of the assistant secretary's private correspondence with the administrators of relief. Nor had there been any attempt to deny the Irish executive the discretion to press ahead with works the Treasury had suspended. Goulburn regretted that Lincoln had failed to understand this, he tartly observed to Peel, but it could not have been clearer if he had composed the minute himself. Difficult as it was to reconcile subordinate departments to effective Treasury control, he added, "it is an odious duty but I have endeavoured to exercise the control for the public interest in as little irksome a manner to those who are affected by it as I can." And looking down the road to that inevitable day when they would be accused in the Commons of "prodigality" in financing works of little practical value, he suggested that it would then be helpful at least to be able to demonstrate that the works had been essential and that local proprietors had refused to contribute to them. "Surely you can have no difficulty in giving us an assurance on these points, subject always to your acting on your discretion if the case be one of urgent necessity," he wrote pacifyingly to the agitated Lincoln. After all, the pressure to open the government depots was only just beginning to be felt, for substantial quantities of Indian meal had continued to be imported on private accounts. Similarly, there was ample evidence of public works being initiated more in response to local lobbying than to genuine necessity.[36]

Even this modified policy was too cautious and deliberate for Peel and Lincoln, both of whom were showing signs of panic at the mounting unrest among the hungry. On 15 April the chief secretary reported attacks on mills, bakeries, and convoys of flour. If Trevelyan was allowed "to be the judge" of what was to be done, Lincoln complained, then the danger was frightful. He overturned the assistant secretary's veto of the purchase in London of another cargo of Indian corn for immediate shipment to Dublin. And he directed Routh to buy four hundred tons of oatmeal in Ireland; it was impossible to leave the government stores in their present state, he asserted, "for we are obliged now to give out to a considerable extent in many places." Simultaneously, at Lincoln's urging, Peel was exerting heavy pressure on Goulburn. As evidence that policy could not be governed by "ordinary considerations," the prime minister pointed to the excited state of the residents of County Galway and to reports that it would be difficult to restrain them unless a depot was immediately established there.[37]

Goulburn authorized additional purchases of Indian corn in England, but he again arranged to have them procured privately in order not to raise the price on the strength of government intervention. The expenditures on food purchases eventually exceeded £180,000, though two-thirds of this sum was recovered in sales. Goulburn urged

Lincoln to avoid making oatmeal purchases near the distressed areas lest this push up the price there or be interpreted as encouragement to fresh disorders, and he continued to press him to seek contributions from the principal proprietors. He also arranged for another vessel to be placed at the chief secretary's disposal, both to ferry supplies and to serve as a troop transport. Finally, he clipped Trevelyan's wings. "I shall be obliged to you to show this letter and all my subsequent letters to you to Lord Lincoln," the chastened assistant secretary wrote to Routh, "and you will then at once ascertain what his lorship's wishes are on any point of information or suggestion which they may contain." Furthermore, Lincoln was now given the freedom to sanction works, despite Treasury hesitations, if he considered them imperative. In short, truly effective Treasury control of the relief program was now surrendered. "You may operate without hesitation on your credit," Graham advised the viceroy on 25 April 1846, "and if it be exhausted it shall be renewed. And with respect to works it is more prudent to grant assistance in doubtful cases than to undertake long inquiries, which may indefinitely postpone the relief, where most required, until it is too late." The Irish executive was soon sanctioning as necessary many of the works that the Treasury had earlier suspended. For Goulburn, who had struggled long and hard to advance and defend the cause of Treasury control, this amounted to a severe reverse. Further, by clinging to procedures that were intended to prevent waste and abuse – and there was plenty of evidence of both – he had exposed himself and his department to the charge of lack of compassion.[38]

As additional supplies of food arrived in Ireland and as reports circulated of abundant provisions in the hands of private merchants, Treasury minds began to hope that it would be safe by the autumn "to break up our Establishment as well as dispose of the meal at the different Depots and settle the accounts." Without denying "the existence of real and extensive distress and the necessity of relieving it," there was a suspicion at the Treasury that the demand at government stores was "mainly owing to the sales from them being made too indiscriminately, and, above all, *at too low a price*." Thus in some places the depots had been opened for sales to all comers. In others, local merchants had given voice to the fear that the government was going to lower prices and make issues without limit. Routh was firmly reminded that the government stocks were to be sold and that the means to purchase them was to come from private subscriptions, government donations, and relief works. Similarly, the price ought to be set with an eye to the prevention of abuse, the conservation of supplies, and the maintenance of private trade. Indeed, Baring's report in June that a fleet of ships had arrived loaded with corn, and his prediction that the price on the west coast of Ireland would fall to £10 a ton, excited overconfidence that the government would soon be relieved of all difficulties. The time had arrived, the Treasury concluded, to allow dealings in the provisions trade to "return to their ordinary channels."[39]

Summing up the achievements of the Peel administration's relief policies in Ireland at a time when their necessity was being challenged in England, Trevelyan claimed that in the north of the island the population had been rescued from severe distress. In the south, "there must have been appalling starvation but for the assistance afforded by the Government, either directly by means of Money, Meal or employment, or indirectly by the stimulus and organization which has been given to private effort." One of the senior officers much closer to the scene was more specific. The opening of depots and the issuing of Indian corn or meal to relief committees had lowered food prices. Local subscriptions and government donations had served to provide the needy with food. Yet his estimate of 12,000 labourers daily employed on projects supervised by the Board of Works, independent of the employment offered by individual proprietors, and his claim that the workhouse population had grown by a similar number did suggest the limited nature of the crisis in June 1846. This in turn cast Goulburn's resistance to frantic activity in a somewhat more defensible light. His natural inclination as chancellor to keep expenditures to the minimum in order to check waste and abuse, his far from baseless suspicion that some proprietors were exploiting the crisis for private gain, his long-standing anxiety not to allow Irish poverty to become a permanent charge on the other parts of the United Kingdom, and his personal caution and conservatism all persuaded him to intervene only warily and with an apparent lack of true compassion. His was a Treasury mind. Nevertheless, he and his colleagues, with whatever misgivings, had handled successfully and even generously the partial failure of the potato crop in 1845. There had been no hidebound allegiance to the minimal state. Unforeseen was the extent to which the availability of other foodstuffs and their continuing export nourished a genocidal conspiracy thesis, which was first systematically advanced by the anglophobic John Mitchel. His sinister interpretation of government policy has shaped both popular culture and even historical accounts of the disaster. But the immediate political price proved to be no less startling. The Conservative party was sundered and the government destroyed.[40]

There was a valedictory tone to the financial statement which Goulburn delivered in the Commons on 29 May 1846. The eye-catching details of the budget had already been introduced by Peel and passed by the House. What Goulburn offered was a review of the administration's record. Duties had been reduced on 727 articles and repealed on 503 more, he reported. For the most part they concerned, either directly or indirectly, the food, clothing, and comfort of the people. Resources were showing continuing elasticity; revenues were buoyant; the funded and unfunded debt had been reduced by £7,000,000; the annual carrying charges had already been cut by £1,500,000 and the saving would exceed £2,000,000 within a few years; the resort to the temporary expedient of deficiency bills had been minimized; and the Exchequer balances were flourishing. General prosperity was to be gauged from the doubling of deposits in savings banks, the increased consumption of excisable goods, a significant decrease in the incidence of crime, and the growth of education. Finally, Goulburn dwelt on the dramatic spurt in church construction. "The ardour with which this object is pursued, and the equal ardour with which congregations rush to them for instruction" was, in his mind, "conclusive evidence of the improvement in the moral and religious habits of the people." These were all the results, he claimed, of the prudent and progressive policies pursued by the Peel government. Others were less lavish in their praise. The *Times* described the nation's economic progress as "satisfactory" and complained of the seeming permanence of the income tax. Yet it did admit to being sanguine of the ultimate success of Peel's policy of free trade now that he had freed the article of first necessity – bread. Less than one month later, within hours of the Corn Bill clearing the Lords, the protectionists took their revenge by combining with the Whigs and O'Connell to defeat Peel on the Coercion Bill.[41]

CHAPTER THIRTEEN

Peelite

Peel had prepared his colleagues for the inevitability of resignation if they were defeated on the Coercion Bill. Moreover, there was not any realistic prospect of a dissolution producing a majority "agreeing with the Government in general principles of Policy." This analysis was endorsed, without a dissenting voice, by the cabinet when it met on 26 June 1846, and the following evening the prime minister tendered his resignation to the queen. Yet there had already been some intrigue by a faction that included Ellenborough, who had entered the cabinet in December following his recall from India, to press Peel and Graham to resign in order to allow the rest of the ministers to reunite with the protectionists. Although this plan came to naught, within two weeks of Peel's departure from office Goulburn was approached to serve as the leader of a reunited Conservative party in the Commons. There was never any likelihood of his accepting such an offer. His resentment of the political bargain which the protectionists had struck with the Whigs to oust Peel remained too strong, nor was he prepared to acquiesce in their proscription of some of his fellow Peelites. Above all, he still looked to his friend for leadership and was fully prepared to allow the course of events to reunite the party. Personal loyalty and gradualism remained his watchwords.[1]

When Goulburn returned to London in mid-August, following a brief absence to arrange the letting of Betchworth (which he was now so hard pressed to keep up that he could rarely afford to live there), he was immediately consulted by Lord John Russell on the state of Ireland. The situation had deteriorated alarmingly, the new prime minister explained. Certainly, distress was especially severe in the northwest of the island. Unwilling to commit himself, the former chancellor responded evasively. After all, the Whigs had not scrupled to assail as wasteful and inefficient the relief program which they had inherited.

He pleaded lack of detailed knowledge of the current crisis and re-marked that Peel and he had never intended their measures to be per-manent. More ominously, he questioned whether, in view of the failure of the potato crops in England and Scotland, it would be possible to apply public funds exclusively to relief in Ireland. In truth, profoundly distrustful as ever of Whigs, Goulburn suspected that they were schem-ing to overcome British resistance to larger expenditures in Ireland by embarking in England on measures of "a very radical character under the name of social improvement." This prospect did not fire his enthu-siasm for more aid to Ireland.[2]

Goulburn passed the balance of the summer and the early autumn of 1846 on the Welsh island of Anglesey in another fruitless quest for a cure for his wife's chronic ill health, and from this vantage point he watched with deepening pessimism the developments a mere sixty miles away across the Irish Sea. He did not see how the crisis there was to be met, and he looked for little beyond confusion and ever-greater expenditure. Ironically, the Whigs were at that very moment steeling themselves to do battle with the "system of terror" that was now afflict-ing that desperate land and for which they held the "excessive" gener-osity of the Peel government responsible. They intended to be harder taskmasters. Employment on public works was to be reduced, as were sales from food depots, while the works sanctioned by the Board of Works were to be charged to local taxpayers. But events quickly over-took them. The Whig chancellor of the exchequer, Charles Wood, gave his predecessor a chilling account of Ireland when he called on him at Portman Square in November. The previous month had seen the number of persons employed by the board quadruple, and they had reopened food depots that had earlier been closed. Goulburn concluded that the Whigs had made the "great mistake" of endeavour-ing to apply to a general famine the same means by which he and his colleagues had attempted to relieve "an extensive but yet only a partial dearth." It was simply impossible "to make new roads for ever or to employ upon them for successive years a large proportion of the popu-lation." Nor was he optimistic of the Treasury ever recovering the ad-vances it had already made for public works. "But the rapid rise in the price of every species of grain," which could probably have been checked if the government had prohibited its export from Ireland, did induce him, over the objections of Peel, to depart from the Corn Law settlement which they had so recently effected at such personal and political cost. When Russell moved the suspension for a limited period of all remaining duties on imported corn, Goulburn supported him. He feared that any attempt to maintain them, or the Navigation Laws – especially following their suspension by the French – would simply see the cereals intended for Britain diverted to France or other distressed countries.[3]

On the other hand, Goulburn agreed with Peel that they should do all in their power to convince the Whigs to resist Lord George Bentinck's proposal that £16 million be made available in the form of advances to finance a massive program of railroad construction in Ireland. Although he had earlier identified "bona fide" railways as possible engines of relief, Goulburn suspected that this expensive plan had been concocted by George Hudson, the railway king, and Robert Stephenson, the engineer. "The pretence for it was the relief of distress in Ireland," he remarked privately. "The effect would be to raise the value of all shares in Irish railroads now at a great discount to a premium & thus realize to the fortunate holders a large sum of money." Moreover, precious little of the money would finance employment, especially in the short term. Alarmed by Russell's "weak and vacillating" response to Bentinck, Goulburn took upon himself the task of exposing the absurdity of the proposal, and he succeeded in extracting from the prime minister a statement that he opposed a grant of money for this purpose. Not that this allayed Goulburn's fears. Russell's evident irresolution promised to expose him to renewed and perhaps irresistible pressure exerted by "the railway people," by the entire body of Irish members, and by Bentinck's followers. But Lord John eventually threatened to resign if defeated on this issue, and a number of Irish repealers joined the Peelites in an odd alliance to help sustain him.[4]

Goulburn also went to Charles Wood's defence during the budget debate when the chancellor was criticized by English members for seeking to meet the escalating costs of relief with loans rather than with "taxes specifically applicable to Ireland." He cast his support in providential terms. The "great and overwhelming calamity" that had visited Ireland arose from "the dispensation of a far higher Power" than man, and this "evil" was not to be palliated by any human agency, he argued. On the other hand, the bounty of Providence might do much in the next harvest to restore prosperity; therefore, a large taxation on that unfortunate country might not be required and in the prevailing circumstances would be utterly unproductive. Britain's "first duty" was to extend assistance to the poor and the starving. Ireland's obligation was to repay at least a portion of the loans raised to finance relief. But Goulburn's old fear that vast sums were being wasted and that Irish poverty would yet be the ruin of Britain was never far from his mind, and it led him to endorse the Whig revisions of the Irish Poor Law in 1847. These measures transferred the cost of relief to the Irish. Guardians were now obligated to provide either workhouse accommodation or outdoor relief to all the destitute poor in their unions, while the government promised to act decisively to enforce payment of the poor rates. Clearly, this action would not answer the needs of the Irish, for the workhouses were already overcrowded and unhealthy, and the general population was already weighed down by debt. Nor can it be denied that Goulburn and other supporters of this fateful decision were motivated by a desire for economy rather than by the spirit of humanity.[5]

Meanwhile, in the Commons, general support of the Whigs against the protectionists was very much the chosen path of Peel. Yet he continued to turn a deaf ear to Goulburn's appeals for his active leadership of the more than one hundred free trade Conservatives. "I neither contemplate the return to office nor will I undertake to reorganize a party in opposition to the Government," Peel wrote in December 1846. He remained embittered by the conduct of the landed interest whose influence he believed he had preserved by his policies, and he harshly and speciously criticized Goulburn's sensible suggestion that they position themselves as a third force in the House. Goulburn was far from convinced by his friend's arguments. Certain that Peel would ultimately be driven to resume office by "the force of circumstances" and fearful that if left leaderless their followers would drift away to Stanley and the protectionists, Goulburn welcomed the news that the small group of Peelites with whom he was acting had taken it upon themselves to hold their forces together. Then, in the spring of 1847, the evident lack of enthusiasm among protectionists for Bentinck's leadership in the Commons rekindled Goulburn's hopes of the party's reunification. Peel again doused them. Thin-skinned as ever, he repeated that he would never ally with persons who in the last session had "either openly preferred or covertly sanctioned accusations against me that were equally injurious to my Character, and destitute of Truth."[6]

The Peelites managed to pass the sternest test of their viability as an independent force. Almost ninety of them were returned to the Commons in the general election of 1847, doing well in the few direct contests with protectionists. Goulburn had faced a stiff challenge at Cambridge, where his identification with Peel and his dislike of Tractarianism worked to his disadvantage. In the end, he narrowly survived with the assistance of the Whigs, who themselves remained in office. Gloomily, he predicted that they would continue to be dependent on Radicals or Peelites for a working majority at the very time when the nation's need was for "a strong government." Ireland remained a peculiarly acute problem. There, the burden of the new Poor Law appeared to be driving some Conservatives into the arms of repealers. Meanwhile, the crumbling of many proprietors under the weight of "overgrown incumbrances" and the poor rates was threatening a social change that would dissolve the bonds between higher and lower orders and thus compound the difficulty of government. "But in a country where there is so little on which the Government can depend either for the adoption of what is right or the prevention of what is wrong, the difficulty appears to me almost insurmountable," Goulburn concluded ominously in a letter to Peel. He was, in truth, preparing to wash his hands of Ireland even as other difficulties pushed this concern into the background.[7]

Goulburn had forwarded this sombre assessment to Peel from the serenity of Tunbridge Wells, where both Janes were taking the cure, his daughter's health having collapsed under the strain of caring for his wife. During the Restoration period, the Earl of Rochester had described the spa as "the rendezvous of fools, buffoons and praters, Cuckolds, whores, citizens, their wives and daughters," but it had long since acquired a more sedate and Victorian reputation, with one visitor likening it to a large convent with everyone asleep and in their own beds before midnight. This calm was disturbed during the autumn of 1847 by reports of a deepening national commercial depression and heightening anxiety in the City. On a brief visit to the capital at the beginning of October, Goulburn discovered that banks were refusing to accept stock and exchequer bills as security for loans. The Bank of England contributed to the instability and confusion by first lowering and then suddenly raising interest rates. Rumours of imminent and startling insolvencies heightened the panic. Under mounting pressure for action as the threat of large-scale unemployment in the manufacturing districts increased, and as one provincial branch of the Bank of England reported a run on its gold deposits, the Whigs turned to Peel for aid. He agreed to support a suspension of the Bank Act's restrictions on currency issues, and the crisis abated. Goulburn acquiesced in this decision. Although he feared that a dangerous precedent might have been established, he conceded that "the present benefit may outweigh the evil of a bad precedent" and accepted the absence of fresh demands for violations of the Bank Act as proof "that the suffering arose from alarm than from any real want of money." Nevertheless, he absented himself from the Guildhall banquet in November. "To be alone in the glory of the Bank Bill of 1844 in which I still do glory," he explained to a friend, "would not have been an enviable position." However, he and other supporters of the measure were able to use their dominance of the Commons committee appointed to investigate the crisis to vindicate the act. The committee accepted Goulburn's analysis that the "excess of Railway speculation" had caused a "derangement," which the failure of the potato crop had then aggravated.[8]

In the midst of the panic, Goulburn reminded Peel that one particular commercial class was experiencing peculiar difficulties that deserved special legislative attention – West India planters. Goulburn had continued to supervise from afar the management of Amity Hall even during his years as chancellor, but his success in restoring the nation's finances had not extended to his own. "I am almost weary of advancing money for the cultivation of an Estate which produces nothing in return," he had informed his attorney even before his return to the Exchequer in 1841. To restore its profitability, either the costs of production had to be reduced or the yield greatly increased. With the hope of saving on labour, Goulburn sanctioned the use of "any mechancial improvement" that could be introduced at "a moderate expense." He revived his earlier suggestion of allowing labourers to work some of the lands of the estate in return for a share of the canes, but the attorney rejected this form of sharecropping as impractical. It would be difficult to persuade the labourers to enter into an arrangement from which they would not derive any income for a full year, he explained. Then again, to hand over to them the fruits of an entire year's labour would be tantamount to inviting them not to return to work until they had spent their money; or it might give them the opportunity to invest in a small business as a more attractive way of earning their living. Finally, he fancied that former slaves would never accept less than one-half of the crop they produced as payment for their labour, and this would amount to an inflation of the current wages.[9]

Bitterly disappointed by the continuing losses despite the good crops of 1842 and 1843, which ought to have returned a profit, Goulburn eventually replaced his attorney with a "man of sense and decision," who was willing to accept 10 per cent of the net profits as payment for his services. The new manager, Lewis MacKinnon, brought fresh energy and purpose to the position. He obtained Goulburn's permission to employ a few of the East Indian "coolies" who were being imported on assisted passage schemes, the costs being recovered by a tax on their employers. A "few of these people accustomed in their own country to work hard for moderate wages would be valuable both for the aid they would give us and the example they would set," observed MacKinnon. He subsequently reported that the East Indians were giving "great satisfaction" and were working well with the black labourers, but that they possessed a fondness for rum. In another effort to increase production, MacKinnon made greater use of fertilizers, especially guano, and increased the acreage in canes. "If we can by attention to the cultivation of the land ever again raise the crops to their former average," Goulburn commented in the autumn of 1845, "I do not despair of again rendering the Property to a degree productive." As a result, 1846 opened on a somewhat more optimistic note. The attorney predicted that his owner would make a good profit.[10]

Confident that his property was at last in capable hands and that the world consumption of sugar was rising faster than the supply, and believing that the Russell administration would facilitate labour immigration to Jamaica and would also take steps to bring colonial rum into free competition with British spirits, Goulburn joined with his fellow Peelites in assisting the Whigs to pass the Sugar Act of 1846. It provided for the progressive equalization of the duties on colonial and all foreign-grown sugar. Goulburn's support was conditional, however. It turned on the enactment of "other measures of compensation" to provide "the great security against the foreign Slave Trade by bringing the produce of the West Indies into competition with slave-grown sugar." When the Whig government privately consulted him, he pressed for the equalization also of duties on rum and British spirits. "I believe that we shall gain more under that arrangement than we shall lose by the admission of foreign sugar," he explained to MacKinnon. Although the government did not give the West Indians the generous terms Goulburn had been led to expect, he remained sanguine that the consumption of rum would rapidly increase. Also welcome was Wood's move to open the breweries to colonial sugar.[11]

Goulburn expected the price of British colonial sugar to fall briefly and for foreign sugar then to rise in price to a level remunerative to planters such as himself. Furthermore, the advantage of the new system was its settled character: "We know now therefore on what we have to depend and we must exert ourselves to improve our agriculture and our manufacture both of which are still most lamentably defective." Brimming with ideas for cooperative ventures with neighbouring estates – such as a division of labour between cane cultivation and sugar production, and irrigation projects to overcome the chronic insufficiency of well water – Goulburn called for the abandonment of old prejudices and a course of gradual improvements. It was imperative "that a beginning of a better system should be made." Nevertheless, his optimism quickly evaporated. Prices continued to fall with the rapid growth in imports from Cuba and Brazil, and the reports from Amity Hall were of fresh setbacks instead of cooperative ventures to work the land more effectively.[12]

Shortages of water and fuel, and mechanical breakdowns frequently stopped the steam engine; the wings of the breeze mill were ripped off by a storm; the still and the worm were chronically troublesome; and when all the machinery was functioning, production was disrupted by a strike. Yet Goulburn showed no weakening of his commitment to his peoples' welfare. His attitude towards them was paternal, prudent, and pragmatic. He continued to accept that the provision of medical care for those injured while working on the estate was "so much a matter of duty that it scarcely requires approval." He did not blame labour for the recurrent setbacks. On the basis of the information reaching him, he concluded that low productivity resulted more from the ignorance and idleness of supervisors than from the laziness of former slaves. Similarly, he instructed MacKinnon to handle all strikes with "temper and kindness" as well as with firmness. The need for labour during crop was too important for it to be lost or put at risk by any "imprudence or violence of temper." Meanwhile, Goulburn sanctioned the hiring of more "coolies" in a successful effort to persuade the traditional workforce to moderate their demands. And he fretted over the quantity and quality of the sugar produced, and voiced dismay that carelessness resulted in the rum being smoked and the still damaged beyond repair. "If greater care be not taken of Machinery when supplied it is impossible that any Estate can be productive," he wearily commented.[13]

Goulburn had hoped that a free population would rapidly multiply, thereby creating the pressure to find the means of subsistence, which would ensure a reliable and manageable supply of labour. This hope proved as illusory as that of profits, and it was as misplaced as his belief that slavery in Cuba and Brazil would not long outlast emancipation in the British Empire. The commercial crisis of 1847 added to Goulburn's troubles, for colonial produce was dumped on the market by houses in difficulty, further depressing prices. Not suprisingly, he now regretted his acceptance of the Sugar Act of 1846. It had been "wrong," he complained to Peel. It violated the principle of free trade "so long as the West Indies were subject to limitations as to labour from which foreign countries were exempt." But Peel refused to be a party to any attempt to modify the act through the maintenance of a "reasonable" differential duty. Demoralized, Goulburn initially accepted his decision. "I presume therefore that we must submit to our fate as one of those inflictions of Providence which by weaning us from the things of this world are mercifully intended to prepare us for another," he observed to his old friend Ripon. His desperation was such, however, that he soon allied with Bentinck and the protectionists in a campaign to secure assistance for hard-pressed sugar producers. They secured the appointment of a committee on which he served and whose report he largely prepared. The principal recommendation called for the restoration for a period of six years of a significant differential duty in favour of colonial sugar. The government declined to go that far, but it did slow the pace of equalization and it provided a substantial loan to spur schemes of indentured immigration. Subsequently, the Whigs extended additional assistance in the form of lower rum duties. Although these concessions fell short of Goulburn's demands, he was sufficiently encouraged to renew his search for profits from Amity Hall. Increased energy and rigid economies, including "judicious communication" with the labourers to obtain their "willing assent" to wage reductions, were all solutions that sprang to his mind. Additional encouragement came in the form of difficulties for Cuban and Brazilian producers, who were squeezed by depressed prices and rising production costs. Nevertheless, there was precious little cheer in the final estate accounts for 1847. Expenditures had again exceeded revenues.[14]

To maintain the nation's fiscal stability, Goulburn supported the Whigs on the renewal of the income tax. An expected deficit in 1848 of at least £3 million plainly demanded this resolute action, yet Goulburn's patience with Russell and his ministers was by now exhausted. Hard-hearted as the Whigs had been in Ireland, Goulburn considered them far too improvident. He persuaded himself that they were seeking to buy the support of Irish members with large advances for "useless public works" and were thereby "inducing the Irish to depend too much upon Parliament for remedies which can only be derived from their own energy and moral improvement." He opposed the decision to make an additional £1 million available to Ireland in the form of advances. The amount involved already exceeded £8 million, he calculated. He believed that a better policy would be to vote money in Supply for specific projects and thus avoid encouraging "improvident expenditures." He objected to Wood's proposals to advance inexpensive loans to spur railway construction, insisting that the selective nature of this assistance excited legitimate suspicions of partiality. As for the attempted Irish rebellion in 1848, he laid it at the door of the Whigs' long accommodation with agitation. "It would seem to be a just reflection on the present Government that they should have to reap the fruit of the arrangement which they have for so many years given to agitation and rebellion," he observed privately of ministers who had for so long been associated with the recently deceased O'Connell. "It is if political lessons were ever attended to a good lesson to future statesmen to be careful how they aggravate public evils with a view to the advancement of local or private interests." Sadly absent here was any expression of private sympathy for the multiplying victims of the famine. Publicly, however, he did express sorrow "that the course he was now adopting might seem like a want of feeling for the distress of Ireland."[15]

The nation was cursed with the "great evil" of "a weak Government kept in power not by their own merit but by the division of their opponents," Goulburn observed in August 1848. Although "there never was a fairer opportunity to attack," the Peelites found themselves in the "anomalous position of fearing to turn out" ministers of whom they did not approve. The new Parliament had opened in November with the protectionists seemingly more bitterly hostile to the Peelites than ever. Yet Bentinck's alienation of many of his followers – as much by his religious liberalism on the admission of Jews as by his failings as their chief – soon prompted his resignation from the leadership. Goulburn, who was still regarded as closer to the protectionists in sentiment than any of his senior colleagues, was immediately approached to take Bentinck's place. He again declined the offer, observing that his acceptance would surely create a schism in their ranks and that his objective was to effect a reunion of all Conservatives. This could only be achieved, he reasoned, by harmony on the important questions that came before the House. Thus, when he and Gladstone met with a pair of protectionist representatives later in the session, their discussions immediately foundered on the issue of commercial policy. In short, in the summer of 1848, Conservative reunion seemed no nearer than at any other time over the past two years.[16]

Goulburn returned to Tunbridge Wells from a visit to Drayton in September somewhat more optimistic that Peel was finally overcoming his "repugnance" at the thought of returning to office. He fancied that the "most rancorous part of personal hostility" to the former prime minister would be buried with Bentinck, who had died unexpectedly, and that many protectionists might now be induced to return "to their former connexions." Instead, the vituperative Disraeli soon emerged as *de facto* leader of the protectionists in the Commons, and Goulburn gloomily concluded that his earlier fears of a disintegrating Conservative party opening the door to democracy and radicalism had been realized. He watched with dismay Palmerston's liberal response to the eruption on the Continent of popular disorders and revolution. Closer to home, Ireland threatened to sink into "a winter of continued outrage on life and Property more difficult to suppress if not more dangerous than actual insurrection." Britain itself appeared to be doomed to a winter of severe distress. Goulburn anticipated Radical efforts to introduce "under the name of Reform great democratic changes utterly subversive if successful of a monarchical constitution," which he considered essential for "the real prosperity of nations." He equated democracy with extravagance. The public, he complained, was unwilling to curtail "enjoyments and luxuries" by judicious reductions, and the Whigs' "system" of attempting to appease the disaffected by "limited acquiescence" in their views would "no longer do." The one ray of light in the enveloping gloom was the certainty that the country would inevitably and gratefully turn to honest and able men as the only defence against disorder. But Goulburn waited in vain for Peel and himself to be summoned to the nation's rescue. The Whig government staggered on, and the Peelites continued to behave with a conspicuous lack of cohesion as their disenchantment deepened with Peel's conduct in steadily sustaining the Whigs.[17]

Cursed with the gout in his toes, which condemned him to a couch, and all too aware of the distressing regularity with which his early friends were dying – and with his conservatism plainly hardening even faster than his arteries – Goulburn was losing his appetite for politics by 1849. September found him established at Lower Walmer on the Kent coast, seeking refuge from another outbreak of cholera and a restoration to health of his wife and daughter. At least he had the company of his brother Edward and was able to dine at the nearby castle with Wellington. He discovered that his and the duke's views on public affairs still coincided. "As my only cause for alarm for this Country is the undue growth of the Democratic power," he reminded Ripon a few weeks later, "I am certainly not without anxiety for the future." This fear, no less than the heightened awareness of his mortality, encouraged him to devote ever more of his time to the affairs of the church.[18]

"Every day convinces me more and more that our only hope of permanent tranquillity or prosperity is the increasing to the utmost extent the means of sound religious education," he confided to Peel in January 1849. Convinced that the "only available means" to fund such a program was "the property of the Church," he was as resolute as ever in his protection of it from potential predators. He had automatically returned to the Ecclesiastical Commission (which the Whigs had enlarged in 1840) with his appointment as chancellor of the exchequer, and he remained one of the eight permanent lay commissioners following the fall of the Peel government, faithfully travelling up to London on Thursdays to attend meetings. In the Commons, he took every opportunity to emphasize the progress of church reform since 1835: a significant increase in the number of benefices and of resident clergy; a less impressive but worthwhile improvement in the stipends of lower-paid clergy; and the promise of a great improvement in the management of church property "with the view to the better promotion of the religious instruction of the country." Privately, Goulburn worried that many of Russell's episcopal and clerical appointees were infected with German theology, which in his opinion was "calculated to undermine not the Church of England merely but Christianity itself."[19]

Suddenly, in September 1849, the commission was visited by scandal. Charles Murray, its capable and masterful secretary, was revealed to have misappropriated some £6,000. He had used the money to speculate disastrously in railroad shares. Murray's frank admission of his crime, the evidence that he had intended to repay the monies from his expected profits, the valuable service he had long rendered, and his desperate attempts at restitution all led his employers to treat him with humanity. He was permitted to emigrate with his family to Australia, where he rebuilt his life and his fortune. Yet Murray's fate was less important to Goulburn than the impact his misconduct might have on the Ecclesiastical Commission. The commission had long been unpopular among the lower clergy, dominated as it was by bishops who did not appear to be above using it to advance their own interests. Furthermore, they had evidently failed to supervise the secretary and a permanent staff whose power had increased with the "scale and perplexity" of the commission's work. So Goulburn feared that the secretary's fall from grace would provide the excuse for the government, or Parliament, to absorb the commission's funds if not wind it up altogether. The *Times* was predicting its demise. Instead, the Murray affair helped to expedite a reform that proved eminently satisfactory to Goulburn.[20]

The cumbersome and inefficient commission of 1840 was, to all intents and purposes, replaced by three estates commissioners and "by a small, full-time, professional" board on which they constituted a majority. Indeed, two of them had to be present for any business to be transacted. They had "absolute charge of the whole of the Commissioners' property" but might undertake any other business that the full board delegated to them. In short, the commission was finally to be provided with coordination and a controlled strength. Two of the three were to be paid, one of them being nominated by the crown and the other by the archbishop of Canterbury. Goulburn was Archbishop Sumner's choice. The two men were alike in their orthodoxy tinged with evangelicalism and in their conservatism. Goulburn agreed to accept the position for two reasons. "In the first place I think I may be of more use there than anywhere else," he explained to his elder son. "In the next the addition to my income of 1,000 pounds a year without vacating my seat in Parliament is under present circumstances very convenient as enabling me to continue my present mode of life without risk of adding to my debt." And while he assured his son that there was no danger of his overworking himself, Goulburn established an unmatched record of attendance at the Estates Committee's weekly meetings. Together with his two colleagues, he provided the commission with stable and efficient managment. Although they still lacked sufficient means to raise the stipends of many of the lower clergy to a truly adequate level, they were soon distributing £70,000 annually to the incumbents of small livings. No longer was the commission regarded "as a mere machine for bishops' palaces." And they continued to hope that the ongoing cathedral reform would eventually arm them with the necessary monies. For it was a melancholy truth, one observer commented, "that great improvements cannot be effected without a liberal command of funds."[21]

While Goulburn viewed the reconstruction of the Ecclesiastical Commission as both important and worthwhile, it paled in significance – like all other developments in 1850 – on the death of Peel. In a common enough accident, Peel was thrown by his horse. Tragically, the stumbling animal struck him in the back and he suffered severe internal injuries. Goulburn was in Cambridge at the time, but the alarming reports in the press brought him hurrying back to London on 2 July. The attending physicians admitted that they had been unable to determine the precise nature of the injuries and that the patient's exhaustion and high fever were ominous. Peel did get some sleep that day with the aid of opium and took some nourishment, but the fever remained extremely high and he died late the same evening. Goulburn, as his friend of more than forty years and as one of the executors of his estate, was deputed by the family to reject on their behalf the Whigs' offer of a public funeral. This he did gracefully and with an affecting simplicity. "And if I were to attempt to enter upon other topics," he explained to the House, "the wound his friends have received is too recent to admit of their being touched upon, and the tongue would fail to utter what the heart is too full to express."[22]

His serving as a pallbearer at the funeral at Drayton on 9 July by no means ended Goulburn's personal anguish. There was the severe emotional strain of dealing with a distraught widow. "Pray write as often as you can to me, and Pray write me all you can to try and comfort me," she begged two months after Peel's death. More than a year later, she was still expressing her appreciation of his "kind feeling heart," which permitted her to pour out her "flood of Sorrow." Goulburn was also thrust into the role of mediator between widow and heir, and then between Peel's sons when they fell to squabbling over a piece of property. The experience "has more than ever satisfied me as to the real difficulty of making a will which shall after being reduced to technical language give effect to the wishes of the Testator," he wearily remarked to a fellow executor. He was obliged to travel frequently to Drayton to sort through Peel's papers – which included household accounts and bank statements for almost thirty years – carefully extracting and returning the personal letters from Lady Peel and the children. Finally, he distributed legacies and attempted to settle with creditors. The most importunate of these was Dr Louis Foucart, the Glasgow physician who had witnessed Peel's accident and had remained in attendance on him even after death. Foucart complained that the combination of an ill-ventilated room and decomposition had seen him fall victim to "diarrhoea of the Cholera type," which had kept him away from his practice for six weeks. Thus, by way of additional recompense, he sought an appointment as an assistant surgeon in the East India Company. An enraged Goulburn declined to continue the correspondence.[23]

What was to become of the Peelites without Peel? Disraeli had come to suspect that both Peel and Stanley saw "old Goulburn" as the one person behind whom most Conservatives in the Commons would be willing to reunite, but there was little likelihood of his now providing the leadership that Peel had refused to offer. Although Goulburn believed that it might yet be possible to "create and maintain a party which would draw to itself much that [was] protectionist and command the confidence of the Country," he looked to a younger generation, such as Graham, Gladstone, and Herbert, to undertake this task. What was required, he insisted, was a common set of policies with respect to finance, commerce, and religion. Otherwise, the Peelites would disintegrate and be individually absorbed either by the Whigs or the protectionists. His prediction proved all too accurate. Evidently, he did not see himself in the role of leader. He was too old, too insecure with respect to those essentials of natural leadership – rank and station – too poor, and certainly too conservative for many younger Peelites. "I fear the growing Radicalism of the Whigs on the one side and Protectionists on the other," he admitted to one of them in October, "and should desire as far as my wishes go to stem the progress of that march towards Democracy which the Reform Bill originated and which every new political event unless managed with great prudence as well as firmness assists." Similarly, he stood apart from the other senior Peelites on the issue of religious tolerance.[24]

Goulburn had opposed in 1847 Russell's attempt to remove from Roman Catholic clerics some of the restrictions placed on them in 1829, and he continued to resist efforts to admit Jews to a Christian Parliament. Then, in September 1850, the Pope announced the establishment of an English episcopacy, complete with territorial titles, and elevated Nicholas Wiseman to the rank of cardinal as well as archbishop of Westminster. An injudicious pastoral letter issued by the new cardinal, coupled with the public claim by John Henry Newman, one of the Tractarian converts to Catholicism, that God was leading England back to the true church, merely restoked the fires of anti-Catholicism. The flame of intolerance was fanned by several factors: the tide of Irish immigration, which had increased significantly during the famine; the traditional belief that Catholic values were inconsistent with those of the English, a belief which the politics of the previous two decades had served merely to intensify; and the disarray within Protestant ranks. Personally, Goulburn had watched with dismay the defection to Rome of persons of social prominence. It was "becoming so much the fashion to exalt unduly the necessity of a Church authority that persons entirely forget to examine what the doctrine of the Church is to whom they are prepared to give implicit obedience," he observed. The Church of England founded its articles on what was written in or might be proved from Scripture and thus "was intended to embrace in the same fold men who on minor points entertained different opinions." Here was additional evidence of Goulburn's drift away from evangelicalism – which had become narrower and more rigid, less pastoral, and less tolerant – and towards the "Broad Church" with its advocacy of "the fullest toleration of all within the pale." Further, this party could now lay claim to the mantle of "the originators of ecclesiastical reform, and the pioneers of moral progress," which had once belonged to the evangelicals.[25]

The defender of the church was the role the prime minister reserved for himself. Russell enjoyed a well-deserved reputation for religious toleration and had initially treated with indifference the papal rescript, but on 4 November 1850 he suddenly issued an inflammatory public letter to the bishop of Durham. He denounced the Pope's "insidious" and "insolent" "aggression" on "our Protestantism" and his "pretension to supremacy over the realm of England," and concluded with references to the "immortal martyrs of the Reformation" and "mummeries of superstition." While Russell's political intent was clearly to prevent the Tory protectionists from placing themselves at the head of outraged Protestant opinion, he was also actuated by a desire to exert pressure on the pontiff to be more cooperative in Ireland, especially on the controversial issue of the "Godless" colleges, and by a determination to strike against the Tractarians, whom he considered to be the church's enemy within.[26]

Although Goulburn was privately contemptuous of Russell's pandering to a religious intolerance which he would evidently find "difficult to subdue and impossible to gratify," he soon found himself publicly at odds with most of his fellow Peelites. Goulburn did not agree with those of them who claimed to be unable to see any difference between the new English Roman hierarchy and that which had long been implicitly recognized in Ireland, or between a papal assumption of authority in England and that claimed by the Free Church and Presbyterians in Scotland. If "we submit to this Papal edict," he reasoned, "we do in fact abandon all idea of the Queen's supremacy and open the door to the regular Establishment in this Country of what never before existed, a jurisdiction of infinite power unconnected with the Government and under Foreign Controul." On the other hand, he saw in Russell's published letter further evidence "of a disposition on the part of some persons to ascribe the Pope's conduct to Puseyism alone and instead of endeavouring to bring back this enemy within take a course of bitterness calculated to drive them out of the Pale." He remained convinced that many of the Tractarians might yet be recovered. The majority were little inclined to the essential doctrines of Roman Catholicism, he opined, "though in ignorance of or regardless of the danger of adopting Popish forms of worship and ceremonial (which by the by the Liturgy allows) they appear to a casual spectator to be the assistants of Rome." His attempts to recruit the intensely evangelical Ashley on behalf of this inclusive policy failed. Ashley took the opposite tack, and Goulburn worried that an effort would soon be launched to make changes to the Liturgy, ostensibly to expunge "whatever savoured of Popery" but which would lead to consequences no one could foretell.[27]

The bill that Russell introduced in February 1851 merely prohibited Catholic clerics under pain of fine from assuming ecclesiastical titles. Goulburn criticized the prime minister for having aggravated the hostile feelings that had existed in the country following the papal announcement, and he lamented the "prejudicial effect" that was likely to be produced by the discrepancy between the measure now brought forward and the excitement to which Russell had contributed. Yet he was the only senior Peelite to vote for the bill, satisfied as he was that the spiritual needs of the Roman Catholic population had not required the creation of a hierarchy that trespassed "upon the sovereign power of the Queen, upon the Protestantism of England, and upon our Established Church." Certainly, the Catholics had been imprudently arrogant in their dismissive references to the Church of England. But Goulburn's association with the protectionists on this emotional issue did not presage closer cooperation with them. Thus, when a group of Irish members immediately took revenge on Russell for the Ecclesiastical Titles Bill by helping to defeat him on another measure, thus causing him to resign, Goulburn played a significant role in frustrating Stanley's admittedly irresolute attempt to form a government. The emissary who came to solicit his support departed convinced that he should not himself join with Stanley. Similarly, Herries declined to accept the office of chancellor of the exchequer out of fear of Goulburn. As Disraeli later recalled, a terrified Herries gave the impression "that our monetary affairs were in a critical state, and that Goulburn would eat us alive if we presumed to touch them." After a week of manoeuvring, Stanley threw up his hands and Russell resumed office.[28]

One year later, Russell's government again fell. This time the defeat was engineered by Palmerston in revenge for his dismissal from the Foreign Office. A more determined Stanley, who was now Earl of Derby, formed an administration to which most of the Peelites agreed to give "a fair trial." Yet their influence was diminishing, a fact that was illustrated by the return of fewer than fifty of them in the general election held during the summer of 1852. Significantly, those most closely identified with ecclesiastical liberalism had been the hardest pressed at the polls. Nevertheless, Gladstone and Goulburn played large if unequal roles in demolishing the budget that Disraeli introduced as chancellor, and the Peelites were a small but important element of the majority that turned out the Conservatives in December. Goulburn was one of the senior Peelites who then gathered for a dinner meeting at Sidney Herbert's to discuss policy even as Lord Aberdeen was preparing to visit the queen to receive his commission to form a coalition administration with the Whigs. However, Goulburn was the only senior Peelite omitted from the new cabinet. He was disqualified by age, by his profound distrust of the Whigs, and by his conservative rigidity. "All I am determined upon," he had advised Aberdeen a few months earlier, "is to maintain the principles of Commercial and Fiscal policy which we when in power established because I consider that policy to be in the strictest sense conservative." This stand separated him from Aberdeen, who was of the opinion "that all Government in these times, must be a Government of progress; conservative progress if you please; but we can no more be stationary than reactionary." Unlike Goulburn, he saw no growing threat of democracy. "Perhaps there is even less than at any former period," he judged.[29]

As an emeritus, Goulburn was consulted often by Gladstone, the new chancellor, whose promotion to this office he welcomed enthusiastically. Illness prevented him from being present in the House to witness the triumph of Gladstone's 1853 budget. "But I feel that in the 69th year of my age and the 46th of unbroken Parliamentary service," he explained, "I must be content to be rather an admirer of others than a fellow labourer with them." Goulburn was to give the coalition loyal support until it fell early in 1855, primarily as a result of the mismanagement of the Crimean War, in which his eldest son was fighting. He then urged the Peelites to join the administration that Palmerston was asked to form, for they had a duty "to obviate the danger of a very weak Government," to restrain Palmerston in foreign affairs, and to maintain what "little coherence exists in the Party." Unfortunately, the four most prominent Peelites resigned almost immediately in protest to the appointment of a parliamentary committee to inquire into the conduct of the war.[30]

Distressed as he had been by the passing of Wellington in 1852, Goulburn had found solace in the knowledge that the duke had died "before extreme old age had impaired his mental faculties or deprived him of the power of bodily exertion." He was to share this same good fortune. He travelled down to Folkestone in the spring of 1855 to take the sea air. He visited Dover to examine the new harbour and pier, and alarmed his son Freddy with talk of taking a steamer over to France. Indeed, he was provoked into a rare display of irritation by his son's querying the wisdom of a solitary holiday and by his evident doubt that Goulburn was as strong as he imagined. Yet there were grounds for anxiety. Goulburn had long been troubled by weak lungs and had suffered a series of "attacks." Nevertheless, he appeared to be in good health that autumn, which he spent at Betchworth. Then, at year's end, he made his annual visit to Cambridge, and there he caught cold and quickly developed pleurisy. On 7 January 1856 he suddenly began to weaken, and he died five days later. He "yielded up his last breath without the slightest struggle, and in a calm and confident expectation of the reward which we know awaited him," his younger son informed a friend.[31]

Goulburn's death received little attention, for like many another old politician, he had quickly faded from the public mind once he quit the public scene. Yet he was a man who saw his own life almost exclusively in terms of his public career, perhaps because he had been one of the more successful politicians of his generation. Raised in a world threatened by the revolutionary upheaval in France, and ever aware of his want of true rank and station, for he belonged by birth only to the fringe of the ruling class, he had quickly embraced as a young man the reassuring conservative values of order, stability, and tradition. It was an attachment reinforced by his evangelical convictions in matters of faith. Indeed, he embarked on a career of public service as something of a vocation. Unlike George Canning, whose origins were far humbler, and unlike Robert Peel, Goulburn neither dazzled his contemporaries with his oratorical or intellectual brilliance nor acquired a personal following. Nor was he driven by ambition. If he had not had influential patrons, he might have passed his public life in the backbench wilderness. There was thus a strong element of good fortune in the launching of his career. He owed much to Matthew Montagu, who first took him in hand, packed him off to his own college at Cambridge, and then encouraged him to enter Parliament, where he enrolled the young Goulburn in Spencer Perceval's following.

If political connections brought Goulburn the reward of junior office, he seized the opportunity to impress. First at the Home Office and then in the Colonial Department, he proved himself. His was not a glittering performance, but it was a solid one. He exhibited that good sense, industry, integrity, and discretion which earned him the much-valued reputation as a "man of business." This ensured his retention by Liverpool, a distant relation, following Perceval's assassination. As under-secretary for war and colonies, Goulburn not only managed a far-flung empire with the assistance of a miniscule staff but also laid the foundations of the modern Colonial Office. He performed the thankless task – given his superiors' less than resolute support – of negotiating an unsatisfactory peace with the Americans in 1814. Loyal and discreet, honourable and able, a stalwart of the church of England, he was first invited to go to Ireland as chief secretary in 1818 and eventually accepted this promotion three years later. His hesitation was rooted in another of his insecurities – the seemingly irreversible decline in his personal income.

Goulburn's fear that he lacked the means to afford high office was overcome with the aid of a modest pension, but he was rarely free of money worries for the remainder of his life. He had purchased one of the trappings of the ruling class in 1816, a country house and estate, but whenever he was out of office he could ill afford its upkeep, and he was eventually reduced to leasing it and living in more humble rental accommodation. This state of genteel poverty may explain why Goulburn left a lifetime of public service without the traditional reward of rank. He lacked the income to maintain the necessary state. He had received little personal compensation other than a modest pension and the office of church estates commissioner. There is no evidence that Goulburn resented the absence of public recognition, though on at least one occasion his wife voiced her bitterness. He accepted his fate, no doubt reassured that this was what God had ordained for him. Equally, even more so than Peel, his was the "honour of the unadorned name."

A lack of recognition, even an undervaluing of his role in a succession of Tory governments, was also the result of Goulburn's willingness to serve in the shadow of greater men. This, at least, was how he somewhat apologetically explained to his children his failure to leave to them a name. At the Home and Colonial offices he had made himself indispensable to his superiors – Richard Ryder and Earl Bathurst, respectively. This was not some calculated obsequiousness; it was a form of filial attachment to older men. In the case of Wellington, it was a matter of hero-worship. Goulburn's relationship with Peel was more complex, for they were of the same age. He early recognized Peel's political brilliance and increasingly deferred to him as the man selected by destiny and providence to lead the forces of conservatism. They shared a bureaucratic attitude towards government, being dedicated to professionalism and efficiency in administration. They shared an unconscious arrogance that they were far better qualified than their political adversaries to exercise power in the national interest. Similarly, to the extent that they were reformers, it was to preserve existing institutions by guarding them from damaging criticism. When Goulburn was finally compelled to choose between Peel and Wellington, he aligned himself with the younger man. During the 1830s, he patiently supported and loyally defended Peel's Fabian policy of slowly rebuilding popular support and creating a more coherent party structure, even though his own instinct was to ally with the Ultras and to be more aggressive in assaults on the Whigs. In important policy matters, Goulburn invariably suppressed his own private doubts once a decision had been taken and publicly gave wholehearted support to his leader. He rallied to Wellington and Peel on Catholic emancipation, and he endorsed the latter's controversial efforts to conciliate Ireland. That Goulburn's personal loyalty to Peel was the touchstone of his conduct, taking precedence over all other considerations, was most evident during the debate on the repeal of the Corn Laws. He recognized and privately warned that this action was a serious political mistake. Peel was putting at risk the only party that was plugging the dykes against radicalism and democracy, but Goulburn remained true to his closest political friend rather than to his own opinions. The price he paid for this measure of loyalty was that he was written off as a mere functionary, one of Wellington's "parasites" and Peel's *alter ego*. In fact, he was one of the major political figures of the era.

What colleagues valued in Goulburn was not only his intense loyalty and administrative efficiency, welcome as these qualities were, but a spotless character and personal integrity. He was one of those administrators who demonstrated, following the end of the French wars, that a minimal state was not inconsistent with efficiency and effectiveness. There was, however, a costly personal price to be paid in the form of bone-wearying days of labour and separation from his family. Goulburn proved to be fully as capable and cautious a chancellor as Wellington had expected, implementing a characteristically moderate version of liberal Toryism. After Peel reappointed him to this office in 1841, Goulburn played a large if discreet role in the formulation of the successful economic policy on which Peel's reputation was made. To the extent that good finance was "the first necessity of national prosperity," Henry Goulburn had a strong claim to a share of the credit for the triumph of the mid-1840s. Significantly – and characteristically – the first lord introduced the most dramatic budgets; he left to Goulburn the more humdrum statements of economic and fiscal policy. Not that Goulburn ever resented this supporting role. He did, however, baulk at the massive program of relief which the prime minister appeared to envisage in response to the failure of the potato crop in Ireland – a resistance that reflected his Treasury mind and an awareness of the partial nature of the crop failure in 1845 and early 1846. Under pressure, Goulburn modified his restricted notion of government intervention in such crises and surrendered the principle of Treasury control that he had so long upheld. Nevertheless, the conviction that much of the money advanced or granted to finance relief works was being wasted or misappropriated, a belief rooted in his own experience and nurtured by more recent reports from Ireland, saw him adopt a less charitable position once he was out of office and somewhat freer of Peel's influence. His old fear that Irish poverty might bankrupt Britain resurfaced with the total failure of the potato, especially when the Whigs seemed content merely to extend the already expensive policies for which he had been partially responsible. Yet Goulburn did not advance a compassionate alternative, despite his acknowledgment that the "first duty" of the nation was to provide assistance to the poor and starving. And to the extent that his sterner attitudes towards Irish relief subsequently placed him in the same camp as the Whigs, he must share some of the responsibility for the tragedy that overtook Ireland. However, the subsequent accusation that the British had pursued a genocidal policy was even less true of Goulburn than it was of his Whig successors. Moreover, today, when democratic politicians are redefining social welfare programs in terms of what the state can afford as distinct from what the impoverished and underprivileged may need, Goulburn's mid-nineteenth-century response to the distress in Ireland may appear a little less reprehensible. Similarly, as one distinguished historian of Ireland has mordantly observed, the British were more efficient in delivering relief to the starving Irish in the mid-nineteenth century than the United Nations has been in providing it to starving Africans in the late twentieth century.[32]

Goulburn's rectitude was rooted in faith. His early evangelicalism moderated over time as he moved towards the *via media*, or "Broad Church," though this was not a difficult transition for such an instinctively orthodox man, who had never belonged to one of the parties within the church. Thus he ultimately tempered his once inflexible sabbatarianism in response to social considerations, and he wished to attract Tractarians back into the fold, not drive them beyond the pale. He remained throughout his life, however, a consistent champion of the established church and undoubtedly found some comfort in the census returns of 1851, which indicated that the church was making something of a recovery. Goulburn's zeal in its defence had plainly been heightened by the political compromises he had accepted with respect to the emancipation of all dissenters, Protestant and Catholic, and the erosion of the rights of the established church in both Britain and Ireland. Fittingly, he ended his days as one of the three estates commissioners. "Our Church has lost in him a firm and *sensible* defender," the bishop of Durham commented on learning of Goulburn's death.[33]

Goulburn was challenged morally as few of his friends and colleagues were. He had inherited a sugar estate worked by an army of slaves, and they were long his principal source of income, an income that assured him of his social and political position. He grew to manhood to the rising drumbeat of the campaigns for the abolition of the slave trade and the amelioration of slavery, though these crusades were briefly compromised by their identification with a political radicalism that Goulburn always scorned. While this association temporarily afforded him some intellectual protection from the demands of humanitarianism, and while it may have excited suspicion of the cause in his conservative mind, his conduct as an absentee proprietor was shaped by the cumulative pressures under which he laboured. In an enlightened age and as a devout churchman, he wished his property to be worked in a progressive manner. Furthermore, the abolition of the slave trade dictated, as its advocates intended, that greater attention be given to the welfare of slaves. Their numbers had to be sustained by natural reproduction now that fresh importations had been banned. Yet good intentions were for too long overborne by the demands of production and profit and the mysteries of disease. This compromise with materialism and mortality was eased for the evangelical Goulburn by his commitment to amelioration and his willing acceptance of a racial caricature that depicted blacks as licentious and irresponsible. Nor can his dramatic elevation of human priorities, following his brother's devastating report on conditions at Amity Hall, be entirely divorced from his fear of public embarrassment. Responsible as he was for the implementation of the program of amelioration, he could ill afford as under-secretary for the colonies to be exposed as an owner who tolerated a hard-driving management of his own property.

Goulburn failed to acknowledge the inevitablity and desirability of emancipation until the mid-1820s. In one sense this was not surprising, for until then the gradualism to which he was wedded as a conservative had been the main thrust even of the abolitionists. Privately, he lived to regret that he had compromised with the evil of slavery for so long and had failed to speak out against the institution. The desire to protect his income, and thus his family's future, induced a moral blindness on this issue. The energy and persistence with which he sought to defend himself from Macaulay's attacks in 1826 and 1831 reflected a realization that his personal honour had been successfully impugned. Belatedly, he sacrificed much, especially income, in the name of humanity. Similarly, he behaved in an exemplary fashion during the difficult period of apprenticeship and following the premature dismantling of that system. Of course, he was still motivated in part by self-interest. He was anxious to attach labourers to Amity Hall, and he waged a long and depressingly unsuccessful battle during the last decade of his life to operate the estate profitably through enlightened labour policies. Like many another life, Goulburn's petered out in obscurity, genteel poverty, and disappointment. For all of his achievements in public life, he feared that the disintegration of the Conservative party had opened the door to democracy. He had failed to protect from erosion the privileged position of the established church. He had failed the moral test set by slavery. He had failed to leave his family a name. He had failed to put his plantation back on its feet as a profitable enterprise and thus pass it on to his heirs as a valuable asset. Perhaps, therefore, his providential interpretation of the outbreak of a cholera epidemic in Jamaica reflected a more general pessimism. It would seem, he observed mordantly, "that it was the intention of God to complete the ruin which the folly of man has commenced."[34]

Notes

PREFACE

1 John Kenyon, *The History Men: The Historical Profession in England since the Renaissance* (London, 1983), 271–2; Richard Brent, "Butterfield's Tories: 'High Politics' and the Writing of Modern British History," *Historical Journal* 30 (1987): 952; Elizabeth Chapin Furber, ed., *Changing Views of British History: Essays on Historical Writing since 1939* (Cambridge, Mass., 1966), 260; Michael Bentley, *Politics without Democracy: Great Britain, 1815–1914, Perception and Preoccupation in British Government* (Oxford, 1984), 378.

2 Kenyon, *History Men*, 287.

3 Richard Schlatter, ed., *Recent Views on British History: Essays on Historical Writing since 1966* (New Brunswick, N.J., 1984), 274; Peter Jupp, *Lord Grenville 1759–1834* (Oxford, 1985); E.A. Smith, *Lord Grey 1764–1845* (Oxford, 1990); John Derry, *Charles Earl Grey, Aristocratic Reformer* (Oxford, 1992); E.A. Wasson, *Whig Renaissance: Lord Althorp and the Whig Party 1782–1845* (New York, 1987); D.D. Olien, *Morpeth: A Victorian Public Career* (Washington, D.C., 1983); Richard Brent, *Liberal Anglican Politics: Whiggery, Religion and Reform 1830–1841* (Oxford, 1987); Peter Mandler, *Aristocratic Government in the Age of Reform: Whigs and Liberals, 1830–1852* (Oxford, 1990); Ian Newbould, *Whiggery and Reform, 1830–1841: The Politics of Government* (Stanford, 1990); Jonathan Parry, *The Rise and Fall of Liberal Government in Victorian Britain* (New Haven, 1993), 1; Martin J. Wiener, "The Unloved State: Twentieth-Century Politics in the Writing of Nineteenth-Century History," *Journal of British Studies* 33 (1994): 291; Brent, "Butterfield's Tories," 945–6; F.M.L. Thompson, ed., *The Cambridge Social History of Britain 1750–1950*, vol. 3. *Social Agencies and Institutions* (Cambridge, 1990): 8–9.

4 Francis Bamford and Duke of Wellington, eds., *Journal of Mrs Arbuthnot 1820–1832*, 2 vols. (London, 1950) 1:129–30; Ford K. Brown, *Fathers of the Victorians: The Age of Wilberforce* (Cambridge, 1961), 359; Boyd Hilton, *The Age of Atonement: The Influence of Evangelicalism on Social and Economic Thought, 1795–1865* (Oxford, 1988), 226; see also Norman Gash's review of Hilton's book in *English Historical Review* 104 (1989): 136–40; John Walsh, Colin Haydon, and Stephen Taylor, eds., *The Church of England c.1689–c.1833: From Toleration to Tractarianism* (Cambridge, 1993), 337.

CHAPTER ONE

1 For Goulburn's scant interest in his antecedents, see his handwritten memoirs, Acc 304/68, in the Goulburn Papers, Surrey Record Office (SRO), Kingston upon Thames; for the Chester Goulburns, see George Ormerod, *The History of the County Palatine and City of Chester*, 3 vols. (London, 1882), 2:666–72; Register of Jamaican Landholders 1754, in Public Record Office (PRO), London, Colonial Office (CO) 142/31; J.R. Ward, *British West Indian Slavery 1750–1834: The Process of Amelioration* (Oxford, 1988), 85.

2 F.W. Pitman, *The Development of the British West Indies 1700–1763* (New Haven, 1917), 120–4; for the development of the estate and the provisions of the various wills of the early Goulburns, see SRO, Acc 304/59/3A; also G.S. Ramlackhansingh, "Amity Hall 1760–1860: The Geography of a Jamaican Plantation," MSC thesis, University of London, 1966, 9–16.

3 Edward Long, *The History of Jamaica, or General Survey of the Antient and Modern State of That Island*, 3 vols. (London, 1774), 2:247–9.

4 R.A. Austen Leigh, ed., *Eton College Lists 1678–1790* (Eton, 1907), 163, 167, 172, 176; R.A. Austen Leigh, *The Eton College Register 1753–1790* (Eton, 1921), xix–xxi, 223; Goulburn memoirs, SRO, Acc 304/68.

5 SRO, Acc 304/59/3A.

6 Sir Bernard Burke, *A Genealogical and Heraldic History of the Landed Gentry of Great Britain and Ireland*, 2 vols. (London, 1894), 1:796; R.R. Nelson, *The Home Office 1782–1801* (Durham, N.C., 1969), 164; Goulburn memoirs, SRO, Acc 304/68.

7 Deposition of John Walker Heneage, in PRO, Chancery Records, C12/474/22; Thomas Hughes to M. Goulburn, 5 February 1790, and M. Goulburn to Hughes, 16 February 1790, SRO, Acc 304/59/3A.

8 George Clinch, *Marylebone and St. Pancras: Their History, Celebrities, Buildings and Institutions* (London, 1890), 17–20; Goulburn memoirs, SRO, Acc 304/68.

9 Mrs Paget Toynbee, ed., *The Letters of Horace Walpole, Fourth Earl of Oxford*, 16 vols. (Oxford, 1904), 9:28–9; M. Goulburn to Hughes, 1 February 1790, SRO, Acc 304/59/3A; Goulburn memoirs, SRO, Acc 304/68.

10 The details of Munbee's finances are to be found in PRO, C12/197/24, PRO, C12/474/22, and SRO, Acc 304/59/3A; Craggs to Hughes, 3 October 1794, SRO, Acc 304/53; M. Goulburn to Thomas Gairdner, 4 January 1791, SRO, Acc 426.

11 Craggs to M. Goulburn, 16 January 1794, SRO, Acc 304/54; Goulburn memoirs, SRO, Acc 304/68.

12 Daniel Lysons, *The Environs of London, Being an Historical Account of the Towns, Villages, and Hamlets within Twelve Miles of the Capital* (London, 1811), vol. 2, pt. 1, 1–12; Goulburn memoirs, SRO, Acc 304/68.

13 SRO, Acc 304/59/3A; Craggs to S. Goulburn, 22 December 1796, and S. Goulburn to Craggs, 2 May 1798, SRO, Acc 304/53; *Quarterly Review* 30 (1824): 278.

14 S. Goulburn to Craggs, 5 November 1800, and Nethersole to Craggs, 3 September 1799, SRO, Acc 304/54; Craggs to Goulburn, 10 July, 10 September 1800, SRO, Acc 304/53.

15 Geoffrey H. White, ed., *The Complete Peerage* (London, 1949), 11:73; Henry B. Wheatley, *London Past and Present*, 3 vols. (London, 1891), 3:110; Mrs Godfrey Clark, ed., *Gleanings from a Portfolio*, 3 vols. (Edinburgh, 18〔8), 3:60–2.

16 Clinch, *Marylebone and St. Pancras*, 60–2; Peter Cunningham, *A Handbook for London Past and Present*, 2 vols. (London, 1849), 2:670; John Summerson, *Georgian London*, new ed. (London, 1988), 124–7; *Gentleman's Magazine* 223 (1867): 464–71.

17 *Quarterly Review* 10 (1814): 31–41; *Gentleman's Magazine* 223 (1867): 467.

18 Denis Gray, *Spencer Perceval: The Evangelical Prime Minister, 1762–1812* (Manchester, 1963), 47.

19 James Torne, *Handbook to the Environs of London* (London, 1876), 269–73; Richard Rush, *A Residence at the Court of London*, pb. ed. (London, 1987), 147; Craggs to S. Goulburn, 13 February 1801, SRO, Acc 304/51; Goulburn memoirs, SRO, Acc 304/68.

20 W.W. Rouse Ball and J.D. Venn, eds., *Admissions to Trinity College Cambridge 1546–1900*, 5 vols. (London, 1911–16), 4:3; D.A. Winstanley, *Unreformed Cambridge: A Study of Certain Aspects of the University in the Eighteenth Century* (Cambridge, 1935), 186–7, 197, 208.

21 Goulburn memoirs, SRO, Acc 304/68.

22 Goulburn memoirs, SRO, Acc 304/68; quoted by C.A. Bayly, *Imperial Meridian: The British Empire and the World, 1780–1830* (London, 1989), 114–15.

23 See L.E. Elliot-Binns, *The Early Evangelicals: A Religious and Social Study* (London, 1953), 353–65; Marcus L. Loane, *Cambridge and the Evangelical Succession* (London, 1952), 185; Ford K. Brown, *Fathers of the Victorians: The Age of Wilberforce* (Cambridge, 1961), 295; Henry Reeve, ed., *The Greville Memoirs: A Journal of the Reigns of King George IV and King William IV*, 3 vols. (London, 1874), 3:129.

24 Hugh Evan Hopkins, *Charles Simeon at Cambridge* (London, 1977), 65; Loane, *Evangelical Succession*, 212, 190–1; Boyd Hilton, *The Age of Atonement: The Influence of Evangelicalism on Social and Economic Thought, 1795–1865* (Oxford, 1988), 9; Arthur Pollard and Michael Hennell, eds., *Charles Simeon (1759–1836)* (London, 1959), 26, 29, 162–4, 168.

25 For Goulburn's requests to God, see SRO, Acc 304/66; Pollard and Hennell, *Simeon*, 164; Ian Bradley, *The Call to Seriousness: The Evangelical Impact on the Victorians* (New York, 1970), 19–20; R.A. Soloway, *Prelates and People: Ecclesiastical Social Thought in England 1783–1852* (London, 1969), 79; see Owen Chadwick's assessment of Peel in his *Victorian Church*, 2 vols. (London, 1966–70), 1:101.

26 John Kenneth Severn, *A Wellesley Affair* (Tallahassee, 1981), 96; Goulburn memoirs, SRO, Acc 304/68; Kenneth Bourne, *Palmerston: The Early Years, 1784–1841* (New York, 1982), 42–3, 40–1; Kenneth Bourne, ed., *The Letters of the Third Viscount Palmerston to Laurence and Elizabeth Sulivan 1804–1863*, Camden Fourth Series, 23 (London, 1979), 8–9.

27 Goulburn memoirs, SRO, Acc 304/68; William Howitt, *The Northern Heights of London* (London, 1869), 266, 240.

28 Goulburn memoirs, SRO, Acc 304/68.

29 *The Blueviad: A Satyrical Poem* (London, 1805); *The Pursuit of Fashion* (London, 1810); for the debts of Edward Goulburn, see SRO, Acc 304/81; Goulburn memoirs, SRO, Acc 304/68.

30 William Albery, *A Parliamentary History of the Ancient Borough of Horsham 1295–1885* (London, 1927), 195–229; Frank O'Gorman, *Voters, Patrons, and Parties: The Unreformed Electoral System of Hanoverian England 1734–1832* (Oxford, 1989), 34–5; J.V. Beckett, "The Making of a Pocket Borough: Cockermouth 1722–1756," *Journal of British Studies* 20 (1980): 140–3; Bourne, *Palmerston*, 65–6.

31 Bourne, *Palmerston*, 65–6, 68–71; Albery, *Parliamentary History of Horsham*, 195–7.

32 Albery, *Parliamentary History of Horsham*, 233, 235, 238; Goulburn memoirs, SRO, Acc 304/68.

33 Goulburn to Peel, 5 November 1832, British Library (BL), Add. Ms. 40333; Hilton, *Age of Atonement*, 12; Bradley, *Call to Seriousness*, 165; Diana Davids Olien, *Morpeth: A Victorian Public Career* (Washington, 1983), 22; Goulburn memoirs, SRO, Acc 304/68; Bruce Coleman, *Conservatism and the Conservative Party in Nineteenth-Century Britain* (London, 1988), 18, 10; Gray, *Spencer Perceval*, 111.

34 Goulburn memoirs, SRO, Acc 304/68; Gray, *Spencer Perceval*, 53, 27, 15, 35–6, 93, 20–1; Thomas Pinney, ed., *The Letters of Thomas Babington Macaulay*, vol. 2 (Cambridge, 1974), 45; see Perceval Papers, BL, Add. Ms. 49182; Henry Brougham, *Historical Sketches of Statesmen Who Flourished in the Time of George III* vol. 1 (London, 1855), 323–4; Coleman, *Conservatism*, 35, 22.

35 H. Goulburn to R. Peel, 3 October 1847, BL, Add. Ms. 40445; J.C.D. Clark, *English Society 1688–1832: Ideology, Social Structure and Political Practice during the Ancien Regime*, reprint ed. (Cambridge, 1988), 200; Thomas Philip Schofield, "Conservative Political Thought in Britain in Response to the French Revolution," *Historical Journal* 29 (1986): 604, 618; Trevor McGovern, "Conservative Ideology in Britain in the 1790s," *History* 73 (1988): 241–2.

36 H.T. Dickinson, *Liberty and Property: Political Ideology in Eighteenth Century Britain* (London, 1977), 280; Schofield, "Conservative Political Thought," 621; Ian Christie, *Stress and Stability in Late Eighteenth Century Britain: Reflections on the British Avoidance of Revolution* (Oxford, 1984), 163.

37 Schofield, "Conservative Political Thought," 621; Dickinson, *Liberty and Property*, 285; McGovern, "Conservative Ideology," 246–7; Christie, *Stress and Stability*, 183–4; Brian Jenkins, *Era of Emancipation: British Government of Ireland 1812–1830* (Montreal, 1988), 17–19; Clark, *English Society*, 246.

38 F.M.L. Thompson, ed., *Cambridge Social History of Britain 1750–1950*, vol. 3, *Social Agencies and Institutions* (Cambridge, 1990), 322; Hilton, *Age of Atonement*, 205; David Hempton, *Methodism and Politics in British Society 1750–1850* pb. ed. (London, 1987), 183; Goulburn to C. Wordsworth,

3 February 1826, Lambeth Palace Library (LPL), London, Ms. 2150; Peter Mandler, "Tories and Paupers: Christian Political Economy and the Making of the New Poor Law," *Historical Journal* 33 (1990): 88, 86–7, 91.

39 Frank O'Gorman, *The Emergence of the British Two-Party System 1760–1832* (London, 1982), 51, 56; Hilton, *Age of Atonement*, 205; Philip Harling and Peter Mandler, "From 'Fiscal-Military' State to Laissez-faire State, 1760–1850," *Journal of British Studies* 32 (1993): 62–6; Michael Bentley, *Politics without Democracy: Great Britain, 1815–1914* (Oxford, 1984), 64.

40 Goulburn memoirs, SRO, Acc 304/69; Wilbur Devereux Jones, *"Prosperity" Robinson: The Life of Viscount Goderich, 1782–1859* (New York, 1967), 29–32; *Letters of the Earl of Dudley to the Bishop of Llandaff* (London, 1841), 195–6, 250–1; Rush, *Residence at the Court of London*, 59.

41 Hilton, *Age of Atonement*, 16–17, 94; Mandler, "Tories and Paupers," 86, 91; Harding and Mandler, "From 'Fiscal-Military' State of Laissez-faire State," 45, 54; P.J. Cain and A.G. Hopkins, "Gentlemanly Capitalism and British Expansion Overseas 1. The Old Colonial System, 1688–1850," *Economic History Review*, 2nd ser., 39 (1986): 514–15.

42 Goulburn memoirs, SRO, Acc 304/68.

43 Peter Jupp, ed., *Letter-Journal of George Canning 1793–1795*, Camden Fourth Series, 41 (London, 1991), 55; Roland Thorne, ed., *The House of Commons 1790–1820*, 5 vols. (London, 1986), 2:44; Goulburn memoirs, SRO, Acc 304/68; *Courier*, 25 February 1809; A. Aspinall, *The Later Correspondence of George III*, 5 vols. (Cambridge, 1970), 5:210.

44 Aspinall, *Later Correspondence of George III*, 5:225.

45 H. Goulburn to E. Goulburn, 3 July 1809, H. Goulburn to S. Goulburn, 7 July 1809, and H. Goulburn to S. Goulburn, 4 December 1809, SRO, Acc 304/61.

46 H. Goulburn to S. Goulburn, 6, 15 July 1809, SRO, Acc 304/61; Goulburn memoirs, SRO, Acc 304/68; Goulburn kept a detailed daily account of his visit to the peninsula, see Peninsular diary SRO, Acc 304/33.

47 H. Goulburn to S. Goulburn, 15 July 1809, SRO, Acc 304/61; Peninsular diary, 16–18 July 1809, SRO Acc 304/33.

48 H. Goulburn to S. Goulburn, 22, 27 July 1809, SRO, Acc 304/61.

49 H. Goulburn to S. Goulburn, 1 August 1809, SRO, Acc 304/61; Peninsular diary, 31 July, 5 August 1809, SRO, Acc 304/33; Norman R. Bennett, "The Golden Age of the Port Wine System, 1781–1807," *International History Review* 12 (1990): 241–2.

50 Peninsular diary, 9, 11, 16, 18, 20 August 1809, SRO, Acc 304/33; Goulburn memoirs, SRO, Acc 304/68.

51 Severn, *Wellesley Affair*, 49–54.

52 Peninsular diary, 20 July, 12, 21, 24 August 1809, SRO, Acc 304/33; H. Goulburn to S. Goulburn, 13 August, 23, 30 September 1809, SRO, Acc 304/61; Charles Esdaile, "War and Politcs in Spain 1808–1814," *Historical Journal* 31

(1988): 296–8; Charles Esdaile, "Wellington and the Military Eclipse of Spain, 1808–1814," *International History Review* 11 (1989): 58, 63–4.

53 Peninsular diary, SRO, Acc 304/33; see also Gerald Newman, *The Rise of English Nationalism: A Cultural History 1740–1830* (New York, 1987); H. Goulburn to S. Goulburn, 22 October 1809, SRO, Acc 304/61.

54 Goulburn memoirs, SRO, Acc 304/68; Peninsular diary, 29 August – 21 September 1809, SRO, Acc 304/33; H. Goulburn to S. Goulburn, 13 September 1809, SRO, Acc 304/61.

55 H. Goulburn to S. Goulburn, 23 September 1809, SRO, Acc 304/61; Goulburn memoirs, SRO, Acc 304/68; Peninsular diary, 23, 27 September and 2, 3 October 1809, SRO, Acc 304/33; H. Goulburn to S. Goulburn, 4, 20, 30 October 1809, SRO, Acc 304/61.

56 H. Goulburn to S. Goulburn, 22 October 1809, SRO, Acc 304/61.

57 Peninsular diary, 1 November 1809, SRO, Acc 304/33; H. Goulburn to S. Goulburn, 27 November 1809, SRO, Acc 304/61.

58 H. Goulburn to S. Goulburn, 4 December 1809 and 12 February 1810, SRO, Acc 304/61; Peninsular diary, 1, 24 December 1809, and 11 January, 18 February 1810, SRO Acc 304/33.

CHAPTER TWO

1 Angus Calder, *Revolutionary Empire: The Rise of the English-Speaking Empires from the Fifteenth Century to the 1780s* (London, 1981), 314–15, 323–4, 321–2, 328; Richard S. Dunn, *Sugar and Slaves: The Rise of the Planter Class in the English West Indies, 1624–1713*, pb. ed. (New York, 1973), 149, 40–5; Noel Deer, *The History of Sugar,* 2 vols. (London, 1949), 1:30.

2 For a brief discussion of the attractions of sugar, see Sidney W. Mintz, *Sweetness and Power: The Place of Sugar in Modern History* (New York, 1985); Richard B. Sheridan, *Sugar and Slavery: An Economic History of the British West Indies 1623–1775* (Baltimore, 1973), 21, 24–30; Seymour Drescher, *Econocide: British Slavery in the Era of Abolition* (Pittsburg, 1977), 52; Edward Long, *The History of Jamaica, or General Survey of the Antient and Modern State of that Island,* 3 vols. (London, 1774), 1:435.

3 Long, *History of Jamaica,* 1:435; Dunn, *Sugar and Slaves,* 151, 21, 165; L.J. Ragatz, *The Fall of the Planter Class in the British Caribbean, 1763–1833* (New York, 1928), 132; Sheridan, *Sugar and Slavery,* 342–7, 353.

4 Sheridan, *Sugar and Slavery,* 208; Long, *History of Jamaica,* 2:71, 1:454; Cynric R. Williams, *A Tour through the Island of Jamaica ... in the Year 1823* (London, 1826), 197; M. Goulburn to Thomas Gairdner, 4 January 1791, Surrey Record Office (SRO), Kingston upon Thames, Acc 426.

5 Robin Blackburn, *The Overthrow of Colonial Slavery* (London, 1988), 84; John Stewart, *An Account of Jamaica and Its Inhabitants* (London, 1808), 127–8.

6 Stewart, *An Account of Jamaica*, 129.

7 Ibid., 132; Long, *History of Jamaica*, 1:439–40, 448–9, 451; for a more modern account that developed these criticisms, see Ragatz, *Fall of the Planter Class*, 54–63.

8 B. Edwards, *The History, Civil and Commercial, of the British Colonies in the West Indies*, 5 vols. (1819), 2:287–8, 306; Mintz, *Sweetness and Power*, 49; Drescher, *Econocide*, 43.

9 M.G. Lewis, *Journal of a West Indian Proprietor 1815–17*, ed. Mona Wilson (London, 1929), 90–1; Dunn, *Sugar and Slaves*, 190–1; Sheridan, *Sugar and Slavery*, 108–10; Mintz, *Sweetness and Power*, 49; Michael Craton and James Walvin, *A Jamaican Plantation: The History of Worthy Park 1670–1970* (London, 1970), 101.

10 Sheridan, *Sugar and Slavery*, 112, 269; Dunn, *Sugar and Slaves*, 198, 207–8; for lists of supplies, see SRO, Acc 304/51.

11 J.R. Ward, "The Profitability of Sugar Planting in the British West Indies, 1650–1834," *Economic History Review*, 2nd ser., 31 (1978): 198–9; R.B. Sheridan, "The Wealth of Jamaica: A Rejoinder," *Economic History Review*, 2nd ser., 21 (1968): 51, 46; Craton and Walvin, *Jamaican Plantation*, 118; Orlando Patterson, *The Sociology of Slavery: An Analysis of the Origins, Development and Structure of Negro Slave Society in Jamaica* (London, 1967), 27; J.R. Ward, *British West Indian Slavery 1750–1834: The Process of Amelioration* (Oxford, 1988), 40–2; Robert William Fogel, *Without Consent or Contract: The Rise and Fall of American Slavery* (New York, 1989), 61.

12 In 1770 fully 90 per cent of Jamaica's exports were sugar products, but as coffee became a more important crop, this percentage declined to 75 per cent in 1790 and to 67 per cent by the late 1820s. See David Eltis, *Economic Growth and the Ending of the Transatlantic Slave Trade* (Oxford, 1987), 32; Drescher, *Econocide*, 16, 52; Calder, *Revolutionary Empire*, 632; for an account of the formation of the West Indian lobby, see Lillian M. Penson, "The London West India Interest in the Eighteenth Century," *English Historical Review* 36 (1921): 373–92; Michael Duffy, *Soldiers, Sugar and Seapower: The British Expeditions to the West Indies and the War against Revolutionary France* (Oxford, 1987), 17; Judith Blow Williams, *British Commercial Policy and Trade Expansion 1750–1850* (Oxford, 1972), 9; Ward, "The Profitability of Sugar Planting," 207.

13 Ward, "The Profitability of Sugar Planting," 207; Ragatz, *Fall of the Planter Class*, 297; Herbert S. Klein, *African Slavery in Latin America and the Caribbean* (New York, 1986), 92; Patterson, *Sociology of Slavery*, 27; Penson, "The London West Indian Interest," 385.

14 Mintz, *Sweetness and Power*, 29–30, 32; David Brion Davis, *Slavery and Human Progress* (New York, 1984), 65–8; Dunn, *Sugar and Slaves*, 167; Ward, *British West Indian Slavery*, 10–11; Calder, *Revolutionary Empire*, 450–1; Herbert S.

Klein, "The English Slave Trade to Jamaica, 1782–1808," *Economic History Review,* 2nd ser., 31 (1978): 25.

15 Davis, *Slavery and Human Progress,* 73; Dunn, *Sugar and Slaves,* 224–5, 239–44.

16 See in particular Michael Craton, *Testing the Chains: Resistance to Slavery in the British West Indies* (Ithaca, 1982) (the quotation is from page 15); R.B. Sheridan, "The Wealth of Jamaica in the Eighteenth Century," *Economic History Review,* 2nd ser., 18 (1965): 296.

17 Blackburn, *Overthrow of Colonial Slavery,* 20; Edwards, quoted by R.B. Sheridan, *Doctors and Slaves: A Medical and Demographic History of Slavery in the British West Indies 1680–1834* (Cambridge, 1985), 185, 100; Michael Craton, *Searching for the Invisible Man: Slaves and Plantation Life in Jamaica* (Cambridge, Mass., 1978), 97–9; Ward, *British West Indian Slavery,* 176–7; James Walvin, *Black Ivory: A History of British Slavery,* pb. ed.(London, 1993), 119, 147; Orlando Patterson, *Slavery and Social Death: A Comparative Study* (Cambridge, Mass., 1982), 133.

18 Ward, *British West Indian Slavery,* 130–1; Sheridan, *Doctors and Slaves,* 188–90, 200–3, 228, 247; Dunn, *Sugar and Slaves,* 324; Craton, *Searching for the Invisible Man,* 87, 94–5; Stewart, *An Account of Jamaica,* 223; Long, *History of Jamaica,* 2:269.

19 Craton, *Searching for the Invisible Man,* 55, 119; Sheridan, *Doctors and Slaves,* 135, 171, 177, 276, 95, 43, 70–1, 45–6, 229; Ward, *British West Indian Slavery,* 160–1.

20 Seymour Drescher, *Capitalism and Antislavery: British Mobilization in Comparative Perspective* (London, 1986), 13, 26–8, 34–9; James Oldham, "New Light on Mansfield and Slavery," *Journal of British Studies* 27 (1988):45–68; Calder, *Revolutionary Empire,* 685–8.

21 James Walvin, ed., *Slavery and British Society 1776–1846* (London, 1982), 5; G.R. Mellor, *British Imperial Trusteeship 1783–1850* (London, 1951), 39, 41–2; James Walvin, *England, Slaves and Freedom 1776–1838* (London, 1986), 100; Drescher, *Capitalism and Antislavery,* 43.

22 Mellor, *Imperial Trusteeship,* 16; for the influence of the evangelicals, see in particular Roger Anstey, *The Atlantic Slave Trade and British Abolition 1760–1810* (Atlantic Highlands, 1975); for the influence of Benezet, see C. Duncan Rice, *The Rise and Fall of Black Slavery* (Baton Rouge, 1975), 200, 212–17; for the significance of Wesley's conversion, see Walvin, *England, Slaves and Freedom,* 103; Christine Bolt and Seymour Drescher, eds., *Anti–Slavery, Religion, and Reform: Essays in Memory of Roger Anstey* (Hamden, 1980), 20; David Eltis and James Walvin, eds., *The Abolition of the Atlantic Slave Trade: Origins and Effects in Europe, Africa and the Americas* (Madison, 1981), 27, 33, 6–7.

23 Walvin, *England, Slaves and Freedom,* 107; Walvin, *Slavery and British Society,* 52–8, 23–5; Rice, *Rise and Fall of Black Slavery,* 218–20; Drescher, *Capitalism*

and Antislavery, 78; Eltis and Walvin, *Abolition of the Atlantic Slave Trade,* 64–5.

24 Drescher, *Capitalism and Antislavery,* 69, 73, 58–9; Anstey, *Atlantic Slave Trade and British Abolition,* 266; Mellor, *Imperial Trusteeship,* 47; Blackburn, *Overthrow of Colonial Slavery,* 145; Walvin, *Black Ivory,* 22; Eltis and Walvin, *Abolition of Atlantic Slave Trade,* 221–9.

25 Blackburn, *Overthrow of Colonial Slavery,* 146–7; Anstey, *Atlantic Slave Trade and British Abolition,* 278; Walvin, *Slavery and British Society,* 8–11, 123–8, 144; Bolt and Drescher, *Antislavery, Religion and Reform,* 22–3, 102–14; Frank J. Klingberg, *The Anti-Slavery Movement in England: A Study in English Humanitarianism* (New Haven, 1926), 104–5.

26 Patterson, *Sociology of Slavery,* 77–8; Anstey, *Atlantic Slave Trade and British Abolition,* 286–7, 290; Ragatz, *Fall of the Planter Class,* 268–9.

27 Calder, *Revolutionary Empire,* 688–9; Walvin, *England, Slaves and Freedom,* 82; Blackburn, *Overthrow of Colonial Slavery,* 154–7; Anstey, *Atlantic Slave Trade and British Abolition,* 149, 295; Mellor, *Imperial Trusteeship,* 61; Eltis and Walvin, *Abolition of Atlantic Slave Trade,* 270; Fogel, *Without Consent or Contract,* 213.

28 Drescher, *Econocide,* 13, 71, 73, 98; Klein, "English Slave Trade to Jamaica," 28; Patterson, *Sociology of Slavery,* 78; Ragatz, *Fall of the Planter Class,* 284; Eltis and Walvin, *Abolition of the Atlantic Slave Trade,* 271–2.

29 Anstey, *Atlantic Slave Trade and British Abolition,* 343, 341, 344–5, 275, 347, 357; Peter Jupp, *Lord Grenville 1759–1834* (Oxford, 1985), 356.

30 See Abraham D. Kriegel, "A Convergence of Ethics: Saints and Whigs in British Antislavery," *Journal of British Studies* 26 (1987): 423–50 (the quotation is from page 438); Jupp, *Grenville,* 356–8.

31 Anstey, *Atlantic Slave Trade and British Abolition,* 394–5; Drescher, *Econocide,* 178–9; Drescher, *Capitalism and Antislavery,* 90–1; Jupp, *Grenville,* 388–91; Ragatz, *Fall of the Planter Class,* 277.

32 Craggs to M. Goulburn, 8 August, 1 September 1793, SRO, Acc 304/53.

33 M. Goulburn to Craggs, 6 November 1793, SRO, Acc 304/52; Craggs to S. Goulburn, 28 February 1797, SRO, Acc 304/54.

34 Craggs to S. Goulburn, 22 December 1796, SRO, Acc 304/53; Craggs to S. Goulburn, 15 February 1797, SRO, Acc 304/53; Craggs to S. Goulburn, 28 February, 5 June, 17 August, 20 September, 11 October 1797, SRO, Acc. 304/54; Craggs to S. Goulburn, 6 August, 18 October, 23 October 1798, SRO, Acc 304/53; Craggs to S. Goulburn, 1 February, 28 July, 11 October, 28 November 1799, SRO, Acc 304/54.

35 Craggs to S. Goulburn, 20 February, 18 March, 19 June, 13 August, 10 September 1800, SRO, Acc 304/53; Craggs to S. Goulburn, 16 July 1801, and Craggs to H. Goulburn, 6 August, 4 September 1801, SRO, Acc 304/51; S. Goulburn to Craggs, 18 November 1800, SRO, Acc 304/53; H. Goulburn to Craggs, 3 June 1801, SRO, Acc 304/51.

36 Falconer to S. Goulburn, 3 October 1801, 10 February 1802, and Samson to S. Goulburn, 30 October 1801, SRO, Acc 304/51; "A friend of Humanity" to S. Goulburn, 1 November 1801, and Craggs to S. Goulburn, 19 September 1799, SRO, Acc 304/54.

37 Moir to S. Goulburn, 10 April, 1 May, 1802, SRO, Acc 304/54; Samson to S. Goulburn, 8 April, 30 September 1802, and S. Goulburn to Samson, n.d.[1802], 4 August 1802, SRO, Acc 304/52.

38 Samson to S. Goulburn, 7 August, 3 September, 24 December 1802, SRO, Acc 304/54; S. Goulburn to Samson, 6 October 1802, SRO, Acc 304/54; Moir to S. Goulburn, 23 December 1802, SRO, Acc 304/54; Samson to S. Goulburn 19, 20 May 1803, SRO, Acc 304/53.

39 S. Goulburn to J. Edwards, 3 November 1802, SRO, Acc 304/52; S. Goulburn to Shand, 3 November 1802, SRO, Acc 304/54; Falconer to Goore, 3 September 1802, and Goore to S. Goulburn, 28 October 1802, 24 October 1803, 17 March 1804, SRO, Acc 304/52; Samson to H. Goulburn, 3 August 1804, SRO, Acc 304/51.

40 Samson to S. Goulburn, 5 March, 24 December, 1802, SRO, Acc 304/54; Samson to S. Goulburn, 14 January 1803, SRO, Acc 304/53; Samson to S. Goulburn, 8 March, 13 July, 1804, SRO, Acc 304/51; H. Goulburn to Samson, 29 June 1804, and Samson to H. Goulburn, 3 August 1804, SRO, Acc 304/51; Samson to H. Goulburn, 25 January, 15 March, 10 May, 7 June, 25 June, 1 August 1805, SRO, Acc 304/53.

41 H. Goulburn to Samson, 5 November 1805, SRO, Acc 426.

42 H. Goulburn to Samson, 5 November 1805, SRO, Acc 426; Samson to H. Goulburn, 18 January 1806, SRO, Acc 304/53.

43 H. Goulburn to Samson, 1 April, 28 June 1806, and 6 January 1807, SRO, Acc 426.

44 Samson to H. Goulburn, 13 March 1807, and 13 November, 12 December 1806, SRO, Acc 304/53.

45 Report on slaves, 1807, SRO, Acc 304/59; Samson to H. Goulburn, 25 April, 10 September 1808, SRO Acc 304/53; ibid., 15 June 1809, SRO, Acc 304/51.

46 H. Goulburn to Samson, 28 August 1810, 10 September 1811, SRO, Acc 416.

47 Samson to H. Goulburn, 23 November 1810, SRO, Acc 304/52.

48 Samson to S. Goulburn, 5 March, 15 October 1802, SRO, Acc 304/54; Samson to S. Goulburn, 19 May, 10 September 1803, SRO, Acc 304/53; Samson to H. Goulburn 26 April 1804, SRO, Acc 304/51; Samson to H. Goulburn, 15 March 1805, SRO, Acc 304/53; Craggs to M. Goulburn, 8 August 1793, SRO, Acc 304/53; Samson to H. Goulburn, 15 December 1803, and 12 January, 9 November 1804, SRO, Acc 304/51; ibid., 10 May 1805, SRO, Acc 304/53; H. Goulburn to Samson, 29 June 1804, SRO, Acc 304/51.

49 Goore to H. Goulburn, 25 May 1805, SRO, Acc 304/52; accounts submitted to Chancery, SRO, Acc 304/51; see also SRO, Acc 304/52; G.S. Ramlackhansingh, "Amity Hall 1760–1860: The Geography of a Jamaican Plantation," MSC thesis, University of London, 1966, 318.

50 Goore to S. Goulburn, 24 October 1803, SRO, Acc 304/52; H. Goulburn to Samson, 30 April, 5 June, 3 July 1805, and 7 April 1808, SRO, Acc 426.

51 Samson to H. Goulburn, 1 August, 28 October, 20 December 1805, 23 April, 18 June, 9 October 1806, 19 August, 11 December 1807, and 6 March, 16 June, 8 December 1808, SRO, Acc 304/53; ibid., 17 May, 20 July 1810, GP, Acc 304/52.

CHAPTER THREE

1 Roland Thorne ed., *The House of Commons 1790–1820*, 5 vols. (London, 1986), 4:78, 2:395; Montagu to Dudley Ryder, n.d. [July 1783], Sandon Hall (SH), Stafford, Harrowby Mss. vol. 8.

2 George Leveson Gower, *Hary-O: The Letters of Lady Harriet Cavendish, 1796–1809* (London, 1940), 305, 312; H. Goulburn to J. Goulburn, n.d. [1824], Surrey Record Office (SRO), Kingston upon Thames, Acc 304/67; E.A. to Mrs Montagu, 3 December 1811, SRO, Acc 304/31; Lady Grovesnor to Mrs Montagu, 4 December 1811, SRO, Acc 304/31; Laura Waldegrave to Mrs Montagu, 5 December 1811, SRO, Acc 304/31; William Montagu to Jane Montagu, 5 October 1811, SRO, Acc 304/31; S. Goulburn to H. Goulburn, n.d.[December 1811], SRO, Acc 304/31.

3 E.A. to Mrs Montagu, 3 December 1811, Susan Bathurst to Jane Montagu, n.d. [December 1811], and Lady Grovesnor to Mrs Montagu, 4 December 1811, SRO, Acc 304/31; F.M.L. Thompson, *English Landed Society in the Nineteenth Century*, pb. ed. (London, 1963), 16; J. Montagu to H. Goulburn, 6 December 1811, SRO, Acc 304/67; Goulburn memoirs, SRO, Acc 304/68.

4 Dennis Gray, *Spencer Perceval: The Evangelical Prime Minister, 1762–1812* (Manchester, 1963), 141; abstract of marriage settlement, 18 December 1811, SRO, Acc 304/52; for details of Goulburn's income in 1811, see SRO, Acc 304/24; Nethersole to H. Goulburn, 11 September 1811, SRO, Acc 304/52; Goulburn memoirs, SRO, Acc 304/68.

5 Peter Jupp, ed., *The Letter-Journal of George Canning 1793–1795* (London 1991), 274; see SRO, Acc 1180/18; Goulburn to J. Goulburn, 2 July 1812, SRO, Acc 304/31; J. Goulburn to H. Goulburn, 14 October 1813, SRO, Acc 304/67; Stewart to J. Goulburn, n.d. [1812], SRO, Acc 304/31; Goulburn memoirs, SRO, Acc 304/68.

6 Goulburn memoirs, SRO, Acc 304/68; Ryder to Yorke, 28 October 1809, Hardwicke Papers, British Library (BL), Add. Ms. 45038; Gray, *Spencer Perceval*, 273–4.

7   See R.R. Nelson, *The Home Office 1782–1801* (Durham, N.C., 1969), 6–7, 19, 21–2, 83, 125, 136, 139–41; J.C. Sainty, *Home Office Officials 1782–1870* (London, 1975), 1–3; Elizabeth Sparrow, "The Alien Office, 1792–1806," *Historical Journal* 32 (1990): 362.

8   F.M.L. Thompson, ed., *Cambridge Social History of Britain 1750–1950*, vol. 3 (Cambridge, 1990), 1, 8; John Rule, *The Vital Century: England's Developing Economy 1714–1815* (London, 1992), 285; Philip Harling and Peter Mandler, "From 'Fiscal-Military' State to Laissez-faire State, 1760–1850," *Journal of British Studies* 32 (1993): 54; Nelson, *Home Office*, 39, 67, 41, 27, 43.

9   Thompson, *Cambridge Social History*, 3:8; Henry Parris, *Constitutional Bureaucracy: The Development of British Central Administration since the Eighteenth Century* (London, 1969), 109, 43–4; Goulburn memoirs, SRO, Acc 304/68; Thorne, *House of Commons 1790–1820*, 2:168–9; Sainty, *Home Office Officials*, 3.

10 Nelson, *Home Office*, 53; Goulburn memoirs, SRO, Acc 304/68; Gray, *Spencer Perceval*, 289–98; M.W. Patterson, *Sir Francis Burdett and His Times (1770–1844)*, 2 vols. (London, 1931), 1:240–88.

11 Torrens to Goulburn, 4 September 1810, Public Record Office (PRO), Home Office (HO) 50/547; Goulburn to Peel, 2 January 1811, PRO, War Office (WO) 1/776; Goulburn to Freeling, 23 March 1811, PRO, HO 43/19; Goulburn to Manley, 5 October 1811, 20 April 1812, PRO, HO 43/19.

12 Clive Emsley, *British Society and the French Wars, 1793–1815* (London, 1979), 132; J.W. Fortescue, *A History of the British Army*, 13 vols. (London, 1899–1930), 7:334, 10:183–5.

13 For Goulburn's correspondence on volunteers, see PRO, HO 57/87, 88; for militia recruiting, see PRO, HO 50/422; memorandum on recruiting, [n.d.], SH, Harrowby Mss., 1235a; for the requests concerning the Militia Acts, see PRO, HO 50/245; Goulburn memoirs, SRO, Acc 304/68.

14 Goulburn memoirs, SRO, Acc 304/68; Castlereagh to Ryder, 20 April [1811], SH, Harrowby Mss., vol. 97; Duke of York to Ryder, 17 July, 5 August 1811, PRO, HO 50/420; *Quarterly Review* 6 (1811): 409.

15 Emsley, *British Society and the French Wars*, 153–8.

16 Ryder to Maitland, 7 May 1812, PRO, HO 43/20; J.L. Hammond and Barbara Hammond, *The New Town Labourer 1760–1832: The New Civilization*, reprint ed. (New York, 1967), 81–2.

17 Ryder to Fitzwilliam, 12 May 1812, PRO, HO 43/20; Goulburn to Carden, 15 May 1812, and Goulburn to Lt. Col. South Hants Militia, 15 May 1812, PRO, HO 43/20; Merry to Goulburn, 15 April, 15 May 1812, PRO, HO 50/424.

18 Goulburn memoirs, SRO, Acc 304/68; *Morning Chronicle*, 12, 19 May 1812; Henry Brougham, *Historical Sketches of Statesmen Who Flourished in the Time of George III*, vol. 1 (London, 1855), 329.

19 Christopher Hibbert, *George IV*, pb. ed. (London, 1976), 388–92; Ryder to Yorke, 29 May 1812, BL, Add. Ms. 45038; Goulburn memoirs, SRO, Acc 304/68.

20 *Morning Chronicle*, 9, 11 June 1812; *Quarterly Review* 6 (1811): 409; Norman Gash, *Mr. Secretary Peel: The Life of Sir Robert Peel to 1830*, 2nd ed. (London, 1985), 88–90; Brian Jenkins, *Era of Emancipation: British Government of Ireland 1812–1830* (Montreal, 1988), 57.

21 For a helpful and brief survey of the historiography of imperialism, see P.J. Cain and A.G. Hopkins, *British Imperialism: Innovation and Expansion 1688–1914* (London, 1993), 5–16, 56–7; Jonathan Parry, *The Rise and Fall of Liberal Government in Victorian Britain* (New Haven, 1993), 23; Paul Knaplund, *James Stephen and the British Colonial System 1813–1847* (Madison, 1953), 3; Klaus E. Knorr, *British Colonial Theories 1570–1850* (Toronto, 1944), 176–83, 207–11, 246; *Quarterly Review* 6 (1811): 497; C.A. Bayly, *Imperial Meridian: The British Empire and the World, 1780–1830* (London, 1989), 146–9, 160; for the anti-French character of British nationalism, see Gerald Newman, "Anti-French Propaganda and British Liberal Nationalism in the Early Nineteenth Century: Suggestions towards a General Interpretation," *Victorian Studies* 18 (1974–75): 385–418; *Quarterly Review* 39 (1829): 215.

22 Knorr, *British Colonial Theories*, 223–5, 261–5; Bernard Semmel, *The Rise of Free Trade Imperialism: Classical Political Economy, the Empire of Free Trade and Imperialism, 1750–1850* (Cambridge, 1970), 44–7; John Manning Ward, *Colonial Self-Government: The British Experience 1759–1856* (London, 1976), 218; R. Koebner, *Empire* (Cambridge, 1961), 291–2.

23 *Quarterly Review* 5 (1811): 416; Ward, *Colonial Self-Government*, 218–19; Knorr, *British Colonial Theories*, 245–6; Cain and Hopkins, *British Imperialism*, 97, 44; Philip A. Buckner, *The Transition to Responsible Government: British Policy in British North America 1815–1850* (Westport, Conn., 1985), 22–3.

24 Bayly, *Imperial Meridian*, 162, 195; Buckner, *Transition to Responsible Government*, 17–21, 47.

25 D.J. Murray, *The West Indies and the Development of Colonial Government* (Oxford, 1965), 102, 1–4; A.G.L. Shaw, "British Attitudes to the Colonies ca. 1820–1850," *Journal of British Studies* 9 (1969): 89, 92; Cain and Hopkins, in *British Imperialism*, argue that greater central control was asserted during this period (see 96–7); Ward, *Colonial Self-Government*, 82–3, 86.

26 Murray, *The West Indies*, 93–4; Ward, *Colonial Self-Government*, 90–1; D.M. Young, *The Colonial Office in the Early Nineteenth Century* (London, 1961), 201.

27 Young, *Colonial Office*, 253, 124–46, 155.

28 Ibid., 21, 15–17, 4; Murray, *The West Indies*, 114–15; Henry Reeve, ed., *The Greville Memoirs*, 3 vols. (London, 1874), 3:116; Charles Duke Yonge, *The Life and Administration of Robert Banks, Second Earl Liverpool*, 3 vols. (London, 1868), 1:309–10.

29 Young, *Colonial Office*, 18–19, 52–3, 91–2; Henry Taylor, *Autobiography*, 2 vols. (London, 1874), 1:40–3; Goulburn memoirs, SRO, Acc 304/68; *Greville Memoirs*, 3:115.

30 Charles J.F. Bunbury, ed., *Memoir and Literary Remains of Lieutenant-General Sir Henry Bunbury* (London, 1968), 58–9.

31 Goulburn memoirs, SRO, Acc 304/68; Goulburn to Peel, 23 September, 2, 6, 7 October 1812, BL, Add. Ms. 40221; Goulburn to Peel, 15 October, 6, 14 November 1812, BL, Add. Ms. 40222.

32 Goulburn to Peel, 13 September 1813, BL, Add. Ms. 40230; Goulburn to Peel, 3 January 1814, BL, Add. Ms. 40233.

33 J.C. Sainty, *Colonial Office Officials 1784–1870* (London, 1976), 9; Goulburn memoirs, SRO, Acc 304/68; Buckner, *Transition to Responsible Government*, 30, 16, 93; Murray, *The West Indies*, 117; Young, *Colonial Office*, 169, 177, 179; the most careful examination of the handling of Colonial Office business remains that of Helen Taft Manning, *British Colonial Government after the American Revolution* (New Haven, 1933), 481–3.

34 *Parl. Deb.*, 1st ser., 36:68; *Parl. Deb.*, 1st ser., 32:1251–2, 1257; Parry, *Rise and Fall of Liberal Government*, 34.

35 Peel to Goulburn, 12 August 1812, SRO, Acc 304/35; for secret service accounts, see SRO, Acc 304/32, Acc 304/33, and PRO, WO 1/926; William Doyle, *The Oxford History of the French Revolution* (Oxford, 1989), 282–3.

36 Peel to Goulburn, 12 August 1812, SRO, Acc 304/35.

37 *Quarterly Review* 6 (1811): 497–8; Peel to Goulburn, 12 August 1812, SRO, Acc 304/35.

38 Peel to Goulburn, 12 August 1812, SRO, Acc 304/35.

39 Goulburn to Peel, 16 September 1812, BL, Add. Ms. 40221; Goulburn memoirs, SRO, Acc 304/68; D.B. Swinfen, *Imperial Control of Colonial Legislation 1813–1865: A Study of British Policy towards Colonial Legislative Powers* (Oxford, 1970), 21, 4; Manning, *British Colonial Government*, 493; Knaplund, *James Stephen*, 12; Young, *Colonial Office*, 58.

40 Order in council, PRO, CO 295/28; Monro to Bathurst, 11 September 1812, PRO, CO 295/28; Woodford to Bathurst, 14 September, 18 October 1813, PRO, CO 295/30; Woodford to Bathurst, 12 November 1813, PRO, CO 295/31; Stephen to Bathurst, 24 August 1813, PRO, CO 295/31.

41 Stephen to Bathurst, 24 August 1813, PRO, CO 295/31; Woodford to Bathurst, 4 January, 18 March 1814, PRO, CO 295/32; A. Meredith John, "The Smuggled Slaves of Trinidad, 1813," *Historical Journal* 31 (1988): 365–75; *Parl. Deb.*, 2nd ser., 7:1843–4.

42 Resolutions of the "General Meeting of Planters, Merchants ... Trinidad," 13 February 1812, PRO, CO 295/28; Woodford to Bathurst, 1, 6 July, 13 August 1813, PRO, CO 295/29; Woodford to Bathurst, 12 November 1813, PRO, CO 295/31; Woodford to Bathurst, 4 January, 19 February 1814, PRO, CO 295/32.

43 Woodford to Bathurst, 7 July 1813, PRO, CO, 295/29; Woodford to Bathurst, 3 August 1813, PRO, CO 295/30; Woodford to Bathurst, 4 January 1814, PRO, CO 295/32; Manning, *British Colonial Government*, 514–21, 495–501; Young, *Colonial Office*, 184–9; Murray, *The West Indies*, 102; *Parl. Deb.*, 1st ser., 27:340–1, 377, 436–8; Goulburn memoirs, SRO, Acc 304/68.

44 Gaillard Hunt, ed., *The Writings of James Madison*, vol. 8 (New York, 1909), 192–200; James Ketcham, *James Madison*, pb. ed. (London, 1990), 528–9; J.C.A. Stagg, *Mr. Madison's War: Politics, Diplomacy, and Warfare in the Early American Republic 1783–1830* (Princeton, 1983), 110–17; Paul A. Varg, *New England and Foreign Relations 1789–1850* (Hanover, 1983), 52; Roger H. Brown, *Republic in Peril: 1812* pb. ed. (New York, 1971), 131–76.

45 J. Mackay Hitsman, *The Incredible War of 1812: A Military History* (Toronto, 1965), 24–5, 27–8; Philip P. Mason, ed., *After Tippecanoe: Some Aspects of the War of 1812* (Toronto, 1963), 30, 14; Prevost to Liverpool, 18 May 1812, PRO, CO 42/146; James M. Banner, Jr, *To the Hartford Convention: The Federalists and the Origins of Party Politics in Massachusetts, 1789–1815* (New York, 1970), 306–7; Varg, *New England and Foreign Relations*, 62–3; Robert Allen Rutland, *James Madison: The Founding Father* (London, 1987), 225; Ketcham, *James Madison*, 537; Prevost to Liverpool, 15 July 1812, PRO, CO 42/147.

46 Mason, *After Tippecanoe*, 17–23; Brock to Liverpool, 29 August 1812, PRO, CO 42/524.

47 Gregory Evans Dowd, *A Spiritual Resistance: The North American Indian Struggle for Unity, 1745–1815* (Baltimore, 1992), 27, 119; J. Leitch Wright, Jr, *Britain and the American Frontier 1783–1815* (Athens, 1975), 20–5, 29; Brock to Liverpool, 29 August 1812, PRO, CO 42/524.

48 Mason, *After Tippecanoe*, 67, 34; Brock to Liverpool, 29 August 1812, PRO, CO 42/524; Brock to his brothers, 18 September 1812, PRO, CO 42/523.

49 *Edinburgh Review* 19 (1812): 308; Historical Manuscripts Commission, *Report on the Manuscripts of J.B. Fortescue, Esq., Preserved at Dropmore* (London, 1927), 10:124, 286; Liverpool to Prevost, 15 May 1812, PRO, CO 43/23; Donald R. Hickey, *The War of 1812: A Forgotten Conflict* (Chicago, 1989), 42–3, 31–2; *Edinburgh Review* 20 (1812): 233; *Morning Chronicle*, 26 June 1812; Bathurst to Prevost, 4 July 1812, PRO, CO 43/23; Frank A. Updike, *The Diplomacy of the War of 1812*, reprint ed. (Gloucester, Mass., 1965), 60, 136–41.

50 *Edinburgh Review* 21 (1812): 457, 462, 460; Bradford Perkins, *Castlereagh and Adams: England and the United States 1812–1823* (Berkeley, 1964), 15; *Quarterly Review* 8 (1812): 202–3; Clifford L. Egan, *Neither Peace Nor War: Franco-American Relations 1803–1812* (Baton Rouge, 1983), 176; Lawrence Kaplan, "France and the War of 1812," *Journal of American History* 57 (1970): 36–41; Wright, *Britain and the American Frontier*, 155–7; Philip Coolidge Brooks, *Diplomacy of the Borderlands: The Adams-Onís Treaty*

of 1819, reprint ed. (New York, 1970), 34–6; Goulburn memoirs, SRO, Acc 304/68.

51 Bathurst to Prevost, 10 August, 1, 10 October, 8 December 1812, PRO, CO 43/23; Bathurst to Brock, 16 November 1812, PRO, CO 43/40; Goulburn to Peel, 6 October 1812, BL, Add Ms. 40221.

52 Bathurst to Prevost, 10 August, 1, 10 October, 8 December 1812, PRO, CO 43/23; Bathurst to Brock, 16 November 1812, PRO, CO 43/40; Goulburn to Peel, 6 October 1812, BL, Add. Ms. 40221; Goulburn memoirs, SRO, Acc 304/68.

53 Brock to Liverpool, 29 August 1812, PRO, CO 42/524; Prevost to Bathurst, 5 October 1812, PRO, CO 42/147; Wright, *Britain and the American Frontier*, 69–72; Bathurst to Brock, 16 November 1812, PRO, CO 43/40; Bathurst to Prevost, 9 December 1812, PRO, CO 43/23; Prevost to Bathurst, 19 March 1813, PRO, CO 42/150.

54 Bathurst to Prevost, 16 November 1812, PRO, CO 43/23; Prevost to Bathurst, 17 October 1812, PRO, CO 42/147; Prevost to Bathurst, 21 November 1812, PRO, CO 42/148; Bathurst to Prevost, 9 December 1812, PRO, CO 43/23; Sheaffe to Bathurst, 5 April, 13 May 1813, PRO, CO 42/324; Prevost to Bathurst, 22 September 1813, PRO, CO 42/151.

55 Bathurst to Prevost, 5 November, 12 March, 15 December 1813, PRO, CO 43/23; Prevost to Bathurst, 9 May 1814, PRO, CO 42/156; Drummond to Bathurst, 3 July 1814, PRO, CO 42/355; Prevost to Bathurst, 6 November 1814, PRO, CO 42/157; Mason, *After Tippecanoe*, 56–7.

56 Bathurst to Prevost, 12 January 1813, PRO, CO 43/23; Bathurst to Beckwith, 18 March 1813, PRO, CO 43/23; Banner, *Hartford Convention*, 313–14.

57 Prevost to Bathurst, 21 April 1813, PRO, CO 42/150; Bathurst to Prevost, 11 February, 12 March, 1 July, 13 August 1813, PRO, CO 43/23; Prevost to Bathurst, 15 September 1813, PRO, CO 42/151.

58 Bathurst to Prevost, 15 December 1813, 20 January, 14 April, 3 June 1814, PRO, CO 43/23.

59 Bathurst to Prevost, 3 June, 11 July, 1814, PRO, CO 43/23.

60 Georgiana, Lady Chatterton, *Memorials Personal and Historical of Admiral Lord Gambier*, 2 vols. (London, 1861); Perkins, *Castlereagh and Adams*, 58–9; J.Q. Adams to Monroe, 5 September 1814, Dept. of State, Ghent, in National Archives (NA), Washington, 36/1.

61 Castlereagh to Baring, 8 October 1813, Goulburn Papers, University of Michigan (UM), Ann Arbour, microfilm, reel 1; C.J. Bartlett, *Castlereagh* (London, 1966), 119–30, 133–4; Henry Adams ed., *The Writings of Albert Gallatin*, 3 vols. (Philadelphia, 1879), 1:618–19.

62 Raymond Walters, *Albert Gallatin: Jeffersonian Financier and Diplomat* (New York, 1957), 259; Ketcham, *James Madison*, 481–4; Steven Watts, *The Republic Reborn: War and the Making of Liberal America 1790–1820* (Baltimore,

1987), 207; Merrill Petersen, *The Great Triumvirate: Webster, Clay, Calhoun* (New York, 1987), 4–18, 39–45; Robert V. Remini, *Henry Clay, Statesman for the Union* (New York, 1991); Castlereagh to Liverpool, 28 August 1814, BL, Add. Ms. 38259.

63 James F. Hopkins et al., eds., *The Papers of Henry Clay*, 2 vols. (Lexington, 1959–61), 1:913–14, 919, 947–8; Goulburn to K. Montagu, 31 July 1814, SRO, Acc 304/40.

64 Elizabeth Donnan, ed., "The Papers of James A. Bayard 1796–1815," *American Historical Association Annual Report* 2 (1913): 205, 215, 228–9; *Writings of Gallatin*, 1:540–4, 611–12.

65 Castlereagh to commissioners, 28 July 1814, UM, Goulburn Papers, reel 1; see also draft instructions, 28 July 1814, PRO, Foreign Office (FO) 5/101; *Papers of Clay*, 1:954–9, 963–5; Daniel George Lang, *Foreign Policy in the Early Republic: The Law of Nations and the Balance of Power* (Baton Rouge, 1985), 72–3, 115–16.

66 Goulburn to K. Montagu, 31 July 1814, SRO, Acc 304/30; Diary of John Quincy Adams, 3, 5 July, 7 August 1814, Massachusetts Historical Society (MHS), Adams Papers, microfilm, reel 32; Goulburn to Peel, 30 October 1814, BL, Add. Ms. 40240.

67 Goulburn to K. Montagu, 11 September, 4 October 1814, SRO, Acc 304/30; Goulburn to S. Goulburn, 18, 25 October 1814, SRO, Acc 304/61; Goulburn to Peel, 30 October 1814, BL, Add. Ms. 40240.

68 Goulburn to K. Montagu, 4 October 1814, SRO, Acc 304/30.

69 Adams to Monroe, 5 September 1814, NA, 36/1; Wellington, *Supplementary Despatches, Correspondence, and Memoranda: Field Marshal Arthur Duke of Wellington, K.G., 1794–1818*, 15 vols. (London 1858–72), 9:452–4, 189–91, 217; Goulburn to Peel, 30 October 1814, BL, Add. Ms. 40240; Goulburn to K. Montagu, 11 September 1814, SRO, Acc 304/30; Goulburn to Bathurst, 16 September 1814, UM, Goulburn Papers, reel 1.

70 Adams to Monroe, 5 September 1814, NA, 36/1; Wellington, *Supplementary Despatches*, 9:177; Donnan, "Papers of Bayard," 316; Castlereagh to commissioners, 14 August 1814, UM, Goulburn Papers, reel 1.

71 Diary of J.Q. Adams, 1 September 1814, MHS, Adams Papers, reel 32; Goulburn to Bathurst, 16 September 1814, UM, Goulburn Papers, reel 1.

72 Goulburn to Castlereagh, 24 August [1814], and Castlereagh to Goulburn, 28 August 1814, UM, Goulburn Papers, reel 1; Wellington, *Supplementary Despatches*, 9:189–91, 217, 287; *Writings of Gallatin*, 1:638, 640; Historical Manuscripts Commission, *Report on the Manuscripts of Earl Bathurst* (London, 1923) (hereafter *HMC: Bathurst*), 294–5; Bathurst to Goulburn, 4, 5 October 1814, UM, Goulburn Papers, reel 1; *Papers of Clay*, 1:989, 982–6.

73 Castlereagh to Liverpool, 28 August 1814, BL, Add. Ms. 38259; *HMC: Bathurst*, 286–9, 284–5; Bathurst to Prevost, 27 August, 15 October 1814, PRO, CO 43/23.

74 Liverpool to Castlereagh, 2 November 1814, BL, Add. Ms. 38572; Bathurst to Goulburn, 6 December, 15, 21 November 1814, UM, Goulburn Papers, reel 1; Wellington, *Supplementary Despatches*, 9:436–7; *Parl. Deb.*, 1st ser., 29:376–85, 368–76.

75 Bathurst to Goulburn, 21 November, 6, 19 December 1814, UM, Goulburn Papers, reel 1; Diary of J.Q. Adams, 12 December 1814, MHS, Adams Papers, reel 32.

76 A.L. Burt, *The United States, Great Britain, and British North America from the Revolution to the Establishment of Peace after the War of 1812* (New Haven, 1940), 371; *Courier*, 27 December 1814; *Papers of Clay*, 1:1007; Donnan, "Papers of Bayard," 366.

77 *Morning Chronicle*, 27 December 1814; Perkins, *Castlereagh and Adams*, 134, 131; Canning to Liverpool, 14 January 1815, BL, Add. Ms. 38193; Bathurst to Goulburn, 19 December 1814, UM, Goulburn Papers, reel 1; for a statement of the importance of the treaty unqualified by even a hint of British understatement, see Paul Johnson, *The Birth of the Modern World Society 1815–1830* (New York, 1991), 41; J. Goulburn to W. Montagu, 24 December 1814, SRO, Acc 304/64.

78 *Morning Chronicle*, 9, 10, 16, 21 March 1815; *Parl. Deb.*, 1st ser., 30:500–18, 531–2.

CHAPTER FOUR

1 Goulburn memoirs, Surrey Record Office (SRO), Kingston upon Thames, Acc 304/68; H. Goulburn to K. Montagu, 28 June 1815, SRO, Acc 304/30.

2 Goulburn to K. Montagu, 28 June 1825, SRO, Acc 304/30; Goulburn memoirs, SRO, Acc 304/68; Goulburn to Bathurst, 4 August 1812, British Library (BL) Loan 57/22; Bathurst to Lowe, 12 September 1815, Lowe Papers, BL, Add. Ms. 20114; Julian Park, ed. and trans., *Napoleon in Captivity: The Reports of Count Balmain, Russian Commissioner, on the Island of St. Helena 1816–1820*, reprint ed. (New York, 1971), 15, 22.

3 Minute, 11 May 1815, Public Record Office (PRO), London, FO 5/109; J.Q. Adams to Monroe, 23 February 1815, National Archives (NA), Washington, M30/15; James F. Hopkins et al., eds., *The Papers of Henry Clay*, 2 vols. (Lexington, 1959–61) 2:22.

4 Diary of J.Q. Adams, 12, 28 February 1815, Massachusetts Historical Society (MHS), Adams Papers, reel 32; Clay and Gallatin to Monroe, 18 April 1815, NA, 36/1; *Papers of Clay*, 2:12, 18–22, 24–5, 38–9.

5 J.Q. Adams to Monroe, 9 May 1815, NA, M30/15; *Papers of Clay*, 2:25, 23.

6 Minute of the conference of 11 May 1815, PRO, FO 5/109.

7 See the minute of this conference, 11 May 1815, PRO, FO 5/109; *Papers of Clay*, 2:28–37.

8 J. Q. Adams diary, 27 May, 7 June 1815, MHS, Adams Papers, reel 32.

9 J.Q. Adams diary, 24, 27 May, 7 June 1815, MHS, Adams Papers, reel 32; British comissioners to Castlereagh, 7 June 1815, PRO, FO 5/109; *Papers of Clay*, 2:40–3.

10 J.Q. Adams diary, 9, 19, 20, 23 June 1815, MHS, Adams Papers, reel 32; *Papers of Clay*, 2:40–59, 26; British commissioners to Castlereagh, 4 July 1815, PRO, FO 5/109; Robinson to Castlereagh, 19, 21 June 1815, PRO, FO 5/109.

11 J.Q. Adams diary, 3 July 1815, MHS, Adams Papers, reel 32; Henry Adams, ed., *The Writings of Albert Gallatin*, 3 vols. (Philadelphia, 1879), 1:650; Adams to Monroe, 19 September 1815, NA, M30/15.

12 J. Goulburn to K. Montagu, 1 August 1815, SRO, Acc 304/30; H. Goulburn to Peel, 2 September 1815, BL, Add. Ms. 40333; H. Goulburn to K. Montagu, 28 June, 20 September 1815, SRO, Acc 304/30.

13 Goulburn memoirs, SRO, Acc 304/68; H.E. Malden, *The Victorian History of the County of Surrey* (London, 1911), 3:166–9; for specifications of the house and estate, see SRO, Acc 304/68.

14 Goulburn memoirs, SRO, Acc 304/68; H. Goulburn to J. Goulburn, n.d. [July 1816], and 28 September 1816, SRO, Acc 304/61.

15 See Goulburn's account books, SRO, Acc 304/24.

16 Goulburn memoirs, SRO, Acc 304/68; Robert Isaac Wilberforce and Samuel Wilberforce, *The Life of William Wilberforce*, 5 vols. (London, 1838), 4:176–7, 182–9, 192–7; Richard Sheridan, *Doctors and Slaves: A Medical and Demographic History of Slavery in the West Indies, 1680–1834* (Cambridge, 1985), 230.

17 Samson to Goulburn, 1, 30 March, 9 August 1811, 12 June, 29 October, 7 December 1812, 29 January, 20 February, 18 March, 23 April, 21 May, 20 July 1813, and 9 March 1815, SRO, Acc 304/51.

18 Samson to Goulburn, 14 May, 20 September 1811, and 20 February, 12 March 1812, SRO, Acc 304/51.

19 Slave returns, 1811, SRO, Acc 304/51; Samson to Goulburn, 24 June, 20 September 1811, 20 February 1812, and 20 February, 18 March, 28 April 1813, SRO, Acc 304/51; Orlando Patterson, *The Sociology of Slavery* (London, 1967), 106–9.

20 Goulburn to Samson, 3 August 1813, Samson to Goulburn, 15 October 1813, Goulburn to Samson, 25 October 1814, Samson to Goulburn, 12 January, 11 August, 6 October 1815, and 28 March 1816, SRO, Acc 304/51.

21 Samson to Goulburn, 28 March 1816, 10 February 1814, 21 April, 9 June 1815, Goulburn to Samson, 25 October 1814, and Samson to Goulburn, 10 December 1813, SRO, Acc 304/51.

22 Richards to Goulburn, 27 November 1812, and Samson to Goulburn, 29 October 1812, SRO, Acc 304/51; Goulburn memoirs, SRO, Acc 304/68; Richards to Goore, 12 July 1817, SRO, Acc 304/51.

23 Samson to Goulburn, 16 October, 7 November 1817, and 20 February, 18 April, 9 July, 6 August 1818, SRO, Acc 304/51; Richards to Goulburn 8 May 1819, SRO, Acc 304/51.

24 Goulburn to Samson, 9 January 1818, Samson to Goulburn, 20 February 1818, and Richards to Goulburn, 9 March 1818, SRO, Acc 304/51; Goulburn memoirs, SRO, Acc 304/68.

25 F. Goulburn to H. Goulburn, 22 February 1818, SRO, Acc 304/51; in 1814, for example, seventy barrels of herring were shipped to Amity Hall. See the lists of supplies, SRO, Acc 304/51.

26 Richards to Goulburn, 5 September 1818, 16 January 1819, SRO, Acc 304/51.

27 Richards to Goulburn, 5 September 1818, 7 February 1819, SRO, Acc 304/51.

28 Richards to Goulburn, 5 September 1818, 16 January 1819, SRO, Acc 304/51; G.S. Ramlackhansingh, "Amity Hall 1760–1860: The Geography of a Jamaican Plantation," MSC thesis, University of London, 1966, 319, 145; see annual slave return, 1819–22, SRO, Acc 304/51; Richards to Goulburn, 9 January 1821, SRO, Acc 304/51; Goulburn memoirs, SRO, Acc 304/68.

29 Peel to Whitworth, 19 March 1817, Whitworth Papers, Centre for Kentish Studies (CKS), Maidstone; Goulburn memoirs, SRO, Acc 304/68.

30 Peel to Goulburn, 19 March [1820], SRO, Acc 304/35; George Peel, ed., *The Private Letters of Sir Robert Peel* (London, 1920), 32; H. Goulburn to J. Goulburn, 26 January 1819, SRO, Acc 304/31.

31 Goulburn memoirs, SRO, Acc 304/68.

32 Goulburn to Bathurst, 30 July 1821, Bathurst Papers, on loan to British Library (BL Loan) 57/13; H. Goulburn to J. Goulburn, n.d. [1819], SRO, Acc 304/61; H. Goulburn to J. Goulburn, n.d. [1819], SRO, Acc 304/64; H. Goulburn to J. Goulburn, 23 February 1820, SRO, Acc 304/64; see also the fees paid to Knighton, SRO, Acc 304/24.

33 See, for example, Goulburn to Bathurst, 4, 5, 6, 8 December 1815, BL Loan 57/10; Goulburn to Bathurst, 10, 15 January 1816, BL Loan 57/11; Goulburn to Bathurst, n.d. [1819], BL Loan 57/12; Goulburn to Bathurst, 5, 8 August 1820, 26 December 1820, 26, 30 July 1821, n.d. [October 1821], 23 November 1821, BL Loan 57/13; Historical Manuscripts Commission, *Report on the Manuscripts of Earl Bathurst* (London, 1923) (hereafter *HMC: Bathurst*), 408, 504–5; 508, 506–7; 517–19, 524–5; Wilbur Devereux Jones, *"Prosperity" Robinson: The Life of Viscount Goderich, 1782–1859* (New York, 1967), 83–6; PRO, CO 168/4; H. Goulburn to J. Goulburn, n.d. [1816], SRO, Acc 304/61.

34 P.J. Cain and A.G. Hopkins, *British Imperialism: Innovation and Expansion 1688–1914* (London, 1993), 103; D.M. Young, *The Colonial Office in the Early Nineteenth Century* (London, 1961) 90; D.J. Murray, *The West Indies and*

the Devlopment of Colonial Government 1801–1834 (Oxford, 1965), 150–1; J. Holland Rose, A.P. Newton, and E.A. Berzians, eds., *Cambridge History of the British Empire*, vol. 2 (Cambridge 1961), 285; *HMC: Bathurst*, 519; C.A. Bayly, *Imperial Meridian: The British Empire and the World 1780–1830* (London, 1989), 197–9; *Parl. Deb.*, 2nd ser., 5:1140; Goulburn memoirs, SRO, Acc 304/68.

35 Philip Harling and Peter Mandler, "From 'Fiscal-Military' State to Laissez-faire State," *Journal of British Studies* 32:52–3; *Parl. Deb.*, 1st ser., 33:900–1, 36:64–9, and 32:1251–7; *British Sessional Papers* [1816], 13:132–3.

36 Goulburn to Bathurst, 17 August 1819, BL Loan 57/12.

37 John P. Halstead, *The Second British Empire: Trade, Philanthropy, and Good Government, 1820–1890* (Westport, Conn., 1983), 21; *Quarterly Review* 14 (1815/1816): 38.

38 Robert Hughes, *The Fatal Shore: The Epic of Australia's Founding*, pb. ed. (New York, 1988), 301.

39 Bathurst to Bigge, 6 January 1819, PRO, CO 202/9; Bathurst to Macquarie, 19 May 1813, 3 February 1814, PRO, CO 202/7; *Parl. Deb.*, 1st ser., 39:488, 1134.

40 John Manning Ward, *Colonial Self-Government: The British Experience 1759–1856* (London, 1976), 132; Bathurst to Macquarie, 10 November 1812, and Goulburn to Davey, 19 October 1812, PRO, CO 202/7; *Parl. Deb.*, 1st ser., 39:491–2.

41 Bathurst to Macquarie, 23 November 1812, 3 February 1814, PRO, CO 202/7.

42 Bathurst to Macquarie, 23 November 1812, 3 February 1814, PRO, CO 202/7; ibid., 30 January 1817, PRO, CO 202/8; *Parl. Deb.*, 1st ser., 39:490–1.

43 Bathurst to Macquarie, 9 April 1816, PRO, CO 202/8; ibid., 23 November 1812, PRO, CO 202/7; ibid., 12 May 1818, PRO, CO 202/8; *Parl. Deb.*, 1st ser., 33:989.

44 Hughes, *Fatal Shore*, 150–1; *Parl Deb.*, 1st ser., 39:488–90.

45 Ward, *Colonial Self-Government*, 132; Bathurst to Bigge, 6 January 1819 (see also the supplementary instructions of the same date), 24 April, 25 September 1819, and 10, 15 July 1820, PRO, CO 202/9; Helen Taft Manning, *British Colonial Government: After the American Revolution* (Hamden, 1933), 539.

46 Bathurst to Prevost, 15 September 1814, PRO, CO 43/23; Drummond to Bathurst (see particularly Goulburn's draft response), 18 January 1815, PRO, CO 42/356; Goulburn to Stuart, 30 July 1818, PRO, CO 43/57.

47 Prevost to Bathurst, 18 March, 1 April 1815, PRO, CO 42/161; Bathurst to Sherbrooke, 1 July 1816, PRO, CO 43/24; *Parl. Deb.*, 1st ser., 32:1253.

48 Drummond to Bathurst, 12 July 1814, PRO, CO 42/355; Goulburn to Peel, 21 January 1815, BL, Add. Ms. 40242.

49 H.J.M. Johnston, *British Emigration Policy 1815–1830* (Oxford, 1972), 19–21; *HMC: Bathurst*, 324; Goulburn to Peel, 28 November 1815, BL, Add. Ms. 40249; ibid., 20 February 1816, BL Add. Ms. 40253; Goulburn to Campbell, 15 April 1816, PRO, CO 43/53.

50 Bathurst to Sherbrooke, 4 October 1816, and 14 April, 13 May, 5 September, 10 November 1817, PRO, CO 43/24; Goulburn to Campbell, 25 July 1816, and Goulburn to Leary, 24 March 1817, PRO, CO 43/54; Goulburn to commissioners of the navy, 15 May 1817, and Goulburn to Lushington, 13 August 1817, PRO, CO 43/55; Bathurst to Sherbrooke, 5 September 1817, PRO, CO 43/24.

51 Bathurst to Vansittart, 4 January 1817, Goulburn to Watson, 23 January 1817, and Goulburn to Leary, 24 March 1817, PRO, CO 43/54; Goulburn to commissioners of the navy, 21, 26 June 1817, PRO, CO 43/55; Goulburn to Harrison, 6 December 1817, PRO, CO 43/56; Goulburn to Peel, 18 December 1817, BL, Add. Ms. 40272; Goulburn to Peel, March 1818, BL, Add. Ms. 40275; Goulburn to Richmond, 4 July 1818, PRO, CO 43/24; Bathurst to Sherbrooke, 5 February 1817, PRO, CO 43/24.

52 Goulburn to Peel, 22 May 1818, BL, Add Ms. 40277; Goulburn to Hamilton, 21 November 1816, PRO, CO 43/54; *HMC: Bathurst*, 451; Richmond to Bathurst, 11 August 1818, PRO, CO 42/179; Richmond to Bathurst, 27 March 1818, BL Loan 57/12; *HMC: Bathurst*, 461.

53 Richmond to Bathurst, 11 August 1818, PRO, CO 42/179; Goulburn to Cooke, 18 September 1816, PRO, CO 43/53; Sherbrooke to Bathurst, 16 December 1816, PRO, CO 42/67; Richmond to Bathurst, 10 November 1818, PRO, CO 42/179; Goulburn to Harrison, 19 March 1819, PRO, CO 43/57; Kenneth Bourne, *Britain and the Balance of Power in North America 1815–1908* (London, 1967), 36; Bowles to Bathurst, 17 December 1819, BL Loan 57/12.

54 Bourne, *Britain and the Balance of Power in North America*, 9, 6–7, 10, 12–15, 28; A.L. Burt, *The United States, Great Britain and British North America* (New Haven, 1940), 399–408; Prevost to Bathurst, 15 March 1815, PRO, CO 42/161; Bathurst to Sherbrooke, 9 September 1816, PRO, CO 43/24; *Quarterly Review* 39 (1829): 227; François Couzet, *Britain Ascendant: Comparitive Studies in Franco-British Economic History* (Cambridge, 1990), 240; Judith Blow Williams, *British Commerical Policy and Trade Expansion 1750–1850* (Oxford, 1972), 238.

55 See J.H. Power, *Richard Rush: Republican Diplomat 1780–1859* (Philadelphia, 1942); Hughes to Monroe, 20 August 1818, Library of Congress (LC), James Monroe Papers, reel 7; Rush to Monroe, 22 April, 10 May 1818, LC, Monroe Papers, reel 6; Rush to Monroe, 10 February 1819, LC, Monroe Papers, reel 7.

56 Rush to Monroe, 9 July 1818, LC, Monroe Papers, reel 7; Power, *Richard Rush*, 39; *Writings of Gallatin*, 2:67; Gallatin to Rush, 13 July 1818, NA,

M34/21; Gallatin to Adams, 10 August 1818, NA, M34/21; Rush to Monroe, 13 August 1818, LC, Monroe Papers, reel 7; Rush to Adams, 15 August, 1818, NA, M30/19; Gaillard Hunt, ed., *The Writings of James Madison*, vol. 8 (New York, 1909), 415; Gallatin to Adams, 7 November 1818, NA, M34/21.

57 Power, *Richard Rush*, 117; Bradford Perkins, *Castlereagh and Adams: England and the United States 1812–1823* (Los Angeles, 1964), 260; Gallatin memorandum, 22–3 August 1818, LC, Albert Gallatin Papers, microfilm copy, reel 31; Castlereagh to Robinson and Goulburn, 24 August 1818, PRO, FO 5/138.

58 Rush memorandum, 10 November 1818, LC, Monroe Papers, reel 7; Castlereagh to Robinson, 8 October 1818, PRO, FO 5/138; Rush to Monroe, 1, 17 October 1818, LC, Monroe Papers, reel 7.

59 Gallatin memorandum, 16 October 1818, LC, Gallatin Papers, reel 31; Rush memorandum, 10 November 1818, LC, Monroe Papers, reel 7; Gallatin memorandum, 19 October 1818, LC, Gallatin Papers, reel 31.

60 Rush memorandum, 10 November 1818, LC, Monroe Papers, reel 7.

61 Bathurst to Macquarie, 23 November 1812, 19 May 1813, and 3 February 1814, PRO, CO 202/7; ibid., 4 December 1815, PRO, CO 202/8; Bathurst to Brownrigg, 23 January 1813, PRO, CO 55/62; 10 May and 20, 30 August 1815, PRO, CO 55/63; Bathurst to Farquar, 5 April, 10 October, 23 December 1813, PRO, CO 168/2.

62 Liverpool to Bathurst, 17 January 1815, BL Loan 57/9; *Parl. Deb.*, 1st ser., 32:1044–5; see, for example, Bathurst to Brownrigg, 29 March 1816, PRO, CO 55/63.

63 *British Sessional Papers* 14 (1821): 209–41; *Parl. Deb.*, 1st ser., 40:272; 2nd ser., 2:4.

64 Bathurst to Brownrigg, 5 July 1817, PRO, CO 55/63; CO circular, 24 February 1817, PRO, CO 29/30; Bathurst to Farquar, 9 August 1817, PRO, CO 168/3; Bathurst to Brownrigg, 20 March 1820, and 20 August, 20 June 1817, PRO, CO 55/63; Bathurst to Sherbrooke, 13 July 1816, PRO, CO 43/24; Bathurst to Brownrigg, 10 March 1820, PRO, CO 55/63.

65 Bathurst to Sherbrooke, 7 June, 14 July 1816, PRO, CO 43/24; Bathurst to Dalhousie, 11 September 1820, PRO, CO 43/25; Bathurst to Sherbrooke, 19 June 1816, PRO, CO 43/24; Bathurst to Brownrigg, 25 July 1818, 30 January 1819, PRO, CO 55/63.

66 Bathurst to Hall, 5 June, 15 July 1818, PRO, CO 168/3; Bathurst to Darling, 10 September 1818, PRO, CO 168/3; Bathurst to Farquar, 26 September 1818, PRO, CO 168/3.

67 Bathurst to Macquarie, 4 December 1815, PRO, CO 202/8; ibid., 24 March 1820, PRO, CO 202/9; Bathurst to Brownrigg, 23 January, 17 December 1813, PRO, CO 55/62; ibid., 10 May 1815, PRO, CO 55/63; ibid., 30 July

1814, PRO CO 55/62; Bathurst to Somerset, 30 January 1817, PRO, CO 49/12.

68 Goulburn to Harrison, 6 December 1817, PRO, CO 43/56.

69 Goulburn to Harrison, 6 December 1817, PRO, CO 43/56; Peel to Goulburn, 7 February 1815, SRO, Acc 304/35; Johnston, *British Emigration Policy*, 25, 29, 52–3; Goulburn to Sweeney, 4 March 1818, PRO, CO 43/56; Goulburn to Taylor, 7 March 1818, PRO, CO 43/56; Goulburn to Spilsbury, 4 February 1819, PRO, CO 43/56; Bathurst to Maitland, 6 May 1820, PRO, CO 43/41; Bathurst to Dalhousie, 17 March, 10 August 1821, PRO, CO 43/25.

70 Goulburn to Harrison, 6 December 1817, PRO, CO 43/56; Bathurst to Somerset, 28 July 1817, PRO, CO 49/12; Johnston, *British Emigration Policy*, 32; Goulburn to Newcastle, 5 September 1819, University of Nottingham Library (UNL), Newcastle Papers, Nec 5, 155; Bathurst to Somerset, 20 July, 6 November 1819, PRO, CO 49/12; Bathurst to Donkin, 2 December 1820, PRO, CO 49/12.

71 Bathurst to Somerset, 6 November 1819, PRO, CO 49/12; Johnston, *British Emigration Policy*, 40–1; Ralph Elphick and Hermann Giliomee, *The Shaping of South African Society 1652–1840* (Middletown, Conn., 1989), 475; Stanley Trapido, "From Paternalism to Liberalism: The Cape Colony, 1800–1834," *International History Review* 12 (1990): 87; Goulburn to Newcastle, 5 September 1819, UNL, Newcastle Papers, Nec 5, 155; James Sturgis, "Anglicisation at the Cape of Good Hope in the Early Nineteenth Century," *Journal of Imperial and Commonwealth History* 11 (1982–83): 5–32; Goulburn to Somerset, 10 April 1821, PRO, CO 49/12.

72 Bathurst to Macquarie, 13 May 1820, PRO, CO 202/9; Bathurst to Brownrigg, 5 April, 17 December 1813, and 30 July 1814, PRO, CO 55/62; John Walsh, Colin Haydon, and Stephen Taylor, eds., *The Church of England c.1689–c.1833: From Toleration to Tractarianism* (Cambridge, 1993), 251; Goulburn to Glennie, 21 July 1816, PRO, CO 55/63.

73 Bathurst to Brownrigg, 20 June 1817, 30 November 1819, PRO, CO 55/63; Goulburn to Slater, 30 November 1818, 25 August 1819, PRO, CO 168/5; Goulburn to Farquar, 13 April 1819, PRO, CO 168/3; Bathurst to Darling, 6 August 1819, PRO, CO 168/3; Goulburn to Darling, 18 September 1819, PRO, CO 168/3.

74 Bathurst to Sherbrooke, 2 July 1816, 17 June 1817, PRO, CO 43/24; Bathurst to Bishop of Quebec, 21 April 1818, PRO, CO 43/41; ibid., 27 April 1819, PRO, CO 43/57

75 Bathurst to Smith, 2 April 1818, PRO, CO 43/41; Bathurst to Bishop of Quebec, 27 April 1819, 15 August 1818, PRO, CO 43/57; Bathurst to Richmond, 20 August 1818, PRO, CO 43/24; Goulburn to Hall and Reddie, 17 March 1817, PRO, CO 43/54; Goulburn to Bathurst, 9 September 1819, BL Loan 57/22.

76 Bathurst to Woodford, 24 June 1816, PRO, CO 296/5; CO circular, 7 April 1817, PRO, CO 29/30; Bathurst to Woodford, 8 November 1817, 20 January 1820, PRO, CO 296/5.

77 CO circular, 7 April 1817, PRO, CO 29/30; Manchester to Bathurst, 30 May, 23 October 1817, PRO, CO 137/144; Combermere to Bathurst, 20 August 1817, PRO, CO 28/86; CO circular, 8 April 1819, PRO, CO 29/30; Manchester to Bathurst, 17 April 1819, PRO, CO 137/148; see also his private dispatch of the same date.

78 Manchester to Bathurst, 6 February 1819, but see particularly Goulburn's minute on this disaptch, PRO, CO 137/148; Bathurst to Manchester, 11 May 1819, PRO, CO 138/47; Patterson, *Sociology of Slavery*, 207.

79 Manchester to Bathurst, 10 July 1819, PRO, CO 137/148; CO circular, 7 March 1821, PRO, CO 29/30.

80 *Morning Chronicle*, 4 June 1816; *Edinburgh Review* 19 (1811–12): 147; *Edinburgh Review* 25 (1815): 323.

81 Wilberforce, *Life of Wilberforce*, 4:243–4, 249–53, 263–4; Sir George Stephen, *Anti-Slavery Recollections*, reprint ed. (London, 1971), 10; James Walvin, *England, Slaves and Freedom, 1776–1838* (London, 1986), 128; *HMC: Bathurst*, 353.

82 Wilberforce, *Life of Wilberforce*, 4:284–6, 304, 292; *Morning Chronicle*, 28 June 1816; *HMC: Bathurst*, 415; see also 414–19.

83 Wellington, *Supplementary Despatches, Correspondence, and Memoranda: Field Marshal Arthur Duke of Wellington, K.G., 1794–1818*, 15 vols. (London, 1858–72), 9:225, 227ff; Betty Fladeland, "Abolitionist Pressures on the Concert of Europe, 1814–1822," *Journal of Modern History* 38 (1966): 355–73; *Edinburgh Review* 24 (1814–15): 109, 121; Walvin, *England, Slaves and Freedom*, 126; Seymour Drescher, *Capitalism and Antislavery: British Mobilization in Comparative Perspective* (New York, 1987), 91.

84 *HMC: Bathurst*, 352; Bathurst to Farquar, 25 January, 23 December 1813, PRO, CO 168/2; ibid., 31 May 1814, PRO, CO 168/3.

85 Bathurst to Woodford, 24 February 1816, PRO, CO 296/5; Goulburn to Woodford, 23 May 1816, 1 December 1817, PRO, CO 296/5; Bathurst to Farquar, 5 March 1816, PRO, CO 168/3; Bathurst to Somerset, 6 September 1816, PRO, CO 49/10; *Quarterly Review* 8 (1812):392.

86 Codd to Leith, 25 April 1816, PRO, CO 28/85; CO circular, 28 June 1816, PRO, CO 29/30.

87 Manchester to Bathurst, 20 December 1816, PRO, CO 137/142; *HMC: Bathurst*, 428–31, 432.

88 Manchester to Bathurst, 21 June 1817 (see Goulburn's comments on this dispatch), PRO, CO 138/46; Goulburn to Murray, 6 February 1817, PRO, CO 138/46; Goulburn to Harrison, 25 February 1817, PRO, CO 138/46; Goulburn to Hobhouse, 28 July 1817, PRO, HO 30/3; Bathurst to Farquar, 3 January, 1 April, 2 June 1817, PRO, CO 168/3; Goulburn to Clive,

8 September 1818, PRO, CO 168/5; Goulburn to Hall, 20 March 1819, PRO, CO 168/5; Goulburn to Harrison, 25 March, 13 May 1819, PRO, CO 168/5; Goulburn to law officers, 18 April 1820, PRO, CO 168/5.

89 Bathurst to Manchester, 17 March, 7 April 1817, PRO, CO 138/46; Goulburn to Shand, 20 November 1817, PRO, CO 168/46; Bathurst to Combermere, 6 February 1818, PRO, CO 29/30; D. Eltis, "The Traffic in Slaves between the British West Indian Colonies, 1807–1833," *Economic History Review*, 2nd ser., 15 (1972): 55–64.

90 F.J. Klingberg, *The Anti-Slavery Movement in England: A Study in English Humanitarianism* (New Haven, 1926), 161–5; David Eltis, *Economic Growth and the Ending of the Transatlantic Slave Trade* (Oxford, 1987), 86; *Parl. Deb.*, 1st ser., 38:296–308, 842–6, 1205.

91 Hibbert to Holland, 24 February 1819, Holland House Papers, BL, Add. Ms. 51820; *Parl. Deb.*, 1st ser., 40:976–8 *British Sessional Papers* 18 (1819).

92 CO circular, 15 September 1819, PRO, CO 29/30; Goulburn to Darling, 10 February 1820, PRO, CO 168/6; Bathurst to Darling, 20 February 1820, PRO, CO 168/6; Bathurst to Farquar, 17 April, 31 August 1820, and 30 August 1821, PRO, CO 168/6.

93 Goulburn to Bathurst, n.d. [December 1821], BL Loan 57/13; Bathurst to Moody and Dougan, 30 November 1821, PRO, CO 29/30.

94 Goulburn memoirs, SRO, Acc 304/68; Walsh, Haydon, and Taylor, *Church of England*, 255.

95 P.J. Cain and A.G. Hopkins, "Gentlemanly Capitalism and British Expansion Overseas: 1. The Old Colonial System 1688–1850," *Economic History Review*, 2nd ser., 39 (1986): 522.

96 Goulburn memoirs, SRO, Acc 304/68; *Parl. Deb.*, 1st ser., 38:297; Philip A. Buckner, *The Transition to Responsible Government: British Policy in British North America 1815–1850* (Westport, 1985), 38; J.C. Beaglehole, "The Colonial Office, 1782–1854," *Historical Studies, Australia and New Zealand* 1 (1940–41): 179; Manning, *British Colonial Government*, 510; Young, *Colonial Office*, 33, 45; Harling and Mandler, "From 'Fiscal-Military' State," 46.

CHAPTER FIVE

1 For a full discussion of Liverpool's difficulties, see Norman Gash, *Lord Liverpool* (London, 1984), 151–69; Elie Halevy, *The Liberal Wakening (1815–1830)*, pb. ed. (London, 1987), 116.

2 Plunket to Charles Wynn, 2 May [1821], National Library of Wales (NLW), Aberystwyth, Coed-y-Maen Mss.; Gash, *Liverpool*, 166–7, 181.

3 Brian Jenkins, *Era of Emancipation: British Government of Ireland 1812–1830* (Montreal, 1988), 160–3, 166; Liverpool to Talbot, 29 November 1821, British Library (BL), Add. Ms. 38290; Historical Manuscripts Commission,

Report on the Manuscripts of Earl Bathurst (London, 1923) (hereafter *HMC: Bathurst*), 522.

4 A. Aspinall, ed., *Correspondence of Charles Arbuthnot, 1808–1850*, Royal Historical Society, Camden Third Series, 65 (London, 1941), 45; Goulburn to Liverpool, 26 November 1821, BL, Add. Ms. 38290; Goulburn to Bathurst, n.d. [December 1821], BL Loan 57/13; Liverpool to Goulburn, 26 November 1821, Surrey Record Office (SRO), Kingston upon Thames, Acc 426/6; H. Goulburn to Peel, 25 January 1822, BL, Add. Ms. 40328; Goulburn diaries, 1827, SRO, Acc 304/24.

5 Goulburn memoirs, SRO, Acc 304/68; *HMC: Bathurst*, 523–4; E. Montagu to J. Goulburn, 14 December 1821, SRO, Acc 304/61; *Parl. Deb.*, 2nd ser., 4:1537–38; Francis Bamford and Duke of Wellington, eds., *Journal of Mrs Arbuthnot 1820–1832*, 2 vols. (London, 1950), 1:218; Maurice R. O'Connell, ed., *The Correspondence of Daniel O'Connell*, 8 vols. (Dublin, 1972–81), 2:366.

6 Goulburn diaries, 1821, SRO, Acc 304/24; Peel to H. Goulburn, n.d. [December, 1821], SRO, Acc 304/35; Goulburn memoirs, SRO, Acc 304/68; H. Goulburn to Sidmouth, 21 December 1821, Sidmouth Papers, Devon Record Office (DRO), Exeter; Goulburn to Bathurst, 31 December 1821, BL Loan 57/13.

7 H. Goulburn to Peel, 6 January 1822, BL, Add. Ms. 40328; Jonah Barrington, *Historic Memoirs of Ireland*, 2 vols. (London, 1835), 2:346.

8 Peel to H. Goulburn, 2 January 1822, SRO, Acc 304/35; H. Goulburn to Peel, 21 January 1822, BL, Add. Ms. 40328.

9 Jenkins, *Era of Emancipation*, 165; Historical Manuscripts Commission, *Report on the Manuscripts of J.B. Fortescue, Esq., Preserved at Dropmore* (London, 1927), 10:428–29; Buckingham and Chandos, *Memoirs of the Court of George IV 1820–1830 from Original Family Documents*, 2 vols. (London, 1859), 1:250, 247; *Times*, 22 December 1821.

10 *Morning Chronicle*, 12 December 1821; *Times*, 18 December 1821; Lord Charles Colchester, ed., *The Diary and Correspondence of Charles Abbot, Lord Colchester*, 3 vols. (London, 1861), 3:242; Earl of Ilchester, *The Journal of the Hon. Henry Edward Fox (afterwards the Fourth and Last Lord Holland) 1818–1830* (London, 1923), 90–1.

11 Jenkins, *Era of Emancipation*, 10; Peel to Gregory, n.d. [1822], BL, Add. Ms. 40334; Charles Stuart Parker, ed., *Sir Robert Peel from His Private Papers*, 3 vols., (reprint New York, 1970), 1:309.

12 Christine Colvin, ed., *Maria Edgeworth: Letters from England, 1813–1844* (Oxford, 1971), 287; Saxton to Wynn, 13 January 1822, NLW Coed-y-Maen Mss.

13 Lady Gregory, ed., *Mr. Gregory's Letter-Box, 1813–1835* (London, 1898), 209; Gregory to Peel, 2 February 1822, BL, Add. Ms. 40334.

14 Goulburn to Gregory, 27 February 1822, SRO, Acc 304/69; Gregory to Goulburn, 3 April 1822, SRO, Acc 304/69; D.A. Chart, *Ireland from the Union to Catholic Emancipation* (London, 1910), 181.

387 Notes to pages 136–41

15 H. Goulburn to J. Goulburn, 4 February 1823, SRO, Acc 304/65; H. Goulburn to J. Goulburn, [February] 1824, SRO, Acc 304/67.

16 H. Goulburn to J. Goulburn, 2 February 1825, SRO, Acc 304/67; H. Goulburn to J. Goulburn, [1826], SRO, Acc 304/64.

17 H. Goulburn to J. Goulburn, n.d. [1824], SRO, Acc 304/67; H. Goulburn to J. Goulburn, n.d. [1826], Acc 304/65; H. Goulburn to J. Goulburn, n.d. [March 1824], SRO, Acc 304/67; Herbert Maxwell, ed., *The Creevey Papers: A Selection from the Correspondence and Diaries of the Late Thomas Creevey, M.P., 1768–1838*, 2 vols. (London, 1903), 2:75; Croker to Blomfield, 8 August 1822, BL, Add. Ms. 52471.

18 H. Goulburn to J. Goulburn, 1 March 1824, SRO, Acc 304/67; J. Goulburn to H. Goulburn, n.d. [1824], SRO, Acc 304/67; H. Goulburn to J. Goulburn, 1 March 1824, SRO, Acc 304/67; H. Goulburn to J. Goulburn, 18 March 1823, SRO, Acc 304/65; H. Goulburn to J. Goulburn, 21, 22 February 1825, SRO, Acc 304/67; Derek Beales and Geoffrey Best, eds., *History, Society and Churches: Essays in Honour of Owen Chadwick* (Cambridge, 1985), 224.

19 H. Goulburn to J. Goulburn, 7 April 1824, SRO, Acc 304/67; H. Goulburn to J. Goulburn, 26 February 1823, SRO, Acc 304/65; H. Goulburn to J. Goulburn, n.d. [1826], SRO, Acc 304/66.

20 H. Goulburn to Harry Goulburn, 17 February, 24 March 1824, SRO, Acc 304/66.

21 J. Goulburn to H. Goulburn, n.d. [1828], SRO, Acc 304/67; R. Mayor to Harry Goulburn, January 1824, SRO, Acc 304/66; H. Goulburn to J. Goulburn, 18 February 1824, SRO, Acc 304/67; H. Goulburn to J. Goulburn, n.d. [October, 1825], SRO, Acc 304/64; H. Goulburn to J. Goulburn, n.d. [1826], SRO, Acc 304/67; Harry Goulburn to J. Goulburn, 9 October 1825, SRO, Acc 304/64; H. Goulburn to Harry Goulburn, 20 March 1826, SRO, Acc 304/66.

22 Goulburn to Bathurst, 31 December 1821, BL Loan 57/13; H. Goulburn to J. Goulburn, 18 February 1825, SRO, Acc 304/67; H. Goulburn to J. Goulburn, 4, 12, 26 February 1823, n.d. [1823], SRO, Acc 304/65.

23 H. Goulburn to J. Goulburn, 12 February 1823, SRO, Acc 304/65; ibid., 4 March 1824, 2 February 1825, SRO, Acc 304/67; ibid., n.d. [1826], SRO, Acc 304/64; ibid., 15 May 1824, SRO, Acc 304/67; ibid., 15, 18, 19, 23 February 1825, SRO, Acc 304/67; ibid., 17 February 1824, SRO, Acc 304/67; ibid., 26 February 1823, SRO, Acc 304/63.

24 H. Goulburn to Harry Goulburn, n.d., SRO, Acc 304/67; H. Goulburn to J. Goulburn, 25 January 1825, SRO, Acc 304/67; H. Goulburn to J. Goulburn, 19 March 1826, SRO, Acc 304/64; H. Goulburn to J. Goulburn, 11 March 1824, SRO, Acc 304/67; H. Goulburn to J. Goulburn, n.d., SRO, Acc 304/64; H. Goulburn to J. Goulburn 28 February 1825, SRO, Acc 304/67.

25 Jenkins, *Era of Emancipation*, 160–1; *Times*, 20, 18 December 1821; *Parl. Deb.*, 2nd ser., 6:1479; Peel to Goulburn, 2 January 1822, SRO, Acc 304/35.

26 *Parl. Deb.*, 3rd ser., 37:938; Goulburn to Peel, 26 November 1824, BL, Add. Ms. 40330; H. Goulburn to Fred Goulburn, n.d. [October 1825], SRO, Acc 304/66; *Parl. Deb.*, 2nd ser., 6:1483; H. Goulburn to J. Goulburn, 21 February 1825, SRO, Acc 304/67; H. Goulburn to Peel, 18 January 1822, BL, Add. Ms. 40328.

27 H. Goulburn to J. Goulburn, 21 February 1825, SRO, Acc 304/67; Colchester, *Diary*, 3:270; Saxton to Wynn, 8, 28, 13 January 1822, NLW, Coed-y-Maen Mss.; Saxton to Wynn, 3 November 1822, NLW, Coed-y-Maen Mss.; W. Torrens McCullagh, *Memoirs of the Right Honourable Richard Lalor Sheil*, 2 vols. (London, 1855), 1:280.

28 Saxton to Wynn, 3 November, 27 December 1822, NLW, Coed-y-Maen Mss.; Gregory to H. Goulburn, 21 July 1822, SRO, Acc 304/70; Gregory to H. Goulburn, 7 May 1823, SRO, Acc 304/71; Peel to H. Goulburn, 7 April 1823, BL, Add. Ms. 40329.

29 Saxton to Wynn, 28 January 1822, NLW, Coed-y-Maen Mss.; A. Aspinall, ed., *The Diary of Henry Hobhouse (1820–1827)*, 81; Peel to H. Goulburn, 2, 18 January 1822, SRO, Acc 304/35; H. Goulburn to Peel, 7 January 1822, BL, Add. Ms. 40328; Parker, *Peel*, 1:305; Gregory to Goulburn, 16 February, 22 March 1822, SRO, Acc 304/69; H. Goulburn to Peel, 6 January 1822, BL, Add. Ms. 40328.

30 Wellesley to Sidmouth, 3 January 1822, BL, Add. Ms. 37298; H. Goulburn to Peel, 26 January 1822, PRO, HO 100/203; H. Goulburn to Peel, 30 January 1822, BL, Add. Ms. 40328.

31 Saxton to Wynn. 19 December 1821, NLW, Coed-y-Maen Mss.; H. Goulburn to Peel, 18, 21 January 1822, BL, Add. Ms. 40328; Peel to H. Goulburn, 21 January 1821, SRO, Acc 304/35; Wellesley to Peel, 31 January 1822, BL, Add. Ms. 37298; Wellesley to Peel, 3 February 1822, BL, Add. Ms. 40324.

32 Wellesley to Peel, 29 January 1822, BL, Add. Ms. 37298; H. Goulburn to Hobhouse, 1 February 1822, PRO, HO 100/203; Peel to H. Goulburn, 24 January [1822], SRO, Acc 304/37; *Parl. Deb.*, 2nd ser., 6:104–10, 114–30, 185–8.

33 Gregory to H. Goulburn, 18 February 1822, SRO, Acc 304/69; H. Goulburn to Wellesley, 28 February 1822, BL, Add Ms. 37298; Gregory to H. Goulburn, 3, 13, 20, 26 April 1822, SRO, Acc 304/69; Gregory to H. Goulburn, 5, 19, 22 March 1822, SRO, Acc 304/69; Wellesley to Peel, 1 May 1822, BL, Add. Ms. 37299.

34 *Parl. Deb.*, 2nd ser., 6:1505–34; H. Goulburn to Wellesley, 23 April 1822, BL, Add. Ms. 37299; H. Goulburn to Peel, 4 May 1822, BL, Add. Ms. 40328; *London Quarterly Review* 124 (1868):137.

35 H. Goulburn to Wellesley, 15 April 1822, BL, Add. Ms. 37299; *Parl. Deb.*, 2nd ser., 7:852–73; Jenkins, *Era of Emancipation*, 198–9; Stanley H. Palmer,

Police and Protest in England and Ireland 1780–1850 (Cambridge, 1988), 240–3; Cloncurry to Holland, 18 June 1822, Holland House Papers, BL, Add. Ms. 51573.

36 Wellesley to Goulburn, 16 June 1822, SRO, Acc 304/44; Palmer, *Police and Protest*, 243–4.

37 Jenkins, *Era of Emancipation*, 199; H. Goulburn to Peel, 22 November 1822, BL, Add. Ms. 40328; H. Goulburn to Peel, 9 September 1822, BL, Add. Ms. 40328; Peel to Wellesley, 24 February 1823, BL, Add. Ms. 37300; Cloncurry to Holland, 18 June 1822, BL, Add. Ms. 51573; Goulburn to Peel, 30 December 1829, BL, Add. Ms. 40333.

38 Wellesley to Peel, 14 February 1822, BL, Add. Ms. 37298; H. Goulburn to Wellesley, 26 February, 5 March 1822, BL, Add. Ms. 37298; Wellesley to H. Goulburn, 23 February, 21 March 1822, SRO, Acc 304/44; Liverpool to Wellesley, 22 March 1822, BL, Add. Ms. 37298.

39 Donald Harmon Akenson, *The Church of Ireland: Ecclesiastical Reform and Revolution, 1800–1885* (New Haven, 1971), 103; H. Goulburn to Wellesley, 13, 22 February, 10 March 1822, BL, Add. Ms. 37298; *Parl. Deb.*, 2nd ser., 7:1030–4.

40 *Parl. Deb.*, 2nd ser., 7:1039; Buckingham to Wynn, 8 October 1822, NLW, Coed-y-Maen Mss.; H. Goulburn to Peel, 1 December 1822, BL, Add. Ms. 40328; Wellesley to H. Goulburn, 21 September 1822, SRO, Acc 304/36.

41 Liverpool to Peel, 9 October 1822, BL, Add. Ms. 40304; Wellesley to H. Goulburn, 21 September 1822, SRO, Acc 304/36.

42 H. Goulburn to Peel, 16 October 1822, BL, Add. Ms. 40328; Gregory to H. Goulburn, 12 April 1822, William Gregory Papers, Emory University Library (EUL), Atlanta; H. Goulburn to Peel, 18 November 1822, BL, Add. Ms. 40328; Wellesley to Liverpool, 18 November 1822, BL, Add. Ms. 37300; Wellesley to Peel, 21 November 1822, BL, Add. Ms. 37300.

43 Wynn to Plunket, 4 December 1822, NLW, Coedy-Maen Mss.; Liverpool to Wellesley, 9 December 1822, BL, Add. Ms. 37300; H. Goulburn to Peel, 13 December 1822, BL, Add. Ms. 40328; H. Goulburn to Peel, 8, 21 January 1822, BL, Add. Ms. 40329.

44 Goulburn to Wellesley, 2, 16 April 1822, BL, Add. Ms. 37298; Stephen Baxter, *England's Rise to Greatness 1660–1763* (London, 1983), 65–6; Boyd Hilton, *The Age of Atonement: The Influence of Evangelicalism on Social and Economic Thought, 1795–1865* (Oxford, 1988), 93; *Parl. Deb.*, 2nd ser., 7:472

45 R.R. Pearce, *Memoirs and Correspondence of the Most Noble Richard Marquis Wellesley*, 3 vols. (London, 1846), 3:350–1; Wellesley to Peel, 22 May 1822, BL, Add. Ms. 37299; Wellesley to Peel, 31 January 1822, BL, Add. Ms. 37298; H. Goulburn to Wellesley, 2, 16 April 1822, BL, Add. Ms. 37299; Gregory to H. Goulburn, 28 March, 17 April 1822, SRO, Acc 304/69.

46 H. Goulburn to Gregory, 20 April 1822, EUL, Gregory Papers; Goulburn to
     Wellesley, 7 April 1824, BL, Add. Ms. 37302; *Parl. Deb.*, 2nd ser., 7:148, 156;
     Journal of Mrs. Arbuthnot, 1:165; Hilton, *Age of Atonement*, 93; Charles Duke
     Yonge, *The Life and Administration of Robert Banks, Second Earl of Liverpool*,
     3 vols. (London, 1968), 3:168.

47 *Parl. Deb.*, 2nd ser., 7:670, 698; Power Tuam to H. Goulburn, 5 June 1822,
     EUL, Gregory Papers; Power Tuam to Gregory, 12 June 1822, EUL, Gregory
     Papers; H. Goulburn to Gregory, 10 June 1822, EUL, Gregory Papers;
     Wellesley to H. Goulburn, 16 June 1822, SRO, Acc 304/44; Goulburn to
     Wellesley, 19 June 1822, BL, Add. Ms. 37299.

48 H. Goulburn to Gregory, 18 June, 11 July 1822, EUL, Gregory Papers; H.
     Goulburn to Wellesley, 19 June 1822, BL, Add. Ms. 37299.

49 H. Goulburn to Gregory, 15 July 1822, and Gregory to H. Goulburn,
     16 July 1822, SRO, Acc 304/70; H. Goulburn to Peel, 17 August 1822, BL,
     Add. Ms. 40328.

50 Commissioners for Relief of the Poor to H. Goulburn, 17 August 1822,
     PRO, HO 100/206; Buckingham to Wynn, 8 October 1822, NLW, Coed-y-
     Maen Mss.; H. Goulburn to Peel, 7 September 1822, PRO, HO 100/206;
     Mary E. Daly, *The Famine in Ireland* (Dublin, 1986), 41.

51 Wellesley to Sidmouth 5 January 1822, DRO, Sidmouth Papers;
     Wellesley to Peel, 15 July 1822, BL, Add. Ms. 37299; Peel to Wellesley,
     21 July 1822, BL, Add. Ms. 37299; Goulburn to Peel, 2 November 1822,
     BL, Add. Ms. 40328; Peel to Wellesley, 11 November 1822, BL, Add.
     Ms. 37300; H. Goulburn to Peel, 16 September 1822, BL, Add. Ms.
     40328.

52 Peel to Wellesley, 21 July 1822, PRO, HO 100/207; H. Goulburn to Peel,
     2 November 1822, BL, Add. Ms. 40328; Wellesley to Peel, 7 November
     1822, BL, Add. Ms. 37300; Saxton to Wynn, 13 November 1822, NLW,
     Coed-y-Maen Mss.

53 Saxton to Wynn, 16 December 1822, NLW, Coed-y-Maen Mss.; R. Hunter to
     Sidmouth, 18 December 1822, DRO, Sidmouth Papers; Talbot to Gregory,
     20 December 1822, EUL, Gregory Papers.

54 H. Goulburn to Peel, 15 December 1822, BL, Add. Ms. 40328; Plunket to
     Wellesley, 23 December 1822, BL, Add. Ms. 37300; Peel to H. Goulburn,
     26 December 1822, SRO, Acc 304/36; H. Goulburn to Peel, 1, 22 January
     1823, BL, Add. Ms. 40329; Buckingham to Wynn, 26 January 1823, NLW,
     Coed-y-Maen Mss.

55 Saxton to Wynn, 16 December 1822, NLW, Coed-y-Maen Mss.; Bucking-
     ham, *Memoirs*, 1:420; J. Goulburn to H. Goulburn, n.d [February 1823],
     SRO, Acc 304/67.

56 H. Goulburn to Peel, 3 January 1823, BL, Add. Ms. 40329; Gregory to H.
     Goulburn, 16 February 1823, SRO, Acc 304/69; H. Goulburn to Wellesley,
     17 February 1823, BL, Add. Ms. 37300; J. Goulburn to H. Goulburn, n.d.

[February 1823], SRO, Acc 304/67; H. Goulburn to J. Goulburn, 26 February 1823, SRO, Acc 304/65.

CHAPTER SIX

1 H. Goulburn to J. Goulburn, 6, 8, 22 February 1823, Surrey Record Office (SRO), Kingston upon Thames, Acc 304/67; Peel to Wellesley, 22 February 1823, British Library (BL), Add. Ms. 37300; Goulburn to Wellesley, 23 February 1823, BL, Add. Ms. 37300; *Parl. Deb.* 2nd ser. 8:8, 204–28, 461; Gregory to Goulburn, 14 March 1823, SRO, Acc 304/72; Maurice R. O'Connell, ed., *The Correspondence of Daniel O'Connell*, 8 vols. (Dublin, 1972–81), 2: 452; Hereward Senior, *Orangeism in Ireland and Britain 1795–1836* (London, 1966), 208–9.

2 *Parl. Deb.*, 2nd ser., 8:495–8; Irish Hierarchy to Wellesley, 6 March 1823, Public Record Office (PRO), HO 100/208; Lord Charles Colchester, ed., *The Diary and Correspondence of Charles Abbot, Lord Colchester,* 3 vols. (London, 1861), 3:285; Goulburn to Wellesley, 8 March 1823, BL, Add. Ms. 37300.

3 Brian Jenkins, *Era of Emancipation: British Government of Ireland 1812–1830,* (Montreal, 1988), 202–4; *Parl. Deb.*, 2nd ser., 8:497–8 and 9:366, 372–3, 990; Goulburn to Wellesley, 10 June 1823, BL, Add. Ms. 37301; A. Aspinall, ed., *The Letters of King George IV, 1812–1830,* 3 vols.(Cambridge, 1938), 3:308–9; H. Goulburn to J. Goulburn, 31 January [1824], SRO, Acc 304/67; *Blackwood's Magazine* 25 (1829):194.

4 Wellesley to Peel, 27 April 1823, BL, Add. Ms. 37301; Wellesley to Peel, 18 May 1823, PRO, HO 100/209; Plunket to Wynn, 15 November 1823, National Library of Wales (NLW), Coed-y-Maen Mss.; Aspinall, *Letters of George IV,* 3:297; Stanley H. Palmer, *Police and Protest in England and Ireland 1780–1850* (Cambridge, 1988), 246–7, 249, 264; Jenkins, *Era of Emancipation,* 206–7; *Parl. Deb.*, 2nd ser., 9:1276, 1283–7.

5 Goulburn to Wellesley, 13 May 1823, BL, Add. Ms. 37301; Wellesley to Goulburn, 15 May 1823, SRO, Acc 304/44; Goulburn to Peel, 15 November 1823, BL, Add. Ms. 40329; Peel to Goulburn, 28 October 1823, Goulburn to Peel, 22 October, 7 November 1823, BL, Add. Ms. 40329; Peel to Goulburn, 19 November 1823, SRO, Acc 304/36.

6 H. Goulburn to J. Goulburn, 4, 7 February 1824, SRO, Acc 304/67; *Parl. Deb.*, 2nd ser., 10:183, 852–7, 1453–63; *Parl. Deb.*, 2nd ser., 11:425; E.A. Wasson, "The Coalitions of 1827 and the Crisis of Whig Leadership," *Historical Journal* 20 (1977): 594; Goulburn to Peel, 16 April 1824, BL, Add. Ms. 40330.

7 *Parl. Deb.*, 2nd ser., 11:654, 685; Buckingham and Chandos, *Memoirs of the Court of George IV, 1820–1830,* 2 vols. (London 1859), 2:72–4; *Parl. Deb.*, 2nd ser., 11:1329–30.

8 *Parl. Deb.*, 2nd ser., 10:837–8, 1406–7; Goulburn to Dr Murray, 27 March 1824, SRO, Acc 304/33.

9 Goulburn to Murray, 27 March 1824, SRO, Acc 304/33; H. Goulburn to J. Goulburn, 31 March, 20 May 1824, SRO, Acc 304/67; Goulburn to Peel, 13 April 1824, BL, Add. Ms. 40330.

10 Gregory to Goulburn, 28 May, 1 April, 13, 20 June 1824, SRO, Acc 304/73.

11 Francis Bamford and Duke of Wellington, eds., *Journal of Mrs. Arbuthnot 1820–1832*, 2 vols. (London, 1950), 1:311, 317–18; *Parl. Deb.*, 2nd ser., 11:596; Goulburn to Gregory, 7 June 1824, Gregory Papers, Emory University Library (EUL), Atlanta.

12 Gregory to Goulburn, 22 June 1824, PRO, HO 100/212; Goulburn to Peel, 5 July 1824, BL, Add. Ms. 40330.

13 Goulburn to Peel, 31 August 1824, BL, Add. Ms. 40330.

14 Goulburn to Peel, 15 December 1824, BL, Add. Ms. 40330; Goulburn to Peel, 22 September 1824, PRO, HO 100/200.

15 Clancarty to Liverpool, 18 November 1824, BL, Add. Ms. 40304; Wellesley to Peel, 2 December 1824, PRO, HO 100/211; Goulburn to Peel, 16 November 1824, SRO, Acc 304/37; Jenkins, *Era of Emancipation*, 216–17.

16 Gregory to Peel, 25 February 1824, BL, Add. Ms. 40344; Gregory to Goulburn, 20 March 1824, SRO, Acc 304/73; Goulburn to Wellesley, 26 March 1824, BL, Add. Ms. 37302; David Plunket, *The Life and Letters and Speeches of Lord Plunket*, 2 vols. (London, 1867), 2:145–6; Goulburn memoirs, SRO, Acc 304/68; Henry Brougham, *Historical Sketches of Statesmen*, 2 vols. (London, 1855), 2:255; Peel to Goulburn, 14 April 1824, SRO, Acc 304/35; Goulburn to Peel, 20 April 1824, BL, Add. Ms. 40330.

17 Goulburn to Peel, 27 October 1824, SRO, Acc 304/35; the description of the association as a "Popish Parliament" was William Gregory's, see Gregory to Goulburn, 16 May 1824, SRO, Acc 304/73; Goulburn to Peel, 14 December 1824, BL, Add. Ms. 37303.

18 *Journal of Mrs. Arbuthnot*, 1:356–57; Wellington to Peel, 3 November 1824, SRO, Acc 304/35; Peel to Goulburn, 6 November 1824, SRO, Acc 304/35; Wellesley to Peel, 10 December 1824, BL, Add. Ms. 37303.

19 Peel to Goulburn, 15 December 1824, BL, Add. Ms. 40330; Peel to Wellesley, 18 December 1824, BL, Add. Ms. 37303; Wellesley to Peel, 19 January 1825, BL Add Ms. 37303; Grenville to Wynn, 26 January 1825, NLW, Coed-y-Maen Mss.; H. Goulburn to J. Goulburn, 5, 9 February 1825, SRO, Acc 304/67; Goulburn to Wellesley, 1 February 1825, BL, Add. Ms. 37303; Buckingham, *Memoirs of the Court of George IV*, 2:210; *Parl. Deb.*, 2nd ser., 12:182, 185.

20 H. Goulburn to J. Goulburn, 11, 19, 12 February 1825, SRO, Acc 304/67; *Parl Deb.*, 2nd ser., 12:318, 200, 691–2; Broughton, *Recollections of a Long Life*, 5 vols. (London, 1909–10), 3:85–8.

21 H. Goulburn to J. Goulburn, 19, 22, 21, n.d. [26] February 1825, SRO, Acc 319/67.

22 For the hearings of the select committee, see *Parl. Papers*, 1825, vol. 9; O'Connell, *Correspondence*, 3:9, 127–9.

23 H. Goulburn to J. Goulburn, 2 March 1825, SRO, Acc 304/25; Buckingham, *Memoirs of the Court of George IV*, 2:229; *Journal of Mrs. Arbuthnot*, 2:380; Liverpool to Peel, 10 March 1825, BL, Add. Ms. 40305; Gregory to Goulburn, 6 March 1825, SRO, Acc 304/74.

24 Gregory to Goulburn, 6, 16, 22 March, 24 April 1825, SRO, Acc 304/74; Peel to Gregory, 21 March 1825, BL, Add. Ms. 40344; Gregory to Peel, 25 March 1825, BL, Add. Ms. 40344.

25 *Parl. Deb.*, 2nd ser., 13:73, 329; O'Connell, *Correspondence*, 3:150, 152; Broughton, *Recollections*, 3:93–8.

26 Jenkins, *Era of Emancipation*, 230; G.I.T. Machin, "The Catholic Emancipation Crisis of 1825," *English Historical Review* 78 (1963): 476–79; *Journal of Mrs. Arbuthnot*, 1:392–401; Goulburn to Gregory, 19 May 1825, EUL, Gregory Papers.

27 Gregory to Goulburn, 7 May 1825, SRO, Acc 304/74; Buckingham, *Memoirs of the Court of George IV*, 2:192; O'Connell, *Correspondence*, 3:173; Gregory to Goulburn, 17, 23 May, 5 June 1825, SRO, Acc 304/74; Goulburn to Gregory, 19, 27 May 1825, EUL, Gregory Papers.

28 Goulburn to Wellesley, 25 June 1825, SRO, Acc 304/43; Wellesley to Goulburn, 27 June 1825, SRO, Acc 304/43.

29 Donald Akenson, *The Irish Education Experiment: The National System of Education in the Nineteenth Century* (Toronto, 1970), 96–8; Goulburn to Wellesley, 6, 10 June 1825, SRO, Acc 304/43.

30 Goulburn to Peel, 19 September 1825, SRO, Acc 304/43; Goulburn to Wellesley, 18 August 1826, SRO Acc 304/43.

31 Wellesley to Goulburn, 17 July, 27 June, and n.d. [October] 1825, SRO, Acc 304/44; Wellesley to Peel, 26 September 1825, PRO, HO 100/214; Goulburn to Peel, 13 October, 15 November 1825, BL, Add. Ms. 40331; O'Connell, *Correspondence*, 3:197.

32 Augustus Granville Stapleton, *George Canning and His Times* (London, 1859), 253–6; Wynn to Spring Rice, n.d. [October 1825], 27 October 1825, NLW, Coed-y-Maen Mss.; Wellesley to Peel, 29 December 1825, BL, Add. Ms. 37303; Goulburn to Peel, 31 December 1825, BL, Add. Ms. 40331; Peel to Wellesley, 3 January 1826, BL, Add. Ms. 37304.

33 Goulburn to Peel, 2 January 1826 1826, BL, Add. Ms. 40332; *Journal of Mrs. Arbuthnot*, 2:2, 6, 9–10, 21; Boyd Hilton, "The Political Arts of Lord Liverpool," *Transactions of the Royal Historical Society*, 5th ser., 38 (1988): 148.

34 Goulburn to Peel, 4 February 1826, BL, Add. Ms. 37304; *Journal of Mrs. Arbuthnot*, 2:10–11; H. Goulburn to J. Goulburn, 12 February 1826, SRO, Acc 304/64.

35 *Parl. Deb.* 2nd ser., 14:128–9, 426–7, and 15:3–11, 15, 81, 227.

36 *Parl. Deb.*, 2nd ser., 14:544–9; George O'Brien, *Economic History of Ireland from the Union to the Famine* (New York, 1921), 160.

37 *Journal of Mrs. Arbuthnot*, 2:16–17, 24; H. Goulburn to J. Goulburn, 29 April, 4 May 1826, SRO, Acc 304/65; H. Goulburn to J. Goulburn, 2 June 1826, SRO, Acc 304/64.

38 Wellesley to Liverpool, 12 January 1826, BL, Add. Ms. 38301; Gregory to Goulburn, 4, 5, 12 May 1826, SRO, Acc 304/76; Wellesley to Peel, 13 May 1826, PRO, HO 100/216.

39 Thomas Pinney, ed., *The Letters of Thomas Babington Macaulay*, vol. 1 (London, 1974), 181; *Journal of Mrs. Arbuthnot*, 2:26; Kenneth Bourne, *Palmerston: The Early Years, 1784–1841* (New York, 1982), 241.

40 Bourne, *Palmerston*, 246, 242, 241; Goulburn to Herries, 26 November 1826, Herries Papers, BL, Add. Ms. 57401.

41 H. Goulburn to J. Goulburn, 20 December 1825, SRO, Acc 304/64; H. Goulburn to J. Goulburn, 24 May 1826, SRO, Acc 304/65; Bourne, *Palmerston*, 247, 243, 246; Z. Macaulay to Goulburn, 2 June 1831, SRO, Acc 304/33.

42 Macaulay to Goulburn, 2 June 1831, SRO, Acc 304/33; George Stephen, *Anti-Slavery Recollections*, 2nd. ed. (London, 1971), 65; Macaulay to Godfrey, president of Queen's College, n.d. [February] 1826, SRO, Acc 304/33; H. Goulburn to J. Goulburn, 26 February 1826, SRO, Acc 304/64.

43 Macaulay to Goulburn, 2 June 1831, SRO, Acc 304/33; H. Goulburn to J. Goulburn, 2, 3 March 1826, SRO, Acc 304/64.

44 Goulburn to Godfrey, 15 May 1826, SRO, Acc 304/33.

45 H. Goulburn to J. Goulburn, n.d. [1826], 14, 29 May, n.d. [May 1826], n.d. [June 1826], 3, 16 June 1826, SRO, Acc 304/65.

46 Henry Lytton Bulwer, *The Life of Henry John Temple, Viscount Palmerston, with Selections from His Diaries and Correspondence*, 3 vols. (London, 1870–74), 1:167–9; Bourne, *Palmerston*, 245, 248; Goulburn diaries, 1826, SRO, Acc 304/24.

47 Bulwer, *Viscount Palmerston*, 1:167–9; Bourne, *Palmerston*, 245, 248; Goulburn diaries, 1826, SRO, Acc 304/24; J.Goulburn to H. Goulburn, 22 February [1827], SRO, Acc 304/67; H. Goulburn to J. Goulburn, 28 January 1825, and n.d., SRO, Acc 304/65; Bathurst to Darling, 10 September 1826, SRO, Acc 304/32.

48 H. Goulburn to J. Goulburn, 21 June 1826, SRO, Acc 304/65; *Journal of Mrs. Arbuthnot*, 2:31, 34; G.I.T. Machin, *The Catholic Question in English Politics 1820 to 1830* (Oxford, 1964), 84–5; Gregory to Goulburn, 22, 24, 26 June 1826, SRO, Acc 304/76; Wellesley to Goulburn, 28 June 1826, SRO, Acc 304/44.

49 Charles Stuart Parker, ed., *Sir Robert Peel from His Private Papers*, 3 vols., reprint (New York, 1970), 2:415; *Journal of Mrs. Arbuthnot*, 2:34; Peel to Liverpool, 12 July 1826, BL, Add. Ms. 40305.

50 Goulburn to Peel, 25 July 1826, BL, Add. Ms. 40332.

51 Peel to Wellington, 31 July 1826, BL, Add. Ms. 40306; Peel to Goulburn, 31 July 1826, SRO, Acc 304/38; Hunt to Fitzgerald, 7 August 1826, Spring Rice Collection, John Rylands University Library (JRU), Manchester; Wellesley to Goulburn, 7 August 1826, SRO, Acc 304/43; Peel to Wellesley, 11 August 1826, SRO, Acc 304/38; Goulburn to Wellesley, n.d. [August] 1826, SRO, Acc 304/43; Wellesley to Peel, 27 August 1826, PRO, HO 100/216.

52 Peel to Goulburn, 17 August 1826, SRO, Acc 304/38; Goulburn to Peel, 25 August 1826, SRO, Acc 304/38; Wellesley to Peel, 27 August, 4 September 1826, PRO, HO 100/216.

53 Goulburn to Peel, 11 October 1826, PRO, HO 100/216.

54 Goulburn to Peel, 13 September 1826, BL, Add. Ms. 40332; Goulburn to Peel, 10 October 1826, PRO, HO 100/216; Peel to Goulburn, 20 October 1826, SRO, Acc 304/38; Parker, *Peel*, 1:421–2.

55 *Parl. Deb.*, 2nd ser., 16:44–8, 89; Peel to Goulburn, 15 December 1826, BL, Add. Ms. 40332; O'Connell, *Correspondence*, 3:283; Goulburn to Peel, 17, 20, 23 December 1826, 24 January 1827, BL, Add. Ms. 40332.

56 H. Goulburn to J. Goulburn, 10, 13 February 1827, SRO, Acc 304/65.

57 H. Goulburn to J. Goulburn, 17, 20 February 1827, and n.d., SRO, Acc 304/65; Christopher Hibbert, *George IV* pb. ed. (London, 1976), 718.

58 J. Goulburn to H. Goulburn, 20 February 1827, SRO, Acc 304/67; H. Goulburn to J. Goulburn, 22, 23, 24, 25 February 1827, SRO, Acc 304/65.

59 *Parl. Deb.* 2nd ser., 16:825; *Journal of Mrs. Arbuthnot*, 2:86; H. Goulburn to J. Goulburn, 5, 8, 14, 21, 22 March 1827, SRO, Acc. 304/65; Goulburn to Gregory, 19 March 1827, EUL, Gregory Papers.

60 Wellington to Londonderry, 20 April 1827, McGill University Library (MUL), C1/14, Henry Hardinge Papers; Louis J. Jennings, ed., *The Croker Papers*, 3 vols. (London, 1885), 1:189; R.W. Davis and R.J. Helmstadter, eds., *Religion and Irreligion in Victorian Society* (London, 1992), 31; Wasson, "Coalitions of 1827," 587–600; Robert Stewart, *The Foundation of the Conservative Party 1830–1867* (London, 1978), 3, 33; Goulburn to Gregory, 14 April 1827, EUL, Gregory Papers.

61 Goulburn memoirs, SRO, Acc 304/68; Goulburn to Wellesley, 20 March 1822, BL, Add. Ms. 37298; Goulburn to Wellesley, 16 May 1822, BL, Add. Ms. 37299; Goulburn to Wellesley, 3 June 1822, SRO, Acc 304/43; Goulburn to Peel, 2 January 1826, BL, Add. Ms. 40332; Parker, *Peel*, 1:60; P.J. Cain and A.G. Hopkins, *British Imperialism: Innovation and Expansion 1688–1914* (London, 1993), 23.

CHAPTER SEVEN

1 For the low opinion of Goderich and his government, see Ellenborough to Hardinge, 12, 16 August [1827], Arbuthnot to Hardinge, 14 August 1827, anon to Hardinge, n.d. [17 August 1827], and Wellington to Hardinge, 24 August 1827, all in McGill University Library (MUL), C1/14, Henry Hardinge Papers.

2 Charles Stuart Parker, ed., *Sir Robert Peel from His Private Papers*, 3 vols., reprint (New York, 1970), 2:22; Christoper Hibbert, *George IV* (London, 1976), 734–5; H. Goulburn to J. Goulburn, 11 January 1828, Surrey Record Office (SRO), Kingston upon Thames, Acc 304/64; Parker, *Peel*, 2:28–9.

3 Goulburn memoirs, SRO, Acc 304/68; H. Goulburn to J. Goulburn, 12 February 1824, SRO, Acc 304/67; H. Goulburn to J. Goulburn, n.d. [1823], SRO, Acc 304/65; Wellington to Goulburn, 9 January 1827, SRO, Acc 304/34; Robert Stewart, *The Foundation of the Conservative Party 1830–1867* (London, 1978), 12.

4 Parker, *Peel*, 2:29; Huskisson to Grenville, 11 January 1828, Huskisson Papers, British Library (BL), Add. Ms. 38754; A. Aspinall, ed., *The Letters of George IV 1812–1830*, 3 vols. (Cambridge, 1938), 3:362–3; Wellington, *Despatches, Correspondence, and Memoranda of Arthur Duke of Wellington (New Series) 1819–1832*, 8 vols. (London, 1867–1880), 4:187; Huskisson to Wellington, 17 January 1828, BL, Add. Ms. 38754; Wellington to Huskisson, 17 January 1828, BL, Add. Ms. 38754.

5 Grant to Huskisson, 17 January 1828, BL, Add. Ms. 38754; Palmerston to Huskisson, n.d. [17 January 1828], BL, Add. Ms. 38754; Huskisson to Granville, 25 January 1828, BL, Add. Ms. 38754; Huskisson to Seaford, 25 January 1828, BL, Add. Ms. 38754; Francis Bamford and Duke of Wellington, eds., *Journal of Mrs. Arbuthnot 1820–1832*, 2 vols. (London, 1950), 2:158–60; Henry Reeve, ed., *The Greville Memoirs*, 3 vols. (London, 1874), 1:108.

6 For the development of the office of chancellor and of Treasury power, see David Kynaston, *The Chancellor of the Exchequer* (Lavenham, 1980), Henry Roseveare, *The Treasury: The Evolution of an Institution* (London, 1969), and Norman Chester, *The English Administrative System 1780–1870* (Oxford, 1981); Norman Gash, *Pillars of Government, and Other Essays on State and Society c.1770–c.1880* (London,1986), 30; Kynaston, *Chancellor of Exchequer*, 7–8, 10–12; Denis Gray, *Spencer Perceval: The Evangelical Prime Minister, 1762–1812* (Manchester, 1963), 94; Roseveare, *The Treasury*, 114.

7 Gray, *Spencer Perceval*, 306–7; Roseveare, *The Treasury*, 123; J.R. Torrance, "Sir George Harrison and the Growth of the Bureaucracy in the Early Nineteenth Century," *English Historical Review* 83 (1968): 58–9; Henry Roseveare, *The Treasury: The Foundations of Control* (London, 1968), 86–93.

8 Sidney Buxton, *Finance and Politics: An Historical Study, 1783–1885*, 2 vols.,
  reprint (New York, 1966), 1:8, 12–14; John Ehrman, *The Younger Pitt*, vol. 1
  (London, 1969), 260–9; Frank W. Fetter, *The Economist in Parliament,
  1780–1868* (Durham, N.C., 1980), 11–12, 111–28; Patricia James, *Population Malthus: His Life and Times* (London, 1979), 245–8; Sydney Checkland,
  British Public Policy 1776–1939: An Economic, Social and Political Perspective
  (Cambridge, 1983), 16–17.

9 P.J. Cain and A.G. Hopkins, *British Imperialism: Innovation and Expansion
  1688–1914* (London, 1993), 79; Boyd Hilton, *Corn, Cash, and Commerce:
  The Economic Policy of the Tory Governments 1815–1830* (Oxford, 1977), 55–
  61, 48, 304–7, 176, 202–9, 215–19; A. Brady, *William Huskisson and Liberal
  Reform* (London, 1928), 111–27; Cain and Hopkins, *British Imperialism*, 39.

10 Boyd Hilton, *Age of Atonement: The Influence of Evangelicalism on Social and
  Economic Thought, 1795–1865* (Oxford, 1988), 36–7, 69; Jonathan Parry,
  The Rise and Fall of Liberal Government in Victorian Britain (New Haven,
  1993), 23, 43; Philip Harling and Peter Mandler, "From 'Fiscal-Military'
  State to Laissez-faire State, 1760–1850," *Journal of British Studies* 32 (1993):
  52; John Rule, *The Vital Century: England's Developing Economy 1714–1815*
  (London, 1992), 290.

11 Hilton, *Corn, Cash, Commerce*, 211–12; Frank W. Fetter, *The Development of
  British Monetary Orthodoxy 1797–1875* (Cambridge, Mass., 1965), 107–8,
  120–2; Fetter, *The Economist in Parliament*, 98; W. Marston Acres, *The Bank of
  England from Within, 1694–1900*, 2 vols. (London, 1931), 2:426–8, 454.

12 Hilton, *Corn, Cash, Commerce*, 200, 302, 20–8; Barry Gordon, *Economic Doctrine and Tory Liberalism, 1824–1830* (London, 1979), 43, 52, 56; Brady,
  Huskisson, 65, 67.

13 Kynaston, *Chancellor of Exchequer*, 113; Northbrook, ed., *Journals and Correspondence of Francis Thornhill Baring, Lord Northbrook*, 2 vols. (London,
  1902), 1:142, 145, 155; Wilbur Devereux Jones, *"Prosperity" Robinson: The
  Life of Viscount Goderich, 1782–1859* (New York, 1967), 173, 92; Henry Parris, *Constitutional Bureaucracy: The Development of British Central Administration
  since the Eighteenth Century* (London, 1969), 47; Louis J. Jennings, ed., *The
  Croker Papers*, 3 vols. (London, 1885), 1:403–4; *Greville Memoirs*, 2:49; *Parl.
  Deb.*, 2nd ser., 18:1311; J. Goulburn to C. Cane, 29 January [1828], SRO,
  Acc 304/64.

14 *Parl. Deb.*, n.s., 21:1168–82, 1311–15, and 19:1206–13; Wellington, *Despatches*, 2nd ser., 5:23; Harling and Mandler, "From 'Fiscal-Military' State,"
  53.

15 *Parl. Deb.*, 2nd ser., 19:990–2, 987; Hilton, *Age of Atonement*, 222; Harling
  and Mandler, "From 'Fiscal-Military' State," 65; B.A. Corry, *Money, Savings
  and Investment in English Economics, 1800–1850* (London, 1962), 25, 71.

16 Kynaston, *Chancellor of Exchequer*, 20; Hilton, *Age of Atonement*, 7; *Parl. Deb.*,
  2nd ser., 18:423–4, 446; Treasury minute books, 11 January 1828, Public

Record Office (PRO), T29/277; Aspinall, *Letters of George IV*, 3:391; Hilton, *Corn, Cash, Commerce*, 241, 249; Edward Herries, *Memoir of the Public Life of the Rt. Hon. John Charles Herries*, 2 vols. (London, 1880), 2:90; *Parl. Deb.*, 2nd ser., 18:1311 and 19:731; Lord Colchester, ed., *A Political Diary 1828–1830, by Edward Law, Lord Ellenborough*, 2 vols. (London, 1881), 1:134; Jennings, *Croker Papers*, 1:407, 419; Ernest Taylor, ed., *The Taylor Papers* (London, 1913), 306; Wellington, *Despatches*, n.s., 4:389–97, 416.

17 *British Sessional Papers* 5 (1828): 548–59, 6–8; ibid., 7 (1829): 4–43; Roseveare, *Treasury Control*, 159–60; Roseveare, *The Treasury*, 137.

18 Hilton, *Corn, Cash, Commerce*, 252–5; *British Sessional Papers* 5 (1828): 565–7.

19 For a brief discussion of Wellington's deficiencies, see John Keegan, *The Mask of Command* (New York, 1987), 141ff; Norman Gash, ed., *Wellington: Studies in the Military and Political Career of the First Duke of Wellington* (Manchester, 1990), 122–7, 117–19; Jennings, *Croker Papers*, 1:405; *Political Diary, Lord Ellenborough*, 1:4, 20–1, 30–1, 34–5; *Greville Memoirs*, 1:126–7; Henry Lytton Bulwer, *The Life of Henry John Temple, Viscount Palmerston, with Selections from His Diaries and Correspondence*, 3 vols. (London, 1870–74), 1:216, 219; Huskisson to Goderich, 12 February 1828, BL, Add. Ms. 38755; Herbert Maxwell, ed., *The Creevey Papers: A Selection from the Correspondence and Diaries of the Late Thomas Creevey, M.P., 1768–1838*, 2 vols. (London, 1903), 2:145.

20 A.W. Ward and G.P. Gooch, eds., *The Cambridge History of British Foreign Policy, 1783–1919*, reprint ed. (New York, 1970), 2:95ff; Neville Thompson, *Wellington after Waterloo* (London, 1986), 75–6; *Political Diary, Lord Ellenborough*, 1:36, 39–40, 42–4, 46; Norman Gash, *Mr. Secretary Peel: The Life of Sir Robert Peel to 1830*, 2nd ed. (London, 1985) 464; G.F.A. Best, "The Constitutional Revolution, 1828–1832," *Theology* 62 (1959): 228; R.W. Davis and R.J. Helmstadter, eds., *Religion and Irreligion in Victorian Society* (London, 1992), 31; Jennings, *Croker Papers*, 1:412.

21 Hilton, *Corn, Cash, Commerce*, 287–90; Bulwer, *Viscount Palmerston*, 1:231–44; Goulburn to Peel, 18, 30 March, and n.d [March] 1828, BL, Add. Ms. 40333; Peel to Goulburn, 29 March [1828], SRO, Acc 304/39; Goulburn to Huskisson, n.d. [March 1828], BL, Add. Ms. 38755; *Political Diary, Lord Ellenborough*, 1:49–73; *Journal of Mrs. Arbuthnot*, 2:174–9.

22 Jennings, *Croker Papers*, 1:415; *Political Diary, Lord Ellenborough*, 1:76; Gordon, *Economic Doctrine and Tory Liberalism*, 57; Hilton, *Corn, Cash, Commerce*, 290–1; Peel to Goulburn, 18 August 1828, SRO, Acc 304/39; Goulburn to Peel, 20 August 1828, BL, Add. Ms. 40333.

23 For a discussion of the crisis, see *Political Diary, Lord Ellenborough*, 1:106–17; Bulwer, *Viscount Palmerston*, 1:233, 253–8; Jennings, *Croker Papers*, 1:409, 413, 420.

24 Bulwer, *Viscount Palmerston*, 1:219, 259–70; *Political Diary, Lord Ellenborough*, 1:115, 111, 113–14; Parry, *Rise and Fall of Liberal Government*, 51.

25 Wellington, *Despatches*, n.s., 4:461–2; *Political Diary, Lord Ellenborough*, 1:118, 127.

26 Thompson, *Wellington after Waterloo*, 89–90, 82; Croker to Hardinge, 2 June 1828, MUL, C1/16, Hardinge Papers; Kenneth Bourne, *The Letters of the Third Viscount Palmerston to Laurence and Elizabeth Sulivan, 1804–1863* (London, 1979), 206–7; *Political Diary, Lord Ellenborough*, 1:143, 145–6; Jennings, *Croker Papers*, 1:426.

27 *Political Diary, Lord Ellenborough*, 1:80; for a brief analysis of the economy, see Arthur D. Gayer, W.W. Rostow, and Anna Jacobson Schwartz, *The Growth and Fluctuation of the British Economy 1790–1850: An Historical, Statistical, and Theoretical Study of Britain's Economic Development*, 2 vols. (Oxford, 1953), 1:211–35.

28 Gordon, *Economic Doctrine and Tory Liberalism*, 123–6; Hilton, *Corn, Cash, Commerce*, 238; Bank of England Committee of Treasury, 30 April, 14 May 1828, Archives of the Bank of England (ABE), G8/23; *Parl. Deb.*, 2nd ser., 19:980–92.

29 Wellington, *Despatches*, n.s., 4:564; *Parl Deb.*, 3rd ser., 7:1032–5; *Parl. Deb.*, 2nd ser., 19:1652–64; Cain and Hopkins, *British Imperialism*, 89; Gordon, *Economic Doctrine and Tory Liberalism*, 114–15.

30 *Parl. Deb.*, 2nd ser., 19:1664, 1670, 1674–82; *Times*, 12 July 1828.

31 Harling and Mandler, "From 'Fiscal-Military' State," 69; *Parl. Deb.*, 2nd ser., 19:1682–6; Emmeline W. Cohen, *The Growth of the British Civil Service 1780–1939*, reprint ed. (London, 1965), 63–4; Treasury minute, 4 August 1829, PRO, T172/918.

32 *Political Diary, Lord Ellenborough*, 1:173, 184–7, 207, 212; Peel to Goulburn, 17 September [1828], SRO, Acc 304/39.

33 *Political Diary, Lord Ellenborough*, 1:241; Wellington to Goulburn, 14 September 1828, SRO, Acc 304/34; Wellington, *Despatches*, n.s., 4:653, 656: Wellington to Goulburn, 16 September 1828, SRO, Acc 304/34; Wellington, *Despatches*, n.s., 4:629–30, 640.

34 Peel to Goulburn, 4 August [1828], n.d. [August 1828], SRO Acc 304/40; *Political Diary, Lord Ellenborough*, 1:159–63, 169, 176; Elizabeth Longford, *Wellington: Pillar of State* (London, 1972), 69.

35 Longford, *Wellington: Pillar of State*, 69; *Greville Memoirs*, 1: 138; Wellington, *Despatches*, n.s., 4:653, 656; Parker, *Peel*, 2:53.

36 Goulburn to Peel, 9 September, 14 November 1828, BL, Add. Ms. 40333.

37 *Journal of Mrs. Arbuthnot*, 2:229, 231–2; Owen Chadwick, *The Victorian Church*, 2 vols. (London, 1966–70), 1:9, 17; Parry, *Rise and Fall of Liberal Government*, 54; Parker, *Peel*, 2:82; *Political Diary, Lord Ellenborough*, 1:300; Walter Alison Phillips, ed., *The History of the Church of Ireland from the Earliest Times to the Present Day*, 3 vols. (Oxford, 1933), 3:294.

38 Parker, *Peel*, 2:89; *Parl. Deb.*, 2nd ser., 20:263; *Political Diary, Lord Ellenborough*, 1:358, 365.

39 *Parl. Deb.*, 2nd ser., 20:1128–37; *Political Diary, Lord Ellenborough,* 1:412.

40 John Wolffe, *The Protestant Crusade in Great Britain, 1829–1860* (Oxford, 1991), 19–23; Gash, *Mr. Secretary Peel,* 587; Goulburn to Peel, 9 July 1829, BL, Add. Ms. 40333; *Parl. Deb.*, 2nd ser., 24:88, 853, 74.

41 Stewart, *Foundation of the Conservative Party,* 43–4, 48; Bruce Coleman, *Conservatism and the Conservative Party in Nineteenth-Century Britain* (London, 1988), 46; Parry, *Rise and Fall of Liberal Government,* 54–5.

42 Gordon, *Economic Doctrine and Tory Liberalism,* 126; Peel to Goulburn, 14 January 1829, SRO, Acc 304/39; Gayer, Rostow, and Schwartz, *Growth and Fluctuations of British Economy,* 1:211, 213, 215; Gash, *Mr. Secretary Peel,* 601, 603,

43 *Parl. Deb.*, 2nd ser., 21:1168–82; Diaries of Harry Goulburn, 8 May 1828, SRO, Acc 304/67; *Parl. Deb.*, 2nd ser., 20:338, 449; Hilton, *Corn, Cash, Commerce,* 255.

44 *Parl. Deb.*, 2nd ser., 21:1183–5, 1186, 1255–6; Denis Le Marchant, *Memoir of John Charles Viscount Althorp, Third Earl Spencer* (London, 1876), 229–32; Kynaston, *Chancellor of the Exchequer,* 113–4.

45 *Parl. Deb.*, 2nd ser., 21:1311–15, 1570, 1598, 1543; Hardinge to Taylor, 20 January 1830, MUL, C2/4, Hardinge Papers; Wellington, *Despatches,* n.s., 6:125; Wellington to Goulburn, 19 October 1829, SRO, Acc 304/34; Hay to Hardinge, 12 May 1829, MUL, C2/1, Hardinge Papers; Goulburn to Babbage, 20 November 1829, BL, Add. Ms. 37184, Babbage Papers; Babbage to Goulburn, 24 November 1829, BL, Add. Ms. 37184; Anthony Hyman, *Charles Babbage: Pioneer of the Computer* (Princeton, 1982), 49; Henry Parris, *Constitutional Bureaucracy: The Development of British Central Administration since the Eighteenth Century* (London, 1969), 276; Wellington to Goulburn, 30 August 1830, SRO, Acc 304/34; Wellington, *Despatches,* n.s., 6:124–5.

46 Lewis Melville, ed., *The Huskisson Papers* (London, 1931), 310–14; *Quarterly Review,* 43 (1830):304; Wellington, *Despatches,* n.s., 6:407–8, 417–18, 502–3, 507–8, 222–3, 265–6: A. Aspinall, ed., *Correspondence of Charles Arbuthnot, 1808–1850,* Royal Historical Society, Camden Third Series, 65 (London, 1941), 122–3, 125–7.

47 Greville *Memoirs,* 1:266; Thompson, *Wellington after Waterloo,* 99: *Parl. Deb.*, 2nd ser., 22:89–91, 94, 155–60, 166; *Journal of Mrs. Arbuthnot,* 2:331.

48 *Parl. Deb.*, 2nd ser., 22:90, 165, 386–7, 502, 744–53; *Correspondence of Arbuthnot,* 124.

49 Herries to Goulburn, 29 July 1829, BL, Add. Ms. 57401; Wellington, *Despatches,* n.s., 6:393, 5:21–3.

50 Wellington, *Despatches,* n.s., 5:27; Wellington and Goulburn to governor and deputy governor of Bank of England, 16 February 1830, ABE, M5/201.

51 Committee of Treasury, 22 February 1830, ABE, G8/24; governor and deputy governor to Wellington and Goulburn, 23 February 1830, ABE, M5/

201; memoranda of interviews, 23, 27 February, 10 March 1830, ABE M5/
201; Wellington and Goulburn to governor and deputy governor, 6 March
1830, ABE, M5/201.

52 Memoranda of interviews, 16, 23, 29 April 1830, ABE, M5/201; Goulburn
to Palmer, 27 April 1830, ABE, M5/201; Palmer to Goulburn, ABE, G23/
53, secretary's letterbooks.

53 Wellington, *Despatches*, n.s., 5:23; *Political Diary, Lord Ellenborough*, 2:203–4;
Hilton, *Corn, Cash, Commerce*, 260; Lucy Brown, *The Board of Trade and the
Free Trade Movement, 1830–1842* (Oxford, 1958), 8–9; Kynaston, *Chancellor
of the Exchequer*, 89; *Political Diary, Lord Ellenborough*, 2:203–6, 208–13; *Journal of Mrs. Arbuthnot*, 2:335, 343–5.

54 *Parl. Deb.*, 2nd ser., 23:301–22; *Parl. Deb.*, 2nd ser., 24:27.

55 *Parl. Deb.*, 2nd ser., 23:331, 923–30; Taylor, *Taylor Papers*, 316–17; *Parl. Deb.*,
2nd ser., 23:1418–23; Le Marchant, *Althorp*, 236.

56 *Political Diary, Lord Ellenborough*, 2:216–17; *Parl. Deb.*, 2nd ser., 23:896–904;
Peel to Goulburn, 14 October 1828, SRO, Acc 304/39; *Parl. Deb.*, 2nd ser.,
24:959, 1399–40.

57 Jennings, *Croker Papers*, 2:60; Peel to Goulburn, 6 April 1830, BL, Add. Ms.
40333; Parker, *Peel*, 2:151.

58 Goulburn to Peel, n.d. [4 May 1830], BL, Add. Ms. 40333; *Political Diary,
Lord Ellenborough*, 2:237; *Parl. Deb.*, 2nd ser., 24:696, 750; Goulburn to Peel,
11 May 1830, BL, Add. Ms. 40333.

59 Gash, *Mr. Secretary Peel*, 632; *Political Diary, Lord Ellenborough*, 2:269; *Parl.
Deb.*, 2nd ser., 25:22; *Greville Memoirs*, 1:269–71.

60 *Parl. Deb.*, 2nd ser., 25:315–22, 535–42; *Political Diary, Lord Ellenborough*,
2:270, 274, 276–7, 295–6; *Parl. Deb.*, 2nd ser., 25:830.

61 *Political Diary, Lord Ellenborough*, 2:277; *Journal of Mrs. Arbuthnot*, 2:355;
Gash, *Mr. Secretary Peel*, 634–5; *Political Diary, Lord Ellenborough*, 2:289–90,
295; *Journal of Mrs. Arbuthnot*, 2:366, 372–3.

62 *Political Diary, Lord Ellenborough*, 2:346; memorandum of interview,
14 September 1830, ABE, M5/201.

63 *Parl. Deb.*, 2nd ser., 24:64–7; Parris, *Constitutional Bureaucracy*, 249; Roseveare, *The Treasury*, 137; Cohen, *Growth of British Civil Service*, 66; Wellington, *Despatches*, n.s., 6:564.

CHAPTER EIGHT

1 Lord Colchester, ed., *A Political Diary 1828–1830, by Edward Law, Lord
Ellenborough*, 2 vols. (London, 1881), 2:308–12; Henry Reeve, ed., *The
Greville Memoirs*, 3 vols. (London, 1874), 2:3, 12; Herbert Maxwell, ed.,
*The Creevey Papers: A Selection from the Correspondence and Diaries of the Late
Thomas Creevey, M.P., 1768–1838*, 2 vols. (London, 1903), 2:211–
12.

2   Buckingham and Chandos, *Memoirs of the Courts and Cabinets of William IV and Victoria*, 2 vols. (London, 1861), 1:43–5; *Greville Memoirs*, 2:25; Michael Staunton, *Hints for Hardinge* (Dublin, 1830), 39–40, 54; Wellington, *Despatches, Correspondence, and Memoranda of Arthur Duke of Wellington (New Series) 1819–1832*, 8 vols. (London, 1867–80), 7:72–3, 80–1, 112; *Political Diary, Lord Ellenborough*, 2:333; Bruce Coleman, *Conservatism and the Conservative Party in Nineteenth-Century Britain* (London, 1988), 50; Robert Stewart, *The Foundation of the Conservative Party, 1830–1867* (London, 1978), 53; Kenneth Bourne, ed., *The Letters of the Third Viscount Palmerston to Laurence and Elizabeth Sulivan 1804–1863* (London, 1979), 240.

3   Francis Bamford and Duke of Wellington, eds., *Journal of Mrs. Arbuthnot 1820–1832*, 2 vols. (London, 1950), 2:381; *Edinburgh Review* 51 (1830): 571, 577; ibid., 52 (1830): 265, 267, 272; Jonathan Parry, *The Rise and Fall of Liberal Government in Victorian Britain* (New Haven, 1993), 57; *Political Diary, Lord Ellenborough*, 2:362–3.

4   Neville Thompson, *Wellington after Waterloo* (London, 1986), 103–4; J. Goulburn to Cane, n.d. [1830], Surrey Record Office (SRO), Kingston upon Thames, Acc 304/65; J. Goulburn to Harry Goulburn, n.d. [September 1830], SRO, Acc 304/66; A. Aspinall, ed., *Correspondence of Charles Arbuthnot, 1808–1850* (London, 1941), 131; *Political Diary, Lord Ellenborough*, 2:362; Norman Gash, *Mr. Secretary Peel: The Life of Sir Robert Peel to 1830*, 2nd ed., (London, 1985), 643; *Journal of Mrs. Arbuthnot*, 2:389–91, 393–5; Henry Lytton Bulwer, *The Life of Henry John Temple, Viscount Palmerston, with Selections from His Diaries and Correspondence*, 3 vols. (London, 1870–74), 1:362–3; Michael Brock, *The Great Reform Act* (London, 1973), 113; *Edinburgh Review*, 52 (1830): 278.

5   Wellington, *Despatches*, n.s., 7:295, 130–2, 314–15; for the growing significance of public opinion, see Parry, *Rise and Fall of Liberal Government*; *Political Diary, Lord Ellenborough*, 2:383, 388; Peel to Hardinge, 6 October 1830, McGill University Library (MUL), C2/7, Henry Hardinge Papers.

6   *Political Diary, Lord Ellenborough*, 2:388, 390, 403; Arthur D. Gayer, W.W. Rostow, and Anna Jacobson Schwartz, *The Growth and Fluctuations of the British Economy 1790–1850: An Historical, Statistical, and Theoretical Study of Britain's Economic Development*, 2 vols. (Oxford, 1953), 2:240–1; Goulburn to Peel, 17 August 1830, SRO, Acc 304/40; Peel to Hardinge, 14 October 1830, MUL, C2/7, Hardinge Papers; *Times*, 3 November 1830; Brock, *Great Reform Act*, 117.

7   Brock, *Great Reform Act*, 121, 76–9; Wellington, *Despatches*, n.s., 7:352–3; John Keegan, *The Mask of Command* (New York, 1987), 162; *Political Diary, Lord Ellenborough*, 2:426, 414, 416; *Parl. Deb.*, 2nd ser., 18:1416; *Blackwood's Magazine* 27 (1830): 722–3.

8   *Journal of Mrs. Arbuthnot*, 2:400–1, 402; *Political Diary, Lord Ellenborough*, 2:427, 429, 431; Gash, *Mr. Secretary Peel*, 651; *Times*, 13 November 1830;

Broughton, *Recollections of a Long Life*, 6 vols. (London, 1910), 4:63; Wellington, *Despatches*, n.s., 7:361; *Correspondence of Arbuthnot*, 132; Parry, *Rise
and Fall of Liberal Government*, 70.

9 Goulburn to Gregory, 3 December 1830, Emory University Library (EUL),
   William Gregory Papers; J. Goulburn to Harry Goulburn, n.d. [November
   1830], SRO Acc 304/31.

10 Goulburn to Gregory, 3 December 1830, EUL, Gregory Papers; J. Goulburn
   to Harry Goulburn, n.d. [December 1830], J. Goulburn to Harry Goulburn, n.d. [November/December 1830], J. Goulburn to Harry Goulburn,
   2 December 1830, Edward Goulburn to Harry Goulburn, n.d. [January
   1831], and Freddy Goulburn to J. Goulburn, n.d. [November 1830], SRO
   Acc 304/31.

11 Goulburn to Gregory, 3 December 1830, EUL, Gregory Papers; Bourne,
   Palmerston-Sulivan Letters, 230; Harry Goulburn to W. Jackman, n.d. [1829],
   SRO, Acc 304/33; Goulburn to Harry Goulburn, 13 October 1830, SRO, Acc
   304/31; Goulburn to Harry Goulburn, 30 November 1831, SRO, Acc 304/
   67; J. Goulburn to Harry Goulburn, 27 October 1830, SRO, Acc 304/31.

12 *Greville Memoirs*, 2:71; Peter Mandler, *Aristocratic Government in the Age of Reform: Whigs and Liberals 1830–52* (Oxford, 1990), 122, 124; E.A. Smith,
   Lord Grey 1764–1845 (Oxford, 1990), 10–11; E.A. Wasson, *Whig Renaissance: Lord Althorp and the Whig Party, 1782–1845* (New York, 1987), 73–80,
   84; Ellis Archer Wasson, "The Great Whigs and Parliamentary Reform,
   1809–1830," *Journal of British Studies* 24 (1985): 434–64; Mandler, *Aristocratic Government*, 8; Richard Brent, *Liberal Anglican Politics: Whiggery, Religion and Reform, 1830–1841* (Oxford, 1987), 43–7, 52–3; John A. Phillips,
   "The Many Faces of Reform: The Reform Bill and the Electorate," *Parliamentary History* 1 (1982): 115; John Milton-Smith, "Earl Grey's Cabinet and
   the Objects of Parliamentary Reform," *Historical Journal* 15 (1972): 63–6.

13 Stewart, *Foundation of the Conservative Party*, 6; Goulburn to Peel, 3 October
   1847, British Library (BL), Add. Ms. 40445; J. Goulburn to Harry Goulburn, n.d. [December 1830], SRO, Acc 304/31; R.A. Soloway, *Prelates and
   People: Ecclesiastical Social Thought in England 1783–1852* (London, 1969),
   83–4; *A Portion of the Journal Kept by Thomas Raikes Esq.*, 4 vols. (London,
   1856), 1:113–14.

14 H. Goulburn to J. Goulburn, 26 January 1819, SRO, Acc 304/31; E. Jones-
   Parry, ed., *Correspondence of Lord Abderdeen and Princess Lieven*, 2 vols., Camden Third Series (London, 1938–39), 1:81–2; Angus Hawkins, "'Parliamentary Government' and Victorian Political Parties, c.1830–c.1880,"
   English Historical Review 104 (1989): 652; Parry, *Rise and Fall of Liberal Government*, 76, 72; G.F.A. Best, "The Whigs and the Church Establishment in
   the Age of Grey and Holland," *History* 45 (1960): 117–18; Frank O'Gorman, *Voters, Patrons and Parties: The Unreformed Electoral System of Hanoverian
   England, 1734–1832* (Oxford, 1989), 245, 199, 207–15; John A. Phillips

and Charles Wetherell, "The Great Reform Bill of 1832 and the Rise of Partisanship," *Journal of Modern History* 63 (1991): 624–7; *Times*, 18 November 1830.

15 Harry Goulburn to J. Goulburn, 17 November 1830, SRO, Acc 304/64; J. Goulburn to Harry Goulburn, 22 August 1831, H. Goulburn to Harry Goulburn, n.d. [July 1831], and J. Goulburn to Harry Goulburn, 14 September 1831, SRO, Acc 304/67; H. Goulburn to J. Goulburn, 13 February 1832, SRO, Acc 304/65.

16 H. Goulburn to J. Goulburn, 5 February 1831, SRO, Acc 304/65; Parry, *Rise and Fall of Liberal Government*, 105; F.M.L. Thompson, ed., *The Cambridge Social History of Britain, 1750–1950*, vol. 3, *Social Agencies and Institutions* (Cambridge, 1990), 3:15; Buckingham, *Memoirs of William IV and Victoria*, 1:212; Lucy Brown, *The Board of Trade and the Free Trade Movement 1830–1842* (Oxford, 1958), 46; Denis Le Marchant, *Memoir of John Charles Viscount Althorp, Third Earl Spencer* (London, 1876), 276–86; Ellenborough Journals, 11, 12 February 1831, Public Record Office (PRO), 30/12/28/2; John Brooke and Julia Gandy, eds., *The Prime Ministers' Papers: Wellington, Political Correspondence, vol. 1, 1833–November 1834* (London, 1975), 309; Philip A. Buckner, *The Transition to Responsible Government: British Policy in British North America, 1815–1850* (Westport, 1985), 22.

17 *Parl. Deb.*, 3rd ser., 2:418–25; *Times*, 12, 15 February 1831; *Greville Memoirs*, 2:113, 117; Sidney Buxton, *Finance and Politics: An Historical Study, 1783–1885*, 2 vols., reprint (New York, 1966), 1:34; Brown, *Board of Trade*, 48; Ellenborough Journals, 21, 24 February 1831, PRO, 30/12/28/2.

18 Le Marchant, *Althorp*, 286; H. Goulburn to J. Goulburn, n.d [15 February 1831], SRO, Acc 304/65; A. Aspinall, ed., *Three Early Nineteenth Century Diaries* (London, 1952), 10; Ellenborough Journals, 26 February 1831, PRO, 30/12/28/2; Louis J. Jennings, *The Croker Papers*, 3 vols. (London, 1885), 2:105; *Greville Memoirs*, 2:80, 95; Stewart, *Foundation of the Conservative Party*, 58, 70–2; H. Goulburn to J. Goulburn, 4 February 1831, SRO, Acc 304/65; *Correspondence of Arbuthnot*, 135–7.

19 Ellenborough Journals, 26 February 1831, PRO, 30/12/28/2; Broughton, *Recollections*, 4:98; for the weaknesses of the old system, see Brock, *Great Reform Act*, 18ff; John Prest, *Lord John Russell* (Columbia, S.C., 1972), 40–5.

20 *Greville Memoirs*, 2:121–3; Ellenborough Journals, 2 March 1831, PRO, 30/12/28/2; Wasson, *Althorp*, 207–9; Norman Gash, *Sir Robert Peel: The Life of Sir Robert Peel after 1830* (London, 1972), 10; H. Goulburn to J. Goulburn, 4 February 1831, SRO, Acc 304/65; H. Goulburn to J. Goulburn, 2 March 1831, SRO, Acc 304/66; J. Goulburn to Harry Goulburn, 5 March 1831, SRO, Acc 304/66.

21 Ellenborough Journals, 3 March 1831, PRO, 30/12/28/2; Gash, *Sir Robert Peel*, 12–13; Brock, *Great Reform Act*, 163; H. Goulburn to J. Goulburn,

9 March 1831, SRO, Acc 304/66: *Parl. Deb.*, 3rd ser., 3:279–86; Monteagle to Lady Holland, n.d. [March 1831], BL, Add. Ms. 51573.

22 H. Goulburn to J. Goulburn, 9 March 1831, SRO, Acc 304/66; Ellenborough Journals, 10 March 1831, PRO, 30/12/28/2; *Greville Memoirs*, 2:130; Brock, *Great Reform Act*, 173; *Greville Memoirs*, 2:130; H. Goulburn to J. Goulburn, 19 March 1831, SRO, Acc 304/66; H. Goulburn to J. Goulburn, 16 March 1831, SRO, Acc 304/65; H. Goulburn to Harry Goulburn, 19 March 1831, SRO, Acc 304/66.

23 H. Goulburn to J. Goulburn, n.d. [23 March 1831], SRO, Acc 304/65; Philip Ziegler, *King William IV* (London, 1973), 182–5; H. Goulburn to Harry Goulburn, 23 March 1831, SRO, Acc 304/66; Brock, *Great Reform Act*, 179, 182–9; Wellington, *Despatches*, n.s., 7:423–6; *Correspondence of Arbuthnot*, 141; Gash, *Sir Robert Peel*, 14.

24 Ellenborough Journals, 25 March 1831, PRO, 30/12/28/2; *Parl. Deb.*, 3rd ser., 3:1190; H. Goulburn to Harry Goulburn, 27 April 1831, SRO, Acc 304/66: *Times*, 2, 5 April 1831.

25 *Times*, 2 April, 4 May 1831; *Parl. Deb.*, 3rd ser., 27:241, 38:1241, and 55:726.

26 Parry, *Rise and Fall of Liberal Government*, 60; Resolutions of the General Meeting of the Anti-Slavery Society, 23 April 1831, SRO, Acc 304/33; Members of the University of Cambridge ..., 28 April 1831, SRO, Acc 304/33; Goulburn to Bayley, 6 November, 19 December 1831, SRO, Acc 304/54; Bourne, *Palmerston-Sulivan Letters*, 249: Aspinall, *Three Early Nineteenth Century Diaries*, 91; J. Goulburn to Harry Goulburn, n.d. [April 1831], SRO, Acc 304/66; for the 1831 election expenses, see SRO, Acc 304/24; Cunningham to Goulburn, 10 May 1831, and Goulburn to Cunningham, 14 May 1831, SRO, Acc 304/32.

27 Goulburn to Pringle, 19, 25 May 1831, Pringle to Goulburn, 20, 27 May 1831, Macaulay to Pringle, 30 May 1831, Goulburn to Cunningham, 25 May 1831, Cunningham to Goulburn, 30 May, 4 June 1831, Goulburn to Cunningham, 10 June 1831, Cunningham to Goulburn, 14 June [1831], Macaulay to Goulburn, 2, 10 June, 10, 16, 21, 25 July, 1 November 1831, Goulburn to Macaulay, 6 June, 7, 13, 20, 30 July, 4 August 1831, Wildman to Goulburn, 30 June 1831, and Goulburn to Wildman, 15 November 1831, SRO, Acc 304/33.

28 Goulburn to Smith, 2 August 1831, Smith to Goulburn, 9 February 1832, and Bishop of Jamaica to Goulburn, 19 March 1832, SRO, Acc 304/33.

29 Wellington to Goulburn, 11 May 1831, SRO, Acc 304/67; Robert Stewart, *Party and Politics, 1830–1852* (New York, 1989), 24; Gash, *Sir Robert Peel*, 18; John A. Phillips, *The Great Reform Bill in the Boroughs: English Electoral Behaviour 1818–1841* (Oxford, 1992), 297–8; Stewart, *Foundation of the Conservative Party*, 82; Brock, *Great Reform Act*, 199; Wellington, *Despatches*, n.s., 7:451.

30 *Times*, 21 May 1831; Charles Stuart Parker, ed, *Sir Robert Peel from His Private Papers*, 3 vols., reprint (New York, 1970), 2:186–7.

31 Goulburn to Peel, 2 June 1831, BL, Add Ms. 40333; Peel to Goulburn, 5 June 1831, SRO, Acc 304/40; Peel to Herries, 2, 7 June 1831, BL, Add Ms. 57402; Aspinall, *Three Early Nineteenth Century Diaries*, 91; Norman Gash, *Politics in the Age of Peel* (London, 1952), 395.

32 H. Goulburn to J. Goulburn, 17 June 1831, SRO, Acc 304/65; Brock, *Great Reform Act*, 215; Wasson, *Althorp*, 220; *Parl. Deb.*, 3rd ser., 5:613, 707–9, 875–6, 879, 1150; J. Goulburn to Harry Goulburn, 12 August 1831, SRO, Acc 304/67.

33 Gash, *Sir Robert Peel*, 21; J. Goulburn to Harry Goulburn, 5 August 1831, SRO, Acc 304/67; Peel to Goulburn, 17, 26 August 1831, SRO, Acc 304/40; Peel to Hardinge, 13 September 1831, MUL, C1/9, Hardinge Papers.

34 *Parl. Deb.*, 3rd ser., 6:1409–11 and 7:60–1; Prest, *Lord John Russell*, 49–50; Wasson, *Althorp*, 225; H. Goulburn to J. Goulburn, 4 October 1831, SRO, Acc 304/65; Thompson, *Wellington after Waterloo*, 118.

35 *Parl. Deb.* 3rd ser., 8:386–90; *Times*, 13 October 1831; Wellington, *Despatches*, n.s., 7:563; Brock, *Great Reform Act*, 248, 257.

36 Brock, *Great Reform Act*, 259, 240, 265; Smith, *Lord Grey*, 269; Thompson, *Wellington after Waterloo*, 121; Parker, *Peel*, 2:194–6; H. Goulburn to Harry Goulburn, 30 November 1831, SRO, Acc 304/67.

37 Brock, *Great Reform Act*, 266; *Parl. Deb.*, 3rd ser., 9:631; Peel to Goulburn, 21 December 1831, SRO, Acc 304/40; Goulburn to Peel, n.d. [December 1831], 28 December 1831, BL, Add Ms. 40333.

38 Peel to Goulburn, n.d. [December 1831/January 1832], SRO, Acc 304/40.

39 Gash, *Sir Robert Peel*, 25; H. Goulburn to J. Goulburn, 25 January 1832, SRO, Acc 304/65; *Parl. Deb.*, 3rd ser., 7:82, 97, 1032–5, and 9:1285–94; *Correspondence of Arbuthnot*, 154.

40 *Parl. Deb.*, 3rd ser., 9:671, 689–91, 694, 720, 748, 987–8, 759.

41 *Parl. Deb.*, 3rd ser., 10:47, 222; ibid., 9:812–17; ibid., 10:228; ibid., 11:855–7.

42 Wasson, *Althorp*, 240–1; Ziegler, *William IV*, 205–14; Brock, *Great Reform Act*, 282–92.

43 Thompson, *Wellington after Waterloo*, 123–4; *Correspondence of Arbuthnot*, 159; *Times*, 9 May 1832; Brock, *Great Reform Act*, 293–7; Gash, *Sir Robert Peel*, 29; Ellenborough Journals, 11, 12 May 1832, PRO, 30/12/28/3.

44 [John Wade], *The Extraordinary Black Book: An Exposition of Abuses in Church and State* (London, 1832), 537, 246–7; Jennings, *Croker Papers*, 2:163.

45 Goulburn to Wordsworth, 15 May 1832, Correspondence of Christopher Wordsworth, in Lambeth Palace Library (LPL), Ms. 1822; H. Goulburn to J. Goulburn, 8, 11, 15 May 1832, n.d. [May 1832], SRO, Acc 304/65; Goulburn to Peel, n.d. [December 1831], BL, Add. Ms. 40333; Goulburn memoirs, SRO, Acc 304/68.

46 Goulburn to Wordsworth, 15 May 1832, LPL, Ms. 1822; H. Goulburn to J. Goulburn, 15 May 1832, SRO, Acc 304/65; Stewart, *Party and Politics*, 32–3; Phillips, *Great Reform Bill in the Boroughs*, 2.

47 Wasson, *Althorp*, 260; H. Goulburn to J. Goulburn, 21 June 1832, SRO, Acc 304/65; *Greville Memoirs*, 2:301; *Correspondence of Arbuthnot*, 161; H. Goulburn to J. Goulburn, July 1832, SRO, Acc 304/65; 25 February 1832, SRO, Acc 304/64.

48 Harry Goulburn to J. Goulburn, 11 November 1831, SRO, Acc 304/65; Richard J. Evans, "Epidemics and Revolutions: Cholera in Nineteenth-Century Europe," *Past and Present* 120 (1988): 135, 132; Elizabeth Burton, *The Early Victorians at Home, 1837–1861* (Newton Abbott, 1973), 201; Harry Goulburn to J. Goulburn, 30 November 1831, SRO, Acc 304/65.

49 J. Goulburn to Harry Goulburn, 22 August, 12 September 1832, 31 March 1831, SRO, Acc 304/66; Harry Goulburn to Edward Goulburn, 13 March 1832, SRO, Acc 304/65; H. Goulburn's requests to God, SRO, Acc 304/66; Wellington to Goulburn, 19 August 1833, SRO, Acc 304/34.

50 H. Goulburn to J. Goulburn, 14, 15 February 1832, SRO, Acc 304/65; *Greville Memoirs*, 2:279.

51 J. Goulburn to Jane Goulburn, n.d. [1832], J. Goulburn to Harry Goulburn, 27 July 1832, SRO, Acc 304/66; H. Goulburn to J. Goulburn, 15 February 1832, SRO, Acc 304/65; ibid., 23 July 1832, SRO, Acc 304/33; Owen Chadwick, *The Victorian Church*, 2 vols. (London, 1966–70), 1:36–7; J. Goulburn to Harry Goulburn, 31 August [1832], SRO, Acc 304/66.

52 H. Goulburn to Harry Goulburn, 12 August 1832, SRO, Acc 304/66.

53 Peel to Goulburn, 2 November 1832, SRO, Acc 304/40; Goulburn to Peel, 5 November 1832, BL, Add Ms. 40333.

54 Peel to Goulburn, 25, 14 December 1832, SRO, Acc 304/40; for the interest in slavery, see Gladstone's comments on his contest in Newark, in John Brooke and Mary Sorenson, eds., *Prime Ministers' Papers: W.E. Gladstone*, vol. 2, *Autobiographical Memoranda, 1832–1845* (London, 1972) 13; for Goulburn's election expenses, see SRO, Acc 304/24; Harry Goulburn to H. Goulburn, 22 November 1832, SRO, Acc 304/66; Goulburn to Peel, 12 December 1832, BL, Add Ms. 40333; Stewart, *Foundation of the Conservative Party*, 84–5.

CHAPTER NINE

1 Goulburn to Herries, 4 January 1833, British Library BL, Add. Ms. 57401; Goulburn to Peel, 5 November 1832, BL, Add. Ms. 40333; Peel to Goulburn, 3 January 1833, Surrey Record Office (SRO), Kingston upon Thames, Acc 304/40.

2 Goulburn to Herries, 4 January 1833, BL, Add. Ms. 57401; John Brooke and Julia Gandy, eds., *Prime Ministers' Papers: Wellington, Political Correspon-*

dence, vol. 1, *1833-November 1834* (London, 1975), 16–18, 74; A. Aspinall, ed., *Correspondence of Charles Arbuthnot, 1808–1850* (London, 1941), 165–6; Ellenborough Journals, 29 January 1833, Public Record Office (PRO), 30/12/28/4.

3 Henry Reeve, ed., *The Greville Memoirs*, 3 vols. (London, 1874), 3:27, 2:353; Norman Gash, *Sir Robert Peel: The Life of Sir Robert Peel after 1830*, 2nd ed. (New York, 1986), 44; Melville to Goulburn, 8 February 1833, SRO, Acc 304/46; E.A. Wasson, *Whig Renaissance: Lord Althorp and the Whig Party, 1782–1845* (New York, 1987), 248; H. Goulburn to J. Goulburn, 22, 23 February 1833, SRO, Acc 304/64; Olive J. Brose, *Church and Parliament: The Reshaping of the Church of England 1828–1860* (Stanford, 1959), 21; H.C.G. Matthew, *Gladstone, 1809–1874* pb. ed. (Oxford, 1988), 5, 29; *Parl. Deb.*, 2nd ser., 25:95, 99.

4 *Random Recollections of the House of Commons* (London, 1835), 122–4; Bruce Coleman, *Conservatism and the Conservative Party in Nineteenth-Century Britain* (London, 1988), 121–3; John Walsh, Colin Haydon, and Stephen Taylor, eds., *The Church of England c.1689–c.1865: From Toleration to Tractarianism* (Cambridge, 1993), 354–5, 337; Owen Chadwick, *The Victorian Church*, 2 vols. (London, 1966–70), 1:62.

5 Goulburn memoirs, SRO, Acc 304/68; Jonathan Parry, *The Rise and Fall of Liberal Government in Victorian Britain* (New Haven, 1993), 100; *PMP: Wellington*, 1:106; John A. Phillips, *Great Reform Bill in the Boroughs: English Electoral Behaviour 1818–1841* (Oxford, 1992), 272–3, 278; Parry, *Rise and Fall of Liberal Government*, 15; David Hempton, *Methodism and Politics in British Society 1750–1850*, pb. ed. (London, 1987), 185, 206; G.F.A. Best, "The Constitutional Revolution of 1828–32," *Theology* 62 (1959): 229–31; Chadwick, *Victorian Church*, 1:23.

6 For the church and its problems, see Peter Virgin, *The Church in the Age of Negligence: Ecclesiastical Structure and Problems of Church Reform, 1700–1840* (Cambridge, 1989); Desmond Bowen, *The Idea of the Victorian Church: A Study of the Church of England 1833–1889* (Montreal, 1968); G.F.A. Best, *Temporal Pillars: Queen Anne's Bounty, the Ecclesiastical Commissioners, and the Church of England* (Cambridge, 1964); Walsh, Haydon, and Taylor, *Church of England*, 1–64, 265–82; *Edinburgh Review*, 98 (1853): 141–3; G.I.T. Machin, *Politics and the Churches in Great Britain, 1832 to 1868* (Oxford, 1977), 6; William Law Mathieson, *English Church Reform 1815–1840* (London, 1923), 62; Chadwick, *Victorian Church*, 1:25–7, 38–9; Brose, *Church and Parliament*, 7–21; Elizabeth Burton, *The Early Victorians at Home, 1837–1861* (Newton Abbott, 1973), 62.

7 Philip Ziegler, *King William IV* (London, 1971), 242; Brose, *Church and Parliament*, 47; Richard Brent, *Liberal Anglican Politics: Whiggery, Religion and Reform 1830–1841* (Oxford, 1987), 25–8.

8 Goulburn's notes on Irish education, 1832, SRO, Acc 304/33; *Parl. Deb.*, 3rd ser., 14:660–1; Stanley to Goulburn, 22 July, 2 August 1832, SRO, Acc

304/45; Wasson, *Althorp*, 274; Walter Alison Phillips, ed., *The History of the Church of Ireland from the Earliest Times to the Present Day*, 3 vols. (Oxford, 1933), 3:297; Edward Brynn, *The Church of Ireland in the Age of Catholic Emancipation* (New York, 1982), 246.

9 H. Goulburn to J. Goulburn, 13, 15, 16 February 1832, SRO, Acc 304/45; Wasson, *Althorp*, 274; Phillips, *Church of Ireland*, 3:297; Brynn, *Church of Ireland*, 246; for a detailed of account of Stanley's bill, see Brynn, *Church of Ireland*, 251ff; Chadwick, *Victorian Church*, 1:56–7; R.W. Davis and R.J. Helmstadter, *Religion and Irreligion in Victorian Society* (London, 1992), 33.

10 *PMP: Wellington*, 1:93; Brynn, *Church of Ireland*, 275–7, 280; *Parl. Deb.*, 3rd ser., 15:588–91.

11 Peel to Goulburn, 18 April, 19 June [1833], SRO, Acc 304/40; Aberdeen to Goulburn, 13 May 1833, SRO, Acc 304/46; Goulburn to Peel, 26 April 1833, BL, Add Ms. 40333; *Parl. Deb.*, 3rd ser., 17:1145–8 1389, 1400; Brose, *Church and Parliament*, 111; Brynn, *Church of Ireland*, 282–4; Chadwick, *Victorian Church*, 1:58–9; Charles Stuart Parker, ed., *Sir Robert Peel from His Private Papers*, 3 vols., reprint (New York, 1970), 2:221–3; Goulburn to Peel, 25 June 1833, BL, Add Ms. 40333.

12 J. Goulburn to E. Goulburn, 25 July 1833, SRO, Acc 304/31; *PMP: Wellington*, 1:248, 284–5; Wasson, *Althorp*, 285; Brynn, *Church of Ireland*, 286–9.

13 For a brief discussion of the amelioration policy of the Tory governments, see John Manning Ward, *Colonial Self-Government: The British Experience 1759–1865* (London, 1976), 96–102; *Quarterly Review* 32 (1825): 531–2, 536–9.

14 Robin Blackburn, *The Overthrow of Colonial Slavery* (London, 1988), 428; Brent, *Liberal Anglican Politics*, 265; B.W. Higham, "The West India 'Interest' in Parliament, 1807–1833," *Historical Studies* 13 (1967): 4; James Walvin, ed., *Slavery and British Society 1776–1846* (London, 1982), 35; *Greville Memoirs*, 2:29; James Walvin, *England, Slaves and Freedom 1776–1838* (London, 1986), 161–5; J.R. Ward, *British West Indian Slavery 1750–1834: The Process of Amerlioration* (Oxford, 1988), 276; *Times*, 28 May 1831; Parry, *Rise and Fall of Liberal Government*, 97.

15 Orlando Patterson, *The Sociology of Slavery* (London, 1967), 79; Bayley to Goulburn, 12 March, 14 April, 6 July, 6 August, 15 October 1825, 1 January, 14 February, 6 May, 12 November 1826, Goulburn to Bayley, 24 August 1826, and Bayley to Goulburn, 5 September 1829, SRO, Acc 304/54.

16 Goulburn to Bayley, 12 July, 10 September 1828, 26 January 1829, 26 June 1830, Bayley to Goulburn, 29 September 1827, 22 November 1828, 5 September, 13 March 1829, 11 September 1830, Goulburn to Bayley, 6 November 1830, 17 August 1831, and Amity Hall slave returns, 1 January 1826 to 1 January 1830, SRO, Acc 304/54.

17 Goulburn to Bayley, 17 August 1831, SRO, Acc 304/54.

18 Olwyn M. Blouet, "Earning and Learning in the British West Indies: An Image of Freedom in the Pre-Emancipation Decade 1823–1833," *Historical Journal* 34 (1991): 395; Thomas Pinney, ed., *The Letters of Thomas Babington Macaulay*, vol. 2 (London, 1974), 103, 118.

19 Michael Craton, *Testing the Chains: Resistance to Slavery in the British West Indies* (Ithaca, 1982), 291ff; B.W. Higmam, *Slave Populations of the British Caribbean, 1807–1834* (Baltimore, 1984), 227–30; Patricia T. Rooke, " 'The World they Made': The Politics of Missionary Education to British West Indian Slaves, 1800–1833," *Caribbean Studies* 18 (1978–80): 55, 61; Thomas C. Holt, *The Problem of Freedom: Race, Labor, and Politics in Jamaica and Britain, 1832–1938* (Baltimore, 1992), 14–17.

20 William Green, *British Slave Emancipation: The Sugar Colonies and the Great Experiment 1830–1865* (Oxford, 1976), 35–44; Herbert S. Klein, *African Slavery in Latin America and the Caribbean* (New York, 1986), 93; Higmam, *Slave Population*, 230; *Parl. Deb.*, 3rd ser., 8:177–9, 347–8; Richard B. Sheridan, "The West Indian Sugar Crisis and British Slave Emancipation, 1830–1833," *Journal of Economic History* 21 (1961): 539–40; H. Goulburn to J. Goulburn, 7 March 1833, SRO, Acc 304/64; Samuel Redgrave, *A Dictionary of Artists of the English School*, reprint ed. (Bath, 1970), 332.

21 Goulburn to Bayley, 10 March 1832, SRO, Acc 304/54; Edith F. Hurwitz, *Politics and the Public Conscience: Slave Emancipation and the Abolitionist Movement in Britain* (London, 1973), 52; D.J. Murray, *The West Indies and the Development of Colonial Government 1801–1834* (Oxford, 1965), 191–2; Goulburn to Bayley, 29 May 1832, SRO, Acc 304/54; Goulburn to Bishop of Jamaica, 30 May 1832, SRO, Acc 304/33; Bayley to Goulburn, 6 July 1832, SRO, Acc 304/52.

22 See the *Report from the Select Committee on the Extinction of Slavery throughout the British Dominions* (1832), *British Parliamentary Papers,* Irish Universities Press edition, *Slave Trade,* vol. 2, Session 1831–32 (Shannon, 1968); for a brief but helpful analysis of its work, see Blouet, "Earning and Learning," 400–7; Ashley to Goulburn, 18 August 1832, Goulburn to Ashley, 5 October 1832, SRO, Acc 304/58; Holt, *Problem of Freedom*, 43–7; Colonial Office cabinet minute, 7 January 1833, BL, Add. Ms. 51820.

23 Izhak Gross, "The Abolition of Negro Slavery and British Parliamentary Politics 1832–33," *Historical Journal* 23 (1980): 67–71, 73–84; *Greville Memoirs*, 2:371; *Parl. Deb.*, 3rd ser., 18:110–11; for Goulburn's revealing comment, see SRO, Acc 304/66; Bruce M. Taylor, "Our Man in London: John Pollard Mayers, Agent for Barbados, and the British Abolition Act, 1832–1834," *Caribbean Studies* 16 (1976–77): 60–84.

24 Gross, "Abolition of Negro Slavery," 85; John Brooke and Mary Sorenson, eds., *Prime Ministers' Papers: W.E. Gladstone*, vol. 2, *Autobiographical Memoranda, 1832–1845* (London, 1972), 5; *PMP: Wellington*, 1:306, 230, 282; Douglas Hall, *Five of the Leewards 1834–1870: The Major Problems of the Post-*

Emancipation Period in Antigua, Barbados, Montserrat, Nevis and St. Kitts (Barbados, 1971), 16.

25 Peel to Goulburn, 16 August 1833, SRO, Acc 304/40; Goulburn to McPherson, 31 August 1833, SRO, Acc 304/58; McPherson to Goulburn, 29 August, 13 November, 19 December 1833, Goulburn to McPherson, 29 January 1834, McPherson to Goulburn, 1 March 1834, SRO, Acc 304/58.

26 McPherson to Goulburn, 26 July, 14 August 1834, and Goulburn to McPherson, 1 October 1834, SRO, Acc 304/58; Emancipation Assessments and Awards, Treasury Papers, PRO, T71/696, T71/858.

27 Goulburn to Peel, 27 November 1833., BL, Add. Ms. 40333; Brynn, *Church of Ireland*, 289–95; Brent, *Liberal Anglican Politics*, 74–5, 257, 184–6; Chadwick, *Victorian Church*, 1:80–1.

28 G.F.A. Best, "The Whigs and the Church Establishment in the Age of Grey and Holland," *History* 45 (1960): 105; *Parl. Deb.*, 3rd ser., 22:590–2, 913–14; ibid., 24:671–3; ibid., 25:646–8; Goulburn memoirs, SRO, Acc 304/68; Chadwick, *Victorian Church*, 1:88–9.

29 Brynn, *Church of Ireland*, 295–6, 300–1; *Parl. Deb.*, 3rd ser., 23:451–4; Goulburn to Peel, 24 May 1834, BL, Add. Ms. 40333; Goulburn memoirs, SRO, Acc 304/68.

30 Parker, *Peel*, 2:243–4; E.A. Smith, *Lord Grey 1764–1845* (Oxford, 1990), 305; Goulburn to Peel, 28 May 1834, BL, Add. Ms. 40333; Neville Thompson, *Wellington after Waterloo* (London, 1986) 137–9; *Times*, 10, 12 June 1834; Carola Oman, *The Gascoyne Heiress: The Life and Diaries of Frances Mary Gascoyne-Cecil, 1802–1839* (London, 1968), 117–21.

31 Brynn, *Church of Ireland*, 304–7; *Greville Memoirs*, 3:96; Gash, *Sir Robert Peel*, 74; Smith, *Grey*, 305–6; Philip Ziegler, *Melbourne: A Biography of William Lamb, 2nd Viscount Melbourne* (London, 1976), 168–76; *Parl. Deb.*, 3rd ser., 25:483–88, 522–5; Northbrook, ed., *Journals and Correspondence of Francis Thornhill Baring, Lord Northbrook*, 2 vols. (London, 1902), 1:106–7.

32 *Greville Memoirs*, 3:100; Peel to Hardinge, 27 May [1834], MUL, C22/13, Hardinge Papers; Knatchbull to F. Knatchbull, 15 July 1834, in Centre for Kentish Studies (CKS), Maidstone, U951/251, Edward Knatchbull Papers; *PMP: Gladstone*, vol. 1, *Autobiographica*, 56; Gash, *Sir Robert Peel*, 75; Norman Gash, *Aristocracy and People, Britain 1815–1865* (Cambridge, Mass., 1979), 175–6; *PMP: Wellington*, 1:693.

33 Peel to Goulburn, 22 August, 25 September [1834], SRO, Acc 304/40; Gash, *Sir Robert Peel*, 78–80; *Correspondence of Arbuthnot*, 188; Henry Lytton Bulwer, *The Life of Henry John Temple, Viscount Palmerston, with Selections from His Diaries and Correspondence*, 3 vols. (London, 1870–74), 2:207; *Greville Memoirs*, 3:148; R.J. Olney and Julia Melvin, eds., *Prime Ministers' Papers: Wellington*, vol. 2, *Political Correspondence, November 1834–April 1835* (London, 1986), 549.

34 *Greville Memoirs*, 3:155; *PMP: Wellington*, 2:159, 45, 130–1; Goulburn to
   Peel, 8 December 1834, BL, Add Ms. 40333; Ellenborough Journals,
   10 December 1834, PRO, 30/12/28/5; H. Goulburn to J. Goulburn,
   10 December 1834, SRO, Acc 304/64.

35 Ellenborough Journals, 11, 12, 13 December 1834, PRO, 30/12/28/5;
   Knatchbull to F. Knatchbull, 13, 15 December 1834, CKS, U951/251,
   Knatchbull Papers.

36 Norman Gash, *Pillars of Government, and Other Essays on State and Society
   c.1770–c.1880* (London, 1986), 98–107; *Quarterly Review* 53 (1835): 266;
   Donald Read, *Peel and the Victorians* (Oxford, 1987), 67–71; Richard Davis,
   "Toryism to Tamworth: The Triumph of Reform, 1827–1835," *Albion* 12
   (1980): 132–46.

37 Gash, *Sir Robert Peel*, 95–7; *Greville Memoirs*, 3:178; *A Portion of the Journal
   Kept by Thomas Raikes Esq.*, 4 vols. (London, 1856), 1:312; Herbert Maxwell,
   ed., *The Creevey Papers: A Selection from the Correspondence and Diaries of the Late
   Thomas Creevey, M.P., 1768–1838*, 2 vols. (London, 1903), 2:302; J.B. Atlay,
   The Victorian Chancellors, 2 vols. (London, 1906), 1:112–13; Ellenborough
   Journals, 24, 27, 30 December 1834, PRO, 30/12/28/5; Peel to Goulburn,
   1 January 1835, BL, Add. Ms. 40333.

38 Ian Newbould, "Whiggery and the Growth of Party 1830–1841: Organization and the Challenge of Reform," *Parliamentary History* 4 (1985): 146,
   153; Norman Gash, "The Organization of the Conservative Party, 1832–
   1846, Part 1: The Parliamentary Organization," *Parliamentary History* 1
   (1982): 137–59, and "Part 2: The Electoral Organization," *Parliamentary
   History* 2 (1983): 131–52; Goulburn to Hardinge, 26 January 1835, MUL,
   C2/14, Hardinge Papers; *PMP: Wellington*, 2:318, 428; M.R.D. Foot, ed.,
   The Gladstone Diaries (Oxford, 1968), 2:147; Phillips, *Great Reform Bill in the
   Boroughs*, 283; *Times*, 13 January 1835.

39 *Poor Man's Guardian*, 30 January 1835; *Companion to the Newspaper*, February
   1835; Read, *Peel and the Victorians*, 74–5; Peel to Herries, 11 January
   [1835], BL, Add. Ms. 57402; ES to Hardinge, 19 January 1835, MUL C2/
   14, Hardinge Papers.

40 A. P. Donajgrodzki, "Sir James Graham at the Home Office," *Historical Journal* 20 (1977): 98–9; Peel to Goulburn, 3 December 1834, BL, Add. Ms.
   40333; J.R. Torrance, "Sir George Harrison and the Growth of the Bureaucracy in the Early Nineteenth Century," *English Historical Review* 83 (1968):
   74; Goulburn to Peel, 2, 4 January 1835, BL, Add. Ms. 40333; J. Goulburn
   to Cane, 3 February 1835, SRO, Acc 304/65.

41 Deposition of Thomas Keane, 13 December 1834, and Gossett to Home
   Office, 17 December 1834, with Goulburn's minute, PRO, HO 100/245;
   Goulburn to Lords Justices, 24 December 1834, PRO, HO 100/245.

42 Report of Archbishop Beresford, PRO, HO 100/245; Goulburn to Haddington, 10 January 1835, PRO, HO 100/246.

43 Haddington to Goulburn, 10 January 1835 (see also the private letter of the same date), SRO, Acc 304/46; Goulburn to Peel, 14 January 1835, BL, Add. Ms. 40333; Peel to Goulburn, 15 January 1835, SRO, Acc 304/40; Ellenborough Journals, 19 January 1835, PRO, 30/12/28/5.

44 Haddington to Goulburn, 11, 12, 14 February 1835, SRO, Acc 304/46; Ellenborough Journals, 13, 14, 16 February 1835, PRO, 30/12/28/5.

45 Goulburn to Peel, 12, 13 January 1835, BL, Add. Ms. 40333; Peel to Goulburn, n.d. [January 1835], SRO, Acc 304/40; Chadwick, *Victorian Church*, 1:143; Mathieson, *English Church Reform*, 124–5; Mills and Alison to Goulburn, 7 January 1835, PRO, HO 102/42; Phillips to Stuart, 10 January 1835, PRO, HO 103/7; Mansfield to Goulburn, 1 January 1835, PRO, HO 61/14; Talbot to Goulburn, 10 January 1835, PRO, HO 44/28; Goulburn to Talbot, 13 January 1835, PRO, HO 43/46; Goulburn to Desborough, 23 February 1835; and Goulburn to Cartwright, 22 January 1835, PRO, HO 43/46.

46 Goulburn to Peel, n.d. [January 1835] and 15 January 1835, BL, Add. Ms. 40333; Parker, *Peel*, 2:282–3; Louis J. Jennings, ed., *The Croker Papers*, 3 vols. (London, 1885), 2:263; *Parl. Deb.*, 3rd ser., 32:164; Mathieson, *English Church Reform*, 68–9; Canterbury to Peel, 13 January 1835, BL, Add. Ms. 40333; Best, *Temporal Pillars*, 296–300; Brose, *Church and Parliament*, 132; Gash, *Aristocracy and People*, 177.

47 Ellenborough Journals, 6, 11, 13, 14, 16, 21 February 1835, PRO, 30/12/28/5; Peel to Goulburn, 5 January 1835, SRO, Acc 304/40; Abraham D. Kriegel, "The Politics of the Whigs in Opposition, 1834–1835," *Journal of British Studies* 7 (1967): 76–7, 82–5; *Greville Memoirs*, 3:218–9; Brent, *Liberal Anglican Politics*, 85.

48 *Greville Memoirs*, 3:213–14; *Parl. Deb.*, 3rd ser., 26:64–7, 287–8, 537–9, 615, and 27:149; Haddington to Goulburn, 15 March, n.d. [March] 1835, SRO, Acc 304/46; John Wolffe, *The Protestant Crusade in Great Britain 1829–1860* (Oxford, 1991), 85.

49 Ellenborough Journals, 25 March 1835, PRO, 30/12/28/5; *PMP: Wellington*, 2, 563, 561–2; Oman, *Gascoyne Heiress*, 158; Parker, *Peel*, 2:292–4, 301–2.

50 *Parl. Deb.*, 3rd ser., 27:691–701; *Times*, 3, 8 April 1835; Ellenborough Journals, 26 March, 3 April 1835, PRO, 30/12/28/5; Goulburn to Wordsworth, 8 April 1835, LPL, Ms. 1822.

51 David Close, "The Formation of a Two-Party Alignment in the House of Commons between 1832 and 1841," *English Historical Review* 84 (1969): 260–1; Wolffe, *Protestant Crusade*, 85.

CHAPTER TEN

1 Henry Reeve, ed., *The Greville Memoirs*, 3 vols. (London, 1874), 3:255; Philip Ziegler, *Melbourne: A Biography of William Lamb, 2nd Viscount Mel-*

bourne (London, 1976), 189, 201; Rosslyn to Ellenborough, 20, 21 April 1835, Public Record Office (PRO), 30/12/29; Ellenborough Journals, 12, 13 April 1835, PRO, 30/12/29/5; *Greville Memoirs*, 3:256; John Brooke and Mary Sorensen, eds., *Prime Ministers' Papers: W.E. Gladstone* vol. 2, *Autobiographical Memoranda, 1832–1845* (London, 1972), 49; E. Jones-Parry, ed., *Correspondence of Lord Aberdeen and Princess Lieven*, 2 vols. (London, 1938–39), 1:29; D.G. Southgate, *The Passing of the Whigs, 1832–1886* (London, 1962), 61–3; Peter Mandler, *Aristocratic Government in the Age of Reform: Whigs and Liberals, 1830–1852* (Oxford, 1990), 158–61; Peel to Goulburn, 5 May [1835], Surrey Record Office (SRO), Kingston upon Thames, Acc 304/40.

2 Jonathan Parry, *The Rise and Fall of Liberal Government in Victorian Britain* (New Haven, 1993), 3, 153; F.M.L. Thompson, ed., *The Cambridge Social History of Britain, 1750–1950*, vol. 3, *Social Agencies and Institutions* (Cambridge, 1990), 18, 21; Edward Brynn, *The Church of Ireland in the Age of Catholic Emancipation* (New York, 1982), 316–18; Norman Gash, *Sir Robert Peel: The Life of Sir Robert Peel after 1830*, 2nd ed. (New York, 1986), 137; *Parl. Deb.*, 3rd ser., 29:894–903, 1115–16.

3 Parry, *Rise and Fall of Liberal Government*, 15; Thompson, *Cambridge Social History*, 3:21; G.I.T. Machin, *Politics and the Churches in Great Britain 1832 to 1868* (Oxford, 1977), 10; Gash, *Sir Robert Peel*, 132–5; Goulburn to Peel, 11 August 1835, British Library (BL), Add. Ms. 40333; Charles Stuart Parker, ed., *Sir Robert Peel from His Private Papers*, 3 vols., reprint (New York, 1970), 2:314–15; Owen Chadwick, *The Victorian Church*, 2 vols. (London, 1966–70), 1:109; Goulburn to Peel, 22, 26 August 1835, BL, Add. Ms. 40333.

4 Goulburn to Peel, 26, 22, 28 August 1835, BL, Add. Ms. 40333; Parker, *Peel*, 2:316–17.

5 Gash, *Sir Robert Peel*, 138–9; *Greville Memoirs*, 3:304–5; Neville Thompson, *Wellington after Waterloo* (London, 1986), 162; Jones-Parry, *Aberdeen-Lieven Correspondence*, 1:38; Parker, *Peel*, 2:224–5; Goulburn to Peel, n.d. [31 December 1835], SRO, Acc 304/40.

6 Peel to Goulburn, 3, 6 January 1836, SRO, Acc 304/40; Parker, *Peel*, 2:319; Goulburn to Peel, 7 January 1836, BL, Add Ms. 40333; Gash, *Sir Robert Peel*, 140–3; H. Goulburn to J. Goulburn, 5 February 1836, SRO, Acc 304/64.

7 Gash, *Sir Robert Peel*, 144–7; H. Goulburn to J. Goulburn, n.d. [March 1836], SRO, Acc 304/64; Lord Sudley, trans. and ed., *The Lieven-Palmerston Correspondence, 1828–1856* (London, 1943), 117; John Prest, *Lord John Russell* (Columbia, S.C., 1972), 106–7.

8 Prest, *Lord John Russell*, 104–5; *Parl. Deb.*, 3rd ser., 32:1093–6; ibid., 33:787; ibid., 34:132–5, 145; ibid., 43:971–2; ibid., 44:434–8; see Peter Mandler, "Cain and Abel: Two Aristocrats and the Early Victorian Factory Acts," *Historical Journal* 27 (1984): 83–109; for an extended discussion of roman-

tic Tories, see R.L. Hill, *Toryism and the People, 1832–1846* (London, 1929), and more recently, David Eastwood, "Robert Southey and the Intellectual Origins of Romantic Conservatism," *English Historical Review* 104 (1989): 308–31.

9 Machin, *Politics and Churches*, 57–9; Goulburn to Peel, 16 August 1836, BL, Add. Ms. 40333; Nicholas Edsall, *The Anti-Poor Law Movement, 1834–44* (Manchester, 1971), 27–8, 31; H. Goulburn to Harry Goulburn, 16 August 1836, SRO, Acc 304/66.

10 David Newsome, *Godliness and Learning: Four Studies on a Victorian Ideal* (London, 1961), 1–3, 11–13; H. Goulburn to J. Goulburn, 26 February 1836, SRO, Acc 304/65; H. Goulburn to Harry Goulburn, 31 October 1835, 16 August 1836, SRO, Acc 304/66.

11 Parker, *Peel*, 2:325; Goulburn to Peel, 2 September 1836, BL, Add. Ms. 40333; Ziegler, *Melbourne*, 245; *Greville Memoirs*, 3:376–7.

12 Peel to Goulburn, 12 September 1836, SRO, Acc 304/40; Wellington to Goulburn, 19 December 1836, SRO, Acc 304/34; Goulburn to Peel, 20 December 1836, BL, Add. Ms. 40333; Prest, *Lord John Russell*, 112–13.

13 Parry, *Rise and Fall of Liberal Government*, 137–8; J.P. Ellens, "Lord John Russell and the Church Rate Conflict: The Struggle for a Broad Church, 1834–1868," *Journal of British Studies* 26 (1987): 233–41; *Parl. Deb.*, 3rd ser., 37:930–1, 368, 370, 372; ibid., 38:1400–4; ibid., 42:848–57; Jones-Parry, *Aberdeen-Lieven Correspondence*, 1:60.

14 Gash, *Sir Robert Peel*, 159–62; *Parl. Deb.*, 3rd ser., 37:938, 934, 939; D.D. Olien, *Morpeth: A Victorian Public Career* (Washington, D.C., 1983), 164.

15 Jones-Parry, *Aberdeen-Lieven Correspondence*, 1:60, 66–7; *Greville Memoirs*, 3:394; Ellens, "Russell and the Church Rate Conflict," 241; John A. Phillips, *The Great Reform Bill in the Boroughs: English Electoral Behaviour 1818–1841* (Oxford, 1992), 152–4; Bruce Coleman, *Conservatism and the Conservative Party in Nineteenth-Century Britain* (London, 1988), 58–9; Edsall, *Anti-Poor Law Movement*, 63–6; Goulburn to Peel, 28 July 1837, BL, Add. Ms. 40333.

16 Peel to Goulburn, 21 August 1837, SRO, Acc 304/40; Gash, *Sir Robert Peel*, 197; Jones-Parry, *Aberdeen-Lieven Correspondence*, 1:78, 85–6.

17 For Goulburn's financial affairs in 1837, see SRO, Acc 304/25; for his correspondence concerning his brother's estate, see SRO, Acc 304/13; for his club memberships, see SRO, Acc 304/24; Lawrence Goldman, "The Origins of British 'Social Science': Political Economy, Natural Science and Statistics, 1830–1835," *Historical Journal* 26 (1983): 587–616; M.J. Cullen, *The Statistical Movement in Early Victorian Britain* (New York, 1975), 85–7, 92, 175n62.

18 Goulburn to E. Goulburn, Jr, 21 December 1837, SRO, Acc 304/31; for the background of the rebellion, see Helen Taft Manning, "The Colonial Policy of the Whig Ministers, 1830–37," pts 1 and 2, *Canadian Historical Review* 33 (1952): 203–36, 341–68; John Manning Ward, *Colonial Self-Government:*

The British Experience, 1759–1865 (London, 1976), 38ff; *PMP: Gladstone,* 2:91–3; Goulburn to Peel, 21 January 1838, BL, Add. Ms. 40333.

19 Goulburn to Peel, 21 January 1838, BL, Add. Ms. 40333; Peel to Goulburn, 24 January [1838], SRO, Acc 304/40; Ward, *Colonial Self-Government,* 63; Graham to Hardinge, 22 January 1838, McGill University Library (MUL), C2/17, Henry Hardinge Papers.

20 Parker, *Peel,* 2:367; for Goulburn's attitude towards the censure motion, see his memorandum, n.d., SRO, Acc 304/33; *PMP: Gladstone,* 2:94–100; Jones-Parry, *Aberdeen-Lieven Correspondence,* 1:101.

21 Goulburn to Edward Goulburn, Jr, 19 May 1838, SRO, Acc 304/31; Gash, *Sir Robert Peel,* 205–7; Olien, *Morpeth,* 171–4; *PMP: Gladstone,* 2:109; Walter Ailson Phillips, ed., *The History of the Church of Ireland from the Earliest Times to the Present Day,* 3 vols. (Oxford, 1933), 3:300; Peter Virgin, *The Church in the Age of Negligence: Ecclesiastical Structure and Problems of Church Reform, 1700–1840* (Cambridge, 1989), 209–10, 102.

22 *PMP: Gladstone,* 2:103–5; Thomas C. Holt, *Problem of Freedom: Race, Labour, and Politics in Jamaica and Britain 1832–1938* (Baltimore, 1992), 104–5; see Izhak Gross, "Parliament and the Abolition of Negro Apprenticeship 1835–1838," *English Historical Review* 6 (1981): 560–76.

23 William Green, *British Slave Emancipation: The Sugar Colonies and the Great Experiment, 1830–1865* (Oxford, 1976), 130–61; D. Hall, *Five of the Leewards, 1834–1870* (Barbados, 1971), 24–5, 28, 31; Holt, *Problem of Freedom,* 63.

24 McPherson to Goulburn, 23 February, 22 July 1835, 9 January 1836, 20 May 1837, SRO, Acc 304/58; Goulburn to McPherson, 13 April, 7 September 1835, SRO, Acc 304/58; McPherson to Goulburn, 10 December 1835, Goulburn to McPherson, 29 January 1836, and McPherson to Goulburn 20 May 1837, SRO, Acc 304/58; McPherson to Goulburn, 30 June, 28 July 1838, SRO, Acc 304/57.

25 Goulburn to McPherson, 1 December 1837, McPherson to Goulburn, 8 February 1838, and Goulburn to Mcpherson, 1 April 1838, SRO, Acc 304/57.

26 Goulburn to McPherson, 30 July 1838, SRO, Acc 304/57.

27 McPherson to Goulburn 28 July, 11 August, 6 September, 17 December 1838, and 17 January, 21 February, 5 April, 12 June 1839, SRO, Acc 304/57; Goulburn to McPherson, 9 April, 15 November 1839, SRO, Acc 304/57.

28 H. Goulburn to E. Goulburn, Jr, 19 May, 5 June 1838, SRO, Acc 304/31; Goulburn to Peel, 13 October 1838, BL, Add. Ms. 40333.

29 Ziegler, *Melbourne,* 283–6; Gash, *Sir Robert Peel,* 210–11; Graham to Hardinge, 14 January 1839, MUL, C2/17, Hardinge Papers; *Parl. Deb.,* 3rd ser., 45:63–4; H. Goulburn to E. Goulburn, Jr, 10, 14 February, 1, 26 March 1839, and H. Goulburn to J. Goulburn, 2 March 1839, SRO, Acc 304/31.

30 H. Goulburn to E. Goulburn, Jr, 14 February, 26 March 1839, SRO, Acc 304/31.

31 H. Goulburn to E. Goulburn, Jr, 14 February 1839, SRO, Acc 304/31; *Parl. Deb.*, 3rd ser., 46:1261–7 and 47:902–13.

32 Gash, *Sir Robert Peel,* 222–5; Ziegler, *Melbourne,* 290–8; Parker, *Peel,* 2:390–2, 400–1.

33 Peel to Hardinge, 7 December 1838, MUL, C2/17, Hardinge Papers; M. G. Wiebe, J.B. Conacher, John Matthews, and Mary S. Millar, eds., *Benjamin Disraeli's Letters,* vol. 3, *1838–1841* (Toronto, 1987), 171, 173; *Parl. Deb.*, 3rd ser., 47:1041–50.

34 H. Goulburn to E. Goulburn, Jr, 1 June 1839, SRO, Acc 304/31.

35 Goulburn to Gladstone, 7 April 1838, BL, Add. Ms. 44162; Ian D. C. Newbould, "The Whigs, the Church, and Education, 1839," *Journal of British Studies* 26 (1987): 332–46; Richard Brent, *Liberal Anglican Politics: Whiggery, Religion and Reform 1830–1841* (Oxford, 1987), 219–29, 250–1; *Parl. Deb.*, 3rd ser., 48:789–90; Machin, *Politics and Churches,* 64–8.

36 *Parl. Deb.*, 3rd ser., 34:636–44, 42:1401–9, and 43:778, 1086.

37 Arthur D. Gayer, W.W. Rostow, and Anna Jacobson Schwartz, *The Growth and Fluctuations of the British Economy, 1790–1850,* 2 vols. (Oxford, 1953), 1:242; Lucy Brown, *The Board of Trade and the Free Trade Movement, 1830–1842* (Oxford, 1958), 58–9; *Parl. Deb.*, 3rd ser., 48:1365–75.

38 Elizabeth Burton, *The Early Victorians at Home, 1837–1861* (Newton Abbott, 1973), 23; Ziegler, *Melbourne,* 300–1; *A Portion of the Journal Kept by Thomas Raikes Esq.,* 4 vols. (London, 1856), 3:355; *Parl. Deb.*, 3rd ser., 48:1373–5, and 49:277–84, 624–5; A. Aspinall, ed., *Correspondence of Charles Arbuthnot, 1808–1850* (London, 1941), 206.

39 H. Goulburn to E. Goulburn, Jr, 20 July 1839, SRO, Acc 304/31; Goulburn to Peel, 31 July 1839, BL, Add. Ms. 40333; Goulburn diaries, 1839, SRO, Acc 304/25; *Disraeli Letters,* 3:226.

40 Goulburn to Peel, 11, 20 November 1839, BL, Add. Ms. 40333.

41 Peel to Goulburn, 15 December 1839, SRO, Acc 304/40; Goulburn to Peel, 20 December 1839 and 4 January 1840, BL, Add. Ms. 40333; for Goulburn's deficit calculations, see Goulburn to Peel, n.d. [12/13 January 1840] and 15 January 1840, BL, Add. Ms. 40333.

42 Gash, *Sir Robert Peel,* 239, 242–3; *Correspondence of Arbuthnot,* 215–16; J. Goulburn to E. Goulburn, Jr, 13 [February] 1840, SRO, Acc 304/31; Jones-Parry, *Aberdeen-Lieven Correspondence,* 1:132.

43 *Parl. Deb.*, 3rd ser., 53:610 and 54:149–51; Prest, *Lord John Russell,* 164; Gash, *Sir Robert Peel,* 245; Goulburn to Peel, 13, 24 June 1840, BL, Add. Ms. 40333; *Correspondence of Arbuthnot,* 219; Goulburn to Peel, 23 October 1840, BL, Add. Ms. 40333.

44 Goulburn to Peel, 23 October 1840, BL, Add. Ms. 40333; Turner to Goulburn, 4, 16 January 1840, and Goulburn to Turner, 31 March 1840, SRO, Acc 304/57.

45 J.F.A. Ajayi, *Christian Missions in Nigeria 1841–1891: The Making of a New Elite* (London, 1965), 10–16; Brent, *Liberal Anglican Politics*, 175, 284–9; Goulburn to Gladstone, 9 December 1840, BL, Add. Ms. 44162.

46 Gayer, Rostow, and Schwartz, *Growth and Fluctuation of British Economy*, 1:276–303; Thompson, *Wellington after Waterloo*, 199; Henry Lytton Bulwer, *The Life of Henry John Temple, Viscount Palmerston, with Selections from His Diaries and Correspondence*, 3 vols. (London, 1870–74), 3:39–40; *Correspondence of Arbuthnot*, 226–7; Graham to Hardinge, 18 January 1841, MUL, C1/3, Hardinge Papers.

47 Graham to Hardinge, 18 January 1841, MUL, C1/3, Hardinge Papers; Prest, *Lord John Russell*, 173; Brown, *Board of Trade*, 195, 209, 214–21; Ian Newbould, *Whiggery and Reform, 1830–41: The Politics of Government* (Stanford, 1990), 302–4; Brent, *Liberal Anglican Politics*, 292–3; C. Duncan Rice, "'Humanity Sold for Sugar': The British Abolitionists' Response to Free Trade in Slave-Grown Sugar," *Historical Journal* 13 (1970): 412.

48 *Parl. Deb.*, 3rd ser., 57:1309–13 and 56:586–96, 1147; *PMP: Gladstone*, 2:131–4; *Parl. Deb.*, 3rd ser., 58:236–46; Gash, *Sir Robert Peel*, 257–8.

49 *PMP: Gladstone*, 2:142–7.

50 Brent, *Liberal Anglican Politics*, 298; Newbould, *Whiggery and Reform*, 306–8; Robert Stewart, *Party and Politics, 1830–1852* (New York, 1989), 61; Graham Davis, *The Irish in Britain 1815–1914* (Dublin, 1991), 151; Wendy Hinde, *Richard Cobden: A Victorian Outsider* (New Haven, 1987), 91; Jones-Parry, *Aberdeen-Lieven Correspondence*, 1:174; *PMP: Gladstone*, 2:152–5; Ellenborough Journals, 24 August 1841, PRO, 30/12/28/7; Thomas Pinney, ed., *Letters of Thomas Babington Macaulay*, vol. 3 (London, 1976), 387.

CHAPTER ELEVEN

1 Goulburn to Herries, 14 July 1841, British Library (BL), Add. Ms. 57401; David Close, "The Formation of a Two-Party Alignment in the House of Commons between 1832 and 1841," *English Historical Review* 84 (1969): 269; Robert Stewart, *The Foundation of the Conservative Party 1830–1867* (London, 1978), 154–5; Angus Hawkins, "'Parliamentary Government' and Victorian Political Parties, c.1830–c.1880," *English Historical Review* 104 (1989):654–5; Bruce Coleman, *Conservatism and the Conservative Party in Nineteenth-Century Britain* (London, 1988), 93–6, 100–5, 112–13; Donald Read, *Peel and Victorians* (Oxford, 1987), 6–8.

2 A. Aspinall, ed., *Correspondence of Charles Arbuthnot, 1808–1850* (London, 1941), 231; Gladstone to Peel, 22 July 1841, BL, Add. Ms. 44275; Peel to Goulburn, 28 July, 3 August 1841, Surrey Record Office (SRO), Kingston upon Thames, Acc 304/40; Goulburn to Peel, 5 August 1841, BL, Add. Ms. 40333.

3 Norman Gash, *Sir Robert Peel: The Life of Sir Robert Peel after 1830*, 2nd ed. (New York, 1986), 275–8; M.G. Wiebe et al., eds., *Benjamin Disraeli's Letters,*

vol. 3, *1838–1841* (Toronto, 1987), 334, and vol. 4, *1842–1847* (Toronto, 1989), 14; Goulburn to Peel, 31 July 1841, BL, Add. Ms. 40333; T. Wemyss Reid, *The Life, Letters and Friendships of Richard Monckton Milnes, First Lord Houghton*, 2 vols. (London, 1890), 1:270; Goulburn to Wordsworth, 1 September 1841, Lambeth Palace Library (LPL), Ms. 1822; David Kynaston, *The Chancellor of the Exchequer* (Lavenham, 1980), 23.

4 *Parl. Deb.*, 3rd ser., 66:762 and 84:58; Goulburn to Peel, 21 November 1842, BL, Add. Ms. 40443; Goulburn to Peel, 6 January 1845, BL, Add. Ms. 40445.

5 Goulburn to Peel, 24 October 1845, BL, Add. Ms. 40445; Stanley to Goulburn, 7 March, 5 May [1842], SRO, Acc 304/45; Jennifer Hart, "Sir Charles Trevelyan at the Treasury," *English Historical Review* 75 (1960): 92–110; Edward Hughes, "Sir Charles Trevelyan and Civil Service Reform, 1853–5," *English Historical Review* 64 (1949): 53–5; F. Darrell Munsell, "Charles Edward Trevelyan and Peelite Irish Famine Policy, 1845–46," *Societas* 1 (1971): 302–3; Joseph M. Hernon, Jr, "A Victorian Cromwell: Sir Charles Edward Trevelyan, the Famine and the Age of Improvement,"*Eire/ Ireland* 22 (1987): 16–19; Trevelyan to Goulburn, 31 January 1842, in University of Newcastle Library (UNEW), Trevelyan Letterbooks, 1:148–55, Trevelyan Papers; Trevelyan to Larpent, 23 December 1840, UNEW, Trevelyan Letterbooks, 1:16–17; Graham to Goulburn, 9 September 1841, in Bodleian Library (BOD), Oxford, Ms. film 116, Graham Papers; Peel to Goulburn, 20 April [1843], SRO Acc 304/41.

6 Goulburn to Herries, 11 September 1841, Herries to Goulburn, 12, 17 September 1841, Goulburn to Herries, 27 September 1841, and Herries to Goulburn, 28 September 1841, BL, Add. Ms. 57401; *Parl. Deb.*, 3rd ser., 59:828–35, 842–7; Northbrook, ed., *Journals and Correspondence of Francis Thornhill Baring, Lord Northbrook*, 2 vols. (London, 1902), 1:183.

7 *Parl. Deb.*, 3rd ser., 60:1377–87; *Times*, 28, 29 October, 2 November, 6, 20 December 1841, 4, 17 January 1842; Goulburn to Peel, 24 December 1841, BL, Add. Ms. 40443; *Parl. Deb.*, 3rd ser., 66:420–27, 447.

8 Sidney Buxton, *Finance and Politics: An Historical Study, 1783–1885*, 2 vols., reprint (New York, 1966), 1:43; Charles Stuart Parker, ed., *Sir Robert Peel from His Private Papers*, 3 vols., reprint (New York, 1970), 2:493.

9 *Parl. Deb.* 3rd ser., 28:767–8 and 57:563–4; Goulburn to Peel, 22 July 1841, BL, Add. Ms. 40443; *Parl. Deb.*, 3rd ser., 77:577.

10 Parker, *Peel*, 2:491–4; Stanley to Graham, 5 August 1841, BOD, Ms. film 112, Graham Papers; Peel to Queen, 4 November 1841, in Royal Archives (RA), Windsor, film 95709/1, Peel Papers; Peel to Goulburn, 20 October 1841, SRO, Acc 304/40.

11 Francis Edwin Hyde, *Mr. Gladstone at the Board of Trade* (London, 1934), 15–16; Charles Stuart Parker, *Life and Letters of Sir James Graham, 1792–1861,*

2 vols. (London, 1907), 1:309; Goulburn to Peel, 20 November 1841, BL, Add. Ms. 40469.

12 Gash, *Sir Robert Peel*, 303–4; *Parl. Deb.*, 3rd ser., 77:573; Wilbur Devereux Jones, *"Prosperity" Robinson: The Life of Viscount Goderich, 1782–1859* (London, 1967), 241–3; Hyde, *Gladstone at Board of Trade*, 59–60; Herries to Peel, 8, 29 November 1841, BL, Add. Ms. 57402.

13 Bernard Semmel, *The Rise of Free Trade Imperialism in Classical Political Economy: The Empire of Free Trade and Imperialism 1750–1850* (Cambridge, 1970), 149; John Brooke and Mary Sorensen, eds., *Prime Ministers' Papers: W.E. Gladstone*, vol. 2, *Autobiographical Memoranda, 1832–1845* (London, 1972), 172, 166–71; Gladstone to Goulburn, 13 November 1841, SRO, Acc 304/46.

14 Norman Gash, "The Organization of the Conservative Party, 1832–1846, Part 2, The Electoral Organization," *Parliamentary History* 2 (1983): 143; *A Portion of the Journal Kept by Thomas Raikes Esq.*, 4 vols. (London, 1856), 4:193; Malmesbury, *Memoirs of an Ex-Minister*, 2 vols. (London, 1884), 1:139; Peel to Queen, 8, 17, 25 February 1842, RA, film 95709/1, Peel Papers; Goulburn to Peel, n.d [23 January 1842], BL, Add. Ms. 40443.

15 Goulburn to Peel, 3 February [1842], BL, Add. Ms. 40443; *Edinburgh Review* 97 (1853): 267–94; Goulburn to Gladstone, 17 February 1842, BL, Add. Ms. 44162; Herries to Goulburn, 7 March 1842, BL, Add. Ms. 57401; Peel to Queen, 10, 23, 24 March 1842, RA, film 95709/1, Peel Papers; Peel to Goulburn, 25 March 1842, BL, Add. Ms. 40443.

16 *Parl. Deb.*, 3rd ser., 61:860–75; ibid., 62:102–20, 1269–70; ibid., 63:1035–42; Finch to Saurin, 30 March 1842, BL, Add. Ms. 40443.

17 *Parl. Deb.*, 3rd ser., 63:1039; Eddy to Peel, 9 May 1842, and Goulburn to Peel, 27 August, 11 November 1842, BL, Add. Ms. 40443.

18 Peel to Queen, 11, 24 May 1842, RA, film 95709/1, Peel Papers; *PMP: Gladstone*, 2:109; *Parl. Deb.*, 3rd ser., 63:1545–9, 1155–62; Peel to Queen, 9, 29 June, 12, 23 July, and 6, 9, 10 August 1842, RA, film 95709/1, Peel Papers.

19 Lund to Goulburn, 14 October 1841, BL, Add. Ms. 40443; Wendy Hinde, *Richard Cobden: A Victorian Outsider* (New Haven, 1987), 107–8, 110; Graham to Brougham, 21 August 1842, BOD, Ms. film 113; Peel to Queen, 20 May and 13, 16 August 1842, RA, film 95709/1; Hardinge to Goulburn, 5 October 1842, SRO, Acc 304/42; Graham to Hardinge, 1 September 1842, McGill University Library (MUL), C3/3, Henry Hardinge Papers.

20 Graham to Hardinge, 1 September 1842, MUL, C3/3, Hardinge Papers; Gash, *Sir Robert Peel*, 351–2; A.P. Donajgrodski, "Sir James Graham at the Home Office," *Historical Journal* 20 (1977): 110–11; Parker, *Graham*, 1:333–6; Goulburn memorandum, n.d. [1842], BOD, Ms. film 114.

21 Gash, *Sir Robert Peel*, 360–1; Goulburn to Peel, 17 November 1842, BL, Add. Ms. 40443; *PMP: Gladstone*, 2:185; Kenneth Bourne, ed., *The Letters of*

the Third Viscount Palmerston to Laurence and Elizabeth Sulivan, 1804–1863
(London, 1979), 275; Peel to Goulburn, 13 October 1842, BL, Add. Ms.
40443.

22 Peel to Goulburn, 6 October 1842, SRO, Acc 304/42; Goulburn to Peel, 7,
18, 28 October 1842, BL, Add. Ms. 40443; Peel to Goulburn, 20 October
[1842], SRO, Acc 304/41.

23 Peel to Queen, 14, 16, 17, 18 February, and 5, 7 March 1842, RA, film
95709/2.

24 *Times*, 9, 10 March 1842; Peel to Queen, 27 March 1842, RA, film 95709/
2.

25 *Parl. Deb.*, 3rd ser., 68:1391–414 and 70:1401.

26 Goulburn to Wordsworth, 26 September 1842, LPL, Ms. 1822; Harry Goulburn to Jackman, 30 August 1842, SRO, Acc 304/33; Harry Goulburn to J.
Goulburn, 26 October 1842, SRO, Acc 304/67; Diaries of Jane Goulburn,
January–April 1843, SRO, Acc 304/64; J. Goulburn to H. Goulburn,
19 March and n.d. 1843, SRO, Acc 304/67; H. Goulburn to Harry Goulburn, 22 March, 4 April 1843, SRO, Acc 304/66.

27 Diaries of Jane Goulburn, 21 May 1843, SRO, Acc 304/64; J. Goulburn to
H. Goulburn, n.d. [21 May 1843], SRO, Acc 304/67; for his son's last days,
see Goulburn's notes, 7, 8 June 1843, SRO, Acc 304/65; Harry Goulburn
to F. Goulburn, 8 June 1843, SRO, Acc 304/30.

28 J. Goulburn to H. Goulburn, n.d. [June 1843], SRO, Acc 304/67; see also
Diaries of Jane Goulburn, June–December 1843, January–April 1844, SRO,
Acc 304/64; see also SRO, Acc 304/27.

29 Goulburn to Peel, 9 June 1843, BL, Add. Ms. 40443; *PMP: Gladstone*,
2:191–2, 204, 206–8; David Hempton, *Methodism and Politics in British Society 1750–1850*, pb. ed. (London, 1987), 166, 171; *Parl. Deb.*, 3rd ser.,
70:213–19; A.C. Howe, "Free Trade and the City of London, c.1820–
1870," *History* 77 (1992): 397–8; Goulburn to Bonham, n.d. [October
1843], BL, Add. Ms. 40617; Goulburn to Peel, 23 October 1843, BL, Add.
Ms. 40444.

30 Peel to Queen, 25 October 1843, RA, film 95709/2; Peel to Goulburn, 19,
30 October 1843, Goulburn to Peel, n.d., and 20, 31 October 1843, BL,
Add. Ms. 40534.

31 Goulburn to Peel, 21 January 1842, 1 December 1841, BL, Add. Ms.
40443; Goulburn to Peel, 1 May 1845, BL, Add. Ms. 40445; Geoffrey
B.A.M. Finlayson, *The Seventh Earl of Shaftesbury, 1801–1885* (London,
1981), 164.

32 Goulburn to Peel, 10 January 1842, BL, Add. Ms. 40443; P.J. Welch, "Blomfield and Peel: A Study in Cooperation between Church and State, 1841–
1846," *Journal of Ecclesiastical History* 12 (1961): 78; Goulburn memorandum, n.d. [December 1842], BL, Add. Ms. 40444; Peel to Graham,
22 December 1842, BOD, Ms. film 124; *PMP: Gladstone*, 2:186–9; Gash, *Sir*

Robert Peel, 381–3; Goulburn to Peel, 12 February 1843, BL, Add. Ms. 40444; Parker, *Peel*, 2:567.

33 Peel to Queen, 25 September 1843, RA, film 95709/2; Arthur D. Gayer, W.W. Rostow, and Anna Jacobson Schwartz, *Growth and Fluctuation of the British Economy 1790–1850*, 2 vols. (Oxford, 1953), 1:304–39; E. Jones-Parry, ed., *Correspondence of Lord Aberdeen and Princess Lieven*, 2 vols. (London, 1938–39) 1:223–4.

34 Peel to Goulburn, 25 March 1843, BL, Add. Ms. 40444; Kynaston, *Chancellor of the Exchequer*, 114; Goulburn to Herries, 28 February 1844, BL, Add. Ms. 57401; Peel to Queen, 6, 7 March 1844, RA, film 95709/2; *Times*, 9 March 1844; *Parl. Deb.*, 3rd ser., 74:730–48.

35 Oliver MacDonagh, *Early Victorian Government, 1830–1870* (London, 1977), 65–8; *PMP: Gladstone*, 2:159; Hinde, *Cobden*, 140; A.B. Erickson, *The Public Career of Sir James Graham* (Oxford, 1952), 222–3; Peel to Queen, 19 March 1844, RA, film 95709/2.

36 *PMP: Gladstone*, 2:252–4; Erickson, *Graham*, 224; Gash, *Sir Robert Peel*, 443; Peel to Queen, n.d. [11 May 1844], RA, film 95709/2; J. Goulburn to H. Goulburn, 21 May [1844], SRO, Acc 304/67.

37 *PMP: Gladstone* 2:252; 202–6, 222; for O'Connell's campaign, see Kevin B. Nowlan, *The Politics of Repeal: A Study in Relations between Great Britain and Ireland, 1841–1850* (London, 1965), and Oliver MacDonagh, *The Emancipist: Daniel O'Connell, 1830–47* (London, 1989), 219–40.

38 Hardinge to Graham, 23 May 1843, MUL, C3/7, Hardinge Papers; Trevelyan to Byham, 12 October 1843, UNEW, Trevelyan Letterbooks, 3:111–2; Peel to Graham, 15 October [1843], BOD, Ms. film 116; Peel to Goulburn, 10 September [1843], BL, Add. Ms. 40444; Peel to Goulburn, 4 December [1843], SRO, Acc 304/41; Gash, *Sir Robert Peel*, 384, 402–5, 410, 412; Donal A. Kerr, *Peel, Priests and Politics: Sir Robert Peel's Administration and the Roman Catholic Church in Ireland, 1841–1846* (Oxford, 1982), 65, 68, 80, 87, 106, 115–17.

39 *PMP: Gladstone*, 2:228–44.

40 Goulburn memorandum, 10 March 1844, BOD, Ms. film 114.

41 *PMP: Gladstone*, 2:220–1; Goulburn to Peel, 6 April 1844, BL, Add. Ms. 40444.

42 Peel to Goulburn, 8 April 1844, SRO, Acc 304/41.

43 *Times*, 29 April 1844; *Parl. Deb.*, 3rd ser., 74:360–85; *Times*, 1 May 1844; J. Goulburn to E. Goulburn, 28 April, 1 May 1844, SRO, Acc 304/31.

44 F.W. Fetter, *The Development of British Monetary Orthodoxy, 1797–1875* (Cambridge, Mass., 1965), 177–8, 181; *Parl. Deb.*, 3rd ser., 75:810; Goulburn to Peel, 17 November 1842, BL, Add. Ms. 40443; Lionel Robbins, *Robert Torrens and the Evolution of Classical Economics* (London, 1958), 93.

45 Robbins, *Torrens*, 97–8, 101; *Parl. Deb.*, 3rd ser., 75:810–11; *PMP: Gladstone*, 2:227.

46 Goulburn to Cotton, 16 January 1844, Cotton to Peel, 19, 26 January 1844, Archives of the Bank of England (ABE), M5/206; Cotton to Peel, 2 February, 1844, Goulburn to Cotton, 17 February, 11 March 1844, ABE, M5/205; Goulburn to Cotton, 20, 26, 29 April, 2, 4, 11 May 1844, and Cotton to Goulburn, 27 April 1844, ABE, M5/206; Cotton and Heath to Goulburn, 30 April 1844, ABE, M5/207.

47 Goulburn to Gladstone, 5 May 1854, BL, Add. Ms. 44162; Howe, "Free Trade and the City of London," 398–9; John Clapham, *The Bank of England*, 2 vols. (Cambridge, 1944), 2:178–81; David Kynaston, *The City of London*, vol. 1, *A World of Its Own 1815–1890* (London, 1994), 127; Gash, *Sir Robert Peel*, 431–7.

48 Goulburn memorandum, n.d. [September 1843], BL, Add. Ms. 40470.

49 *Parl. Deb.*, 3rd ser., 74:1279 and 75:434, 927–8; Gash, *Sir Robert Peel*, 445–6.

50 Gash, *Sir Robert Peel*, 447; *PMP: Gladstone*, 2:261; H. Goulburn to E. Goulburn, 15 June 1844, SRO, Acc 304/31.

51 *PMP: Gladstone*, 2:262–5; Peel to Queen, 17 June 1844, RA, film 95709/2; *Parl. Deb.*, 3rd ser., 75:1035–8; Stewart, *Foundation of the Conservative Party*, 188.

52 For a discussion of Peel's concept of leadership in this context, see D.R. Fisher, "Peel and the Conservative Party: The Sugar Crisis of 1844 Reconsidered," *Historical Journal* 18 (1975): 279–302; also Robert Stewart, "The Ten Hours and Sugar Crises of 1844: Government and the House of Commons in the Age of Reform," *Historical Journal* 12 (1969): 35–57; Thomas Pinney, ed., *Letters of Thomas Babington Macaulay*, vol. 4 (Cambridge, 1977), 195.

CHAPTER TWELVE

1 Goulburn to Peel, 14 November 1844, British Library (BL), Add. Ms. 40444; Goulburn to Peel, 25 August 1842, BL, Add. Ms. 40443; Peel to Queen, 11 January 1845, Royal Archives (RA), Windsor, film 95709/3; Peel to Goulburn, 11 January 1845, Surrey Record Office (SRO), Kingston upon Thames, Acc 304/42; Somerset to Goulburn, 18 September 1844, BL, Add. Ms. 40444.

2 Goulburn to Peel, 12 September 1844, BL, Add. Ms. 40444; Muriel E. Chamberlain, *Lord Aberdeen: A Political Biography* (London, 1983), 331ff.; E. Jones-Parry, ed., *Correspondence of Lord Aberdeen and Princess Lieven*, 2 vols. (London, 1938–39), 1:231–2; Charles Stuart Parker, ed., *Sir Robert Peel from His Private Papers*, 3 vols., reprint (New York, 1970), 3:197; Peel to Goulburn, 7 December [1844], SRO, Acc 304/41; Goulburn to Peel, 15 September 1844, BL, Add. Ms. 40444; Goulburn to Peel, 29 December 1844, BL, Add. Ms. 40556.

3 Goulburn to Peel, 12 September, 18 October 1844, BL, Add. Ms. 40444.

4 Goulburn to Peel, 16 October, 7 November 1844, BL, Add. Ms. 40444.

5 Peel to Goulburn, 23 October, 17 December [1844], SRO, Acc 304/41; Goulburn memorandum, n.d. [December 1844], BL, Add. Ms. 40444.

6 Peel to Goulburn, 22 December [1844], SRO, Acc 304/41; Peel to Goulburn, n.d. [February 1845], SRO Acc 304/42; Peel to Queen, 11 February 1845, RA, film 95709/3.

7 Norman Gash, *Sir Robert Peel: The Life of Sir Robert Peel after 1830*, 2nd ed. (New York, 1986), 465; *Parl. Deb.*, 3rd ser., 78:335–6, 224–6, 474–86, and 77:1149–51, 1247–60, 1258, 573–81, 786–91; Peel to Queen, n.d. [April 1845], RA, film 95709/3; Gash, *Sir Robert Peel*, 467.

8 Henry Lytton Bulwer, *The Life of Henry John Temple, Viscount Palmerston, with Selections from His Diaries and Correspondence*, 3 vols. (London, 1870–74), 3:174; Donal A. Kerr, *Peel, Priests and Politics: Sir Robert Peel's Administration and the Roman Catholic Church in Ireland, 1841–1846* (Oxford, 1982), 151, 265–6; Goulburn to Peel, 6, 16 January 1845, BL, Add. Ms. 40445; John Wolffe, *The Protestant Crusade in Great Britain, 1829–1860* (Oxford, 1991), 116–18; D.G. Paz, "Popular Anti-Catholicism in England, 1850–1851," *Albion* 11 (1979): 338.

9 John Brooke and Mary Sorensen, eds., *Prime Ministers' Papers: W.E. Gladstone*, vol. 2, *Autobiographical Memoranda, 1832–1845* (London, 1972); 271–2, 275–6; Wolffe, *Protestant Crusade*, 198–200; *Times*, 11 June 1845; G.I.T. Machin, "The Maynooth Grant, the Dissenters and Disestablishment, 1845–1847," *English Historical Review* 82 (1967): 61–3; Peel to Queen, 11 April 1845, RA, film 95709/5; *A Portion of the Journal Kept by Thomas Raikes Esq.*, 4 vols. (London, 1856), 4:422–4.

10 *Parl. Deb.*, 3rd ser., 79:781–97; *Times*, 17 April 1845; for the response of the Central Anti-Maynooth Committee, see RA, film 95709/5; Wolffe, *Protestant Crusade*, 271; *Times*, 20, 30 May 1845; Robert Stewart, *Party and Politics 1830–1852* (New York, 1989), 75; Jones-Parry, *Aberdeen-Lieven Correspondence*, 241.

11 Parker, *Peel*, 3:177; Kerr, *Peel, Priests and Politics*, 297ff: Bulwer, *Viscount Palmerston*, 3:176; Parker, *Peel*, 3:273.

12 Goulburn to Peel, 21, 24 October, 25 August, 21 October 1845, BL, Add. Ms. 40445; F.M.L. Thompson, ed., *Cambridge Social History of Britain, 1750–1850*, vol. 3, *Social Agencies and Institutions* (Cambridge, 1990), 25; Goulburn to Cotton, 9 October 1845, Archives of the Bank of England (ABE), M5/206; *Parl. Deb.*, 3rd ser., 83:132–3; Arthur D. Gayer, W.W. Rostow, and Anna Jacobsen Schwartz, *The Growth and Fluctuation of the British Economy 1790–1850*, 2 vols. (Oxford, 1953) 1:332.

13 Peel to Queen, 28, 31 August 1845, RA, film 95709/3; Redcliffe Salaman, *The History and Social Influence of the Potato*, rev. ed., with introduction by J.G. Hawkes, pb. ed. (Cambridge, 1970), 286; R.F. Foster, *Modern Ireland 1600–1972* (New York, 1988), 319–20.

14 *Parl. Deb.*, 3rd ser., 85:61 and 91:914; Trevelyan to Blake, 3 February 1842, University of Newcastle Library (UNEW), Trevelyan Letterbooks, 2:157–9; Trevelyan to Eliot, 28 September 1841, Trevelyan to Lucas, 30 April 1842,

Public Record Office (PRO), T14/28; Goulburn to Peel, 8, 18, 21 October,1845; 7 November 1849, BL, Add. Ms. 40445.

15 Gash, *Sir Robert Peel,* 535; Peel to Goulburn, 18 October 1845, SRO, Acc 304/42; Parker, *Peel,* 3:224–5; Peel to Graham, 15 October [1845], Bodleian Library (BOD), Ms. film 120; Thomas Wemyss Reid, *Memoirs and Correspondence of Lyon Playfair,* reprint ed. (Jemimaville, 1976), 98–9; W.E. Vaughan, ed., *A New History of Ireland: Ireland under the Union,* vol. 1, *1801–1870* (Oxford, 1989), 274–6.

16 Goulburn to Peel, 21 October 1845, BL, Add. Ms. 40445.

17 Parker, *Peel,* 3:225; Graham to Heytesbury, 31 October, 1 November 1845, BOD, Ms. film 116; Goulburn to Peel, 21 October 1845, BL, Add. Ms. 40445; Peel to Queen, 6 November 1845, RA, film 95709/5.

18 Graham to Heytesbury, 7 November 1845, BOD, Ms. film 120; Vaughan, *Ireland under the Union,* 1:280; Goulburn to Peel, 11 November 1845, BL, Add. Ms. 40445; Lord Mahon and Edward Cardwell, eds., *Memoirs of the Right Honourable Sir Robert Peel,* 2 vols. (London, 1857), 2:173–4.

19 Goulburn memorandum, November 1845, BOD, Ms. film 121; Trevelyan to Routh, 28 November 1845, UNEW, Trevelyan Letterbooks, 5:190–1.

20 Goulburn memorandum, November 1845, BOD, Ms. film 121; Peel to Queen, 27 November 1845, RA, film 95709/5; Goulburn to Peel, 27 November 1845, BL, Add. Ms 40445.

21 Goulburn to Peel, [27 November 1845], BL, Add. Ms. 40445; Parker, *Peel,* 3:281; Mahon and Cardwell, *Memoirs of Peel,* 2:174ff; Peel to Queen, 3, 4, 5 December 1845, RA, film 95709/5; *Parl. Deb.,* 3rd ser., 84:49; Queen to Peel, 13 December 1845, Peel to Queen, 15 December 1845, Queen to Russell, 16 December 1845, Russell to Queen, 16 December 1845, Queen to Peel, 18 December 1845, Russell to Queen, 19, 20 December 1845, and Prince Albert memorandum, 20 December 1845, RA, film 95709/5; John Prest, *Lord John Russell* (Columbia, 1972), 201–7; D.G. Southgate, *The Passing of Whigs, 1832–1886* (London, 1962), 129; Thomas Pinney, ed., *Letters of Thomas Babington Macaulay,* vol. 4 (Cambridge, 1977), 278–9; for an account of Russell's conduct, see F.A. Dreyer, "The Whigs and the Political Crisis of 1845," *English Historical Review* 80 (1965): 514–37.

22 *Times,* 22 December 1845; Gash, *Sir Robert Peel,* 614; Boyd Hilton, "Peel: A Reappraisal," *Historical Journal* 22 (1979): 585–614; William O. Aydelotte, "The Country Gentlemen and the Repeal of the Corn Laws," *English Historical Review* 82 (1967): 40–60; Ellenborough to Brougham, 23 December 1845, PRO, 30/12/21/12; Betty Kemp, "Reflections on the Repeal of the Corn Laws," *Victorian Studies* 6 (1962–63): 189–204; S. Fairlie, "The Nineteenth-Century Corn Law Reconsidered," *Economic History Review,* 2nd ser., 18 (1965): 562–75; D.C. Moore, "The Corn Law and High Farming," *Economic History Review,* 2nd ser., 18 (1965): 544–61; Robert Stewart, *The Foundation of the Conservative Party, 1830–1867* (London, 1978), 324; Peel to

Queen, 21, 22, 23 December 1845, and Prince Albert memorandum, 25 December 1845, RA, film 95709/5.

23 Goulburn to Gladstone, 22 December 1845, BL, Add. Ms. 44162; Louis J. Jennings, *The Croker Papers*, 3 vols. (London, 1885), 3:61–2; *Parl. Deb.*, 3rd ser., 84:64–5, 45–9; *Times*, 20 June 1846.

24 Jackman to Goulburn, 22 December 1845, Goulburn to Peel, 25 December 1845, and n.d. [December 1845], BL, Add. Ms. 40445.

25 Parker, *Peel*, 3:294; Prince Albert memorandum, 25 December 1845, RA, film 95709/5; Peel to Queen, 14 January 1846, RA, film 95709/4; Gash, *Sir Robert Peel*, 569–72; Prince Albert memorandum, 27 January [1846], RA, film 95709/4.

26 *Parl. Deb.*, 3rd ser., 84:54–67, 85:60–4, and 86: 837–44; *Times*, 19 May 1846; Peel to Queen, n.d. [25 February], [1 March 1846], RA, film 95709/4.

27 Trevelyan to Routh, 23 December 1845, 24 January 1846, UNEW, Trevelyan Letterbooks, 5:208–9, 268–9; Cecil Woodham-Smith, *The Great Hunger: Ireland 1845–1849*, pb. ed.(New York, 1980), 62; Goulburn to Peel, 13 August 1846, BL, Add. Ms. 40445; Trevelyan to Routh, 5 February 1846, UNEW, Trevelyan Letterbooks, 6:4; Trevelyan to Routh, 3 February 1846, UNEW, Trevelyan Letterbooks, 5:285–92.

28 Trevelyan to Hewetson, 24 December 1845, UNEW, Trevelyan Letterbooks, 5:218–9; Trevelyan to Routh, 24 December 1845, 4 February 1846, UNEW, Trevelyan Letterbooks, 5:219–20, 295–305.

29 Trevelyan to Routh, 4 February 1846, UNEW, Trevelyan Letterbooks, 5:295–305; Trevelyan to Routh, 3 January 1846, UNEW, Trevelyan Letterbooks, 5:233–6; Trevelyan to Routh, 30 April 1846, UNEW, Trevelyan Letterbooks, 6:221–2; Trevelyan to Perceval, 26 May 1846, UNEW, Trevelyan Letterbooks, 6:296.

30 A.R. Griffiths, "The Irish Board of Works in the Famine Years," *Historical Journal* 13 (1970): 634–5; Trevelyan to Jones, 15 January 1846, UNEW, Trevelyan Letterbooks, 5:249–52; F. Darrell Munsell, "Charles Edward Trevelyan and Peelite Irish Famine Policy, 1845–1846," *Societas* 1 (1971): 301; *Parl. Deb.*, 3rd ser., 83:433, 638; Trevelyan to Paymaster Civil Services, 27 February 1846, PRO, T14/29; Trevelyan to Fremantle, 26 February 1846, UNEW, Trevelyan Letterbooks, 6:53–61.

31 Trevelyan to Routh, 14 March 1846, UNEW, Trevelyan Letterbooks, 6:101–3; Trevelyan to Clanricarde, 17 March 1846, Trevelyan to Lincoln, 21 March 1846, PRO, T14/30; Graham to Heytesbury, 6 February 1846, BOD, Ms. film 121; *Parl. Deb.*, 3rd ser., 84:1001–2.

32 *Times*, 14 March 1846; Thomas Campbell Foster, *Letters on the Condition of the People of Ireland*, 2 vols. (London, 1847), 2:622; *Parl. Deb.*, 3rd ser., 85:61–3; Prince Albert memorandum, 29 March 1846, RA, film 95709/6.

33 Routh to Coffin, 23, 26, 27 February 1846, PRO, War Office (WO) 63/132; Routh to Hewetson, 13 February 1846, PRO, WO 63/132; Routh to Coffin,

20 February 1846, PRO, WO 63/132; Trevelyan to Routh, 4 March 1846, UNEW, Trevelyan Letterbooks, 6:74–7; Routh to Coffin, 17 March 1846, PRO, WO 63/132; Trevelyan to Routh, 3 April, 28 March 1846, UNEW, Trevelyan Letterbooks, 6:152–3, 141–3; Routh to Trevelyan, 4 April 1846, PRO, WO 63/132.

34 Routh to Trevelyan, 6 March 1846, PRO, WO 63/132; Lincoln to Goulburn, 1 April 1846, University of Nottingham Library (UNL), Nec 9233, Newcastle Papers; Treasury minute, 3 April 1846, PRO, T29/496.

35 Goulburn to Lincoln, 3 April 1846, UNL, Nec 9237; Trevelyan to Pennyfather, 4 April 1846, PRO, T14/30; Lincoln to Goulburn, 10 April 1846, UNL, Nec 9234/2; Charles Stuart Parker, *Life and Letters of Sir James Graham, 1792–1861* (London, 1907), 2:38; Peel to Goulburn, 10 April 1846, BL, Add. Ms. 40445; Peel to Goulburn, 25 April 1846, Acc 304/42.

36 Goulburn to Peel, 12, 13, 15 April 1846, BL, Add. Ms. 40445; Goulburn to Lincoln, 15 April 1846, UNL, Nec 9241; Mary E. Daly, *The Famine in Ireland* (Dublin, 1986), 71, 75.

37 Lincoln to Goulburn, 15 April 1846, UNL, Nec 9235/1; Peel to Goulburn, 15 April 1846, BL, Add. Ms. 40445.

38 Goulburn to Lincoln, 17 April 1846, UNL, Nec 9242; Goulburn to Lincoln, 18 April 1846, UNL, Nec 9243; Goulburn to Lincoln, 21 April 1846, UNL, Nec 9244; Lincoln to Goulburn, 19 April 1846, UNL, Nec 9236; Trevelyan to Routh, 18 April 1846, UNEW, Trevelyan Letterbooks, 6:178–83; Parker, *Life and Letters of Graham*, 2:38; Trevelyan to Pennyfather, 24 April, 5 May 1846, PRO, T14/30.

39 Trevelyan to Routh, 29 April, 2 May 1846, UNEW, Trevelyan Letterbooks, 6:213–16, 233–4; Trevelyan to Routh, 3, 12, 25 June 1846, UNEW, Trevelyan Letterbooks, 7:16–20, 38–9, 62–7.

40 Trevelyan to Cropper, 3 June 1846, UNEW, Trevelyan Letterbooks, 7:21–2; Twistleton to Graham, 10 June 1846, BOD, Ms. film 122; Graham Davis, *The Irish in Britain 1815–1914* (Dublin, 1991), 14–15, 22–6.

41 *Parl. Deb.*, 3rd ser., 86:1429–52; *Times*, 30 May 1846; Peel to Prince Albert, n.d. [29 May 1846], RA, film 95709/4; *Times*, 5 June 1846.

CHAPTER THIRTEEN

1 Peel memorandum, 21 June 1846, Peel to Queen, 26 June 1846, and Prince Albert memorandum, 28 June 1846, Royal Archives (RA), Windsor, film 95709/4; John Brooke and Mary Sorensen, eds., *Prime Ministers' Papers: W.E. Gladstone*, vol. 3 (London, 1981), 30–1; Goulburn to Peel, 20 June 1846, British Library, (BL), Add. Ms. 40445.

2 Goulburn to Peel, 13 August, 15 October 1846, BL, Add. Ms. 40445.

3 Goulburn to Peel, 15 October 1846, BL, Add. Ms. 40445; Reddington memorandum, 25 October 1846, and Prince Albert memorandum,

6 November 1846, RA, film 95709/6; W.E. Vaughan, ed., *A New History of Ireland: Ireland under the Union*, vol. 1, *1801–1870* (Oxford, 1989), 294–5, 297; Goulburn to Peel, 24 November 1846, BL, Add. Ms. 40445; Peel to Goulburn, 14 August, 17 October, 21, 29 November 1846, Surrey Record Office (SRO), Acc 304/42; *Parl. Deb.*, 3rd ser., 89:222.

4 Goulburn to E. Goulburn, Jr. 5 February 1847, SRO, Acc 304/31; *Parl. Deb.*, 3rd ser., 89:1310–17; Brian Jenkins, *Sir William Gregory of Coole* (Gerrards Cross, 1986), 70–1.

5 *Parl. Deb.*, 3rd ser., 90:369–71; Peel to Goulburn, 27 August [1847], SRO, Acc 304/42; *Parl. Deb.*, 3rd ser., 91:913–4; Vaughan, *Ireland under the Union*, 1:320.

6 Goulburn to Peel, 19 December 1846, BL, Add. Ms. 40445; Peel to Goulburn, 20 December 1846, SRO, Acc 304/42; Goulburn to Peel, 24, 31 December 1846, BL, Add. Ms. 40445; Herbert to Goulburn, 13 December 1846, SRO, Acc 304/45; Goulburn to Aberdeen, 12 December 1846, BL, Add. Ms. 43196; Peel to Goulburn, 3 April 1847, SRO, Acc 304/42.

7 Robert Stewart, *The Foundation of the Conservative Party, 1830–1867* (London, 1978), 229; Goulburn to Peel, 4 August 1847, BL, Add. Ms. 40445; Henry Gunning, *Reminiscences of the University, Town and County of Cambridge from the Year 1780*, 2 vols. (London, 1854), 1:xvi–xvii; Goulburn to Peel, 24 August 1847, BL, Add. Ms. 40445.

8 David M. Vieth, ed., *The Complete Poems of John Wilmot, Earl of Rochester* (New Haven, 1968), 73; Lewis Melville, *Society at Royal Tunbridge Wells in the Eighteenth Century and After* (London, 1912), 198; Goulburn to Peel, 27 September, 3 October 1847, BL, Add. Ms. 40445; Peel to Goulburn, 28 October 1847, SRO, Acc 304/42; Norman Gash, *Sir Robert Peel: The Life of Sir Robert Peel after 1830*, 2nd ed. (New York, 1986), 627–31; Goulburn to Ripon, 30 October 1847, BL, Add. Ms. 40877; Goulburn to Cardwell, 9 November 1847, Public Record Office (PRO), 30/48, Cardwell Papers; Goulburn to Cotton, 12 February 1848, Archives of the Bank of England Archives (ABE), M5/206.

9 Goulburn to Peel, 23 October 1847, BL, Add. Ms. 40445; Goulburn to Turner, 27 August 1840, SRO, Acc 304/57; Goulburn to Watson, 13 June 1842, SRO, Acc 304/57; Goulburn to Turner, 1 October 1841, SRO, Acc 304/57; Goulburn to Watson, 1 May 1843, SRO, Acc 304/57; MacKinnon to Goulburn, 22 July 1844, SRO, Acc 304/56.

10 Goulburn to Watson, 1 March 1844, SRO, Acc 304/56; Estridge to Goulburn, 29 October 1844, SRO Acc 304/35; Goulburn to MacKinnon, 14 December 1844, SRO, Acc 304/56; Douglas Hall, *Free Jamaica 1838–1865: An Economic History* (New Haven, 1959), 52–3; Goulburn to MacKinnon, 28 August 1845, and MacKinnon to Goulburn, 5 December 1844, 14 April 1845, 21 July, 20 January 1846, SRO, Acc 304/56.

11 Goulburn to MacKinnon, n.d. [September 1846], SRO, Acc 304/56; *Parl. Deb.*, 3rd ser., 88:262–3; Goulburn to Peel, 19, 24, 25 November 1846, BL, Add. Ms. 40445; *Parl. Deb.*, 3rd ser., 89:304–7; Goulburn to MacKinnon, 29 March 1847, SRO, Acc 304/55; Goulburn to Peel, 27 September 1847, BL, Add. Ms. 40445.

12 Goulburn to MacKinnon, n.d. [autumn 1846], SRO, Acc 304/56; Goulburn to Peel, 27 September 1847, BL, Add. Ms. 40445.

13 MacKinnon to Goulburn, 5, 21 January, 9 March, 6 April, 22 July 1847, 22 March 1848, SRO, Acc 304/55; Goulburn to MacKinnon, 1 June 1846, SRO, Acc 304/56; Goulburn to MacKinnon, 1 March 1847, 30 September 1847, 29 August 1851, 30 September, 16 October 1847, SRO, Acc 304/55.

14 Goulburn to Peel, 23 October 1847, BL, Add. Ms. 40445; Peel to Goulburn, 28 October 1847, SRO, Acc 304/42; Goulburn to Ripon, 30 October 1847, BL, Add. Ms. 40877; *Parl. Deb.*, 3rd ser., 96:150–60; Noel Deer, *The History of Sugar*, 2 vols. (London, 1949), 2:438–9; *Parl. Deb.*, 3rd ser., 99:1344–58 and 100:555–8, 366–71; Goulburn to MacKinnon, 16 October 1847, 30 April, 15 July, 14 October 1848, SRO, Acc 304/55.

15 Goulburn to Ripon, 24 January 1848, BL, Add. Ms. 40877; *Parl. Deb.*, 3rd ser., 97:192–7; Goulburn to Ripon, 25 July 1848, BL, Add. Ms. 40877; *Parl. Deb.*, 3rd ser., 100:490–5; Goulburn to Ripon, 5 August 1848, BL, Add. Ms. 40877; Goulburn to Jane Goulburn, 27 September 1848, SRO, Acc 304/30; *Parl. Deb.*, 3rd ser., 107:64.

16 Goulburn to Ripon, 24 August 1848, 16 November 1847, BL, Add. Ms. 40877; Stewart, *Foundation of the Conservative Party*, 231–2; J.B. Conacher, *The Peelites and the Party System, 1846–1857* (Newton Abbott, 1972), 19; Charles Stuart Parker, *Life and Letters of Sir James Graham, 1792–1861*, 2 vols. (London, 1907), 2:63; Gladstone memorandum, 12/48, BL, Add. Ms. 44777.

17 Goulburn to Cardwell, 1, 19, 27 October 1848, PRO, 30/48; Goulburn to Peel, 6 January 1850, BL, Add. Ms. 40445; Goulburn to Ripon, 6 December 1848, BL, Add. Ms. 40877; Goulburn to Cardwell, 1 October 1848, PRO, 30/48; Stewart, *Foundation of the Conservative Party*, 239.

18 Goulburn to Gladstone, 19 March 1849, BL, Add. Ms. 44162; Goulburn to Ripon, 24 January 1848, BL, Add. Ms. 40877; *Parl. Deb.*, 3rd ser., 103:824–9; Conacher, *Peelites and the Party System*, 53; Goulburn to E. Goulburn, Jr, 12 September 1849, SRO, Acc 304/31; Goulburn to Ripon, 12 September 1849, 18 January 1850, BL, Add. Ms. 40877.

19 Goulburn to Peel, 16 January 1849, BL, Add. Ms. 40445; Goulburn to Harrowby, 3 November 1849, Harrowby Mss, vol. 37, Sandon Hall, Stafford. Goulburn to Ripon, 6 December 1848, BL, Add. Ms. 40877; *Parl. Deb.*, 3rd ser., 100:1093–4 and 94:379–85, 654; Goulburn to Peel, 13, 29 September

1849, BL, Add. Ms. 40445; Goulburn to Ripon, 30 September 1849, BL, Add. Ms. 40877.

20 Goulburn to Peel, 29 September 1849, BL, Add. Ms. 40445; G.F.A. Best, *Temporal Pillars: Queen Anne's Bounty, the Ecclesiastical Commisssioners, and the Church of England* (Cambridge, 1964), 383–4, 389–92; Peel to Goulburn, 6 October [1849], SRO, Acc 304/42; Goulburn to Ripon, 30 September 1849, BL, Add. Ms. 40877; Kenneth A. Thompson, *Bureaucracy and Church Reform: The Organizational Response of the Church of England to Social Change, 1800–1965* (Oxford, 1970), 62–5.

21 Best, *Temporal Pillars*, 393–7, 414–19; Goulburn to E. Goulburn, Jr, 11 August 1850, SRO, Acc 304/31; Robert S. Dell, "Social and Economic Theories and Pastoral Concerns of a Victorian Archbishop," *Journal of Ecclesiastical History* 16 (1965): 196–207; Thompson, *Bureaucracy and Church Reform*, 73–4; *Edinburgh Review* 97 (1853): 88, 84.

22 Donald Read, *Peel and the Victorians* (Oxford, 1987), 266–8; Goulburn to Ripon, 3 July [probably misdated] 1850, BL, Add. Ms. 40877; *Parl. Deb.*, 3rd ser., 112:896–8.

23 Lady Peel to Goulburn, 30 July, 28 August 1850, 7 October 1851, SRO, Acc 304/9; Goulburn to Frederick Peel, 22 September 1851, and Goulburn to Sir Robert Peel, 3 October 1850, 2 February 1851, SRO, Acc 304/9; Goulburn to Cardwell, 21 August, 5 October 1850, PRO, 30/48; for correspondence concerning Foucart, see SRO, Acc 304/6.

24 William Flavelle Monypenny and George Earle Buckle, *The Life of Benjamin Disraeli, Earl of Beaconsfield*, 6 vols. (London, 1910–12), 3:260; Goulburn to Cardwell, 5 October 1850, PRO, 30/48; Conacher, *Peelites and the Party System*, 71.

25 *Parl. Deb.*, 3rd ser., 91:791–7 and 116:401–4; Goulburn to Cardwell, 5 September 1850, PRO, 30/48; Goulburn to Ripon, 16 December 1850, BL, Add. Ms. 40877; *Edinburgh Review* 98 (1853): 168–9; for a recent account of the "papal aggression" crisis, see Gerald Parsons, ed., *Religion in Victorian Britain*, vol. 4, *Interpretations* (Manchester, 1988), 115–34.

26 Jenkins, *Gregory*, 112–13; Wolffe, *Protestant Crusade*, 243–5; G.I.T. Machin, "Lord John Russell and the Prelude to the Ecclesiastical Titles Bill, 1846–51," *Journal of Ecclesiastical History* 25 (1974): 277–95.

27 Goulburn to Ripon, 15 November, 16 December 1850, BL, Add. Ms. 40877.

28 *Parl. Deb.*, 3rd ser., 115:60–6; Monypenny and Buckle, *Disraeli*, 3:293–4; Stewart, *Foundation of the Conservative Party*, 247.

29 Conacher, *Peelites and the Party System*, 94ff; G.I.T. Machin, *Politics and the Churches in Great Britain, 1832 to 1868* (Oxford, 1977), 241; *Parl. Deb.*, 3rd ser., 123:907–8, 1402–12; Goulburn to Aberdeen, 27 August 1852, and Aberdeen to Goulburn, 2 September 1852, BL, Add. Ms. 43196; J.B. Conacher, *The Aberdeen Coalition, 1852–1855* (Cambridge, 1968), 13, 28.

30 Conacher, *The Aberdeen Coalition*, 13, 28; Goulburn to Gladstone,
   27 January, 24 May, 13, 20 June, 6, 16 July, 19 August, 3 October 1853,
   5, 24 May, 3 December 1854, BL, Add. Ms. 44162.

31 Goulburn to Gladstone, 21 September 1852, BL, Add. Ms. 44162; F. Goulburn to E. Goulburn, n.d. [May 1855], SRO, Acc 304/31; Goulburn to J.
   Goulburn, 29 May 1855, SRO, Acc 304/31; F. Goulburn to Cardwell,
   18 January [1856], PRO 30/48.

32 *Edinburgh Review* 97 (1853): 269. Donald Harmon Akenson, *The Irish Di-
   aspora: A Primer* (Toronto, 1993), 19.

33 Dalby to F. Goulburn, 18 January 1856, SRO, Acc 304/23.

34 Goulburn to Ripon, 16 December 1850, BL, Add. Ms. 40877.

Index